The sordid union between Intelligence and
Organized Crime that gave rise to Jeffrey Epstein

ONE NATION UNDER
BLACKMAIL

VOL. 1

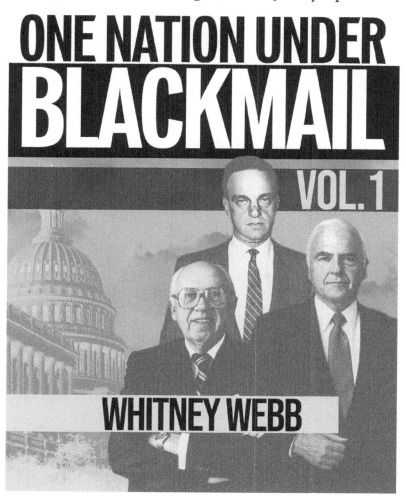

WHITNEY WEBB

One Nation Under Blackmail: The Sordid Union Between Intelligence and Crime that Gave Rise to Jeffrey Epstein, Volume One.

Published by:
Trine Day LLC
PO Box 577
Walterville, OR 97489
1-800-556-2012
www.TrineDay.com
trineday@icloud.com

Library of Congress Control Number: 2022945071

Webb, Whitney
One Nation Under Blackmail: The Sordid Union Between Intelligence and Crime that Gave Rise to Jeffrey Epstein, Volume One.—1st ed.
p. cm.

Epub (ISBN-13) 978-1-63424-303-2
Print (ISBN-13) 978-1-63424-301-8
1. Epstein, Jeffrey, -- 1953-2019. 2. Epstein, Jeffrey, -- 1953-2019 -- Friends and associates. 3. Extortion -- United States 1940-2022. 3. Organized Crime -- United States. 5. Organized Crime -- Canada. 6. Intelligence services -- United States. 7. Espionage. 8. POLITICAL SCIENCE / Corruption & Misconduct. 9. Truthfulness and falsehood -- Political aspects. 10. Espionage -- Israel -- United States. 11. Sex scandals -- Political aspects -- United States. 12. TRUE CRIME / Sexual Assault. I. Title
First Edition

PEOPLE ON COVER: Willaim Casey, Roy Cohn, & Robert Keith Gray

FIRST EDITION
10 9 8 7 6 5 4 3

Distribution to the Trade by:
Independent Publishers Group (IPG)
814 North Franklin Street
Chicago, Illinois 60610
312.337.0747
www.ipgbook.com

PUBLISHER'S FOREWORD

PROSPERO: *But you, my brace of lords, were I so minded,*
I here could pluck his highness' frown upon you
And justify you traitors: at this time
I will tell no tales.

SEBASTIAN: *The devil speaks in him.*

– William Shakespeare, The Tempest, Act 5, Scene 1

I want something embarrassing! Something sexual! Little boys, midg-
ets, that sort of thing! Cows! I don't give a goddamn!

– Sam Elliott as Kermit Newman, *The Contender*

"Where's my Roy Cohn?"

– Donald Trump, *New York Times*, January 4, 2018

Why do folks lie, cheat and steal? Is it simply the survival of the fittest? What about our rule of law and the hoary moral codes left to us? Are they worth the paper they are printed on? Will we ever learn?

Whitney Webb takes us on a hidden history excursion – beyond the realm of the gatekeepers – delving into a deep netherworld where disgraceful actions seemingly trump noble principles. *One Nation Under Blackmail: The Sordid Union Between Intelligence and Crime that Gave Rise to Jeffrey Epstein* is a *tour de force*. A deep exposé into how the world actually works.

I will never forget my introduction to this underworld: a "talk" with my "spooky" father and his professor friend from Vanderbilt. It was a reality beyond my ken, way further than my teen-age experience. So I simply went on with growing up, but looking in the dark corners.

My education was through reading, magazine articles and books – so many books. There was much going on in the late 1960s and '70s. My father and his friend had talked about an activity I call "CIA-Drugs," and about "political forces," using psychological warfare to move agendas.

It soon became apparent that within this milieu there were many players: intelligence agencies and their operatives, criminal gangs, secret societies, bag men, money launderers, financial institutions and governments.

As my studies into intelligence matters and protocols progressed, I became aware of "honey-traps" and the use of blackmail to compromise individuals and stilt honest political discourse. It floored me that there were, it appeared, federal agents running interference to some of the operations. Where was the country and the values I had been taught? How did we get here?

"It's far more constructive to work for the church than to work for the Central Intelligence Agency. When you work for the CIA the ends justify the means," my father was quoted in a local paper a few years before his passing.

Immoral methods skew our futures and lead to imbalance. Leaving us ruled by "rich men who are not quite respectable."

British historian Eric Hobsbawm opined, "He [Roy Cohn] made his legal and political career in a milieu where money and power override rules and law – indeed where the ability to get, and get away with, what lesser citizens cannot, is what proves membership of an elite."

A corrupt elite debasing our future. Trying to bully us into their depravity. With this book and others we can become educated and empowered to right our ship-of-state.

Whitney has done her homework and *One Nation Under Blackmail* shows with great alacrity the past actions, present situations, and future problems that we face. And *must* deal with in order to fulfill our founder's aspirations, foster current needs, and forsee our children's future.

A blackmailer believes that they are "in control," but secrets can cut many ways, and ultimately we are in the driver's seat. What will we do?

Onwards to the Utmost of Futures!
Peace,
R.A. "Kris" Millegan
Publisher
TrineDay
August 18, 2022

Contents

ACKNOWLEDGMENTS

First and foremost, I'd like to extend my deepest and sincerest thanks to Ed Berger, without whom this book would not have been possible. Ed contributed amazing, in-depth and original research to several key parts of this book and his contributions were and are invaluable. If you enjoy historical deep dives about the intersection of organized crime networks, corporate power and intelligence agencies, please consider listening to and supporting his podcast: The Pseudodoxology Podcast Network at https://www.patreon.com/wydna

I also want to thank my amazing assistant Star Parsons for helping keep my website afloat while I worked on this book and for painstakingly formatting all the many, many citations within this book. I also owe much to my publisher Kris Millegan for his infinite patience and understanding, as this book was delayed several times, and for his support of my work. Also, an important thank you to Johnny Vedmore who made some important contributions to this book and whose original past reporting on the Epstein case was key to developing important parts of this book.

In addition, this work, and my journalistic career in general, would not have been possible if not for Mnar Muhawesh and the team at MintPress News. Mnar and the MintPress team first gave me the space and platform necessary to develop my journalistic work and provided me with the support I needed to publish my original, four-part series on which this book is based. Thank you so much for believing in me and for supporting my work from the very beginning – I owe you all so much.

I also would like to thank my amazing babysitters, Fresia Retamal and Patricia Guzmán, for taking great care of my little ones so that I could put in the time to write this book.

Last but not least, I would like to extend my deepest, heartfelt thanks to all of my supporters, specifically the thousands of readers who financially support my work, allowing me to be 100% independent. Without your support, this book would not have happened and I cannot thank you enough for your help in financing this book as well as in supporting and sharing my other work, both online and in print.

Introduction, Volume 1

The July 2019 arrest of Jeffrey Epstein and his subsequent death that August brought national as well as international attention to a sex ring where certain members of the power elite sexually abused and exploited female minors and young women. Epstein's death, officially ruled a suicide, has been treated skeptically by many, for a variety of reasons. Regardless of the real circumstances of his death, it has led to scores of Americans embracing the view that his death was both intentional and necessary to protect his powerful co-conspirators and the full extent of his covert and illegal activities.

Even if one chooses not to entertain such disconcerting possibilities, it is quite apparent that most of those who aided or enabled Epstein will never see the inside of a prison cell. Though Ghislaine Maxwell is now serving a 20 year sentence, others known to have been intimately involved in his illegal activities continue to enjoy protection from the so-called "sweetheart deal," or plea deal that followed Epstein's first run-in with the law for his sex trafficking activities in the mid-2000s. In addition, Ghislaine Maxwell's recent trial saw information involving third parties redacted, leading many to believe that the public will never know the names of the "johns" or clients, who benefitted from the sex trafficking activities of Epstein and Maxwell and who were potentially blackmailed by them.

Yet, for both Jeffrey Epstein and Ghislaine Maxwell, there is much more to the story. This became apparent when it emerged that Alex Acosta, then-serving as Secretary of Labor in the Trump administration, had disclosed to the Trump transition team that he had previously signed off on Epstein's "sweetheart deal" because Epstein "had belonged to intelligence." Acosta, then serving as US attorney for Southern Florida, had also been told by unspecified figures at the time that he needed to give Epstein a lenient sentence because of his links to "intelligence." When Acosta was later asked if Epstein was indeed an intelligence asset in 2019, Acosta chose to neither confirm or deny the claim.

Other hints of a connection between Epstein and intelligence subsequently emerged, with reporting from a variety of sources that Epstein was affiliated with the CIA, Israeli intelligence, or both. Despite the implications and significance of these connection(s) to intelligence, most of mainstream media declined to dig deeper into these claims, instead largely focusing on the salacious aspects of the Epstein case. The narrative soon became that Epstein was an anomaly, the sole mastermind of an industrial sex trafficking enterprise and a talented con artist. Even his closest associates and benefactors, like retail billionaire Leslie Wexner, have been taken at their word that they knew nothing of Epstein's crimes, even when there is considerable evidence to the contrary.

Indeed, it was later stated by Cindy McCain, wife of former Senator John McCain, that "we all knew what he [Epstein] was doing" at an event in January 2020, where she also claimed that authorities were "afraid" to properly apprehend him. If he was such an anomaly and a stand-alone con artist – how was he singlehandedly able to intimidate the law enforcement apparatus of an entire nation for decades? The claim that Epstein did not have powerful backers and benefactors stands on incredibly shaky ground.

Oddly enough, mainstream reporting on Epstein was once relatively open about his alleged intelligence ties, with British media reporting as early as 1992 and throughout the early 2000s that Epstein had ties to both US and Israeli intelligence. In addition, also in the early 1990s, Epstein's name was mysteriously dropped from a major investigation into one of the largest Ponzi schemes in history even though he was labeled the mastermind of that swindle in grand jury testimony. Around the same time, subsequently released White House visitor logs show that Epstein visited the Clinton White House 17 times, accompanied on most of these visits by a different, attractive young woman. Reporting on those visitor logs was largely done by a single media outlet, Britain's The Daily Mail, with hardly any American mainstream media outlets bothering to investigate these revelations about Epstein and a former US president.

Why was Epstein so heavily protected from justice for decades – in connection to both his sex trafficking crimes and his financial crimes? Why have the once commonly reported intelligence connections of Jeffrey Epstein now been relegated to "conspiracy theory" despite evidence to the contrary? If powerful Senators knew what Epstein was doing to young women and girls – who else knew and why wasn't something done?

This two-volume book endeavors to show why Jeffrey Epstein was able to engage in a series of mind-boggling crimes for decades without incident. Far from being an anomaly, Epstein was one of several men who, over the past century, have engaged in sexual blackmail activities designed to obtain damaging information (i.e. "intelligence) on powerful individuals with the goal of controlling their activities and securing their compliance. Most of these individuals, including Epstein himself, have their roots in the covert world where organized crime and intelligence have intermingled and often cooperated for the better part of the last 90 years, if not longer. Perhaps most shockingly, these men are all interconnected to various degrees.

Following the formal establishment of the organized crime-intelligence in World War II through what is today remembered as Operation Underworld, the relationship between these two entities has since become so intertwined and so symbiotic that, today, it is nearly impossible to know where one ends and the other begins. As this book will show, many of the biggest scandals and events of the last century have not only been tied to these networks, but many of them also have counted with the involvement of sex traffickers and blackmailers, Epstein among them. Publicly, these men have been powerful lawyers, businessmen and lobbyists. Their more clandestine and shadowy activities, though a matter of record, are often known only to those who are well read on certain historical events or in the field of "deep politics."

In order to understand Jeffrey Epstein and his activities in their full context, one must understand his powerful contacts and the structures that protected him. Those structures and those networks did not begin with Jeffrey Epstein and they also did not die with him. In revealing his broader milieu, and that of his past associates and clients, one is left not only with a damning indictment of Jeffrey Epstein, but a damning indictment of American institutions, particularly those involved in "national security" matters and law enforcement. We cannot properly address the crimes of Jeffrey Epstein, nor prevent them being committed by others in the future, unless we grapple with the covert power structures that have long wielded blackmail, bribes and assassinations as their weapons of choice to corrupt and control public institutions while manipulating and looting the public.

Jeffrey Epstein was not an anomaly and his activities represent just the tip of the veritable iceberg.

Whitney Webb, 8/14/22

"Who are these people? They are the group that is popularly called the Enterprise. They are in and outside [the] CIA. They are mostly Right Wing Republicans, but you will find a mix of Democrats, mercenaries, ex officio Mafia and opportunists within the group. They are CEOs, they are bankers, they are presidents, they own airlines, they own national television networks. They own six of the seven video documentary companies of Washington, DC and they do not give a damn about the law or the Constitution or the Congress or the Oversight committees except as something to be subverted and manipulated and lied to.

They abhor sunlight and love darkness. They deal in innuendo and character assassination, and planted stories, the incomplete thought and sentence. They burn and shred files if caught, they commit perjury, and when caught they have guaranteed sinecures with large US corporations.

If you let them, they will take over not only [the] CIA but the entire government and the world, cutting off dissent, free speech, a free media, and they will cut a deal with anyone, from [the] Mafia to Saddam Hussein, if it means more power and money. They stole $600 billion from the S & L's and then diverted our attention to the Iraqis. They are ripping off America at a rate never before seen in history. They flooded our country with drugs from Central America during the 1980s, cut deals with Haro in Mexico, Noriega in Panama, and the Medillin and Cali cartels, and Castro, and recently the Red Mafia in the KGB.

They ruin their detractors and they fear the truth. If they can, they will blackmail you. Sex, drugs, deals, whatever it takes."

–Former CIA officer and Iran-Contra whistleblower Bruce Hemmings,
circa 1990

CHAPTER 1

THE UNDERWORLD

OF SPIES AND CROOKS

At 2:30 in the afternoon on February 9th, 1942, a fire broke out onboard the *Normandie*, a ship that was then in the process of being converted into a troop transporter in New York City's harbor. As the flames roared, winter winds fanned the flames, spiraling the fire up, and then down onto the ship's top decks. Within hours, the *Normandie* began to lean to her port side, weighed down by the water that was being dumped onto the boat by fire crews. Soon, the ship capsized and an expensive, unprecedented salvage operation was mounted. Despite these efforts, repairing the ship was soon found to be too complicated and too costly, and the *Normandie* was scrapped in 1946.

Investigations into the destruction of the *Normandie* quickly revealed that the cause of the disaster had been incompetence and carelessness. Yet, nevertheless, rumors grew that it had been the work of German saboteurs, who were intent on disrupting America's early war efforts. Proponents of these theories argued that the alleged saboteurs sought to break down the country's logistical capabilities through attacks in ports and harbors as well as factories and other strategic, industrial locations. William B. Herlands, the then-New York Commissioner of Investigation, summed up the spirit of the times when he said, "We are faced with a grave national emergency.... A blackout was imposed over the ... waterfront area within the Third Naval district, which included New York and New Jersey. Many of our ships were being sunk by enemy submarines off the Atlantic Coast ... and the outcome of the war hung in the balance."[1]

Management and regulation of these critical harbors and coastlines was the responsibility of the Office of Naval Intelligence (ONI). An ONI inquiry was opened in May 1942 into potential saboteurs and Nazi agents operating in the ports and the possibility of U-boat movements off the east coast. The man tasked with overseeing this inquiry was C. Radcliff

Haffendon.[2] Several of the agents assigned to work under Haffendon had previously worked with Thomas E. Dewey, the US State Attorney who later served as governor of New York. Dewey was best known for his prosecution of organized crime, and through these contacts, Haffendon learned of the role played by gangsters and other criminal elements on the New York City waterfront. Dewey's chief of staff, attorney Frank Hogan, suggested to Haffendon and the ONI that they speak with a man named Joseph "Joe Socks" Lanza.

Lanza was officially a "business agent for the United Seafood Workers Union." He was also a mobster in his own right and was known as the "rackets boss of the Fulton Fish Market ... in downtown New York City."[3] Yet, compared to the stature of other criminal figures in the city, Lanza was a small-fry, and he knew it. As a result, he ended up telling the ONI that they would have better luck higher up the food chain. He suggested either Meyer Lansky, who controlled the longshoreman's union, or Frank Costello, a gambling figure with numerous interests throughout the waterfront. But to get to them, Lanza told Haffendon, he would need to first speak to Charles "Lucky" Luciano.

Luciano, at the time, was locked away in prison, having been put there by Thomas Dewey. A delicate series of negotiations were subsequently launched in what is now known as "Operation Underworld." This operation, which the government was forced to reluctantly acknowledge after decades of public denials, involved the recruitment of high-level organized crime figures for work with American intelligence services, justified by war-time necessity. Not long after Operation Underworld had been given the go-ahead, Luciano agreed to the ONI's requests, and his prison cell soon became a hub for meetings between him and his criminal associates, meetings in which they would coordinate counter-intelligence activities with the Navy.

Despite Operation Underworld's initial and relatively narrow objectives, the scope of the operation organically expanded. Before long, Luciano and his colleagues – Meyer Lansky, chief among them – were helping the ONI cultivate intelligence for the Allied invasion of Sicily. Lower ranking mob figures and immigrants were frequently brought to Haffendon's offices for questioning. Names and contact information for friendly Sicilians, many of whom were Mafia figures, were provided to ONI agents for use in the military campaign. While the resulting collaborations between the Mafia and the military on the beaches and in the villages of Sicily have slipped into legend, the legacy of Operation Underworld has endured and undeniably forever altered the United States of America, and beyond. Indeed, Operation Underworld was the beginning of the creation of a new underworld entirely, one built on the cooperation, if not outright symbiosis, between organized crime and American intelligence.

SHADOWY ALLIANCES

Lucky Luciano was born in Sicily in 1897 and arrived on American shores in 1906. At a young age, he formed his own gang, which offered protection to Jewish immigrants from Italian and Irish organized crime elements in exchange for small fees. This protection, unsurprisingly, was tantamount to extortion, and the money he accrued allowed him to begin expanding into other rackets – including, notably, prostitution. Early on, he met and formed an alliance with another young gangster named Frank Costello, an immigrant from Calabria, Italy. Together, the two consolidated their power by taking control of the numerous environs now considered typical of organized crime: prostitution, narcotics, and even organized labor in New York City's docks.

As their business expanded, so too did their revenue. Soon, Luciano and his cohorts were being propelled to the heights of power in New York City. Thomas Dewey once commented that Luciano's "business was far-flung and brought in a colossal revenue. This was estimated to be far, far in excess of $12 million a year."[4] Key to Luciano and Costello's operation was the fact that it had overcome the traditional bifurcation of organized crime into ethnic enclaves. For the first time, in Luciano's growing criminal empire, Italian, Jewish, and Irish criminal networks intermingled and cooperated with one another. However, this early cooperation lacked the cohesion and integration that the networks born out of Luciano's and Costello's enterprise would develop in the years to come.

Joining Luciano and Costello in their criminal enterprise was Meyer Lansky and his close friend, Benjamin "Bugsy" Siegel. Lansky was well-connected in Jewish mob circles, and he, along with Siegel, had amassed significant wealth during the Prohibition era. Lansky, whose long shadow is cast across the entire history of organized crime in the twentieth century, was something of a visionary. Various accounts paint him as the intellectual architect behind the multi-ethnic organized crime model that Luciano successfully pursued. Lansky was also instrumental in bringing mob groups into the world of gambling, helping set up casinos in the Caribbean that would be utilized to wash the money generated by their various vices and rackets. Perhaps most important

3

of all was that Lansky had also helped develop the use of a complex banking network, which he adopted in an effort to avoid the fate of Al Capone. After all, Capone had not been taken down for murder or extortion, but for tax evasion.

This Luciano-Costello-Lansky-Siegel alliance was the basis of what subsequently became known as the National Crime Syndicate. Far from the well-organized image of the Mafia often promoted by the media, the National Crime Syndicate operated loosely at best – and, according to some commentators, did not actually exist in any meaningful way. Such arguments might be going a step too far, although they are worth considering. The National Crime Syndicate might be best understood as a social network – a sprawling, faction-filled web of associations and organizations that either collaborated or competed, depending on the situation or the spoils.

In 1936, this emerging crime network took what, at first glance, appeared to be a major blow following the arrest and successful prosecution of Luciano by Thomas E. Dewey in a spectacular, if not sensational, trial. Luciano's apparent downfall came via an assault on New York City's prostitution rackets, which his organization firmly controlled. As Alfred McCoy summarizes, "Dewey's investigators felt that the forced prostitution charge would be more likely to offend public sensibilities and secure a conviction."[5] A handful of prostitutes who worked in Luciano's brothels testified against him, and a New York court quickly sentenced the gangster "to a thirty-to-fifty year jail term."

Dewey's role in this affair is quite interesting. Six years later, when he ran to secure the presidential nomination for the Republican Party, he joined forces with John Foster Dulles, the brother of Allen Dulles – best known for his role as the first civilian head of the CIA in the early years of the Cold War. Dulles, a member of the "internationalist" camp of American politics that typified the attitudes of the elite "Eastern Establishment," impressed upon Dewey the importance of overcoming the isolationist factions of the Republican Party.[6,7] What Dulles got in exchange for his steering of Dewey in pursuit of political power was his own rise through the ranks of the party, ultimately culminating in his service as President Dwight D. Eisenhower's Secretary of State.

Even more curious was an investment that Dewey made, during the 1950s, in an entity called the Mary Carter Paint Company, later renamed Resorts International. Mary Carter was controlled by the Crosby family, and its operations were overseen by the most practical-minded of the family's sons, James Crosby. Mary Carter was deeply tied to organized crime networks.[8,9] It worked closely in developing businesses in the Bahamas, hand-in-hand with a number of Meyer Lansky frontmen, while James' brother, Peter Crosby, was a notorious confidence man with an impressive roster of criminal contacts. It had also been widely rumored that Mary Carter was a CIA front company.[10]

THE OSS

Lurking in the background of Operation Underworld, which had seen the ONI directly recruit Luciano, was the Office of Strategic Services (OSS), the wartime forerunner to the CIA and America's first robust national intelligence organization. The precise role that the OSS played in the affair isn't exactly clear. According to George White, a notorious agent of the Federal Bureau of Narcotics who had been recruited into the OSS, he had been propositioned by an organized crime associate to enlist Luciano in exchange for a pardon – but this was a bridge too far. An alliance between the OSS and "a person of Luciano's reputation 'would be a very naive way of doing business' … White maintained that he felt it was outrageous to entertain … [the] proposition, 'even for the OSS' who were willing to do almost anything."[11]

White would make these statements in the course of Federal testimony, and, in all likelihood, he was lying to protect the OSS. According to Richard Harris Smith, an historian of the OSS, Earl Brennan, an OSS officer in Italy, was kept in the loop regarding negotiations between Luciano and the ONI.[12] Meanwhile, Assistant District Attorney Murray Gurfein, who handled the legal end of the Luciano negotiations, subsequently went to Europe to serve as a colonel in the OSS.

The OSS was many things, operating in many different theaters. In Europe, it ran a fairly unsuccessful paramilitary campaign. However, in the China-Burma-India theater, its military operations achieved remarkable results. When it came to spycraft, its supporters gushed with praise, while its detractors regarded the tales later woven by its veterans as worthy of skepticism. The OSS was frequently – and accurately – seen as a social club. While its ranks did boast a great many military officers and figures from other government agencies like the FBI and the FBN, its leadership and higher-ranking administrative posts tended to be secured by the sons of the country's wealthiest elite. In London, Madrid, Geneva, Paris and elsewhere, posts were held by members of the Mellon family of Pittsburgh, the family behind the Gulf Oil fortune. Heirs of the Morgan family also secured positions within the agency, as did members of the DuPont and the Vanderbilt families.

"Only the Rockefellers were conspicuously absent" from the OSS, writes Richard Harris Smith, adding that "Nelson [Rockefeller] headed his own agency, the Coordinator of Inter-American Affairs."[13] David Rockefeller, Nelson's brother, also reportedly ran his own intelligence apparatus during the war.[14]

The agency itself was something of brainchild – at least partially – of General William J. Donovan, a prominent New York City anti-trust lawyer and veteran of World War I. Along with figures like Dewey and Dulles, Donovan was the consummate "Eastern Establishment" insider. He maintained a deep preoccupation with organization and rationalization, which filtered into his work defending the trusts and combines that dotted the corporate landscape of his day. He was also a firm internationalist when it came to his political outlook. During the inter-war years, Donovan had acted as an agent for various corporate interests, and had even traveled to Russia on behalf of the Morgans to collect information on the developments of the Bolshevik Revolution.[15]

In the course of his wartime intelligence work, Donovan was first appointed by President Roosevelt to head the Office of the Coordinator of Information (COI), which was intended to help coordinate the scattered intelligence outfits and military organizations that communicated infrequently and cooperated even less. COI was the seed from which the OSS would later spring. Under Donovan's direction, it became a clearinghouse for military and political propaganda. This was in no small part thanks to Donovan's close friend, a British intelligence operative named William Stephenson.

Stephenson was the wartime head of a British intelligence unit in the United States, headquartered in New York City and known as the British Security Coordination (BSC). He reported to Stewart Menzies, who was then serving as the head of MI6. Menzies had tasked Stephenson with "establish[ing] relations on the highest possible level between the British SIS [the Secret Intelligence Service, another name for MI6] and the U.S. Federal Bureau of Investigation."[16] Stephenson and the BSC operated from an office located in Rockefeller Center's International Building, which was also the home of numerous, other BSC front organizations. Stephenson also worked closely with other British intelligence agencies, including MI6 itself and the Special Operations Executive (SOE), which had begun its life as Section D of MI6.

In agreement with Menzies' mandate, Stephenson developed a close working relationship with J. Edgar Hoover, who seemed to be enthusiastic about being a liaison to British intelligence on matters concerning the war in Europe (at this stage, the US had yet to enter the conflict). Reportedly, the BSC "provided the FBI with over 100,000 confidential reports," while Hoover kept the British in the loop with American reports on German naval movements and the like.[17] The relationship between Hoover and Stephenson would ultimately break down by 1941. Soon after, Stephenson began to cultivate William Donovan, who increasingly challenged Hoover's position as the sole conduit between the Americans and the British. When Donovan was appointed by Roosevelt as the Coordinator of Information – and subsequently formed the OSS – an intense bureaucratic struggle erupted between Hoover and his rivals. As will be discussed in greater detail in the next chapter, this struggle allegedly led Donovan to coordinate with organized crime kingpins, namely Meyer Lansky, to blackmail Hoover in an effort to bring him to heel.

Stephenson did more than simply cultivate Donovan. In 1940, he reported back to his handlers in England that "There is no doubt we can achieve infinitely more through Donovan than through any other individual.... He is very receptive ... and can be trusted to represent our needs in the right quarters and in the right way in the U.S.A."[18] Donovan's COI and OSS were, in all actuality, the offspring of these British-led efforts, and a great deal of the decisions Donovan made were influenced by figures tied to Stephenson's BSC. Before the COI was up and running, for example, Donovan conferred closely with Robert Sherwood, a playwright, ardent interventionist and close confidant of President Roosevelt. "On June 16th, 1941," writes Thomas Mahl, "Sherwood sent to Donovan a list of people he thought he could trust, 'for the work we discussed ... yesterday evening at your home.'"[19] At the time, Sherwood was working closely with the BSC – even sending them copies of speeches he had written for the president prior to Roosevelt receiving them.[20]

As efforts were undertaken to get the American intelligence apparatus up and running, the BSC undertook a propaganda campaign aimed at garnering support for such an institution. Mahl, in his book *Desperate Deception*, shows how BSC assets seeded the idea throughout the mass media, which in turn was circulated up to the heights of political power. One characteristic incident took place in May 1941, just a month prior to Donovan's meeting with Sherwood. It was on 9th of that May that:

Vincent Astor, FDR's friend and New York area coordinator of intelligence, sent the president a clipping from the *New York Herald Tribune* that was probably a plant to build the consensus for voices calling for the plan British intelligence wanted. The *Herald Tribune* … was BSC's favorite outlet for planted articles. Moreover, the putative author, George Fieling Eliot, was a devoted British sympathizer, one of the most influential people in the BSC front Fight for Freedom, and a favorite vehicle for planted articles. Citing the threat from fifth columnists and enemy agents, Eliot pointed out with alarm at the lack of a coordinator for the FBI, ONI, and G-2 intelligence.[21]

The idea of a "fifth column" was a prime component of BSC propaganda, and would later be adopted by the OSS itself. It was used to attack isolationist holdouts against American entry into the war, and was also used to generate fear and create an atmosphere of distrust among the general public. The term originated during the course of the early phase of the Spanish Civil War of the 1930s, and was used to describe something like a domestic military-in-waiting. The fifth column was purported to be composed of enemy agents and their sympathizers, with a mandate towards sabotage and other violent activities. According to Mahl, one of the strongest promoters of the notion of a Nazi fifth column active in America was a Chicago journalist and close associate of Donovan named Edgar Ansel Mowrer – who was subsequently identified as an asset of British intelligence.[22]

The fifth column, however, was simply an exaggerated threat. Axis sabotage efforts within the United States did occur, but were limited and ultimately ineffectual. Yet, this reality didn't matter to the BSC and its American allies, as the promotion of fifth column fears had a legitimizing function for their activities. It formed the very justification and popular base of support for the creation and expansion of the emerging, organized intelligence apparatus.

It also spawned events like Operation Underworld. After all, it was the specter of fifth column activity that had first prompted the collaboration between the ONI and organized crime elements. Even more incredibly, it seems that the legitimization gained by intelligence services through BSC propaganda ultimately benefited these criminal networks as well. At the war's end, naval intelligence began a campaign to have Luciano released from prison – and at the beginning of 1946, the very man who had put Luciano away, Thomas Dewey, commuted the mobster's sentence in exchange for his deportation to Italy. In the year or two that followed, numerous other gangsters – perhaps as many as a hundred – were deported and joined him.

Luciano's deportation was the beginning of an effort to cement in place a powerful organized crime network that was transnational in scope and wedded to the American intelligence services. Indeed, even though Luciano was no longer physically in the United States, he and his ilk continued to guide organized criminal activities from abroad while also establishing new rackets during their exile in the "Old World." Deported alongside Luciano, for instance, was Frank Coppola, the powerful Detroit mob boss who had been something of a mentor to Jimmy Hoffa, the mob-linked head of the Teamsters union (the use of the Teamsters' pension fund for organized crime-linked financing recurs throughout this book). By the 1960s, Hoffa and the Teamsters were working closely alongside the CIA, particularly on efforts to assassinate Fidel Castro, who had seized many of the mob's casinos during the course of the Cuban revolution. Coppola himself was linked to American intelligence: he "was said to have been behind a 1947 May Day massacre in Sicily, allegedly financed by former OSS chief William Donovan, in which eight people were killed and thirty-three wounded; 498 people, mostly left-wingers, were killed in 1948 alone."[23]

Also deported was Silvestro "Silver Dollar Sam" Carolla, a Sicily-born mobster who had arrived in New Orleans, Louisiana, in the early 1900s and had become the city's boss. He was particularly close to the interests of New York City organized crime. In the 1930s, Carolla had worked with Costello and Luciano to provide New Orleans with slot machines under the watchful eye of their ally, Huey Long. The gambling operation was so successful that it soon attracted the attention of Lansky, and plans were put in motion to establish "centers of communication and money laundering operations to be used by the underworld, on a national scale, in New Orleans."[24] This included the opening of "three big Las Vegas-style gambling casinos" across Louisiana, and the introduction of a new, rising star in the underworld into this partnership.

That rising star was Carlos Marcello. Soon, Marcello was managing the whole of the Louisiana casino operation. When Carolla was deported to Sicily, Marcello was tapped to take his place – and so began the reign of one of the most powerful crime bosses of the twentieth century. "... [I]t was said," wrote John Davis in his book *Mafia Kingfish*, "Frank Costello sent his blessing from New York, and Sam Carolla sent word from Palermo that he approved Carlos' selection as caretaker-boss until he, Silver Dollar Sam, returned from exile."[25]

In Italy, Carolla linked up with Luciano in developing what was reported by American law enforcement to be a large-scale drug network. As will be discussed in Chapter 3, this network spanned the Middle East, Europe, and the United States, and one particularly well-oiled pipeline of this network – one that connected Lebanon to Sicily to Marseilles – was infamously known as the "French Connection." Curiously, Carolla and Luciano turned up in Mexico in 1948 to oversee the development of a drug smuggling operation in that country. While Mexico had its own domestic drug production, it was also a key transshipment point for the flow of heroin, refined from opium produced in the East. Here, we again find the fingerprints of cooperation between intelligence services and organized crime.

THE DRUG CONNECTION AND "OPERATION X"

The story of China's Green Gang is complicated, partially due to the mixing of fact with rumor and legend. Yet, it is undeniable that their rise was a consequence of the rapid transformations that shook Chinese society in the early twentieth century. However, the Green gang itself began long before the twentieth century dawned, originating as a secret society with roots stretching back to Luoism, a folk religion that followed the teachings of Buddhist mystic Luo Menghong. During the late 1700s, this particular branch of Luoism had become a powerful force among boatmen whose trade was the transport of grain and other foodstuffs. Fearful of their growing power, authorities stepped in to suppress this network, driving it underground. Once bitterly ensconced in the margins of society, these Luoists began engaging in smuggling and formed alliances with other smuggling groups. Soon, they consolidated their power and became a formidable force in the world of crime.

Under the leadership of Du Yuesheng, the Green Gang helped bring to power the Kuomintang (KMT), later known as the Nationalist Chinese, under the direction of Chiang Kai-Shek.[26] Chiang himself was not a member of the Green Gang, but his political mentor and protector, General Ch'en Ch'i-mei, had been. Between the 1920s and 1930s, the Green Gang was fully integrated with the government of Shanghai, and became a primary source of power for the KMT. They "relied on the Green Gang to conduct counter-espionage activities and gather political intelligence," and called upon the resources of the organization to suppress trade unionists and communists.[27]

The Green Gang financed its activities through the cultivation and sale of opium – an activity that was fully sanctioned by Chiang and the KMT. Prior to the KMT's rise to power, Chinese opium production was unorganized, distributed among many different warring figures. Under Chiang, however, a "suppression" was carried out with the ostensible goal of wiping out the opium trade in the name of public health. Behind the scenes, however, the KMT was doing quite the opposite: the "suppression" of opium production was actually an integrated effort to centralize it, placing production, distribution and ultimately control of the substance in the hands of a joint KMT-Green Gang monopoly.[28]

Support for the KMT opium monopoly came from Western modernizers – including the Rockefeller Foundation, which had set up shop in China during the 1910s with the creation of the China Medical Board.[29] Through this apparatus, the Rockefeller Foundation undertook efforts to promote "modern science," develop medical education programs, and set up hospitals. It is likely that the foundation's support for opium monopolization was intricately bound up with their health crusade, since opium had important, wide ranging medicinal applications.

At the same time, it was also part of a larger tendency among internationalists like the Rockefellers to seek the regulation and control of the global drug trade. After the First World War, the nascent League of Nations formed an Advisory Committee on the Traffic of Opium and Other Dangerous Drugs. It worked closely with the Rockefeller Foundation's International Health Board, the "parent" of the China Medical Board. The overarching imperative of the League's efforts for global drug regulation was to rationalize the production of opium and other precursors and to consolidate drug refining and distribution within a series of select major pharmaceutical corporations.

Under Chiang's leadership, China simultaneously kowtowed to the League's initiatives while using the monopolization drive to cement itself at the center of drug production for both the criminal underworld and the "legitimate" overworld. A full-blown narco-state was in the process of being formed, as opium cultivation came to be the central focus of the government's revenue-raising programs. As Jonathan Marshall noted:

> "In the central provinces of China, especially in Hubei and Hunan, nearly every government organization has come to depend on opium revenue for maintenance," observed one expert. "Even law courts, Tangpus (Kuomintang organizations), and schools are

no exception." Thus in one locality, authorities charged one picul of opium $320 for general taxes, $32 for Communist suppression, $3.20 for national revenue, $1.50 for the Chamber of Commerce, $2.50 for Special Goods (opium) Association fees, $2.50 for the Hsih-tsun Girl's School, and $7.00 for protection fees. Later, highway maintenance and more school taxes were added. When the opium finally reached Hankou, monopoly authorities added another $920 tax. The original cost of the opium was only $400.[30]

It was in this context that American organized crime figures arrived on China's shores and began to organize an intensely lucrative global narcotics trading network. Among the first was Arnold Rothstein, who acted as a mentor to Lansky, Luciano, and Costello. He dispatched a series of frontmen to China: Sidney Stajer, Jacob Katzenberg, and George Uffner.[31] Uffner would later be described by Federal investigators as a longtime friend of Costello, while Katzenberg was a high-level figure in New York City's Jewish crime syndicates. These syndicates, according to Alfred McCoy, "controlled much of New York's heroin distribution." Katzenberg – himself a Lansky flunky as much as a Rothstein frontman – was involved with a secret heroin processing laboratory in the city, which was refining opium flowing from Asia.[32]

Hans Derks, in his encyclopedic *History of the Opium Problem: The Assault on the East, 1600-1950,* suggests that the connections between American organized crime and the KMT/Green Gang-dominated Chinese opium trade more than likely involved the complicity of Western – predominantly Anglo-American – economic interests in the region.[33] He singles out in particular the powerful Sassoon family.

Nicknamed the "Rothschilds of the East," the Sassoons had emerged as economic administrators in Iraq before organizing one of the dominant opium trading complexes in the East. It is said, writes Derks, "that 'one fifth of all opium brought into China was shipped on the Sassoon fleet.' Thanks to opium they became not only the wealthiest family in India, but also the largest real estate dealers in Shanghai."[34] The family also became integrated into the world of oil: they invested heavily, at various times, in Britain's Burmah Oil and the Anglo-Iranian Oil Company (a subsidiary of Burmah that eventually became British Petroleum), among others.

During the 1800s, the Sassoons competed for dominance of the opium trade with Jardine-Matheson, one of the great Anglo-Hong Kong trading houses that has been firmly controlled by the prominent Keswick family. Over time, the interests of the Sassoons and the Keswicks intermingled and became part of a vast network winding its way through Hong Kong, Shanghai, and elsewhere. This is by no means ancient history: as late as 2013, the *Financial Times* reported that Lord James Sassoon, having just finished a stint serving as the Commercial Secretary to the Treasury in the government of UK Prime Minister David Cameron, became an executive director of the Jardine-Matheson board.[35]

These dynastic-corporate structures not only influenced the shape of the international drug trade during the twentieth century, but also the evolution of Western intelligence services during and after World War II. Take, for example, the offspring of Henry Keswick, who served as one of the most powerful heads of Jardine Matheson and the controller of numerous affiliated entities (such as the Hong Kong and Shanghai Banking Corporation, the Hong Kong & Whampoa Company, and the Shanghai Municipal Council). Two of Henry's sons, John Henry Keswick and William Johnston "Tony" Keswick, served in the Chinese theater as part of the UK's Special Operations Executive. In addition to the SOE, John Henry Keswick served as the personal aide to Lord Mountbatten, the Supreme Allied Commander of the Southern Asia Theater.[36]

Tony Keswick, meanwhile, crossed paths with Federal Bureau of Narcotics (FBN) veteran and OSS operative Garland Williams. When the OSS was still being organized and efforts were underway to expand its paramilitary capacities, Williams was dispatched by Preston Goodfellow – "a former Hearst executive and publisher of *Brooklyn Eagle*" who had become William Donovan's special assistant – to meet with the SOE officer. "After meeting the British spymaster Keswick," writes Douglas Valentine, "Williams returned to Washington with the SOE's training manuals and helped establish OSS training schools in Maryland and Virginia."[37]

After the war came to an end, Tony Keswick returned to the world of corporate affairs, taking up a position running one of the family's correspondent companies in London. He also served, for a time, as a governor of the Hudson's Bay Company in Canada. As discussed in the next chapter, the Hudson's Bay Company was central to the rise of the Bronfman family, who have long straddled the murky line between "legitimate" corporate enterprises and the criminal underworld. In turn, the Bronfmans, as will be illustrated at length in this book, would be important to the rise of the network that later enabled the illicit activities of Jeffrey Epstein.

Through his acquisition of the SOE manuals from Keswick, Garland Williams played an essential role that paralleled – and was almost certainly framed by – the higher level cooperation between William Donovan and William Stephenson. At the same time, Williams appears to have operated at the intersection of the American intelligence services, still in their infancy, and the networks of American organized crime.

In his book *Deep Politics and the Death of JFK*, Peter Dale Scott theorizes that there existed a formation that he provisionally dubs "Operation X." Williams, and other veterans of the FBN that were brought into the OSS and the CIA, are identified as players in this apparatus:

> …the intelligence-mob collaboration established with Operation Underworld did not end after World War II. On the contrary, postwar narcotics operations overseas were subordinated to anti-Communist activities; and they were used as a cover for ongoing use of mob assets, above all drug traffickers, around the world. In developing these post-war mob contacts, White and his FBN associates, notably his former supervisor Garland Williams, and his protégé Charles Siragusa, even while formally back in the FBN hierarchy, 'functioned as a counterintelligence unit, attached to the CIA and, at times, the Army'.… In the 1950s and 1960s it would appear that the FBN systematically subordinated the prosecution of drug cases to a second, hidden agenda, the use of traffickers as agents against communism.[38]

One example that Scott cites is the "selective arrests made by George White in a 1959 heroin case involving the anti-Communist (and pro-Kuomintang) Hip Sing tong or gang."[39] White, an agent for the FBN and OSS who was a contractor for the CIA after the war, had busted a heroin ring operating out of San Francisco that tracked back to these pro-KMT gangster elements – and then subsequently identified the heroin as originating from Chinese Communists.[40] Interestingly, White himself had a history with the Hip Sing tongs. "In 1936 he infiltrated the notorious Hip Sing Tong brotherhood of Seattle by masquerading as a drug dealer," leading to a massive sting operation that nabbed some thirty drug smugglers and their associates.[41]

It is worth saying a bit more about George White, who was no stranger to courting the services of organized crime figures to bolster the early American intelligence apparatus. The research carried out by the late Hank Albarelli has shown that White cultivated a protégé named Pierre Laffite, who he had recruited into the CIA as a "special employee" in June 1952.[42] Twenty years prior, Lafitte worked in France for Jean Voyatzis, "the greatest importer of manufactured Chinese opium into Europe" and a figure of considerable interest to the FBN.[43] Later, Lafitte turned up in Cuba in the company of Amleto Battisti y Lora, a Corsican expat who had partnered with Meyer Lansky in a Havana hotel. Battisti, according to a 1955 FBI memo, was "for many years ... known unofficially as the numbers king of Havana."[44]

When White brought Lafitte to the CIA, the FBN agent was himself being recruited by Sidney Gottlieb, a chemist who was working at the Agency's Office of Technical Service. There, Gottlieb oversaw the CIA's research into potential "truth drugs," which in time expanded into a sweeping inquiry that dealt with the effects of drugs, shock therapy and sensory deprivation, hypnosis and even more esoteric currents on the human mind. The most famous of these programs, MK-ULTRA, saw the CIA become the largest consumer of LSD, which it used to experiment on witting and unwitting subjects. The subjects included soldiers, patients in psychiatric hospitals, prisoners (sometimes organized crime figures), and private citizens. Under Gottlieb's directions, CIA-run "safehouses" were established in New York City and San Francisco, where unsuspecting people were dosed with hallucinogenic substances while being monitored from behind two-way mirrors.

Gottlieb was impressed by White's street smarts and his inclinations towards the other side of the law – traits that were necessary for the covert drug program. As one of Gottlieb's Agency employees later stated, "We were Ivy League, white middle class. ... We were naive, totally naive about this, and he felt pretty expert. He knew the whores, the pimps, the people who brought in the drugs.... He was a pretty wild man."[45] Under the alias of "Morgan Hall," White maintained a safehouse in Greenwich Village, New York City, where he supplied unsuspecting people with LSD and other substances. In order to lure people into his web, he deployed false life stories – "He posed alternatively as a merchant seaman or a bohemian artist, and consorted with a vast array of underworld characters, all of whom were involved in vice, including drugs, prostitution, gambling and pornography."[46]

In 1955, Harry J. Anslinger, the commissioner of the FBN, transferred White to San Francisco to fill a vacant post as the FBN district supervisor for the city. This was by no means the end of his work with Gottlieb and the CIA. Instead, he was granted control of MK-ULTRA Subproject 42 – or, as White called it, "Operation Midnight Climax." Midnight Climax involved a safehouse, much like the one set up in New York City, which was then decked out with electronic surveillance equipment. Prostitutes were then enlisted, who would lure unsuspecting clients back to the "pad," where they would then be slipped LSD. John Gittinger, a Harvard psychologist who was on the CIA payroll – best known perhaps for developing the Personality Assessment System – later admitted in Congressional testimony that the Agency "was interested in the combination of certain drugs with sex acts. We looked at the various pleasure positions used by prostitutes and others.... Some of the women, the professionals, we used, were very adept at this practice."[47]

White wasn't alone in obscuring the role of the KMT in the drug trade. This was also the *modus operandi* of Harry Anslinger, the FBN commissioner who served as boss to both George White and Garland Williams. Although Anslinger – like Donovan – was a bitter enemy of J. Edgar Hoover, he rode the rising tide of McCarthyism in the US, and identified China as the number one threat to public order.[48] The Chinese Communist Party, he claimed in the media and in official FBN reports, was overseeing vast opium fields and had trained thousands of agents to distribute heroin within the West. Per Anslinger, Chinese opium production totaled "more than 4,000 tons ... a year," with the "profits from the smuggling [being] used to finance the activities of the Communist Party and the obtain strategic raw materials."[49]

Importantly, Anslinger did not have any agents located in Asia in the post-war years, with FBN posting taking place at a fairly late date in 1962.

The claims made by Anslinger in the 1950s were sourced from intelligence provided by the KMT itself and, in the early years, by the intelligence apparatus of General Douglas MacArthur's military command in post-war Japan. Overseeing this intelligence web was MacArthur's protégé, a fascist sympathizer named General Charles Willoughby. Willoughby, as will be discussed in Chapter 5, would later become a player in the so-called China Lobby, a domestic political pressure network that supported the KMT and hardline Cold War politics.

It is doubtful that the misdirection being deployed by Anslinger, White, and others in their milieu was for propagandistic purposes alone. Scott's "Operation X" thesis suggests a dual function. First, it bolstered Cold War propaganda efforts, which roughly followed the same template as the "fifth column" propaganda of the OSS during World War II. Second, it helped hide the roles of certain individuals, organizations, and networks that worked in tandem with Western intelligence services, militaries, governments, and businesses in the global drug trade. During this period, investigations into organized crime in America were soft-pedaled, if they took place at all, in part thanks to coercion and blackmail, particularly the blackmailing of FBI director J. Edgar Hoover. This also worked to obscure the role of the KMT in the drug trade due to the historical unity of American organized crime with Asian drug traffickers, forged in the inter-war period.

There is the stark possibility that this unity was maintained, well into the post-war epoch, through the efforts of American intelligence services themselves. This would result from the long-term effects of the OSS apparatus that had been set up in the China-India-Burma theater during the war. That apparatus had been concentrated around a powerful unit called Detachment 101 (which, incidentally, had been set up with the aid of Garland Williams). Many of the most notorious intelligence operatives and soldiers who dotted the landscape of the late 20th century can trace their roots back to this OSS theater – and many of them will appear throughout this book. Those who served there included E. Howard Hunt, later a CIA coup-master who achieved infamy during Watergate. Another was John Singlaub, a major player in the Iran-Contra affair. There was also Paul Helliwell, soon to become one of the architects of convoluted shadow banking strategies and a primary node between the worlds of intelligence and organized crime.

In 1943, William R. Peers – who would later lead the CIA's first training program – became the head of OSS Detachment 101 after his predecessor, Carl F. Eifler, was injured. Peers subsequently became the head of all OSS operations in the China-Burma-India theater, and personally oversaw commando operations carried out by KMT troops against Chinese Communist forces. Peers later reflected on his OSS years in an autobiography and, while discussing payment issues needed to finance the OSS' operations in Asia, made a startling disclosure:

> Simply stated, paper currency and even silver were often useless, as there was nothing to buy with money; opium, however, was the form of payment everybody used. Not to use it as a means of barter would spell an end to our operations. Opium was available to agents who used it for a number of reasons, from obtaining information to buying their own escape. Any indignation felt was removed by the difficulty of the effort ahead. If opium could be useful in achieving victory, the pattern was clear. We would use opium.[50]

The OSS activities in Burma would lay the groundwork for the country to subsequently act as an essential node in early Cold War activities against Communist elements in Asia. Importantly, after Chinese Communists drove the KMT out of the mainland and into Taiwan, Burma became one of their main outposts. There, the CIA organized a secret army with prospective plans to stage an invasion of China. "Although the KMT was to fail in its military operations," writes Alfred McCoy, "it succeeded in monopolizing and expanding ... the opium trade."[51] He continues:

> The KMT shipped the opium harvests to northern Thailand, where they were sold to General Phao Siyanan of the Thai police, a CIA client. The CIA had promoted the Phao-KMT partnership to secure a rear area for the KMT, but this alliance soon became a critical factor in the growth of Southeast Asia's narcotics traffic. With CIA support, the KMT remained in Burma until 1961, when a Burmese army offensive drove them into Laos and Thailand. By this time, however, the Kuomintang had already used their control over the tribal populations to expand Shan state opium production by almost 500 percent – from less than 80 tons after World War II to an estimated 300-400 tons by 1962.[52]

The CIA's Burma-Thailand support for the KMT was code-named "Operation Paper."[53] One of the architects of the operation was a close associate of Thailand's General Phao named Willis Bird – later nicknamed Mr. Opium. Bird, during World War II, had served with OSS in the Burma-China-India theater. After the end of the conflict, he remained in the region as a supplier to the Thai military and police. Whether or not Bird was an on-the-books asset of the CIA isn't clear, though he certainly was a middleman for moving supplies that had been obtained via Agency financing.

These supplies arrived in Thailand by way of a company called South East Asia Supply Corporation, most frequently referred to simply as SEA Supply.[54] Willis Bird acted as SEA Supply's Bangkok office manager under the direction of Sherman Joost – a veteran of OSS Detachment 101. SEA Supply was not set up in Thailand, however. The business was instead registered in Miami, Florida by OSS-veteran-turned lawyer and banker Paul Helliwell. At the same time that Helliwell was handling the legal end of SEA Supply's activities, he was also acting as consul for the Thai government in the US. In this capacity, he was closely linked to General Phao and the network of politicians who supported him.[55]

SEA Supply worked closely with Civil Air Transport (CAT), the CIA's first proprietary airline. The roots of CAT were planted during the Second World War, when Claire Chennault organized the Flying Tigers, a volunteer aviation unit set up to provide support for the KMT in China in their fight against Japan. With ranks drawn from the US military, the Flying Tigers trained at bases in Burma, which acted as a logistics hub for their airlift. Chennault had long standing ties to the KMT: since the late 1930s, Chennault had served as a military advisor to Chiang Kai-Shek and his brother-in-law, the powerful Nationalist Chinese banker and diplomat T.V. Soong.

Besides his links to the KMT leadership and to the US military, Chennault maintained an impressive array of contacts. His lawyer was Thomas Corcoran, a top advisor in President Roosevelt's New Deal brain trust. Corcoran was close to Helliwell, and both worked together to promote Chennault's aviation plans when the war ended. Back in America, Chennault fell in with the so-called China Lobby, the network of politicians, businessmen, and other players who lobbied for support for the KMT as the only viable group who could oppose the Chinese communists. He set up and managed an impressive airlift of "American relief supplies in China" – with the supply flight contracts going to Chennault, of course.[56] Central to this effort was the 1946 creation of a new airline called Civil Air Transport that Chennault had co-founded with Whiting Willauer.[57] Willauer would go on to be US ambassador to Costa Rica and was also later involved in the 1954 CIA-led coup in Guatemala. When the KMT retreated to the island of Formosa (now Taiwan), Chennault used CAT to run arms and medical supplies to National Chinese fighters.

CAT was brought into the world of special operations thanks to the efforts of Helliwell. He had brought Chennault and the aviation company to the attention of Frank Wisner, then the head of a covert body called the Office of Policy Coordination (OPC). Within several years, the OPC was incorporated into the CIA, cementing in place a militarized command structure governing the dark arts of the clandestine services. By 1950, CAT was a full-fledged CIA proprietary airline, operating under the auspices of a holding company set up by the Agency called Airdale Corp [58] Later, Airdale Corp was renamed Pacific Corp, and CAT would become Air America.

Air America was the CIA's premier airline, and remained active from the 1950s into the 1970s. It was finally dissolved in the wind-down of the Vietnam War, though many of its assets were sold off and absorbed into a CIA-linked firm called Evergreen International Aviation. Meanwhile, several Flying Tigers pilots went on to create the air freighter firm Flying Tiger Line, a major commercial cargo airline that also operated military contract services and engaged in covert operations. Flying Tiger Line would later have a major presence at the Rickenbacker airfield near Lockbourne, Ohio. CAT's later incarnation, Southern Air Transport, would relocate there in the early 1990s, a few years after Flying Tiger Line was absorbed into Federal Express. The airline's relocation was thanks, in part, to Jeffrey Epstein and had chiefly relocated to manage cargo for Leslie Wexner's The Limited (see chapter 17).

Connections to organized crime appear in nearly every corner of this web. Take, for instance, Margaret Chung, an "attending physician" for Chennault's Flying Tigers. A member of the Hip Sing tong, she made "frequent trips" to Mexico City in the 1940s in the company of Virginia Hill – an inside player in organized crime circles with close ties to the likes of Bugsy Siegel and Meyer Lanksy.[59] During this period, Hill "became intimate with a number of Mexico's top politicians, army officers, diplomats, and police officials," which likely facilitated the activities of her friends in the underworld.[60] Hill was also particularly close to the Chicago Outfit during this time, the significance of which will become clear shortly.

As mentioned above, Mexico had become an important base of operations for the drug smuggling network of Costello and Carolla. Given their ties to Meyer Lansky, it is certainly possible that Hill's own appearance in Mexico was connected to these earlier activities. Importantly, Mexico had also become a vital transshipment point for the KMT's own drug trafficking during this same period. Does the presence of Margaret Chung alongside Hill, then, suggest that the KMT's drug operations in Mexico directly intersected with those of Lansky and his milieu? Given the history of Lansky associates working with the KMT and the Green Gang, it is certainly possible, if not likely.

The structure of this apparently intricate network can be developed further when considering that Civil Air Transport, one of the successors to the Flying Tigers, was, by 1960, flying in and out of Laotian territory controlled by the Hmong tribesmen. The tribesmen were a major supplier of opium destined for refinement into heroin (the CIA's covert support for the Hmong is discussed in Chapter 5). Airstrips for CAT's flights were built by Bird and Sons, a "private engineering firm" controlled by "the CAT representative in Bangkok," William H. Bird.[61] Bird was the cousin of Willis Bird of the OSS and of Helliwell's SEA Supply.

There was also the case of Helliwell himself. By this point, he had become a prominent player in Republican politics. He was, for example, a delegate for Dwight Eisenhower as he strove to clinch the Republican Party presidential nomination. Helliwell had also been a leader in the Florida chapter of Citizens for Eisenhower. That chapter was subsequently accused of "being taken over by professionals who refuse[d] to work with the regular GOP leaders and who are accountable to no one for the finances they collect."[62] Members of this cadre of operators aside from Helliwell included Curt Landon and James Guilmartin. Together, these three men were tightly-connected co-conspirators amassing unaccountable power:

> Landon is a substantial client of Helliwell's law firm; Guilmartin is a partner of Helliwell's and Guilmartin is married to Landon's daughter. We find these men closely allied by business and marriage who, if their plan succeeds, will find themselves in a position of enormous power in Florida and responsible to no recognized Republican authority.[63]

While Helliwell was making waves in the world of politics and in the world of covert operations, he was also making a foray into the world of Florida insurance. He was the consul for, and later secretary, then chairman, of American Bankers Life Assurance, located in Miami. Importantly, Helliwell utilized the offices of American Bankers Life as the hub for many of his activities. The Florida Thai consulate, for instance, was located at the same address as the insurance company – as was SEA Supply.

In addition to this important CIA linkage, American Bankers Life also shared important connections – one of which was Helliwell himself – with Miami National Bank. Founded with a loan from the Teamster pension fund, Miami National "was identified in 1969 as having served between 1963 and 1967 as a conduit through which 'hot' syndicate money was exported by Meyer Lansky's couriers and 'laundered' through the interlocking Exchange and Investment Bank in Geneva."[64] The importance of Lansky's Geneva bank will be discussed in Chapter 3.

Helliwell's ventures, and specifically his banking endeavors, were probably related to the flow of heroin that originated as KMT opium and then passed through the hands of American organized crime figures. In his book *Hot Money and the Politics of Debt*, offshore banking expert R.T. Naylor writes that "South Florida is ... a major refuge for Latin American flight money, which pours into the Florida banking system and local real estate. The flight capital-into-real estate business is an old one. In the 1950s and 1960s, Kuomintang money from Thailand and Burma came via Hong Kong to be washed in Lansky-related property firms."[65]

THE SUPERMOB

The global drug trade is a massive business, and the offshore banking system that enables it is even bigger. Although most imagine drug networks, their controllers and their users as existing on the fringes of society, in reality, the massive amounts of capital that result from the production and distribution of illicit drugs occupy a central place within the global economic system. Consider a statement made in 2009 by Antonio Maria Costa, who was then the head of the UN Office on Drugs and Crime. According to Costa, proceeds from the drug trade were an important source of liquidity for cash-starved banks at the height of the 2008 economic crisis. The amounts absorbed by the banking system were enough to prevent some banks from collapsing: "Inter-bank loans were funded by money that originated from the drugs trade and other illegal activities.... There were signs that some banks were rescued that way."[66]

In 2000, *Le Monde Diplomatique* suggested that the global drug trade was a billion dollar a year business – an incredibly low estimate. Seventeen years later, the Global Financial Integrity Project estimated that worldwide drug trafficking revenue stood somewhere between $426 to $652 billion annually.[67] In the same report, the overall revenue of illicit activities was posited to be $2.2 trillion. The UN Office on Drugs and Crime, meanwhile, estimated that money laundering activities – encompassing the washing of illicit drug revenue and more – make up anywhere from 2 to 5% of global GDP, at around $800 billion to $2 trillion.[68] This, again, is almost certainly a conservative estimate. In 2012, $21-$32 trillion was estimated to be sloshing through the offshore banking system.[69] This number would have only increased in the wake of the earlier 2008 financial crisis.

When such immense sums of money are being generated, it isn't left to idle in bank accounts in the Caymans, Bermuda, the City of London, or wherever. The end destination of a money washing process is to transform dirty money into seemingly-clean investment capital. Journalist Michael Ruppert, in his book *Crossing the Rubicon*, cites cases where companies have tapped illicit money flows in order to borrow money at a lower interest rate than they would receive from major banking institutions.[70] The conversion of dirty or hot money into "credit capital" (capital that begins as a line of credit issued by a lending institution) is made easier by bank secrecy laws in tax havens, which makes it possible for legitimate and illegitimate pools of capital to intermingle freely.

Catherine Austin Fitts and Chris Sanders have gone even further by suggesting that there is a positive correlation between the upwards trajectory of stock market performance and the consistent ballooning of the drug trade. While there are a number of factors that impact stock market performance – such as easy money injected into the economy by the central banks of various countries – Fitts and Sanders write that:

> It may seem strange to think of a positive correlation between narcotics trafficking and the stock market, but consider ... the proceeds of crime need to find a way into legitimate, that is, legal, channels or they are worthless to the holders. If one further imagines that the banking system earns a fee of one per cent for handling this flow (rather low considering that money laundering is a seller's market) then the profits for banks from this activity are of the order of $5 to $10 billion. Applying Citigroup's current stock market multiple of 15 or so to this yields a market capitalisation of anywhere from $65 to $115 billion. One can thus readily see the importance of the illegal drug trade to the financial services industry.[71]

Another tactic for washing money is the "capital-into-real estate" operations that Naylor referred to in relation to KMT drug money flows in Florida. Indeed, it seems that the explosive growth of the world economy in the decades following World War II opened up countless investment opportunities where the funds from drugs and other sources of capital for organized crime would be socked away. It was this period, after all, that saw the great ballooning of real estate markets and the high tech industry, along with the modern tourism industry that spawned everything from destination resorts in "exotic" locales to the sparkling lights of Las Vegas casinos.

In his book *Power Shift*, Kirkpatrick Sale argues that the **post-war** era was characterized by a rising "Southern Rim" that came to confront the traditional seat of American economic and political power in the northeast. The Southern Rim was made of the southern states, portions of the Midwest and the Sunbelt – a large expanse that stretched from Florida to California. The Rim's ascendancy, he argues, was connected to the opening up of vast real estate opportunities, related in part to tourism and retirement, to the oil and gas industries, and to the delirious growth of defense-related industries under the new Cold War paradigm.

Sale suggests that organized crime, so often associated with the American northeast, found a remarkable range of new opportunities in the Southern Rim, thus propelling these networks to previously inconceivable heights of power and influence. The blossoming trade of opium and heroin, clearly spurred and protected by the CIA, fit snuggly into these series of developments. Sale writes that:

> Smuggling – especially of heroin, in which the trade grew steadily more lucrative after the opening up of Asia's golden triangle in 1948 – tilted to the South, taking advantage of the enormous Rim coastline and the porous Mexican border, along which whole networks of "Latin connections" and "Mexican connections" were developed.... And everywhere in the booming Rim, millions of dollars were placed in legitimate investments, chiefly in those high-risk operations where venture capital is hard to come by – oil exploration, for example, and land speculation – and in those large-scale businesses where sizable amounts of capital are necessary – corporate farming, for example, technological manufacturing, and, above all, real estate development.[72]

The observations and arguments made by Kirkpatrick Sale, Michael Ruppert, and Catherine Austin Fitts neatly dovetail with the complicated yet organized history detailed by Gus Russo in his book *Supermob*. The term "Supermob," per Russo, refers to a close-knit circle of Jewish and Italian mobsters and businessmen who arose in the corruption-ridden corridors of Chicago and who then installed themselves in California and elsewhere. What makes the "Supermob" unique is that it was particularly stark and fairly unmasked example of how criminal networks, political power, and "legitimate" commercial activity mixed together in the period of explosive economic and cultural growth in the wake of World War II.

A key player in this group was Jake Avery, who started off as a political fixer in Chicago's 24th Ward. He acted as a precinct captain, and managed to swing the dominant political orientation of the ward from the Republican to the Democratic Party. He was later praised by Franklin D. Roosevelt for his efforts to make his district "the best Democratic ward in the country."[73] By 1928, Avery was the ward chairman – and a budding associate of organized crime. He forged an alliance with the gangster Al Capone, and the two worked together to elevate Anton Cermak to the mayor's office.

On the business side of things, one of Avery's closest associates was Henry Crown, who later became a major figure in the Hilton hotel company, the dominant controlling interest in the major defense contractor General Dynamics, and the owner of the Empire State Building. He subsequently sold the iconic building to Lawrence Wien, a New York City lawyer and real estate developer who was helping manage the assets of the Desert Inn in Las Vegas, which was controlled by mobster Moe Dalitz and, as will be noted in Chapter 4, tied up with the affairs of the infamous lawyer Roy Cohn.

Crown was also in business with David G. Baird, who ran a trio of foundations closely tied to organized crime and that moved CIA money. David Baird and his foundations will also be discussed in Chapter 4. Crown's son, Lester, would later join the "Mega Group," which was co-founded by Leslie Wexner and Charles Bronfman in 1991 and is discussed in detail in Chapter 14.

Henry Crown's business empire first began with his company Material Services Corporation, a supplier of concrete and other materials for construction companies. During World War II, Crown took leave from Material Service to serve in the Army Corps of Engineers. During this same period, the company benefited greatly from Crown's relationship with Jake Avery. As Russo writes, Avery, who had also joined the armed services, "managed to become, with no small thanks to friends in the Roosevelt administration, the overseer of countless international post exchange (PX) facilities on military bases. Soon, the military was supplying these PXs with goods purchased from buddy Col. Crown's Material Service Corporation."[74]

In 1959, Material Services Corporation merged with General Dynamics, which – at the time – was a producer of bomber aircraft, ballistic missile systems and other cutting-edge technologies for the American military. Crown received 20% equity in the company, making him the controlling stakeholder, and his right-hand man, Patrick Hoy, was installed as vice president of the corporation. Hoy had earlier been president of the Hotel Sherman in Chicago, a popular watering hole for various denizens of the city's organized crime community.[75] Since General Dynamics' board was populated by a cross-section of individuals tied to the Cold War military and intelligence structures, this chain of ownership and associates is a surprisingly straightforward instance of mutual collusion between these spheres and the criminal underworld. In 1966, after leaving General Dynamics, Hoy became vice chairman of the Penn-Dixie Cement Company – the CEO of which, Jerome Castle, "was an admitted 'old friend' of New York crime boss Frank Costello."[76]

Avery, Crown, and Hoy were all close to an important Chicago lawyer named Sidney Korshak. The Korshak family had grown up with the Averys, and just like Jake Avery, Sidney Korshak forged an early working relationship with Al Capone. Even before he was officially an attorney, Korshak's side gig, while he was in law school, had been to act as an advisor to the infamous gangster. His subsequent law partner, Edward King, was the "lawyer for Capone's heir Frank Nitti," before setting off for "greener pastures in New York," where he worked for Meyer Lansky himself.[77] Lansky and Korshak also did business together, as partners in the Acapulco Towers Hotel. Notably, the magazine *New West* stated in 1976 that Korshak was the "logical successor to Meyer Lansky."[78]

Like Crown's business associate Lawrence Wein, Korshak had ties to mobster Moe Dalitz's circles. According to Russo, Korshak lent his considerable legal talents to helping arrange frontmen for organized crime interests in Las Vegas hotels and casinos. "[T]he hoods," he writes, needed owners of record whose IRS statements reflected legitimate wealth. The obvious first choice was ... Moe Dalitz."[79] Dalitz, his criminal background, and his webs of associations will be discussed mainly in Chapter 4.

Another associate of the "Supermob" was Julius Caesar Stein, an "ophthalmologist and musician" that abandoned "his medical career to book dance bands and singers into speakeasies and nightclubs on Chicago's South Side."[80] In 1924, he founded the Music Corporation of America (MCA) as an umbrella company for his booking efforts; reportedly, Al Capone owned a secret piece of the company. While this cannot be confirmed, it is true that Capone and Stein had a cozy relationship, with the gangster ensuring that Chicago's bars, clubs, and music halls directed their business towards Stein and MCA.[81]

In 1936, Stein brought a man into the MCA fold who would go on to fundamentally shape the character and direction of the American entertainment industry forever – Lew Wasserman. Unsurprisingly, Wasserman already boasted a background in mob circles: he had been the publicist for Cleveland, Ohio's Mayfair Casino, which was controlled by Moe Dalitz's network. Dalitz and Wasserman maintained life-long ties – Wasserman would even marry Edith Beckerman, the daughter of Dalitz's lawyer, Henry Beckerman.[82] Wasserman knew Beckerman from his days at the Mayfair Casino: Beckerman's name was listed on the club's liquor license.[83] Wasserman's and MCA's connections to organized crime are discussed in greater detail in chapters 9 and 10.

Soon, the Chicago mob began its slow creep into Los Angeles, moving into Hollywood and adjacent industries. The man who started off their advance was Johnny Roselli, who would later land in Las Vegas as the Chicago mob's frontman in the casino business. He was placed in charge of skimming operations, which, as will be discussed in Chapter 3, moved money into offshore banks in the Caribbean that were themselves controlled by representatives of Meyer Lansky. Perhaps it was his intimate familiarity with this world that helped Roselli become the CIA's mafiosi of choice when it came to recruiting organized crime figures for its covert assassination plots against Fidel Castro in Cuba.

Through the operations that took shape in California, massive amounts of illicit money began to be dumped into "above-board" industries. Real estate was a particularly hot commodity, and the architect of many of the investments made by the "Supermob" was a protégé of Avery and Korshak named Paul Ziffren. Ziffren's granddaughter would later marry Lew Wasserman's grandson, bringing these families even closer together. Ziffren acted as the LA representative of Hilton Hotel interests, and he was the source of the seed capital that launched Store Properties Inc., a real estate holding company whose ostensible owner was a man named Sam Genis. Genis was most likely a conduit for enabling the flow of organized crime money into real estate. Per Russo, Genis was:

> ... a known associate of mob bosses Longy Zwillman, Doc Stacher, Frank Costello, Joey Adonis, and Meyer Lansky. Genis' criminal record showed that he had been arrested for bad checks in Florida, embezzlement in New York, and mail fraud and securities law violations in Georgia.... By 1957, Store Properties had bought thousands of acres of land in over three hundred transactions worth $20 million in Los Angeles alone. When Store's other California purchases are factored in (in San Bernardino, Fresno, Oakland, and San Francisco), the estimate approaches $100 million. Then there were the additional investments in such states as Arizona, Utah, Colorado, Oklahoma, Florida, Illinois, and New York.[84]

Genis, interestingly, was the member of an organized circle of businessmen who helped provide the start-up capital for the Committee on the Present Danger (CPD), an early Cold War-pressure group set up to build public support for the militarization plan that had been drawn up by NSC 68. NSC 68 was a National Security Council policy paper that called for the remarkable expansion of the US' military budget. Naturally, the CPD counted among its members many representatives of defense contracting companies, a field that, as noted above with the case of Crown, Hoy, and General Dynamics, was becoming increasingly infiltrated by elements of organized crime.

The organizers behind this California group (CPD) were the movie producer Samuel Goldwyn and industrialist Floyd Odlum. Odlum, a shadowy figure who is now largely forgotten, was the man behind the towering Atlas Corporation, through which he invested heavily into a vast array of aviation companies, film studios, real estate, and natural resources. Atlas Corporation would later gain lucrative government contracts; in particular for its interests in uranium mining inside the United States and abroad. Odlum's interests were certainly diverse: through Atlas, his money seeped into Hilton hotels, into the United Fruit Company, and into Pan Am. Atlas also controlled Convair, the aircraft manufacturer and defense contractor, which it sold to General Dynamics in 1953. As part of the deal, Atlas received large amounts of General Dynamic stock and a representative on the company's board. Odlum and Harry Crown, in other words, were directly affiliated.[85]

Other associates of the California group backing the formation of the CPD were a number of film industry figures, including future president Ronald Reagan. Reagan was a MCA man through and through, having been represented by the company when it bought out the agency that had previously represented him in 1940. "Based on the success of King's Row in 1942," wrote Dan Moldea in his book on MCA, *Dark Victory*, "[Lew] Wasserman renegotiated Reagan's contract with Warner Brothers, obtaining a deal that paid Reagan $3,500 a week for seven years. The deal gave Reagan the distinction of being Wasserman's first 'million-dollar client.'"[86]

As will be noted again in Chapter 10, the rise of Reagan to the heights of political power in the United States was facilitated in large part by Wasserman and MCA. At the same time, Reagan was vital to the survival and success of MCA in Hollywood. At the behest of Wasserman, Reagan ran for, and won, the presidency of the powerful Screen Actors Guild (SAG). At the time, Reagan was also acting as an FBI informant, reporting to the bureau on leftists in Hollywood. Once in charge of the SAG, Reagan began to change the rules to benefit his benefactors. SAG had previously restricted companies like MCA – that is, talent agencies – from becoming producers. However, in 1952, Reagan granted the company a special waiver. MCA thus gained "an insurmountable edge over competing agencies in Hollywood" and "began to exponentially increase its hold over the entertainment industry."[87]

Later, when Reagan secured the governorship of California in 1966, MCA's hidden hand was again lurking in the background. The co-chairman of his campaign was Taft Schreiber, the long-running vice president of MCA, while the company's founder Jules Stein went to work arranging funding. According to Moldea, a "standing joke in Hollywood was that 'MCA even had its own governor.'"[88] MCA had actually hedged its bets in that election. Running against Reagan was the incumbent Pat Brown, who was being backed by Wasserman and Korshak. Henry Denker, a playwright and producer with numerous Hollywood connections, stated that:

> MCA was divided into two groups. There was a Democratic group and a Republican group. They always wanted to have a hand in the White House, no matter which party was there. When Reagan was doing the General Electric show, somebody came up with the idea that he would promote GE to the plants, make visits. These appearances were very successful. They saw how the workers loved him, and somebody at MCA said, 'Hey, he could be governor of the state.' In show business you go with what's working – that's an old maxim.[89]

After being defeated by Reagan, Pat Brown took a directorship at Investors Overseas Services (IOS), an international mutual fund with connections to Meyer Lansky. He had been brought to the fund by James Roosevelt, one of the sons of former President Franklin D. Roosevelt. James, it seems, had organized crimes ties of his own, as he had done business with Store Properties, the mob-controlled real estate company that had been set up by Ziffren and Genis. Also partnered alongside Roosevelt in Store Properties was James Swig, who would serve earlier as "Pat Brown's statewide finance chairman in his successful California gubernatorial campaign."[90]

The Roosevelt boys seemed to have a penchant for fostering ties to the underworld. James' brother, John Roosevelt, had arranged for Jimmy Hoffa to get a job at Bache & Company, a New York City securities and stock brokerage that "handled about 25 percent of the [Teamster Pension's] funds $160 million dollar investments."[91] The president of Bache & Co., incidentally, was Frank T. Ryan, a veteran of the OSS, who was partnered with the spymaster William Donovan and other veterans of US and British wartime intelligence in the World Commerce Corporation (WCC). WCC itself was capitalized by a handful of firms, including Bache & Co. itself and Floyd Odlum's Atlas Corporation, which was represented on the WCC board by Odlum's brother-in-law, L. Boyd Hatch.[92]

With this set of ties, the specter of intelligence connections begins to emerge once again. It is no surprise, then, that there is a direct line running from the Chicago-Los Angeles "Supermob" to the networks that were simultaneously being organized by Paul Helliwell.

KINGS OF THE CASTLE

On the forty-fifth page of the most-well known of Jeffrey Epstein's two black contact books are the names and numbers of two individuals from the same prominent Chicago family: Nicholas and Thomas Pritzker. Epstein listed two addresses, five phone numbers and one email address for Nicholas; for Thomas, he had two addresses, one email, and twelve phone numbers ranging from his main office number to his farm to his emergency contact line. Under Nicholas Pritzker, Epstein placed the name "Hyatt Development Corp" – the Hyatt hotel company had been taken over by the Pritzker family late in the 1950s – while under Thomas he cryptically noted "Numero Uno."

The Pritzkers have long been a potent force in local, state and national politics. Penny Pritzker, a cousin to Thomas (and a board member of the Council on Foreign Relations), had met Barack Obama in the early 1990s, and the future president's political career has long relied on lucrative donations made by her and her family. Obama repaid his debt by making Penny Pritzker a member of the President's Economic Recovery Advisory Board. During Obama's second term, Penny was nominated – and confirmed – as his Secretary of Commerce.

Penny's brother J.B. Pritzker, meanwhile, served as the co-chair of Hillary Clinton's 2008 campaign before working to broker an agreement between Clinton and Obama. In 2019, he was elected Governor of Illinois. The third sibling, Anthony Pritzker, has avoided taking public office, but maintains a post on the advisory board of the Center for Asia Pacific Policy at the RAND Corporation.

Travel up the family tree and one begins to find that the Pritzker family's wealth and influence might have originated in darker corners. Take Abram Nicholas Pritzker, grandfather to Nicholas, Thomas, Penny, J.B. and Anthony. One of three sons of Nicholas J. Pritzker, Abram had worked with his brothers at the family law firm, Pritzker & Pritzker, where he specialized in business law. In the 1930s, he decided to dip into the world of business himself, and he and his brother Jack invested in a string of companies across Chicago. One of these was Hyatt, which would help the family secure lasting influence. As was the case with Henry Crown, the Pritzkers had to deal with the Hotel and Restaurant Employees Union – where Sidney Korshak was the labor negotiator.

Then, there was the case of the Frontier Finance. As Gus Russo writes:

> Jack Clarke, a renowned Chicago private investigator, recently re-
> called what he heard on the streets: "Frontier Finance was used and
> owned by the Pritzkers as a holding company and is believed to
> be the secret to the origins of the family's involvement with crimi-
> nals. Pritzker lent to immigrants 'five for seven,' or five dollars lent
> against seven dollars repayment with interest. It was started on
> the West Side and the Pritzkers let the mob run it for them. This
> company office was where the mob held their meetings." Frontier
> Finance was a state-licensed loan company, with a number of legit
> investors, such as the postmaster of Chicago, a former chairman of
> the Cook County Republican Party, and a retired Chicago police
> captain. But curiously, the president of the firm was Frank Buccieri,
> brother of the notorious Fiore "Fifi" Buccieri, one of the Outfit's
> top gambling bosses and a dreaded "juice" collector.[93]

Another Abram Pritzker venture was the Franklin Investment Company, which later went on to dominate the hotel business in Columbus,
Ohio. It had been set up with the aid of Paul Ziffren, who acted as a partner in the venture. Joining them was a friend of Abram named Arthur
Greene. Described by the Chicago Crime Commission as the "brains of
all the Chicago rackets," Greene – a close associate of the aforementioned
James Roosevelt – was reported to have facilitated investments on behalf
of Meyer Lansky. Additionally, "Greene somehow figured in the California expansion of Jules Stein's MCA, through a relative named Edwin
Greene" – a vice president at MCA.[94]

The Pritzker family employed Burton Kanter to serve as the tax attorney for their burgeoning empire, and Kanter gained a spot on the Hyatt
board. Kanter would, in time, boast connections to powerful operatives
from international criminal networks – not to mention the CIA and Israel's Mossad. Yet, earlier on, Kanter received massive kickbacks from
Abram Pritzker after Kanter arranged for the family to take over a San
Francisco hotel built by Prudential Financial (Kanter, in characteristic
fashion, opted not to pay any taxes on his gains).[95] As part of the deal,
Kanter had arranged for secret payments to be made to Prudential executives. What's remarkable about this story is that it took several decades to
unravel: Kanter and Pritzker had put this scheme in motion in the 1970s,
but it was not revealed until 2007.

Kanter was deeply connected to the world of mob-linked business. In
1968, for example, he was listed as the agent for the La Costa Club near San

Diego. La Costa, for all intents and purposes, was built for and by organized crime figures. Gene Ayres and Jeff Morgan, writing in the *Oakland Tribune*, noted that "La Costa's original developers include Allard Roen, who was convicted in 1962 on stock fraud charges, and Morris Barney 'Moe' Dalitz, who, with Roen, was part of the old-time Cleveland gambling crowd."[96]

Ayres and Morgan then added that "Among La Costa's visitors have been Chicago 'politicians' Marshall Korshak [brother of Sidney Korshak] and Jake Avery; St. Louis attorney Morris Shenker, a legal defender of James Hoffa.... One man who reportedly spends more time at La Costa than anyone else is Allen Dorfman, the Chicago insurance magnate who wields tremendous influence over the Teamsters Central State Pension Fund".[97] La Costa itself managed to tap into $62 million in Teamster pension fund loans.[98] Importantly, a close associate of Kanter named Stanford Clinton – himself a partner at the Pritzker & Pritzker law firm and Hyatt board member – was a trustee for the fund.[99]

Other Kanter ventures were located far from the windswept cityscapes of Chicago and the sunny, beach-adjacent plains of Southern California. He was also connected to a most curious bank located in the Bahamas: Castle Bank and Trust. When the IRS came knocking on Castle's door, Kanter told them he was merely a tax consultant to the bank. That was a lie – he was one half of the bank's top management, and he was shepherding money from his various clients into its coffers. The Pritzker family itself would later be revealed to be the bank's largest depositors, while a number of people tied closely to them maintained accounts there as well. Stanford Clinton held money in Castle, as did the actor Tony Curtis, a close friend of Sidney Korshak.[100] Playboy's Hugh Hefner was there as well; he intriguingly "planned to join with a Pritzker company in an Atlantic City casino venture."[101]

Castle maintained accounts for the usual crew of organized crime suspects. Morris Kleinman, Sam Tucker and Lou Rothkopf, as well as major parts of the Cleveland mob scene that surrounded Moe Dalitz, held money in Castle. However, accounts vary as to whether or not Dalitz himself had money there.[102] Kleinman, whose attorney was Kanter, was reportedly a secret co-owner in the bank. Either way, his accounts in Castle reflected his hidden interest in a company called Karat Inc., which operated the Stardust Casino in Las Vegas. The Stardust itself was owned by Lodestar Inc., a company controlled by Dalitz.

Authorities had been put on the trail of Castle Bank in 1971 after a man named Allan George Palmer and several of his associates were busted flying marijuana from Florida to Oakland, California. Palmer was subsequently revealed to have been "a major producer of LSD, mescaline, and THC" in the San Francisco Bay area since around 1968.[103] Palmer fell under the scrutiny of the San Francisco IRS office, which was then leading a program against drug money networks. That office soon discovered that the dealer had used the then-unknown Castle Bank, whose services he accessed via American National Banker & Trust Company in Chicago. Palmer, it seems, had been brought to Castle via Roger S. Baskes, Kanter's brother-in-law and a partner in his law firm.

This was not the only LSD-related banking taking place at Castle. Accounts were also maintained by William Mellon Hitchcock, a scion of the Mellon family, who will appear again in connection with the UK's Profumo Affair in Chapter 4. Hitchcock was one of the financial backers of the Brotherhood of Eternal Love, the so-called "hippie mafia" that produced and distributed psychedelics on an international scale.[104] Given that they were based in Orange County, California, it is possible that Palmer's ring was part of their operation – though that cannot be confirmed at this time.

The San Francisco IRS requested aid from the IRS intelligence apparatus in Chicago, which promptly tracked down Castle's information. They found a card that listed the bank's principals, several of whom were revealed to have been fictitious characters. At the top of the list was Kanter and his partner, the other half of Castle's management: Paul Helliwell. Alan Block writes that "Kanter and Helliwell had known each other since the late 1950s, having met while working on a deal between a Kanter client and one of Helliwell's."[105]

Castle Bank was a melding of worlds. On the one hand, there was Kanter's specialty in offshore trusts and his connections to both the city's political power centers and the sprawl of its "supermob". On the other hand, there was Helliwell – the Republican Party insider, intelligence veteran (and continued intelligence asset), and an offshore specialist in his own right with intimate connections to the blossoming heroin traffic coming out from Southeast Asia. Together, they organized a complicated money laundering operation that silently moved the funds of powerful gangsters, politicians, businessmen, and intelligence services around the globe.

When Castle was first established, it was a just a paper company – a company that existed only as a legal entity, with no officers, infrastructure or business activity to speak of. It sat for three years from when it was registered in 1964 until 1967, when it was finally activated. A physical headquarters was established in Nassau and a law firm – that of a British expat living in Argentina named Anthony James Tullis Gooding – was retained. Shortly thereafter, the number of accounts at the bank began to balloon. Banking relations were then established with banks in the United States; namely, Bank of Perrine and Bank of Cutler-Ridge.

Bank of Perrine and Bank of Cutler-Ridge were small, Florida-based institutions that were intimately interconnected. They shared relationships not only with Castle Bank, but with one another as well. Both had the same chairman – Paul Helliwell – and they were also owned by the same sets of holding companies, HMT Corporation and later Florida Shares, Inc. The shares of these companies were owned by Helliwell and his circle of associates, with one being a mysterious figure by the name of E.P. Barry. Helliwell and Barry had known each other since their days together in the OSS, though the details of the particulars of their relationship are murky. Barry had spent time in the Middle East during his clandestine service, but, by the end of the war, he was serving as the head of OSS' X-2 Vienna branch (i.e. the OSS counterintelligence division).[106]

Following the war, Barry remained in Europe and became immersed in the world of Zurich banking. Through Barry and his connection to Helliwell and HMT/Florida Shares, a number of connections can be found. As will be discussed in Chapter 3, Barry, at the same time that he was involved with these Florida banks, could also be found at the ground floor of Inter Maritime Bank, which was controlled by a close friend of future CIA director William J. Casey and a businessman-underworld operator named Bruce Rappaport (Casey, also an OSS veteran, was reportedly close to Barry as well).

Another bank, discussed in later chapters, is the Bank of World Commerce, a Lansky-controlled bank that helped move casino skim and other "hot money" funds abroad. According to Tom Farer, Bank of Perrine had banking relations with the Bank of World Commerce in addition to Castle Bank and Trust.[107] What was taking shape, in other words, appears to have been an elaborate "daisy chain" of offshore banks.

One of the early ventures that Castle engaged in was a convoluted land fraud that netted millions and intimately involved Kanter. The fraud was carried out under the auspices of a company called International Computerized Land Research (ICLR). Gooding, the British-Argentine attorney who represented Castle, registered the company, and Kanter appears to have kept the company afloat financially, in addition to it using the services of Castle Bank. Thanks to the Bahamas' bank secrecy structures, Kanter was able to obscure his position as hidden partner in ICLR.

ICLR was run by James McGowan and James Farrara, the latter of whom was a "fairly sleazy operator with a criminal record stretching back to 1926 when he was fined for running a whorehouse. He spent some time in prison in the 1930s and 1940s for violations of the Mann Act, having to do with transporting women across state lines for immoral purposes."[108] ICLR was just one, albeit the largest and most complex, in a string of companies this pair had formed in order to hawk low-value California land at a high price to unsuspecting investors in Europe and Asia. "The promotional material," reads one press report, "lists Nassau, Okinawa, Hong Kong, Zurich, and Munich as sites of real estate agencies representing ICLR."[109]

Like Kanter's elaborate kickback schemes on behalf of the Pritzkers, authorities took decades to untangle the web left by ICLR. When indictments were finally brought against McGowan and Farrara in 1982, the *Los Angeles Times* reported that the duo stood accused of running a "far-flung land sales empire" that defrauded "buyers of more than $15 million over a 17-year period. 'The $15 million is a very conservative number,' said Assistant U.S. [Attorney] Gary Feess."[110] Given that Kanter and his associates effectively structured ICLR, provided it with financing, took a financial stake in the company, and provided it with banking services, there are obvious questions as to the ultimate purpose – and destination – of this pilfered money.

Castle Bank wasn't only a repository and conduit for money belonging to tax-evading billionaires, shady businessmen, drug dealers and land fraudsters. It seems some of their other clients wielded a different kind of power that helped grant the bank its knack for evading official inquiry. First, a sweeping IRS probe into Castle that had unearthed an expansive network dedicated to tax evasion was shut down. In addition, the list of names of Castle clients investigators had obtained was declared to have been found through illegal means. Then, a Department of Justice probe into the bank was dropped in 1977. Three years later, in 1980, the real circumstances of this obstruction were revealed:

> It now appears that pressure from the Central Intelligence Agency, rather than any legal problem, was what caused the Justice Department to drop what could have been the biggest tax evasion case of all time. Moreover, the supposed legal obstacle to using the Castle Bank Depositors' list was questionable at best – the government

already had in its possession the same list, legally obtained – What caused the Justice Department to back off seems to have been the CIA's argument that pursuit of the Castle Bank would endanger "national security."[111]

According to an unnamed Federal source, Castle Bank was "one of the CIA's finance channels for operations against Cuba." Helliwell – and presumably Castle – was purportedly involved with the Agency in "financing a series of covert forays between 1964 and 1975 against Cuba by CIA operatives working from Andros Island," one of the many islands located in the Bahamas not too far from Florida's southernmost coastline. Declassified CIA files show that, going back to the pre-Bay of Pigs invasion era, Andros was used as a staging ground for the CIA's cadres of Cuban exiles that the Agency had armed and trained to fight against Castro. Later, in the 1980s, Andros would serve as one of the transshipment points for Colombian cocaine flowing into the United States by way of Nicaragua. Involved in this particular channel was a figure who will be addressed at length in future chapters, Robert Vesco.[112]

Endnotes

1   Alfred W. McCoy, *The Politics of Heroin: CIA Complicity in the Global Drug Trade: Afghanistan, Southeast Asia, Central America, Colombia*, Rev. ed (Chicago: Lawrence Hill Books : Distributed by Independent Publishers Group, 2003), 31.

2   The role of Haffendon is discussed at length in Rodney Campbell, *The Luciano Project: The Secret Wartime Collaboration of the Mafia and the U.S. Navy* (New York: McGraw-Hill, 1977).

3   McCoy, *The Politics of Heroin*, chap. 1.

4   Campbell, *The Luciano Project*, 76.

5   McCoy, *The Politics of Heroin*, 30.

6   Priscilla M. Roberts in "The American 'Eastern Establishment': A Challenge for Historians" describes the concept as encompassing "A body of individuals committed to what are often loosely term 'internationalist' policies, men drawn from the leading financial and business institutions, law firms, Ivy League universities, major philanthropic foundations, and communications media of the East Coast, who take a particular interest in and have a substantial impact upon the direction of twentieth century foreign affairs." From the *SHAFR Newsletter*, XIV, December 1983, 9.

7   Richard H. Immerman, *John Foster Dulles: Piety, Pragmatism, and Power in U.S. Foreign Policy* (Rowan & Littlefield Publishers, 1998), 23-24.

8   Donald Janson, "Resorts Head Tells of Dropping Partner," *New York Times*, January 17, 1979, https://www.nytimes.com/1979/01/17/archives/resorts-head-tells-of-dropping-partner.html.

9   Joan Cook, "James M. Crosby, 58, Founder of Hotel and Casino Concern," *New York Times*, April 12, 1986, https://www.nytimes.com/1986/04/12/obituaries/james-m-crosby-58-founder-of-hotel-and-casino-concern.html.

10   Sally Denton and Roger Morris write that the Mary Carter Paint Company "was widely considered to be a CIA front that laundered money to the Cuban exile army in the early 1960s." Sally Denton and Roger Morris, *The Money and the Power: The Making of Las Vegas and Its Hold on America, 1947-2000*, 1st ed (New York: Alfred A. Knopf, 2001), 284, https://archive.org/details/moneypowermaking00dent.

11   John C. Williams, "Covert Connections: the FBN, the OSS, and the CIA," *The Historian*, Vol. 53, No. 4, Summer, 1991, 668.

12   Richard Harris Smith, *OSS: The Secret History of America's First Central Intelligence Agency* (Guilford, Conn: Lyons Press, 2005), 80.

13   Smith, *OSS*, 14.

14   David Rockefeller's wartime intelligence activities is discussed in David Rockefeller, *Memoirs* (New York: Random House, 2003).

15   Richard B. Spence, *Wall Street and the Russian Revolution, 1905-1925*, ePub (Oregon: Trine Day LLC, 2017), 507-08. Spence notes that when Donovan returned to New York City in October 1920, another passenger on the same ship was William Wiseman, the British spymaster who maintained a post in New York City during World War I (sort of a model for the later activities of William Stephenson and the British Security Coordination during World War II). In 1920, Wiseman went to work for Kuhn Loeb, and two years later became head of the New York & Foreign Development Corporation – a "spin-off" of Kuhn Loeb set up to "capitalize on Eastern European opportunities."

16   Thomas E. Mahl, *Desperate Deception: British Covert Operations in the United States, 1939-44*, ePub (Washington [D.C.]: Brassey's, 1998), 44.

17   Curt Gentry, J. *Edgar Hoover: The Man and the Secrets* (New York, N.Y.: Norton, 2001), 265–66.

18   Smith, *OSS*, 29.

19   Mahl, *Desperate Deception*, 65.

20   David Ignatius, "How Churchill's Agents Secretly Manipulated the U.S. Before Pearl Harbor," *Washington Post*, September 17, 1989, https://www.washingtonpost.com/archive/opinions/1989/09/17/how-churchills-agents-secretly-manipulated-the-us-before-pearl-harbor/0881f7a8-7c9d-49d0-8338-eac3be333134/

21   Mahl, *Desperate Deception*, 64.

22   Mahl, *Desperate Deception*, 96

23   Peter Dale Scott, *Deep Politics and the Death of JFK* (University of California Press, 1996), 174.

24   John H Davis, *Mafia Kingfish: Carlos Marcello and the Assassination of John F. Kennedy* (New York: New American Library, 1989), 50.

25   Davis, Mafia *Kingfish*, 59.

26   For an excellent overview of this history, see Shiu Hing Lo, *The Politics of Controlling Organized Crime in Greater China*, 2016.

27   Lo, *Controlling Organized Crime*, 12.

28   The most in-depth treatment of the KMT's opium monopoly efforts is Jonathan Marshall, "Opium and the Politics of Gangsterism in Nationalist China, 1927–1945," *Bulletin of Concerned Asian Scholars*, No. 8, Vol. 3, 1976.

29   On the Rockefeller Foundation and the KMT, see Marshall, "Opium and the Politics of Gangsterism," 21. On the activities of the China Medical Board, see the "Rockefeller Foundation Annual Report," 1922, https://www.rockefellerfoundation.org/wp-content/uploads/Annual-Report-1922-1.pdf .

30   Marshall, "Opium and the Politics of Gangsterism," 22.

31   Marshall, "Opium and the Politics of Gangsterism," 30.

32   McCoy, *The Politics of Heroin*, 27.

33   Hans Derks, *History of the Opium Problem: The Assault on the East, ca. 1600-1950* (Boston: Brill, 2012), 689.

34   Hans Derks, *History of the Opium Problem*, 93.

35   George Parker, "Lord Sassoon to Join Jardine Matheson," *Financial Times*, January 3, 2013, https://www.ft.com/content/1a7c4e5c-55ad-11e2-bbd1-00144feab49a.

36   "All the World's a Fair, Parts 1-4," January 3, 2021, Pseudodoxology Podcast Network, https://patreon.com/posts/45747840.

37   Douglas Valentine, *The Strength of the Wolf: The Secret History of America's War on Drugs*, ePub (London: Verso, 2004), 44.

38   Scott, *Deep Politics and the Death of JFK*, 167-68.

39   Scott, *Deep Politics and the Death of JFK*, 168.

40   Valentine, *Strength of the Wolf*, 195.

41   "Guide to the George White Papers," https://oac.cdlib.org/findaid/ark:/13030/tf6k40059b/.

42   H. P Albarelli, *Coup in Dallas: The Decisive Investigation Into Who Killed JFK* (NY: Skyhorse Publishing, 2021), 94.

43   Albarelli, *Coup in Dallas*, 101.

44   "NRO, Mafia, Organization A/O Membership, BKG, Criminal Act, Method of Operation, Legitimate Enterprises, Polit Act, Cuba," FBI Memo, October 11, 1955, https://www.archives.gov/files/research/jfk/releases/docid-32301903.pdf.

45   Stephen Kinzer, *Poisoner in Chief: Sidney Gottlieb and the CIA Search for Mind Control* (New York: Henry Holt and Company, 2019), 123.

46   Kinzer, *Poisoner in Chief*, 126.

47   H. P. Albarelli, *A Terrible Mistake: The Murder of Frank Olson, and the CIA's Secret Cold War Experiments*, 1st ed (Oregon: Trine Day, 2009), 744.

48   Jonathan Marshall, "Cooking the Books: The Federal Bureau of Narcotics, the China Lobby and Cold War Propaganda, 1950-1962," *The Asia-Pacific Journal* 11, no. 37 (September 15, 2013), https://apjjf.org/-Jonathan-Marshall/3997/article.pdf.

49   Marshall, "Cooking the Books."

50   Bertil Lintner, *Burma in Revolt: Opium and Insurgency Since 1948* (Routledge, 2019), 62.

51   McCoy, *The Politics of Heroin*, 162.

52   McCoy, *The Politics of Heroin*, 162.

53   Peter Dale Scott, "Operation Paper: The United States and Drugs in Thailand and Burma," *The Asia-Pacific Journal* 8, no. 44 (November 1, 2010), https://apjjf.org/-Peter-Dale-Scott/3436/article.pdf.

54   Lintner, *Burma in Revolt*, 104.

55   See, for example, "20 Children," *Miami Herald*, November 20, 1954, https://miamiherald. newspapers.com/image/618421882.

56   Peter Dale Scott, *The War Conspiracy: The Secret Road to the Second Indochina War* (Indianapolis: The Bobbs-Merril Company, Inc., 1972), 7, https://archive.org/details/warconspiracys00scot.

57   John Prados, *Safe for Democracy: The Secret Wars of the CIA* (Chicago: Ivan R. Dee, 2009), 125.

58   Prados, *Safe for Democracy*, 196-197.

59   Valentine, *Strength of the Wolf*, 44.

60   Ed Reid, *The Mistress and the Mafia: The Virginia Hill Story* (Bantan Books, 1972), 42.

61   Scott, *The War Conspiracy*, 207.

62   "GOP 'Regulars' Hit At 'Harmful' Tactics In State Ike Group," *Tampa Bay Times*, August 25, 1952.

63   "GOP Regulars' Hit."

64   Scott, *The War Conspiracy*, 241.

65   R.T. Naylor, *Hot Money and the Politics of Debt* (Linden Pub, 1988), 292.

66   Rajeev Syal, "Drug Money Saved Banks in Global Crisis, Claims UN Advisor," *The Guardian*, December 12, 2009, https://www.theguardian.com/global/2009/dec/13/drug-money-banks-saved-un-cfief-claims.

67   "Transnational Crime Is a $1.6 Trillion to $2.2 Trillion Annual 'Business', Finds New GFI Report," *Global Financial Integrity*, March 27, 2017, https://gfintegrity.org/press-release/transnational-crime-is-a-1-6-trillion-to-2-2-trillion-annual-business-finds-new-gfi-report/.

68   "Money Laundering," United Nations : Office on Drugs and Crime, https://www.unodc. org/unodc/en/money-laundering/overview.html.

69   "Super Rich Hold $32 Trillion in Offshore Havens," Reuters, July 22, 2012, https://www. reuters.com/article/us-offshore-wealth-idUSBRE86L03U20120722.

70   Michael C. Ruppert, *Crossing the Rubicon: The Decline of the American Empire at the End of the Age of Oil* (New Catalyst Books, 2004), 60.

71   Chris Sanders and Catherine Austin Fitts, "The Black Budget of the United States: The Engine of a 'Negative Return Economy'," *World Affairs* 8, no. 2 (April-June 2004), 29-30.

72   Kirkpatrick Sale, *Power Shift: The Rise of the Southern Rim and Its Challenge to the Eastern Establishment* (Random House, 1975), 86.

73   Gus Russo, *Supermob: How Sidney Korshak and His Criminal Associates Became America's Hidden Power Brokers*, 1st U.S. ed (New York: Bloomsbury, 2006), 16.

74   Russo, *Supermob*, 20.

75   On Patrick Hoy at the Hotel Sherman, see the *Chicago Tribune*, July 22, 1957, 52. Interestingly, the operator of the Hotel Sherman was famed hotelier Ernie Byfield. Byfield's son, Ernie Byfield Jr., served in the OSS. After he passed away, his wife remarried to Robert McNamara in 2004. "Ex-U.S. Defense Secretary Remarries," AP News, September 16, 2004, https://apnews.com/article/7a9915a3b31cd47f699e07c586224518.

76   Jonathan Marshall, *Dark Quadrant: Organized Crime, Big Business, and the Corruption of American Democracy: From Truman to Trump*, Additional Endnotes (Lanham: Rowman & Littlefield, 2021), 28, https://rowman.com/WebDocs/Dark_Quadrant_Extra_Notes.pdf.

77   Russo, *Supermob*, 37.

78   "New West," *New West Communications*, 1976, Volume 1, p. 27, https://www.google.com/books/edition/New_West/6SkcAQAAIAAJ?hl=en&gbpv=0.

79   Russo, *Supermob*, 202.

80   Jane Applegate, "The History of MCA," *Los Angeles Times*, November 27, 1990, https://www.latimes.com/archives/la-xpm-1990-11-27-fi-5451-story.html.

81   Russo, *Supermob*, 43.

82   Mike Barnes, "Edie Wasserman, Wife of Lew Wasserman, Dies at 95," *The Hollywood Reporter*, August 18, 2011, https://www.hollywoodreporter.com/news/general-news/edie-wasserman-wife-lew-wasserman-225101/.

83   Russo, *Supermob*, 204.

84   Russo, *Supermob*, 100.

85   Marshall, *Dark Quadrant*, 252-253.

86   Dan E. Moldea, *Dark Victory: Ronald Reagan, MCA, and the Mob* (New York, N.Y: Viking, 1987), 37.

87   Russo, *Supermob*, 231.

88   Moldea, *Dark Victory*, 254.

89   Russo, *Supermob*, 306.

90   Russo, *Supermob*, 100.

91   Scott, *Deep Politics and the Death of JFK*, 285.

92   "Trading Unit Bridges Foreign Exchange Gap", *Los Angeles Times*, September 24, 1947; "Foreign Trade: Idealism, Inc.," TIME, October 6, 1947, https://content.time.com/time/subscriber/article/0,33009,779340,00.html.

93   Russo, *Supermob*, 68-9.

94   Russo, *Supermob*, 93.

95   David Cay Johnston. "Court Upholds Tax Evasion Ruling," *New York Times News Service*, February 4, 2007.

96   Gene Ayres and Jeff Morgan, "Pension Fund Loans Buy Luxury," *Oakland Tribune*, September 23, 1969.

97   Ayres and Morgan, "Pension Fund."

98   Russo, *Supermob*, 67.

99   Lee Dembart, "Teamster Pension Chiefs May Quit," *New York Times*, October 13, 1976, https://www.nytimes.com/1976/10/13/archives/teamster-pension-chiefs-may-quit-11-trustees-of-teamsters-pension.html.

100   Russo, *Supermob*, 440.

101   Penny Lernoux, *In Banks We Trust*, 1st ed (Garden City, N.Y: Anchor Press/Doubleday, 1984), 80.

102   Alan A. Block and Constance A. Weaver, *All Is Clouded by Desire: Global Banking, Money Laundering, and International Organized Crime* (Connecticut: Praeger, 2004), 45.

103   Alan A. Block, *Space, Time & Organized Crime*, 2nd ed (New Jersey: Transaction Publishers, 1994), 354.

104   Martin A Lee and Bruce Shlain, *Acid Dreams: The Complete Social History of LSD: The CIA, the Sixties, and Beyond* (New York: Grove Press, 2007), 245.

105   Block and Weaver, *All is Clouded By Desire*, 40.

106   Block and Weaver, *All is Clouded By Desire*, 35.

107   Tom J. Farer, *Transnational Crime in the Americas: An Inter-American Dialogue Book* (New York: Routledge, 1999), 67.

108   Block and Weaver, *All is Clouded By Desire*, 42.

109   Subcommittee of the Committee on Government Operations, Oversight Hearings Into the Operations of the IRS, 1975, 917.

110   Victor Merina, "Two Promoters Indicted in Southland Land Fraud," *Los Angeles Times*, October 5, 1982.

111   Jim Drinkhall, "CIA Helped Quash Major, Star-Studded Tax Evasion Case," *Washington Post*, April 24, 1980, https://www.washingtonpost.com/archive/politics/1980/04/24/cia-helped-quash-major-star-studded-tax-evasion-case/a55ddf06-2a3f-4e04-a687-a3dd87c32b82/.

112   "Fugitive Vesco Indicted In Drug Conspiracy," *New York Times*, April 18, 1989, https://www.nytimes.com/1989/04/18/us/fugitive-vesco-indicted-in-drug-conspiracy.html.

Chapter 2

Booze and Blackmail

The Whisky Men

Per his own account, Samuel Bronfman had never planned to become one of North America's top liquor magnates, having previously aspired to a career in law. Nevertheless, true to his family's last name, which means "whisky man" in Yiddish, he and his brothers went on to build a liquor empire that would rocket the Bronfmans into the upper echelons of the Western business elite, though the road they traveled to get there was hardly elegant.

While the Bronfmans are now remembered as scions of Canada's upper class, this was certainly not the case when Samuel's parents – Mindel and Yechiel Bronfman – brought the family to Canada from Bessarabia, now part of modern-day Moldova and Ukraine, in 1889. They had left as part of a wave of Jewish immigrants fleeing the anti-Semitic pogroms of czarist Russia, leaving behind a somewhat profitable tobacco farming business.

In Bessarabia, they had been relatively well off and had emigrated to Canada along with two of their servants and their personal rabbi. However, Canada, particularly Manitoba where the Bronfmans eventually settled, was poorly suited for tobacco farming, forcing Yechiel to labor on Canadian railroads and in sawmills before moving into the sale of firewood and the trading of livestock and fish. It would be their trading of horses that would eventually lead them to begin work in the hospitality sector and, subsequently, the liquor business.[1]

The Bronfmans' beginnings, particularly following their arrival in Canada, stand in such stark contrast to their current reputation that even Sam's sons, Edgar and Charles, were kept in the dark by their own father regarding the family business' early days. "He would never tell us any of the early history," Edgar Bronfman would later remember of his father. A Bronfman biographer – former senior editor at *The Economist*, Nicholas

Faith – would also write that "underlying the family's riches was a deep sense of shame as to their origins" and that Sam's generation had "shared an absolute refusal to tell their offspring anything about their life before their arrival in the Promised Land," i.e., Canada.

Part of the reason for this secrecy, even within the family and between father and son, was likely related to the personal struggle of many immigrants, some of whom choose to turn their back on their lives prior to immigrating and strive to establish and prove their connections to the new land in which they find themselves. Indeed, Sam Bronfman went to great lengths to do just that, publicly claiming for much of his late life that he had been born on March 4, 1891 in Brandon, Manitoba, Canada, obfuscating both his real date and place of birth – February 27, 1889, Bessarabia.[2] Michael Marrus, one of Bronfman's more sympathetic biographers, would write that Sam Bronfman never truly "abandoned his enthusiastic identification with the country in which his career began, and [his attempts to obfuscate his place of birth] is perhaps the most significant indication of his obsession with the respectability he associated with Canadian citizenship."[3]

While Sam Bronfman was undoubtedly ill at ease with his status as an immigrant, there is another factor that may explain his unwillingness, and that of his seven siblings, to discuss the family's "early days" and, specifically, the chain of events and eventual alliances with unsavory characters that would lead them to the top of Canada's business elite.

At some point in the early 1890s, as he sampled spirits in a dingy saloon after selling off some horses, Yechiel Bronfman mulled the merits of leaving behind a life of hard labor in favor of the intertwined businesses of hospitality and liquor sales. Sam Bronfman would later claim that it was actually he who had convinced his father to move into hospitality and bartending, though most biographers doubt this, given Sam's age at the time.[4] Regardless, it would be over a decade before the Bronfman family patriarch and his eldest sons managed to scrape together the funds necessary to realize Yechiel's dreams.

The Bronfmans had saved enough money to lease their first Canadian hotel, the Anglo-American Hotel in Emerson, Manitoba, by 1903.[5] Soon, they acquired several more hotels in Yorkton, Saskatchewan and later in Winnipeg and beyond, building a small yet profitable network of hotels prior to the onset of World War I. The dramatic shift in the family's fortune was largely thanks to the business acumen of Sam's brother Harry, who managed to stave off the financial damage and legal trouble caused by the gambling and other "unseemly" habits of their older brother, Abe.

Sam Bronfman formally joined the new family business in 1907, though he would later regale some of his biographers with tales of how he had been the original "dynamo" behind the family's success in hospitality, despite considerable evidence to the contrary. What is notable, however, is the fact that, not long after Sam formally became involved in hotel management, the family's hotels were targeted by a series of unfortunate accusations, including when they went to renew their liquor license in Yorktown in 1908. Locals had alleged that the Bronfmans were guilty of violating local liquor laws and condoning illegal gambling in their inns.[6] The latter is particularly likely given the well-known gambling habits of Abe Bronfman, which were known to have threatened the family business on more than one occasion.

The same year that Sam joined the family's hotel business, the organization that would eventually bring "Prohibition" to Canada also emerged, the Social and Moral Reform Council. A joining of the leadership of various Protestant churches, the Women's Christian Temperance Union, the Royal Templars of Temperance and other like-minded groups, the Social and Moral Reform Council was born out of a far-reaching Protestant religious movement of the period, known as the "Social Gospel" movement, that sought to "fight social evils," particularly those caused or exacerbated by rapid urbanization and industrialization.[7] For groups like the Social and Moral Reform Council, liquor quickly became a main target.

The Council and its allies managed to successfully appeal to many Canadians, both those who shared and lacked their religious zeal, as bars and saloons were often disliked for other reasons aside from their "moral depravity," such as their often far-reaching stenches and the fact that around a third of criminal prosecutions at the time were related to drunkenness.[8] Though the Temperance movement in Canada deeply divided its population, it got the boost it needed to become common policy with the onset of the First World War.

In Canada, Prohibition was initially a provincial matter, with a handful of provinces having enacted Prohibition laws prior to the war. Yet, once the curtain of war had fallen, many Canadians came to believe that banning the sale, trade and manufacture of alcohol would aid the war effort. As a result, most Canadian provinces enacted some sort of alcohol ban prior to Canada's short-lived federal ban, enacted near the end of the war in 1918 and expiring a year after hostilities ended.[9] The impact of Prohibition on Canada's liquor industry was substantial and felt long after it was repealed, with 75% of its breweries having closed by 1928. However,

Prohibition was conveniently fortuitous for some, the Bronfmans chief among them.

Given the provincial nature of Prohibition in Canada prior to its brief stint as a federal policy, the differences between the Temperance laws of various provinces provided numerous loopholes that the Bronfmans were able to exploit to great effect. So successful were the Bronfmans at aptly working in the gray area of the varied and often temporary gaps between provincial laws that author Peter Newman remarked in his biography of the Bronfmans, *Bronfman Dynasty: The Rothschilds of the New World,* "Sometimes it almost seemed that the American Congress and the Canadian federal and provincial legislatures must have secretly held a grand conclave to decide one issue: How they could draft anti-liquor laws and regulations that would help maximize the Bronfman brothers' bootlegging profits."[10]

In one example, during World War I, the three eldest Bronfman brothers (Abe, Harry, and Sam) exploited the fact that Manitoba and Ontario, while prohibiting the sale of liquor within the province, allowed alcohol to be imported. The brothers set up several mail-order liquor businesses throughout these two provinces and profited handsomely, that is until the ban on interprovincial trading would go into effect in 1918 with federal Prohibition.

However, federal Prohibition also came with a loophole, which allowed alcohol to be sold for "medicinal purposes." This prompted Harry Bronfman to create a wholesale drug company that permitted him to import alcohol in bulk and provide it to area pharmacies. He placed its offices next door to one of the family's ritzier hotels, the Balmoral, and its business model involved offering doctors a bonus for each liquor prescription they wrote if that prescription was fulfilled by a pharmacy whose liquor was furnished by the Bronfmans.[11]

Canadian writer Mordecai Richler would later allege that the initial license for Harry's new enterprise, named the Canada Pure Drug Company, was acquired by a well-placed bribe to a prominent politician.[12] Other family biographers, like Michael Marrus, called the firm "a thinly disguised liquor outlet that soon pumped more whiskey into retail drugstores than any other wholesaler in Saskatchewan."[13] The company also benefitted from the corruption of the province's liquor commission, which allowed a percentage of the liquor it seized to be sold back to Harry Bronfman, who then resold it an exorbitantly marked-up price.

Subsequent government investigations that were part of a Royal Commission would further allege that the Bronfman family "drug" company was "never engaged in the drug business, but confined its activities to the sale of alcohol in the western provinces," adding that the company imported hundreds of thousands of gallons of alcohol from the United States.[14] Out of the Bronfman brothers, it had been Sam who was sent to travel across Canada and the United States, which allowed him to build a vast network that included numerous American and Canadian distilleries and bootleggers. This network would, in a few years, prove essential to the Bronfmans, especially Sam, once Prohibition arrived in Canada's southern neighbor, the United States.

THE MANY FRIENDS OF MR. SAM

Beyond the complicity of corrupt officials and doctors, a driving force behind the Bronfman family's Prohibition era success was their ties, forged by Sam, to the Hudson's Bay Company, long a dominant force in Canada's economy backed by the political and economic elite of England since its founding in the 1600s. According to Nicholas Faith, Hudson's Bay Company "trusted him [Sam] implicitly after he had refused to make any profit on a couple of thousand cases of Dewar's whisky that Hudson's Bay wanted to buy back from him." However, in the cutthroat and often extremely violent world of bootlegging in Canada, "implicit trust" was unlikely to have been granted from just a single act.

More likely was the fact that Hudson's Bay Company had long been the dominant force in Canada's liquor industry and had every intention of continuing to operate its liquors business during Prohibition. The Bronfmans were sure to have caught their attention early on, not just through their mail order business, but because Harry Bronfman had quickly gained a reputation as "the king of bootleggers" who was able to easily skirt the law due to his contacts with corrupt local and provincial officials. His brother Sam sought to focus the entire family business on liquor early on in Prohibition, which would have made him a critical contact for any business seeking to clandestinely deal with the Bronfmans' sale of spirits during this period.[15]

The Hudson's Bay Company's import of liquor into Canada by various means during Prohibition greatly aided the business of several distillers in England and Scotland. Many of those British distillers boasted close ties to the royal family and England's political elite, like Dewar's. These companies risked losing a considerable amount of income if their ability to export spirits to Canada had been entirely cut off, especially at a time when drinking in England was on the wane. The British government itself was clearly aware of these concerns and made the promotion of exports, liquor in particular, a key policy aimed at offsetting the country's considerable war debts.[16]

Direct ties of the company to bootlegging in Canada emerged when British Colombia's Prohibition Commissioner, Walter Findlay, was caught engaging in and profiting from the illegal liquor trade. At his trial, the existence of "a liquor delivery service run by the Hudson's Bay Company" that sent alcohol to private addresses and spanned the nation was revealed, despite Findlay's refusal to testify.[17]

Whatever the real story was behind the ties that were forged between Sam Bronfman and the Hudson's Bay Company, the dominant distillers of England and Scotland that held great sway over the company's liquor subsidiary would be critical to Bronfman's success during and after Prohibition, and he to theirs.

Soon after the conclusion of Canadian prohibition, Prohibition went into effect in the United States in January 1920. The Bronfmans, now largely under Sam's leadership, continued to import American liquor at incredible quantities, but at a much cheaper rate given that the new law had made it essentially worthless in its country of origin. That imported liquor was then mixed with raw alcohol and water. This degradation allowed the Bronfmans to ship a much larger quantity of the liquor than they had purchased back into the United States.[18] Such was the story of the Bronfman family's initial entry into the distilling business.

As stock from American distilleries began to run out in 1923, the Bronfmans built a distillery near Montreal. They named their newest venture Distillers Corporation Limited, the same name as the then-unrelated and significantly more prestigious Scottish company that included the top five whisky and gin producers in the British Isles. The name the Bronfmans had chosen was no coincidence, as the "audacious" name Sam had chosen for the family's first distillery succeeded in attracting the near-immediate attention of the Scottish firm. The Bronfman family subsequently formed a joint venture with the elite of Scotland's and England's liquor industry, thereby uniting the two companies that shared the name Distillers Corporation Limited. Their union also allowed the Bronfmans to secure the exclusive rights to import many of the top brands from "across the pond."[19] Roughly a decade later, in the 1930s, Samuel Bronfman purchased and built a number of distilleries in Scotland, further deepening his ties to the liquor barons of the "Old World."

The ability of the Bronfmans to secure this deal at the time likely owed to Sam's pre-existing ties to the Hudson's Bay Company, which had previously imported many of the brands united under the British Distillers Company Limited. Another potential factor was the "chance" meeting between one of the Bronfman's "middlemen," Lewis Rosenstiel, and Winston Churchill in 1922. A year later, Bronfman traveled to Kentucky, where Rosenstiel was based at the time, and purchased an ailing distillery, the components of which were then shipped North and used to create the Bronfman's first distillery.

Churchill had deep family and personal ties to the Hudson's Bay Company and, from 1919 to 1922, he was in charge of Britain's Colonial Office.[20] In this capacity, Churchill refused to use British authority or influence to interfere with the liquor trade in any British colony, including in British-dominated "Rum Row" where the Bronfmans were also active. Churchill argued that England was not obligated to enforce the laws of another nation, and would later call Prohibition as a policy "an affront to the whole history of mankind."[21] Churchill would later emerge as a key investor in America's post-Prohibition liquor industry, which Bronfman and Rosenstiel would quickly come to dominate.[22]

As the Bronfman family's clout in the liquor industry grew after Prohibition, Sam Bronfman would later manage to personally meet Queen Elizabeth II of England and he would even create a Canadian whisky, Crown Royal, to specifically commemorate her visit to Canada in 1939.

Five years after creating the successful joint venture with Distillers Company Limited, the Bronfman's Distillers Corporation Limited purchased Joseph E. Seagram's and Sons Limited and their distillery in Waterloo, Ontario. The merged company became Seagram Company Limited, or Seagram's, and would serve as the Bronfman family's financial vehicle, not just for their ever-expanding liquor empire, but their subsequent interests in chemicals, oil, and entertainment.

Though his British and Scottish connections were important to his and Seagram's success, Sam Bronfman's rise as a global liquor baron also depended significantly on the ties he had forged, often through his "middlemen," with more unsavory actors, namely key figures in North American organized crime. Many of them still live on in American urban legend and were discussed at length in the previous chapter, including Charles "Lucky" Luciano, Moe Dalitz, Abner "Longy" Zwillman, Meyer Lansky, and members of Detroit's Purple Gang, among others.

Much of the Bronfmans' early involvement in bootlegging took place across the Saskatchewan-North Dakota border in "boozoriums" where their liquor could be purchased in Canada and then moved to their final destination in the United States. Yet, the murder of a Bronfman broth-er-in-law turned associate, and the promise of more lucrative markets for Bronfman booze soon drew their attention elsewhere.

"We were late starters in the two most lucrative markets – on the high seas and across the Detroit River. What came out of the border trade in Saskatchewan was insignificant by comparison," Bronfman once told Ca-nadian journalist Terence Robertson. Despite being late to the game, "this was when we started to make our real money," Bronfman recounted.[23]

The bootlegging operation of the Bronfmans would later extend far be-yond the Canadian-US border, with the family establishing warehouses and fronts throughout the Caribbean and Mexico. They were encircling their main market – the United States – like prey.

Of course, with great profit came great risk, and though they avoided major legal trouble for their ties to bootlegging operations during Ameri-can Prohibition, it caught up with them soon after. In 1934, the Bronfman brothers were charged with conspiracy "to violate the statutes of a friend-ly country" and for evading taxes on liquor that they had exported out of Canada.

Soon after the charges were announced, Sam Bronfman allegedly or-dered the destruction of thousands of documents aimed at "shielding their early operations from inquisitorial eyes" and Bronfman-owned companies tied to smuggling and their assets would mysteriously vanish. As a result, the case against the Bronfmans ran into an insurmountable roadblock and the four Bronfman brothers were acquitted on all charges by the summer of 1935. They even managed to settle with US authori-ties, negotiating a $3 million settlement with the Treasury Department, a mere fraction of what they had gained during American Prohibition.

Most of Bronfman's mob associates during American Prohibition were members of, or somehow tied to, the National Crime Syndicate. This Syn-dicate, described in detail in the previous chapter, was subsequently de-fined by the 1950s Senate investigative body, the Kefauver Committee, as a confederation of organized crime interests then dominated by the Ital-ian-American mafia and the Jewish-American mob. During the Kefauver Committee's investigation, some of the biggest players in the American Mafia named Bronfman as a central figure in their bootlegging operations.

Though Sam was careful to distance himself as much as possible from prominent criminals, he did have a somewhat cozy relationship with Meyer Lanksy, with Lansky's wife later recounting how Bronfman had thrown lavish dinner parties for her husband. The relationship appears to have begun in 1923 when Lansky bought Sam prized tickets to the boxing championship between Jack Dempsey and Luis Firpo in New York, likely a gesture aimed at gaining Sam's favor, or perhaps returning one. Subsequently, Lansky would, among other thing, offer exclusive protection of Bronfman's booze shipments.

In his old age, Lansky, apparently bitter that Bronfman had managed to launder his post-Prohibition reputation into that of an "upstanding" member of North American aristocracy, would remark "Why is Lansky a 'gangster' and not the Bronfman and Rosenstiel families? I was involved with all of them in the 1920s, although they do not like to talk about it and change the subject when my name is mentioned."[24]

The ties between the Bronfman family business and organized crime may explain why some past efforts to chronicle the rise of the Bronfmans were ill-fated, particularly during Sam Bronfman's lifetime. The first person who attempted to write a biography of Samuel Bronfman, Terence Robertson, had traveled to New York to investigate Bronfman and the then-sprawling corporate empire of Seagram's. While in New York, he had allegedly concluded the book, but had telephoned a journalist colleague back in Canada, distraught. In that phone call, Robertson claimed to have "found out things about Sam, they didn't want me to write about."

Robertson would call a second colleague, stressing that his "life had been threatened and we would know who was doing the threatening but that he would do the job himself." After receiving the frantic call and fearing that Robertson's life was in danger, the second journalist called the New York police, who quickly responded, only to find Robertson dying of barbiturate poisoning, to which he succumbed. Robertson's lengthy interviews with Bronfman were never published, but still exist in manuscript form.

Subsequent attempts to author a biography of Sam Bronfman and his family's rise to prominence also failed to make it to publication, such as the effort made by former editor of the Canadian edition of *TIME* magazine, John Scott, and another made by Canadian journalist Erna Paris. However, some books on the Bronfman family did emerge once Sam had reached old age, such as an account of the family by Peter Newman and a novel by Mordecai Richler believed to have been inspired by the Bronfmans. The Bronfmans apparently did not take kindly to their portrayal by either Newman or Richler, both of whom were Jewish, prompting the family behind Seagram's to allege that both authors were "anti-Semitic Jews." The Bronfman clan has always been sensitive to critical reports, given that their longstanding efforts to develop their reputation as elite "philanthropists" are marred by the evidence of the symbiotic relationship between their family business and organized crime.

THE MIDDLEMEN

Aside from these more personal ties, also crucial to the success of Seagram's and the Bronfman family enterprise during this period were an assortment of "middlemen." Two of these men were particularly essential to the Bronfman business – Joseph Reinfeld and the aforementioned Lewis "Lew" Rosenstiel. The two men were of extremely different temperaments, with Reinfeld being described as "a jovial, avuncular Jewish immigrant from Poland" whereas Rosenstiel was described as "loud, opinionated and domineering."

Reinfeld served as a close advisor to Sam Bronfman as well as an important business associate as he was the principal purchaser of Seagram's Whiskey. It was also Reinfeld who convinced Sam to "build up inventory" prior to and during Prohibition, which would help Bronfman secure a significant portion of the post-Prohibition liquor market. He also managed much of the in-person dealings with crime-linked individuals on Bronfman's behalf, which was key to Bronfman's winning strategy to mitigate legal risks and prevent further damage to his social reputation.

The end result saw Reinfeld buy large amounts of Seagram's liquor, mainly at Rum Row, while ensuring that the Bronfmans did not have to directly deal with their final, crime-linked customers. However, in at least one instance, Reinfeld actually brought Sam Bronfman, and his family business, into close contact with a notorious mobster. By 1923, the Reinfeld syndicate was half-owned by Longy Zwillman, who Reinfeld sent to negotiate directly with Sam Bronfman. Bronfman was reportedly very impressed with Zwillman, then in his early 20s, calling him "well-behaved" and "studious looking," adding that "you'd never guess he was a *shtarker*."[25]

Reinfeld's operation during Prohibition was massive, and massively profitable for Bronfman. Government investigators later revealed that Reinfeld had "imported nearly 40 percent of all the illicit alcohol consumed in the United States during Prohibition." Retired US Treasury agents later testified that the Bronfman family were Reinfeld's main supplier, while also alleging that much of Reinfeld's ill-gotten profits had been laundered in Canada, some of it allegedly laundered with the help of Seagram's employees. The use of Canadian institutions as laundries for Reinfeld is not only plausible but likely, given the intimate involvement of the Royal Bank of Canada in Rum Row, the same place where Reinfeld had received his shipments of Bronfman liquor. [26] The Bronfmans themselves were known to operate a network of shell companies, some registered to fictitious individuals and linked to a series of both domestic and foreign bank accounts. This network facilitated the family's own "elaborate money laundering operations," according to Canadian historian Stephen Schneider.

The close association between Bronfman and Reinfeld would later come back to haunt them both, particularly when Reinfeld's longtime bodyguard, James Rutkin, testified in front of the Kefauver Committee in the early 1950s. Rutkin would tell all regarding the "early days" of the Bronfman family business, including the relationships of both Bronfman and Reinfeld with mobsters like Zwillman and Lansky. Some Bronfman family biographers, like Nicholas Faith, have alleged that Rutkin sought to use his testimony in a failed attempt to blackmail the Bronfmans, threatening to reveal more if he was left uncompensated.

Among Rutkin's claims regarding the Bronfmans, several pertained to the family's hotel business in Canada that had preceded their liquor empire. Rutkin, describing the Bronfmans as "four brothers from Montreal," teased the Kefauver Committee, stating first that "if you want to find out more about the [Bronfman owned] hotels, you can ask the Canadian Mounted Police, and they will tell you about the little hotels, and you can use your imagination." He later added that these hotels serviced people who slept "very fast," and that the same room would be rented "quite a few times during the night," implying that the hotels were in fact brothels.[27] Several Bronfman family biographers also mention these accusations, which had dogged the family since their earliest days in the hotel business. Some believe that Sam Bronfman tacitly confirmed that this was the case many years after Rutkin first made these claims, when he remarked "If they were [brothels], they were the best in the West!"[28]

Nevertheless, in the early 1950s at the time of the Kefauver hearings, the Bronfmans alleged that Rutkin's claims were "absurd," and they declined to pony up any of the "hush money" that Rutkin was rumored to have been seeking. Yet, despite their best efforts, Rutkin's testimony, which received considerable publicity due to the televised broadcast of the hearings, created a whirlwind of rumors that refused to be snuffed out for some time, at least until Rutkin turned up dead, having allegedly slit his own throat with a borrowed razor in 1956.[29]

Lewis Rosenstiel, the other most prominent of Sam Bronfman's Prohibition Era "middlemen," saw his relationship with the Seagram's chairman take a completely different trajectory than that of Bronfman and Reinfeld. As Prohibition neared its end, Rosenstiel and Bronfman would grow into bitter rivals, despite continuing to share many of the same contacts in the North America's criminal underworld.

The Chairman

While Sam Bronfman struggled with his would-be biographers, no biography was ever written of his one-time middleman and later chief rival, Lewis Rosenstiel. Of those books and other writings that do touch on Rosenstiel's history and demeanor, few are favorable. For instance, a 1959 piece in *Esquire* offers one of the more favorable accounts, calling Rosenstiel "intelligent, articulate and extraordinarily aggressive," adding that he often "slopes in his chair, plays with his tongue as he speaks, and utters his strong opinions with a growl, expressing dislike and contempt for anyone who might disagree."[30]

Others, like Bronfman biographer Nicholas Faith, describe Rosenstiel as "loud, opinionated and domineering," a "hulking figure who favored amber-tinted glasses, which he rarely removed, and large cigars to go with his status as one of the wealthiest men alive."[31] The *New York Times* obituary for Rosenstiel uses similar terms, referring to the liquor baron known to many simply as "the Chairman" as having been "a domineering man with [a] quick temper."[32]

Official accounts of Rosenstiel's past and how he built his company Schenley into a corporate behemoth seem oddly sanitized, not unlike the official accounts of the Bronfman family's early days that decline to mention the darker side of their business model that was particularly important to their activities prior to the repeal of American Prohibition.

Born in 1891 in Cincinnati, Ohio, Rosenstiel – thanks to an unfortunate injury during a football match in his teenage years – dropped out of high school and went to work for his uncle at the Susquemac Distilling Company in Milton, Kentucky in 1907. Rosenstiel worked on largely menial tasks at the facility, including as a "pinhooker" rolling barrels in warehouses and as a belt splicer. His fortunes shifted dramatically from those humble beginnings during the era of American Prohibition, with little being known of his life during the period, aside from him allegedly leaving the tedious tasks of his uncle's distillery behind to become a "whisky broker."

According to official accounts, Rosenstiel turned to selling shoes and bonds once Prohibition set in, with his prior line of work in the distilling and sale of spirits drying up. Yet, somehow, the young Rosenstiel accumulated enough money to afford a vacation to the French Riviera in 1922. It was during that vacation that he would be lucky enough to score a "chance" meeting with Winston Churchill, "who advised him to prepare for the return of liquor sales in the United States," per the *New York Times*.[33] There is little, if any, context given in official accounts as to how or why a high-school dropout turned distillery worker and shoe salesman would have attracted the attention of a notorious elitist and member of the British aristocracy like Churchill.

As the story goes, Rosenstiel spent the next ten years of his life dutifully following Churchill's advice. He somehow convinced one of the most powerful banks on Wall Street, Lehman Brothers, to offer him a massive loan to finance his acquisition of closed distilleries and to accumulate aged whisky inventories for the yet-to-materialize date of repeal. Again, no official explanation is offered as to how an elite banking institution like Lehman Brothers would grant someone with Rosenstiel's background such a large amount of capital based merely on advice he had received from a British politician, suggesting there is more to the story.

Returning to the official narrative of Rosenstiel's rise, we are told that Rosenstiel then incorporated Schenley Distillers Company in the wake of Repeal in 1933. He was conveniently well-placed to become "the most powerful figure in the distilled spirits business," all thanks to his having heeded Churchill's advice and thanks to a remarkable patience that he was never known to have possessed during any other point in his life.[34] Indeed, per these same official sources, *impatience*, rather than patience, was one of Rosenstiel's most well-known traits, with his characterization by media as a "domineering man with a quick temper" being one of many examples.

Of course, as should be clear to the reader, this narrative conveniently obfuscates any hint of illegality in Rosenstiel's Prohibition era dealings and fails to mention Rosenstiel's documented ties to organized crime figures or his role as a prominent purchaser of Bronfman liquor alongside Joseph Reinfeld and other Seagram's "middlemen." Years later, James P. Kelly, chief investigator for the Interstate and Foreign Commerce Committee of the New York House of Representatives, testified under oath that Rosenstiel had been part of an "underworld consortium" that bought Bronfman liquor and sold it throughout the United States during Prohibition.[35]

Key figures in this consortium, aside from Rosenstiel, included Meyer Lansky as well as Joe Fusco, an associate of Al Capone, and Joe Linsey, a

Boston-based criminal associated with Joe Kennedy's bootlegging operations. Kelly added that Rosenstiel was "particularly close" to Lansky, and it later emerged that they had "owned points together" in mob-operated businesses. He was also reportedly close to Frank Costello, who was said to have attended a business meeting alongside Rosenstiel "to give [the meeting's attendees] a message that Rosenstiel was one of their people."[36]

One of Rosenstiel's ex-wives, Susan Kaufman, later told journalist Anthony Summers that, in Summers' words, "living with Rosenstiel was to live with the command structure of organized crime." Kaufman's testimony to Summers includes numerous, specific, and very detailed allegations of the various meetings between her ex-husband and organized crime figures she witnessed during their marriage, including business meetings where Rosenstiel was given "thousands and thousands and thousands of dollars in bundles of cash" from Lansky.

After Prohibition, Fusco and Linsey took their operations into the legal and legitimate business world, just as Rosenstiel had done. They set up legitimate companies in Chicago and Boston, respectively, to market Schenley products. As a result, Rosenstiel maintained his links to the criminal underworld long after publicly transitioning from bootlegger to businessman. Frequent dinner guests at Rosenstiel's home in the years and decades after Prohibition included legendary figures of American organized crime, including Frank Costello, Sam Giancana, Santo Trafficante and Meyer Lansky. Lansky was known to address Rosenstiel as "Supreme Commander," a name that Roy Cohn, Rosenstiel's attorney and close friend, also used for the liquor baron.[37]

Rosenstiel's transition from bootlegger to businessman very nearly included a direct partnership with Sam Bronfman. In 1929, as the end of Prohibition neared, Bronfman invested $585,000 in a Rosenstiel-owned distillery producing "medicinal spirits" and had acquired a 20% stake in Rosenstiel's company. Per Sam, however, he concluded after visiting Rosenstiel's distillery that it was "a piece of junk and ... on the inside it was even worse" and he was allegedly offended at the inferiority of his whisky production method. It's unclear if this was the actual motive for their falling out, but, regardless, their subsequent business and personal rivalries became legendary.

According to Nicholas Faith's account of Bronfman's life, the falling out with Rosenstiel, whatever the cause, took a tremendous emotional toll on the two men before it descended into a decades-long, acrimonious spat. Faith asserts that Bronfman's failure to reach an agreement with

Rosenstiel "really hit him, for he came down with severe flu" soon after calling off any possibility of a partnership. Despite being gravely ill, Bronfman told Rosenstiel that "we have nothing to discuss" when the latter had arrived to attempt to salvage a deal. Terence Robertson's manuscript, as cited by Faith, states that Rosenstiel "all but wept as he begged 'for just a minute with my friend.'"[38]

Their feud would subsequently escalate to such an extent that it would transcend business competition, with a 1959 article in *Esquire* noting that neither man "appears willing to sacrifice profit to do the other in the eye." Rosenstiel was known to refer to Bronfman and his business as "unscrupulous alien competition," with alien in this instance meaning foreign, i.e. Canadian.[39] Bronfman, for his part, was known to become angry rather quickly when Rosenstiel's name or business came up, saying he had "no admiration" for the man, and would frequently refer to him as "Rosenschlemiel," with "schlemiel" meaning something along the lines of simpleton or a born loser in Yiddish.[40] It was also alleged that Bronfman's lavish Seagram building in New York City had been planned to make "Rosenstiel's 1930s-style offices in the Empire State Building look just a little shabby in their luxury."[41]

THE KING OF BOURBON AND BLACKMAIL

Though both men had legendary tempers and a legendary feud to match, Bronfman and Rosenstiel had major differences in character, particularly in how they managed their respective businesses and in their personal lives. One of these differences was the fact that Sam Bronfman did not share Rosenstiel's obsession with blackmail.

Indeed, reports of Rosenstiel's behavior at his company's offices, as cited by Nicholas Faith, included Rosenstiel having placed "bugging devices" throughout his offices. Per Faith, he would treat his employees "like dirt, sacking them at a moment's notice" and then go "to the toilet to leave them time to compromise themselves by talking in his absence." Those employees were "compromised" as their conversations were recorded by the devices that Rosenstiel had strewn about the premises.

Additional assertions made in court and under oath by one of Rosenstiel's ex-wives held that Rosenstiel had also placed microphones throughout his home in order to record conversations that took place at social events he hosted for the alleged purpose of obtaining potential blackmail against his guests. In addition, several sources reported to the 1971 New York State Legislative Committee on Crime that Rosenstiel's Manhattan home had been "wired from roof to basement with hidden microphones, so that he could spy on visitors and staff."[42]

The system in Rosenstiel's home had been installed by Fred Otash, an infamous private detective who had used electronic means to spy on the Kennedy family, Marilyn Monroe, and others. Otash later said that Rosenstiel's home "was rigged to tape conversations for hours on end." Otash had a penchant for blackmail himself, particularly sexual blackmail – he had once attempted to entrap John F. Kennedy using a call girl named "Sue Young" in the lead-up to the 1960 presidential election.[43] As we'll see shortly, Rosenstiel was also involved in a broader effort to obtain this variety of blackmail, which may explain why he had sought out the California-based Otash to bug his New York home.

Some of the sources that discuss Rosenstiel's interest in blackmail also claim that Rosenstiel was bisexual. According to Nicholas Faith, discussions about Rosenstiel's bisexuality among Schenley office employees were frequent enough for Rosenstiel to be referred to as "Rosie" around the office. Additional evidence for these claims later came from Rosenstiel's fourth wife, Susan Kaufman.

Per Kaufman, whose previous marriage had collapsed because her first husband had been homosexual, she soon discovered that she had made a similar mistake in marrying Rosenstiel. Rosenstiel was reportedly uninterested in having sex with his new wife, but "went to great expense to have her dress up in clothes that made her look like a little girl."[44] He would later be discovered in bed with one of his lawyers, Roy Cohn, and shrugged it off to his wife by asking for some more "alone time" with his attorney. Kaufman remembered responding, "I've never seen Governor [Thomas] Dewey in bed with you," as Dewey was also one of his attorneys at the time, and she walked out.[45]

Kaufman remembered the young Cohn, who was best known for his infamous stint as Joe McCarthy's chief counsel during the height of the Red Scare, as flaunting his homosexuality whenever he was around Kaufman, openly caressing a former congressional associate in front of her and describing the homosexual antics of a close friend of his and Rosenstiel's – Cardinal Spellman, one of the most powerful figures in the Catholic Church in North America. Cohn reportedly was so open with her because her first husband "had been gay and I must have understood because I'd stayed with him for nine years," Kaufman later stated.[46]

In 1958, Kaufman accompanied her husband Lewis Rosenstiel to a "party" hosted by Cohn at the Plaza Hotel in New York. Kaufman recalled entering through a side entrance and taking an elevator to the 2nd or 3rd floor; her husband knew the way well enough that she "had the impression [he] had been there before." The suite was one of the largest available at the hotel and it was "all done in light blue." Inside the suite were Cohn and another figure closely associated with both Cohn and Rosenstiel: FBI Director J. Edgar Hoover. To Kaufman's surprise, Hoover was wearing women's clothes and wig, with Cohn introducing him as "Mary" in a bout of barely concealed laughter. "Mary" was also incidentally the nickname widely used among New York Catholic clergy for Cardinal Spellman, who was also alleged to attend other parties hosted by Cohn in the Plaza's "blue suite."[47]

After being served a few drinks, Kaufman recalled seeing "a couple of boys come in, young blond boys. I'd say about eighteen or nineteen. And then Roy [Cohn] makes the signal we should go into the bedroom."[48] Sexual activities between the "young blond boys," Cohn and Hoover ensued, with Kaufman declining to participate after being urged to do so by her then-husband. The Rosenstiels then left, leaving the boys alone with Cohn and Hoover. Cohn later laughed about the incident to Kaufman, saying that "Mary Hoover" attends his parties regularly and that he would make sure to "arrive at the Plaza first with his clothes [the female clothes allegedly used by Hoover at the parties] in a suitcase."[49]

Per her testimony, Kaufman was repulsed by the whole affair, but ended up attending another of these parties at the Plaza after Rosenstiel bribed her with "an expensive pair of earrings from Harry Winston's."[50] The events of that evening played out as they had the time before, but the Rosenstiels later quarreled, and she never attended any more Cohn-hosted parties at the Plaza hotel.

These allegations made by Kaufman resulted in considerable efforts to discredit her testimony, especially during the 1971 New York State Legislative Committee on Crime. Kaufman had agreed to serve as a witness for the State regarding her ex-husband's ties to organized crime figures. The very week that she was due to testify, Kaufman was hit with an "attempted perjury" charge that was regarded as unprecedented and bizarre by lawyers and outraged the Committee's Chairman and Chief Counsel. Kaufman still testified, but mostly behind closed doors, in executive session. Her testimony – several decades later – still remains sealed.

Members of the Committee believed at the time that the "attempted perjury" charges had been instigated by Lewis Rosenstiel himself in order to prevent his wife from testifying, as he had previously used similar tactics to protect his corrupt dealings.[51] This "attempted perjury" charge has since been used by some authors to discredit Kaufman's later testimony regarding her ex-husband and his associates.

However, the former Chief Counsel of the Crime Committee, New York Judge Edward McLaughlin, and Committee investigator William Gallinaro found Kaufman to be "an exceptionally good witness."[52] McLaughlin later told journalist and Hoover biographer Anthony Summers, "I thought her absolutely truthful.... The woman's power of recall was phenomenal. Everything she said was checked and double checked, and everything that was checkable turned out to be true." Additional evidence corroborating Kaufman as a witness came from two male witnesses who supported the astonishing allegations of Hoover's habit of cross-dressing, with those witnesses having learned of the former FBI director's habit at a different time and place than the events described by Kaufman. They also had no knowledge of Hoover and the "blue suite" parties in New York.

In addition, Kaufman told Anthony Summers that she possessed photographs showing Hoover in the company of Lewis Rosenstiel's organized crime associates. Though Summers did not see these pictures personally, they were confirmed as authentic and had been seen by journalist Mary Nichols of the *Philadelphia Enquirer*. Nichols told Summers "She did have suitcases of photographs that she had hauled away from her marriage to Lewis Rosenstiel. The ones I saw showed Hoover, lawyer Roy Cohn and Rosenstiel, at all sorts of social events with mobsters."[53]

There is also evidence that, not only did these parties at the Plaza hotel take place, but that they were used to obtain sexual blackmail, with Kaufman asserting that her husband possessed pictures of Hoover wearing women's clothes and that those images had been passed to Rosenstiel's associate, mobster Meyer Lansky.[54] Journalist and author Anthony Summers has noted that, given Rosenstiel's interest and ability to have his residences and businesses bugged, "[Rosenstiel] was quite capable of having the sex sessions at the Plaza bugged or arranging for Edgar to be photographed in his female costumes."[55]

In addition, New York attorney John Klotz, tasked with investigating Roy Cohn for a case well after Kaufman's testimony, independently found evidence of the "blue suite" at the Plaza Hotel and its role in a sex extortion ring after combing through local government documents and information gathered by private detectives. It allegedly involved minors as well as young men aged eighteen and older. Klotz later summarized his findings, telling journalist and author Burton Hersh:

Roy Cohn was providing protection. There were a bunch of pe-
dophiles involved. That's where Cohn got his power from – blackmail.[56]

Further confirmation of Rosenstiel's and Cohn's activities in the
"blue suite," later determined to be Suite 233, comes from statements
made by Cohn himself to former NYPD detective and ex-head of the
department's Human-Trafficking and Vice-Related Crimes Division,
James Rothstein. Rothstein later told John DeCamp – a former Nebraska state senator who investigated the Franklin scandal of the 1980s –
that Cohn had admitted to being part of a sexual blackmail operation
targeting politicians with minors during a sit-down interview with the
former detective.

Rothstein told DeCamp the following about Cohn:

> Cohn's job was to run the little boys. Say you had an admiral, a gen-
> eral, a congressman, who did not want to go along with the pro-
> gram. Cohn's job was to set them up, then they would go along.
> Cohn told me that himself.[57]

Rothstein later told Paul David Collins, a former journalist turned researcher, that Cohn had also identified this sexual blackmail operation as
being part of the anti-communist crusade of the time.[58]

The fact that Cohn, per Rothstein's recollection, stated that this sex
blackmail ring was part of the anti-communist crusade coupled with
Hoover's involvement in these "blue suite" events suggests that elements
of the government, including Hoover's FBI, may have been connected at
a much broader level to the operation in a way that transcended Hoover's
own personal involvement.

Rothstein confirmed his statements to both DeCamp and Collins in
an interview with me that was conducted in early 2020. He additionally
told me that Cohn had told him that his role in this ring had originally come about because he himself had been entrapped and blackmailed,
leading Rothstein to feel some sort of sympathy for Cohn.

For those that may find it hard to believe that such an operation would
take place with the involvement of the FBI director, there are also other, related allegations to consider – that American intelligence operatives
and organized crime had competed and then collaborated to blackmail
Hoover years before Kaufman witnessed these events at the Plaza hotel
beginning in 1958.

Lansky was credited with obtaining compromising photos of FBI Director J. Edgar Hoover sometime in the 1940s, which showed "Hoover in some kind of gay situation," according to a former Lansky associate, who also said that Lansky had often said of Hoover, "I fixed that sonofabitch." Meyer Lansky's widow also later claimed that her husband had acquired "hard proof of Hoover's homosexuality and used it to neutralize the FBI as a threat to his own operations."[59] The photos showed Hoover engaged in sexual activity, specifically oral sex, with his long-time friend, FBI Deputy Director Clyde Tolson.[60] There is considerable, separate evidence from the period that the close, professional relationship between Hoover and Tolson was also intimate and that this was an "open secret" in Washington.[61]

At some point, these photos fell into the hands of CIA counterintelligence chief James J. Angleton, who later showed the photos to several other CIA officials, including John Weitz and Gordon Novel.[62] Both Weitz and Novel later stated that the pictures they had seen showed Hoover engaged in oral sex on a man who Angleton identified as Tolson; however, only Hoover's face was recognizable in the photographs.[63] Angleton also claimed that the photos had been taken in 1946.[64] Angleton was in charge of the CIA's relationship with the FBI as well as Israeli intelligence until he left the agency in 1972. Angleton was also a CIA figure who had pushed for the Agency to forge ties with Meyer Lansky, raising the possibility that Angleton could have received the photo from Lansky.

However, Anthony Summers, in *Official and Confidential: The Secret Life of J. Edgar Hoover*, has argued that it was not Lansky, but William Donovan, the director of the OSS, who obtained the original photos of Hoover and either he, or another person at the OSS or early CIA, had later shared them with Lansky. Summers also states that "To [gangster Frank] Costello and Lansky, the ability to corrupt politicians, policemen and judges was fundamental to Mafia operations. The way they found to deal with Hoover, according to several mob sources, involved his homosexuality."[65]

With the mobster associates of Rosenstiel being under significantly more pressure during the 1950s, in large part thanks to the Kefauver Committee, it's possible that Hoover's appearances at The Plaza Hotel may have served as additional "insurance" for these interests.

Hoover, for his part, was likely already used to the realities of being blackmailed by this point, given that his private sex life had been known to the mob and US intelligence community for years. He likely saw the opportunity to partake in the scheme as a means of amassing his own, massive collection of blackmail. With thick dossiers on friend and foe alike, Hoover's office contained "secret files" on numerous powerful people in Washington and beyond, files he used to gain favors and protect his status as FBI director for as long as he wished. Even former OSS veterans like Richard Helms have made such claims, alleging that Hoover "played 'a very skillful game' with knowledge of the sexual habits of prominent people."[66]

Further evidence for this comes from journalist and author Burton Hersh who alleges in his book *Bobby and J. Edgar: The Historic Face-Off Between the Kennedys and J. Edgar Hoover That Transformed America* that Hoover had also been tied to Sherman Kaminsky, who helped run a sexual blackmail operation in New York that involved young male prostitutes.[67] Kaminsky claimed to have been New York-bred, but federal investigators later stated he was originally from Baltimore. Some reports claim Kaminsky had ties to Israel, having served in the Israel Defense Forces.[68]

The ring, which was called "The Chickens and the Bulls" by the NYPD, targeted prominent men who were closeted homosexuals throughout the United States, many of them married with families. Among those who had been blackmailed were a Navy admiral, two generals, a US congressman, a prominent surgeon, an Ivy League professor and well-known actors and television personalities.[69] That operation was busted and investigated in a 1966 extortion probe led by Manhattan District Attorney Frank Hogan, though the FBI quickly took over the investigation and photos showing Hoover and Kaminsky together soon disappeared from the case file.[70] Kaminsky successfully avoided arrest for 11 years, having "disappeared" from a New York courthouse undetected during his sentencing hearing.[71]

Why would Hoover have been involved with the activities of Kaminsky? There are only a few possibilities. One possibility is that Hoover had been blackmailed by Kaminsky, though it's more likely that Kaminsky instead had ties to figures in organized crime that had already blackmailed Hoover long before. Another possibility is that Hoover was cozy to a second sexual blackmail operation targeting closeted homosexual men because he sought to pad his own library of blackmail for personal and professional gain.

What does seem clear is that Hoover was well aware of the power that amassing blackmail afforded and was willing to indulge in taboo behavior at the "blue suite" because he was no longer concerned about being extorted or manipulated with sexual blackmail in ways that would end his career or destroy his public image. He had fallen in with the very crowd that had reportedly blackmailed him, later developing a symbiotic relationship with that same network.

The most obvious, and troubling, symptom of this symbiosis was Hoover's reluctance to tackle organized crime as FBI director. Hoover repeatedly declined to use the Bureau to target organized crime networks, referring to organized crime as a "local" problem in which the FBI did not need to intervene for most of his nearly fifty year stint as the top law enforcement administrator in the country.[72]

According to congressional crime consultant Ralph Salerno, Hoover's apparent aversion to targeting organized crime networks, such as those in which Rosenstiel and Lansky figured prominently, "allowed organized crime to grow very strong in economic and political terms, so that it became a much bigger threat to the wellbeing of this country than it would have been if it had been addressed much sooner."[73]

BUSINESS AS USUAL

Other aspects of Hoover's symbiotic relationship with these organized crime-tinged networks can also be seen in Hoover's ties to Rosenstiel, and Rosenstiel's close associate Roy Cohn, in the "above-board" worlds of "legitimate" business and politics.

Most records place the beginning of Hoover's relationship with Rosenstiel as occurring in the 1950s, the same decade that that Hoover was allegedly attending Rosenstiel's blackmail parties. Rosenstiel's FBI file, obtained by Anthony Summers, cites the first Rosenstiel meeting as taking place in 1956.[74] After requesting that meeting, Rosenstiel was granted a personal face-to-face meeting with the director in a matter of hours, a rare feat. However, Summers notes that there is evidence that the two men had met much earlier, as Hoover was on record showing an unusual concern in the FBI's handling of Rosenstiel's criminal links as early as 1939.[75]

The "blue suite" parties and blackmail may also explain the uncharacteristic ease with which a young Roy Cohn was able to meet with J. Edgar Hoover upon his arrival as a young man in Washington DC in 1952, an event that has puzzled Cohn's biographers. Roy Cohn's account of how he was able to meet Hoover in person, deemed "improbable" by Cohn biographer Nicholas von Hoffman, involves Hoover calling Cohn after the latter had unsuccessfully sought to go through the normal channels to communicate with the FBI Director.[76] Cohn, only in his mid-20s, had been seeking Hoover's aid in gathering support for a controversial pre-sentment, which alleged communist subversion among United Nations staff.

Hoover, who is supposed to be talking to Cohn for the first time per "official" accounts, is alleged to have said "Roy, are you trying to see me?" To that, Cohn claimed to have responded "You're darn right I'm trying to see you. It's been rather difficult." Hoover then offered, "Whenever you want to see me, you just pick up the phone and ask for me and you'll be able to see me." "Well, when can I see you?" Cohn had asked, with the director then saying, "Come on over." Per Cohn, he was then seated in front of Hoover within ten minutes. Von Hoffman, who notes elsewhere in his Cohn biography that some of Cohn's unlikely stories "do turn out to be true," notes that the story is improbable, in part, because the only tie he could find between Cohn and Hoover at the time was a connection to George Sokolsky, the director of the American Jewish League Against Communism.

Also unlikely, per Von Hoffman, was Hoover's alleged urging to Roy that "When you want to see me, call me directly. Don't go through chan-nels ... [The Justice Department] is monitoring your calls at your own office across the way." Von Hoffman states that this degree of frankness "with a junior whom he had only recently met" is at odds with Hoover's reputation "as one of the most adept of mountain goats in negotiating the trails and passes of the federal bureaucracy." Von Hoffman asks, "Would merely sharing a political outlook on the dangers of communism be enough to seduce Hoover, who was never indiscreet, into such indiscre-tions as advising Roy, all else failing, to threaten to quit and back it up by calling a press conference if there were no other way to shake the present-ment loose?"

Von Hoffman concludes that Cohn's story was inaccurate, though he notes that "Roy's account of what Hoover told him is a story that some-body with a dangerous secret to hide might tell."[77] However, in the context of the "blue suite" parties at the Plaza hotel, it's certainly possible that both Cohn's account of his first "official" meeting with Hoover and his harboring of "a dangerous secret" are both true. This is supported from press reports of the same period that claim that, soon after "Cohn caught Hoover's eye" in Washington DC, Hoover "showered Cohn with compliments and notes and photographs."[78] Author Burton Hersh similarly asserts that, soon after meeting, Hoover and Cohn "traded favors, effusive compliments, gifts and elaborate private dinners. It quickly became 'Roy' and 'Edgar.'"[79]

The "official" story also holds that the only bond initially shared between Rosenstiel and Cohn, as it is alleged with Hoover and Cohn, was a shared commitment to anti-communism, which has similarly left biographers and observers of their relationship puzzled by "improbable" anecdotes similar to that described above. Yet, in an era where the Red Scare raged alongside the so-called Lavender Scare (which targeted homosexuals with the same fervor as the Red Scare targeted communists), the bonds forged between a group of men who shared their forbidden passions in a milieu of secretive orgies, blackmail, and organized crime, would have fostered a much stronger sense of camaraderie.

The surprising closeness shared among Rosenstiel, Cohn and Hoover can be seen in other arrangements. For instance, soon after meeting Hoover "officially" for the first time in 1956, Hoover sent Rosenstiel flowers when the latter fell ill. A year later, Rosenstiel was heard telling Hoover "Your wish is my command" during a meeting.[80] That same year, Louis B. Nichols, Hoover's "Number 2" at the Bureau for decades, was hired to become executive vice president of Rosenstiel's empire of Schenley. Around this time, it was reported that Rosenstiel had "bought large quantities of books about Hoover and distributed them as gifts."[81] In addition, Rosenstiel had also bought no less than 25,000 copies of *Masters of Deceit*, a book written by Hoover about how to fight communism in the United States, which he sent "to schools around the country."[82]

A few years later, in 1965, Nichols incorporated the J. Edgar Hoover Foundation. Rosenstiel was the principal contributor, giving the foundation 1000 shares of Schenley stock. Nichols also gave a smaller, yet unknown amount of Schenley shares to the foundation, while the American Jewish League Against Communism, of which Roy Cohn was now president, gave $500 to help start the foundation. A year later, the Dorothy H. and Lewis Rosenstiel Foundation gave $50,000 to the foundation. In 1968, the Rosenstiel Foundation gave an additional $1 million to the foundation that was made in the form of bonds of the Glen Alden Corporation, which took over Schenley industries that same year. A 1969 report in the *Washington Post* later noted that "nearly everyone directly associated with Nichols in the Hoover Foundation is or was connected with either the FBI or Schenleys. The report also noted that, despite lofty promises regarding the foundation's activities, it spent hardly any money at the time the *Washington Post*'s report was published in 1969, suggesting that something about the foundation's activities during that period was odd.[83]

Around this same period, Rosenstiel began to retire, selling his controlling interest to Glen Alden in 1968 and resigning as chairman and CEO of Schenley. While it seemed that Cohn would serve as Rosenstiel's successor in matters of blackmail, it seems another man served as his successor in matters of business. Per Rosenstiel's *New York Times* obituary, around the time he sold his control of Schenley to Glen Alden and retired, he also sold his Manhattan town house, bugged for blackmail, to Israeli-American businessman Meshulam Riklis.[84] Riklis was then an "influential figure" at Glen Alden, whose rise had been regarded with skepticism by Wall Street and the press. Indeed, Riklis had absorbed so many companies, including Glen Alden/Schenley in 1972, into his Rapid-American Corporation that he was forced to defend himself publicly, insisting that the fuel for his corporate takeovers involved "no mystery money, no unnamed associates, no Swiss-bank money."[85]

Endnotes

1   Peter C. Newman, *Bronfman Dynasty: The Rothschilds of the New World* (Toronto: McClelland and Stewart, 1978), 66–68.

2   Michael R. Marrus, *Samuel Bronfman: The Life and Times of Seagram's Mr. Sam* (Hanover: Published by University Press of New England [for] Brandeis University Press, 1991), 15.

3   Marrus, *Samuel Bronfman*, 22.

4   Nicholas Faith, *The Bronfmans: The Rise and Fall of the House of Seagram*, 1st ed (New York: St. Martin's Press, 2006), 217–18.

5   Eli Yahri, "Seagram | The Canadian Encyclopedia," February 13, 2012, https://www.thecanadianencyclopedia.ca/en/article/seagram-company-limited.

6   Stephen Schneider, *Iced: The Story of Organized Crime in Canada* (Mississauga, Ont: Wiley, 2009), 199.

7   Richard Allen, "Social Gospel | The Canadian Encyclopedia," February 7, 2006, https://www.thecanadianencyclopedia.ca/en/article/social-gospel; Leona Anderson, Bryan Hillis, and Margaret Sanche, "The Encyclopedia of Saskatchewan | Details," n.d., https://esask.uregina.ca/entry/religion.jsp.

8   Faith, *The Bronfmans*, 28.

9   John M. Bumsted, *The Peoples of Canada*, Fourth edition (Don Mills, Ontario: Oxford University Press, 2014), 218–19.

10   Newman, *Bronfman Dynasty*, 74.

11   Daniel Okrent, *Last Call: The Rise and Fall of Prohibition*, First Scribner hardcover ed (New York: Scribner, 2010), chap. 10.

12   Faith, *The Bronfmans*, 34-5.

13   Marrus, *Samuel Bronfman*, 68.

14   Schneider, *Iced*, 200.

15   Faith, *The Bronfmans*, 34-5.

16   Okrent, *Last Call*, chap. 12.

17   Jesse Donaldson, "On BC Day, a Look at Five Wacky Stories from the Province's Past," The Tyee, August 5, 2019, https://thetyee.ca/Culture/2019/08/05/BC-Day-Provincial-Past-Wacky-Stories/.

18   Okrent, *Last Call*, chap. 11.

19   Davin de Kergommeaux, "Whisky Heroes: Sam Bronfman, Seagram | Scotch Whisky," March 21, 2019, https://scotchwhisky.com/magazine/whisky-heroes/24781/sam-bronfman-seagram/.

20   James W. Muller, "Two Churchills and the Hudson's Bay Company," APSA 2009 *Toronto Meeting Paper* (Rochester, NY: Social Science Research Network, September 3, 2009), https://papers.ssrn.com/abstract=1451764.

21   Okrent, *Last Call*, chap. 12.

22   Thomas Maier, "Prohibition and Profit: The Secret Kennedy-Churchill-Roosevelt Deals," *TIME*, October 21, 2014, https://time.com/3529756/kennedy-churchill-roosevelt-investment-deal/.

23   Faith, *The Bronfmans*, 132.

24   Schneider, *Iced*, 203.

25   Faith, *The Bronfmans*, 64.

26   Okrent, *Last Call*, chap. 12.

27   *Investigation of Organized Crime in Interstate Commerce*, Hearings before the Special Committee to Investigate Organized Crime in Interstate Commerce (1950, 1951), p. 544, https://archive.org/details/investigationofo07unit/page/544/mode/2up.

28   Schneider, *Iced*, 199.

29   Faith, *The Bronfmans*, 65.

30   Martin Mayer, "The Volatile Business," *Esquire*, August 1959, https://classic.esquire.com/article/1959/8/1/the-volatile-business.

31   Faith, *The Bronfmans*, 65.

32   Leonard Sloane, "Lewis Rosenstiel, Founder Of Schenley Empire, Dies," *New York Times*, January 22, 1976, https://www.nytimes.com/1976/01/22/archives/lewis-rosenstiel-founder-of-schenley-empire-dies.html.

33   Sloane, *Lewis Rosenstiel Dies.*

34   Sloane, *Lewis Rosenstiel Dies.*

35   Nicholas Gage, "Ex-Head of Schenley Industries Is Linked to Crime 'Consortium,'" *New York Times*, February 19, 1971, https://www.nytimes.com/1971/02/19/archives/exhead-of-schenley-industries-is-linked-to-crime-consortium.html.

36   Anthony Summers, *Official and Confidential: The Secret Life of J. Edgar Hoover* (New York: Pocket Star Books, 1994), 285, https://archive.org/details/officialconfide000summ.

37   Summers, *Official and Confidential*, 287.

38   Faith, *The Bronfmans*, 98-99.

39   Mayer, *The Volatile Business.*

40   Faith, *The Bronfmans*, 64.

41   Mayer, *The Volatile Business.*

42   Summers, *Official and Confidential*, 297.

43   M.A. Jones, "Potential Criminal Informant (PCI) Sue Young, Hollywood, Calif., Call Girl" (Archives.gov, July 26, 1960), https://www.archives.gov/files/research/jfk/releases/docid-32304320.pdf.

44   Summers, *Official and Confidential*, 291.

45   Summers, *Official and Confidential*, 292.

46   Summers, *Official and Confidential*, 292.

47   Lucian K. Truscott IV, "I Was Groped by a Man Called 'Mary': The World Changes but Not the Catholic Church," *Salon*, February 9, 2019, https://www.salon.com/2019/02/09/i-was-groped-by-a-man-called-mary-the-world-changes-but-not-the-catholic-church/.

48   Summers, *Official and Confidential*, 293.

49   Summers, *Official and Confidential*, 293.

50   Summers, *Official and Confidential*, 294.

51   Summers, *Official and Confidential*, 515.

52   Summers, *Official and Confidential*, 515.

53   Summers, *Official and Confidential* 516.

54   Michael Newton, *The Mafia at Apalachin*, 1957 (Jefferson, N.C: McFarland, 2012), 117.

55   Summers, *Official and Confidential*, 297.

56   Burton Hersh, *Bobby and J. Edgar: The Historic Face-off between the Kennedys and J. Edgar Hoover That Transformed America* (New York: Basic Books, 2008), 88.

57   John W. DeCamp, *The Franklin Cover-up: Child Abuse, Satanism, and Murder in Nebraska* (Lincoln, Neb: AWT, 1992), 179.

58   Terry Melanson, "The Ghost of Roy Cohn – Conspiracy Archive," August 24, 2014, https://www.conspiracyarchive.com/2014/08/24/the-ghost-of-roy-cohn/.

59   Jerome A. Kroth, *Conspiracy in Camelot: The Complete History of the Assassination of John Fitzgerald Kennedy* (New York: Algora Pub, 2003), 233, https://books.google.cl/books?id=VStz_I0QcB0C.

60   "New Book Pictures J. Edgar Hoover as Drag Queen," UPI, February 6, 1993, https://www.upi.com/Archives/1993/02/06/New-book-pictures-J-Edgar-Hoover-as-drag-queen/1064728974800/.

61   Many of the key pieces of evidence for Hoover's relationship with Tolson, as well as Hoover's closeted homosexuality, can be found in this article published by the UK's *The Guardian*: Anthony Summers, "The Secret Life of J Edgar Hoover," *The Guardian*, December 31, 2011, https://www.theguardian.com/film/2012/jan/01/j-edgar-hoover-secret-fbi.

62   "J. Edgar Hoover Was Homosexual, Blackmailed by Mob, Book Says," *Los Angeles Times*, February 6, 1993, https://www.latimes.com/archives/la-xpm-1993-02-06-mn-1078-story.html.

63   Summers, *Official and Confidential*, 280.

64   Jerome A. Kroth, *Conspiracy in Camelot: The Complete History of the Assassination of John Fitzgerald Kennedy* (New York: Algora Pub, 2003), 233.

65   Summers, *Official and Confidential,* 276.

66   Mark Riebling, *Wedge: From Pearl Harbor to 9/11: How the Secret War Between the FBI and CIA Has Endangered National Security,* 1st Touchstone ed. (New York: Simon & Schuster, 2002, n.d.), 131.

67   Hersh, *Bobby and J. Edgar,* 88.

68   William McGowan, "The Chickens and the Bulls," *Slate,* July 11, 2012, https://slate.com/human-interest/2012/07/the-chickens-and-the-bulls-the-rise-and-incredible-fall-of-a-vicious-extortion-ring-that-preyed-on-prominent-gay-men-in-the-1960s.html.

69   McGowan, "The Chickens and the Bulls."

70   Hersh, *Bobby and J. Edgar,* 88.

71   Ronald Smothers, "Seize 11-Year Fugitive in Homosexual Blackmail Case," *New York Times,* January 14, 1978, https://www.nytimes.com/1978/01/14/archives/seize-11year-fugitive-in-homosexual-blackmail-case.html.

72   Summers, *Official and Confidential,* 517.

73   Summers, O*Official and Confidential,* 517.

74   Summers, *Official and Confidential,* 516.

75   Summers, *Official and Confidential,* 516.

76   Nicholas Von Hoffman, *Citizen Cohn,* 1st ed (New York: Doubleday, 1988), 123–24.

77   Von Hoffman, *Citizen Cohn,* 123-125.

78   Maxine Cheshire, "The Director," *Washington Post,* 1969, http://jfk.hood.edu/Collection/Weisberg%20Subject%20Index%20Files/H%20Disk/Hoover%20J%20Edgar%20Foundation/Item%2005.pdf.

79   Hersh, *Bobby and J. Edgar,* 133-134.

80   Summers, *Official and Confidential,* 516.

81   Cheshire, "The Director."

82   Summers, *Official and Confidential,* 289.

83   Cheshire, "The Director."

84   Sloane, *Lewis Rosenstiel Dies.*

85   "CORPORATIONS: The Rapid Riser – *TIME,*" June 6, 1960, https://web.archive.org/web/20111007012745/http://www.time.com/time/magazine/article/0,9171,874162-1,00.html.

CHAPTER 3

ORGANIZED CRIME
AND THE STATE OF ISRAEL

STATE-BUILDING

In its July, 1971 obituary for Samuel Bronfman, the *New York Times* wrote that, after World War II, the liquor baron had "helped finance a secret purchase of Canadian weapons for troops of the Haganah."[1] Additional details on Bronfman's role in that purchase, beyond its brief mention by the *Times*, are rather difficult to come by. Peter Newman, in his otherwise exhaustive *The Bronfman Dynasty*, writes that Sam "personally underwrote life insurance policies for Canadian pilots recruited to help Israel fight its 1948 war of independence."[2] However, it is also known that, a few years after Israel's creation, in 1951, Bronfman would play a leading role in a similar, "secret purchase" for the Haganah's successor, the Israel Defense Force (IDF). In that case, Bronfman specifically answered the call of Israel's Shimon Peres, taking Peres to Ottawa, Canada to negotiate the transfer for $2 million worth of weapons to Israel. Bronfman then raised funds to cover the entire cost of the sizable arms cache.[3]

Yet, aside from that little is known of his earlier role in arming Zionist paramilitaries prior to Israel's founding. As Newman noted, Bronfman preferred to remain tight-lipped on "Zionist matters," despite his position as head of the Canadian Jewish Congress – an example of the family's characteristic "quiet manipulation." Regardless of the exact nature of Bronfman's activities in this area, his connection to the Haganah was not unique for those in his social circles. Yet, even outside of Bronfman's contacts, efforts to aid the Zionist paramilitary group, which would later form the backbone of the IDF, were already indicative of a wider tendency in pro-Zionist activism that swept across Canada, America, Latin America and beyond during the late 1940s.

What was at stake was the creation of Israel itself, as a sovereign political entity independent of the British, who, until 1948, had controlled Mandatory Palestine in accordance with treaties set up at the end of World War I. When the British Mandate ended in May 1958, Israel declared itself independent, and immediately entered into conflict with the Palestinians and a coalition of Arab forces. Those fighting to create Israel were able to assert themselves so forcefully largely because of the careful groundwork that had been laid out in advance by a number of individuals and groups, many of them working in the shadows.

Such was the historical mission of the Haganah ("Defense"), an organized Zionist paramilitary network that had been set up by the Jewish Agency – an activist branch of the World Zionist Organization (WZO). The Jewish Agency, under the leadership of David Ben-Gurion, oversaw the creation of numerous towns, villages, communal outposts and defense groups in Mandatory Palestine. The Jewish Agency would later atrophy, only to be relaunched by one of Leslie Wexner's mentors, Max Fisher, in 1970.

The formation of the Haganah in 1920 was a major step forward towards the formation of the Israeli state. Vital to its functioning was the training and arms provided by the British military. Major General Orde Charles Wingate, who had been dispatched to help administer British control over the territories, worked closely with the Haganah. Wingate even organized joint British Army-Zionist paramilitary commando units dedicated to patrolling and suppressing Arab elements in the region. These were called the Special Night Squads.

In 1945, the Haganah began its effort to stockpile weapons, ammunition, aircraft, non-lethal supplies, and machine tools sourced from around the globe. In the US, Ben-Gurion reached out to a close associate, Zionist activist Rudolf Sonneborn, who had traveled to Palestine years earlier to survey the construction of Jewish villages on behalf of the World Zionist Organization.[4] Under the leadership of Sonneborn, eighteen or so Jewish millionaires and billionaires were recruited into bankrolling the supply effort. Thus, the Sonneborn Institute, as it was known, was born.

The Institute, an activist collaboration of Zionist millionaires and billionaires that pursued specific, Zionism-related causes, would later serve as sort of a model for the "Mega Group," founded years later by Leslie Wexner and Charles Bronfman in 1991. The Sonneborn Institute's chief asset was a Haganah operative named Yehuda Arazi. During World War II, he served as a soldier in the Jewish Brigade, a British army unit that recruited its fighters from the immigrant populations living in Mandatory

Palestine. By 1945, he was an old hand at gun-running. Indeed, Arazi "had been active smuggling arms for the Haganah into Palestine from Europe since 1938."[5] Through these efforts, he developed an impressive roster of contacts, many of whom were tapped to set up front companies through which the Sonneborn Institute and the Haganah could carry out their activities. Ricky-Dale Calhoun wrote that:

> [One] Arazi associate was Leonard Weisman, who was probably a member of the Sonneborn group. Weisman was a 34-year-old from Pittsburgh who had made a fortune in scrap metals and construction materials. His businesses included Materials Redistribution Company, a firm that dealt in scrap machinery; Paragon Design and Development Corporation, a company that traded in building materials; and Pratt Steamship Lines. A fourth Weisman company, Foundry Associates, Inc., existed only on paper. All assisted in the purchase and illegal export of arms from the United States."[6]

Other front companies were organized by Nahum Bernstein, an attorney in New York City, that were used to source weapons and/or construct them from spare parts, and then export them overseas. Bernstein's name can be found on the corporate registrations of firms like Machinery Processing and Converting Company, which "provided cover for the purchase and illegal export of arms-making machines as well as armaments," and Oved Trading Company, which supplied "legal cover for buying and transporting explosives."[7]

There was also a trio of interlaced companies: Materials for Palestine, Inland Machinery and Metal Company, and the Eastern Development Company. Materials for Palestine was a charity through which money could be raised, while Inland Machinery actively shipped armaments and lethal munitions. Eastern Development, meanwhile, "exported legal nonmilitary goods and machinery to Palestine as relief supplies." There is a possibility that Paul Helliwell, discussed in Chapter 1, had some connection to this company, as he was listed as the attorney for the similarly named Eastern Development Corporation. According to a 1951 article in the *Miami News*, this Eastern Development was doing business in Florida, but had been formed in Pittsburgh.[8] As mentioned above, Leonard Weisman, the probable Sonneborn group member who worked with Arazi to create fronts for arms exporting, was also from Pittsburgh.

The potential presence of Helliwell in this mesh leads naturally to another question: was organized crime also involved in these efforts? Unlike the mysteries around Eastern Development, the role of organized crime in covertly arming the Haganah is well-documented. As these unofficial arms trade networks spread across the US, gangsters and mobsters – many of whom actively identified with the Zionist cause – threw their hats into the ring. Early on, Arazi forged ties with Meyer Lansky, requesting aid in maritime transit for the arms. Lansky, in turn, contacted two of his associates who controlled New York City's docks and the longshoremen's union, Albert Anastasia and Joe Adonis. The trio then "helped Israeli agents conceal the arms purchased for Israel, while arms bound for Egypt mysteriously fell overboard."[9] Lansky's close associate, Bugsy Siegel, met with Reuven Dafne, a representative of the Haganah looking to raise funds. Dafne, as the story goes, told Siegel that the Zionists were looking to unshackle themselves from British rule and that the path to do this was to fight. Siegel told Dafne "I'm with you," and for several weeks afterwards, the Haganah would receive suitcases "filled with $5 and $10 dollar bills – $50,000 in all."[10]

Besides Lansky, one of the more active mobsters in the flow of arms was Joseph "Bayonne Joe" Zicarelli. According to files obtained from the Federal Bureau of Narcotics, Zicarelli was "alleged to have been involved in the traffic of arms and munitions sold to the government of Israel."[11] It was one of many destinations for Zicarelli's arms: he also brokered arms sales to Cuba, Mexico, Venezuela, the Dominican Republic, and Nicaragua. The latter, as will be discussed shortly, was also active in the acquisition of arms for Israel. Zicarelli was close to Carmine Galante, a key player in the Bonanno mafia family, who would later become one of Roy Cohn's main clients from the criminal underworld. Allegedly, Zicarelli had been the subject of a feud between Charles Tourine of the Genovese family and Galante, with each wanting to recruit him into their crime family.[12] Galante won out, and it was under his watch that Zicarelli's lucrative arms trade flourished. At one point in the 1950s, Zicarelli was dispatched to Montreal by Galante to work with the Canadian mobster Vincenzo Cotroni. Together, Zicarelli and Cotroni organized the import of large sums of heroin into the country, as part of the Canadian wing of the French Connection.

Zicarelli was also alleged to be a close business associate of Lewis Rosenstiel. Rosenstiel's fourth wife Susan Kaufman testified that Zicarelli had been a secret partner in New Jersey warehouses owned by Schenley Industries, Rosenstiel's company. She further alleged that Rosenstiel had meetings with Zicarelli and Meyer Lansky.[13] The connection to Schenley signals Zicarelli's penchant for involving himself in quasi-legitimate businesses that acted as both "above-board" profit-turners and as fronts for less-than-reputable activities. Another one of these businesses was ABCO Vending, a cigarette vending machine company that was controlled by Zicarelli and Galante. Joining them there was Irwin "Steve" Schwartz, who later became infamous in the 1970s for his involvement in costly stock manipulation schemes. FBN files describe Schwartz as representing "the Galante-Zicarelli interests in the arms traffic, promotion and sale of worthless stocks and securities, and the cigarette vending business," before adding that "Since 1946 Schwartz has been engaged in the traffic of arms, a good portion of which have been obtained from Communist Bloc nations and shipped first to Israel and later to Cuba. Associated with Schwartz in these ventures were Irving Schindler and Adolf Schwimmer."[14]

Adolph "Al" Schwimmer was the founder of Israel Aircraft Industries, one of the country's great military contractors known today as Israel Aerospace Industries (IAI). During the 1930s, he worked for Lockheed and TWA, and, after World War II broke out, he was affiliated in some capacity with the US Air Transport Command. Schwimmer would remain active down through the decades, with a tendency to crop up in various Cold War-era covert operations. Perhaps most notoriously, he emerged as a key player on the Israeli side of the Iran-Contra Affair, and by some accounts was the individual who conceived of the "arms-for-hostages" plot at the center of Oliver North's complicated web. As for IAI, it would become owned, years later, by Israel's richest man Shaul Eisenberg. Under Eisenberg, IAI would have close ties to Israeli intelligence, from which he drew most of the company's senior staff.[15]

In his work securing materials for the Haganah, Schwimmer worked closely with Irvin "Swifty" Schindler. Schindler owned an airfreight company called Service Air, which Schwimmer relocated to California with funds from the Haganah. Together, Schwimmer and Schindler utilized the company as a means of acquiring aircraft and aircraft parts to be shipped to Palestine. Yet, with an embargo in place due to President Truman's declaration of neutrality, Service Air was prohibited from sending them overseas. Schwimmer and Schindler, aided by Arazi, turned to the Haganah's contacts in Panama. Soon, "legal ownership of the airplanes was transferred to the newly established Panamanian national airline LAPSA, allowing the aircraft to be legally flown to Panama" and from there they were moved abroad.[16]

In Chapter 7, which details the Iran-Contra Affair, Israel's close-knit relationship with Panama is mentioned in greater detail. Yet, the origins of this relationship began here, with the efforts of the Haganah to arm Zionist forces in Palestine following World War II. It wasn't, however, the only country in that region to have similar connections to Israel. Many of the people discussed in this chapter, like Bayonne Joe Zicarelli, were actively working with anti-communist forces in the Dominican Republic, Cuba, and elsewhere at the same time that they were working with the Haganah. One particularly important anti-communist force that was collaborating with the Haganah was the Somoza regime in Nicaragua.

The special relationship between the Zionist cause and Somoza's Nicaragua was largely due to the heavy presence of United Fruit, the New York-Boston banana trading company whose influence in Latin America was to be fundamentally intertwined with the CIA's activities in the region.[17] In 1933, United Fruit had fallen under the control of Samuel Zemurray, whose Cuyamael Fruit Company – a favorite of top Wall Street firms like Lehman and Goldman Sachs – had merged with the company several years prior. Zemurray, during the 1940s, was a big backer of Zionist causes. He aided the supply of arms to the Haganah, and reportedly helped the organization acquire the *SS Exodus*, a steamship used to ferry refuges to Palestine, in 1946. United Fruit, which later became United Brands, is discussed throughout this book due to its persisting intelligence connections as well as the fact its main leadership later included members of Leslie Wexner's inner circle and his two main mentors, Max Fisher and A. Alfred Taubman.

By 1947, as Truman's embargo began to be enforced, Nicaragua started providing arms to the Haganah. Somoza reportedly profited directly from this venture: he "received 3.5. percent commission on all arms purchases made by the Haganah under Nicaraguan aegis."[18] A decade later, Israel returned the favor when Shimon Peres negotiated an arms deal with Somoza that transformed Israel's emergent military-industrial complex into the primary supplier of weapons for Nicaragua.[19] As will be discussed in Chapter 7, Israel was active in arming and training the Nicaraguan Contras, the US-backed paramilitary forces that opposed the Sandinista government, which had toppled the Somoza regime in the late 1970s. The entry of Israel into this conflict was guaranteed by this precise history – and the Reagan administration, as part of its propaganda campaign, was quick to paint the new, Sandinista-led government as violently anti-Semitic.

The relationship between the Haganah and Latin America wasn't sole-ly dependent upon the graces of Zemurray and United Fruit. Reportedly, Haganah officers called upon the services of Sam Kay, a Florida business-man and real estate developer, who had extensive contacts in Panama, Batista's Cuba, and elsewhere. FBI files describe Kay as a "reputed inter-national gangster," and one of his close business associates was the Miami Beach hotel impresario Morris Lansburgh, who was himself a frontman for Meyer Lansky. Kay would later be linked to Florida mob boss Santo Trafficante, though the two were purported to have had a falling out that would almost cost Kay his life.

It was at this point where the Zionist interests melded with organized crime's real estate ventures, casino operations, and slush funds at the door of the Caribbean. Soon, these connections would truly begin to sprawl outwards and become truly intercontinental in scope.

THE HOT MONEY WEB

"During the Second World War," writes Jim Hougan, Tibor Rosen-baum "became a hero for the resistance through his activities on behalf of the Jews. Using 'Istvan Lukacs' as a *nom de guerre*, he carried out a series of Mission Impossible rescues. In one instance he posed as a high-ranking Nazi officer, entered a concentration camp, and under 'ad-ministrative pretext' obtained the release of thirty doomed prisoners."[20] His subsequent activities, however, were less than heroic.

With high-level connections secured through his position as a delegate for the World Zionist Congress, Rosenbaum set up his Geneva bank, In-ternational Credit Bank (ICB). ICB regularly moved money for Mossad and for Israel's Ministry of Defense. The British *Sunday Times* later report-ed in 1975 that "as much as [90%] of the Israeli Defense Ministry's exter-nal budget flowed ... through Rosenbaum's bank."[21] It also moved money for organized crime. In 1967, an exposé in *LIFE* magazine fingered ICB as the recipient of large sums of money skimmed off by the mob from the casinos they owned in Las Vegas, the Caribbean, and elsewhere.[22]

Overseeing the complex chains of inter-bank relations and transfer chains that enabled this "hot money" to flow around the globe was a series of banking institutions controlled by Meyer Lansky frontmen.The set-up was essentially as follows: casino skim (as well as profits generated by the drug trade and other organized crime rackets) was moved into two key offshore banks, the Bank of World Commerce (BWC) and Atlas Bank, the latter of which was a subsidiary of Rosenbaum's ICB. The funds would then be moved to accounts held by ICB in Geneva, where they would be converted into loans and investments to complete the money laundering loop. As will be discussed shortly, some of these funds may have been used to finance real estate investments that were made by people connected to American and Israeli intelligence.

The organizer of Atlas, on behalf of ICB, was Sylvain Ferdmann. The exposé in *LIFE* described Ferdmann as a "Swiss citizen who is an international banker and economist," before adding that "US authorities have marked Ferdmann a fugitive ... accused of interfering with the federal inquiry into the skimming racket."[23] Working alongside Ferdmann and Rosenbaum was a coterie of Lansky's closest allies. Sitting on the board of ICB itself was Ed Levinson and John Pullman. Levinson, who was partnered with Lansky in the Miami International Airport Hotel, ran the "mob-controlled Fremont Hotel-Casino in Las Vegas."[24] Levinson was also tight with Clifford Jones, the lieutenant governor of Nevada between 1947 and 1954 who was also an alleged associate of Meyer Lansky.[25]

Sitting alongside Levinson on the ICB board was John Pullman, Lansky's personal financial advisor. Pullman was also close to Lou Chesler, having become acquainted with the Canadian businessman in the 1940s. He subsequently introduced Chesler into Lanksy's orbit. Soon, Chesler began managing Lansky's interests in the Bahamas – including the development of hotels and casinos. At the same time, Pullman was organizing the Bank of World Commerce, the partner bank to Atlas Bank and correspondent bank to ICB.

Levinson and Pullman also sat on the board of BWC. An IRS report aptly described this bank as having been set up to maintain "a liquid supply of funds to be used for setting up new gambling casinos in the Caribbean wherever and whenever the opportunity presents itself."[26] They were joined on the board by Benjamin Siegelbaum, a money courier for Lansky and a prominent figure in organized crime circles in his own right. Besides BWC, Siegelbaum held posts at the Exchange and Investment Bank, a sort of Geneva-based counterpart bank to Rosenbaum's ICB. R.T. Naylor, in his book *Hot Money and the Politics of Debt*, writes that, for a time, Exchange and Investment Bank was Lansky's preferred financial institution – at least until his role in the bank was accidentally exposed by Chase Manhattan. This occurred after the bank found two of their employees using accounts there to spirit away embezzled funds. It was at this point that Lansky shifted the bulk of his business to Rosenbaum's bank.

Aside from Geneva banking, Siegelbaum also dabbled in Florida real estate. His money backed one of the state's large landowners, Major Realty, which had been co-founded in part by a Florida entrepreneur named Max Orovitz. Orovitz was, as Jonathan Marshall points out, "a legitimate businessman and an honored Jewish philanthropist, but no stranger to criminals."[27] He was partnered with Lou Chesler in both Florida real estate (albeit via Chesler's General Development Company, not Major Realty) and in development projects in the Bahamas that ultimately spawned Resorts International, which was previously Mary Carter Paint and had been linked to both the mob, to former New York governor Thomas Dewey and to Paul Helliwell's Castle Bank.

Orovitz was part of what was known as the "Miami Group" – a circle of organized crime-linked Jewish businessmen with holdings across various economic sectors in Florida and in Israel. Members of the Miami Group established Dan Hotels, a luxury hotel chain with locations in Israel and India, and also set up "Israel's first successful oil drilling company, Israel Oil Ventures."[28] Israel Oil Ventures expanded its capacities considerably in 1960, when it purchased Israel-American Oil Corp – an oil venture that was intimately tied to organized crime via its holding in another oil firm, Rimrock Tidelands. A subsidiary of Rimrock Tidelands, Rimrock International, was of interest to a Senate investigation into "international narcotics traffic." This was because Rimrock International's managing director was Santo Sorge, who was described in the Senate report as "one of the most important Mafia leaders" and a liaison between American and Sicilian mafia clans.[29]

Compared to its fellow dark money conduits, Atlas Bank – later renamed the "Atlas Trust" – is something of a mystery. It not only sat at the intersection of Geneva-bound money flows, but was also tied to hot money from the Middle East. According to Alan Block, Atlas "was united in some shadowy way with Intra Bank in Beirut, Lebanon," which maintained its own offshore entity in the Bahamas called Intra Bahamas Trust Ltd.[30]

Intra Bank was formed in 1951 by Yousef Beidas, a Christian Palestinian refugee who had been born into a prominent banking family. Just over a decade later, what began as a modest operation ballooned into a sprawling empire, at which point Beidas forged agreements with leading American banks. These included Bank of America and Chase Manhattan, and Beidas then placed branches of Intra Bank in the world's important hotspots for hot money: London, Geneva, and the Caribbean. At home, in Lebanon, Intra held "20% of the country's total deposits" and "56[%] of all the country's banking assets."[31] There was also a deep relationship between Intra Bank and illicit activities of all types. As Jonathan Marshall notes:

> Smugglers of all sorts availed themselves of Intra Bank's services. It was a prime depository for many of the world's leading arms traffickers, who received financing from Lebanese traders for illegal weapons sales in the Southern Arabian peninsula (Yemen and Aden), Cyprus, Sudan, Nigeria, Rhodesia, South Africa, and Kurdish communities in the Middle East. Wealthy Arabs with too many petrodollars on their hands, looking for a savvy bank in the region to look after their wealth, fattened its deposits further. ... Lebanon was prized as a "haven for cash for anybody with a balance to hide – U.S. tax evaders, oil-rich sheiks who want to lay something by for the rainy day of revolution, and assorted racketeers and purveyors of stolen or smuggled wealth from all over the world," observed *LIFE* magazine in 1967.[32]

Naturally, this sort of environment made Intra Bank an attractive financial institution for the CIA, and the bank helped transform Beirut into a core hub for the Agency's covert operations in the Middle East. Marshall reports that Beidas in particular had a "personal touch" when it came to dealing with the CIA – he was even seen "taking CIA officers into his private office to handle their checks."[33] Sitting on the board of directors of Intra Bank was Kamal Adham, the head of Saudi intelligence and a cousin of the infamous arms dealer Adnan Khashoggi – a later key player in Iran-Contra, the BCCI affair, and numerous other covert activities. According to the Congressional BCCI Report, Adnan "was the CIA's principle liaison for the entire Middle East from the mid-1960s through 1979."[34]

Intra Bank was identified by American law enforcement as being a major laundromat and source of funding for the global drug trade, a sizable portion of which was based in Lebanon. This was thanks to the country's position as a key node in the famed French Connection, as Lebanon was a major source of hashish, raw opium, and even refined heroin that was destined for black markets in Europe and North America.

This node of the international drug trade was largely controlled by Sami Khoury and his partner, Omar Makkouk. They had forged close ties to the Lebanese political establishment and law enforcement community, generating an atmosphere of generalized corruption that gained Khoury the nickname of "the Untouchable." Khoury's ties soon expanded overseas. According to a CIA report, Corsican organized crime figures allied with Khoury had made inroads into "the highest levels of French government, industry and society, including the cabinet, police, and military."[35]

Khoury also enjoyed protection from Israel. James Attie, an agent of the Federal Bureau of Narcotics (FBN) assigned to the Middle East, reported that the drug lord had provided thousands of guns to Israel, and that the country had "provided the contacts and money that enabled Khoury to move narcotics across Europe."[36] Intriguingly, another figure implicated by the FBN in the flow of drugs from Lebanon to Europe was the banker Edmond Safra, whose connection to BCCI, Iran-Contra, and figures like Robert Maxwell and Jeffrey Epstein is discussed in Chapter 7.[37] Safra was also a Zionist with strong ties to Israel. For instance, during the 1980s, he served on the board of overseers of B'nai B'rith International, seated alongside figures like Edgar M. Bronfman and Max Fisher.

One of Intra Bank's most lucrative holdings was the Casino du Liban, a gambling establishment outside of Beirut. The casino was a hot-spot for the international jet-set as well as a meeting place for various figures from the underworld who regularly rubbed shoulders with elites. According to Jonathan Marshall, the Casino du Liban "was a favorite playground for Saudi sheiks and rich Arab businessmen, such as Adnan Khashoggi.... It was also a favorite gathering place for foreign businessmen, diplomats and spies."[38] Jim Hougan, meanwhile, writes that the casino, at its height, was "said to be the biggest gambling emporium in the world – dwarfing the Sands, the Dunes, the Flamingo, and Monte Carlo."[39]

At the Casino du Liban, gambling concessions were held by Marcel Francisci, the leader of the Corsican underworld. In the 1940s, Francisci allied himself with Sami Khoury, and, prior to his murder in 1968, he forged a close working relationship between French and Italian gangsters. "Mr. Heroin," as he was known by American authorities, "was the man with the international perspective." As a result of his other connections to Francisci and others, Khoury did perhaps more than anyone to maintain the French connection drug pipeline.[40] Francisci was also a partner with Meyer Lansky, who was likewise known to haunt the Casino du Liban from time to time.[41]

Intra Bank's peculiarities make a little more sense when one considers that, for bankers and organized criminals alike, there is often money to be made on both sides of any given conflict. After all, this was a bank that had been founded by someone who had fled the Haganah's activities in Palestine – and a casino that, according to Jim Hougan, would siphon money off to finance the Palestine Liberation Organization (PLO).[42] Yet, at the same time, Zionist-aligned gangsters, bankers and other figures were caught up in its web. This apparent contradiction was ultimately indicative of a trend that would grow in the 1970s and 1980s: a "behind-the-scenes" alignment between the ruling elites of Arab societies, enriched by the petrodollar system, and the Israeli business class and security apparatus. This tension-filled, often contradictory and ever-shifting alignment was of considerable interest to the US, which often found itself serving as the mediator between these two forces. The US, of course, would use that role as its pivot-point in its attempts to dominate the Middle East. This environment was fertile soil for crooks, businessmen and operatives of all types – many of whom were interlaced with the command structures of Western (and sometimes Eastern) intelligence services.

BANKERS AND TANKERS: THE WORLD OF BRUCE RAPPAPORT

While he was President Ronald Reagan's director of the CIA, William Casey, maintained – much to the chagrin of many in the Agency – an informal intelligence apparatus composed of his close friends and associates. Nicknamed the "Hardy Boys," this group lacked CIA clearances but its members "had their own back door, so to speak, into Langley. They would ride upstairs in Casey's own elevator."[43] Among this clique was Max Hugel, who managed to be appointed deputy director of the CIA before his history of dubious stock trading caught up with him. Hugel makes a brief appearance later, in Chapter 10.

Other members, who will also be discussed in later chapters of this book, included John Shaheen and Robert B. Anderson. Shaheen, an oil trader, played a role in the October Surprise affair, while Robert B. Anderson's career veered from being a prominent figure in the Eisenhower administration to being disbarred for money laundering in 1980s. One of Casey's most important friends, however, was Bruce Rappaport.

Across the latter half of the twentieth century, Rappaport left a string of business deals that were mind-numbing in their complexity and tied to fraud, intelligence-linked bust-out operations, and backroom dealings, all of which was facilitated by a sophisticated web of interlocking shipping companies, banks, oil companies, mines, and numerous other holdings. Rappaport and Casey were sometimes co-participants in these activities, some of which predated Casey's time at the CIA. During the 1980s, they were also known to be golfing buddies, and made frequent visits together to the Deepdale Golf Club on Long Island.

"When Rappaport visited Deepdale," writes Alan Block, the author of an exhaustive study on his life and times, "his chauffeur was often Louis Filardo, an alleged associate of New York area mobsters."[44] By the late 1980s – if not earlier – he was tied to Russian organized crime interests, including Semion Mogilevich, the "boss of bosses" of Russian crime syndicates who makes several appearances later in this book. With a position on the FBI's top 10 most wanted list, Mogilevich is described by the bureau as a leader in "weapons trafficking, contract murders, extortion, drug trafficking, and prostitution on an international scale."[45] Interestingly, it is quite possible that Rappaport had been introduced to Mogilevich by none other than Robert Maxwell, who, by the late 1980s, had become a key business partner of Mogilevich's and facilitated Mogilevich's entry into the Israeli and US financial systems. Another contact of Mogilevich's crime networks was the aforementioned banker Edmond Safra, who was acquainted with both Maxwell and Rappaport.[46]

Rappaport's origins are murky, though a few facts are known. He was born in Haifa, Palestine, in 1922 to a family that had settled there from Ukraine. At some point he earned a law degree, and spent time as a judge after Israel's founding. He also served in the IDF, achieving the rank equivalent to major. His military career, however, had begun before the formation of the state of Israel in 1948.

Rappaport has stated that he spent a portion of World War II fighting with the British Army, who dispatched him to Africa. He may have been a member of the African Auxiliary Pioneer Corps, later shortened to the African Pioneer Corps. The Corps had existed from 1941 until 1946, and had started off as a logistic support unit that gradually expanded to include combat capabilities. Many of the African Pioneers were attached to the Ninth Army, one of the British field armies that was part of the Middle East Command. Rappaport was also reportedly a member of the Special Interrogation Group (SIG), the British commando group made up Jewish volunteers from Mandatory Palestine. SIG recruited heavily from the ranks of the Haganah, the Irgun and the Special Night Squads.

After the war, Rappaport joined the 6th Airborne Division, another British Army outfit. This was an airborne infantry division that had been deployed to Palestine in the late 1940s, and worked closely with Jewish groups in the region to administer the territories until Israel's creation in 1948. The 6th Airborne, which had a fairly significant casualty rate among its personnel, worked to regulate and balance the competing interests of Jewish and Arab factions in the region, while also laying the logistical groundwork for the steady influx of refugees from Europe.

During his time with the 6th Airborne, Rappaport helped organize Israel's military police. Soon, however, he began to focus more on his another of his interests – the world of criminal enterprises and covert operations. According to Alan Block, a Scotland Yard report provided some of the earliest known information on Rappaport's shadier activities, charging that "in the early 1950s, Rappaport and Teddy Kollek, who became the charismatic mayor of Jerusalem, devised a scam on construction materials serious enough to produce warrants."[47] Israeli newspapers reported a similar story, but sometimes Paul Kollek – Teddy's brother – was instead identified as Rappaport's partner. Regardless of which Kollek was actually involved, Rappaport's proximity to the Kollek brothers points to his own proximity to the centers of power in nascent Israel. This connection is also one that leads back to the Haganah and the inter-mixing of intelligence and organized crime: Teddy Kollek, in the 1940s, "ran the day-to-day operations of the arms procurement" in New York for the Haganah, which brought him into contact with the city's criminal elements.[48] His close contacts included Al Schwimmer and Yehuda Arazi, and he worked with the two in delivering aircraft to Israel by way of intermediaries in South America.

Kollek's activities put him on the radar of British intelligence and their interest in him was multi-fold. On the one hand, he was treated with suspicion: "His phone was bugged, his bags were searched" and his movements were consistently tracked.[49] On the other hand, he was actively courted by MI5 – first indirectly, and then later directly. Kollek's main contact with British intelligence was through an MI5 officer named Simkin. The two had a mutual friend, Ben Aharon, who was reportedly an ardent Bolshevik who would subsequently become head of the Histadrut, the centralized body that coordinated Israel's trade unions. Aharon's wife, Miriam, worked for the Shai, the intelligence apparatus of the Haganah.

After his scam with one of the Kollek brothers went bust, Rappaport fled Israel. Over the course of his lifetime, he held passports for numerous countries: he was listed as a citizen of Panama, Costa Rica, Israel, and Switzerland. It was the latter location where he settled down in the early 1950s. Early support for his Swiss ventures came from the Société Générale de Surveillance (SGS), a Geneva-based multinational that provides inspection and verification services for international trade.[50] Besides SGS, another entity that helped Rappaport launch his early activities was

Swiss-Israel Trade Bank, headquartered in Geneva. According to Rappaport, he knew Swiss-Israel's owner, who provided him with loans.[51] Interestingly, the bank's original founder and owner – likely who Rappaport was referring to – was Gideon Persky.[52]

Gideon was the brother of Shimon Peres, the leading Israeli Labor Party politician who would later serve as both president and prime minister of the country and become a close friend of Robert Maxwell and, later, his daughter Isabel. Years later, Ehud Barak, who would later serve as Israel's Defense Minister and Prime Minister, alleged that Shimon Peres had been the person who had originally introduced him to Jeffrey Epstein.[53] Shimon, a veteran of the Haganah, had joined the IDF towards the end of the 1940s, and was appointed by David Ben-Gurion as the chief purchaser of munitions for Israel's military. By 1953, Shimon headed Israel's Ministry of Defense. According to Jonathan Nitzan and Shimshon Bichler, Shimon's control over defense spending greatly benefited the businesses of his brother.

That Swiss-Israel helped prop up Rappaport is significant, as it was effectively a Mossad front in Europe.[54] Overseeing the bank's daily operations was Yehuda Assia, who was actively on the Mossad payroll. Under his direction, the bank both raised funds for the bank and acted as a conduit for the financing of its international operations. It was also utilized to raise money for the construction of nuclear reactors that played a major role in Israel's covert construction of nuclear weapons. Avner Cohen, in his book *Israel and the Bomb*, writes that Ben-Gurion and Shimon Peres "conducted [the management of funds] outside the official state budget," and had enlisted the aid of an American-Jewish fundraiser and businessman named Abraham Feinberg to locate private donors.[55] Feinberg ran American Bank & Trust, a subsidiary of Swiss-Israel.[56]

There are other lines running from Swiss-Israel to the worlds of organized crime and – unsurprisingly – to Helliwell's banking complex. Prior to his relocation to Geneva to take over the operations of Swiss-Israel, Yehuda Assia spent World War II in Thailand, where he met General Phao Sriyanonda.[57] During the 1950s, Phao spent a considerable amount of time in Geneva, where he lived with Assia. As mentioned in Chapter 1, Phao was closely connected to Helliwell, and stood at a nexus of American intelligence's complicity in the opium trade during the post-war period.

In 1960, Assia was contacted by Irving Davidson – a powerful lobbyist whose clients included the CIA, the Teamsters, Texas oil giant Clinton

Murchison, and the state of Israel – concerning a Bahamian bank called Guarantee Trust Company.[58] Guarantee Trust was run by a major supporter of Israel named Abe Multer and was one of the offshore entities that handled hot money flows from the Teamsters pension fund and from other organized criminal activities, such as the skim from casinos. The vice chairman of the bank was Leonard Bursten, a former director of Miami National Bank – which, as previously mentioned in Chapter 1, had been founded with the aid of a loan from the Teamster pension fund and had employed the services of Paul Helliwell's law firm.

With these early ties, Rappaport's empire began to expand in all directions, interlocking with shipping and financial interests all over the world. This process began in 1959, with the creation of International Maritime Services and International Maritime Supplies Company Limited. The latter company was closely linked to a shipping concern in the UK called Wilson (London & International) Limited, which was soon joined by a trio of major maritime companies. These were, per Alan Block, "a Dutch company, N.S. Frank & Zoon, N.V.; the American Maritime Supply Service Inc., based in Chicago; and the Italian Maritime Supplies Co. Ltd. Rappaport noted with glee that with three other firms buying into International Maritime … it would be possible to have a shipping clientele of 161 firms that will cover the entire world."[59]

In those early years, Rappaport formed what would be a lifelong connection to the Kulukundis family, a Greek shipping clan who had set up shop in the United States and in Great Britain. Michael Kulukundis was the co-organizer of International Maritime Supplies, and court documents show that, as early as 1961, the pair were using the company to run scams and loot the coffers of unsuspecting businesses.[60] At the same time, the Kulukundis family advanced their own shipping interests through London & Overseas Freighters, which, in time, would boast an impressive fleet of tankers that played a significant role in the global oil trade. Some of the affairs of the Kulukundis family will be discussed in Chapter 6.

In the early 1960s, Inter Maritime Supplies owned a stake in London & Overseas Freighters. It is worth mentioning that London & Overseas was formed by the Kulukundis family with their cousins, the Mavroleon family. As will be noted in Chapter 15, the Mavroleons were themselves connected to the circles around Jeffrey Epstein and Ghislaine Maxwell. For several years, Ghislaine Maxwell dated Gianfranco Cicogna, whose mother had been married to the patriarch of the Mavroleon family – and original founder of London & Overseas – Basil "Bluey" Mavroleon. Contact information for Bluey Mavroleon and his son, Nicholas Mavroleon (Gianfranco's half-brother), can be found in Epstein's black book of contacts.

It wasn't until 1965 that Rappaport set up the institution that would later stand at the center of his complex network of firms and money conduits: Inter Maritime Bank (IMB). IMB, writes Block, "had A and B shareholders." The various holders of Class B stock were representatives of banking institutions that were in business with Rappaport. These included Klaus Uilke Polstra, representing Bank M. van Embden, and Rolando Zoppi, representing Weisscredit, a bank in the Swiss Canton of Ticino. Nestled near the border of Switzerland and Italy, Weisscredit was identified by the US State Department as a bank utilized by numerous Italians involved with organized crime to hide their money from financial authorities in their home country.[61] Zoppi would wind up with a five-year prison sentence in 1975 when Weisscredit lost some $150 million of depositors' money due to "fraud and mismanagement in high-risk speculative operations."[62]

Another holder of Class B stock was David Hodara, from the Swiss financial outfit Sofigest. Sofigest would later be involved in the strange affairs of Investors Overseas Services, an international mutual fund and capital flight apparatus with ties to Tibor Rosenbaum and Meyer Lansky. Later, Sofigest would emerge in Brazil, where it was involved in everything from a joint venture with Fiat to frauds perpetuated by the infamous Naji Nahas.

When it came to the holders of Class A stock, things were a bit more limited. The bulk was held by Rappaport himself, albeit filtered through various other companies that he either owned or controlled. The rest were held by E.P. Barry – the OSS veteran who, as mentioned in Chapter 1 was one of the primary figures in Paul Helliwell's Florida banking network. In fact, at the same time that Barry was involved with HMT/Florida Shares, the holding company for some of Helliwell's banks, he came to hold IMB Class A shares. This link to the world of Helliwell would endure: one of Rappaport's chief financial allies, and an architect of a large number of his ventures, was Helliwell's banking partner Burton Kanter, also an affiliate of the mob.

Over the decades, there has been a slow and steady trickle of news articles in major publications that examine Bruce Rappaport. In 1988, the *New York Times* published on Rappaport entitled "A Secret Emperor of Oil and Shipping."[63] The article described how Rappaport had:

> [...]developed a reputation for both openness and secrecy. On one hand, Mr. Rappaport – who is said by some associates to be a

billionaire – sponsors golf and tennis tournaments and gives huge sums to a host of charities, especially medical and Jewish ones. On the other hand, former and current business associates say Mr. Rappaport is involved in hundreds of companies, registered in remote places like Liberia and Panama, to run his banking, shipping and oil empire.[64]

The appearance of Rappaport in Liberia is particularly interesting. It was there that he had established one of his many Inter Maritime outfits; in this case, it was Inter Maritime Owners Corporation of Monrovia. Liberia was a favorite for owners of shipping companies: besides the low tax rates, the astoundingly lax regulation, and the degree of bank secrecy, the country boasts a robust flags of convenience system, which "allows ship owners to register their vessels in an alternative sovereign to their place of origin."[65] Liberia's shipping registry system also has some unique characteristics: it was managed not in Liberia itself, but was overseen by International Bank, located in Washington DC. The longtime controller of International Bank, George Olmsted, would end up on the periphery of the BCCI affair, discussed later in Chapter 7.

Rappaport wasn't a lone figure in this network with ties to Liberia; in fact, there is every indication that Liberia was of immense importance to a number of individuals that have been discussed in this chapter. Tibor Rosenbaum, for example, was listed as the managing director of Swiss-Liberian Finance Corporation in 1954. That year, Swiss-Liberian Finance Corporation provided a multi-million dollar line of credit to help capitalize the Bank of Liberia Inc. – a development bank partially controlled by the Liberian government.[66] Other capital inflows for the Bank of Liberia came from the Bank of Monrovia and the Liberian Trade and Development Corp (TRADEVCO). The Bank of Monrovia had first been owned by the Firestone Tire & Rubber Company before it was acquired by the First National City Bank, an institution controlled by the Rockefeller family.[67] TRADEVCO, meanwhile, was controlled by a group of Italian banks.

Tax banking laws and the flags of convenience system certainly helped attract people to Liberia. Another may have been the lucrative diamond trade: during the 1950s, the country became the primary transshipment point for the flow of diamonds from countries like Sierra Leone to diamond cutting hubs.[68] Many of these hubs were located in Antwerp and in Israel. In Israel, one of the major banks involved in the financing of the diamond cutting industry was Bank Leumi, which opened offices and branches in Liberia early on. The board of Bank Leumi reportedly interlocked with that of Rosenbaum's ICB – while Rosenbaum himself was affiliated with Kupat Am Bank, a subsidiary of Bank Leumi.

Serving as honorary counsel to Liberia in this period was a man named Louis Mortimer Bloomfield. He was a powerful Canadian attorney with an exhaustive roster of connections to all sorts of elite figures and institutions, starting with the law firm he belonged to: Phillips & Vineberg of Montreal. Through its senior co-partner Lazarus Phillips, it was connected to the Royal Bank of Canada. Libbie and Frank Park, in their classic study of the Canadian elite establishment, *The Anatomy of Big Business*, show that this bank was one of the commanding institutions in Canada, and acted as a conduit for the entry of foreign capital originating in the US, the UK and Belgium.[69]

The firm was also closely tied to the Bronfman family. Peter Newman writes in *The Bronfman Dynasty* that "Because of the many family feuds, two of Montreal's best lawyers – Lazarus Phillips and Philip Vineberg – have become ex officio members of the family, charged with arbitrating among its several factions."[70] It has been alleged that Bloomfield himself did work on behalf of the Bronfmans. While this is by no means outside the realm of possibility, it is difficult to find evidence to confirm this particular claim. What is known and extensively documented, however, is Bloomfield's ties to a mysterious entity in Rome that was tied to American, Italian, French, and Israeli intelligence networks – as well as to international organized criminal actors and their banks.

MOSSAD GOES TO ROME

In 1967, Gershon Peres, a brother of Shimon Peres, joined the board of Centro Mondiale Commerciale (CMC), the Italian subsidiary of Permindex – a world trade center organization headquartered first in Basel and then in Rome and made famous by New Orleans district attorney Jim Garrison's investigation into the assassination of John F. Kennedy.[71] Ostensibly, the purpose of Permindex-CMC was to maintain what was effectively a permanent world's fair – a centralized site where businessmen could display their wares, deals could be made, and important corporations could maintain offices. On the back end, however, Permindex-CMC was tied into various covert networks. What first placed Garrison on the trail of Permindex, for example, was the presence of Clay Shaw, an apparent CIA contract agent, on their board.[72]

87

Italian journalist Michele Metta, who recovered a cache of CMC corporate documents, has shown that Permindex-CMC was plugged into the Italian state security apparatus, and also had a curious series of connections to Israel.[73] One of CMC's founders, Georges Mandel (also known as Giorgio Mantello), was affiliated with the Banque pour le Commerce Suisse-Amerique Centrale, which was identified as having "supplied cover employment for [Israeli Intelligence Service] agents."[74] Another CMC board member, Alberto Forte, subsequently became managing director of Banque Belgo-Centrade – a subsidiary of the Mossad-linked Swiss-Israel Trade Bank.[75]

Louis Mortimer Bloomfield has often been described as the founder of Permindex, and sometimes as its dominant shareholder. This seems to be an inaccurate picture of his role in the complex, as Bloomfield was Permindex's attorney. In this capacity, he was responsible for coordinating all the different players involved, who were scattered across multiple continents. He does not appear to have owned stock of his own in Permindex or CMC. Instead, he acted as a proxy for particular interests, effectively hiding their identities. Their stock was held in his name, and he occupied their spots on the board.

With the links between Permindex-CMC and the world of intelligence, it is unsurprising that rumors have circulated for decades that Bloomfield was, during the Second World War, a member of the OSS. There is little to corroborate this claim, though he did serve in the Royal Canadian Army Service Corps, achieving the rank of major in August 1946. Correspondences in his archive show that he was in communication with the British spymaster William Stephenson, who at the time was active in Canadian industry and finance. Bloomfield did hold membership in a number of elite organizations, including the Most Venerable Order of the Hospital of St. John of Jerusalem – a British chivalric order established by royal charter in the 1880s as something of a Protestant counterpart to the Catholic Sovereign Military Order of Malta (better known as the Knights of Malta). He eventually became both the attorney for and president of the Order's Quebec Council.

Bloomfield was also attached to a number of Zionist organizations. He served as honorary counsel to the World Jewish Congress, and was active in building up the Canadian branches of the Histadrut, Israel's trade union complex.[76] In addition to organized labor, Bloomfield's concerns involved maritime commerce as well. He was president of the Canadian wing of the Israel Maritime League, set up in the late 1940s to "make the people of Israel 'sea-conscious.'"[77] The Israel Maritime League and the Histadrut were tightly connected: along with the Jewish Agency, the three organized Zim Shipping, the major transport concern that was a key supplier of weapons and supplies to Israel in the early days of the state's existence.[78]

Later in life, Bloomfield corresponded with George H.W. Bush, including while Bush was serving as director of the CIA.[79] The letters indicate that the two first met at a meeting at the Canadian embassy in Beijing in 1975. Bloomfield appears to have had a long-running fascination with China, having traveled there as early as 1966 (if not earlier). After that particular trip, he gave public addresses calling for the normalization of diplomatic relations with the country and for increased trade relations between the East and the West. As Maurice Phillips – the first to explore the contents of Bloomfield's archives – points out, Bloomfield's position on China predated that of President Richard Nixon and Henry Kissinger by a number of years.[80]

Another prominent figure in touch with Bloomfield was Tibor Rosenbaum. Permindex documents show that Rosenbaum and his International Credit Bank were deeply involved with Permindex and CMC. A July 12th, 1961, memo from Bloomfield to Rosenbaum discusses an adjacent project, headed by CMC's founder Georges Mantello, called Marina Reale.[81] Registered in Panama, Marina Reale was a holding company utilized by Permindex's principals to acquire real estate. Just as with Permindex itself, Bloomfield acted as a proxy for shareholders whose names remain unknown. The communication between him and Rosenbaum, however, identifies some of the other parties with interests tied up in Marina Reale. Among these were Dov Biegun, a leading figure in the World Zionist Organization who became the national secretary for the National Committee for Labor Israel. Much like Bruce Rappaport and Robert Maxwell, Biegun spent World War II in the British Army. According to his obituary, he "served in intelligence operations in France, Holland and Norway."[82]

Another investor in Marina Reale – and one who received his shares directly from Mantello – was "Nate Dolin of Cleveland, Ohio." Dolin achieved notoriety in 1970 when a firm he was connected to, Realty Equities, ran a fraud scheme in conjunction with Rosenbaum's ICB.[83] Interestingly, Dolin had a business relationship with the Lansky-connected mobster Moe Dalitz going back to the 1940s, when they both owned shares of the Cleveland Indians sports team.[84]

There were other big names involved in Permindex-CMC's real estate deals. Communiqués found in Louis Bloomfield's archival papers show that his law partner Stanley Vineberg was keeping a close eye on these developments, and perhaps even had a role in these transactions that super-seded that of Bloomfield.[85] These same cables identified a French compa-ny called Compagnie Financière as holding a 10% stake in one of the real estate ventures. Compagnie Financière had been set up in 1953 by Fran-cois Pereire, a scion of the famed French banking family, and Edmond de Rothschild, who exerted dominant control over the institution. Today, Compagnie Financière is known as the Edmond de Rothschild Group.

Rothschild was also a business partner of Tibor Rosenbaum: the two had organized the Israel Corporation, "Israel's largest investment com-pany," designed to "encourage large-scale private investment in Israel."[86] When it was discovered in 1974 that Rosenbaum had bilked the company to the tune of $60 million dollars, the Israeli government linked up a small handful of the country's leading banks "to participate in efforts to prevent its liquidation."[87] One of these banks was Bank Leumi.

Rothschild himself appears all over Bloomfield's correspondences, and was clearly intimately involved with Permindex-CMC's activities. One ca-ble from Bloomfield to Abraham Friedman at the Israel Continental Oil Corporation in Tel-Aviv requested that Friedman discuss matters relevant to the Italian real estate deals with Rothschild. Intriguingly, the *Oil and Petroleum Year Book* identifies Israel Continental Oil as having been set up in Canada in 1952, while Canadian government records show that Louis Bloomfield's nephew, Bernard Bloomfield – mentioned earlier as a director of International Credit Bank's subsidiary, Atlas Bank – was the oil producer's president.[88]

According to the *Jewish Telegraph Agency*, a year after Israel Continental Oil was founded, it became a player in a consortium of oil firms looking to drill "near the Dead Sea and in other sections of Israel."[89] Other partners in this consortium included Husky Oil Company, which was affiliated with the aforementioned mob-linked Rimrock Tidelands oil company, and New Continental Oil Company, with which Israel Continental Oil set up joint ventures in Canada. The president of New Continental was Frank Kaftel, an organized crime associate and stock manipulator orig-inally from Cleveland, the stomping grounds of Moe Dalitz and CMC investor Nate Dolin.[90] Federal Bureau of Narcotics documents identified Kaftel as a close associate of "Bayonne Joe" Zicarelli – the aforementioned mobster and businessman who had been involved in the running of arms to Israel.[91]

Another Canadian-based oil concern active in the Israel petroleum industry of the early 1960s was Tri-Continental Pipelines, where Edmond de Rothschild, Francois Pereire, and Louis Bloomfield could all be found.[92] Galina Nikitina, in her political and economic history of the state of Israel, notes that Tri Continental was part of a group that controlled a pipeline from Eilat to Haifa – the basis for the larger "Trans-Israel Pipeline" that linked Israel and Iran – alongside the Miami Group and the Palestine Economic Corporation (PEC).[93] The Miami Group, as mentioned above, maintained ties to organized crime interests and was also connected to the family of companies that was partnered with the Israel Continental Oil Corporation. PEC, on the other hand, was a primary conduit for the investment of American capital into nascent Israeli industries. To quote Nikitina:

> [...]described as the largest American private investor in Israel, [PEC] was formed in 1926 as an instrument through which American Jews could render material assistance to production enterprises in Palestine. In only the period from 1950 to 1959 its capital increased 70 percent. PEC assets totalled 19,300,000 dollars in 1961. It has numerous daughter companies, banks and agencies, and shares in other companies. Having grown to gigantic proportions, PEC has its tentacles in all the key branches of Israel's economy.
>
> PEC is linked with leading financial and industrial monopolies in the USA, such as the Wall Street bankers Lehman Brothers, Kuhn, Loeb and Company (one of the eight largest financial groups in the USA), the Mellon group of Pittsburgh, the Cabot Lodge group of Boston, and the Hanna group of Cleveland.[94]

This particular network of individuals and institutions is complex and convoluted; yet, what is clear is that there was something of an Israel-Italy-France-Canada axis that was tied directly into hot money networks in the Caribbean, to the flow of capital from the west into Israel itself, and to the outflows of raw materials (like diamonds) from the "third world." Once this foreign investment – generally from American and Canadian sources – was in Israel, it went to work building up various industries. It appears, then, that the logical successor to the earlier efforts to raise money, supplies, and weapons for the Zionist paramilitary groups in Mandatory Palestine was now all about building up the capacities of the new state.

As for the more narrow case of Permindex-CMC itself, it is clear how this "world trade center" would have been beneficial for engendering international capital flows and business arrangements of this very nature. At the same time, however, the links between these entities and intelligence services, like the CIA, the Italian special services and Mossad, also suggests a more covert imperative.

Michele Metta, in his book on Permindex, notes that, in the early 1960s, special arrangements were made between Israel and Italy to support the OAS – the French paramilitary group – in Algeria, in return for Italian oil companies getting access to Algerian crude.[95] While the geopolitical implications of this arrangement are wide-ranging, it was also intimately connected to CMC. Leading these secret negotiations was former Italian prime minister Fernando Tambroni, whose son-in-law, Micucci Cecchi, sat on the board of CMC.[96] On the side of the OAS, the negotiations were reportedly handled by the paramilitary leader Jacques Soustelle.[97]

This particular angle emerged during the investigation into the mysterious death of Enrico Mattei, whose plane exploded in October 1962. Mattei was the head of ENI, the dominant oil and gas firm in Italy that supplied, among other things, petroleum to NATO and the US Sixth Fleet. In the early 1960s, however, Mattei had embarked on something of a path different from the status quo of Cold War politics. He sought to sign oil agreements with the Soviet Union, and with Algerian and Egyptian interests who were, at the time, opposed to Israel.

With such a pivot taking place, theories that Mattei's death was less than accidental have existed for decades and have also led to multiple official inquiries into the incident. Italian journalist Fulvio Bellini turned over information allegedly identifying the real culprits to one of these inquiries headed by the judicial magistrate Vincenzo Calia. "I think to understand the death of Enrico Mattei," Bellini told Calia, "you need to follow the trail to Jacques Soustelle. This was the man given the job of doing Operation Mattei with around one hundred thousand dollars from Montreal, through Permindex."[98]

And what, then, of the connections to organized crime networks? One possibility is that, through its connection with Tibor Rosenbaum's International Credit Bank, Permindex-CMC was involved with money laundering activities. In one of the earliest exposés of Permindex-CMC, published by investigative journalist Mario Ugazzi in the now-defunct *Paese Sera*, a company called the Italo-American Hotel Corporation (IAHC) was identified as an affiliate of CMC (Metta, meanwhile, describes IAHC as a subsidiary of CMC).[99] IAHC was dedicated to high-end real estate development in various locations in Rome. One of its big projects was the Hotel du Lac, curiously located next to ENI's headquarters.[100]

Financing for IAHC's projects came from Banca Nazionale del Lavoro (BNL) – a bank that, as will be discussed in Chapter 7, was tied to notorious banks like BCCI and Banco Ambrosiano and also played a role in the flow of weapons to Iraq in the 1980s. The money that BNL handled, however, came from a variety of other sources in Geneva and Lichtenstein. One of these sources was none other than ICB. While this is to be expected given Rosenbaum's numerous ties to Permindex-CMC, it does raise questions about the ultimate provenance of this money. Given that ICB was moving the hot money being poured into its correspondent banks into the Caribbean, it is possible that, via these various companies, this money was being put into Italian real estate ventures.

Such conclusions are at best speculative. Yet, what is certain and undeniable is that much of the wartime OSS and CIA as well as Israel's intelligence services operated in close proximity to, and were effectively indistinguishable from, organized crime. What's unique in Israel's case, however, is that such collusion was baked in at the very foundations of, not only its intelligence service, but the origins of the state itself.

Endnotes

1   "Samuel Bronfman Dead at 80; Founded Distillers Corporation," *New York Times*, July 11, 1971, https://www.nytimes.com/1971/07/11/archives/samuel-bronfman-dead-at-80-foundeddistillers-corporation-his.html.

2   Peter C. Newman, *Bronfman Dynasty: The Rothschilds of the New World* (Toronto: McClelland and Stewart, 1978), 46.

3   "Samuel Bronfman," Entrepreneur, October 10, 2008, https://www.entrepreneur.com/article/197618.

4   Wolfgang Saxon, "Rudolf Sonneborn Dies at 87; A Zionist Leader in the US," *New York Times*, June 4, 1986, https://www.nytimes.com/1986/06/04/obituaries/rudolf-sonneborn-dies-at-87-a-zionist-leader-in-the-us.html.

5   Ricky-Dale Calhoun, "Arming David: The Haganah's Illegal Arms Procurement Network in the United States, 1945-49," *Journal of Palestine Studies* 36, no. 4 (July 1, 2007): 22–32, https://doi.org/10.1525/jps.2007.36.4.22.

6   Calhoun, "Arming David," 25.

7   Calhoun, "Arming David," 26.

8   "Marina Request Rouses Protest," *Miami News*, October 31, 1958.

9   Robert Rockaway, "Gangsters for Zion," *Tablet*, April 18, 2018, https://www.tabletmag.com/sections/arts-letters/articles/gangsters-for-zion.

10   Michael Feldberg and American Jewish Historical Society, *Blessings of Freedom: Chapters in American Jewish History* (NJ: KTAV Publishing House, 2002), 223.

11   "Federal Bureau of Narcotics Memo on Joseph Zicarelli," Doug Valentine Drug War documents, April 1, 1961, http://archive.org/details/DougValentineDrugWarDocuments.

12   Scott M. Deitche, *Garden State Gangland: The Rise of the Mob in New Jersey* (Lanham: Rowman & Littlefield, 2018), 84.

13   Jonathan Marshall, *Dark Quadrant: Organized Crime, Big Business, and the Corruption of American Democracy: From Truman to Trump,* ePub (Lanham: Rowman & Littlefield, 2021), 107.

14   Valentine, "Memo on Joseph Zicarelli."

15   Gordon Thomas and Martin Dillon, *Robert Maxwell, Israel's Superspy: The Life and Murder of a Media Mogul* (New York: Carroll and Graf, 2003), 54.

16   Calhoun, "Arming David," 30.

17   See, for example, Ignacio Klich, "Latin America, the United States and the Birth of Israel: The Case of Somoza's Nicaragua," *Journal of Latin American Studies* 20, no. 2 (November 1988): 389–432, https://doi.org/10.1017/S0022216X00003047.

18   Calhoun, "Arming David," 27.

19   Margo Gutierrez, "Israel in Central America," Middle East Research and Information Project, June 1986, *https://merip.org/1986/05/israel-in-central-america/*.

20   Jim Hougan, *Spooks: The Haunting of America: The Private Use of Secret Agents* (New York: Morrow, 1978), 172.

21   Hougan, *Spooks,*172.

22   Sandy Smith, "Monsters in the Marketplace: Money, Muscle, Murder," *Life*, September 8, 1967.

23   Smith, "Monsters."

24   Marshall, *Dark Quadrant*, 204.

25   Dennis Eisenberg, Uri Dan, and Eli Landau, *Meyer Lansky: Mogul of the Mob* (New York: Paddington Press, 1979), 266.

26   Marshall. *Dark Quadrant*, 247-48.

27   Jonathan Marshall, "Nixon's Caribbean Milieu, 1950–1968," *Dark Quadrant Appendix,* https://rowman.com/WebDocs/Dark_Quadrant_Appendix_Nixon-Caribbean.pdf.

28   Marshall, "Nixon's Caribbean Milieu."

29   Peter Dale Scott, *Deep Politics and the Death of JFK* (University of California Press, 1996), 202-5.

30   Alan A. Block, *Masters of Paradise: Organized Crime and the Internal Revenue Service in the Bahamas* (Routledge, 1991), 51.

31   R. T. Naylor, *Hot Money and the Politics of Debt* (New York: Linden Press, 1987), 34; Jonathan Marshall, *The Lebanese Connection: Corruption, Civil War, and the International Drug Traffic* (California: Stanford University Press, 2012), 49.

32   Marshall, *The Lebanese Connection*, 50.

33   Marshall, *The Lebanese Connection*, 53.

34   Sen. John Kerry and Sen. Hank Brown, *The BCCI Affair: A Report to the Committee on Foreign Relations*, 102nd Congress 2nd Session US Senate, December 1992, 299.

35   Marshall, *The Lebanese Connection*, 43.

36   Marshall, *The Lebanese Connection*, 134.

37   Douglas Valentine, *The Strength of the Wolf: The Secret History of the War on Drugs*, ePub (Verso, 2004), 407.

38   Marshall, *The Lebanese Connection*, 47.

39   Hougan, *Spooks*, 213.

40   Henrik Krüger, *The Great Heroin Coup: Drugs, Intelligence & International Fascism* (Montreal: Black Rose Books, 1980), 88.

41   Valentine, *The Strength of the Wolf*, 261.

42   Hougan, *Spooks*, 213.

43   Jonathan Beaty and S.C. Gwynne, *The Outlaw Bank: A Wild Ride Into the Secret Heart of BCCI* (Ramjac Inc, 1991), 309.

44   Alan A. Block and Constance Weaver, *All is Clouded by Desire: Global Banking, Money Laundering, and International Organized Crime*, (Praeger, 2004), 27.

45   "Top Ten Fugitives - Global Con Artist and Ruthless Criminals," FBI, October 2009, https://www.fbi.gov/news/stories/2009/october/mogilevich_102109.

46   The use of Safra's Republic National Bank by Russian organized crime interests, some of which involving Mogilevich, is discussed in Constance and Weaver, *All is Clouded By Desire*; Robert I. Friedman, *Red Mafiya: How the Russian Mob Invaded America* (Little, Brown & Company, 2000).

47   Block and Weaver, *All is Clouded by Desire*, 8.

48   Rockaway, "Gangsters for Zion."

49   Marc Goldberg, "Teddy Kollek: The British Spy Who Never Was," *Tablet*, December 15, 2020.

50   "Baruch Rappaport, the man who founded and continues to support the Faculty of Medicine at the Technion, speaks for the first time in the media," *Hayadan*, October 19, 2004.

51   "Baruch Rappaport."

52   Jonathan Nitzan and Shimshon Bichler, *The Global Political Economy of Israel* (Pluto Books, 2002), 116.

53   Noga Tarnopolsky, "Ehud Barak: I Visited Epstein's Island But Never Met Any Girls," *The Daily Beast*, July 15, 2019, https://www.thedailybeast.com/israels-ehud-barak-i-visited-epsteins-island-but-never-met-any-girls.

54   "Yehuda Assia Banker to the Mossad, Dies at 99," *Haaretz*, September 3, 2016.

55   Avner Cohen, *Israel and the Bomb* (Columbia University Press, 1998), 70.

56   Jonathan Marshall, "'Bayonne Joe' Zicarelli, Irving Davidson, and Israel," https://rowman.com/WebDocs/Dark_Quadrant_Addendum_to_Chapter_4.pdf

57   American Bank & Trust appeared in the strange story of Argentine financier David Graiver, who controlled the bank at the time of its collapse in 1976. Graiver had maintained a bank in Belgium called Banque pour L' Amerique du Sud (BAS), which according to *Barron's* journalist Richard Karp was simply a money laundering operation. In order to finance BAS, Graiver took control of American Bank & Trust and systematically looted it via the aid of roughly 13 dummy companies set up to create a byzantine maze of money flows. In the end, both BAS and American Bank fell apart, and Graiver allegedly died in a fiery plane crash near Mexico City – though suspicions abounded that he faked his death. It was subsequently revealed that Graiver may have been the banker for the Montoneros, a left-wing Peronist paramilitary organization. See Richard Karp, "Hands Across the Sea: Millions Were Looted from the American Bank & Trust," *Barron's*, December 27, 1976; Steven Rattner, "Financial Intrigue, Mystery Shroud American Bank and Trust Collapse," *New York Times*, September 25, 1976, https://www.nytimes.com/1976/09/25/archives/financial-intrigue-mystery-

shroud-american-bank-and-trust-collapse.html; Karen DeYoung, "'Argentine Watergate': Charges of Guerrilla High Finance," *Washington Post*, April 18, 1977, https://www.washingtonpost.com/archive/politics/1977/04/18/argentine-watergate-charges-of-guerrilla-high-finance/5e3b5b2b-d260-48da-a284-9ea9b4b33825/.

58   Marshall, *Dark Quadrant*, 185-86.

59   Block and Weaver, *All is Clouded By Desire*, 9.

60   See *Atlantic Steamers Supply Co., Inc against Manuel E. Kulukundis*, New York Supreme Court

61   "Margaret P. Grafeld Declassified," US Department of State, May 22, 2009, https://archive.org/details/State-Dept-cable-1977-243051/page/n1/mode/2up?q=Weisscredit&view=theater .

62   "4 Swiss Bankers Convicted," *New York Times*, March 1, 1979, https://www.nytimes.com/1979/03/01/archives/4-swiss-bankers-convicted.html.

63   Steven Greenhouse, "A Secret Emperor of Oil and Shipping," *New York Times*, February 4, 1988, https://www.nytimes.com/1988/02/04/world/a-secret-emperor-of-oil-and-shipping.html

64   Greenhouse, "Secret Emperor."

65   "Liberia's Flags of Convenience," *Al-Jazeera*, November 15, 2011, https://www.aljazeera.com/news/2011/10/15/liberias-flags-of-convenience.

66   "The New Bank of Liberia," *Liberia Today*, Vol. 3-4, 1954, 8.

67   On Bank of Monrovia and First National City Bank, see *Area Handbook for Liberia*, US Government Printing Office, 1964, 340. The influence of the Rockefeller family at First National City came via the presence of James Stillman Rockefeller. He went to work for the bank in 1930s, was elected president in 1952, and became its chairman in 1959. Wolfgang Saxon, "James S. Rockefeller, 102, Dies; Was a Banker and '24 Olympian," *New York Times*, August 11, 2004, https://www.nytimes.com/2004/08/11/business/james-s-rockefeller-102-dies-was-a-banker-and-a-24-olympian.html#:~:text=Rockefeller%20joined%20the%20National%20City,as%20a%20world%20financial%20power.

68   See Ian Smillie, *Blood on the Stone: Greed, Corruption and War in the Global Diamond Trade* (Anthem Press, 2010). FO a historical background on the role of Israel in the global diamond trade and diamond cutting industry, see David De Vries, *Diamonds and War: State, Capital and Labor in British-Ruled Palestine* (Berghahn Books, 2010).

69   Libbie Park and Frank Park, *The Anatomy of Big Business* (Progress Books, 1973), 71-77.

70   Park and Park, *Anatomy of Big Business*, 21.

71   Michele Metta, "Gershon Peres (brother of former Israeli president) was a member of the CMC," Anti-Diplomatico, November 22, 2017, https://www.lantidiplomatico.it/dettnews-esclusivo_ad_gershon_peres_fratello_dellex_presidente_israeliano__stato_membro_del_cmc_il_centro_occulto_della_cia_legato_allomicidio_kennedy/6_22228/; Michele Metta, *On the Trail of Clay Shaw: The Italian Undercover CIA and Mossad Station and the Assassination of JFK* (Independent, 2019), 141–42.

72   For an overview of Jim Garrison's interest in Clay Shaw and Shaw's ties to the CIA, see Joan Mellen, "Clay Shaw Unmasked: The Garrison Case Corroborated" http://joanmellen.com/wordpress/2013/10/21/clay-shaw-unmasked-the-garrison-case-corroborated/2/.

73   One of Metta's most fascinating discoveries is that board meetings of CMC and its subsidiary, the Italo-American Hotel Corporation, were held in the law offices of Robert Ascarelli at 72/A Piazza di Spagna, in Rome. When Licio Gelli was first organizing the infamous P2 Masonic Lodge, which operated as a sort of shadow government within Italy, the early meetings took place in these same law offices. Gelli stated that "In the first phase we celebrated the initiation rituals [to P2] in Ascarelli's office, at number 72 in Piazza di Spagna, on the third floor... As it wasn't a Masonic headquarters, we used a portable temple which we carried in a briefcase that we opened on the table... For each initiation, I provided Ascarelli with the new Freemason's curriculum vitae, so that when the ceremony was finished he could talk to the neophyte about his job and his experiences." Metta, *On the Trail of Clay Shaw*, 39.

74   Metta, *On the Trail of Clay Shaw*, 143.

75   Metta, *On the Trail of Clay Shaw*, 142. One of the directors of Banque Belgo-Centrade was one Arturo Klein, described by Metta as a 'Chilean right-winger'. Interestingly, a heavily-redacted CIA report published in a US Senate Subcommittee on International Operations n assassination

plot against Jimmy Carter. "A Staff Report Concerning Activities of Foreign Intelligence Agencies in the United States," Subcommittee on International Operations, Senate Committee on Foreign Relations, January 18, 1979, 118-122.

76   "Louis M. Bloomfield," *Canadian Jewish Chronicle*, April 7, 1967.

77   "Israel Day Observation Here Monday," *The Gazette* (Montreal), May 25, 1965; Matitiahu Hindes, "Israel and the Sea," *Wisconsin Jewish Chronicle*, September 23, 1949.

78   Bernard Reich and David H. Goldberg, *Historical Dictionary of Israel* (Maryland: Rowman and Littlefield, 2016), 558.

79   Letter from George H.W. Bush to Louis M. Bloomfield, February 11, 1976, https://www.kennedysandking.com/images/2019/kowalski-metta/exhibit-9.pdf.

80   Maurice Phillips, "Revelations from the Bloomfield Archives (4): Permindex, Bloomfield Linked to Freemasons and Rothschilds," *I Have Some Secrets For You*, April 14, 2010, http://somesecretsforyou.blogspot.com/2010/04/revelations-from-bloomfield-archives-4.html.

81   "Cable from Louis M. Bloomfield to Tibor Rosenbaum," July 12, 1961. https://www.kennedysandking.com/images/2019/kowalski-metta/exhibit-8.pdf.

82   "Dov Biegun Dead at 66," *Jewish Telegraphic Agency*, January 22, 1980, https://www.jta.org/archive/dov-biegun-dead-at-66.

83   "Realty Equity Official, Others Indicted on Charges Tied to Sale of Firm's Notes," *Wall Street Journal*, April 14, 1969.

84   Randall Cannon and Michael Gerry, *Stardust International Raceway: Motorsports Meets the Mob in Vegas, 1965-1971* (McFarland, Incorporated, 2018), 346.

85   Maurice Phillips, "The Permindex Papers II: Canadian Attorneys, Venezuelan Corporation, and French Rothschild," *I Have Some Secrets for You*, May 16, 2010, http://somesecretsforyou.blogspot.com/2010/05/permindex-papers-ii.html.

86   "Israeli Corporation - Rosenbaum - International Credit Bank Controversy," Wikileaks (Israel Tel Aviv, September 30, 1974), https://wikileaks.org/plusd/cables/1974TELAV05552_b.html.

87   Clyde H. Farnsworth, "Israeli Investing Scandal Unveiled By Rothschild," *New York Times*, October 19, 1974, https://www.nytimes.com/1974/10/19/archives/israeli-investing-scandal-unveiled-by-rothschild.html.

88   *Oil and Petroleum Year Book*, Volume 58, 1967, p. 58; Report of the Royal Commission Appointed to Inquire Into the Failure of Atlantic Acceptance Corporation, Limited, September 12, 1969, vol. 3, p. 1484, https://archive.org/details/reportofroyatlant03onta.

89   "Seven Oil Companies Prepare to Drill in Israel, Agency Reports," *Jewish Telegraphic Agency*, September 2, 1953, https://www.jta.org/archive/seven-oil-companies-prepare-to-drill-in-israel-agency-reports.

90   Alan Philips, "The Inner Workings of a Crime Cartel," *Macleans*, October 5, 1963, https://archive.macleans.ca/article/1963/10/5/the-inner-workings-of-the-crime-cartel.

91   FBN Memo on Joseph Zicarelli.

92   "Cable from Louis M. Bloomfield to Joseph Kowalaski," June 27, 1959, https://archive.org/details/bloomfield_201907/Tri%20Continental%20Pipe%20Lines/mode/1up.

93   Galina Nikitina, *The State of Israel: A Historical, Economic and Political Study* (Progress Publishers, 1973), 290.

94   Nikitina, *The State of Israel*, 292.

95   Metta, *On the Trail of Clay Shaw*, 167-168.

96   Metta, *On the Trail of Clay Shaw*, 167.

97   Metta, *On the Trail of Clay Shaw*, 167. Further information on the relationship between Israeli intelligence services, Soustelle and the OAS can be found in Sylvia K. Crosbie, *A Tacit Alliance: France and Israel from Suez to the Six Day War* (Princeton University Press, 2015), 140-41. The Italian newspaper *Paesa Sera* reported that Permindex's president, Ferenc Nagy, had helped finance the activities of Soustelle and the OAS. "The Kennedy Conspiracy," *Paesa Sera*, date unknown, http://www.kenrahn.com/Marsh/Scans/Permindex.txt. Ferenc Nagy's papers archives at Colombia University libraries in New York City show extensive correspondence between him and figures like Tibor Rosenbaum, William Donovan, and a "Dr. Rappaport." It is unknown whether or not Dr. Rappaport is Bruce Rappaport.

98   Metta, *On the Trail of Clay Shaw*, 170.

99   Mario Ugazzi, "The Mysterious Activity in Rome of the Businessman Prosecuted for the Kennedy Assassination," *Paese Sera*, date unknown, http://www.kenrahn.com/Marsh/New_Scans/CMC.txt

100   Ugazzi, "The Mysterious Activity in Rome."

CHAPTER 4

ROY COHN'S "FAVOR BANK"

"THE CITY'S PREEMINENT MANIPULATOR"

Roy Cohn, whose public reputation ranged from "boy wonder" to sleazy mob lawyer over the course of his lifetime, was one of the most influential political operators in the country for the better part of three decades. Not only would he serve as Joseph McCarthy's right-hand man during the height of the Red Scare, he would also help secure electoral victories for prominent politicians in New York and beyond, including for US presidents. Years after his death, Cohn's protégé, New York real estate billionaire Donald Trump, would serve as the 45th president of the United States.

Yet, for someone who was so influential, both his admirers and detractors have declined to dig too deeply into his career and dealings, particularly those that are most unsavory. Part of this may owe to Cohn's apparently contradictory nature – he was an anti-communist crusader that closely collaborated with the FBI as well as a close confidant, business associate, and legal counsel to some of the biggest names in organized crime. Perhaps for that reason, Cohn's story is central when detailing the rise of the networks that are the focus of this book.

Roy Cohn was a man once called New York City's "preeminent manipulator," precisely because he was "a one-man network of contacts that have reached into City Hall, the mob, the press, the Archdiocese, the disco-jet set, the courts and the backrooms of the Bronx and Brooklyn where judges are made and political contributions are arranged."[1] In addition, Cohn's ability to manipulate the press, politics and much more may have been partially due to his ability to wield blackmail in a way similar that practiced by his close associate and friend, J. Edgar Hoover. This particular relationship, aspects of which were discussed in Chapter 2, may explain why, long after Cohn's death in 1986, much of the FBI file on Cohn – believed to be over 4,000 pages long in total – has still not been made publicly available despite efforts by Cohn biographers and others over the years.[2]

Cohn's background and the earlier parts of his career serve as a useful window into how the world of "above-board" and "legitimate" business and politics has intermingled with the criminal underworld throughout the decades and how blackmail was critical to Cohn's ability to successfully navigate those murky, grey areas between the legal and the illegal.

AL COHN AND THE NEW YORK MACHINE

Roy Cohn's father, Albert Cohn, was the son of immigrants from Poland, whose limited financial means forced Albert to skip high school. He eventually attended City College, working his way through university, and graduated in 1903. Afterwards, he attended New York Law School, teaching high school classes simultaneously, and became a practicing lawyer in 1908.[3] In 1910, Albert Cohn became heavily involved in the Democratic Party clubhouses based in the Bronx, which involved "attending the once-a-week meetings, working the precincts and winning the district leader's favor," according to Roy Cohn biographer Nicholas von Hoffman.[4] Albert's connections to the Bronx Democrats grew strong enough that he was appointed assistant district attorney for the Bronx by 1917.[5] At this point, Albert or "Al" Cohn sought to become a judge but lacked the money that was necessary to secure such a position. This was because the party required payments from the men it put on the ballot as a form of fundraising, and the more influential the position, the more money was required. Cohn lacked such wealth but continued to ascend through the ranks of New York's legal scene, becoming chief district attorney in 1923 under Bronx County District Attorney Edward Glennon.

Around the time that Al Cohn had gone as far as he could without having the money required for the judgeship he coveted, he met Dora Marcus, the daughter of a wealthy banking family. According to friends of Al Cohn and members of the Marcus family, the relationship between Cohn and Dora Marcus quickly led to an arranged marriage, as Dora "was the ugly duckling daughter they couldn't marry off."[6] According to interviews given by members of the Marcus family, which aired in Matt Tyrnauer's 2019 documentary *Where's My Roy Cohn?*, Dora's father Joseph S. Marcus essentially offered Albert Cohn the money and influence necessary to become a judge in exchange for his marrying Dora.[7] They married in January 1924, and, a year later, Albert Cohn was appointed Bronx County judge by New York governor Al Smith.[8] After their marriage, Al and Dora argued about where to live, with Al initially winning, securing their place in the Bronx. Al's desire to stay in the Bronx was motivated by his desire to stay connected to the political connections he had developed, where he handled the party's "Jewish patronage" on behalf of Bronx party boss Ed Flynn.[9] Al Cohn is regarded as a protégé of Flynn's who came to wield "substantial power in the Democratic Party," according to author Robert Shogan.[10]

In 1921, Cohn created the Pontiac Democratic Club at Flynn's behest in order to weaken the political base of a Flynn rival, Patrick Kane.[11] The club later became hugely influential in local elections. Years later, Roy Cohn would describe his father as Flynn's "chief lieutenant" during this period while his mother Dora would host annual dinner parties at their home in Flynn's honor. As a judge, Al Cohn was incredibly loyal to Flynn and the Democratic Party. According to historian Christopher Elias, "When the party needed Al to rule a certain way for reasons political or personal, he followed through. When they needed his support for a specific candidate, he gave it. When the son of a friend and fellow Democratic operative killed a young woman in an automobile accident, Al made a late-night visit to the police station and 'straightened it out.'"[12]

Al's service to the party and to Flynn paid off, with New York governor Franklin Delano Roosevelt appointing Cohn to the Bronx Supreme Court in 1929, making him Roosevelt's first judicial appointment.[13] At the time and for years afterward, Flynn was one of Roosevelt's most senior strategists. Eight years later, Albert Cohn was appointed to the State Supreme Court's Appellate Division.[14] Like many of the networks already explored in this book, the political machine in which Al Cohn was intimately nestled was interwoven with the city's criminal underworld.

Some modern-day mainstream sources trace the origin of organized crime's influence on New York's Democratic Party to 1931 when Lucky Luciano sent two hired guns to intimidate Harry Perry, the co-leader of Manhattan's 2nd Assembly District, demanding he step down in favor of Albert Marinelli.[15] However, the same crime syndicate had cozy ties with labor unions, a key component of the Democratic Party's power base, going back to the 1920s – an arrangement for which mobster Arnold Rothstein is credited.[16]

Similarly, Marinelli's ties to the mob also dated back to the 1920s, when he owned a trucking company that Lucky Luciano managed during the Prohibition era. Luciano had been responsible for helping Marinelli become the first Italian-American district leader at Tammany Hall well before the incident with Perry, which speaks to organized crime's earlier influence over New York politics through Tammany. Yet, after Perry stepped aside and ceded his position to Marinelli, the National Crime Syndicate's influence on New York City politics, particularly the Democratic Party, became "brazen," according to decades-old reports in *New York* magazine, as the move gave Marinelli – and by proxy, Luciano – control over who was chosen to serve on grand juries as well as the counting of votes in local elections.[17]

The influence of the National Crime Syndicate on top New York politicians was considerable at the time when Albert Cohn was deeply involved in Democratic affairs. For instance, Meyer Lansky is known to have donated to the political campaigns of Al Smith, the governor of New York for much of the 1920s.[18] Smith was a top figure with Tammany Hall, the political powerhouse of New York Democratic politics that controlled Democratic Party nominations and became synonymous with corruption. Smith is regarded as one of the main protégés of Tammany boss Charles M. Murphy, who had worked to improve the organization's reputation until his death in 1924. However, Murphy's success in cleaning up Tammany's public image did not extend long past his death, largely because many of the top names at the organization had remained closely enmeshed with the city's criminal underworld despite his efforts.

During the now-infamous effort of the National Crime Syndicate to rig the Democratic National Convention in 1932 in favor Franklin Delano Roosevelt, it was a tearful Al Smith, who had personally warned Luciano, Lansky, and Costello that Roosevelt would betray them.[19] Smith specifically warned that Roosevelt would break his promise to restrain an official inquiry into criminal activity in New York City, a promise Roosevelt had made to appease organized criminal interests in order to secure his nomination. This anecdote was relayed separately by both Lansky and Luciano.[20] Smith's warning, which the crime bosses had ignored, turned out to be true, as Roosevelt allowed the inquiry, led by Judge Samuel Seabury, to advance after his nomination was cemented. The inquiry soon exposed extensive criminal activity being conducted by Tammany politicians, leading several top officials to resign. Jimmy Walker, the Tammany-backed mayor of New York City and Al Smith's own protégé, not only resigned as mayor but fled to Paris to avoid charges.[21]

Regarding the 1932 convention, Luciano later stated that it was commonly known at the time that his criminal enterprise controlled most of

New York City's delegates to the convention, which speaks to their considerable influence over the party's dealings in the city during that period.[22] Seabury and Roosevelt's combined determination to clean up the Democratic Party's image in New York, however, saw Tammany's influence wane due to its entrenched association with organized crime becoming public knowledge. The National Crime Syndicate's influence on New York politics nevertheless remained strong well past Tammany's fall from grace.

The elder Cohn remained deeply involved in the Democratic political apparatus during this period and, as mentioned, was specifically close to Edward Flynn, who had tightly controlled the Democratic Party in the Bronx since 1922. Flynn, who was another protégé of Tammany Hall boss Charles Murphy but not a Tammany member himself, became favored by Roosevelt in the wake of the Seabury inquiry, supposedly because Flynn had kept his district free of corruption.[23] An argument can be made, however, that Flynn had merely kept his district and his own reputation free from a public association with corruption, as Flynn later moved to protect the mob-linked politician William O'Dwyer. According to Robert Shogan, O'Dwyer was one of the Cohn family's "famous family friends."[24]

The rise of William O'Dwyer, not unlike that of Thomas Dewey, was based on his reputation as a crusader against organized crime, including Meyer Lansky's Murder Inc., and specifically his role in the takedown of syndicate boss Louis "Lepke" Buchalter. It has been disputed, however, as to whether the reality of the Buchalter case was the same as what was publicly reported (i.e., ex-cop O'Dwyer bravely taking on the mob) or, rather, the masking of the consolidation of mob power into fewer hands.

As noted by Sally Denton and Roger Morris in *The Money and the Power*, it was Lansky himself who had arranged for Buchalter to be arrested by the FBI and the Federal Bureau of Narcotics in 1937. Of this alliance, Denton and Morris write that the "betrayal [of Buchalter] at once removed a Lansky rival, gratified Hoover and FBN director Harry Anslinger in their mutual obsession with popular image, and further compromised federal law enforcement, which was growing ever more dependent on informers and double agents for its successes."[25] Both Dewey and O'Dwyer prosecuted Buchalter with great zeal, gaining considerable recognition for themselves in the process.[26] The man they took down, however, had already been consigned to death by both his "friends" and the government before Dewey and O'Dwyer were even involved, which casts doubt on the narrative that Buchalter's prison sentences and eventual death sentence were merely the result of Dewey's and O'Dwyer's prosecutorial abilities.

Further doubt regarding the official story of this incident is raised when one considers that both star prosecutors had their own ties to the same syndicate, with Dewey's ties to Mary Carter Paint/Resorts International having already been noted in Chapter 1. In the case of O'Dwyer, he was meeting with Frank Costello the same year that he secured Buchalter's death sentence.[27] O'Dwyer ran for mayor of New York in 1941 and lost, but he was later elected in 1945, largely on his anticorruption public image. However, an investigation launched by an attorney O'Dwyer had once hired and who was successfully elected to O'Dwyer's old position as Brooklyn District Attorney, Miles McDonald, brought that image – and O'Dwyer's career – crashing down. In 1950, McDonald began investigating Harry Gross, who had been running a multi-million-dollar gambling empire in the city. The investigation into Gross grew rapidly with McDonald discovering a series of other related rackets throughout the city. Most of those rackets led back to one man, James Moran – the man who had served as O'Dwyer's right-hand man when O'Dwyer served as a judge, as a district attorney, and now as the city's mayor.

Once word got out that McDonald was onto Moran, heat started to be applied from the very top, with O'Dwyer denouncing the man he had once hired and calling his investigation a "witch hunt."[28] Soon afterward, Ed Flynn called President Harry Truman and urgently requested a meeting. No formal record of the meeting exists, but it is believed that the topic was the implications that McDonald's investigation would have, not just for New York City but for the Democratic Party and Truman himself. Two days later, Truman met with the head of New York's Democratic Party and a close associate of Flynn's, Paul Fitzpatrick. He then met with Eleanor Roosevelt, whose influence on the New York Democratic Party was still considerable. According to journalist David Samuels:

> What McDonald's investigation would reveal, Flynn and Fitzpatrick knew, was that Mayor O'Dwyer was the frontman for a system of citywide corruption that was administered by Moran, the mayor's closest political associate. Worse, they knew – as the public would find out the following August, from the public testimony of a gangster named Irving Sherman – that O'Dwyer and Moran had been meeting personally with the syndicate boss Frank Costello as far back as 1941. And as a former chairman of the Democratic National Committee, Flynn also knew that the urban political operations that had helped elect Franklin Roosevelt to the presidency four times, and Truman once, were based on a system of unsavory

alliances. Putting O'Dwyer on the stand would put the Democratic Party in New York – and elsewhere – on trial. One way to keep
O'Dwyer safe from McDonald's grand jury was to get him out of
the country.[29]

This is precisely what happened, as Truman appointed O'Dwyer to
be ambassador to Mexico, which allowed O'Dwyer to avoid charges and
further scrutiny. Ed Flynn's close ally and accomplice in helping orchestrate this deal to protect O'Dwyer, Paul Fitzpatrick, thanked Truman in
a letter: "Your recent announcement of the pending appointment of the
Ambassador to Mexico, again proves to me your deep understanding of
many problems and your kindness in rendering assistance…. May I just
say thanks."[30]

Though O'Dwyer had escaped from McDonald's investigation, he was
forced to return to the US from Mexico City to testify before the Kefauver
Committee on his alleged dealings with organized crime in March 1951.
During his testimony, he did not deny having visited Frank Costello's
home in 1941. He also admitted that he had appointed the friends and
relatives of powerful mobsters to public offices and became evasive when
asked how much he had known about their ties to organized crime at the
time. A subsequent report issued by the committee stated that "during
Mr. O'Dwyer's term of office as district attorney of Kings County between 1940 and 1942, and his occupancy of the mayoralty from 1946 to
1950, neither he nor his appointees took any effective action against the
top echelons of the gambling, narcotics, water-front, murder, or book-
making rackets," while his time as mayor had "contributed to the growth
of organized crime, racketeering, and gangsterism in New York City."[31]

Less than a year later, O'Dwyer's right-hand man, James Moran, was
convicted on twenty-three counts of extortion for his role in the corruption McDonald had exposed. If Flynn was indeed a Bronx political boss
who was free of scandal and corruption as some historians claim, it is hard
to justify why he would intervene so dramatically – directly involving the
White House – in order to protect the corruption that had enabled O'Dwyer. Rather, he stepped in to protect the system of "unsavory alliances"
that had given his party its power, including its obvious organized crime
ties. There is also the fact that a young Roy Cohn had been considerably
involved with and worked in O'Dwyer's election campaign, bragging that
he had been the one who had found dirt on O'Dwyer's Republican challenger.[32] The mob connections and the use of "dirt" and blackmail in pol-

itics is something that would later define much of Roy Cohn's career and, ultimately, his legacy.

Uncle Bernie's Bank

Though Roy Cohn was undeniably born into privilege given his father's influence and connections, it can easily be argued that much of Albert Cohn's own success and clout had been due to marrying into the Marcus family. Roy Cohn's mother, Dora Marcus, hailed from an elite family in New York's Jewish community that was later mired in controversy and scandal in connection with their Wall Street activities during the Great Depression.

Dorothy "Dora" Marcus was the daughter of Joseph S. Marcus, who had created the Bank of the United States. Marcus, a Russian-Jewish immigrant, started his career in the garment industry before entering the world of banking, first creating the Public Bank of New York in 1906. He disposed of his interest in that bank in 1912 and chartered the Bank of the United States a year later. One of Marcus' reasons for doing so was apparently related to problems at the Public Bank that had resulted from Marcus' hiring of William Koelsch as cashier. Koelsch's presence at the bank caused "friction" among the bank's directors, according to the *New York Times*.[33]

Marcus, Koelsch, and a business partner of Marcus' named Saul Singer came together to create the Bank of the United States soon afterward, but they had different men officially file the bank's incorporation. This was allegedly done in order to hide their involvement to avoid alerting Public Bank's leadership that Marcus and Koelsch were the real forces behind their new competitor. Marcus' new bank was the subject of immediate controversy, as his new for-profit enterprise was to be located just a stone's throw from Public Bank, leading Public Bank's leadership to complain that "there was no public necessity for such additional banking facilities in that particular block" of the street.[34]

In addition, Public Bank leadership objected to the name of Marcus' new bank, arguing that the name "Bank of the United States" sounded too much like some historical government-linked institutions, such as that which had served as a prototype for a central bank during the days of President Andrew Jackson. This, they argued, could give the false impression of a direct US government connection to Marcus' bank, particularly to the uninformed. This point was made explicit in a letter written on behalf of Public Bank by Samuel I. Frankenstein and sent to the Senate Banking Committee.

Frankenstein, according to a report on the letter published by the *New York Times*, argued that "ignorant foreigners ... would believe that the United States Government was interested in this bank and that it was a branch of the United States Treasury in Washington, and if the bank should fail these poor depositors would bewail the fact that they had entrusted their scant savings to the United States government."[35] He added, "It must be evident to any impartial mind that the motive and purpose in selecting this very peculiar and misleading name for a bank to be located in a neighborhood almost exclusively inhabited by foreigners, especially when so many other appropriate names could have been so easily adopted, was not a laudable one. This name was not selected through pure accident."[36] TIME would prove Frankenstein very prescient.

Despite these concerns, the Bank of the United States was granted its charter by George C. Van Tuyl Jr., NY State Superintendent of Banks, who subsequently became a vice president and later a director of the bank. The Bank of the United States, as Frankenstein had expected, immediately worked to attract business and deposits from the local Jewish immigrant community. Starting with a modest $100,000 in working capital, it experienced moderate growth and had a total of five branches by 1925. Given its Jewish ownership and efforts to cater directly to Jews, it became a point of pride for the New York Jewish community, which "eagerly embraced the new bank, opening savings accounts and borrowing money for fledgling businesses," according to historian Beth S. Wenger.[37]

Legal proceedings were, however, filed against the bank in 1926, requiring an independent examination of the bank's books. The case was dismissed by NY State Supreme Court judge Joseph S. Proskauer, allegedly because the plaintiffs had failed to "make out a case."[38] Yet, there are reasons to doubts Proskauer's objectivity in the case, as he was connected to the same political machine as Albert Cohn. For instance, Proskauer had been appointed by New York governor Al Smith, whose ties to organized crime have already been discussed. Proskauer had also served as Smith's key political advisor during campaigns bankrolled by Lansky, which took place while Proskauer served on the NY State Supreme Court and subsequently the Appellate Court. Proskauer was appointed chair of the New York State Crime Commission in the early 1950s, despite his past conflicts of interest.[39]

That commission had been created at the behest of Governor Thomas Dewey, who, as mentioned in Chapter 1, had released Lucky Luciano from prison after his involvement in Operation Underworld and who was also closely tied to both John Foster Dulles and Allen Dulles. Allen Dulles was serving as CIA director at the time of the commission's activities and as the Agency's ties to organized crime deepened. Soon after the Crime Commission's work was completed, Dewey's former chief assistant, Paul Lockwood, in 1955 became a top executive at Lewis Rosenstiel's mob-linked Schenley Industries, while Dewey himself officially became a business associate of Lansky frontmen in 1958.[40] Lansky had also previously donated to Dewey's unsuccessful bid for the US presidency in 1944.[41] The Proskauer-led Crime Commission was insignificant in terms of its end results, especially in comparison to the impact the Kefauver Committee had had the year before, when Dewey had been called to testify due to his suspected mob ties.[42] This suggests that Proskauer, like Albert Cohn, Ed Flynn and others, could be counted on to protect certain influential actors within the system of "unsavory alliances" that was woven throughout the city.

In addition to Proskauer's own apparent conflicts of interest, there is the added fact that Joseph Marcus had promised Albert Cohn a judgeship in exchange for his marrying his daughter Dora, which further reveals the influence of the Marcus family within legal and judicial circles, as well as with the politicians who appointed judges in New York during this period. Albert Cohn had been appointed as judge for Bronx County by Al Smith a year before this case was brought against Marcus' bank, in 1925.[43]

Joseph Marcus died in 1927, giving his son Bernard K. Marcus – Roy Cohn's "Uncle Bernie" – complete control over the bank's affairs.[44] Bernard Marcus had already been intimately involved with the bank's leadership since 1919, when his father had turned over active management of the bank to him. After his father's death, Bernard was named president of the bank and went on an aggressive acquisitions-and-mergers spree, resulting in the bank growing from five branches in 1925 to sixty two in 1930.[45] Two major mergers took place in 1928 followed by two more in 1929, resulting in the Bank of the United States becoming the third-largest bank in New York City by May 1929.[46] The bank became a member of the Federal Reserve of New York, which was greatly influenced by the Warburg brothers, Felix and Paul. Paul Warburg was the main architect of the privately owned Federal Reserve banking system and a powerful force at the central bank during its early years.[47]

Due to the Bank of the United States' apparent success, Bernard was hailed at the time as "a financial wizard who could make dividends sprout from virtually nothing."[48] Yet, it was soon revealed that Bernard Marcus' wizardry was largely the result of fraud and corruption by the Marcuses and Saul Singer, validating the earlier rationale for having the bank investigated, which had been dismissed by Proskauer. In February 1930, just months after the Black Tuesday stock market crash of October 1929, Bernard Marcus assured shareholders that the bank stood on solid ground.[49] A few months later, the bank began negotiations for its largest merger yet, which would have resulted in their bank managing $1 billion in deposits. The would-be bank was to have been headed by J. Herbert Case, then head of the Federal Reserve Bank of New York, of which the Marcus-run bank was a member.[50] In addition, Goldman Sachs was poised to have "a substantial interest" in the new bank, further underscoring that the merger was set to create another Wall Street behemoth.[51] Terms of the merger were reportedly negotiated in November 1929.[52]

Yet, by December, rumors were proliferating that the Marcus-run bank was insolvent. Nervous investors and depositors, most of whom were Jewish, lined up to withdraw their money on December 10, 1930. By midday, over $2 million had been withdrawn, and tens of thousands of the bank's estimated four hundred thousand clients had gathered outside the doors of the bank's Bronx branch, leading to the police being called to maintain order. The panic quickly spread to other branches, but – by that time – all of the other branches had closed their doors. A massive sell-off of the bank's stock ensued, plunging it to $3 a share, whereas it had stood at $91 the previous year. Bernard Marcus insisted that the bank would reopen following the planned merger. The merger, however, fell through, as clearinghouse banks involved in the deal pulled out after examining the books of the Marcus-run bank.

Superintendent of Banks Joseph Broderick attempted to work with Wall Street's leading bankers to rescue the bank on December 11, 1930, but failed to reach any solution. The governor of New York at the time, Franklin D. Roosevelt, ordered the Bank of the United States closed, which made its failure the largest in US history at the time. An investigation was launched, and the evidence of fraud quickly piled up.

As the investigation began, it became readily apparent that Bernard Marcus and Saul Singer, the bank's vice president, had engaged in illegal activity, including purchasing the bank's stock with depositor funds in order to drive up the stock price.[53] Not only that, but they loaned out over $37 million under suspicious circumstances, including $10 million in mostly unsecured loans to bank directors and their companies, as well as $5.5 million in loans to sixteen insolvent subsidiaries of the bank in the months leading up to its collapse.[54] Marcus and Singer also raided the bank's reserve to finance their own investments in the real estate market.

Public hearings revealed that two months before the bank shut down, officers at the bank had burned a truckload of documents, more than a thousand bundles of papers of bank records, at an incinerator located at the Beresford Apartments, which was owned by a subsidiary of the Bank of the United States.[55] Marcus, in a style that would later be exemplified by his nephew Roy Cohn, fought the investigation of his bank bitterly, even going so far as to refuse to testify and to seek the removal of the lead investigator of the case.[56] Both Marcus and Singer were found guilty of fraud and were sentenced to three years in Sing Sing maximum-security prison, and their appeal was unsuccessful.

According to members of the Marcus family, including Roy's mother Dora, the reason the other banking chieftains of New York had declined to step in to rescue the Bank of the United States had been "anti-Semitism," and editorials appeared in some New York newspapers arguing the same.[57] Per this theory, the Episcopalian J. P. Morgan, the Anglo-Saxon-dominated New York Clearing House, and the German-Jewish bankers – e.g. the Kuhns, Loebs, and Lehmans – had let the Russian-Jewish bankers fail when they could have saved their bank. Dora Marcus referred to these figures as "a dirty anti-Semitic cabal" that sought to destroy her family due to their Russian-Jewish origins.[58]

Other banks, however, have been allowed to fail throughout US history, and "anti-Semitism" was not blamed for those occurrences. In addition, the German-Jewish banking establishment was in part dominated by another powerful family – the Warburgs – with both Felix and Paul Warburg having married into another German-Jewish banking family, the Loebs. In June 1930, just months before the collapse of the Marcus-owned bank, Albert Cohn – Bernard Marcus' brother-in-law – was the guest of honor at a luncheon hosted by Felix Warburg, suggesting that this alleged hatred held by the German-Jewish banking establishment for the Russian-Jewish Marcus family did not exist at the time.[59]

It is perhaps more likely that either the fraud of the Bank of the United States was too enormous or that the German-Jewish banking establishment was disgruntled that such a massive fraud had been perpetrated by a Jewish-owned bank against mostly Jewish depositors. After all, the bank sought to target the Jewish immigrant community through deceptive means from its inception and subsequently committed fraud to rob mostly Jewish immigrants of their money. For example, the bank deliberately advertised its services to the Jewish community in Jewish newspapers and magazines less than a year before its failure at a time when its executives had been engaged in fraudulent activity.[60] In addition, there had been efforts to investigate the bank for fraud earlier, but they had been dismissed with the intervention of Judge Proskauer. That intervention also raises the possibility that powerful interests had been willing to intervene on behalf of the Marcus-owned bank once but would not do so a second time.

Furthermore, Bernard Marcus was pardoned after just twenty-seven months in prison by Herbert Lehman when he was serving as New York governor.[61] Lehman had been one of the judges presiding over Marcus' appeal and was the only one who had argued for the conviction to be overturned.[62] Lehman, who hailed from the German-Jewish Lehman Brothers banking family, was close to Albert Cohn, who had allegedly lobbied Lehman to grant the pardon.[63] If the Lehmans and the rest of the German-Jewish banking establishment had indeed sought to destroy Marcus, it is highly unlikely that Herbert Lehman would have intervened to try to prevent his initial conviction and then intervened again by pardoning Marcus.

The trial and imprisonment of Bernard Marcus had a considerable impact on Roy Cohn, as "Bernie" was his favorite uncle. Roy, like other members of the Marcus family, took the view that the "anti-Semitic cabal" had used Bernard Marcus as a "scapegoat," leading some of his cousins on the Marcus side to claim that it was this view that led Cohn to "fight the establishment."[64] Given other accounts and insights into Roy Cohn's upbringing, it seems more likely that he just resented the law and felt that it should not apply to him, a sentiment apparently shared by Bernard Marcus, as revealed by his conduct during the investigation and trial related to his role as the president of the Bank of the United States.

On Roy Cohn's maternal side, it was not only his grandfather and uncle who were influential figures in New York (despite their very public fall from grace in the 1930s). His maternal grandmother, Celia Cohen Marcus, was the sister of Joshua Lionel Cowen (born Cohen), who cofounded Lionel Corporation, a producer of model railroads and toy trains. The origins of the prominent toy company lie in Cowen's work for Acme Electric Light company, where he began registering patents for lamps and motors in 1899.[65] That same year, Cowen was awarded a $12,000 contract from the US Navy to design and manufacture fuses to ignite submarine mines.[66] Cowen used the money to finance the creation of Lionel Corporation in 1900. Though Cowen is best known as the long-time and founding president of Lionel Corporation, he was also a director of the Bank of United States at the time of its demise.[67]

While his nephew was sent to Sing Sing, Cowen managed to get off light through the help of Fred Piderit, the special deputy banking superintendent charged with overseeing the liquidation of the Bank of the United States.[68] Piderit's son later became a prominent fixture at the New York Federal Reserve.[69] Cowen ultimately settled for $5,000 (about $107,000 in 2022 dollars), despite having personally attended bank directors' meetings during which many of the fraudulent loans had been approved. He testified that he knew nothing of the bank's criminal activities and learned about its many problems from media reports after its closure. Cowen's avoidance of charges in the case further weakens the theory that the prosecution of Bernard Marcus over the bank's collapse was a plot against the Marcus family perpetrated by other Jewish banking families.

Lionel's influence grew and peaked in the early 1950s when it became the world's largest toy manufacturer.[70] Its glory days faded relatively quickly, and by the end of decade, Cowen and his son Lawrence stepped away from the company, selling their shares to none other than Roy Cohn. Cohn's involvement with and role at the company would subsequently be linked to suspect financial activity and organized crime networks. Friends of Cohn's, including former congressman Neil Gallagher, have alleged that Roy persuaded friends and acquaintances to buy Lionel stock while he privately shorted the firm, resulting in Cohn getting rich while those who had invested at his behest took a financial beating.[71] Cohn also "sidestepped" federal regulations in the late 1950s by borrowing large sums from US and foreign sources to buy Lionel stock.[72] At the time, Cohn had already become enmeshed in business interests tied to mob figures such as Moe Dalitz and Tony Salerno.

Regarding other notable claims about Roy Cohn's family tree, it has been alleged by some, including his biographer Nicholas von Hoffman, that his maternal grandmother, Celia Cohen Marcus, was "deranged," suffering from serious mental issues. One of his uncles on his mother's side, Jesse Marcus, was "either mentally retarded or brain-damaged," which the family speculated was due to the misuse of forceps by the doctor who delivered him, while others suspected a congenital condition. Von Hoffman also reported that some members of the Cohn family thought that Roy Cohn's mother needed to be institutionalized, while others thought something similar but believed that being well-to-do made her eccentricities manageable.[73]

Other members of the Marcus family, including Roy Cohn's cousins, have not made such extreme claims but have said that Dora's neurotic and sociopathic tendencies left an undeniable mark on her son. According to one of his cousins, it all started the day Roy Cohn was born in 1927, with Dora telling Al, "This is my baby. I'm going to bring this child up and you're going to have nothing to say about it."[74] Though dominated by his mother and having much less contact with his father, Cohn was aware from a young age of their unhappy marriage and was able to play his parents against each other with ease. Bernard Marcus' wife, Libby Marcus, once stated to biographer von Hoffman that Cohn's parents "saw quite differently in ways of discipline and so forth, so Roy was never said no to. He could always find one person on his side, and that's the one he would use." Cohn's Aunt Libby, added, "I don't think there was any [discipline] between Roy and his mother. It was always in a direction of power, influence, recognition, and there was no chance of Roy ever being stymied because he always, always got his way. … It was not a normal relationship."[75]

This permissiveness was, perhaps, the most lasting impact Cohn's mother had on his character. It was also expressed by one of his law partners, who was anonymously cited by von Hoffman as saying, "His doting mother created a person who was totally free of the rules that you and I or most people go by. What will people think, what's the right thing, what does my religion say about this – Roy played by his own set of rules. Whatever he wanted at any given moment was the right thing."[76]

Roy Rising

From a young age, Roy Cohn was known for being adept at "the trade of human calculus, of deal making, swapping, maneuver, and manipulation."[77] By the time he was twelve, for example, he was using his father's political connections to secure men jobs at the post office, collecting a finder's fee. Those who knew him all agree that he felt more comfortable in the presence of powerful businessmen and New York political powerbrokers than with children his own age. Despite being so different from other children, Roy Cohn developed a few close childhood friends, some of whom would dramatically impact his career trajectory as well as his later ability to manipulate the media for political gain and for the gain of his clients.

These childhood pals of Cohn's included Si Newhouse Jr., who went on to oversee the Conde Nast empire that now includes *Vanity Fair, Vogue, GQ, the New Yorker*, and many other publications; Edwin Weisel Jr., who became assistant attorney general under President Lyndon Johnson and whose father was a prominent lawyer in the movie business; and Generoso (Gene) Pope Jr., who eventually ran the *National Enquirer*. Cohn's Aunt Libby Marcus stated that Roy "had very few contemporary friends, because even as a little boy, if he had a party there would be two youngsters, Generoso Pope [Jr.] and Eddie Weisel, Jr. – those were his two friends. Every time he had a party, he had these two contemporaries and everybody else was somebody in politics or somebody with power. Older. He didn't bother too much [with] people his own age."[78]

Gene, like Roy, had an insatiable interest in politics and, more specifically, the politics of power. He was the favorite son of Generoso Pope Sr., an immigrant who had famously come to the US from Italy essentially penniless and who had risen to the top of New York City's – and then the nation's – concrete industry. Pope Sr. was a controversial man at the time due to his admiration and support for Italian fascism and his ties to Benito Mussolini as well as the Vatican and New York's top mobsters.[79] Pope Sr. was also close to William O'Dwyer, the mob-linked mayor of New York who was also a friend to the Cohn family. Pope Sr. also had the ear of prominent US politicians, including Democratic presidents Franklin D. Roosevelt and Harry Truman as well as Truman's Republican challenger and governor of New York, Thomas Dewey.

Regarding the family's mob ties, Pope Sr. was particularly close to Frank Costello, who he had known since his earliest days in New York and who had shaped the trajectory of his business, Colonial Sand and Stone, by securing the most lucrative city contracts for concrete for Pope's company.[80] The seemingly endless series of sweetheart deals led Colonial to become the largest concrete company in the country and allowed Pope Sr., its head, to become one of the wealthiest, "legitimate" businessmen with intimate organized crime ties.

So close was the tie that Costello – who was the real-life inspiration for Vito Corleone, the main character of the famous Mario Puzo novel *The Godfather* – was chosen to be Gene Pope Jr.'s actual godfather and served as his guide for years. Gene, after a brief stint working in psychological operations for the CIA, got a loan from Costello to construct his own media empire around the *National Enquirer*. Gene Pope Jr.'s son, Paul Pope, described Costello's influence on his family as "like a guardian angel, his power felt but unseen."[81]

The mafioso-style "deals" that brought the Pope family to prominence also became their *modus operandi*. Through his control of the city's concrete industry and the local Italian immigrant voting bloc through his essential monopoly on Italian-language newspapers in New York, Pope was a force that major politicians, and any ambitious politician, could not afford to ignore. He operated through an elaborate system of quid pro quo that was later adopted by Roy Cohn, who called his own version of this system his "favor bank."[82] As Gene Pope Jr. later said of both his and his father's roles in New York – and even national – politics: "We made deals. That's how judges got made, DAs, things like that. That's when you did all your talking. I mean I did everything from fixing parking tickets to making judges."[83]

Cohn, later on in life, reminisced about his closeness to the Pope family, stating that "virtually every Saturday night, we would go out to dinner or have dinner at 1040 Fifth and then Mr. and Mrs. Pope, Gene and I would go see a new Broadway show."[84] According to Gene Pope Jr. and Cohn, Gene Pope Sr. served as a "mentor" to Cohn, whom he admired for his "magnetic personality." Cohn later said that he "learned an awful lot about practical politics" from Pope Sr., including the politics of the "favor bank," and that the mob-linked businessman "had more to do with my incipient political career than any other single person."[85]

Pope Sr. certainly aided Cohn's rise in the world of lawfare, having pulled strings to secure the appointment of Irving Saypol as US Attorney for the Southern District of New York (SDNY), where Cohn subsequently served as assistant attorney. According to Cohn, as cited by his biographer Nicholas von Hoffman, Saypol's appointment as US Attorney was "thanks to the influence of an odoriferous triumvirate" of Pope Sr., Carmine de Sapio of Tammany Hall, and Frank Costello.[86] Saypol's focus on prosecuting Communists led to Cohn's now infamous role in the trial of Julius and Ethel Rosenberg and, shortly thereafter, the McCarthy hearings.

It was Roy Cohn's oddly cozy relationship with J. Edgar Hoover, described in Chapter 2, that was the deciding factor in Cohn's appointment as Joe McCarthy's chief counsel during the controversial anti-Communist hearings. The position had nearly gone to Robert F. Kennedy, who was a lifelong rival and bitter enemy of Cohn's – with Kennedy attempting to nail Cohn on more than one occasion when he was Attorney General during his brother's presidency. Though Cohn was ruthless and seemingly untouchable as McCarthy's counsel, having played a pivotal role in destroying many careers and lives during the parallel "Red" and "Lavender" scares, his antics in relation to his work on the committee eventually led to his downfall after he attempted to blackmail the Army in return for preferential treatment for committee consultant and his rumored lover, David Schine. Notably, shortly before Schine became involved with Cohn and McCarthy, his sister, Renee Schine, married Lester Crown, the future Mega Group member and son of the "Supermob"-linked Henry Crown discussed in Chapter 1.[87]

While Cohn's failed power play with the Army was his most well-known attempt to use blackmail during this period, he was also known to have used blackmail of various sorts to target diplomats, such as Charles Thayer, the US consul general in Munich, Germany, after Thayer's brother-in-law, Charles Bohlen, was nominated for an ambassadorship by Eisenhower. Both Thayer, but especially Bohlen, were hated by the "McCarthyite right" despite there being no solid evidence of communist affiliations in either case.[88] Cohn had learned that, during a stint in Mexico, Thayer had produced a son with a Mexican woman whom he had briefly married and then divorced. Cohn threatened to inform Thayer's aged mother of this long-past affair by shoehorning it into the public confirmation hearings of Charles Bohlen, who had been nominated to serve as US ambassador to the Soviet Union. Thayer, fearing that the news would greatly distress his elderly mother, chose to resign from the State Department.[89]

Cohn also likely used blackmail obtained by other means, given that he had already become involved with the Rosenstiel-linked sexual-blackmail operation during this period. As discussed in chapter 2, this operation was allegedly tied to the anti-Communist "hunt" of the period, and its apparent target, homosexual men, were also being "hunted" due to so-called lavender scare. Ironically, one of the main motives behind the lavender scare was the concern that closeted homosexuals were vulnerable to blackmail. Though the idea was that Communists would use this information to subvert homosexuals in the US government, the evidence suggests that it was this specific anti-Communist group with which Cohn was directly affiliated, who were more adept at blackmailing these men. This group was also subversive, given that their top men, homosexuals such as Hoover and Cohn, where entangled with and compromised by organized crime. After all, it had been Hoover's FBI and the Catholic Church, dominated by Cohn's pal Cardinal Spellman, that had originally backed and legitimized McCarthy and his now infamous witch hunt.[90]

Like Hoover, Cardinal Spellman, the archbishop of New York from 1939 until his death in 1967, was incredibly powerful. As Gene Pope Jr., Roy Cohn's lifelong friend, later recalled: "You couldn't get a job in

New York without Spellman's okay.... Before anybody had a Chinaman's chance, it had to be cleared by Spellman.... He controlled everything with an iron fist, he controlled the legislature, he controlled the city council. He controlled everything."[91] Spellman was very much a control freak, having been known to interpret "any sign of opposition to his will as a sign of Communist subversion."[92] Also like Hoover, Spellman's power was likely the main reason why he was able to keep the facts about his homosexual life under wraps. Spellman's double life not only allegedly involved the "blue suite" parties at the Plaza hotel, but also included private sex parties at his mansion. Even Spellman biographer John Cooney had to acknowledge Spellman's private life, writing, "In New York's clerical circles ... Spellman's sex life was a source of profound embarrassment.... There were stories about his seducing altar boys and choir boys. He had his favorites among handsome young priests and was known to have lovers outside the clergy."[93]

One interesting anecdote shared by Cooney relates to a choir boy who had a relationship with Spellman and who was particularly vocal about it. A man named C. A. Tripp, who later became a sex researcher for the controversial Alfred C. Kinsey, stumbled on this relationship by accident after he met the choir boy, who was bragging about his trysts with Spellman. Tripp was stunned that the powerful Cardinal was not more discreet about his dealings. Tripp asked the boy to ask Spellman why he was not worried that news would get out and harm his reputation. The boy returned several days later and responded: "The archbishop says, 'Who would ever believe *that*?'"[94]

It seems that Spellman was confident that his powerful position would shield him from any real scrutiny, allowing him to carry on his sex life as he saw fit. As Rod Dreher of the *American Conservative* wrote in a 2019 article that detailed various anecdotes about Spellman's double life: "Cardinal Spellman was confident that he would never be outed, and that if someone tried, no one would believe it. And they wouldn't have, until today."[95] As previously noted, Spellman was alleged to have been seen at the "blue suite" parties at the Plaza hotel.

While Spellman and Hoover apparently had similar, and potentially connected, private lives that carried the risk of exposure, it seems that only the latter was blackmailed. Such blackmail was not only wielded by organized crime interests to protect their rackets from FBI meddling, but also by American intelligence agencies. According to David Talbot in *The Devil's Chessboard*, McCarthy's efforts to target CIA analyst and CIA director Allen Dulles' ally William McBundy in mid-1953 led Dulles to put the squeeze on Hoover, who (despite having expressed doubts about McCarthy's campaign at this time) continued to feed the Wisconsin senator and Roy Cohn "a stream of damaging information on his [Hoover's] Washington enemies."[96]

Dulles, himself the subject of a thick dossier kept in Hoover's office that documented his adulterous trysts, made sure the CIA maintained the blackmail on Hoover, including that which had been shared between OSS veterans, most likely James Jesus Angleton, and Meyer Lansky years earlier. As Talbot notes, "The CIA counterintelligence chief [J. J. Angleton] was rumored to occasionally show off photographic evidence of Hoover's intimate relationship with FBI deputy Clyde Tolson, including a photo of Hoover orally pleasuring his longtime aide and companion," while one of Allen Dulles' mistresses was known to refer to Hoover as "the Virgin Mary in pants."[97]

Dulles had also compiled a lengthy dossier on Joe McCarthy's sex life, which included allegations of homosexuality. Talbot details those allegations:

> The senator who relentlessly hunted down homosexuals in government [i.e., McCarthy] was widely rumored to haunt the 'bird circuit' near Grand Central Station as well as gay hideaways in Milwaukee. Drew Pearson got wind of the stories but was never able to get enough proof to run with them. But the less discriminating Hank Greenspun, editor and publisher of the *Las Vegas Sun*, who was locked in an ugly war of words with McCarthy, let the allegations fly. Greenspun had been given access to the Pearson files, and he had picked up his own McCarthy stories involving young hotel bellboys and elevator operators during the senator's gambling trips to Vegas. "Joe McCarthy is a bachelor of 43 years," wrote Greenspun. "He seldom dates girls and if he does, he laughingly describes it as window dressing.... It is common talk among homosexuals who rendezvous at the White Horse Inn [in Milwaukee] that Senator Joe McCarthy has often engaged in homosexual activities."[98]

In the world of Beltway blackmail, these allegations of McCarthy's homosexuality were dismissed by those in Hoover's inner circle, as Hoover had also compiled his own set of secret files on McCarthy's sex life, should he ever need it. Instead, Hoover's secret files were alleged to contain a series of disturbing stories of McCarthy drunkenly groping young girls, which was allegedly so frequent that they had become "common knowl-edge" around the capital.[99] Talbot quotes Walter Trohan, Washington bu-reau chief of the *Chicago Tribune*, who witnessed McCarthy molest one such girl, as saying, "He just couldn't keep his hands off young girls. Why the Communist opposition didn't plant a minor on him and raise the cry of statutory rape, I don't know."[100]

Yet, as previously discussed, it appears that the anti-Communist forces that surrounded McCarthy, as opposed to the "Communist opposition," was the side that most readily engaged in such operations, and it is entirely possible that McCarthy could have been targeted and entrapped by some of his ostensible allies, given that he wielded considerable power and his indiscretions were said to have been widely known in those circles.

For Dulles' part, he didn't need to "plant a minor" on McCarthy, as the compendium of stories of his actions alone was enough to give the CIA director leverage over the senator. As a result, Talbot states, "there was an explosive sexual subtext to the CIA's power struggle with McCarthy, one that was largely hidden from the public but would eventually erupt in the Senate hearings that brought him down."[101] Though it is debatable as to whether McCarthy's struggle with Dulles provoked his undoing, their scuffle did mark his first major failure and was a turning point in his an-ti-Communist campaign. It would be the relationship between Roy Cohn and David Schine, the chief consultant to McCarthy's committee who has been described by one Cold War historian as Roy Cohn's "dumb blonde," that became the deciding factor behind both McCarthy's and Cohn's fall from grace.[102] Though some Cohn biographers have cast doubt on the claims of a romantic relationship between Cohn and Schine, other histo-rians of the period treat it as fact. There is really no way of knowing one way or the other, aside from a series of anecdotes that have been the sub-ject of speculation for, at this point, several decades.

For instance, during Cohn's and Schine's infamous European tour, the German press reported on the two men's "flirtatious antics in a hotel lob-by" while also describing how the pair had left "their hotel room in a sham-bles after a vigorous round of horseplay."[103] Von Hoffman, who dismisses a homosexual relationship between Cohn and Schine in his book *Citizen Cohn*, nevertheless notes some eyebrow-raising stories. One such story that had been reported in *TIME* revolved around how Schine and Cohn "would fly down to Washington from New York on Monday, take adjoin-ing rooms at the Statler Hotel for the week, then fly back on Friday night for a weekend of nightclubbing." On one occasion, the Statler did not have adjoining rooms for the two men, instead only having two single rooms that were not connected. It was Schine, as opposed to Cohn, who then provoked "quite a hassle in the lobby" as he "roared his disapproval."[104]

At the very least, even if there was no sexual relationship, the evidence points to Cohn having been enamored with Schine to the point that he was willing to aim the full force of the McCarthy machine squarely at the Army after Schine, who had been drafted in 1953, was due to be shipped overseas. Cohn's reported response to the news was, "We'll wreck the Army.... The Army will be ruined ... if you pull a dirty, lousy, stinking, filthy, shitty double cross like that."[105] The targeting of the Army did lead to ruin, just not the Army's.

Eventually, and with the full approval of the Eisenhower administration, the Army responded by compiling "the Schine report," which revealed all of the ways that Cohn and McCarthy had sought to blackmail the Army to secure special privileges and favors on Schine's behalf. This led to the now-infamous Army-McCarthy hearings in 1954, which ultimately ended McCarthy's reign and humiliated Cohn to such an extent that it would overshadow him for the rest of his career, long after he left Washington. The intensity of the controversy would also provoke the dissolution of the close relationship between Cohn and Schine. What is undeniable about the whole affair is that it reveals how blackmail, particularly sexual blackmail, had become a major, even if largely invisible, force in American politics.

COHN UNDER FIRE

After the end of McCarthyism, Roy Cohn returned to New York and, thanks to Judge David Peck, joined the Saxe, Bacon & O'Shea law firm in 1957. Peck, a close friend of Roy's father, was also very closely associated with Thomas Dewey and, prior to and after his judgeship, was a lawyer for Sullivan & Cromwell, the Wall Street firm long run by the Dulles brothers.[106] The firm, later renamed Saxe, Bacon & Bolan, came to be dominated by Cohn, for better or for worse. One lawyer who worked there in the early days alongside Cohn has accused him of being the driving force behind the deterioration of its reputation, which declined rapidly in the 1960s.[107] Yet, despite the firm's decline in professional reputation, Roy was making quite a bit of money during this same period, as well as a name for himself.

What could have been good times for Roy Cohn were marred by his ongoing feud with the Kennedys, namely Robert F. Kennedy. "I knew when Bobby Kennedy was lurking nearby, nothing good could happen to me," Cohn was known to have said.[108] He was particularly concerned after learning of John F. Kennedy's plans to run for president, as it would likely mean his "mortal enemy" would be appointed to a powerful position in a future administration. Cohn had done all he could to keep the Kennedys from power by vigorously supporting Lyndon Johnson in the Democratic primary.[109] This involved him lobbying Carmine de Sapio of New York's Tammany Hall to back Johnson.

Yet, the Kennedys were not so easily thwarted, and once Robert Kennedy became Attorney General, the feud became even more acrimonious and particularly dangerous for Cohn. Cohn sought refuge in his powerful connections, which now included even more overt ties to major figures in organized crime. Indeed, the same year that John Kennedy won the presidential election, in 1960, Cohn was the guest of honor at a New Year's Eve party hosted by Moe Dalitz, the Ohio-based gangster who was a close associate of Meyer Lansky and a key figure in the Jewish mob. This same year, Cohn had also begun engaging in illegal financial schemes involving Lionel, his uncle's company.[110] Cohn's control over Lionel had been arranged with the help of Los Angeles accountant Eli Boyer, who – along with Cohn – had invested in a project alongside Dalitz and his associates.[111]

Cohn initially attempted to smooth things over with Kennedy, writing a letter claiming he "harbored no ill will" toward him, a gesture that was ignored.[112] Former congressman Cornelius "Neil" Gallagher, who had met and befriended Roy while representing him in a legal case, later remembered that "Roy was very set back at the fact that Bobby was now named as Attorney General. He was, to put it mildly, very disturbed.... Roy felt, and rightfully so, that they were coming after him. And in fact there was a Get-Roy-Cohn team put together and a Get-Jimmy-Hoffa team put together."[113]

The creation of the "Get-Roy-Cohn" team by the Robert Kennedy-led Justice Department was attested to by Robert Arum, then Assistant US Attorney in New York, while many others have noted the obvious personal hatred that helped fuel Kennedy's efforts to get Cohn. The combined hatred for Cohn shared by Robert Kennedy and Robert Morgenthau, then the US Attorney in New York, resulted in Cohn being taken to court three times over the next few years. He managed to avoid being found guilty in all three cases, thanks to pure luck in at least one instance.

The first case came in 1964, when a grand jury indictment charged Cohn with obstruction of justice for having tried to prevent the indictment of four men in a stock-swindle scheme involving a company called United Dye, as well as perjury for having lied that he had done so. The case focused considerable attention on Cohn's dealings with Moe Dalitz and his associates, particularly those involved in the Desert Inn (discussed in more detail later in this chapter).

During the trial, the allegation was made that Cohn had called Dalitz in June 1962, demanding that the mobster return immediately from a vacation in Europe in order to assist Cohn in intimidating men tied to the United Dye swindle so they would lie under oath to the grand jury investigating the scheme. It also emerged during the case that Cohn, Dalitz, Eli Boyer, and stock swindler Sam Garfield (a close friend of Dalitz's and a central figure in the United Dye scandal) had all been original investors, and thus business associates, in the Sunrise hospital, as had Desert Inn manager Allard Roen, another figure in the United Dye case. Roen was previously discussed in connection with Burton Kanter and the "supermob" in chapter 1. Media reports on the case also noted that Cohn, as previously mentioned, had been the guest of honor at Dalitz's New Year's Eve party in 1960.[114]

Other aspects of the United Dye case, which were ignored or merely glanced over during the trial, are critical for establishing Cohn's ties not just to organized crime during this period but also to organized criminal activity that was intimately enmeshed with a series of CIA assets and other figures of interest in the context of this book. The United Dye web and its organized crime-intelligence links are explored later in this chapter. For now, the focus will be on Cohn and how he fared against the Kennedy-led Justice Department.

Cohn's defense in the case was based on his assertion that the "two Bobbies" – Kennedy and Morgenthau – were after him because of personal vendettas.[115] In the case of Kennedy, it was because Cohn had beat him out to be counsel to Joe McCarthy; for Morgenthau, it was because Cohn had helped target his father, the former treasury secretary, during the McCarthy hearings.[116] Though Cohn had the formidable media empires of the Newhouse family and the Hearst Corporation at his back, his ties to Hoover and Cardinal Spellman also proved useful in this particular legal battle. Spellman's ties to Cohn, writes von Hoffman, were so well known throughout New York that it "enabl[ed] him to put the connection to use in his lawyerly tricks" and served as "Roy's insurance that there would be some political constraints on what Bobby [Kennedy] might do" in his quest to send Cohn to prison, in large part because of the Kennedys' own Catholic connections.[117] Hoover was of more immediate assistance to Cohn at this time, with a lawyer who worked alongside Cohn at Saxe, Bacon & O'Shea claiming that Hoover "gave Roy the government's case, not directly but from FBI agents and witnesses."[118]

Yet, despite all this help, things were not going Cohn's way in the trial, with a single juror holding out for conviction. It later emerged that Cohn and his legal team had done everything they could to have this juror, an African American woman, replaced prior to deliberation, as they assumed that she would surely vote to convict. Unfortunately for this woman juror, her father was killed in a car accident during deliberation, and she was excused from the jury. The judge reluctantly ruled a mistrial as a result of her dismissal.[119]

When the case was retried, it resulted in acquittal. One of the main reasons for this shift was that Cohn's defense lawyer – Frank Raichle – had caught Sam Garfield, a key government witness, in a lie related to his denial that the government had offered him leniency for his role in the United Dye stock swindle if he testified against Cohn. The optics helped Cohn's "vendetta" defense.[120] The second trial Cohn faced, the Fifth Avenue Coach Lines case, saw him charged with "bribery, conspiracy, extortion and blackmail for allegedly bribing a city appraiser to help his client, Fifth Avenue Coach, snare a higher award in a pending condemnation trial."[121]

This trial had a very different trajectory than the United Dye case, particularly when Cohn's defense attorney Joseph Brill had a heart attack in the middle of the case. Brill's heart attack was suspected by some as having been a ploy so that Cohn could serve as his own defense lawyer as the trial drew to a close. While it is debatable if such suspicions were warranted, Cohn becoming his own defense attorney allowed him to offer his own testimony without being cross-examined. It also allowed him to offer "an eloquent seven-hour summation, ending with a protestation of [Cohn's] love for America."[122] That performance saw tears stream down the cheeks of both Cohn and the jurors, who then acquitted Cohn.

The third trial was also related to the Fifth Avenue Coach Lines case and saw Cohn accused of bribery, conspiracy, and filing false reports to the Securities and Exchange Commission. The government's case against Cohn in this instance involved deposits that Cohn had arranged with the money Fifth Avenue Coach received as a result of the condemnation award. One of those two deposits arranged by Cohn, which the government asserted "provoked considerable controversy," was a deposit of five hundred thousand dollars in Geoffrey's Bank in Belgium, which was made the same day that Fifth Coach received the award. One hundred thousand of those funds were then sent to Cohn and deposited in his personal bank account the next day.

Cohn testified that the money was a payment he was owed by A. Newman, "a friend of Cohn's with whom he had certain business dealings" and who was an officer of Geoffrey's Bank.[123] The other "mysterious" deposit made by Cohn was "never fully explained," according to the judge who oversaw the case, despite having been a key point of focus during the trial.[124] Cohn was acquitted when the government's strategy of offering former business associates of Cohn leniency for testifying against him backfired yet again. Nevertheless, the acquittal came with caveats, as the court did find that "Cohn benefitted from the use of Fifth's money to pay the loans made to him by" other directors and that he engaged in a "cover up" of the involvement of two company directors in suspect financial schemes.[125]

The appearance of "A. Newman," or Arno Newman, in this case is worth noting as Newman, who used the last name "Nejman" in Belgium, and his family bank, named for Arno's son Geoffrey, were later tied to illegal arms deals with Israeli intelligence in the 1980s, during roughly the same period as the Iran-Contra affair (see Chapter 7). Some of these deals, gone awry, bankrupted Geoffrey's Bank by 1981, but no legal consequences for the bankruptcy ever befell the Newman/Nejman family.

A key figure in the Mossad-linked smuggling of weapons through Belgium at this time was David Benelie, a Belgian-Israeli dual citizen and an official business partner of the Nejman family. It later emerged that Benelie's real last name was Azulay and that he was the brother of Avner Azulay, who worked closely with Marc Rich, a Mossad-connected commodity speculator and later fugitive. Belgian investigative reporter Willy Van Damme has claimed that both Azulay brothers worked for Mossad.[126]

While these were the three cases brought against Cohn by the "two Bobbies," they were not Cohn's only trials during the period, as he was also indicted for violating banking laws on more than one occasion. However, the conduct of the two Bobbies, particularly that of Robert Morgenthau, in their quest to nail Cohn, ultimately resulted in a flip of the narrative in which Cohn – once seen as an attack dog in McCarthy's witch hunt – now became viewed as a victim of a witch hunt himself. There is some truth to that view, as Cohn's mail had been illegally intercepted during his 1964 trial, and stories that painted Cohn in a negative light were leaked to the press by the government in a clear bid to sway jurors.

Yet, one of the motivating factors behind Kennedy's and Morgenthau's efforts to "get" Cohn, that he was a crooked lawyer with organized crime ties who felt himself to be above the law, was also true. Nevertheless, despite their best efforts, none of the cases stuck, and their failure granted Cohn "an aura of invincibility, respectability, and even sympathy."[127] Though he had garnered some public sympathy, that does not mean that Cohn did not try to get even with his arch nemeses, particularly Bobby Kennedy.

Vendetta Begets Vendetta

One of the many things that Roy Cohn and J. Edgar Hoover shared was having Robert Kennedy as an enemy. Hoover not only subverted the Kennedy-led effort to "get" Roy Cohn by passing Cohn the government's case against him on at least one occasion, he also looked for ways to bring Kennedy down. This was not motivated by Kennedy's efforts to indict Cohn but instead by his efforts as Attorney General to rein in Hoover and bring down the organized crime networks that had first blackmailed Hoover and later formed an "unsavory alliance" with him.[128] According to von Hoffman, regarding Hoover's strategy:

> Hurting Kennedy demanded some ingenuity, for the target was clean on money, far cleaner on sex than his brother, in short not an easy one to bring down. One approach might be to embarrass him with his liberal constituency, to depict him as a ruthless Attorney General indifferent to the Bill of Rights and individual liberty. To put the plan into effect, Roy was needed as a membrane of protection for the Director; others were needed, including Congressman Gallagher who was making a reputation for himself in the House as a civil libertarian, a legislator committed to preventing the government from turning itself, by aid of computers, lie detectors and advanced electronics, into a free-world version of Big Brother.[129]

According to Cornelius "Neil" Gallagher, Cohn called him up and asked him if he would meet with "a friend of ours" who wanted to talk "about some real substantive abuses that are going on in the United States" that could form the basis for a series of Congressional hearings. This "friend" was Sid Zagri, chief lobbyist for the Teamsters Union. At the time that Robert Kennedy instructed his Justice Department to target Cohn he had also had his sights set on the organized crime-linked head of the Teamsters Union, Jimmy Hoffa, meaning that the Teamsters had their own score to settle with the Attorney General.

The meeting with Zagri went forward. Zagri had brought with him a trove of documents that were "aimed at Bobby Kennedy and the strike force concept, the IRS, the uses that Kennedy was making of them," according to Gallagher. Zagri said that he wanted Gallagher to host hearings on the material. When Gallagher asked how he had acquired these "dangerous" documents, Zagri said, "Don't worry about it."[130] In Gallagher's version of what happened, he gave a noncommittal response to Zagri about the possibility of hearings. Zagri responded, stating that he had been promised by Cohn that Gallagher would do the hearings. The meeting went downhill from there and ended when Gallagher angrily ejected Zagri from his office.

Cohn called Gallagher the next day, telling him, "You made a big mistake," to which Gallagher responded that he had not wanted to commit because he was unsure of the documents' authenticity. Cohn then revealed that the documents were authentic, as they had come from the FBI, adding, "They all come from Mr. Hoover and Mr. Deke DeLoach [one of the two top assistants to the director]. Mr. Hoover will consider it a very personal favor if you chair these hearings. He's sick and tired of the bullshit of Bobby Kennedy."[131] Gallagher responded that he wanted to stay out of the brewing battle between Kennedy and Hoover, stating, "I don't agree with what Bobby's doing; I think it's terrible. I don't agree with what Hoover's doing; it's even worse." Cohn promised that if Gallagher did host the hearings both Hoover and Teamster boss Jimmy Hoffa would shower him with favors and aid his reelection efforts. Gallagher was still unwilling to step into the ring. Cohn warned him, "You're going to be sorry.... I know how they [the FBI] work.... If you're not their friend, you're their enemy."[132]

Cohn would repeat the same thing to Gallagher a second time. This next occasion saw Gallagher receive a letter prepared for his signature that demanded that the attorney general at the time, Nick Katzenbach, appear before a Congressional committee with the authorizations for the (illegal) bugging of civil rights activist Martin Luther King Jr. Gallagher asked who had produced this letter for him to sign, since he had never dictated it to anyone. His secretary responded that it had been Roy Cohn. Cohn, when contacted by Gallagher, asserted that Hoover had dictated the letter because "he's sick and tired of Bobby Kennedy proclaiming himself the great liberal when he himself signed the authorizations of his bugging."[133] Gallagher declined to do the director's bidding once more, to which Cohn again replied, "You're going to be sorry.... I told you before, if you're not their friend, you're their enemy. They're gonna get you."[134]

Hoover made good on his threat, and, in 1968, he leaked a story to *LIFE* magazine that tied Gallagher to mobster Joe Zicarelli in the middle of Gallagher's reelection campaign. The story relied on transcripts of taped conversations allegedly between Gallagher and Zicarelli, whose organized criminal activities and role in arms smuggling was discussed in the previous chapter. The FBI later denied the authenticity of these recordings, though some have posited that the tapes might have been authentic, with the FBI only denying their validity to avoid admitting they had illegally wiretapped Gallagher. Given that Gallagher had long been friendly with Cohn, the Zicarelli tie is not outside the realm of possibility, as Zicarelli was an alleged business associate of Lewis Rosenstiel, who was close to Cohn as well as Hoover.

However, the story in *LIFE* is a bit odd for a few reasons. For instance, it failed to establish any benefit to Gallagher from his alleged dealings with the Mafia. It did claim that Gallagher had asked for the Mafia's help in disposing of a dead body, yet Gallagher was not accused of killing him, and the person appeared to have died of natural causes as there were no indications of foul play. The article provided no explanation as to why Gallagher would not have just called a doctor or the police if the man had died of natural causes on his property. The article also asserted that Gallagher's criticisms of the FBI's and the Justice Department's wiretaps were mainly motivated by his purported "alliance" with these Mafia figures. Considering that the FBI itself was later revealed to have been the source of the accusations detailed in the *LIFE* article, as well as Hoover's own conflicts of interest relating to organized crime, the claims about Gallagher in this article are best taken with a grain of salt.[135]

After publication of the *LIFE* story, Gallagher claimed he was again threatened by Hoover, with Roy Cohn again serving as the conduit. Gallagher was told that he had to resign or an even more sensational story would be published, this one involving a man allegedly dying in his bed after fornicating with his wife and with Gallagher again asking for Mafia help in disposing of the body. Gallagher was told by both Roy Cohn and a mutual friend of theirs, Neil Walsh, that Hoover was going to have the story published in *LIFE* unless Gallagher resigned from Congress in the next ten days. According to Cohn, Hoover wanted Gallagher out of Congress because he was "too dangerous" for them, as he had not agreed to Hoover's demands now on two occasions. Walsh summed up the situation by telling Gallagher, "You're not their friend, so you're finished."[136] Needless to say, Gallagher did not take kindly to the threats and delivered a speech on the House floor, exposing Hoover's threats and claiming that the FBI had leaked false information to *LIFE* in a plot against him. Gallagher won reelection despite the FBI director's efforts, but he was indicted in 1972 for perjury and tax evasion.[137]

Regarding Hoover's attempt to blackmail him, Gallagher later stated:

> "The Faustian contracts that were daily made by important parts of the United States media on these kinds of deals, without any recourse as to what the hell they were really building up, has become part and parcel of why we don't have a goddamn presidential candidate around anymore…. You know it's okay to talk about these things, but information is controlled and the bastards [i. e., men like Hoover] have the information, and they use guys like Roy as the interlocutors."[138]

Von Hoffman notes that Gallagher's statement here has "special meaning" given Cohn's subsequent role in similar political power plays, such as those that doomed the vice presidential candidacies of Thomas Eagleton in 1972 and Geraldine Ferraro in 1984.[139] The weaponization of the media, however, was but one of the methods employed by Cohn and allies such as Hoover in their elaborate "favor bank" system.

COHN AND CORBALLY

Roy Cohn served Hoover politically through various means, including by acting as his intermediary in political battles and other power struggles. Cohn and Hoover understood the power of blackmail quite intimately, with both allegedly having been blackmailed themselves, leading to their roles in the Plaza hotel "blue suite" parties. Not only is there evidence of Cohn and Hoover participating in sexual-blackmail rackets alongside Lewis Rosenstiel and (in Hoover's case) Sherman Kaminsky, but there is also evidence of Cohn and Hoover having ties to another sexual-blackmail scandal of the 1960s, one which took place in the United Kingdom and is remembered today as "the Profumo Affair." The key link between Hoover, Cohn, and the Profumo Affair is a man named Thomas Corbally, who used Cohn as a conduit to pass inside information on the scandal to Hoover's FBI as it was unfolding.

Corbally came from a family of private investigators, and his family's detective agency had close ties to organized crime, particularly Meyer

Lansky and his immediate network. These ties were extensive enough that the Corbally family used their detective agency to benefit organized crime interests, which included spying on federal agents in the 1920s and 1930s. As a young man, Thomas Corbally served in World War II in the OSS according to Anthony Summers and Stephen Dorril, though this is disputed by others such as author Steven Snider, who calls the claim a "Corbally embellishment."[140] Corbally does appear to have served in intelligence during the war but in military intelligence via the Army Counterintelligence Corps. He subsequently served in the War Department Detachment, a group whose name has been used interchangeably with the Department of the Army Detachment. The latter was a name used as cover by the CIA in Europe in the immediate post-war period.[141]

In the 1950s, Corbally became a jet-setting private detective who courted the rich and famous, particularly in London and New York. During this period, he met and befriend Roy Cohn, and the two remained close, with Cohn serving as Corbally's attorney over the years. In the 1960s, Corbally began living in London, sharing an apartment with William Mellon Hitchcock of the wealthy Mellon family, who was previously mentioned in Chapter 1. Mellon Hitchcock was the former in-law of David Bruce, an OSS station chief and close ally of William Casey. During the time Corbally and Mellon Hitchcock shared an apartment in London, Bruce was US ambassador to the United Kingdom.

While living together, Mellon Hitchcock and Corbally developed a reputation for throwing "wild parties" or "orgies" for the elite.[142] At the same time, Corbally was courting organized crime networks in the United Kingdom, becoming close to Irish gangster Johnny Francis, who later facilitated the entry of Philadelphia mob boss Angelo Bruno into various businesses in London. Those interests included the Colony Sports Club, where Meyer Lansky associate and Washington, DC-based mobster Joe Nesline held a significant stake.

Both Bruno and Francis worked closely with Ronnie and Reggie Kray, twin brothers and nightclub owners who ran the London-based organized crime gang known as "The Firm" for over a decade. As Stephen Snider and Douglas Thompson have both noted, the Kray brothers "were known to have supplied 'rent boys' [teenage boys] to Lord Boothby [Conservative MP and former Churchill aide] during" the time they were associated with Johnny Francis.[143] Declassified MI5 documents reveal that British intelligence was aware of the Boothby-Kray association that included "sex parties" and "rent boys" at the time these events took place, with those documents also referring to both Boothby and Ronnie Kray as "'hunters' of young men."[144]

Corbally was not only plugged into the more powerful crime networks in the UK, but he was also a member of the Clermont Club, an elite group of gamblers in 1960s London. Many of Clermont's members became extremely powerful during the government of Margaret Thatcher. Several members also later developed close ties to Robert Maxwell, Ghislaine Maxwell's father, and the global arms trade. The Clermont Club was opened by John Aspinall in London's Mayfair district in 1962. Aspinall gave £3,000 to Corbally shortly after he opened the exclusive casino. While he publicly claimed the payment was to settle an old gambling debt with the detective, others associated with the club claimed it was meant as tribute to the organized crime networks that, by that time, were deeply connected to Corbally.

The Clermont Club, as noted in Adam Curtis' documentary series *The Mayfair Set*, acted as a catalyst for the formation of a power nexus around a series of powerful businessmen and politicians who were incredibly influential during Margaret Thatcher's government during the 1980s.[145] At the center of this nexus were figures such as David Stirling, Sir James Goldsmith, and Roland Walter Rowland. Goldsmith later employed Thomas Corbally directly. Lord Boothby was also a member of the Clermont Club.

Stirling and Rowland, in particular, had significant ties to the global arms trade as well as relationships with Saudi weapons dealer Adnan Khashoggi, who later became a client of Roy Cohn as well as Jeffrey Epstein around the same time, as well as a key figure in the Iran-Contra affair. Both Stirling and Rowland also had their own associations with the Iran-Contra operation. Roland Walter Rowland, better known as "Tiny" Rowland, was also a very close associate of Robert Maxwell, as was fellow Clermont Club member and corporate raider James Goldsmith. Goldsmith not only had ties to Maxwell, but also to white collar crime-linked figures including Charles Keating, Michael Milken, and, later, Jeffrey Epstein. Both Keating and Milken were directly connected to the savings and loan scandal of the 1980s that, according to Pete Brewton and others, was largely the result of a collaboration between the CIA and organized crime. The Goldsmith-Epstein connection is revisited in Chapter 11. Another figure at the Clermont Club was Jack Dellal, whose family business later backed Christine Maxwell's homeland-security-focused software venture, Chiliad (see Chapter 21).

In the context of Corbally and the Profumo affair, another very important member of the Clermont Club was a man named Stephen Ward. Ward was an osteopath, who became intimately acquainted with top figures in Britain's aristocracy through W. Averell Harriman. Harriman was the former governor of New York whose Wall Street firm, Brown Brothers Harriman & Co., had been financially entangled with assets of Nazi Germany well after World War II had begun. Harriman's bank employed George H.W. Bush's father Prescott Bush and his maternal grandfather George Herbert Walker. At the time he was promoting Ward, Harriman was an "Ambassador at Large" of the Kennedy State Department.[146]

Ward's friends among the British elite included the Churchills and photographer of the royal family Sterling Henry Nahum.[147] Nahum was particularly close to Lord Louis Mountbatten, Prince Philip's uncle and mentor to Prince Charles.[148] Nahum, Ward, and Lord Mountbatten were attendees of the so-called Thursday Club, which Nahum is said to have founded. Other attendees at the Thursday get-togethers included Prince Philip and the Kray twins.[149] Many of the attendees of the Thursday Club dinners were involved in sex parties, such as those hosted by Corbally and Mellon Hitchcock. Nahum was also a regular host of such parties at his apartment in Piccadilly, some of which featured "girls dressed only in Masonic aprons."[150] Ward regularly attended Nahum's sexually explicit get-togethers as well as analogous events hosted by elite members of British society.

Ward's "talents" were quickly recognized by British intelligence outfit MI6, which had a "reputation for targeting visiting dignitaries in the UK with sexual blackmail operations and recognized Ward's potential in this regard," according to Steven Snider.[151] Ward was first approached by MI6 agent Harold Tracey in 1952 and Tracey cultivated him for years with the help of a close confidant of Ward's, Warwick Charlton. Tracey regularly passed MI6-derived money to Ward via Charlton, but MI6 has since claimed that they never made "operational use" of Ward, despite their known interest and funding.[152]

During the early 1960s, when Corbally and the Clermont Club were becoming established in London, a British politician named John Profumo, who was then serving as the UK's Secretary of State for War, met Christine Keeler. Keeler was a nineteen-year-old model who lived with Stephen Ward, and she began having an affair with Profumo shortly after they met. Keeler was simultaneously having an affair with Eugene Ivanov, a Soviet military attaché and GRU agent in London. Ward allowed Keeler

131

and Ivanov to use his apartment over the course of their affair, and Ivanov had his own ties to Ward, having sought to use Ward as a back channel between the Soviet Union and the UK during the 1962 Cuban Missile Crisis. MI5 began to have concerns that Ivanov was "working" Ward, and Keeler later asserted that Ward was a British and Soviet double agent. Incidentally, Ward was also close to the Astor family and rented a cottage from them. The Astor family's estate at Cliveden was the site of Profumo and Keeler's first meeting, which led to their subsequent affair.

The scandal began only after Keeler, for reasons that are still unclear, told Labour MP John Lewis that she was having affairs with both Ivanov and Profumo. Lewis subsequently informed Profumo's political enemy, Labour MP George Wigg. Wigg, like Ward, was an asset of British intelligence at the time. Between her testimony to Lewis and via him to Wigg, Keeler also told her story to the British press, causing a scandal to erupt around Profumo and leading not only to his resignation but to the breakdown of Harold Macmillan's Conservative government. As an aside, Macmillan's wife was allegedly in a long-term adulterous relationship with the aforementioned Lord Boothby, who was a member of the Clermont Club along with Stephen Ward and tied to the same organized-crime networks as Corbally.

According to Phillip Knightley and Caroline Kennedy in *An Affair of State*, as cited by Steven Snider, it was David Bruce – William Mellon Hitchcock's former in-law and former OSS station chief – who involved Corbally directly in the Profumo affair.[153] According to the authors, Bruce was asked by Macmillan to uncover the truth surrounding Profumo's relationship with Keeler, and Bruce turned to Corbally for information due to Corbally's relationship with Ward, his profession as a private detective, and his close friendship with Mellon Hitchcock. Snider also notes a different account of these events is offered by Anthony Summers and Stephen Dorril in their book *The Secret Worlds of Stephen Ward*. Summers and Dorril assert that it was Ward himself who "dropped in" on Corbally and Mellon Hitchcock, where he confessed everything to them and begged them for help in preventing Keeler's story from going to press.[154]

Whatever the details, Ward, Corbally, and Mellon Hitchcock ultimately met with David Bruce's assistant Alfred Wells, and Ward told Wells how the incidents at the heart of the Profumo affair had transpired. At least a month prior to that meeting and apparently before Keeler had revealed the affair to John Lewis, both Corbally and Mellon Hitchcock had known about Profumo and Keeler via Ward. Bruce's role in these meetings with Wells seems odd, as he sat on this inside information about the affair despite its security implications for the US State Department and the Anglo-American establishment.

Hoover's FBI got the inside scoop from Corbally and began investigating other women of interest in Stephen Ward's circle while the Profumo affair was just beginning. Corbally kept the FBI informed of developments in the scandal through Roy Cohn, Corbally's longtime friend and attorney. In the public release of the FBI case files on the affair, nicknamed the "Bowtie dossier," the information that Cohn gave to the FBI is entirely censored, as is a seventeen-page interview the FBI had with Corbally.[155] One of the reasons for these extensive redactions likely owes to the ties between the other women associated with Stephen Ward and efforts to sexually blackmail John F. Kennedy. Peter Dale Scott discusses this subject in *Deep Politics and the Death of JFK*, drawing partially on the work of Anthony Summers in *Official and Confidential*:

> [Meyer] Lansky had by the 1930s acquired compromising evidence of Hoover's homosexual activities. In the 1950s, Meyer Lansky, and other mob figures such as Sam Giancana, supplied women to John F. Kennedy, some of whom were logged into Hoover's growing files of dirt on the young senator. In the 1960s this deep political equilibrium was threatened by Robert Kennedy's war on organized crime, which alienated Hoover. Feeling increasingly threatened, especially after the Kennedys began to collect their own files on Hoover, both Hoover and the mob began to escalate their collection of Kennedy sexual dirt. At first Hoover gained White House influence by protecting the Kennedys against mob blackmail, but in 1963 Hoover, desperate, began to leak some of his own dirt on Kennedy to the public.
>
> Hoover's sexual dirt on the Kennedys began to surface in late June 1963, after the President's "peace speech" at American University with its appeal, "Let us reexamine our attitude toward the Cold War." On June 20, the United States and the Soviet Union signed an agreement establishing a "hot line" between the Kremlin and the White House.
>
> A week later, there was a flurry of veiled hints linking the President to the Profumo story, such as the Drew Pearson-Jack Anderson column for June 29: "Britishers who read American criticisms of Profumo throw back the question 'What high American official was involved with Marilyn Monroe?'"
>
> On the same day, in a front-page story, the Hearst paper in New York, the *Journal-American*, linked the Christine Keeler-Stephen Ward

sex ring itself to a"'high U.S. aide," one of the biggest names in American politics. Back in 1960, after his election but before his inauguration, the President had slept with two members of the ring, including Mariella Novotny (a former stripper in London's Club Pigalle).[156]

Mariella Novotny, born Stella Marie Capes, met Stephen Ward through her job as a stripper at the Mayfair nightclub The Black Sheep. The owner of that club, Horace Dibben, was a close friend of Ward's who also had an interest in sex parties. Dibben's sex parties were alleged to have a notably occult element, with allegations of "black magic and men in masks" as well as "ritual sadomasochism" based around a master/slave dynamic. Novotny was directly involved in Dibben's occult-themed sex parties, which reportedly attracted prominent individuals in Harold Macmillan's government as VIP guests as well as Stephen Ward.[157]

Novotny was subsequently whisked away from London to New York, where she began working as an upscale prostitute, servicing a lengthy list of powerful men out of four different apartments just months after she arrived. She had been brought to New York through her affair with Harry Alan Towers, a British television producer, and both were charged with operating a sexual-blackmail ring in New York that specifically targeted UN diplomats and other men of influence. John F. Kennedy was also reportedly one of her "clients."

Before she fled the US in 1961, Novotny left her address book, replete with the names and contact information of America's rich and powerful, with the FBI. For "mysterious reasons," the FBI dropped its case against Novotny and Towers and chose to destroy Novotny's address book as well as their files on both Novotny and Towers.[158]

The other woman linked to both Stephen Ward and efforts to sexually blackmail John F. Kennedy was Suzy Chang, a former nurse turned model who moved to London at nineteen. How Chang met Ward is still unknown, though Chang later described Ward as "a good, good, good friend" whom she had met sometime in the early 1950s.[159] Chang was associated with Ward's close friend and Thursday Club founder Sterling Henry Nahum and lived at the Nell Gywne House in London, where another woman working with Ward also lived. William Mellon Hitchcock, Corbally's London roommate, later referred to Chang as "one of Stephen's girls," and Chang later confirmed that she knew Corbally as well.[160]

Novotny is the source of the claim that Chang had sex with John F. Kennedy, which is possible given that Chang was in the US in both 1960 and 1961. Chang acknowledged knowing Kennedy but denied having sex with him. According to Snider, she reportedly denied the affair with "less vigor" as time went by, however.[161] Another noteworthy event that, according to Snider, was more indicative of "shadowy purposes" was Chang's mother hiring the law firm of former OSS chief William Donovan to secure Suzy Chang a visa to the US in 1962.[162] The year 1962 was a critical year for John Kennedy, and it also happened to be the year that the Profumo affair first surfaced.

The first stories on the Profumo affair emerged in the midst of the Cuban Missile Crisis, which may explain why Keeler decided to go public with her story and create a scandal around her lover, costing him his career and setting in motion the destruction of the entire Macmillan government. As previously mentioned, Ivanov had attempted to use Ward as a back channel during the crisis. Not only that, but Ivanov and Ward were also working with Permanent Undersecretary of the British Foreign Office, Harold Caccia, to arrange a summit conference in England to resolve the crisis. The precise timing of the Profumo affair ensured that Ivanov would be rapidly recalled to Moscow, thus scuttling plans for the summit.

In addition, as Peter Dale Scott points out, the reports attempting to link President Kennedy to the Profumo affair only emerged after Kennedy's June 1963 "peace speech." That speech deeply unsettled the anti-Communist network that included Hoover, Cohn, and others, and stories attempting to tie Kennedy to Profumo's scandal were published by the Hearst *Journal-American*. The paper's editor, Guy Richards, was very much involved in this anti-Communist network and had "excellent intelligence contacts," according to Peter Dale Scott, citing Anthony Summers.[163] Summers also noted that the story was published shortly after Richards brought an anti-Communist friend of Keeler's, Michael Eddowes, to the United States.

In addition, Roy Cohn was a longtime close personal friend of Richard Berlin, the top manager of the Hearst newspaper conglomerate, which owned the *Journal-American*.[164] Cohn was notorious for placing stories in Hearst newspapers, as well as publications controlled by his other close friends, such as Si Newhouse, for the benefit of his clients and his network.

The Profumo affair was probably Corbally's most notable tie to a sex-blackmail ring, but it was hardly his only such connection. Years later, Corbally was deeply connected to the so-called Hollywood madam, Heidi Fleiss, as well as a VIP S & M scene in the Hamptons. Corbally claimed, in the case of the latter, to have started that ring, which he said he had "imported" from the UK.[165] He was also said to possess numerous "pictures of various individuals engaged in some rather strange sexual practices that were staples of these parties."[166] Another important association of Corbally's, though not tied necessarily to sexual blackmail, was his connection to Jules Kroll of Kroll and Associates, with many early Kroll employees crediting Corbally for the firm's initial success. Kroll and Associates, long known as the "CIA of Wall Street" and believed by French intelligence to have been an actual front for the CIA, makes a few, yet critically important appearances in the last days of Robert Maxwell and other events related to Maxwell's posthumous legacy in the US, which are discussed in more detail in Chapter 15.

THE UNITED DYE WEB

Another interesting figure in Corbally's close orbit worth exploring is his mentor, John G. "Steve" Broady. Broady was a private investigator who had more than a few run-ins with the law, including for his role in the wiretapping of then mayor of New York William O'Dwyer on behalf of Broady's longtime employer Clendenin Ryan.[167] Ryan was not only Broady's principal sponsor, but also the main financial backer of the International Services of Information Foundation, a private intelligence outfit that had been formed by Ulius Amoss, a veteran of the OSS. Amoss was known, after his service in the OSS, for investing in companies embedded in the country's growing military-industrial complex, some of which were alleged to be CIA fronts for money laundering.[168] Another prominent figure linked to the foundation was Charles Willoughby, Douglas MacArthur's former intelligence chief, who was a trustee.

Clendenin Ryan's son, Clendenin Ryan Jr., was close to a man named Douglas Caddy, who led an anti-Communist group called Young Americans for Freedom (YAF). Clendenin Ryan Jr. and Caddy were roommates at Georgetown University, and the former was "tangentially involved in founding YAF."[169] Another key member of YAF was former CIA officer, *National Review* founder, and close friend of Roy Cohn, William F. Buckley. Caddy's ties to the George Town Club, "established in 1966 for the purpose of bringing together leaders who had an impact on the United States, and the world," via another of his college roommates, Tongsun Park, and the sex blackmail rings that surrounded both that club and the Watergate scandal are discussed in the next chapter.[170]

Another associate of Broady's was Peter Crosby, whose brother – James Crosby – was the chairman of Resorts International (formerly Mary Carter Paint) in the Bahamas. Top investors in Resorts International included the Moody family company American National Insurance Company (ANICO) and Delafield & Delafield. ANICO and the Moody family, specifically Roy Cohn's close friend Shearn Moody Jr., are mentioned in future chapters. Delafield & Delafield is worth noting as it was William Mellon Hitchock's employer.[171]

Peter Crosby was a stock manipulator and associate of organized crime figures who made an appearance in the financial webs surrounding the United Dye stock swindle, the aftermath of which resulted in the indictment of Roy Cohn in the early 1960s. During their "adventures" together in the 1970s, Crosby and Broady were arrested in 1973, though only Crosby went to prison. According to the late journalist Gary Webb, Broady evaded conviction because of his past work for the CIA, an association Broady denied but that was attested to by Crosby associates. Webb, citing reports in the *Kentucky Post*, also noted that the papers confiscated from Crosby and Broady at the time of their arrest showed that the two men dealt "with many of the same men believed by investigators to be part of a nationwide network of confidence men and organized crime figures."[172] Crosby certainly seems to have been part of such a network.

Before his 1973 arrest, for example, he was involved in shady financial dealings with William McCarthy, brother of Texas oil tycoon Glenn McCarthy. Those dealings centered around American Montana Oil & Gas, a dummy corporation through which McCarthy aimed to seize properties then controlled by Ajax Oil Company. Other companies were involved in McCarthy's Ajax takeover plan, including Sundown Oil Company, which counted Paul Roland Jones as a director. Jones was a known figure in Chicago's organized crime scene who had relocated to Texas in 1947 and was implicated in narcotics trafficking.[173] He also, incidentally, had connections to Jack Ruby (born Jacob Rubenstein), the gangster who is now best known for killing Lee Harvey Oswald after the assassination of John F. Kennedy. Ruby also had connections to the Moody family of ANICO. Crosby and McCarthy entered into an arrangement with Satiris "Sonny" Fassoulis as part of this elaborate scheme. Fassoulis also had a business relationship with a man named Alexander Guterma and the Bon Ami company, which played a critical role in the United Dye swindle.

Guterma was a Russian national who came to the United States in the 1950s, arriving first in California before relocating to Florida. There he launched Shawano Corporation and began acquiring other companies by trading Shawano stock. He soon made his way to Las Vegas, where

137

"he found the Vegas mob at the Desert Inn eager to unload the hotel."[174] Guterma "then traded Shawano stock for the little Isle d'Capri Hotel, Bay Harbor Islands, forming the nucleus of United Hotels Inc., which was to dump the Desert Inn on the public if need be.[175] The Desert Inn was very much a focus of Cohn's trial related to United Dye. As previously mentioned, the Desert Inn's manager, Allard Roen, was also in the employ of mobster Moe Dalitz and was a key figure in the United Dye trial. So was Sam Garfield – a lifelong friend of Dalitz.

The government asserted in its case against Cohn that Eli Boyer, the accountant who helped Cohn take control of Lionel Corporation, had been used by Cohn to pipeline threats to Roen to keep him from giving truthful testimony to the grand jury investigating United Dye. Boyer confirmed this in his testimony. In addition, Boyer, Roen, Garfield, Dalitz, and Cohn had all been the original investors together in a venture called Sunrise hospital.[176] In June 1955, Guterma and Sam Garfield as well as Irving Pasternak teamed up to acquire the Franklin County Coal Corporation. That same month, Guterma became an associate of Virgil Dardi, who was then a director at United Dye and subsequently arranged to sell Guterma a large bloc of shares in the company. Guterma then distributed that stock between himself, Garfield, Pasternak, and others. By that September, Guterma had become chairman of the United Dye board, with Dardi serving as its president.[177]

The following year, Guterma took control of a manufacturing company called F. L. Jacobs. The intention of Guterma and his associates was to "loot and divert for their own purposes the assets of F. L. Jacobs and to use its credit as collateral for loans, the proceeds of which were diverted to Guterma's own use and benefit."[178] Soon after, Dardi informed Guterma that the Bon Ami company had 63,000 shares for sale; they then arranged for the purchase of those shares by United Dye via a loan from F. L. Jacobs. Guterma later testified that they had taken control of Bon Ami to "enable Garfield and Pasternak to satisfy the $519,000 obligation owed by them to United Dye." To support Guterma's testimony in the United Dye case, the government "introduced evidence of various 'loan' transactions involving Garfield and Pasternak and, as directors of Bon Ami, Guterma and Dardi," many of which involved United Dye.[179]

When the decision was made to use the United Dye grand jury to "get Cohn," Garfield and Pasternak evaded being sentenced in exchange for their testimony against Cohn and other accomplices. As previously mentioned, their deals to obtain immunity, which were not publicly acknowledged, helped convince a jury to acquit Cohn during the retrial (i. e., the second trial that followed the initial mistrial) of the United Dye case. Guterma had already been found guilty and was serving a four-year prison sentence for having looted millions from F. L. Jacobs when Cohn's case went to trial. He was sentenced in 1961.

Before Guterma was caught and the United Dye swindle unraveled, Guterma and Dardi used Bon Ami company to establish ties with some interesting figures as they obtained a controlling stake in the company. In 1957, Guterma and Dardi entered into negotiations with an entertainment executive named Matthew Fox in which they sought to purchase $5 million worth of spot time for TV commercials for Bon Ami.[180] Bon Ami loaned Fox $115,000, and Fox arranged for Guild Films to supply Bon Ami spot time if Fox defaulted on the loan, which he did.

Fox was much more than a television/movie executive, however, as he had led a CIA front in Indonesia, the American-Indonesian Corporation, until the early 1950s.[181] In that capacity, Fox had controlled extensive rights to develop Indonesia's natural resources and also controlled all Indonesian government buying and selling in the United States.[182] He was also involved in covertly supporting the CIA-backed prime minister of the country, Mohammed Hatta, at the behest of agency intermediaries.[183]

That same year, 1957, Guterma entered into negotiations with Sonny Fassoulis, leading to Fassoulis' acquisition of over 100,000 shares of Bon Ami stock. At the time, 25,000 of these shares were owned by another Guterma-controlled company, the Chatham Corporation. Fassoulis did not have the money for the purchase, however, and sold film rights held by a company he controlled, Icthyan Associates, to Bon Ami to cover the cost. The so-called Icthyan package was intended to "enable Bon Ami to obtain television spot time by transferring the 'Icthyan Package' to Guild Films as credit against the purchase price of a large quantity of television spot time."[184]

Well before Fassoulis and Fox entered the scene as it related to Bon Ami, they appeared to have already been involved in a shadowy financial network that involved Virgil Dardi. In 1953, Fox was the chairman of a company called Pola-Lite, and Fassoulis was its president. Pola-Lite was actually the subsidiary for an intelligence-linked company named Commerce International Corporation that Fassoulis ran.[185] Around the same time, in 1954, it was reported that Matthew Fox was president of C & C Television corporation, a subsidiary of C & C Super Corporation, where Virgil Dardi served as a director. This connects Fassoulis, Fox, and Dardi together years before Guterma and Dardi became involved in the events surrounding the United Dye situation.

Around the same time the United Dye scandal erupted, in the early 1960s, an investigation was launched into the David, Josephine and Winfield Baird Foundation and the Lansing Foundation, both of which were controlled by New York businessman David Baird. The Baird Foundation was listed as owning 24.5 percent of the C & C Television Corporation that Matthew Fox ran, and the foundation also owned significant rights to several other C & C subsidiaries. The Baird Foundation's clients included several organized crime associates, such as Lansky front man Louis Chesler; real estate magnate William Zeckendorf; and Lawrence Wien, another real estate magnate who was a partner in the Dalitz-linked Desert Inn that was tied to the United Dye case. As mentioned in Chapter 1, Wien had bought the Empire State Building from "Supermob" figure Henry Crown.

Other clients of the Baird Foundation included Allen & Co., which later became closely involved with Les Wexner's "mentor" Max Fisher, as well as the director of Maurice L. Rothschild, Nathan Cummings. Cummings was a director of Bon Ami company and was personally involved in selling the controlling stake of that company to United Dye when it was controlled by Guterma and Dardi.[186] Cummings subsequently departed Bon Ami, which opened spots for Guterma and Dardi on its board.

As for David Baird himself, he and Charles Allen of Allen & Co. were known to have dealings with Guterma, even after the Las Vegas mob, specifically the Desert Inn crowd tied to Moe Dalitz, "had exhausted its use" of Guterma in the aftermath of United Dye's unraveling.[187] In addition, Louis Mortimer Bloomfield, attorney for Permindex and whose law firm was deeply enmeshed with the Bronfman family, wrote to Carlo d'Amelio of Permindex's Italian subsidiary in 1961, describing the interest that Permindex had cultivated among American businessmen, specifically David Baird, in their affairs and projects.[188]

Another interesting thread concerning David Baird is related to his client and the *de facto* banker for the Baird Foundation, Serge Semenenko. Semenenko was the vice president of First National Bank of Boston, whose executives were close to the CIA. The Baird Foundation itself was later revealed to be an asset of the CIA's International Organizations Division and, between 1961 and 1964, received $456,800 of agency funds in "pass throughs" that were piped into CIA programs in the Middle East and Africa.[189]

In addition to the direct CIA connection, there is also some level of connection between Baird and Meshulam Riklis. As mentioned in Chapter 2, Riklis took over not only Lewis Rosenstiel's business empire but purchased his blackmail-ready townhouse at around the same time.

Jonathan Marshall, in his article "Wall Street, the Supermob and the CIA," notes:

> Not long after Semenenko left First National, at the height of the 1960s merger mania, he began wheeling and dealing with Baird over the fate of Stanley Warner Corp., a leading theater owner that Baird had advised on financial matters since 1956. The first public hint of their dealings came in November 1967, when New York City newspapers touted Baird's philanthropy by reporting that he was chairing the annual Celebrity Ball of the Variety Club of New York in honor of Democratic Rep. Emmanuel Celler. Vice chairmen for the ball were Semenenko, Stanley Warner Corp. Chairman S. H. Fabian, and Meshulam Riklis, the young, Odessa-born chairman of Glen Alden Corp., a fast-growing conglomerate that was angling to acquire Stanley Warner."[190]

Marshall goes onto reveal that Celler, once the chairman of the House Judiciary Committee, was a "notable friend" of Lewis Rosenstiel. He also notes that David Baird received a $3 million finder's fee for his role in arranging sale of Stanley Warner stock to Riklis' Glen Alden Corporation. Shortly thereafter, Riklis, via Glen Alden, took control of Rosenstiel's Schenley Industries. Incidentally, another Baird associate, Charles Allen of Allen and Co., had previously considered acquiring Schenley before Riklis succeeded in doing so.

Ultimately, this series of serpentine financial connections reveals a dense web linking several organized crime figures, their intermediaries, organized crime–linked businessmen, and intelligence agencies. Some key figures in this network, as mentioned in this and previous chapters, engaged in various forms of blackmail and power plays to ensure the continued growth of both their legal and illegal financial interests. As we shall see, this incestuous web of crime, intrigue, and covert action that was tightly interwoven throughout major events of the 1960s would continue its expansion, largely unimpeded and employing many of the same tactics, throughout the decades that followed.

Endnotes

1   Nicholas Von Hoffman, *Citizen Cohn*, 1st ed (New York: Doubleday, 1988), 414.

2   Von Hoffman, *Citizen Cohn*, 465.

3   Von Hoffman, *Citizen Cohn*, 49.

4   Von Hoffman, *Citizen Cohn*, 49.

5   "Albert Cohn Dies; A Former Justice," *New York Times*, January 9, 1959, https://timesma-chine.nytimes.com/timesmachine/1959/01/09/89104614.html?pageNumber=27.

6   Von Hoffman, *Citizen Cohn*, 50.

7   *Where's My Roy Cohn?*, 2019, [DVD] Directed by M. Tyrnauer, Sony Pictures.

8   "Albert Cohn Marries; First Assistant District Attorney Weds Miss Dorothy Marcus," *New York Times*, January 12, 1924, https://www.nytimes.com/1924/01/12/archives/albert-cohn-marries-first-assistant-district-attorney-weds-miss.html?searchResultPosition=11

9   Von Hoffman, *Citizen Cohn*, 414.

10   Robert Shogan, *No Sense of Decency: The Army-McCarthy Hearings: A Demagogue Falls and Television Takes Charge of American Politics* (Chicago: Ivan R. Dee, 2009), 139.

11   Kenneth T. Jackson, *The Encyclopedia of New York City*, 2nd edition (New Haven : New York: Yale University Press ; New-York Historical Society), 2010, p. 1015.

12   Christopher M. Elias, *Gossip Men: J. Edgar Hoover, Joe McCarthy, Roy Cohn, and the Politics of Insinuation* (Chicago ,The University of Chicago Press, 2021), 120.

13   Michael Whitney Straight, *Trial by Television and Other Encounters*, 1st ed. (New York: Devon Press, 1979), 180; "Justice Albert Cohn Takes Office," *New York Times*, April 3, 1929, http://timesmachine.nytimes.com/timesmachine/1929/04/03/95902552.html?pageNumber=37.

14   "Justice Albert Cohn Promoted," *New York Times*, April 28, 1937, p.17.

15   Nicholas Pileggi, "The Mob and the Machine," *New York Magazine*, May 5, 1986. https://nymag.com/news/features/crime/46610/.

16   David Samuels, "The Mayor and the Mob," *Smithsonian*, October 2019, https://www.smithsonianmag.com/history/mayor-william-odwyer-new-york-city-mob-180973078/.

17   Pileggi, "The Mob and the Machine."

18   Sally Denton and Roger Morris, *The Money and the Power: The Making of Las Vegas and Its Hold on America, 1947-2000*, 1st ed (New York: Alfred A. Knopf, 2001), chap. 1, https://archive.org/details/moneypowermaking00dent.

19   James Cockayne, "How the Mafia Almost Fixed the 1932 Democratic National Convention," *The New Republic*, July 25, 2016, https://newrepublic.com/article/135466/mafia-al-most-fixed-1932-democratic-national-convention; Martin A Gosch and Richard Hammer, *The Last Testament of Lucky Luciano: The Mafia Story in His Own Words* (Enigma Books, 2013), 163.

20   Dennis Eisenberg, Uri Dan, and Eli Landau, *Meyer Lansky: Mogul of the Mob* (New York: Paddington Press : distributed Grosset & Dunlap, 1979), 173; Gosch and Hammer, *Last Testament of Lucky Luciano*, 163-64.

21   Jay Maeder, "Inside Mayor Jimmy (Beau James) Walker's Mighty Downfall," *New York Daily News*, August 14, 2017, https://www.nydailynews.com/new-york/mayor-jimmy-beau-james-walker-mighty-downfall-article-1.792838.

22   Gosch and Hammer, *Last Testament of Lucky Luciano*, 105.

23   "Ed Flynn, the Bronx Boss at FDR's Side," *Irish Echo Newspaper*, March 14, 2012, https://www.irishecho.com/2012/3/ed-flynn-the-bronx-boss-at-fdrs-side.

24   Shogan, *No Sense of Decency*, 122.

25   Denton and Morris, *Money and Power*, chap.1.

26   Bernard Ryan, Jr., "Murder, Inc. Trials: 1941," https://www.encyclopedia.com/law/law-magazines/murder-inc-trials-1941.

27   Samuels, "Mayor and Mob."

28   Samuels, "Mayor and Mob."

29   Samuels, "Mayor and Mob."

30   Samuels, "Mayor and Mob."

31   Samuels, "Mayor and Mob."

32   Von Hoffman, *Citizen Cohn*, 83.

33   "High-Titled Bank Can Hold Its Name," *New York Times*, June 24, 1913.

34   "High-Titled Bank Can Hold Its Name."

35   "High-Titled Bank Can Hold Its Name."

36   "High-Titled Bank Can Hold Its Name."

37   Beth S. Wenger, *New York Jews and the Great Depression: Uncertain Promise* (Syracuse University Press, 1999), 11.

38   "Joseph S. Marcus, Banker, Dies at 65," *New York Times*, July 4, 1927. http://timesmachine.nytimes.com/timesmachine/1927/07/04/120423238.html?pageNumber=15.

39   Rare Book and Manuscript Library, Columbia University, 2005, http://www.columbia.edu/cu/lweb/eresources/archives/rbml/NYSCrimeCommission/.

40   "Paul E. Lockwood, Dewey Aide, Dead," *New York Times*, September 2, 1973, https://www.nytimes.com/1973/09/02/archives/paule-lockwood-dewey-aide-dead-governors-secretary-was-on.html; Joan Cook, "James M. Crosby, 58, Founder of Hotel and Casino Concern," *New York Times*, April 12, 1986, https://www.nytimes.com/1986/04/12/obituaries/james-m-crosby-58-founder-of-hotel-and-casino-concern.html; Donald Janson, "Resorts Head Tells of Dropping Partner," *New York Times*, January 17, 1979, https://www.nytimes.com/1979/01/17/archives/resorts-head-tells-of-dropping-partner.html.

41   Denton and Morris, *Money and Power*, chap.1.

42   "Kefauver to Hear Top Officials Here," *New York Times*, January 24, 1951, https://www.nytimes.com/1951/01/24/archives/kefauver-to-hear-top-officials-here-dewey-and-mayoralty-rivals.html.

43   "Albert Cohn Dies," *New York Times*, January 9, 1951, http://timesmachine.nytimes.com/timesmachine/1959/01/09/89104614.html?pageNumber=27.

44   "Joseph S. Marcus, Banker, Dies at 65," *New York Times*, July 4, 1927, http://timesmachine.nytimes.com/timesmachine/1927/07/04/120423238.html?pageNumber=15.

45   "B.K Marcus Dies; Led Bank of US," *New York Times*, July 18, 1954, http://timesmachine.nytimes.com/timesmachine/1954/07/18/83342783.html?pageNumber=57.

46   "$300,000,000 Merger of Banks Approved," *New York Times*, May 10, 1929, http://timesmachine.nytimes.com/timesmachine/1929/05/10/95947545.html?pageNumber=45.

47   Michael A. Whitehouse, "Paul Warburg's Crusade to Establish a Central Bank in the United States," Federal Reserve Bank of Minneapolis, May 1, 1989, https://www.minneapolisfed.org:443/article/1989/paul-warburgs-crusade-to-establish-a-central-bank-in-the-united-states; Roger Lowenstein, "The Jewish Story Behind the U.S. Federal Reserve Bank," *The Forward*, November 29, 2015. https://forward.com/culture/325447/the-man-behind-the-fed/.

48   "B.K Marcus Dies; Led Bank of US," *New York Times*, July 18, 1954, http://timesmachine.nytimes.com/timesmachine/1954/07/18/83342783.html?pageNumber=57.

49   "President of Bank Reviews Its Growth," *New York Times*, February 2, 1930, http://timesmachine.nytimes.com/timesmachine/1930/02/02/96018687.html?pageNumber=43.

50   "$1,000,000,000 Union of Banks Completed," *New York Times*, November 25, 1930, http://timesmachine.nytimes.com/timesmachine/1930/11/25/102190782.html?pageNumber=9.

51   "$1,000,000,000 Union of Banks Completed."

52   "$1,000,000,000 Union of Banks Completed."

53   John Olszowka et al., *America in the Thirties: America in the Twentieth Century* (NY: Syracuse University Press, 2014), 30.

54   "Bank Heads Face Contempt Action," *New York Times*, February 25, 1931, http://timesmachine.nytimes.com/timesmachine/1931/02/25/100992834.html?pageNumber=4; "Juggling of Loans by Bank Is Shown," *New York Times*, January 24, 1934, http://timesmachine.nytimes.com/timesmachine/1934/01/24/95029871.html?pageNumber=11.

55   Von Hoffman, *Citizen Cohn*, 47; Christopher, Gray, "Streetscapes: The Bank of the United States in the Bronx," *New York Times*, August 18, 1991, https://www.nytimes.com/1991/08/18/realestate/streetscapes-bank-united-states-bronx-first-domino-depression.html.

56   "Marcus Is Arrested as He Defies Steuer," *New York Times*, February 21, 1931, http://times-

machine.nytimes.com/timesmachine/1931/02/21/98323627.html?pageNumber=1; "$50,000,000 Suit Is Filed Against Bank US Officers," *New York Times*, February 12, 1931, http://timesmachine.ny-times.com/timesmachine/1931/02/12/102214836.html?pageNumber=1.

57   Von Hoffman, *Citizen Cohn*, 45; Beth S. Wenger, *New York Jews and the Great Depression: Uncertain Promise* (NY, Syracuse University Press, 1999), 14, https://archive.org/details/newyork-jewsgreat0000weng.

58   Von Hoffman, *Citizen Cohn*, 45.

59   "Justice Cohn Is Honored Here," *New York Times*, June 7, 1930, http://timesmachine.ny-times.com/timesmachine/1930/06/07/96146710.html?pageNumber=9.

60   Wenger, *New York Jews and the Great Depression*, 11.

61   Elias, *Gossip Men*, 109.

62   "Marcus and Singer Must Serve Terms," *New York Times*, March 15, 1933, https://www.nytimes.com/1933/03/15/archives/marcus-and-singer-must-serve-terms-appeals-court-upholds-their.html.

63   Elias, *Gossip Men*, 109.

64   David L. Marcus, "5 Things You May Not Know About My Vile, Malicious Cousin Roy Cohn," *The Wrap*, September 27, 2019, https://www.thewrap.com/roy-cohn-cousin-5-things-to-know/.

65   David B. Green, "1965: Pioneer of Electric Model Trains Dies," *Haaretz*, September 8, 2013, https://www.haaretz.com/jewish/2013-09-08/ty-article/.premium/1965-electric-model-trains-pio-neer-dies/0000017f-f8cc-ddde-abff-fceda8150000.

66   "Joshua Lionel Cowen," Jewish Virtual Library, n.d. https://www.jewishvirtuallibrary.org/joshua-lionel-cowen.

67   "J.L. Cowen Settles Bank of U.S. Suit," *New York Times*, February 27, 1934, https://www.nytimes.com/1934/02/27/archives/jl-cowen-settles-bank-of-us-suit-former-director-eliminated-from.html.

68   "J.L. Cowen Settles."

69   "Fred W. Piderit, Bank Aide, 79, Dies," *New York Times*, June 20, 1961, http://timesma-chine.nytimes.com/timesmachine/1961/06/20/97674643.html?pageNumber=33.

70   "Joshua Lionel Cowen."

71   Von Hoffman, *Citizen Cohn*, 273.

72   Von Hoffman, *Citizen Cohn*, 300.

73   Von Hoffman, *Citizen Cohn*, 52.

74   Von Hoffman, *Citizen Cohn*, 51.

75   Von Hoffman, *Citizen Cohn*, 54.

76   Von Hoffman, *Citizen Cohn*, 68.

77   Von Hoffman, *Citizen Cohn*, 70.

78   Von Hoffman, *Citizen Cohn*, 69.

79   Tate Delloye, "The Godfather of Tabloid: How childhood friend of Roy Cohn and son of an influential political fixer with ties to Mussolini left the CIA to start the National Enquirer with a loan from mob boss Frank Costello," *Mail Online*, November 20, 2019, https://www.dailymail.co.uk/news/article-7687673/national-enquirer-roy-cohn-CIA.html.

80   Delloye, "Godfather of Tabloid."

81   Delloye, "Godfather of Tabloid."

82   Tate Delloye, "Roy Cohn: New Documentary Explores the Man Who Made Donald Trump," *Mail Online*, March 14, 2019, https://www.dailymail.co.uk/news/article-6809557/Roy-Cohn-Donald-Trumps-ruthless-homophobic-attorney-partied-Studio-54-died-AIDS.html.

83   Delloye, "Godfather of Tabloid."

84   Delloye, "Godfather of Tabloid."

85   Delloye, "Godfather of Tabloid."

86   Von Hoffman, *Citizen Cohn*, 82.

87   "Miss Renee Schine Becomes a Bride," *New York Times*, December 29, 1950, http://times-machine.nytimes.com/timesmachine/1950/12/29/82089074.html.

88   Von Hoffman, *Citizen Cohn*, 169.

89   Von Hoffman, *Citizen Cohn*, 168-70

90   David Talbot, *The Devil's Chessboard: Allen Dulles, the CIA, and the Rise of America's Secret Government*, First Harper Perennial edition (New York: Harper Perennial, 2016), 176.

91   Delloye, "Godfather of Tabloid."

92   "Catholic Anti-Communism," *Crisis Magazine*, March 1, 1996, http://www.crisismagazine.com/1996/catholic-anti-communism-2.

93   Von Hoffman, *Citizen Cohn*, 280.

94   Von Hoffman, *Citizen Cohn*, 280-81.

95   Rod Dreher, "Cardinal Mary," *The American Conservative*, February 9, 2019. https://www.theamericanconservative.com/dreher/cardinal-mary-francis-spellman-gay-frederic-martel/.

96   Talbot, *Devil's Chessboard*, 188.

97   Talbot, *Devil's Chessboard*, 188.

98   Talbot, *Devil's Chessboard*, 188.

99   Talbot, *Devil's Chessboard*, 189.

100   Talbot, *Devil's Chessboard*, 189.

101   Talbot, *Devil's Chessboard*, 189.

102   Talbot, *Devil's Chessboard*, 186.

103   Talbot, *Devil's Chessboard*, 187.

104   Von Hoffman, *Citizen Cohn*, 188.

105   Talbot, *Devil's Chessboard*, 192.

106   Von Hoffman, *Citizen Cohn*, 249; Joan Cook ,"David W. Peck, 87, Former Justice And Court Reformer in New York," *New York Times*, August 24, 1990, https://www.nytimes.com/1990/08/24/obituaries/david-w-peck-87-former-justice-and-court-reformer-in-new-york.html.

107   Von Hoffman, *Citizen Cohn*, 250.

108   Von Hoffman, *Citizen Cohn*, 259.

109   Von Hoffman, *Citizen Cohn*, 259-60.

110   Von Hoffman, *Citizen Cohn*, 272, 300.

111   Keith Wheeler and William Lambert, "Roy Cohn: Is He a Liar under Oath?," *LIFE*, October 4, 1963, p. 25, 100; Homer Bigart, "Witness Says Cohn Told Him 'It's No Crime Not to Remember,'" *New York Times*, April 4, 1964, https://www.nytimes.com/1964/04/04/archives/witness-says-cohn-told-him-its-no-crime-not-to-remember.html.

112   Von Hoffman, *Citizen Cohn*, 260.

113   Von Hoffman, *Citizen Cohn*, 261.

114   Wheeler and Lambert, "Cohn: Is He A Liar?," 100.

115   Foster Hailey, "Cohn Scheduled for Trial Today," *New York Times*, March 23, 1964, https://www.nytimes.com/1964/03/23/archives/cohn-scheduled-for-trial-today-he-is-charged-with-perjury-before-us.html.

116   Ken Auletta, "Don't Mess With Roy Cohn, The Man Who Made Donald Trump," *Esquire*, December 1978, https://www.esquire.com/news-politics/a46616/dont-mess-with-roy-cohn/.

117   Von Hoffman, *Citizen Cohn*, 282.

118   Von Hoffman, *Citizen Cohn*, 282-83.

119   Auletta, "Don't Mess with Roy Cohn,"; Von Hoffman, *Citizen Cohn*, 295-96.

120   Von Hoffman, *Citizen Cohn*, 296-97.

121   Auletta, "Don't Mess with Roy Cohn."

122   Auletta, "Don't Mess with Roy Cohn."

123   *Securities & Exchange Commission v. Fifth Ave. Coach Lines, Inc.*, 289 F. Supp. 3 (S.D.N.Y. 1968), *Justia Law*, July 26, 1968, https://law.justia.com/cases/federal/district-courts/FSupp/289/3/1419260/.

124   *Securities & Exchange Commission v. Fifth Ave. Coach Lines.*

125   *Securities & Exchange Commission v. Fifth Ave. Coach Lines.*

126   Willy Van Damme, "Mossad–A safe pass in Belgium," Willy Van Damme's Weblog, Feb-

ruary 27, 2013, https://willyvandamme.wordpress.com/2013/02/27/mossadeen-vrijgeleide-in-bel-gi/.

127 Auletta, "Don't Mess with Roy Cohn."

128 Von Hoffman, *Citizen Cohn*, 284.

129 Von Hoffman, *Citizen Cohn*, 284.

130 Von Hoffman, *Citizen Cohn*, 284-85.

131 Von Hoffman, *Citizen Cohn*, 285-86.

132 Von Hoffman, *Citizen Cohn*, 287.

133 Von Hoffman, *Citizen Cohn*, 331.

134 Von Hoffman, *Citizen Cohn*, 332.

135 Russell Sackett, Sandy Smith, and William Lambert, "The Congressman and the Hood-lum," *LIFE*, August 9, 1968, 20-26.

136 Von Hoffman, *Citizen Cohn*, 333-37.

137 Sam Roberts, "Cornelius E. Gallagher, 7-Term New Jersey Congressman, Dies at 97," *New York Times*, October 22, 2018, https://www.nytimes.com/2018/10/22/obituaries/cornelius-gallagh-er-dead.html.

138 Von Hoffman, *Citizen Cohn*, 341.

139 Von Hoffman, *Citizen Cohn*, 341; Elizabeth Mehren, "A Thirst for Power : Life and Times of Roy Cohn, the Flamboyant Lawyer Who Put Stamp on U.S. History," *Los Angeles Times*, March 18, 1988, https://www.latimes.com/archives/la-xpm-1988-03-18-vw-1638-story.html.

140 Anthony Summers and Stephen Dorril, *Honeytrap - The Secret Worlds of Stephen Ward: Sex, Scandal and Deadly Secrets in the Profumo Affair* (London: Headline, 2013), 249; S. William Snid-er, *A Special Relationship: Trump, Epstein, And the Secret History of the Anglo-American Establishment*, (Independently published, 2020), 332, https://www.amazon.com/gp/product/B08PX93Z1H/.

141 "Klaus Barbie and the United States Government," US Department of Justice, August 1983, 56, https://www.justice.gov/sites/default/files/criminal-hrsp/legacy/2011/02/04/08-02-83bar-bie-rpt.pdf.

142 Snider, *A Special Relationship*, 347.

143 Snider, *A Special Relationship*, 349.; Douglas Thompson, *Stephen Ward, Scapegoat: They All Loved Him* (Chicago: John Blake, 2014), 150.

144 Tom Morgan, "The Spy Files: Lord Boothby's Sordid Sex Parties with Ronnie Kray Revealed in MI5 Files," *The Telegraph*, October 23, 2015, https://www.telegraph.co.uk/news/uknews/11948323/lord-boothby-sex-parties-ronnie-kray-mi5-documents.html.

145 Adam Curtis, "The Mayfair Set: Four Stories about the Rise of Business and the Decline of Political Power," BBC, July-August, 1999, video, https://www.bbc.co.uk/iplayer/episodes/p073k9s0/the-mayfair-set.

146 "William Averell Harriman-People-Department History-Office of the Historian," https://history.state.gov/departmenthistory/people/harriman-william-averell.

147 Snider, *A Special Relationship*, 264-26.

148 Snider, *A Special Relationship*, 268.

149 Rebecca Pocklington, "Secret Society: The Sex, Secrets and Spies Rumours Surrounding Prince Philip's Wild Thursday Club, as Portrayed in The Crown," *The Sun*, February 12, 2020, https://www.thesun.co.uk/news/10930861/prince-philip-thursday-club-the-crown-real-story-inside-sex-secrets-spies/.

150 Snider, *A Special Relationship*, 270-71.

151 Snider, *A Special Relationship*, 288-89.

152 Snider, *A Special Relationship*, 288-89.

153 Snider, *A Special Relationship*, 387.

154 Snider, *A Special Relationship*, 387.

155 Summers and Dorril, *Honeytrap*, 189.

156 Peter Dale Scott, *Deep Politics and the Death of JFK* (University of California Press, 1996), 229-30.

157 Snider, *A Special Relationship*, 356-59.

158   Snider, *A Special Relationship*, 360-63.

159   Snider, *A Special Relationship*, 364.

160   Snider, *A Special Relationship*, 364-65.

161   Snider, *A Special Relationship*, 366.

162   Snider, *A Special Relationship*, 364-66.

163   Snider, *A Special Relationship*, 230.

164   Robert Sherrill, "King Cohn," *The Nation*, August 12, 2009, https://www.thenation.com/article/archive/king-cohn/.

165   Snider, *A Special Relationship*, 345-46.

166   Snider, *A Special Relationship*, 345-46.

167   "Broady Found Guilty In Wiretapping Case," *New York Times*, December 9, 1955, https://www.nytimes.com/1955/12/09/archives/broady-found-guilty-in-wiretapping-case-broady-is-guilty-in-wiretap.html.

168   H. P Albarelli, Leslie Sharp, and Alan Kent, *Coup in Dallas: The Decisive Investigation into Who Killed JFK* (Skyhorse Publishing, 2021), 229-32.

169   Douglas Caddy, "Clendenin J. Ryan - Baltimore Millionaire and CIA Funder," *The Education Forum*, November 18, 2007. https://educationforum.ipbhost.com/topic/11614-clendenin-j-ryan-baltimore-millionaire-and-cia-funder/.

170   "Home - The George Town Club," The George Town Club, https://www.georgetownclub.org/.

171   Alan A. Block, *Masters of Paradise: Organized Crime and the Internal Revenue Service in the Bahamas* (Routledge, 1991), 85-102.

172   Gary Webb, *The Killing Game* (New York: Seven Stories Press, 2014), 106.

173   "House Select Committee on Assassinations Appendix to Hearings," March 1979. Vol. 9, p.518. https://aarclibrary.org/publib/contents/hsca/contents_hsca_vol9.htm.

174   Bock, *Masters of Paradise Island*, 85-102.

175   "Guterma Died Taking Just One More Gamble," *Fort Lauderdale News*, April 9, 1977.

176   Wheeler and Lambert, "Cohn: Is He A Liar?," 100.

177   "*United States of America, Appellee, v. Virgil D. Dardi, Robert B. Gravis, Charles Rosenthal and Charles Berman*, Defendants-Appellants, 330 F.2d 316 (2d Cir. 1964)," Justia Law, March 17, 1964, https://law.justia.com/cases/federal/appellate-courts/F2/330/316/116165/.

178   Hearings, Reports and Prints of the Senate Committee on Banking and Currency, 1964, p.299, https://www.google.com/books/edition/Hearings_Reports_and_Prints_of_the_Senat/9T-c4AAAAIAAJ

179   "*US vs. Dardi*."

180   "Decisions and Reports: Volume 40," Securities and Exchange Commision, 1960, p. 936, https://play.google.com/store/books/details/United_States_Securities_and_Exchange_Commission_D?id=4z2-9QYg4X4C.

181   Jeremy Kuzmarov, *Modernizing Repression: Police Training and Nation Building in the American Century* (Amherst: University of Massachusetts Press, 2012), 101.

182   Chester L. Cooper, *The Lost Crusade: America in Vietnam* (New York: Dodd, Mead, 1970), 52.

183   Kuzmarov, *Modernizing Repression*, 101.

184   "Decisions and Reports," 938.

185   Regarding CIC's intelligence connections: Scott, *Deep Politics*, 168-69; Alfred Friendly, "Four Agencies Probe Act of Chiang's United States Contractor," *Washington Post*, September 10, 1951, printed in P.11066-67. Senate Congressional Record, https://www.congress.gov/bound-congressional-record/1951/09/10.

186   "Memorandum In The Matter of The Bon Ami Company: File No. 1-685," Securities and Exchange Act Release no. 34 - 6677, 1934, p. 3, https://play.google.com/store/books/details?id=Yh-M7AQAAMAAJ.

187   J. C. Louis and Harvey Yazijian, *The Cola Wars*, 1st ed (New York: Everest House, 1980), 302.

188   "Letter from Louis Mortimer Bloomfield to Carlo d'Amelio," January 26, 1961, https://archive.org/details/Damelio.

189   Frances Stonor Saunders, *The Cultural Cold War: The CIA and the World of Arts and Letters* (New Press: Distributed by W.W. Norton & Co, 2000), 298.

190   Jonathan Marshall, "Wall Street, the Supermob and the CIA," *Lobster*, May 2022, https://web.archive.org/web/20211231190726/https://www.lobster-magazine.co.uk/free/lobster83/lob83-wall-street-supermob-cia.pdf

CHAPTER 5

SHADES OF GRAY

THE PR MAN

Today, the Koreagate scandal of the 1970s is largely forgotten, despite the lurid headlines it inspired at the time. Shadowy intelligence operatives, slush funds, kickbacks, complicated schemes to buy political loyalty, and rumors of sex and blackmail were just some of the themes that swirled around Koreagate and the man at its center, Tongsun Park.

As noted in the previous chapter, Park had studied at Georgetown University, where he developed close ties to certain groups of young conservative activists. While there, he was also recruited by the KCIA, the Korean intelligence apparatus. After graduating, Park became a well to-do businessman in the DC area as well as a social gadfly, forming connections with congressmen, senators, and staffers on both sides of the political aisle.

What became known as Koreagate was said to have begun when Chung Il Kwon, South Korea's prime minister, tasked the head of the KCIA, Kim Hyong-uk, with devising an operation to influence political opinion in the United States. The resulting scheme entailed the services of Park, who was then brokering rice sales contracts from the US to South Korea under the auspices of the government's Food for Peace program. Working with Congressman Richard T. Hanna – who represented California, one of America's largest rice-producing states – Park utilized the commissions on these sales to peddle influence. He called upon his impressive network of contacts, who were interwoven throughout the offices of powerful Washington businesses and institutions, as well as the private clubs and backrooms of the capital, to carry out his series of kickbacks and bribes.

Appearing on the periphery of Koreagate – at least as far as the official investigation was concerned – was one of Park's close associates, the powerful lobbyist and Public Relations executive Robert Keith Gray. Across the course of his lengthy and impressive career, Gray was adept at the art of influence peddling. The breadth of his associates ran from Korean CIA operatives such as Park to US CIA agents such as Edwin P. Wilson and soon-to-be CIA director William Casey. Among his other close associates and/or clients were Adnan Khashoggi, Robert Maxwell, the Teamsters, and BCCI (the Bank of Credit and Commerce International), among many others. It all added up to Gray acting as a key node in a shadowy network that was becoming increasingly aligned, and integrated, with the halls of power. Gray's name would often bubble up alongside numerous scandals, with Koreagate being just one. Others would include Watergate, the largely forgotten pageboy scandal of 1982, and the Iran-Contra affair.

Gray hailed from Hastings, a moderately sized industrial town nestled in the Nebraskan countryside, about two and half hours west of Omaha. Early on, he showed an interest in politics and was an avid participant in his high school debate club. After his graduation in 1939, he and several members of his debate club attended Carleton College in Minnesota; his chosen area of study was political science. A year later, with World War II looming on the horizon, the US Navy launched its V-7 program, which was a rapid-training course for naval officers. V-7 worked closely with universities across the United States, and Gray quickly enlisted.

The next couple of years were a whirlwind for Gray. He attended the Navy Supply Corps Midshipmen Officer's School in Newport, Rhode Island, and found time to take business management courses at Harvard. This threefold educational path – politics, business, and adjacency to the military – became defining characteristics of the rest of his long and storied career. Yet, it would be some time before he was able to make a name for himself.

After the war he bounced back to Hastings, where he worked at the naval depot that had been built there. He spent his free time building social capital: he taught business courses at Hastings College and joined many of the city's organizations and social clubs (including the local Masonic lodge).[1]

During this second period in Hastings, Gray became acquainted with Fred Seaton, owner of the *Hastings Tribune* and a powerful figure in Nebraskan politics. Gray then served as a state senator before serving as President Eisenhower's assistant secretary of state for legislative affairs. He brought few things with him to the capital – among them Seaton's contact information. Seaton managed to find Gray a position in the vast

150

complexes of the post-war bureaucracy. He went to work in the Pentagon, serving as a special assistant to Assistant Secretary of the Navy Albert Pratt.

Gray received a promotion in May 1956, which propelled him higher in the strata of power within the Eisenhower administration. He became a special assistant to the White House, acting as deputy to Seaton. Yet, as Susan Trento points outs in *The Power House*, there may have been more to this position than meets the eye. He had been designated as an "excepted appointment," which means that, in lieu of a standard promotion, he had "been simply detailed to the White House from the Navy."[2]

If Gray was still technically working for the Navy while at the White House, it is likely that his new position involved intelligence and security concerns. His primary task was to sift through reams of data in connection with Washington job seekers. "Gray," Trento writes, "was controlling the flow of information about everyone looking for patronage, or political jobs, at a federal level."[3] A significant amount of this information was marked "highly confidential," which gave Gray an inside track on government power.

Soon, he was working under Sherman Adams, Eisenhower's chief of staff. Adams was an early Rockefeller Republican and a master bureaucrat. He was known for regulating access to the president: nobody, it was said, could speak to Eisenhower without Adams' approval. He made up an inner core of Eisenhower cronies that included Floyd Odlum and George Allen – powerful, politically connected businessmen whose interests existed in immediate proximity to the emergent "military industrial complex," as Eisenhower would later call it, as well as the increasingly brazen intersection of intelligence and business interests. This was the world that Gray was easing his way into under the tutelage of Adams.

After the untimely departure of Adams under the cloud of scandal, Gray gained a new mentor – Richard Nixon. This was Gray's introduction into an expanded network of contacts that shaped the trajectory of the rest of his life. In 1960, he went to work on the ill-fated Nixon presidential campaign, perhaps encountering for the first time his future friend William Casey. He also became associated with Clark Clifford in this period; Clifford, a Democratic Party insider and archetypal cold warrior, was one of DC's elite attorneys and had an extensive Rolodex.

Decades later, Clifford was among the numerous US political and business figures implicated in the BCCI scandal, the subject of chapter 7. Beginning in the early 1980s, Clifford served as chairman of the board of

First American Bankshares, a major DC-based bank that had fallen under the secret control of BCCI via their takeover of the bank's parent company. As Edward Jay Epstein has pointed out, First American was a bank used by numerous congressmen and other political figures – control of the bank created possible blackmail opportunities.[4] Shortly after Clifford took control of First American, Gray joined the bank's board of directors.[5]

Following John F. Kennedy's defeat of Nixon in 1960, Gray left government service for a position at Hill & Knowlton (H & K), a major public relations and lobbying firm that had been launched in the 1920s by John Hill and Donald Knowlton. While H & K would become synonymous with the inner conflicts and flashy affairs of the DC Beltway – with clients including everyone from presidential hopefuls to BCCI – in the early days, it was a Cleveland-based company with a particular focus on the local steel industry and the banks that financed it.[6]

In the aftermath of World War II, H & K became a major promoter of the aviation industries that were then benefitting from the fusion of American heavy industry and the US military. John Hill, for example, was a member of the Air Power League, a pressure group formed by a large coterie of businessmen and military officers with the goal of educating the public about aviation and raising support for the construction of "greater airport facilities and air training programs."[7] The league was closely aligned with the Aviation Industries Association (AIA), the major aviation trade association that H & K had taken on as a client. Such connections firmly ensconced H & K within the military-industrial complex, as the *Encyclopedia of Public Relations* makes clear:

> "The [Aviation Industries Association] sought a steady diet of military appropriations for its member companies, and it promoted air safety, travel, and other aspects of civil aviation. After the war ended, military contracts took a nosedive, so the agency focused on convincing the federal government to audit the nation's air policies and its readiness for another war. When both Congress and President Harry S. Truman set up commissions to review air policy, Hill & Knowlton helped industry officials prepare their testimony and publicize the board's findings. Joining with the American Legion, the AIA sponsored a campaign, "Air Power is Peace Power," beginning in 1947."[8]

H & K was also linked, it seems, to the CIA. Robert Crowley, a longtime operator within the Agency's Directorate of Operations, stated that the firm's "overseas offices were perfect 'cover' for the ever-expanding CIA."[9] Crowley would have been in a position to know: he acted as the CIA's "liaison" to the business world, which entailed the use of existing businesses as covers for agents abroad and the creation of proprietary firms to act as fronts.[10] Crowley may even have helped bring a young George H.W.Bush into the CIA's fold, as Bush's Zapata Petroleum served as an Agency front for various Caribbean operations during Crowley's time as an Agency liaison.[11] Gray himself was likely tied directly to these efforts. When Edwin Wilson checked with the CIA's Office of Security prior to adding Gray to the board of a CIA front called Consultants International, "he discovered that Gray had already been cleared by the spy agency – that Gray had previous clearances."[12]

INSIDE THE GEORGE TOWN CLUB

During the 1960s Gray became aligned with a powerful bloc of interests known as the China Lobby. An early Cold War equivalent of today's Israel Lobby, the China Lobby represented the Nationalist Chinese – the Kuomintang (KMT) – and their supporters in Washington. The China Lobby called for US support for Chiang Kai-Shek's government in Taiwan against the Chinese Communists led by Mao Zedong. In its most extreme form, this support entailed militarized intervention in mainland China and elsewhere in Southeast Asia. As scholars such as Peter Dale Scott have shown, many of these activities set in motion a complex chain of events that later cascaded into the Vietnam War.[13]

One of the strongest actors in the China Lobby was Anna Chennault, who cultivated contacts with countless politicians, businessmen, military figures, and intelligence officers. She held positions on the boards of numerous companies and acted as an advisor to various US presidents. She also served as a diplomatic channel to the leaders not only in Taiwan but in South Korea, the Philippines, Japan, and elsewhere. Gray was particularly close to Chennault, though the exact details of how the two first met are unknown.

Anna Chennault's husband had been Claire Chennault, the leader of the First American Volunteer Group – better known as the "Flying Tigers" – during World War II. With ranks drawn from the US military, the Flying Tigers trained at bases maintained in Burma before flying to China to fight Japanese forces alongside the KMT. From the late 1930s, Claire Chennault had served as a military advisor to Chiang Kai-Shek and his brother-in-law, the powerful T. V. Soong.

As previously detailed in Chapter 1, Claire Chennault was a very well-connected man and this included ties to the Roosevelt administration. After the war, the Chennaults became the core members of the China Lobby and, in those early years, managed an impressive airlift of "American relief supplies in China."[14] Central to this effort had been the creation of a new airline called Civil Air Transport (CAT). As previously noted, CAT would later morph into the CIA airline Air America, which would subsequently become the infamous Southern Air Transport.

There were also other airline companies in this mix. As was also noted in Chapter 1, an air freighter called Flying Tiger Lines was set up by a coterie of Claire Chennault's former pilots, and Anna Chennault joined the company as its vice president of international affairs. Evidence suggests that Flying Tiger Lines was also utilized by the CIA, and its board of directors included individuals linked to organized crime.[15] At the same time, Anna acted as a consultant to numerous large aviation concerns, including Pan American, whose interests directly intermingled with those of the CIA's CAT/Air America complex.[16] At any rate, Flying Tiger Lines remained squarely in the fold of the China Lobby and its numerous allies. "Over the years," writes Susan Trento, "Flying Tiger ... would evolve into World Airways, and Gray would become a board member."[17]

Gray's early political mentor, the future president Richard Nixon, was also an ally of the China Lobby. Many journalists and academics have identified Nixon as being a "member" of the lobby, but a 1992 academic paper suggests that his involvement with them was more pragmatic than ideological.[18] He fostered good relations with Chiang Kai-Shek and T. V. Soong, which spilled over into business arrangements during the 1960s, when Nixon temporarily left politics for private law. One of his biggest clients was Pepsi, the Taiwanese interests of which were firmly held by members of Soong's family.[19]

All of this provides a backdrop to the creation of the George Town Club in March 1966. Its main organizers included Gray, Park, and Chennault, along with Henry Preston Pitts, Lawrence Merthan, and General Graves B. Erskine. The Club was officially established "for the purpose of bringing together leaders who had an impact on the United States, and the world, through their work in various business, professional, civic, social and political milieus."[20] Pitts and Merthan, according to the *Washington Post*, worked alongside Gray at H & K at the time of the club's founding.[21] By the time the Koreagate hearings began in the late 1970s, Pitts had left H & K and gone to work for the US Information Agency, the once covert body set up during the Eisenhower administration to direct "public diplomacy" and Cold War propaganda.[22]

Erskine had a lengthy career in the world of intelligence and covert operations. In 1950, he ran the military wing of the Survey Mission to Southeast Asia, which brought him into close contact with the anti-Communist interests that were aligned with the domestic China Lobby. Working closely with representatives of Nationalist China, he developed a military strategy to support KMT fighters in Burma and their allies in Thailand. This was the birth of Operation Paper, which marshaled the resources of CIA operatives such as the mob-linked banker and OSS veteran Paul Helliwell.[23] Arms flowed to Thailand and Burma aboard ships chartered by Sea Supply, a front company organized by Helliwell, while others were procured through the shadowy World Commerce Corporation. Peter Dale Scott has argued that Operation Paper was a key point in the development of US intelligence complicity in the global drug trade – at the very least, it marked a major instance of intelligence's indirect support for drug traffickers.[24]

In 1953, Erskine became the director of Special Operations at the Department of Defense. This put him in charge of an obscure office within the Pentagon that served as the liaison between the armed forces and the CIA. Here, Erskine oversaw an ever-increasing number of covert operations and special wars dotting the globe. Operating under Erskine was the infamous Edward Lansdale, America's architect of guerrilla warfare and psychological operations in the post-war era. When Erskine suffered a heart attack in 1957 and took a protracted leave from the Special Operations office, Lansdale stepped in and ran it in his stead.

The intersection of the George Town Club's membership with China Lobby interests and skilled operators in the world of covert intelligence was apparently unending. The manager of the club, for example, was Norman Larsen. Larsen had previously worked in the Washington offices of the Life Line Foundation, one of the charitable bodies owned by Texas oilman and financier of right-wing causes, H. L. Hunt.[25] Other recipients of Hunt's largess included *Foreign Intelligence Digest*, a private intelligence magazine organized and edited by Douglas MacArthur's former intelligence chief, Charles Willoughby.

While Willoughby operated far from the environs of the George Town Club, numerous authors have highlighted his linkages to the wider China Lobby network. David Clayton, for example, writes that the lobby "was intrinsically tied to advocates of [a foreign policy of] rollback … and to

MacArthur, through his intelligence chief General Charles Willoughby," while Harvey Klehr writes that Willoughby was a "China Lobby ally."[26] And Peter Dale Scott writes that "others who used [Joseph] McCarthy to settle old scores included the Chinese Nationalists of the China Lobby, their spokesman Alfred Kohlberg, and General MacArthur's Prussian-born intelligence chief in Japan, General Charles Willoughby."[27] The expansive nature of this network can also be illustrated by Norman Larsen's membership in the International Youth Federation for Freedom, a "non-profit anti-Communist group" that appears to have had some working relationship with the CIA.[28] The International Youth Federation for Freedom was founded by none other than Tongsun Park, along with his close friend and college roommate Douglas Caddy.

Park, in his Koreagate testimony, makes passing reference to Caddy, noting that Caddy – who would appear later in the course of the Watergate scandal by serving briefly as E. Howard Hunt's attorney – had been the executive director of the Young Americans for Freedom. As noted in the previous chapter, Young Americans for Freedom had been organized by former CIA officer, close friend of Roy Cohn, and *National Review* founder William F. Buckley and counted Charles Willoughby on its advisory board.

When Park mentioned Caddy in his testimony, it was during a line of questioning concerning a man who later figured heavily in the clandestine espionage activities of Robert Maxwell: Senator John Tower. Tower, who was also a member of the George Town Club, had been particularly close to Park. "I was a friend of the [Tower] family," Park stated, before noting Tower's involvement in "helping Young Americans for Freedom, which was founded by one of my closest friends."[29] The "closest friend" alluded to here was Caddy.

A State Department telegram concerning the George Town Club reports that, for the first six years of its existence, the club had operated in the red. Nevertheless, it managed to stay afloat, apparently through the intercession of its owners. The governing board was "divided … equally between the Democratic and Republican parties." The telegram goes on to state that, at the time, Clark W. Thompson had been serving as chairman of the club's board. Thompson was the quintessential moderate Texas Democrat, having served for some three decades as one of the state's representatives. Working both sides was Thompson's forte. For instance, when it came to the issue of school desegregation, he broke with most of his colleagues who opposed it, while he also voted against the Civil Rights Acts of 1957 and 1960.

156

A careful examination of Thompson's affiliations reveals links to the worlds of organized crime and intelligence. Thompson was married to the daughter of William Lewis Moody Jr., a key player in the world of Texas finance and insurance. Moody's flagship firm was American National Insurance Company (ANICO), founded in Galveston, Texas, in 1905. The Moodys were briefly mentioned in the last chapter as Moody's grandson, Shearn Moody Jr., was a close friend and client of Roy Cohn. According to a mutual friend of Cohn's and Moody's, the "eccentric" Moody supplied Cohn with "many little boys of the night," which he also he did for other specific guests who visited his Texas ranch.[30]

Thompson had served on the board and as ANICO's treasurer during the 1920s but departed when he entered politics. At the same time that he was serving as chairman of the George Town Club, he had rekindled ties to the conglomerate and was listed as its official lobbyist.[31] Morris Shenker, best known as Jimmy Hoffa's attorney, was also ANICO's attorney for a time and he helped bring the insurance firm into the mob-dominated world of Las Vegas hotels and casinos. As Sally Denton and Roger Morris write, "ANICO ... funneled untold millions into Las Vegas gambling interests, including $13 million to Shenker himself ... and, most significantly, to Parvin-Dohrmann – the company that owned the Stardust, Aladdin, and Fremont."[32] It certainly helped that E. Parry Thomas, the man credited with establishing the Las Vegas strip, was closely aligned with Marriner and George Eccles, the offspring of a prominent Mormon banking and construction family (e. g., Marriner served as President Roosevelt's Federal Reserve chief). George Eccles maintained a spot on the board of ANICO and nurtured ties to a number of ventures that were, at the very least, adjacent to organized crime.[33]

George Eccles was also affiliated with American Bankers Life Assurance Company, located in Miami, Florida, where the CIA's Paul Helliwell served as its general counsel. Furthermore, the offices of American Bankers Life were used by Helliwell as headquarters for the Agency's SEA Supply operation.[34] In addition to this important CIA linkage, American Bankers Life also connected to Miami National Bank. As discussed in Chapter 1, Miami National "was identified in 1969 as having served between 1963 and 1967 as a conduit through which 'hot' syndicate money was exported by Meyer Lansky's couriers and 'laundered' through the interlocking Exchange and Investment Bank in Geneva."[35]

Clearly, the George Town Club was nestled within a wider network of entities and institutions that were very sensitive to Washington backroom politics, organized crime, and the CIA. Perhaps that is why, as reported in numerous accounts, the CIA became concerned that one of the main figures behind the club was Tongsun Park, a known asset of the Korean CIA. While the KCIA and the CIA were cooperating entities, the KCIA did engage in activities – such as those that later blossomed into the Koreagate scandal – that were seen as compromising US political figures and also seen as potentially disruptive for US geopolitical interests. As a result, the CIA dispatched an agent to monitor the club's comings and goings. That individual was Edwin P. Wilson, a man who would become known as a "rogue" agent roughly a decade later, after he was linked to various terrorist and assassination plots.

A sizable portion of Wilson's early career in the CIA entailed operating undercover as a staffer for the American Federation of Labor and the Congress of Industrial Organizations (AFL-CIO), the large union combine known as a proponent of "business unionism." Since the Agency's inception, the Agency and the AFL-CIO had worked closely together, with the union providing cover for agents and operations, while the CIA often subsidized the activities of the AFL-CIO's foreign wings.[36] Wilson worked in the office of Paul Hall, the head of the AFL-CIO's Maritime Trades Department, which covered unions involved in shipping-related trades and industries. This was the beginning of Wilson's long-running involvement in maritime activities.

After leaving the AFL-CIO, his work for the CIA involved the management of proprietary firms, many of which operated in the world of shipping, freight forwarding, and logistics. One of the first of these was Maritime Consultants, which had been set up in Washington, DC with CIA funds. According to Joseph Trento, "within months he was chartering barges to Vietnam, arranging cover in commercial businesses for CIA agents, and setting up businesses around the world. Using his maritime cover, Wilson did detailed surveys of nearly every port in Africa and the Pacific."[37] One wonders if Wilson's involvement with the George Town Club had less to do with monitoring the activities of Gray, Park, and Chennault and more to do with managing the complexities of these covert maritime operations. It is certainly possible, given Gray's own past with the Navy. In addition, Wilson's business in Vietnam would have gained considerably from contacts with Anna Chennault, who was closely connected to the government and elsewhere in Southeast Asia. At any rate, the arrival of Wilson at the George Town Club marked the beginning of a long association between him and Gray.

There were, for example, their trips to Taiwan, where each had business interests – interests that, in all likelihood, were interrelated. Wilson gained lucrative contracts from the Nationalist Chinese military, while Gray signed on the Taiwanese government as a client. The account was entrusted to George Murphy, an actor who became a US Senator representing California, but, at the time, was an H & K employee. Curiously, Gray routed the work through a separate company that he set up specifically for these purposes, called GM (presumably for Gray-Murphy). Susan Trento writes that "according to Wilson, Gray set up ... GM to handle the Taiwanese account. Since Anna Chennault trusted Murphy, Gray put the senator in charge of GM."[38] Murphy, unsurprisingly, was a member of the George Town Club.

Some of Wilson and Gray's joint activities dovetailed with those of the CIA. Gray was a board member of Consultants International, a firm that Wilson managed from offices adjacent to those of H & K on K Street in the capital. Gray later disavowed knowing Wilson and stated that he had been added to the board of Consultants International without Gray's knowledge. Gray's account is hard to believe and many of those embedded in this network, including H & K employees and Wilson himself, have pushed back against Gray's interpretation of events. At any rate, Consultants International was not simply a consultancy firm. It was also an Agency proprietary firm, set up as a successor to Wilson's earlier CIA front company, Maritime Consulting.[39]

There are plenty of hints and suggestions that Gray, Wilson, Park, and the byzantine web of China Lobby activists and intelligence operatives that circulated around the George Town Club were involved in more than just social networking and the creation of lobbying groups. Eavesdropping and blackmail seem to have been part of the club's covert mandate. Future Reagan national security advisor Richard Allen – who would have known Gray through the involvement of each in the Heritage Foundation – suggested when interviewed by Susan Trento that the club was bugged.[40] Jim Hougan, in his classic *Secret Agenda*, points to even darker possibilities. He writes that he was informed in a letter from Frank Terpil, Wilson's longtime partner, that Wilson had used the club to collect dirt on prominent Washington politicians and businessmen by using it as a place to "arrange trysts for the politically powerful."[41] He quotes from the letter:

> Historically, one of Wilson's Agency jobs was to subvert members
> of both houses [of Congress] by any means necessary.... Certain

159

people could be easily coerced by living out their sexual fantasies in the flesh.... A remembrance of these occasions [was] permanently recorded via selected cameras, I'm sure for historical purposes only. The technicians in charge of filming [were] TSD personnel. The unwitting porno stars advanced in their political careers, some of [whom] may still be in office. You may now realize the total ineffectiveness of the "Watchdog Committees" assigned to oversee clandestine operations.[42]

Former Nebraska state senator John DeCamp, in his work on the Franklin scandal (the subject of chapter 10), alleges that Gray was the "closest friend in Washington" of Harold Andersen, the publisher of the *Omaha World Herald* who was alleged to have played a role in that scandal, which dealt with a politically-connected, nationwide pedophile ring.[43] DeCamp also notes that Andersen was one of the key Nebraskans who was closely tied to the man at the center of Franklin scandal, Larry King, who was also actively aided by George H.W.Bush in rehabilitating his post-scandal image.[44]

DeCamp, who attempted to expose government efforts to sweep the scandal under the rug in *The Franklin Cover-Up*, also asserted that Gray himself was "reportedly a specialist in homosexual blackmail operations for the CIA." DeCamp also wrote that the sexual-blackmail operations in which Gray's associate Edwin Wilson was intimately involved were "apparently continuing the work of a reported collaborator of Gray from the 1950s – McCarthy committee counsel Roy Cohn."[45] Cohn and Gray reportedly knew each other, but the exact nature of their relationship is difficult to discern. They were, however, most certainly intimately acquainted during Ronald Reagan's 1980 presidential campaign, when both men worked closely with William Casey, who was the campaign's manager and subsequently Reagan's CIA director. Shortly after the campaign, Cohn, Gray and Jeffrey Epstein would all take on arms dealer Adnan Khashoggi as a client at the dawn of the Iran-Contra affair.

THE CIA'S BLONDE GHOST

Edwin Wilson ostensibly left the CIA in 1971 under incredibly murky circumstances, though the most common story involves his commercial cover being blown by a Soviet asset. Per the media narrative that was spun during the course of the manhunt for Wilson and his subsequent imprisonment, Wilson is said to have cut ties with the Agency and become a covert private operator for hire – a "rogue." Yet, evidence released not only during his trial but well after its conclusion shows that Wilson remained in close contact with a cadre of CIA officers and officials whose activities, as the 1970s wore on and the Agency was battered by reformists' efforts, took on increasingly strange and frightening forms. This circle was centered around the man known as the "blonde ghost," Theodore "Ted" Shackley.[46]

Shackley, like Wilson, came from a background somewhat different from the usual CIA leadership, which tended to cultivate its upper ranks from the posh world of white-shoe law firms and high finance. He instead hailed from Florida and began his career in the Army; his recruitment into the CIA came after a stint in the Army Counterintelligence Corps. By 1953, he was working under William Harvey at the West Berlin CIA station. Here, Shackley operated at the very frontier of the Cold War: the West Berlin station's activities were carried out under the shadow of the Berlin Wall, and the city was a veritable melting pot of espionage intrigue. While working under Harvey, Shackley may have gotten a taste for the more "exotic" aspects of CIA work. After he returned to the States, Harvey managed a CIA assassination team – with many of its members having been mob hitmen recruited into Agency service under the auspices of the ZR/RIFLE program.

Harvey's assassination activities were woven into Operation Mongoose, the joint CIA-Army covert war against Castro's Cuba. The central hub of the CIA's side of the anti-Castro operations was the Miami station, code-named JM/WAVE. Tucked away in an unassuming building on the extended campus of the University of Miami, the station "employed from 300 to 700 agents and 2,000 to as many as 6,000 Cubans."[47] In 1962 – right as the CIA's Cuban project was spiraling toward its violent apex – Shackley became JM/WAVE's station chief. Joseph Trento asserts that, in this period, Shackley was mentored in the fine of art of covert financial activities by Paul Helliwell: "Helliwell showed Shackley ... the importance of income from Agency fronts. According to numerous case offices who worked at JM/WAVE, Helliwell helped Shackley make certain that fronts like Zenith Technical Enterprises were the perfect cover for JM/WAVE."[48]

These allegations are partially corroborated by other sources. The *Washington Post*, for instance, reported in 1980 that Helliwell "was instrumental in helping to direct a network of CIA undercover operations and 'proprietaries.'"[49] Curiously, one of the only declassified CIA documents to mention Helliwell is a list of files removed from internal circulation in order to avoid turning them over to Watergate investigators.[50] Almost all of the other files in the list deal directly with the CIA's support of anti-Castro Cuban exiles.

JM/WAVE was where Shackley formed close relationships that would shape the rest of his long career, both inside the Agency and out. Chief among Shackley's alliances that were forged via JM/WAVE was with Thomas Clines, who later emerged as a key player in the Iran-Contra conspiracy. Clines served as Shackley's deputy, even after both men stepped beyond the confines of the CIA itself. There was also a score of Cuban exiles: the notorious Felix Rodriguez (known for his involvement in the death of Marxist revolutionary Che Guevara and his own role in Iran-Contra), Rafael Quintero, and Ricardo Chavez. Many of these individuals followed Shackley overseas in 1966, when the "blonde ghost" was made the CIA station head in Vientiane, Laos. It was a perfect spot for a crew that was increasingly adept at "wetworks" (i.e. assassinations) and black operations. This particular station oversaw the Agency's participation in the secret war being waged within Laos and Cambodia.

Vientiane, during this period, was the epicenter of a major illicit trade in contraband, gold, and raw opium, most of it destined for Saigon.[51] Laos boasted a handful of prominent opium merchants with deep ties to the country's political and military establishment. One of these merchants, Ouane Rattikone, had previously commanded the Laotian army, and his drug trafficking operations saw extensive collaboration with Nguyen Cao Ky, the high-ranking commander of the South Vietnamese Air Force. Not only were Ky and his men moving raw opium from Laos on their planes, but Ky was also working closely with the CIA in their secret war efforts such as Operation Haylift, which dropped saboteurs deep into the jungles of North Vietnam.[52] The raw opium was refined into heroin and then moved into Hong Kong, where it was readied for global export.

This circuit was of immense interest to American organized crime figures. In 1965, Meyer Lansky's financial agent John Pullman flew to Hong Kong, reportedly to investigate the burgeoning wartime trade. Several years later, Florida mob boss Santo Trafficante arrived in Hong Kong and soon made his way to Saigon. "Soon after Trafficante's visit to Hong Kong," writes Alfred McCoy, "a Filipino courier ring started delivering Hong Kong heroin to Mafia distributors in the United States. US Bureau of Narcotics intelligence reports in the early 1970s indicated that another courier ring was bringing Hong Kong heroin into the United States through the Caribbean, Trafficante's territory."[53]

The presence of Trafficante is telling. He had been an active support-er of the anti-Castro operations, and after the Agency wound down its JM/WAVE activities, many Cuban exiles trained by the CIA as part of that program went to work trafficking drugs for Trafficante. Was Shack-ley involved in some way with Trafficante's arrival in Southeast Asia? It is possible, as there are plenty of apocryphal stories about Shackley per-sonally introducing Trafficante to Vang Pao, a Laotian heroin warlord, during a 1968 trip to Saigon. While the details of those stories cannot be confirmed, Vang Pao would have had to have known of Shackley, as he commanded the Hmong troops that were being backed and trained by the CIA in Laos.

According to McCoy, the CIA's logistical networks allowed Vang Pao to increase the efficacy of the Laos-South Vietnam opium trade:

> Air logistics for the opium trade were further improved in 1967 when the CIA and USAID … gave Vang Pao financial assistance in forming his own private airline, Xieng Khouang Air Transport. The company's president, Lo Kham Thy, said the airline was formed in late 1967 when two C-47s were acquired from Air America and Continental Air Services. The company's schedule was limited to shuttle flights between Long Tieng and Vientiane that carried relief supplies and an occasional handful of passengers. Financial control was shared by Vang Pao, his brother, his cousin, and his father-in-law…. Reliable Hmong sources reported that Xieng Khouang Air Transport was the airline used to carry opium and heroin between Long Tieng and Vientiane.[54]

This was the crucial context for the formation of a group that would later be known as Shackley's "private CIA." On hand in Laos was Thom-as Clines, and there they soon became acquainted with another future Iran-Contra co-conspirator – Richard Secord. An Air Force pilot, Secord had been detailed to the CIA's Laotian station and he personally knew many of those involved in the traffic of opium via the airways, including the aforementioned Air Marshal Ky.[55] Another figure, who would also later play a key role in the Iran-Contra affair and who also worked with Shackley in Laos was Major John K. Singlaub. Singlaub had served along-side Paul Helliwell in the OSS.

Playing an active role in logistical support for the Agency's secret war was Edwin Wilson. Much of this involved a close working relationship with the head of the Southeast Asian division of the CIA's Air America,

James Cunningham, who also ultimately answered to Shackley.[56] Though Wilson was not stationed in Southeast Asia, he frequently made trips between Washington and Vientiane. There can be little doubt that these jaunts of his were of immense interest to Gray, Park, Chennault, and other members of the China Lobby who populated Wilson's inner stateside circle. The China Lobby, after all, was wired into the world of intelligence and had stumped for the escalation of conflict in Southeast Asia, an escalation that finally erupted into the Vietnam War.

In 1968, Shackley took over the Saigon CIA station, which gave him operational oversight of a vast gamut of operations – including, for a period, the infamous Phoenix Program. The Phoenix Program, while financed by the CIA, operated under the auspices of CORDS (Civil Operations and Revolutionary Development Support). Overseeing CORDS was the CIA's old Southeast Asian hand and bureaucratic mastermind, William Colby. Rumors among the military's in-country brass abounded that Shackley exerted influence over Colby through sexual blackmail. Clearly, Shackley and Wilson, alleged to have been carrying out similar activities at the George Town Club, were quite similar in this regard:

> Colby, then married to his first wife, returned to Vietnam without his family from a stint back in Langley. According to retired US Army Colonel Tullius Accompura, who served in Vietnam, Colby had a girlfriend, a Vietnamese senator's wife. Shackley's colleagues soon realized that Shackley was keeping a book on the private lives of all of his superiors in Vietnam, including Colby and military officers such as General Creighton Abrams, who, according to Accompura, was involved with a Vietnamese woman. If pressed upon an undesirable topic by a colleague, Shackley would warn him off by mentioning any personal entanglements. As John Sherwood put it: "He was good at letting you know he knew, that he had something on you, that he had an edge."[57]

Shackley remained in Saigon until May 1972, when he took over as head of the CIA's Western Hemisphere Division. Since Cuba fell under the rubric of this division, it was something of a return for Shackley to his earlier haunts. Yet, by this point, the anti-Castro operations had largely fallen by the wayside. There was still operational support for Cuban exile groups, many of which were factionalizing into militant terrorist groups such as Coordination of United Revolutionary Organizations (CORU). The Agency's eyes were darting farther south, toward Southern Cone countries like Chile, where socialist leader Salvador Allende had come to power. From his perch at the top of the Western Hemisphere Division, Shackley was on the bureaucratic frontline for the 1973 coup that brought Augusto Pinochet to power in Chile and the parade of dirty wars that ripped across South America.

Even before Shackley left Saigon, his network of contacts was busy making arrangements. Thomas Clines – who would soon be embroiled in the Agency's ventures in Chile – had left Saigon in 1970 and rotated back stateside to spend time at the Naval War College. Joining him there was Richard Secord. Secord, in this period, completed his War College thesis, which had been directed by the "CIA advisor to the president," Clarence Huntley. The prescient title of his thesis was "Unconventional Warfare/ Covert Operations as an Instrument of US Foreign Policy."

Throughout 1971, Clines kept in touch with Edwin Wilson, who was now allegedly operating outside of the CIA's purview. It was at that point that Clines brought Wilson into the realm of naval intelligence by way of a secretive unit known as Task Force 157.

TASK FORCE 157

The groundwork for what became Task Force 157 (TF-157) was laid in 1965 by a memo drafted by President Johnson's secretary of the navy, Paul Nitze. Titled "Instructions for the coordination and control of the Navy's clandestine intelligence collection program," Nitze's program for a naval human intelligence (HUMINT) gathering apparatus had originated with plans made by Admiral Rufus Taylor.[58] Taylor had served in the Office of Naval Intelligence (ONI) as well as the National Security Agency (NSA). In 1966, as this new Navy unit was being prepared for action, he took up a post as deputy director of the Defense Intelligence Agency (DIA). Later that same year, he became deputy of director of the CIA, serving under Richard Helms.

The first iteration of the Navy's HUMINT unit, established in 1966, was the Naval Field Operations Support Group. Author Michael Mc-Clintock suggests that the original template for the unit was Task Force 98, a Navy program that supported the Southeast Asian paramilitary activities carried out by Ed Lansdale and Lucien Conein.[59] By July 1966, the Support Group was given the mandate to establish "a worldwide intelligence collection organization while preserving non-intelligence attributability of collection operations."[60] Internal Navy communiqués and information sharing identified the Support Group by name; soon, to help obscure the organization's activities, it was granted the code-name "Task Force 157."

TF-157's primary focus was "intelligence information on Communist Bloc Naval and shipping information."[61] Subunits were devised and located across the world; many of these were located in ports, adjacent to shipping channels and choke points for maritime traffic, and even out at sea. Just as the CIA deployed commercial covers for their operations, TF-157 set up front companies to charter ships and maintain offices. Listening posts were established, and TF-157 worked closely with the military and the CIA in developing improved navigational maps for the support of military activities. TF-157 even maintained its own international communication system based on encryption technology inherited from the NSA, which was code-named the "Weather Channel."[62]

TF-157's operational autonomy was only partial. It answered to both the Office of Naval Intelligence and the CIA. Though, between the two, the Agency apparently had an edge for nabbing the various projects that TF-157 developed. When it came to organizing the networks of proprietary companies, it was again to the CIA that TF-157 turned. "Ed Wilson is the man you need," the CIA told the task force.[63] Wilson, meanwhile, learned of TF-157 from Thomas Clines, presumably with Ted Shackley lurking not far in the background.[64] Soon enough Wilson was on the TF-157 payroll, making an annual salary of $32,000. Despite his official salary, Wilson quickly became a multimillionaire.

This was because TF-157 allowed him to keep earnings from the commercial fronts he set up, which he operated as legitimate businesses. Two of the new front companies were World Marine Inc. and Maryland Maritime Co. They were registered in DC and were run from the same offices as Consultants International – the same company where Robert Keith Gray sat on the board of directors.[65] There was also Aroundworld Shipping & Charting, based in Houston, Texas, where Wilson spent a considerable amount of time. Whether Aroundworld was tied to TF-157 like World Marine and Maryland Maritime or a CIA-adjacent firm like Consultants International is unknown, but it later played a key role in the activities of Shackley's "private CIA." As Wilson was settling into his new position, TF-157 was becoming embroiled in one of the major foreign policy shifts of the Cold War era. Nixon and Kissinger, as part of a broader geopolitical push for detente – a relaxing of tensions with the Soviet Union and China, alongside curbing the nuclear arms race – were pushing for an opening with China. The initiative was treated with the utmost secrecy: while Alexander Haig was involved in the efforts, the Joint Chiefs of Staff and the CIA were largely boxed out. For Kissinger, the success of these China-focused efforts would require the diplomatic channels and corridors of information to be airtight.

Kissinger appealed to Admiral Thomas H. Moorer, then serving as chairman of the Joint Chiefs of Staff. Moorer had previously been the chief of Naval Operations and thus had had operational involvement with TF-157. Moorer arranged for Kissinger to use the Weather Channel to send encrypted messages and arrange the necessary diplomatic back channels for this impending geopolitical shift. What Kissinger did not seem to realize was that Moorer opposed Kissinger's bureaucratic wrangling and Nixon's overarching imperative of circumventing the usual bastions of political power. Moorer also strongly opposed the initiative itself and was allied with elements of the pro-KMT China Lobby.

THE RADFORD-MOORER AFFAIR

Yeoman Charles Radford barely knew Jack Anderson, the famed muckraking journalist. He was actually more familiar with Anderson's parents, whom he had met during a posting in India in 1970. Radford had been raised Mormon, a faith he shared with the Andersons, and this seems to have kindled a casual friendship between the young naval officer and the older couple. In 1970, Radford briefly crossed paths with Jack Anderson himself, having been invited by his parents to a family reunion. It seemed innocuous enough.

The second time Radford met Anderson was over a year later, in December 1971. Anderson, out of the blue, had contacted Radford and invited him to dinner at the Empress, a Chinese restaurant in which he owned a stake. Radford later told Jim Hougan that the reason he took Anderson up on his offer was "because he was Jack Anderson. He was famous."[66] The dinner took place on a Sunday evening. The following day, Anderson ran in his newspaper column – renowned for the journalist's intrepid pursuit of insider sources in the fast-paced world of DC – an article that contained explosive revelations.

Anderson's column brushed right up against the most sensitive undertaking then being carried out by President Nixon – Henry Kissinger's secret diplomatic negotiations with China. One primary channel being used by Kissinger was Pakistan, which had historically maintained close geopolitical relations with China. Pakistan's president Yahya Khan was especially close to Beijing and had garnered extensive military aid from China

167

in the face of Pakistan's rising hostilities with India. China, likewise, had reason to oppose India. Tensions with the Soviet Union had been escalating steadily since the Sino-Soviet split, and Moscow had thrown its weight behind India. The chessboard was full, and Nixon and Kissinger were stepping carefully into a complex and potentially dangerous position.

Pakistan's conflict with India greatly complicated matters for the administration: outwardly, it took a position of neutrality. In 1971, when martial law was imposed in East Pakistan by President Khan, the White House made an announcement: "The United States does not support or condone this military action." Behind closed doors, however, it was a very different story. Nixon and Kissinger had embarked on a covert path of "tilting" toward Pakistan. President Khan was assured that the administration would "not do anything to complicate the situation … or embarrass him."[67]

What was unfolding was a truly remarkable series of events. Nixon's rise to the Oval Office had been dependent on the support of the domestic China Lobby, and he personally maintained close relations with the KMT's top leadership. The Kissinger-led initiative toward China undermined all of that. In the course of his ongoing negotiations with China, Kissinger was tacitly abandoning the hawkish iterations of a pro-Taiwanese foreign policy. The administration, he said, wasn't looking for a "two Chinas" solution or a "one China, one Taiwan" solution."[68] There was also talk of committing the US military to an exit strategy from Vietnam and a reduction of the US troop presence in the Middle East.

The diplomatic channels of these negotiations were fragile, complex, and, most of all, *secret*. Nixon and Kissinger strove to keep the agenda hidden. The CIA, the State Department, the Joint Chiefs, the China Lobby itself – and even Soviet interests – were recognized as threats to the long-term plan. But Anderson, in his column, nearly scuttled it all. In a single article, he revealed that, despite the carefully calculated public position of neutrality, the "tilt" toward Pakistan was well underway. It threatened to reveal the diplomatic back channel while also putting a question into people's minds: Why, exactly, was the US tilting toward Pakistan?

Journalist Clark Mollenhoff – who served as special counsel to Nixon in 1969 – summed up the implications of Anderson's reporting in a column published on January 22, 1972. "Kissinger's role in the India-Pakistan policy seems to be faulty," he wrote, before adding that "there is a question of why the administration was secretly advocating a 'tilt for Pakistan' when India was able to prove far quicker its overwhelming military superiority."[69] Mollenhoff then sketched out what he saw as the "bigger picture," implicating Nixon and Kissinger's drive toward extreme bureaucratic compartmentalization:

> At both the State and Defense departments, there is hope that President Nixon will view these errors as evidence that some changes are needed in the National Security Council's method of operations. Both departments point out that this isn't the first time the National Security Council decisions haven't been supported by a realistic appraisal of the facts."[70]

Within the corridors of power, Anderson's revelations of the "tilt" strategy set off a firestorm. It was quickly determined that the journalist must have had access to at least three memos – memos that were highly secret and had only been issued to a handful of people. Those people were Kissinger himself, Alexander Haig, Admiral Robert O. Welander (the military assistant for national security affairs to the chairman of the Joint Chiefs of Staff, Admiral Moorer), and Welander's assistant, Yeoman Charles Radford. Welander eliminated himself from suspicion for the leak, as well as Kissinger and Haig. The culprit had to have been Radford; yet, what happened next only increased the strangeness of the case.

Radford, who had acted as a document courier and aide to members of the Joint Chiefs of Staff and the National Security Council, was subjected to a polygraph test by a Pentagon interrogation specialist.[71] When it came to questions concerning the theft of confidential memoranda from diplomatic pouches and burn bags, the yeoman became agitated. "The cause of his concern was a very sensitive operation," writes Colodny, which Radford "could not discuss without the direct approval of Admiral Welander."[72] Welander had initially kicked off the investigation into Radford. With allegations of a secret operation surfacing, however, he moved quickly to try to squash the investigation before it went any further. The attempt did not succeed, and Radford ended up revealing his role in a military-led espionage ring.

The yeoman had pilfered confidential files and made copies of "uncounted documents – just thousands, thousands of documents."[73] He made notes on reports of Kissinger's meeting with Chinese premier Zhou Enlai and other sensitive documents related to the "China initiative." These were then turned over to people working for the Joint Chiefs of Staff, who used them to learn the inner workings of the Nixon-Kissinger strategy, bypassing the carefully constructed blockages on the flow of information within the top tiers of the US government.

Radford would turn the documents over to Admiral Welander who, in turn, gave them to Admiral Moorer. According to Radford, his contribution "put Admiral Moorer in a very powerful position [to] anticipate what Kissinger was going to do and say" in National Security Council meetings.[74] Welander later hinted that Alexander Haig was involved in the ring as well. There was little doubt, he suggested, that Haig had known of Radford's meddling with the diplomatic pouches – and Haig himself had, at times, assigned Radford to accompany Kissinger on diplomatic trips.

According to Radford, the whole operation was designed to thwart a wide-ranging conspiracy that was taking root at the highest levels of the foreign policy establishment. At the center of the conspiracy was Kissinger himself, here appearing as an alleged agent of the Rockefeller family and the institution where the Rockefellers carried so much weight, the Council on Foreign Relations. "The purpose of this alleged conspiracy," writes Jim Hougan, "was to win the Soviets' cooperation in guaranteeing the Rockefellers' 'continued domination' over the world's currencies – in exchange for which, Radford insists, Kissinger was to construct a foreign policy that would ensure eventual Soviet hegemony and a one-world government."[75] The source of his knowledge about this conspiracy, Radford said, was Welander and Moorer.

The accusations being made by Radford echo those being made by the John Birch Society and other groups and actors operating in that same milieu – many of which were also intimately connected to the KMT–China Lobby. (The aforementioned Charles Willoughby, for example, made this world his primary haunt.) Many of the accusations made by John Birch Society affiliates – that Kissinger himself was a Soviet mole – appeared later in the 1970s, with Frank Capell's *Henry Kissinger: Soviet Agent* and Gary Allen's *Kissinger: The Secret Side of the Secretary of State.* (Capell, in the 1960s, had worked for Willoughby's *Foreign Intelligence Digest.*) What makes this important is that Moorer himself had maintained extensive ties to the John Birch Society and related groups. These ideas intensified in the later part of the 1970s and the 1980s, when he became affiliated with the American Security Council, the preferred outpost of military hawks who laid the intellectual groundwork for the so-called Reagan revolution.

There are two puzzling loose threads that are evident when considering the Radford-Moorer affair. The first is that, due to Kissinger's use of the TF-157 Weather Channel, Moorer and the Joint Chiefs were already privy to much of the information concerning the China initiative. Likewise, through Edwin Wilson's arrival at TF-157, there is the distinct possibility that the CIA was also listening in and perhaps, as well, Wilson's KMT–China Lobby friends. It is through the China Lobby, and the incestuous networks of defense hawks, military operatives, and Washington fixers that these two sides met. Was this network the original source of Moorer and Welander's manipulation of Radford?

The second loose thread is that Radford, while admitting to pilfering thousands of pages of sensitive documentation, fervently denied having leaked the documents to Jack Anderson. He disavowed a close association with the journalist, noting that they had only met a handful of times and were distant acquaintances at best. If it is true that Radford had not leaked the documents, who did and for what ends?

A likely answer is that Welander or Moorer or somebody working on behalf of them was responsible for the leak. With the information gained from both the access to the TF-157 channels and through Radford's pilfering, they had an inside look at the "tilt'" strategy and its position within a wide-ranging geopolitical calculus that threatened to shift the entire thrust of the Cold War. Perhaps by hanging their asset Radford out to dry they had hoped to derail Kissinger's process through a calculated leak to Anderson. But what about Anderson himself? His appearance with Radford at the Empress would then suggest that he was at least partially complicit in this plot.

Surprisingly, Anderson boasted longstanding ties to the China Lobby. He seemed particularly close to Anna Chennault: the two had been cofounders of the Chinese Refugee Relief Organization, a pro-KMT humanitarian agency that maintained offices at 1612 K Street. This office was just down the street from Robert Keith Gray's H & K and the offices of Wilson's TF-157 fronts. When the organization was operational, Chennault played the role of president and Anderson served as its secretary.

There is also the fact that a column of Anderson's had been used to hint at John F. Kennedy's connection to the Stephen Ward-connected sex ring that sparked the Profumo Affair. As mentioned in the last chapter, Anderson had co-written in the column "Britishers who read American criticisms of Profumo throw back the question 'What high American official was involved with Marilyn Monroe?'" Which was apparently part of a Hoover-connected effort to use sex blackmail obtained from the broader networks woven throughout the Profumo Affair against Kennedy. This suggests that Anderson's column had, on certain occasions, been weaponized by powerful political factions well before this particular column in the early 1970s.

It is also worth noting that, in the post-Watergate era, Anderson held accounts at – and stock in – Diplomat National Bank in DC, where Anna Chennault sat on the board of directors. The bank was used as a conduit for the Korean CIA and the closely related Unification Church, which – like Anderson – held bank stock.[76] Never one to be far from the action, Tongsun Park "told American friends that he was behind the bank and that [bank chairman Charles] Kim was his agent."[77] This wasn't the only suspect bank that Anderson was connected to. During the 1960s, he owned "complimentary shares" of the District of Colombia National Bank, which had been organized by Democratic Party fixer Bobby Baker and Ed Levinson, a notorious organized crime insider.[78] Joining Anderson at this bank was Arthur Arundel. Arundel – who had served under Edward Lansdale in Southeast Asia – was the son of Pepsi lobbyist Russell Arundel. As mentioned earlier, Pepsi itself was closely tied to the China Lobby and to the KMT itself.

Even the restaurant used to implicate Radford can be found within this matrix. Anderson, as mentioned, had a stake in the establishment – yet so did Anna Chennault. These connections between Anderson and the China Lobby, curiously enough, are known thanks to a dossier on the journalist compiled by the White House "plumbers." Soon enough the "plumbers" would be making history, and Anderson would be there too. There is every indication that he, like so many others in this bizarre world, had foreknowledge of the events that were about to take place, which would later be remembered simply as "Watergate."

BLACK BAGS AND INSIDE JOBS

In April 1972, Jack Anderson received a dossier from William Haddad with information on plans being concocted by the "November group" – "President Nixon's personal advertising agency" – to burglarize the Democratic National Committee (DNC) headquarters at the Watergate and other schemes: surveillance, dirty tricks, and the like.[79] Anderson, for reasons that still remain vague, appears to have effectively suppressed this information, and he later mischaracterized the information that Haddad had provided to him.

Others who were provided information by Haddad took it a little more seriously. A month before Anderson was brought into the fold, Haddad had alerted the DNC's head, Larry O'Brien, who in turn put Haddad in touch with the DNC director of communications John Stewart.[80] In late April, Stewart, Haddad, and Haddad's source, a private investigator named A. J. Woolston-Smith, met in New York City to discuss the accusations. This was roughly a month prior to the first of the break-ins at the Watergate complex.

William Haddad and A. J. Woolston-Smith were by no means strangers to intrigue. Haddad was a longtime political insider within the Democratic establishment and had been particularly close to the Kennedy family. He held various bureaucratic positions, married a Roosevelt daughter, and made a name for himself as a muckraker. It was through the latter role that he became close to Woolston-Smith, whom he employed from time to time. Woolston-Smith had previously worked for Robert Maheu's private detective firm and worked with the CIA on its resettlement programs for Cuban exiles. Maheu himself was no stranger to the CIA's secret wars on Cuba – a background shared by countless individuals interwoven in the Watergate saga – and some investigators have compiled considerable evidence implicating him in the 1968 assassination of Robert F. Kennedy.[81]

Woolston-Smith likely came upon the information concerning the DNC via convoluted networks that snaked across the often incestuous world of private investigators and security firms. As Jim Hougan details, "Woolston-Smith's secretary, Toni Shimon, was the daughter of a Runyonesque former Washington police detective named Joseph Shimon. A convicted wiretapper in his own right, Shimon was the partner of one John Lenn in a detective agency named Allied Investigators Inc. One of the investigators with whom Shimon and Lenn were allied on a part-time basis was Louis James Russell."[82]

Russell supplied tips to Jack Anderson and, in late 1971, was employed by General Security Services. This was the company hired by the DNC to run security at their Watergate offices, and they would have been the ones tasked with handling the information Haddad had provided. Shortly after Haddad notified the DNC of Woolston-Smith's information, Russell resigned from General Security Services and went to work for McCord Associates, the security consulting firm owned by "former" CIA operative James McCord. At that time, McCord was serving as the head of security for the Committee for the Reelection of the President (CRP), the fundraising body for President Nixon's re-election campaign. Russell, too, worked part-time for CRP.

McCord was one of the White House "plumbers," the team put together to plug, prevent, and investigate information leaks, which were endemic in the highly paranoid world of 1970s Washington, DC. Operating alongside him was former FBI agent G. Gordon Liddy and E. Howard Hunt, another CIA veteran. Yet another CIA man in "the plumbers" was Frank Sturgis, who had served alongside Hunt in the Agency's anti-Castro operations. When McCord and Sturgis were arrested in the Watergate DNC offices in July 1972, they were accompanied by a group of CIA-trained Cuban exiles: Virgilio Gonzales, Bernard Baker, and Eugenio Martinez.

There are a few things about McCord's background that are worth mentioning. After a time in the FBI, he joined the CIA, taking a position within the CIA's Office of Security – the in-house body that monitored the internal security of the Agency, ran counterintelligence operations, and provided cover or support for some of the CIA's most sensitive operations. Specifically, McCord was assigned to the Security Research Staff within the Office of Security. There, he honed the craft of electronic eavesdropping, surveillance, and "audio countermeasure programs" to protect sensitive CIA stations and outposts in Europe.[83] These were all of the sorts of techniques that were brought to bear in the course of the Watergate burglary. They also raise some important questions – for example, if McCord was adept at these sorts of affairs, why were the burglaries so remarkably sloppy?

McCord had also served as deputy to Paul Gaynor, the longtime head of the Security Research Staff and a powerful figure within the CIA as a whole. From his commanding place within the Office of Security, Gaynor played an essential role in some of the CIA's darkest projects, such as Project ARTICHOKE – a "special interrogation" program that, with its focus on hypnosis, sensory deprivation, chemical substances, and "psychological harassment" that was the immediate forerunner of the notorious MK-ULTRA program.[84] The groundwork for ARTICHOKE had been laid by an earlier project, BLUEBIRD, described in CIA files as experiments involving "drugs and hypnosis."[85] Jim Hougan writes that Gaynor was reputed to have maintained an extensive array of files on US citizens, with a particular focus on sexual proclivities; these files were known around the Agency as the "fag files."[86] These allegations can be found among the statements made in the 1975 official report of the Rockefeller Commission, an entire section of which is dedicated to the file systems maintained by the CIA's Directorate of Operations. One telling passage of the report reads:

> Miscellaneous files maintained by the Office of Security includes lists of individuals with known or suspected foreign intelligence connections, files associated with handling defectors (some of

whom may now be US citizens), lists of individuals from whom crank calls have been received by the Agency, and lists of persons previously charged with security violations. The Office of Security formerly maintained extensive computer lists of approximately 300,000 persons who had been arrested for offenses related to homosexuality, but these lists were destroyed in 1973.[87]

Gaynor's proclivity for dirt collecting – particularly of the sexual variety – brought him into contact with Roy Blick, the head of the Washington Metropolitan Police's so-called morals squad until he was forced into retirement in the mid-1960s. The morals squad, which today would be called the vice squad, conducted a series of anti-homosexual campaigns under Blick's leadership. According to author Anna Lvovsky, Blick had a penchant for targeting politicians and other people of influence across the Beltway.[88]

His crusading zeal to target homosexuals in the area frequently became the butt of jokes for those in the know. E. Bennett Williams, a DC attorney who appeared in the periphery of the Watergate affair, liked to perform a short routine for the denizens of the after-hours Atlas Club. He would "imitate Blick standing at the urinal for hours, hoping, praying that a 'queer' [Blick's preferred terminology] would come along and grab his penis – so he could make a morals arrest, of course."[89]

Like Gaynor, Blick kept rigorous logs on numerous private citizens. These were recorded on index cards that were stacked high in a safe in Blick's office. According to Lvovsky, "when he left the department, he threatened to keep the key."[90] During the CIA's own information-collection program on homosexuals and other "deviants," police forces across the country were marshaled into the effort, freely turning over their files and working hand in glove with the Agency. Yet, when it came to Roy Blick, who was stationed in the nation's capital, cooperation with the CIA went beyond just file sharing. Numerous declassified files show Blick working closely with the CIA. For example, he made his own contacts at the British embassy available to William Harvey as part of the counterintelligence operation against the Kim Philby spy ring.

The CIA's largest domestic espionage operation, which saw the full cooperation of various police departments and other law enforcement agencies with the Agency, was called Operation CHAOS. It had been initiated during the Johnson years to monitor the growing civil rights and antiwar movements. James Jesus Angleton, the ultraparanoid CIA counterintelligence chief, was the driving force behind CHAOS' inception. Multiple subprograms were created, each tasked with different operational imperatives, and adjacent programs were rallied for support. One such program was called MERRIMAC, which "involved CIA infiltration of antiwar/ peace groups in the Washington, DC area in order to gather … information on the organizations, their members, sources of funds, and plans."[91]

MERRIMAC provided much of the information it harvested to CHAOS. MERRIMAC was run from the CIA's Office of Security. As Shane O'Sullivan points out, McCord was then working as chief of the office's Physical Security Division, which would have brought him into direct cooperation with MERRIMAC and CHAOS.[92] Interestingly, E. Howard Hunt appears to have been delivering "sealed envelopes and packages," believed to contain information on the White House "plumbers," to Richard Ober – one of the top CIA officials, then overseeing Operation CHAOS.[93] O'Sullivan draws other parallels between McCord's post-CIA security firm, McCord Associates, and the CIA's proprietary firms that were involved in MERRIMAC, CHAOS, and more general counterintelligence concerns.

Chief among these was Anderson Security, set up in 1962 to provide support for the Office of Security. Even after MERRIMAC was supposedly terminated in 1968, Anderson Security was, as late as 1971, managing infiltration and espionage of dissident groups in the capital on behalf of the Office of Security.[94] Intriguingly, Hunt seems to have crossed paths with Anderson Security at the same time that he was delivering files to Ober, and he brought them on to carry out security sweeps of the CRP offices.[95] All of this is highly suggestive that lurking within the "plumbers" unit was an apparatus connected to long-running CIA information-collection operations and security matters. The background of James McCord in the Office of Security certainly makes this possible as does Hunt's involvement with Ober and Anderson Security. McCord and Hunt, however, claimed not to have met until their mutual involvement with CRP.

There are reasons to doubt this. Hunt, for example, had been active in the CIA's anti-Castro operations. There he had worked alongside David Atlee Phillips, the eventual chief of the CIA's Western Hemisphere Division, which encompassed the Caribbean and Latin America. In January 1961, McCord was temporarily detailed to Phillips to run a counterintelligence operation against the Fair Play for Cuba Committee, a pro-Castro activist group.[96]

The possibility that McCord and Hunt knew each other because of having operated in the same web of overlapping CIA operations in the 1950s, raises other questions. Why were the "plumbers" being stocked with CIA agents, and why was Hunt turning over information to the CIA? Interestingly, these moves were being made at a time when Richard Nixon – rightfully suspicious of the Agency – was seeking to blunt its power. Early plans were made to exclude Richard Helms, the director of the CIA, from National Security Council meetings.[97] While the administration ultimately backed away from these efforts, the administration had nonetheless engaged in consistent bureaucratic wrangling that induced all sorts of headaches for the CIA. Part of the reason for this, Kissinger later noted, was that Nixon "brought to the presidency ... a belief that the CIA was a 'refuge of Ivy League intellectuals opposed to him.'"[98]

Regardless of whatever else was going on in this dense fog of palace intrigue, the house of cards collapsed on June 17 when police officers arrested McCord, Sturgis, Baker, Martinez, and Gonzalez in the Watergate offices of the DNC. Martinez was found with a key, which he reportedly attempted to conceal by swallowing it.[99] The leader of the arresting officers was Carl Shoffler, a detective in the DC police's Criminal Intelligence Division. Shoffler, incidentally, had been nicknamed "Little Blick" by his fellow officers, presumably for having interests and activities that resembled those of the infamous Captain Roy Blick.[100] It was soon revealed that a previous break-in had taken place, that bugs had been planted in the offices of the DNC, and that McCord had set up a listening post in a rented room in the Howard Johnson Motor Lodge across the street.

The morning after the break-in, the deputy chairman of the DNC, Sam Gregg, called the organization's general counsel, a well-known Washington lawyer named Joseph Califano Jr. Gregg told Califano about the break-in and mentioned that there was photographic equipment in the offices. Califano advised Gregg that the DNC should closely cooperate with the DC police. Califano then hung up the phone and promptly called another of his other top clients. He later said, "I picked up the phone and called Howard Simons who was the managing editor of the *Post*, who was on duty that weekend, and told him there'd been a break-in at the DNC. We didn't know who it was, but it looked suspicious."[101]

That the DNC and the *Washington Post*, soon to be written into history for its coverage of the Watergate affair, had the same general counsel is a surprising coincidence – but it's Califano's deeper history, and the close relations that he had forged in the previous decade, that stretch credulity. At the beginning of the 1960s, he worked for the white-shoe law firm Dewey Ballantine – the "Dewey" being Thomas Dewey – before he was tapped to serve as the special counsel to the Department of Defense's general counsel. A year later, Califano was promoted to become special assistant to US Secretary of the Army, Cyrus Vance. It was during this period that Vance had delved into the world of the CIA and the Army's secret wars.

While serving as assistant to Vance, Califano was deployed to the numerous coordinating bodies that brought the CIA and Army together for covert operations against Castro's Cuba. Internal CIA memoranda and the more recently declassified "Califano papers" illustrate that his involvement with Operation Mongoose would have brought him into contact with a wide-ranging cast of characters, including Edward Lansdale and Ted Shackley. After Mongoose came to a close, Califano was assigned to its successor, the Interdepartmental Coordinating Committee of Cuban Affairs. He worked closely with the Joint Chiefs of Staff, as evidenced by memoranda Califano sent to them outlining "special actions."[102] Califano had his own assistant who worked alongside him through the numerous iterations of the anti-Castro coordinating committees – a young Alexander Haig. Haig later summarized the nature of some of their activities for historian Gus Russo:

> I was part of it, as deputy to Joe Califano and military assistant to General Vance. We were conducting two raids a week at the height of that program against mainland Cuba. People were being killed, sugar mills were being blown up, bridges were demolished. We were using fast boats and mother ships and the United States Army was supporting and training these forces. This was after the Missile Crisis, when the Cuban Coordinating Committee was set up [in 1963]. Cy Vance, the Secretary of the Army, was [presiding] over the State Department, the CIA, and the National Security Council. I was intimately involved.[103]

As late as January 1964, Haig was working with Califano when the lawyer became the Department of Defense's "Executive Agent for Cuban Affairs."[104] His mandate in this position was broad and took place during the general winding down of the Agency's heavy focus on Cuba. He was involved in the management and resettlement of Cuban refugees and helped find homes and employment for scores of CIA-trained exile fighters. This likely would have brought both Califano and Haig into contact with the future private investigator A. J. Woolston-Smith – the same Woolston-Smith who had curious foreknowledge of the Watergate break-ins through his connections to Lou Russell.

And what of the *Washington Post* itself, whose intrepid journalists Bob Woodward and Carl Bernstein so famously broke the case? Originally, Woodward and Bernstein had worked separately, pursuing leads into the murky world of "former" CIA agents and shadowy security units like the plumbers. At the behest of the journal's leadership – including Howard Simons, who had been contacted by Califano on the morning after the break-in – the two journalists began to pool their resources and contacts.

At least, this is the official story. The networks of sources that Woodward and Bernstein cultivated suggests that other dynamics were in play. There was, for example, Robert Bennett, the owner of the public relations firm Robert R. Mullen & Company. Bennett "said … that he [had] been feeding stories to Bob Woodward of the *Washington Post* with the understanding that there would be no attribution … to Bennett."[105] Mullen & Company was also the firm that E. Howard Hunt had gone to work for at the suggestion of CIA director Richard Helms following Hunt's questionable retirement from the CIA. In addition, the firm itself was closely aligned with the CIA. An undated Agency summary, drafted sometime during the Watergate affair, noted that "Robert R. Mullen and Company has been utilized by the [CIA's] Central Cover Staff since 1963. … Mr. Mullen has provided sensitive cover support overseas for Agency employees and he was instrumental in the formation of the Cuban Freedom Committee."[106] The Cuban Freedom Committee was similar to CIA projects like Radio Free Europe and broadcast anti-Castro propaganda to Cuba. In addition, Robert R. Mullen & Company's attorney was Edward Bennett Williams, a partner in the same law firm as Joseph Califano. As an aside, among Williams' clients was Robert Vesco, whose frighteningly intricate history – and peripheral role in Watergate – are discussed in the next chapter.

And what about Woodward himself? Carefully removed from the official Watergate narrative is Woodward's stint, immediately prior to his career as a journalist, in the military. After attending Yale, Woodward had gone into the Navy, where he spent "four years of sea duty as a communications officer."[107] He served under two superiors who would go on to land important positions at the Pentagon. The first of these was Rear Admiral Francis Fitzpatrick, who became the "assistant chief of naval operations for communications and cryptology."[108] The second was Admiral Welander – the top assistant to Moorer and associate of Haig who, as discussed, was a central player in the Radford-Moorer espionage ring. In August 1969, Woodward, still an enterprising young naval officer, arrived in Washington, DC. Because of his expertise in communication systems, the military gave him a post at the Pentagon, where he worked in direct proximity to Fitzpatrick and Welander. As Len Colodny writes:

> Woodward was tasked with overseeing approximately thirty sailors who manned the terminals, teletypes, and classified coding machines at the naval communication center through which all Navy traffic flowed, from routine orders to top-secret messages. It was a sensitive position that afforded Woodward access to more than one hundred communication channels, among them, according to Admiral Fitzpatrick, the top-secret SR-1 channel through which the Navy sent and received its most important messages."[109]

We have already encountered SR-1 under its colloquial name of the Weather Channel, the secret communication system utilized by Task Force 157. Woodward, in other words, was directly linked to the cable traffic of this ultrasecret unit, which became connected in one direction to Edwin Wilson, Robert Keith Gray, and the China Lobby complex and in the other direction to the Joint Chiefs of Staff and the Nixon administration's internal power struggles over East Asian policy and overarching bureaucratic organization. Furthermore, in this position, Woodward would have answered directly to Admiral Thomas Moorer, who not only made SR-1 available to Kissinger but who had also sought to undermine Kissinger's efforts in the China initiative.

According to Colodny's sources, which included Admiral Moorer himself, Woodward also acted as a "briefer," meaning he collected information from a variety of sources for assimilation and subsequent presentation to his commanding officers. Moorer was not the only military official who would have received Woodward's briefings. "On his briefing assignment," writes Colodny, "Woodward was often sent across the river from the Pentagon to the basement of the White House, where he would enter the offices of the National Security Council. There, Woodward would act as briefer to Alexander Haig."[110]

This suppressed connection between Woodward and Haig led Colodny to suggest that Haig was, in fact, the infamous Deep Throat, the mysterious informant who provided Woodward and Bernstein with vital bits and pieces of information. The more recent claims made by Mark Felt, a veteran FBI official, to have been the real Deep Throat has disturbed the Haig thesis. Felt was certainly in a position to have known a lot. His posts at the FBI had included, for example, overseeing the COINTELPRO operations before he became assistant director of the Bureau in 1972. He also had a personal animus against the administration, which had passed over him in appointing a new director after J. Edgar Hoover's death. But, as Colodny's co-author Robert Gettlin has pointed out, certain essential pieces of information that Woodward attributes to Deep Throat simply could not have been known by Felt at that place and time.[111] As a result, it has been posited that Deep Throat was likely a composite of multiple informants.

CALLS GIRLS AND MOBSTERS

The Watergate scandal was one of the great political imbroglios of the latter half of the twentieth century. It collapsed an entire administration, set off a decade of power plays, reform efforts, and bureaucratic changes. It contributed, along with the deeply unpopular Vietnam War and subsequent revelations of government skullduggery, to an overwhelming air of distrust on the part of the American people toward their rulers. Yet, what remains remarkable, despite all of this, is that the rationale for the break-ins has never been satisfactorily explained.

There are an array of competing explanations and interpretations, even from the burglars themselves. According to James McCord, the reason they broke in was to place listening devices in Larry O'Brien's offices. E. Howard Hunt, meanwhile, suggested that the team had been dispatched to the Watergate to unearth evidence of illicit campaign contributions being made to the DNC by Fidel Castro. However, as Jim Hougan has untiringly pointed out time and again, there is no evidence to substantiate either claim.[112] The FBI never found evidence of the purported bugs – which would not have worked anyway. As Hougan writes, "O'Brien's office was part of the interior suite at the DNC and … was shielded from McCord's 'listening post' in the motel across the street from the Watergate."[113]

As for the Castro claims, evidence has never surfaced that the leader of Cuba was funneling money to Democratic politicians, and it is highly unlikely that this is what McCord, Hunt, and company were rummaging for. The most likely repositories for information of this sort – the offices of the DNC treasurer, for example – were left untouched over the course of the break-ins.

There is also the issue of unexplained evidence, the most important of which may be the mysterious key in the possession of Eugenio Martinez. At the time of the burglars' arrest, the lock that matched the key was not discovered. Yet, in the subsequent investigation, it was found that the key fit the lock of the office of Maxine Wells, the secretary to R. Spencer Oliver, whose phone had been tapped. Hougan states that, according to arresting officer Carl Shoffler, photographic equipment "was clamped to the top" of Well's desk."[114] Len Colodny asks: "Why would a Watergate burglar have a key to Wells' desk in his possession, and what items of interest to a Watergate burglar were maintained in Wells' locked desk drawer?"[115]

Intimations that something strange had been afoot involving Oliver's secretaries was reported early on in *Nightmare* by veteran journalist Anthony Lukas. Alfred Baldwin, a former FBI agent hired by McCord to monitor calls being made from Oliver's phone at the nearby listening post, stated that the secretaries were actively using the phone when Oliver, who was frequently away from the office for long stretches of time, was not present. "Some of these conversations," Lukas writes, citing Baldwin, "were 'explicitly intimate.'"[116] Lukas adds that "so spicy were some of the conversations that they have given rise to confirmed reports that the telephone was being used for some sort of call-girl service catering to congressmen and other prominent Washingtonians."[117] Here, Lukas is being deceptive, as the allegations concerning the potential of a Watergate-connected call girl service do not arise on the basis of the phone calls alone. There was, in fact, evidence that several rings were being operated at the nearby Colombian Plaza Apartments, adjacent to both the Watergate and to the motel where McCord's listening post was located. These rings were overseen "by at least two madams, Lil Lori and Helen Henderson"; another woman involved was identified by Hougan as "Tess."[118] He writes:

> Besides their location at the Colombian Plaza Apartments, the prostitutes had at least two things in common. The first was the homogeneity of their clients. With few exceptions, they were professional men – lobbyists, lawyers, stockbrokers, physicians, congressional aides, and real estate developers. They were among the movers and shakers of the capital, and included at least one US senator, an astronaut, a Saudi prince, a clutch of US and KCIA intelligence agents, and a host of prominent Democrats.... According to a 1971 police intelligence report ... "The Watergate Hotel ... was a prime source of their business."[119]

To make matters more complicated, Lou Russell – linked to McCord and other figures nebulously circling around the Watergate affair – was closely acquainted with the proprietors of the call girl ring. Writes Hougan: "According to Russell's friends ... Russell chose to idle away his leisure time in the apartments at the Colombia Plaza. He was a friend to many of the girls, a sometime customer, a free-lance bouncer, and a source of referrals."[120] Russell may, however, have been playing an even more important role at those apartments. Phillip Bailley, a figure of incredible importance to the deeper context of the Watergate saga, encountered Russell there with a set up that included recording equipment, cameras, and two-way mirrors to record the girls' clients.[121]

Who was Phillip Bailley, and why was he so important to these unfolding events? Bailley was a DC lawyer with a predilection for the dark side of life. He presented himself as a well-connected player, an operative in the capital's nighttime world. However, the reality was a bit different – he was, to quote Phil Stanford, a "fledgling lawyer at the bottom of the D.C. legal food chain."[122] A graduate of the local Catholic University of America law school, his self-declared role model was Bobby Baker – the notoriously crooked political fixer of the Democratic establishment of the 1950s and 1960s. Baker himself operated within a constellation of Texas-based businessmen and organized crime figures. It is possible that, after setting his sights on that type of milieu, Bailley decided to begin his ascent into these networks. His preferred clientele included "petty criminals, drug dealers, and prostitutes."[123]

In *Secret Agenda*, Bailley is described as being close to the call girl Jim Hougan dubbed "Tess," which was not her real name.[124] Len Colodny, in *Silent Coup*, identifies Bailley's consort in the call girl ring as Cathy Dieter. To make matters more confusing, Dieter was not the girl's real name either. She was actually Erika "Heidi" Rikan, "a woman who between 1965 and 1966 had performed as a stripper at Washington's Blue Mirror Club in the notorious 14th Street District."[125] Rikan, like Bailley, was well connected. Her best friend was Maureen Biner, who at the time was dating John Dean, the Nixon administration's White House counsel.[126] Dean and Biner later married, and she changed her name to Maureen Dean.

Rikan and Biner had known each other for many years at this point. For a brief period in the late 1960s, Biner was married to George Owen, scout for the Dallas Cowboys. Owen had the inside track to the top Texas power players; his personal friends included the oil heir Clint Murchison Jr.; Bedford Wynne, the offspring of a prominent Dallas family with numerous interests, including oil, real estate, industry, insurance, and law; Bobby Baker; and Gordon McLendon, a prominent radio man and occasional intelligence asset. McLendon's close associates included, interestingly enough, Jack Ruby, the mobster famous for killing Lee Harvey Oswald, and David Atlee Phillips, the CIA officer connected to both E.

Howard Hunt and James McCord.[127] Maureen writes in her autobiography of an extended trip to Lake Tahoe "with a good and new friend I had met through George, Heidi Rikan."[128]

What's interesting here is that, through their mutual relationship with George Owen and the high flyers of Dallas, Texas, Maureen and Rikan were moving into a circle that overlapped considerably with organized crime interests. McLendon's friend Jack Ruby was himself an insider and participant in the Dallas criminal underworld. The Murchison oil and construction interests, meanwhile, deployed as lobbyist Irving Davidson, who also was lobbyist for the CIA, the FBI, Israel, and crime bosses such as Carlos Marcello.[129] The Murchisons also maintained their own ties to Marcello.[130] Rikan continued to maintain her ties to this side of Texas, even after her move to DC. Phil Stanford reports that within her contact book were Wynne, McLendon, Murchison, and others.[131] The roster of names helps to further illustrate the convergence of Texas business interests and organized crime: one of the names, for example, was Fred Black Jr. Black was a close friend and business partner of the controversial Bobby Baker – and also an intimate of Moe Dalitz, Johnny Roselli, and Clifford Jones, the mob-linked lieutenant governor of Nevada.[132] Jones was also an alleged confidant of Meyer Lansky, representing his interests in several Vegas casinos. It might be important, then, that Black – who maintained an apartment in the Watergate – also owned stakes in several Caribbean casinos owned by Jones.

Another name that appeared in Rikan's contact book was Ben Barnes, a Texas real estate major who had served as the state's lieutenant governor between 1968 and 1973. Among Barnes' close circle of contacts was Herman Beebe, and the two, by the 1980s, were linked to a string of collapsed savings and loans – many of which bore the fingerprints of organized crime and intelligence agencies in their demise. Yet, even in the 1960s and 1970s, Beebe was making the rounds. The network of banks and real estate ventures that would lay the groundwork for his later escapades were tightly interwoven with the criminal enterprises of Carlos Marcello.[133]

Just as Rikan maintained her Texas connections after moving to Washington, she also continued her own personal ties to powerful organized crime figures. At the time that she was involved with Phillip Bailley and active in the ring operating across from the Watergate, she was also reportedly the girlfriend of the mob boss of Washington, DC, Joe Nesline.[134]

Born in Washington, DC, in September 1913, Nesline was first arrested in 1931 for "violation of illegal whiskey laws."[135] Over the years, he raked up an immense number of encounters with the law – primarily arrests for his persistent involvement in illicit gambling activities. Nesline's early gambling operations were operated from numerous establishments such as the Spartan Club. Many of his ventures were carried out in partnership with Charles "Charlie the Blade" Tourine. The pair were arrested on June 13, 1963, in a gambling parlor the two had organized in Maryland.

One 1962 FBI report identified Tourine as the "collection man" for Nesline. Nesline and Tourine's gambling interests intertwined with those of Dino Cellini, Meyer Lansky's top casino operator in the Caribbean. Nesline, for example, maintained a stake in the Colony Club in London, which was operated for a time by Dino Cellini.[136] Much earlier, in pre-revolutionary Cuba, Nesline had worked at the Tropicana Club in Havana, where Cellini was acting as manager. At this time, Tourine was managing the nearby Capri. In the wake of Castro's 1959 revolution, Cellini, Tourine, Meyer Lansky's brother Jake, and Florida mob boss Santo Trafficante were imprisoned together in a camp called the Trescornia.[137] In addition, in the early 1960s, Nesline and Tourine co-owned a posh Miami beach house. In 1964, this property was inhabited by Alvin Malnik, a Mafia financier who was something of a protégé of Lanksy's.[138] Malnik, in this same period, was plugged into the web of international banking that the organized crime groups surrounding Lansky used to move the money they reaped from countless real estate interests, the narcotics trade, and the skim from casinos. He was also the counsel for the Allied Empire Corporation, a major stockholder in Lansky's offshore Bank of World Commerce.

Given these sorts of associations, it is perhaps noteworthy that George Owen told Len Colodny that he first met Rikan in the mid-1960s in Antigua.[139] He was visiting the island with his good friends Bedford Wynne and Gilbert Lee Beckley. Beckley, a world-renowned gambler and bookie described by TIME as "a valuable man to the Cosa Nostra," co-owned a hotel on the island called the Miramar, which is where Owen first crossed paths with Rikan.[140] An FBI report states that in 1966, Charles Tourine was dispatched to Antigua "to protect Beckley's interests." The same report states that in addition to Beckley, co-investors in the Miramar included Anthony "Fat Tony" Salerno of the Genovese crime family.

Nesline's DC operations seem to have been enabled by the extensive corruption of the local police force. An FBI report from late May 1962 describes information provided by an informant with intimate knowledge of police involvement with organized crime in the area. The informant's name is withheld in the report – he felt that "his life and that of his family would be placed in jeopardy if knowledge of his interviews and cooperation with the FBI were even suspected by the various members of the Washington DC area gambling element."[141] The report continues: "No gambler operates in the Washington DC area unless he obtains protection from the Metropolitan Police Department."[142] According to the anonymous informant, influence over the gambling rackets was divided up according to the various police precincts, with the "gambling 'backers'" often having to deal "directly with the Captain of the particular precinct."[143] But perhaps some of the most interesting information concerns Roy Blick, the morals squad head who worked so closely with the CIA: "[Redacted] stated that he was told by Mitchell and feels certain that it is true that "Snags" Lewis was paying Inspector Roy Blick and Chief of Police Barnett.... He had been recently advised that "Snags" Lewis, "Billy" Mitchell, and Joe Nesline are currently doing business with Blick."[144]

POTENTIAL MOTIVES

Sometime in 1971, Heidi Rikan came to Phillip Bailley with the idea of using his contacts at the DNC to expand the customer base for the girls at Colombia Plaza.[145] The connection between Bailley and the DNC was Spencer Oliver, and the "thought was someone – perhaps Oliver himself, perhaps another employee – would be able to steer 'high-rolling pols' to [Rikan's] Colombia Plaza operation."[146] According to Bailley, he managed to make contact with someone within the DNC, and the arrangements were made for a call-out line to be set up from the offices. The location of this line was purported to be the phone of Spencer Oliver, though he does not appear to have been the one with whom Bailley was negotiating. As 1971 gave way to 1972, the operation was bearing fruit, reportedly with one client or more a day being set up through the DNC offices. "Other clients," writes Len Colodny, drawing on statements made by Bailley, "included men from the State Department, major hotels in town, a private club, and the Library of Congress."[147]

Unfortunately for Bailley, trouble was looming on the horizon. On April 6, 1972, the DC police and the FBI raided his home. While Bailley was away, tied up in court, the authorities were busy pulling a veritable treasure trove of incredibly incriminating items from his apartment. Among the sex paraphernalia, video-recording equipment, and other such odds and ends were photographs, home movies, ledgers, and contact books. Each of these was taken into police custody and logged as evidence.

The reason for the raid, interestingly enough, was separate from the complex arrangements running at Watergate and the Colombia Plaza Apartments. Bailley was being charged with violating the Mann Act, which is better known as the White-Slave Traffic Act of 1910. The crooked lawyer, it seems, was accused of drugging a university of student, taking pornographic pictures of her and blackmailing her. As the story goes, Bailley threatened to dispatch copies of the photographs to her school's administrators and her parents if she "did not submit to the attentions of his political cronies and business associates. So, she did submit, having sex with fifteen consecutive partners at a party hosted by Bailley in a suburban Maryland house."[148]

Phil Stanford, in his book on Rikan, presents a slightly more complicated story. He identifies the student as Astrid Leflang, who Bailley had attempted to recruit into Rikan's call girl ring.[149] Rikan, however, rejected Leflang on the grounds that she was "too low-class" and not sophisticated enough for the operation she was trying to get up and running. Soon enough, Leflang was feeling snubbed – and began to provide information to the Capitol Police vice squad.[150] Thus began Bailley's legal woes.

Within a month, Assistant US Attorney John Rudy was building a major case against Bailley. By this time, many women had come forward with accusations against the attorney, and lists of potential witnesses were being compiled. Because Bailley's social networks were so broad, there were quite a few to choose from. Nevertheless, the media buzz about Bailley's situation and the seriousness of his crimes was minimal – at least until June 9, when the *Washington Star* ran a front-page story stamped with the headline "Capitol Hill Call Girl Ring Uncovered." "The FBI has uncovered," the article states, "a high-priced call girl ring allegedly headed by a Washington attorney and staffed by secretaries and office workers from Capitol Hill and involving at least one White House secretary."[151] The article seems to be alluding directly to the Rikan call girl ring, while misconstruing just how involved Bailley was with it.

Who exactly tipped off the *Star* is unknown, but it set off alarms elsewhere in DC. Attorney John Rudy received a call from John Dean demanding access to "all documentary evidence involved in the [Bailley] investigation."[152] Rudy and his assistants were personally summoned to the White House. The evidence, including Bailley's contact book, was packed up and brought to Dean. Rudy would later tell Colodny that the main focus of Dean's attention, besides the potential sources for the *Star*'s story, was the black contact book. Many of the individuals in the book were hidden behind aliases, and two of those were "Cathy Dieter" and "Clout." Rudy had taken pains to confirm the identities behind the aliases: Cathy Dieter was Heidi Rikan, while Clout was her good friend and former roommate Maureen Biner. Rudy, at the time, did not know that Dean was dating Biner – or, for that matter, that Biner had moved in with Dean.[153]

The timeframe of these events is telling. The raid on Bailley took place on April 6, 1972, and a day later the CRP provided G. Gordon Liddy with $83,000. On April 12, McCord received a large chunk of this money to purchase electronic surveillance equipment. Hougan notes that it was "three days later, on April 15, that William Haddad wrote to [Jack] Anderson for the first time, informing him of plans to spy on Democrats."[154] The first of the break-ins at the DNC then took place toward the end of May. The *Star* article and John Dean's encounter with Bailley's contact book was June 9. On June 12, Jeb Magruder suggested to Liddy another break-in – ostensibly for the purposes of acquiring the files of DNC chairman Larry O'Brien. Magruder, however, had not concocted the scheme out of whole cloth. It had been Dean's idea.[155] Within five days the police were in the DNC offices making arrests, and Eugenio Martinez was trying to prevent the mysterious key from falling into police hands. From there, it was all downhill for the Nixon administration.

Had Dean ultimately ordered the break-ins to obtain potentially incriminating information related to the Watergate–Colombia Plaza ring, which was connected to his future wife via Heidi Rikan? With the specter of organized crime – chiefly, Rikan's relationship with Joe Nesline – in play and the rumors swirling about high-profile Washingtonians indulging in prostitution, it was certainly an explosive situation. Perhaps Dean was hoping to get out ahead of any revelations that might emerge from the investigation of Bailley and his impending conviction.

There are also other looming questions. Was there a connection between the Watergate call girl ring and the sorts of sexual-blackmail operations alleged to have been carried out by Edwin Wilson? Jim Hougan offers some provocative evidence. For instance, the "trick book" maintained by Lil' Lori (Barbara Ralabate) reportedly contained the names "Ed Wilson" and "Tungsten Park."[156] The "Tungsten Park" was clearly Tongsun Park. Furthermore, he writes that the apartment owned by "Tess" (Heidi Rikan) had been rented in the name of Phillip Bailley but had actually been paid for "by a wealthy defense contractor, a sometime lobbyist on Capitol Hill who owned a huge farm and claimed to 'hail' from Houston, Texas."[157] Each of these descriptions match Edwin Wilson, who had indeed spent time as a lobbyist (covertly working on behalf of the CIA), owned a sprawling farm in Virginia, and managed lucrative defense contracts via the TF-157 front companies – one of which, Aroundworld Shipping & Chartering, operated from Houston, Texas. The implications of this are immense. If Wilson and Park were indeed connected to the Watergate ring, then it was plugged into a network that encompassed the activities of Robert Keith Gray, the George Town Club, the internal politics of Task Force 157, and, ultimately, the forces seemingly aligning themselves against Richard Nixon.

Seen from this point of view, the Watergate incident, which imploded Nixon's presidency, appears less like a sloppy robbery gone awry and more like an elaborate frame-up, followed by a controlled demolition. The specter of the CIA in Watergate continued even into the trials that followed the unveiling of the break-ins, as evidenced by the man who was appointed as the Watergate special prosecutor, Leon Jaworski.

A partner at the Houston-based firm of Fulbright & Jaworski, Jaworski populated numerous boards and maintained affiliations with a wide gamut of powerful interests. He held the position of trustee at the M.D. Anderson Foundation, which had been established in the late 1930s to help build the now-famous medical center in Houston. Sometime towards the end of the 1950s, M.D. Anderson became a conduit for funds originating from the CIA. As trustee, Jaworski was aware of the nature of the funds, and had signed off on it – as had the foundation's president, John Freeman, who was a former partner at Jaworski's firm.[158]

Another Houston-based foundation moving CIA money in this same period was the San Jacinto Fund.[159] Heading the San Jacinto Fund was Ernest Cockrell Jr. – a board member of the wealthy Bank of the Southwest. Jaworski and his law partners could also be found here: a 1977 *Texas Monthly* article describes how "the partners had their closest and most lucrative relationship with the Bank of the Southwest. In addition to serving as the bank's legal counsel, members of the firm dominated the board of directors and occupied the top executive positions."[160] Another bank director was the businessman John de Menil, then the representative of Schlumberger oil interests in America.[161] Schlumberger would later be implicated in the covert support for the anti-Castro Cuban exiles, suggesting yet another CIA element in this network of individuals.[162]

By the time that the Watergate scandal had erupted, Jaworski could be found working closely with a veteran of those same anti-Castro operations, and one who played a prominent role in the events detailed in this chapter: Alexander Haig. The nature of this relationship was so particular that it saw Haig act as a channel for the flow of information to Jaworski, including some which had not been subpoenaed.[163] It seems that Haig was playing a direct, if shadowy, role in shaping the overall thrust of the Watergate prosecution.

THE PAGEBOY SCANDAL

The sordid story rumbling beneath the Watergate fiasco was not the only time that Robert Keith Gray's name would come up in connection with sexual-blackmail rings. As previously mentioned, John De-Camp's 1992 classic book on the Franklin scandal raised the specter of Gray – and his connections to Edwin Wilson – due to his close association with Harold Andersen, the publisher of the *Omaha World Herald* newspaper and a close ally of the man at the city of that particular web, Larry King. Andersen himself stood accused of being a willing participant in King's activities.

Nearly a decade earlier, Gray had surfaced in the course of an investigation into a purported sex-and-drug ring that allegedly operated on Capitol Hill. The scandal made a momentary splash in the media, but it is now merely a footnote. It began when Leroy Williams Jr., a congressional page – pages were high school students employed to fulfill various administrative tasks such as acting as couriers for congressmen – made startling accusations that he "had sex with three House members and procured homosexual prostitutes for a senator."[164] The latter incident was reported as having taken place at the Watergate office complex.[165]

Initial reports suggested that unnamed witnesses came forward with further information on sexual activities between politicians and pages, prostitution rings, and a connected drug ring operating on the Hill. *CBS Evening News* ran the story first on July 30, 1982, and the hints of drug abuse were quickly linked to arrests that had occurred several months earlier. On April 19, Douglas Marshall, Robert Finkel, and Troy Todd had been nabbed by undercover Washington, DC, Metropolitan Police for possession of cocaine; of the three, Marshall and Finkel were charged "with distributing and conspiring to distribute cocaine."[166] Todd and another accomplice, a young woman named Devon Dupres, were subsequently named as "unindicted co-conspirators."

Newspapers described Dupres as "a Georgetown cocktail waitress," though she appears to have been an assistant to Michael O'Harro, the owner of a DC discotheque called Tramps.[167] Others stated that she "reportedly socialized with a California congressman now under investigation by drug agents" and was subsequently entered into the "Justice Department federal witness program" and "moved to an undisclosed location."[168] This odd cast of characters operated a cocaine ring that employed the services of congressional pages, tour guides, and other Hill employees who enjoyed wide-ranging access to members of Congress. Douglas Marshall himself had been a page, while Robert Finkel had worked as an elevator operator in the Capitol. On July 7, Jack Anderson reported that "more than 15 members of congress were customers of a cocaine ring that operated on Capitol Hill, the ringleaders have told narcotics agents."[169] He also appeared on ABC News *Nightline* with Sam Donaldson, publicly linking the cocaine ring with the emerging allegations of prostitution and sexual abuse:

> Donaldson: All right, Jack, tell us about the page setup. Did you actually catch some pages involved as couriers?
>
> Mr. Anderson: There were some pages involved, but the drug scam … changed into a sex scam later. I know very little about the sex angle of it except that the same people were involved. Some of the same people.
>
> Donaldson: But pages were acting as couriers for the dealing of drugs?
>
> Mr. Anderson: That's correct. So were congressional aides.[170]

By the time that Anderson was making these accusations, an FBI investigation and a House Ethics Committee inquiry had formed to assess the possibilities of a sex-and-drugs ring on Capitol Hill. Oddly enough, old Watergate familiar Joseph Califano was put in charge of the inquiry. Califano's team employed a score of lawyers and investigators, including two private investigators – Richard Powers, a former New York City police officer, and John "Jack" Moriarty, a former DC police officer.

Gray's name came up in the inquiry from an anonymous tip, which was handled by Powers, who drafted a memo on it to Califano. The memo quickly disappeared.[171] The lead to Gray arose on July 21, when Ethics Committee counsel Donald Purdy and John Moriarty interviewed yet another figure from the Watergate days, DC police officer Carl Shoffler. Shoffler turned over the extensive information that he had compiled on Gray – his links to Edwin Wilson and the CIA, rumors of his involvement in the use and distribution of narcotics, wild tales of orgies taking place at his home in Rehoboth Beach.

The most alarming allegation made by Shoffler, however, was that a consultant for Diamond Shamrock, a major Texas-based oil and gas concern, and a local photographer personally known to Gray were involved in "a male prostitution service on Capitol Hill."[172] Diamond Shamrock was, at the time, a client of Gray & Co., an independent PR firm set up by Gray in the early 1980s.[173] Several weeks after he provided this information to Purdy and Moriarty, Shoffler was contacted by a security specialist with longtime intelligence ties, Michael Pilgrim.[174] Pilgrim wanted to know if Shoffler had been hired by H & K – Gray had left the firm to start Gray & Co. – to keep tabs on their former executive. Pilgrim, in turn, had been asked to assess Shoffler by Neil Livingstone, yet another strange character from the murky netherworld where intelligence and Beltway subterfuge intersected.

Livingstone, who will be discussed at greater length in the next chapter, was at the time working for Gray at Gray & Co. while also maintaining extensive ties to the circles around Ted Shackley, Thomas Clines, and Edwin Wilson that went back to the mid-1970s. The arrival of Livingstone on the scene raised even more puzzling questions. As Susan Trento asked: "How did Livingstone find out that Shoffler had received allegations about Gray?"[175]

The day after his encounter with Pilgrim, Shoffler was contacted by Thomas Fortuin, Gray's attorney. It was an interesting choice for a lawyer as, in 1981, Fortuin had taken over from Roy Cohn as the chief attorney for Tony Salerno, the boss of the Genovese crime family.[176] These ties may have run deep – Gray was reportedly a friend of Cohn, though – as previously mentioned, the exact nature of their relationship remains vague.

A year after the pageboy scandal first broke, Salerno arranged for the appointment of Jackie Presser as president of the Teamsters Union.[177] Presser was a client and close associate of Gray; the two may have even owned a mysterious company together called Member Services Corporation.[178] Fortuin offered Shoffler the opportunity to interview Gray, with the clarification that Gray would deny the allegations that Shoffler had made to Purdy and Moriarty. He then added that it was Moriarty himself who had turned over the information to Gray's associates. It was an incredible conflict of interest: in addition to working on the Ethics Committee probe, both Moriarty and Powers were moonlighting on behalf of Gray & Co. Powers himself was a longtime associate of Fortuin, who had employed Powers as his own private investigator.[179] In a subsequent meeting with Powers, Shoffler himself was offered a job working for Gray – at a very lucrative salary. Shoffler saw this as an attempted bribe and reported it to the US Attorney. Very soon a sweeping Department of Justice investigation was underway.

On September 28, 1982, the *New York Times* ran an article stamped with the title "Califano suspends 2 investigators in Congress sex and drugs inquiry."[180] These two investigators were identified as Powers and Moriarty. Califano "did not return repeated calls to his office, and Justice Department officials declined to disclose the nature of the charges against Mr. Moriarty and Mr. Powers."[181]

After the Moriarty and Powers debacle, the entire episode came to a close, much more quietly than it had begun. More questions than satisfactory answers were raised. In the final Ethics Committee reported, Califano cited evidence that the US Capitol Police had systematically destroyed documentary records related to drug trafficking on the Hill – including vital documents put together in the critical month of July 1982 when the accusations first began to gain momentum. While the report suggested that disciplinary action in connection with the destruction might be warranted, there was insufficient evidence "to conclude that the records ... contained information important to the Committee's investigation of illicit drug use or distribution of drugs."[182]

The allegations of sexual abuse of pages and homosexual prostitution were also soon swept to the side. Leroy Williams, the page who first came forward, suddenly recanted. He told investigators working on behalf of the Ethics Committee that he "concocted the tale of sexual misconduct and drug use to draw public attention to the pressures of the page system."[183] Importantly, the congressman with whom he had claimed to have had sex – Larry Craig of Idaho – was himself a member of the House Ethics Committee.[184] In 2007, Craig was arrested after propositioning an undercover police officer for sex in the men's restroom of the Minneapolis-Saint Paul International Airport.[185]

Endnotes

1   Susan Trenton, *The Power House: Robert Keith Gray and the Selling of Influence and Access in Washington* (St. Martin's, 1992), 11. https://archive.org/details/powerhouserobert00tren.

2   Trento, *Power House*, 17.

3   Trento, *Power House*, 17.

4   Edward J. Epstein, *Dossier: The Secret History of Armand Hammer* (Random House, 1996), 322.

5   Trento, *Power House*, 370.

6   "Knowlton, Donald Snow," *Encyclopedia of Cleveland History*, May 11, 2018, https://case.edu/ech/articles/k/knowlton-donald-snow; Robert L. Heath, *Encyclopedia of Public Relations* (SAGE Publications, 2013), 418; "Tough Problems Were His Hobby," *Brooklyn Eagle*, April 10th, 1927.

7   Karen Miller, "'Air Power Is Peace Power' The Aircraft Industry's Campaign for Public and Political Support, 1943–1949," *Business History Review*, Vol. 70, no. 3 (1996): 297–327, https://doi.org/10.2307/3117240.

8   Heath, *Encyclopedia of Public Relations*, 419.

9   Trento, *Power House*, 99.

10   Joseph John Trento, *Prelude to Terror : The Rogue CIA and the Legacy of America's Private Intelligence Network* (New York : Carroll & Graf, 2005), p. xvi, http://archive.org/details/preludetoterrorr00tren.

11   "Cryptonym: WUSALINE," https://www.maryferrell.org/php/cryptdb.php?id=WUSALINE.

12   Trento, *Power House*, 106.

13   Peter Dale Scott, *The War Conspiracy: The Secret Road to the Secret Indochina War* (Indianapolis: Bobbs-Merrill, 1972), https://archive.org/details/warconspiracys00scot.

14   Scott, *War Conspiracy*, 7.

15   "Subject: Earl Scheib," *The President John F. Kennedy Assassination Records Collection*, March 1, 1962, FBI Record 124-10328-10003, https://www.archives.gov/files/research/jfk/releases/docid-32313329.pdf.

16   Catherine Forslund. *Anna Chennault: Informal Diplomacy and Asian Relations* (Rowman & Littlefield, 2002), 101.

17   Trento, *Power House*, 98.

18   Glenn Michael Speer, "Richard Nixon's Position on Communist China, 1949-1960: The Evolution of a Pacific Strategy," *CUNY Graduate Center*, 1992, 15-16, https://academicworks.cuny.edu/cgi/viewcontent.cgi?article=2513&context=gc_etds.

19   J. C. Louis and Harvey Z. Yazijan, *Cola Wars: The Story of the Global Battle between the Coca-Cola Company and PepsiCo, Inc* (Everest House, 1980), 115.

20   "Home - The George Town Club," https://www.georgetownclub.org/.

21   Phil McCombs, "Tongsun Park's Club," *Washington Post*, October 16, 1977, https://www.washingtonpost.com/archive/opinions/1977/10/16/tongsun-parks-club/fc4e8ef5-f79b-4a55-b458-25bb6eeea07a/.

22   *Korean Influence Inquiry: Executive Session Hearings Before the Select Committee on Ethics of the United States Senate*, Ninety-fifth Congress, Second Session, 1978. p. 316.

23   Richard M. Gibson, *The Secret Army: Chiang Kai-Shek and the Drug Warlords of the Golden Triangle* (South Tower Singapore: John Wiley & Sons (Asia), 2011), 58-63.

24   Peter Dale Scott, "Operation Paper: The United States and Drugs in Thailand and Burma," no. 2, no. 44 (November 1, 2010), https://apjjf.org/-Peter-Dale-Scott/3436/article.html.

25   "Life Line Tax Status Queried," *Broadcasting: The Businessweekly of Television and Radio*, September 7, 1964, 72.

26   David Clayton, *Imperialism Revisited: Political and Economic Relations Between Britain and China, 1950-54* (Palgrave Macmillan, 1997), 25; Harvey Klehr and Ronald Radosh, *The Amerasia Spy Case: Prelude to McCarthyism* (Chapel Hill: University of North Carolina Press, 1996) 207, https://archive.org/details/amerasiaspycasep0000kleh.

27   Peter Dale Scott, *Deep Politics and the Death of JFK* (University of California Press, 1996), 212.

28   Maxine Cheshire and Charles Babcock, "Tongsun Park and the Korean CIA," *Washington Post*, August 28, 1977, https://www.washingtonpost.com/archive/politics/1977/08/28/tongsun-park-and-the-korean-ciacia-had-reason-to-know-of-parks-ties-to-korean-ciapapers-interviews-show-scope-of-parks-korean-cia-link/99cdbf98-965e-4c6a-a333-f7c146cfc445/.

29   *Korean Influence Inquiry: Executive Hearings Before the Select Committee on the Ethics of the United States Senate*, Ninety-Fifth Congress, Second Session, Vol. 1, (US Government Printing Office, 1978), 152.

30   Nicholas Von Hoffman, *Citizen Cohn* (1st ed. New York: Doubleday, 1988), 364.

31   *Congressional Quarterly Weekly Report 29*: January-December 1971, 1134.

32   Sally Denton and Roger Morris, *The Money and the Power: The Making of Las Vegas and Its Hold on America, 1947-2000*, 1st ed (New York: Alfred A. Knopf, 2001), 316.

33   Scott, *Deep Politics*, 202-5.

34   Peter Dale Scott, *The War Conspiracy: JFK, 9/11, and the Deep Politics of War*, ePub (Sky-horse, 2013), 240.

35   Scott, *War Conspiracy: JFK, 9/11, and the Deep Politics of War*, 241.

36   Kim Scipes, *AFL-CIO's Secret War against Developing Country Workers* (Lexington Books, 2011), 54-60.

37   Trento, *Prelude to Terror*, 40.

38   Trento, *Power House*, 108.

39   Peter Maas, *Manhunt: The Incredible Pursuit of a CIA Agent Turned Terrorist* (Random House 1986), 32.

40   Trento, *Power House*, 181.

41   Jim Hougan, *Secret Agenda: Watergate, Deep Throat, and the CIA* (Random House 1984), 120.

42   Hougan, *Secret Agenda*, 120.

43   John W. DeCamp, *The Franklin Cover-Up: Child Abuse, Satanism, and Murder in Nebraska* (Nebraska: AWT, 1992), 178.

44   DeCamp, *Franklin Cover-Up*, 177.

45   DeCamp, *Franklin Cover-Up*, 179.

46   Jean-Guy Allard, "Philip Agee Versus the CIA," *CounterPunch.org*, January 21, 2008. https://www.counterpunch.org/2008/01/21/philip-agee-versus-the-cia/.

47   Andrea Conception, "The Mystery of the JM Wave," *Distraction*, February 10, 2018, https://www.distractionmagazine.com/the-mystery-of-the-jm-wave/; Peter Dale Scott, "Document: Transnationalised Repression Parafascism and the US," Wikispooks, https://wikispooks.com/wiki/Document:Transnationalised_Repression_Parafascism_and_the_US.

48   Trento, *Prelude to Terror*, 29.

49   Jim Drinkhall, "CIA Helped Quash Major, Star-Studded Tax Evasion Case," *Washington Post*, April 24, 1980, https://www.washingtonpost.com/archive/politics/1980/04/24/cia-helped-quash-major-star-studded-tax-evasion-case/a55ddf06-2a3f-4e04-a687-a3dd87c32b82/.

50   Listing of Traffic Removed from C/WHD Files Watergate File Research, April 24, 1974, https://www.archives.gov/files/research/jfk/releases/2018/104-10095-10326.pdf.

51   Alfred McCoy, *The Politics of Heroin: CIA Complicity in the Global Drug Trade* (Lawrence Hill Books, 2003), 212-13.

52   McCoy, *Politics of Heroin*, 212-13; Frank Browning and Banning Garrett, "The New Opium War," *Wisconsin Historical Society*, p. 6, https://content.wisconsinhistory.org/digital/collection/p15932coll8/id/54609/.

53   McCoy, *Politics of Heroin*, 254.

54   McCoy, *Politics of Heroin*, 318.

55   Richard Secord and Jay Wurts, *Honored and Betrayed: Irangate, Covert Affairs, and the Secret War in Laos* (Wiley, 1992), 20-60.

56   Trento, *Prelude to Terror*, 41.

57   Trento, *Prelude to Terror*, 47.

58   Jeffrey T. Richelson, ed., "The Pentagon's Spies," *National Security Archive*, George Wash-

ington University, May 23, 2001, https://nsarchive2.gwu.edu/NSAEBB/NSAEBB46/.

59   Michael McClintock, *Instruments of Statecraft: U.S. Guerilla Warfare, Counterinsurgency, and Counterterrorism, 1940-1990*, chap. 4, https://www.statecraft.org/chapter4.html.

60   Jeffrey T. Richelson, "Task Force 157: The US Navy's Secret Intelligence Service, 1966-77," *Intelligence and National Security*, Vol. 11, no. 1 (January 1996): 109.

61   Richelson, "Task Force 157," 110.

62   Richelson, "Task Force 157," 122-23.

63   Maas, *Manhunt*, 48.

64   Maas, *Manhunt*, 48; Trento, *Prelude to Terror*, 52.

65   Maas, *Manhunt*, 49.

66   Hougan, *Secret Agenda*, 71.

67   Sajit Gandhi, ed., "The Tilt: The US and the South Asian Crisis of 1971," *National Security Archive*, George Washington University, Dec. 16, 2002, https://nsarchive2.gwu.edu/NSAEBB/NSAEBB79/.

68   Gandhi, "Tilt."

69   Clark Mollenhoff, "Kissinger Doesn't Get High Mark on Anderson Papers," *Courier-Post* (Camden, New Jersey), January 22, 1972.

70   Mollenhoff, "Anderson Papers."

71   David R. Young, "Memorandum for the President Re: Record of Investigation into Disclosure of Classified Information in Jack Anderson Articles December 14 and 16, 1971 on Indian/Pakistan Confrontation," http://nixontapes.org/welander/Young_memo_to_Nixon.pdf .

72   Len Colodny and Robert Gettlin, *Silent Coup: The Removal of the President* (St. Martin's Press, 1992), 22.

73   Colodny and Gettlin, *Silent Coup*, 24.

74   Colodny and Gettlin, *Silent Coup*, 30.

75   Hougan, *Secret Agenda*, 75.

76   R. T. Naylor, *Hot Money and the Politics of Debt* (Linden Pub, 1987), 155-56; Richard Halloran, "Papers Link Bank to K.C.I.A. Aide in Stock Disposal," *New York Times*, Nov. 2, 1977.

77   Richard Halloran, "Inquiry Suggests Korean Agents Tried to Gain Control of Bank in US," *New York Times*, May 31, 1977.

78   Jonathan Marshall, *Dark Quadrant: Organized Crime, Big Business, and the Corruption of American Democracy*, Kindle (Lanham: Rowman & Littlefield, 2021), n. 127, https://rowman.com/WebDocs/Dark_Quadrant_Extra_Notes.pdf.

79   Emma North-Best, "FBI Evidence Points to Journalist Jack Anderson's Role in Watergate," *MuckRock*, Dec. 7, 2017, https://www.muckrock.com/news/archives/2017/dec/07/jack-anderson-watergate/.

80   Hougan, *Secret Agenda*, 79.

81   Lisa Pease, *A Lie Too Big to Fail: The Real History of the Assassination of Robert F. Kennedy*, Kindle (Feral House, 2018), 732–55.

82   Hougan, *Secret Agenda*, 78.

83   Shane O'Sullivan, *Dirty Tricks: Nixon, Watergate, and the CIA*. (La Vergne: Hot Books, 2018), 248.

84   "Memorandum for the Record, Subject: Project Artichoke," National Security Archive, George Washington University, Jan. 31, 1975, https://nsarchive2.gwu.edu/NSAEBB/NSAEBB438/st02.pdf.

85   "Subject: Project Artichoke."

86   Hougan, *Secret Agenda*, 13.

87   *Rockefeller Commission Report* (1975), 249, History Matters Archive, https://history-matters.com/archive/church/rockcomm/html/Rockefeller_0131a.htm.

88   Anna Lvovsky, *Vice Patrol: Cops, Courts, and the Struggle Over Urban Gay Life Before Stonewall* (Chicago: University of Chicago Press, 2021), 106.

89   Evan Thomas, *The Man to See* (Simon & Schuster, 2012), 59-60.

90   Lvovsky, *Vice Patrol*, 106.

91   William Conrad Gibbons, *The US Government and the Vietnam War: Executive and Legislative Roles and Relationships, Part IV* (Princeton University Press, 2014), 857.

92   O'Sullivan, *Dirty Tricks*, 252.

93   O'Sullivan, *Dirty Tricks*, 515.

94   O'Sullivan, *Dirty Tricks*, 251.

95   O'Sullivan, *Dirty Tricks*, 251.

96   O'Sullivan, *Dirty Tricks*, 247-48.

97   Robert M. Hathaway and Russell Jack Smith, *Richard Helms As Director of Central Intelligence* (Center for the Study of Intelligence, 1993), 8, https://archive.org/details/Richard-Helms-CIA.

98   Hathaway and Smith, *Richard Helms*, 9.

99   Hougan, *Secret Agenda*, 202.

100   Hougan, *Secret Agenda*, 232.

101   Joseph A. Califano Jr., "Timothy Naftali interview transcription," *Nixon Library documents*, April 3, 2007, https://www.nixonlibrary.gov/sites/default/files/virtuallibrary/documents/histories/califano-2007-04-03.pdf.

102   Joseph A. Califano Jr., "ICCA: Report on status of implementation of actions designed to counter subversion," Califano Papers (box 2, folder 26), July 18, 1963.

103   Gus Russo, *Live by the Sword: The Secret War against Castro and the Death of JFK* (Bancroft Press, 1998), 163.

104   "Cuban Contingency Planning," Joint Chiefs of Staff Debrief Item Re Cuban Actions, January 23, 1964, https://www.maryferrell.org/showDoc.html?docId=10249.

105   Hougan, *Secret Agenda*, 264.

106   "Entry into Democratic National Headquarters," JFK Assassination Records, NARA Record Number: 104-10256-10268 https://www.maryferrell.org/showDoc.html?docId=161720&relPageId=9

107   Colodny and Gettlin, *Silent Coup*, 70.

108   Colodny and Gettlin, *Silent Coup*, 70.

109   Colodny and Gettlin, *Silent Coup*, 70-71.

110   Colodny and Gettlin, *Silent Coup*, 71.

111   Robert Gettlin, "Author Reflects on Watergate and 'Deep Throat,'" Fredericksburg.com, July 16, 2005, https://fredericksburg.com/town_and_countyother_history/author-reflects-on-watergate-and-deep-throat-robert-co-author-of-silent-coup-1991-watergate/article_b85944c7-3b85-50c4-a339-c184b9386fa1.html.

112   Jim Hougan, "Hougan, Liddy, the Post and Watergate," *Investigative Notes*, June 22, 2011, http://jimhougan.com/wordpress/?p=11.

113   Hougan, "Hougan, Liddy, the Post and Watergate."

114   Hougan, "Hougan, Liddy, the Post and Watergate."

115   Colodny and Gettlin, *Silent Coup*, 63.

116   Anthony J. Lukas, *Nightmare: The Underside of the Nixon Years* (Penguin, 2008), 201.

117   Lukas, *Nightmare*, 201.

118   Hougan, *Secret Agenda*, 115.

119   Hougan, *Secret Agenda*, 115.

120   Hougan, *Secret Agenda*, 116.

121   O'Sullivan, *Dirty Tricks*, 267.

122   Phil Stanford, *White House Call Girl: The Real Watergate Story* (Feral House, 2013), 69.

123   Colodny and Gettlin, *Silent Coup*, 156.

124   Hougan, *Secret Agenda*, 39.

125   Colodny and Gettlin, *Silent Coup*.

126   Colodny and Gettlin, *Silent Coup*.

127   See Scott, *Deep Politics*, 232-35.

128   Maureen Dean and Hays Gorey, *"Mo": A Woman's View of Watergate* (Simon & Schuster, 1975), 40.

129   Marshall, *Dark Quadrant*, 283-86.

130   Peter Brewton, *The Mafia, CIA, and George Bush* (S.P.I. Books, 1992), 98-100.

131   Stanford, *White House Call Girl*, 158n23.

132   Marshall, *Dark Quadrant*, 236-39.

133   Brewton, *Mafia, CIA, and Bush*, 23-26.

134   Colodny and Gettlin, *Silent Coup*, 164.

135   "Report on Joseph Francis Nesline," FBI Criminal Intelligence Program, Miami, November 15, 1963.

136   Scott, *Deep Politics*, 240.

137   *Report of the Select Committee on Assassinations: Findings and Recommendations*, US House of Representatives, Ninety-Fifth Congress, Second Session, March 29, 1979, 154.

138   Alan A. Block, *Masters of Paradise: Organized Crime and the Internal Revenue Service in the Bahamas* (Routledge, 1991) 50.

139   Lindo Minor, "Off the Boards," *Quixotic Joust*, March 30, 2011, https://quixoticjoust.blogspot.com/2011/03/off-boards.html?m=1

140   Minor, "Off the Boards."

141   "Subject: Joseph Shimon," FBI, May 29, 1962, https://www.maryferrell.org/showDoc.html?docId=116549

142   "Subject: Joseph Shimon."

143   "Subject: Joseph Shimon."

144   "Subject: Joseph Shimon."

145   Hougan, *Secret Agenda*, 116-17; Colodny and Gettlin, *Silent Coup*, 130-31.

146   Colodny and Gettlin, *Silent Coup*, 130.

147   Colodny and Gettlin, *Silent Coup*, 136.

148   Hougan, *Secret Agenda*, 112.

149   Stanford, *White House Call Girl*, 78.

150   Stanford, *White House Call Girl*, 106.

151   Colodny and Gettlin, *Silent Coup*, 147.

152   Colodny and Gettlin, *Silent Coup*, 148.

153   Colodny and Gettlin, *Silent Coup*, 149.

154   Hougan, *Secret Agenda*, 111.

155   Colodny and Gettlin, *Silent Coup*, 152.

156   Hougan, *Secret Agenda*, 121.

157   Hougan, *Secret Agenda*, 121.

158   "Leon Jaworski Etex 'Man of the Month,'" *Tyler Courier Times*, November 27, 1960; "Jaworski Reportedly Had Role in Setting Up C.I.A. Aid Conduit," *New York Times*, November 6, 1973.

159   "Texas, Philanthropy, 007, and the Varsity Drag," *Texas Observer*, March 3, 1967.

160   Harry Hurt III, "Have Conscience, Will Travel," *Texas Monthly*, November 1977, 260.

161   Sophy Burnham, "The Manhattan Arrangement of Art and Money," *New York*, December 8, 1969, 38.

162   James DiEugenio, *Destiny Betrayed: JFK, Cuba, and the Garrison Case*, Kindle (New York: Skyhorse Publishing, 2012), 255–58; Russo, *Live by the Sword*, 153.

163   Colodny and Gettlin, *Silent Coup*, 386-396.

164   Andy Davis, "NLR Teen's Allegations Surface in Light of Craig Arrest," *Arkansas Democrat Gazette*, August 31, 2007, https://www.arkansasonline.com/news/2007/aug/31/nlr-teens-allegations-surface-light-craig-20070831/.

165   Robert Pear, "Authorities Meet on Capitol Sex and Drug Inquiry," *New York Times*, July 8, 1982, https://www.nytimes.com/1982/07/08/us/authorities-meet-on-capitol-sex-and-drug-inquiry.html.

166   "Report on the Investigation Pursuant to House Resolution 12 Concerning Alleged Illicit Uses or Distribution of Drugs By Members, Officers, or Employees of the House," House of Representatives, 98th Congress, 1st Session, Report no. 98-559, Nov. 17, 1983, https://ethics.house.gov/

sites/ethics.house.gov/files/Hrpt98-559%20pt.%201.pdf.

167   Robert Gearty and Joseph Volz, "Pol Snorts at Coke Use Rap," *Daily News*, Jan. 22, 1983

168   Robert Gearty and Joseph Volz, "Probe Senator in Coke Case," *Daily News*, Jan. 15, 1983; Gearty and Volz, "Pol Snorts at Coke Use Rap."

169   "Report on the Investigation Pursuant to House Resolution 12," 18.

170   "Report on the Investigation Pursuant to House Resolution 12," 8.

171   Trento, *Power House*, 176.

172   Trento, *Power House*, 177.

173   Sari Horwitz, "Gray & Co.," *Washington Post*, Sept. 6, 1984, https://www.washingtonpost.com/archive/business/1984/09/06/gray-38/7cf190f1-e247-4e06-803b-6c6dcdc6c35a/.

174   Trento, *Power House*, 177.

175   Trento, *Power House*, 177.

176   *Daily Labor Reports*, vols. 21-40, Bureau of National Affairs, 1981, 5.

177   Arnold H. Lubasch, "Mob Figures Chose Teamsters' Chief, Government Says," Nov. 25, 1986, https://www.nytimes.com/1986/11/25/nyregion/mob-figures-chose-teamsters-chief-government-says.html.

178   Trento, *Power House*, 203.

179   Trento, *Power House*, 177-79.

180   Leslie Maitland, "Califano Suspends 2 Investigators in Congress Sex and Drugs Inquiry," *New York Times*, Sept. 26, 1982, https://www.nytimes.com/1982/09/26/us/califano-suspends-2-investigators-in-congress-sex-and-drug-inquiry.html.

181   Maitland, "Califano Suspends 2 Investigators."

182   "Report on the Investigation Pursuant to House Resolution 12," 161.

183   "Leroy Williams, the former page whose tales of sex …," *UPI*, Aug. 27, 1982, https://www.upi.com/Archives/1982/08/27/Leroy-Williams-the-former-page-whose-tales-of-sex/8930399268800/.

184   Davis, "NLR Teen's Allegations Surface."

185   *New York Times*, "Senator, Arrested at Airport, Pleads Guilty," *New York Times*, August 28, 2007, https://www.nytimes.com/2007/08/28/washington/28craig.html.

CHAPTER 6

A PRIVATE CIA

CHANGING TIMES

During the Watergate affair, Henry Kissinger appeared as something of an outsider, even though he had entered the administration as a favored intellectual scion of the Rockefeller-dominated "Eastern Establishment." His positions on the easing of tensions with the Soviet Union, arms reduction, and opening to China put him out of step with the robust, semi-covert network of spooks, lobbyists, power brokers, and businessmen who were oriented toward the Nationalist Chinese, toward rolling back the Soviets through military means, and increasing defense budgets. Until the Watergate scandal, the lines seemed starkly drawn. But, as time wore on, the battles between liberal reformers and hardliners reached a fever pitch, and certain lines seemed to bend and blur.

Kissinger, in particular, appeared to have undergone something of a geopolitical reorientation, retooling his commitments to reflect the new power bloc. In the latter part of the 1970s, he took up a post at the Center for the Institute of International Studies. As Jerry Sanders has noted, the Center and its partner organization, the American Enterprise Institute, "set themselves up in competition with such august bodies as the Council on Foreign Relations and the Trilateral Commission."[1] The Center's director was Ray Cline, an old China Lobby hand, OSS veteran (having served in the China theater alongside notables such as Paul Helliwell, E. Howard Hunt, and John K. Singlaub), and a high-ranking CIA officer. Cline had been a consistent critic of the Nixon-Kissinger policies of detente and opening to China.

To acclimate properly to his new affiliations and associates, Kissinger adopted a harsh line on the ongoing arms reduction talks with the Soviet Union. It was indicative, he said, of a "defeatist consensus" accepted by the "traditional establishment."[2] By this point, a robust network of New Right activist groups, think-tanks, advocacy groups, and their conservative backers had formed to push back against detente policies and arms reduction, calling instead for an increase in military spending and more hawkish orientation toward the Soviets. Many of these were organized from classic centers of power like the American Security Council, an entity described as the "heart and soul of the military-industrial complex,"[3] the Committee on the Present Danger, the Heritage Foundation (where Robert Keith Gray maintained a post), and the AFL-CIO.

New groups such the Conservative Caucus, the Coalition for Peace through Strength, and the Free Congress Foundation also dotted the landscape, drawing on money unleashed by philanthropies such as the Scaife, Olin, and Koch foundations. Other active players in this world included Reverend Moon's Unification Church, which was tied very closely to the China Lobby and to the KCIA. Two of the Unification Church's top US allies were Ray Cline and Alexander Haig.[4] Managing a sizable portion of the Unification Church's promotional campaigns and serving in a secretarial role in many of its front groups was the political direct-mail mastermind Richard Viguerie. A member of the George Town Club, Viguerie was associated with numerous groups during this period, carrying out work on behalf of the Conservative Caucus and the various anti-disarmament campaigns launched by organizations such as the Committee on the Present Danger and its allies. All of these activities were run from Viguerie's headquarters, a building he owned at 7777 Leesburg Pike in Falls Church, Virginia. It was a location that came to play a fundamental role in the world of Ted Shackley, Edwin Wilson, and Thomas Clines.

Reformist efforts, nevertheless, continued to build. One such reformer was Admiral Bobby Ray Inman, who had risen through the ranks to become director of Naval Intelligence in 1974. He followed this with stints as head of the Defense Intelligence Agency, the National Security Agency, and then, briefly, as deputy director of the CIA under William Casey. Inman privileged signal intelligence – intelligence acquired via electronic means as opposed to human intelligence gathering methods – and had a strong distaste for what he perceived as waste, inefficiency, and redundancy within the intelligence community. He was also seen as a something of a moderate, a counterpoint to those fixated on covert operations and assassination programs such as those favored by Shackley and his clique.

In 1976, Task Force 157 was on the chopping block. For Inman, "it was an expensive unit of dubious benefit to the Navy."[5] There were also the rumors and hints that TF-157, via Wilson, had become embroiled in covert operations quite different from its stated mandate. In 1975, for example, Wilson entered into a series of curious business arrangements with Bernie Houghton of Nugan Hand, a bank headquartered in Australia whose management consisted predominately of supposed former US intelligence officials.[6]

Houghton himself was no stranger to the circle of individuals around Wilson, having worked in Vietnam in close proximity to the primary operators in Shackley's secret wars.[7] At the time that Houghton was meeting up with Wilson, the Nugan Hand Bank appears to have been involved in brokering the sale of arms to paramilitaries in South Africa. The financing of the arms was arranged through a web of banks such as Nugan Hand's Hong Kong subsidiary. Yet, when it came to purchasing and shipping the arms, Houghton and his partner, Michael Hand, turned to Edwin Wilson. According to an official Australian government report on the criminal activities of the Nugan Hand Bank:

> There was a number of meetings between Wilson, Houghton, and the others over a relatively short period of time. Subsequently, under the cover of Task Force 157, Wilson placed an order for something like "10 million rounds of ammunition, 3,000 weapons including machine guns, M-1 carbines, and others." The shipment is believed to have left the US from Boston. The End Users' certificate indicated that [Wilson's TF-157 front company] World Marine was the US purchasing agent while the middle company or buyer's agent was an Australian company but not Nugan Hand. The name given as the buyer was Portuguese, and was a name that had been used previously and possibly after by World Marine in other unrelated covert operations.[8]

Rumors also abounded that TF-157 and Nugan Hand were complicit in the destabilization of the Australian government of Gough Whitlam, which was considering closing the CIA's satellite monitoring station called Pine Gap. Alarms about Whitlam's intentions were raised in the halls of the CIA by none other than Shackley; according to Victor Marchetti, a high-ranking CIA officer, Whitlam "caused apoplexy in the White House … a kind of Chile [coup] was set in motion."[9] Likely with these and other incidents in mind, Inman determined that TF-157 was "out of control."[10] Wilson attempted to negotiate with the naval intelligence chief, suggesting that if TF-157 were shut down, perhaps another, more effective organization should be set up (with Wilson getting the lucrative contracts to run it, of course). Shackley also attempted to intercede, suggesting to Inman that shuttering the program and firing Wilson would be the "loss of a major intelligence asset. Inman told Shackley that if he found Wilson so valuable, he could put him back on the CIA payroll."[11]

TF-157 was ultimately shut down, and Wilson was, by all appearances at least, out of the job. At that same moment, events were taking place that would ultimately lead to Wilson's downfall. In December 1975, shortly before Inman's decision to dismantle TF-157 began, Wilson met a former CIA operative named Frank Terpil. Terpil ran a company called Intercontinental Technology, a subsidiary of Stanford Technology – a firm that would feature prominently in the Iran-Contra affair.[12] Stanford's owner was Albert Hakim, an Iranian businessman who acted as a back channel between Iran and Israel.[13]

By the time he met Terpil, Wilson was already familiar with Hakim, as they had been introduced by Richard Secord. Terpil proposed to Wilson a business venture that involved scouring weapons and other sensitive technologies for the government of Muammar Gaddafi in Libya. Terpil had been trading with Libya through a partnership with a Pennsylvania businessman named James McElroy. McElroy, according to Peter Maas, "had been one of the first entrepreneurs to cash in on money-flush OPEC oil nations in Africa and the Middle East. McElroy began supplying them with everything from Pampers to pistols. Gradually Libya became one of his big customers, and from Pampers, it was more and more pistols."[14] But what the Libyans hoped to score, from Terpil and Wilson, was heavier equipment: "C-4 plastic explosives and a Red-Eye Missile."[15]

With the approval of Shackley and Clines, Wilson went to work in Libya. The operation quickly expanded into a training program for Libyan fighters. To carry this out, Wilson and Terpil set up a cover company called Inter-Technology and several other export firms. Former CIA officers like Kevin Mulcahy were brought in to run them, while the secret training school was staffed by former Green Berets.[16] Among the trainers was Eugene Tafoya, "a beefy, acne-scarred thug, widely disliked by his comrades, who after a few glasses of 'flash,' the Libyan equivalent of bathtub gin, would boast about all the people he'd blown away behind enemy lines in Vietnam."[17] Soon enough Tafoya was working as a hitman for Wilson and was outsourced to the Libyan government for an ultimately ill-fated assassination plot against political dissidents living abroad.[18] All the while Wilson reported information back to Shackley and Clines and, reportedly, to the SAVAK – the Iranian intelligence apparatus under the Shah – as well.

At this point, Shackley's star was continuing to rise within the CIA. In January 1976, George H.W.Bush was made President Gerald Ford's director of the CIA, and Shackley was made assistant deputy director for Operations. His coveted position was director of central intelligence, and he fully expected to serve as Bush's successor: "Shackley had been tapped to become CIA director if Gerald Ford had been re-elected president."[19] This, however, never came to pass. Ford didn't win the election and was instead succeeded by President Jimmy Carter. Bush was ousted from his position as director of central intelligence and replaced by a reformist, Admiral Stansfield Turner.

Turner came from outside the world of the CIA. A career military officer, he was a former schoolmate of Carter's and was selected to reorganize the CIA. Large swaths of the Agency dedicated to undercover operations and special warfare were systematically removed, fundamentally changing the character and culture of the CIA. Shackley held on for a while, compartmentalizing what remained in the directorate of Operations and hiding it from the watchful eyes of Carter and Turner.

In 1979, Shackley retired from the CIA to dedicate himself to a series of private business ventures. In reality, these ventures were components of a private intelligence network that he had been designing over the course of several years. The long-term plan was to use this private CIA as the foundation for a rollback of Carter's reforms, when a Republican president would inevitably succeed him. This private network, unsurprisingly, quickly found itself embroiled in a series of international scandals.

Much of Shackley's network was bankrolled with money provided by Wilson. According to FBI memoranda, published as part of a later report by the Congressional Committee Investing the Iran-Contra affair, Wilson provided Clines with a loan to organize a company called International Research and Trade (IRT), which acted as a corporate umbrella for two other Clines-owned companies. These were System Services International (SSI) and API Distributors.

SSI, registered in Bermuda, was later described by Shackley as "designed originally to be a trading company [for] securities." According to his testimony during the Iran-Contra hearings, SSI did very little business.[20] This was soon revealed to be untrue. API Distributors, registered as a Delaware corporation, was organized to act as a supplier for oil companies. One of its primary clients was Pemex, the Mexican state-owned petroleum firm. It set up shop in Houston, Texas, where it shared offices with Wilson's Aroundworld Shipping. API had a tendency to bring into the fold old veterans of the Agency's secret wars. Rafael Quintero and Ricardo Chavez, both old recruits who operated under the auspices of JM/WAVE, were put on the API payroll and dispatched to Mexico, ostensibly to work on the Pemex project.[21]

When questioned about his role in these companies, Shackley offered only vague responses. For SSI, he did some sort of unspecified work, while for API he "worked as a consultant, employee, office manager, trying to get the company off the ground."[22] He told the FBI that he had not played any role whatsoever in IRT, stating that he only had passing knowledge of this Clines-owned parent company. Despite Shackley's efforts to distance himself, numerous figures associated with the private CIA – people like Clines, Wilson, and Richard Secord – "told the FBI and other government agencies that it was quite clear that Shackley was the boss."[23]

Further evidence comes from the curious office arrangement of Research Associates International, the "consultancy and risk analysis" firm Shackley launched in 1979.[24] Just as API Distributors shared office space with Wilson's Aroundworld Shipping, Research Associates International shared offices with SSI and International Research and Trade.[25] RAI's staff included multiple Shackley associates from his CIA days. Directors of the firm included Jim Critchfield, Donald Jameson, and a mysterious "Mr. Ledbetter," who may have actually been Calvin Hicks. If so, Hicks would have known Shackley from his JM/WAVE days.[26]

Research Associates International was formed with a specific focus on the oil industry, and it appears to have only had one, exclusive, client: John Deuss (deceptively spelled as "Dois" in the transcripts of Shackley's Iran-Contra testimony). Deuss, through an expansive corporate web organized around Transworld Oil, moved in the murky world of oil trading where he worked with the likes of the infamous commodity trader (and Mossad asset) Marc Rich. Between 1979, when he first hired Shackley's Research Associates International, and 1993, Deuss dominated South Africa's oil imports, with Transworld Oil accounting "for more than half of South Africa's oil purchases."[27] Aside from Deuss, the other giants of this trade – which was essential for the maintenance of the apartheid regime – were Marc Rich and Marimpex, a German oil-trading company. As will be noted later in Chapter 16, a former "girlfriend" of Epstein's, Francis Jardine, later married John Deuss. Jardine accompanied Epstein to the Clinton White House in September 1994.

Shackley and Deuss intersected through Shackley's massive web of contacts. The introduction between the two was made by Michael Corrie, then serving as president of Transworld Oil. Corrie had run Royal Dutch Shell's Vietnam division, which was one of the major firms tapped by the US military to assist the war effort (though, ironically, a robust black market saw significant amounts of Shell petroleum routed to the Viet Cong). It was there that Corrie and Shackley became acquainted.[28]

There was also the interesting selection of attorneys by Shackley and Clines: the legal legwork for setting up Research Associates International, System Services International, and International Research and Trade was the prestigious Washington-based firm of Shaw, Pittman, Potts & Trowbridge.[29] Terry Reed and John Cummings, in *Compromised*, wrote that the firm was "very much aligned with the CIA" and had "a history of providing criminal defense for intelligence agents."[30] One former CIA officer on the Shaw, Pittman, Potts & Trowbridge payroll at this time was William Barr, the future Attorney General for Presidents George H.W. Bush and, years later, Donald Trump. Barr had worked for the CIA from 1973 to 1977. He joined Shaw, Pittman, Potts & Trowbridge in 1978, but it is unknown if he worked on any of the accounts linked to this private CIA during his time there.

One lawyer at the firm who was known to represent these interests was Barbara Rossotti, who worked as Clines' attorney. Rossotti's name appears in FBI files in connection with what might have been the crown jewel of this entire complex, the Egyptian-American Air Transport and Services Corporation (EATSCO).[31] EATSCO was owned by two corporate entities: 51 percent was held by Tersam, a Virginia company opened by an Egyptian intelligence officer turned businessman, Hussein K. Salem, and 49 percent was held by Clines' SSI. Clines and Salem parked the headquarters of EATSCO at a familiar location: 7777 Leesburg Pike, the same building that was a hub for the emergent New Right networks of Richard Viguerie and his associates.[32] To make these ties more compact, Salem was, throughout this period, living in the Ramada Inn located next to the 7777 Leesburg Pike.

According to Clines, the hotel's bar was a CIA "watering spot."[33] EATSCO functioned as a middleman in arms sales made by the Pentagon to Egypt following the arrangement agreed upon during the Camp David Accords. It inserted itself between the respective militaries and the freight forwarders that were selected to move the cargo. From the get-go, it was clear that this was hardly a normal arrangement. Most Pentagon-related arms sales did not involve "any commercial concern like EATSCO," which makes it somewhat unsurprising that EATSCO became implicated in a scheme to overcharge the Pentagon for the costs of the shipments.[34]

One of EATSCO's men inside the Pentagon – who signed off on the immense prices being demanded by the company – was Richard Secord, the future Iran-Contra co-conspirator. When Wilson's prosecutor, Lawrence Barcella, was put on the trail of EATSCO in the early 1980s, he was paid a visit by yet another future Iran-Contra conspirator – and close friend of Shackley and Clines – Michael Ledeen. According to the *New York Times*, Ledeen suggested to the attorney that "any alleged billing abuses might have gone for a covert operation."[35] EATSCO, in other words, might have been skimming Pentagon money and redirecting it to finance the activities of the private CIA.

Indeed, rumors have abounded that EATSCO was covertly running arms to the Mujahideen in Afghanistan and to CIA-backed fighters in other Cold War hot spots. The fingerprints of Edwin Wilson seemed to be all over EATSCO. Journalists linked a series of major loans to SSI made by Wilson to EATSCO, while handwritten notes made by Eugene Tafoya – the former marine employed by Wilson for wetworks operations – made reference to the company.[36] A security-equipment supplier used by EATSCO called Systems Engineering International Corporation was owned and managed by Donald Lower, the former manager of Wilson's sprawling Virginia farm. Incredibly, Systems Engineering International – like all of the other companies in this complex – drew on the legal resources of Shaw, Pittman, Potts & Trowbridge and operated from an office located adjacent to EATSCO at 7777 Leesburg Pike.[37]

Odd Connections

By the mid-1970s, Edwin Wilson had gained control of Joseph J. Cappucci Associates, an "international firm specializing in the protection of heads of state."[38] The company had been formed by US Air Force Col. Joseph J. Cappucci. He had been no stranger to the world of intelligence: during World War II, he had served as a counterintelligence officer for the Army Air Corps and, after the war, he became a liaison between the new intelligence apparatus of the Air Force and the CIA. He later served as the chief of the Air Force Office of Special Investigations.

How Wilson gained control of Cappucci's company is not clear, nor is there a firm trail of records illustrating the relationship between the two men. What is clear, however, is that it was eventually folded into the byzantine web of the private CIA: Wilson sold his interests in Cappucci to the trio of Thomas Clines, Donald Lowers, and Neil Livingstone (mentioned in the last chapter in connection with Robert Keith Gray and the congressional page boy scandal). The money used to purchase Wilson's shares reportedly came from "US government expropriation funds collected after an airline Livingstone and a partner had purchased was taken over by the Panamanian government."[39] The airline in question was Air Panama.[40]

Livingstone himself had spent time in Panama between 1976 and 1979, and there he had been associated with the notorious Mossad operative Michael Harari.[41] Harari's long and twisting career began with a stint in the Haganah, where he acted as a courier at just thirteen years old, later graduating from their elite fighting corps, the Palmach. After the formation of Israel, he joined the Israel Defense Force and was eventually recruited by Mossad. During the early 1970s, Harari led teams across Europe to hunt and target members of Black September, the Palestinian group responsible for the Munich Olympics massacre. Harari's team had a tendency to leave a trail of dead bystanders and civilians in their wake. Despite this, he was eventually dispatched to serve as head of Mossad's Latin American operations.

Over time, Panama became the primary site of Harari's activities. Livingstone, in an article on the spymaster for the *Washington Post*, wrote that "Panama City had become an intelligence center ... a sort of Latin American version of Beirut or Vienna."[42] Harari became particularly close to Manuel Noriega, then serving as head of the country's intelligence service. Noriega maintained a convoluted intelligence web, simultaneously serving on the payrolls of the CIA and the Cuban intelligence directorate, the Dirección General de Inteligencia. "Noriega's relationship with the DGI," writes Livingstone, "became a valuable pipeline of information on PLO (Palestine Liberation Organization) activities for Harari and his superiors back in Israel."[43]

By the early 1980s, Harari had been detached from the Mossad – at least in an official capacity – and was making a living as an arms dealer and security specialist for Noriega. José Blandón Castillo, a top Noriega advisor who testified to the Senate Foreign Relations Committee's Subcommittee on Terrorism, Narcotics, and International Operations (also known as the Kerry Committee), accused Harari of running a "network" that managed a guns-and-drugs pipeline across Latin America.[44] It was this same logistical network that laid the groundwork for the later Contra-support efforts.

Harari, importantly, was in close contact with Duane Clarridge – the CIA officer who oversaw those initial efforts. Livingstone's tenure at Cappucci was among the first of his post-Panama activities. A contract was signed with the Egyptian government of Anwar Sadat to train the presidential security forces. CIA-trained Cuban exile Felix Rodriguez, who had worked under Shackley at both JM/WAVE and in Vietnam, was brought in to oversee the operation. It was part of the arrangements being organized by Wilson and Clines that had produced the EATSCO deal. Both would later tell journalist Morgan Strong that deals such as these were being made through a kickback arrangement in which large sums of money were to be passed to Sadat via Hosni Mubarak in exchange for the contracts.[45]

EATSCO's primary support apparatus in these various deals was Global International Airways, a Kansas City-based charter airline and cargo carrier founded in the late 1970s by Farhad Azima. An Iranian-born businessman, Azima had launched the company with the ostensible purpose of transporting "cattle from Nebraska to Iran, until the US cut diplomatic ties after the 1979 Islamic Revolution."[46] It was likely that much more than cattle were being ferried on these flights, considering that Azima was reportedly tied to the shah's SAVAK.[47] Azima launched Global International Airways with the aid of a "multi-million dollar loan from the Commercial Credit Corporation."[48] In the beginning, its fleet consisted of one Boeing 707.[49] It quickly grew to be "one of the largest private air carriers in the world, with seventeen 707s, two 727s, and one 747."[50]

Joseph Trento suggests that Azima was a front man for the private CIA, with Global International having actually been designed by James Cunningham, who had worked under Shackley in Laos as the manager of the CIA's Air America.[51] While this particular claim cannot be substantiated, there are hints that this network was present at Global International's inception. For example, at least one of Azima's pilots had previously worked for Air America. Even more suggestive of a connection is the source of Azima's loan – the Commercial Credit Corporation. This was the commercial finance-and-lending subsidiary of the Control Data Corporation (CDC), a supercomputer firm that had operated as a high-profile defense contractor since its inception at the end of World War II. CDC would later make an appearance on the periphery of the PROMIS scandal, also known as the Inslaw affair (the subject of chapter 9).

Around 1976 – shortly before Commercial Credit provided Azima with the start-up capital for Global International Airways – Control Data

Corporation hired Edwin Wilson as a consultant with the hopes of lever-aging the spook's contacts "to unload some outdated computers on Third World countries."[52] The arrangement between the two, however, seems to have been much greater than simple export affairs. Wilson was sub-sequently accused of having bugged the offices of the US Army Materiel Command in order to obtain "inside information ... on bidding and pro-curement plans" on behalf of the corporation.[53]

Before Global International Airways went bust in the mid-1980s, Az-ima ran up huge debts with several financial institutions – most notably Indian Springs State Bank in Kansas, which underwent its own collapse in tandem with Global International. Azima had been brought on as a director for the institution, while its vice president, Anthony Russo, acted as a "financial consultant" for Global International.[54] Russo had previous-ly been a high-profile Kansas City criminal attorney, notorious for rep-resenting members of the Civella crime family. In the investigation that followed the bank's insolvency, it was revealed that Russo had brought Civella interests into the fray. Their accounts at the bank, one state bank-ing examiner found, were "habitually overdrawn."[55] Indian Springs also provided massive loans to the Dunes Hotel and Casino in Vegas, which was at the time under the control of Morris Shenker. Shenker had previ-ously been Jimmy Hoffa's attorney and was no stranger to suspect finan-cial wranglings, as he had been intimately involved with the corruption plaguing the Teamsters pension fund. He personally guaranteed the loan from Indian Springs to the Dunes, while Azima had sponsored it. Global International was at the heart of these business transactions as the airline "had a contract with some Las Vegas hotel-casinos to fly junkets."[56]

Clearly, this emergent network was like an octopus, with far-reaching tentacles reaching out in all directions and intertwined with seemingly le-gitimate businesses. The ghostly traces of this network's presence could be found in all types of corruption. One strange nexus, touched on briefly by journalist Pete Brewton, was the complex of companies set up in Louisi-ana by Charles F. Haynes and Vaughn R. "Bobby" Ross.[57] Ross was a pilot with a military service record, and Haynes was a "timber man." In 1979, they formed Commercial Helicopters, which amassed a fleet of over thirty aircraft in just three years. The primary business of Commercial Helicop-ters was providing transportation to and from the numerous oil rigs that dotted the Gulf of Mexico. Yet, there is also evidence that the company had a strange, darker underbelly. Haynes and Ross, for example, leased he-licopters from Flying Tiger Line, the company that was linked so closely to the China Lobby and to Anna Chennault and Robert Keith Gray. There were also connections to the network of ex-CIA operatives. Brewton notes that Commercial Helicopters "provided parts and services to a helicopter company in Guatemala" called Helicopteros de Guatemala.[58]

Helicopteros was managed by Carl Jenkins, a veteran of the CIA's anti-Castro operations. Operating from outposts in Florida, Mexico, and the Caribbean, Jenkins had been the case officer for a number of important Cuban exiles, including Rafael Quintero and Manuel Artime – both of whom had reappeared in the circles that surrounded Shackley, Clines, and Wilson.[59] Ted Shackley stated, during his questioning as part of the Congressional Iran-Contra inquiry, that he knew Jenkins and had last encountered him in the offices of Thomas Clines, which Jenkins was also using.[60] Given the location and the time frame, this was likely API Distributor's Houston offices, which, as mentioned earlier, were operating from the same offices of Wilson's freight forwarder. Gene Wheaton, a close associate of Jenkins – and one of the early Iran-Contra whistleblowers – told Brewton that he had crossed paths with Ross, having been introduced by the "crowd around Ed Wilson."[61] The 2018 obituary of Ross states that he served a tour in Vietnam from 1969 to 1970, where he was a pilot in the 57th Assault Helicopter Company.[62] During this same year, the 57th was tasked with providing "support to the Military Assistance Command Vietnam Studies and Observation Group in their mission to send reconnaissance teams into Laos and Cambodia to locate and interdict North Vietnamese Army (NVA) infiltration routes and their sources of supply."[63] Ross, in other words, was in direct proximity to the secret war in Laos, the CIA wing of which was being run by Shackley and his cronies.

Wheaton's claim about the business affairs of Ross and Haynes included the allegation that Commercial Helicopters had, in fact, purchased API Distributors. Ross denied to Pete Brewton that this was true – but, oddly enough, Haynes formed a company called API Oil Tools & Supply. While this company, like Commercial Helicopters, was registered in Louisiana, the bulk of its business – leasing "power tongs, an oil drilling tool" – was located in Houston, Texas.[64] Crucial financing for Commercial Helicopters and API Oil Tools & Supply came from Herman Beebe, the financial brain behind a network of banks and savings and loans that sprawled Louisiana, Texas, and other surrounding states. Beebe – who was later implicated in the massive collapse of numerous savings and loans in the 1980s – had long-standing ties to the criminal underworld, some of which went right to the top of the major American Mafia families.

According to Stephen Pizzo, Mary Fricker, and Paul Muolo, Beebe "had been arrested in a New York restaurant with East Coast Mafia boss Carlo Gambino and Florida boss Santo Trafficante" in 1966.[65] He was further linked, by a number of law enforcement sources, to Trafficante's close partner Carlos Marcello, the don of the New Orleans Mafia whose empire extended well into Texas. In 1972, US Customs agents and police raided a Shreveport, Louisiana, warehouse owned by Beebe; inside, explosives and rigging devices that were destined for anti-Castro Cuban groups were found.[66] Though Beebe never faced charges in relation to the incident, numerous conspirators were arrested, among them a close associate of the Gambino family, Murray Kessler. Another was the pilot who had been hired to ferry the explosives – none other than Barry Seal, the infamous drug pilot who operated on the CIA payroll and who would later be implicated in running Colombian cocaine in conjunction with covert Contra-support operations. "Bobby Ross," wrote Brewton, "was a longtime close friend of Barry Seal. 'We grew up together,' Ross said."[67] This raises the possibility that Seal was connected, at a very early stage, to Shackley's network.

BUSH'S WEB

Journalist Pete Brewton, in his study of the savings and loan crisis, reported on the possibility that another – though perhaps related – private-intelligence network was also being formed during this period. The architect of this network was George H.W.Bush. Reportedly, Bush had expressed to Jimmy Carter his willingness to stay on as head of the CIA, only to be rebuffed. Bush subsequently returned to Texas and started anew, alongside his close associates and various business partners.

According to one of Brewton's sources, Bush's main ally was William Blakemore II, an oilman-rancher hailing from Midland, Texas.[68] Buried deep in the voluminous materials compiled as part of official inquiry into the Iran-Contra affair is Blakemore's name: he served as president of the Gulf and Caribbean Foundation, a "philanthropic" body used to move funds raised by private donors to the Nicaraguan Contras.[69]

Another source gave Brewton a different set of names: Walter Mischer, a Houston real estate mogul and banker (and friend of Blakemore), and his son-in-law Robert Corson.[70] In 1991, Corson was found dead in an El Paso motel after being indicted for money laundering and fraud. Those charges connected Corson to a succession of bizarre financial dealings that involved a string of saving and loans, as well as large mainstream banking institutions.[71] Among the sources that Brewton cites is Richard Brenneke, an infamous CIA-adjacent arms dealer and money launderer who became a whistleblower for both the October Surprise and the Iran-Contra affair. "According to Brenneke," Brewton writes, "Corson worked with him in laundering money for the CIA."[72] Interestingly, Brenneke's money-laundering activities were, according to Gordon Thomas, of immense interest to Israeli intelligence, which allegedly studied his methods with the aid of the PROMIS software. PROMIS, and Robert Maxwell's intimate involvement in that operation on behalf of Israeli intelligence, is discussed in greater detail in chapter 9.[73]

Brewton, meanwhile, further suggests the possibility of Corson's involvement with Israeli intelligence: "A Texas law enforcement official who has worked with intelligence agencies confirmed Corson's work for the CIA. This officer said that Corson also did work for the Israelis but may not have known it, because there were several layers of cut-outs between Corson and the Israelis."[74]

Given this possible connection not only to American but Israeli intelligence, there is perhaps significance to the fact that there were direct ties between Walter Mischer and Texas Senator John Tower – the George Town Club member whose activities in the late 1980s were intimately intertwined with those of Robert Maxwell. As will be detailed in chapter 9, Maxwell, an Israeli intelligence asset since the early 1960s, had helped place Tower himself on the payroll of Israel intelligence in the 1980s.

Mischer's ties to Tower came through Mischer's position as something of a political kingmaker. Mischer, according to press reports, had a "virtually unrivaled ability to raise cash for politicians," and he lent his talents to both Democrats and Republicans.[75] While he could often be found backing Democrats like Lloyd Bentsen, he had also "long been a backer of Republican John Tower."[76]

Mischer's rise to the heights of Texan political power came through extensive holdings in construction, manufacturing, real estate and banking. According to his obituary, Mischer, during World War II, had worked as a project manager at Stone & Webster, a major East Coast engineering concern that had become a major defense contractor that, among other things, designed and built the laboratories utilized for the Manhattan Project. During this time, he worked with the company to construct "naval bases in the Caribbean."[77]

After the war, he became entangled with a web of development companies, the most important of which was the Mischer Corporation, which he owned until his death. The Mischer Corporation "own[ed] thousands of acres of prime development land in the Houston area, while affiliated companies do street paving and sell air-conditioning units to home builders."[78] Another Mischer company, organized in partnership with his close friend and colleague Howard L. Terry, was Marathon Manufacturing, which produced heavy industrial equipment. Marathon specialized in oil equipment and offshore drilling platforms, having acquired one of the leading companies in this field, R.G. LeTourneau Inc., in 1970. LeTourneau's first offshore oil platform had been built for Zapata Petroleum, the CIA-linked oil company founded by G.H.W. Bush.[79]

In 1979, Marathon was purchased by Penn Central, a company that, along with its then-owner, Carl Lindner, will be discussed at length in chapter 10. As a result, Mischer and Terry ended up with a significant chunk of Penn stock.[80] In 1986, the pair sold their Penn stock to the tune of $106 million. The most important node of the Mischer complex was Allied Bancshares, a sprawling holding company that Mischer controlled and which owned numerous banks across Texas. Allied's board was stacked with Mischer's close contacts, and provides an inside look at his sprawling "old boy's network," a network quite possibly utilized by Bush after his ouster as CIA director.

Among Allied's board members was the aforementioned Howard Terry, as was Gerald Smith, who was something of Mischer's "right-hand man."[81] Smith's own banking interests extended beyond Texas and into Louisiana, with apparent ties to organized crime and intelligence. Smith was co-owner of a bank with Herman Beebe, the S&L fraudster and mob insider discussed earlier in this chapter.[82] Beebe's own networks of banks and S&Ls were reportedly financed with heavy loans from Allied.

During the 1980s, Allied's co-chairman was one of Mischer's longtime associates, Houston investor Jack T. Trotter. Trotter is described in a 1987 issue of *Texas Monthly* as having been a "[b]ehind the scenes player in setting the course of the Houston business community" with an "enormous network" of "people he has made rich by his deals."[83] Trotter maintained a decades-long business relationship with the powerful Duncan family, lorded over by the patriarch John H. Duncan Sr.[84] Duncan Sr., in the late 1960s, was a director of the Bank of the Southwest – the Texas banking institution discussed in the previous chapter as being linked to a number of CIA funding conduits. Trotter and the Duncan family embarked on a number of business ventures with Gerald D. Hines, another Houston developer and Mischer associate whose impact on Houston can be seen in his ambitious construction projects, including the headquarters of Shell and Pennzoil, as well as the Galleria shopping district (a location that, as we will see in the next chapter, may have played a role in land speculation schemes linked to Iran-Contra).[85] Perhaps significantly, Hines will be encountered again in Columbus, Ohio, as the developer and owner of the building where Leslie Wexner parked his tangled web of real estate and other holding companies, including companies that were mentioned by Columbus police in connection with the murder of his company's tax attorney.

A final Allied director worth mentioning is George A. Butler, then the senior partner at the powerful Houston law firm of Butler, Binion, Rice, Cook and Knapp. Alongside Trotter, he maintained a spot on the board of the Gulf Resources and Chemical Corporation of Houston. Gulf Resources had been founded with the aid of Joseph Patten, a general partner at Bear Stearns. Another Bear Stearns partner named Raphael Bernstein maintained a place on the Gulf board well into the 1980s.[86] Considered a major national security concern due to the role it had played in producing the bulk of the US' lithium supply – essential for, among other things, nuclear weapons – Gulf Resources achieved notoriety in the 1970s when the company's president, Robert H. Allen, smuggled funds via a Mexican subsidiary and bank to Nixon's Committee for the Re-Election of the President. These funds were then utilized by the Plumbers to finance the Watergate break-ins.[87] Allen would, at one time, serve as the campaign finance chair for one of John Tower's senate campaigns.

The movement of the Gulf Resources money towards its ultimate destination was largely facilitated by Bill Liedtke, the founder and president of Pennzoil. Along with his brother, J. Hugh Liedtke, Bill was one of George H.W. Bush's original business partners: they had formed part of the original group that created Zapata Petroleum. In 1959, Bush and the Liedtkes "decided to split Zapata into two companies," with one half becoming Zapata Offshore, and the other half becoming Pennzoil.[88] A 1976 Senate Committee on Interior and Insular Affairs report lists Bill Liedtke as a director of the Bank of Texas.[89] This was almost certainly the Continental Bank of Texas – headquartered in the (Gerald Hines-designed) Shell Plaza in Houston – which had been formed in 1973 through a merger between Continental Bank and the Bank of Texas.[90] The President of the merged bank was Gerald Smith, while the chairman was George Butler. The presence of these two Mischer cronies is no accident, as Continental Bank of Texas was operating under the umbrella of Allied Bancshares.

At the time that Bush was purported to have been organizing his own private intelligence web, he was also making his own forays into the world of banking. On February 23rd, 1977, the *New York Times* reported that he had "been elected a director of First International Bancshares," a large Houston bank holding company.[91] At the same time, he was appointed to the board of its largest holding, First International Bank, and its London merchant bank subsidiary, First National Bancshares Ltd. Russ Baker, in his history of the Bush family, writes that "First International was not your friendly neighborhood bank. Rather it was a Texas powerhouse whose principals reached well beyond banking into the netherworld of intelligence and intrigue."[92] It was particularly close to Saudi interests, which at the time were investing heavily into Houston real estate and industry, a by-product of Texas oil interests taking hold in the Middle East and the Gulf states. FIB reportedly held a "revolving line of credit for Salem bin Laden," while multiple sources have linked it to the Bank of Credit and Commerce International – a powerful and deeply corrupt institution detailed in the next chapter.[93]

Joe L. Albritton, the longtime chairman of Washington, DC's Riggs Bank, maintained a post as director of First International. Riggs was described by the *Wall Street Journal* as having "had a longstanding relationship with the Central Intelligence Agency," and maintained accounts for a number of infamous figures. Among these was Prince Bandar bin Sultan, the Saudi ambassador to the United States from 1983 to 2005 whose contact information would later appear in Jeffrey Epstein's contact book.[94] In early 2005, Riggs pleaded guilty to money laundering charges resulting from an extensive Justice Department inquiry into the bank's activities.[95]

Sitting alongside Bush and Albritton on the board of First International was John Murchison of the Murchison oil family. John Murchison was less known than his counterparts, Clint Murchison Sr. and Jr., but was by no means less prolific when it came to oil and gas holdings and other business concerns. Interestingly, in 1982, John's son John Murchison Jr. was appointed to the board of Gulf Resources and Chemical Corporation following the firm's takeover by a shadowy British businessman-turned-"tax exile" in Switzerland named Alan Clore.[96]

First International appears to have been closely linked to Ling-Temco-Vought (LTV), a major Dallas-based defense contractor that provided the US military with, among other things, light attack aircraft during the Vietnam War. John Murchison was listed among the directors of LTV, as was the independent oilman Edwin L. Cox, also found on the board of

First International.[97] In 1970, LTV's board was run by a prominent Texas businessman named Robert H. Stewart III, who, two years later, would organize First International as a holding company for First National Bank and serve as the institution's long-running chairman.[98]

Much like Walter Mischer, Stewart was incredibly connected both economically and politically. The 1970 *New York Times* announcement of his takeover of the LTV board notes that Senator John Tower was his "very good friend." That same article attributes the following quote to Stewart: "I've always been on the conservative side of politics. Some people refer to me as being a little [to] the right of Louis XIV."[99] He maintained positions on the boards of numerous major corporations, including a position as a director at Pepsi from 1965 through at least 1995. Between the 1960s and 1970s, he was affiliated with Braniff Airways, which for a time was a subsidiary of LTV. During the 1980s, Mischer served on the board of this same aviation company.[100] One important corporate connection for Stewart was his presence at ARCO, formerly known as Atlantic Richfield, in the 1980s. This was the petroleum company of Robert O. Anderson, a close associate of the Rockefeller family who spent time at the Council on Foreign Relations at the same time as George H.W. Bush.[101]

The precise relationship between Anderson and Bush is hard to pin down – but one telling episode involves Atlantic Richfield's role in developing the expansive Trans-Alaskan pipeline system. Service for Anderson's companies was provided by the aviation companies of Phil Bergt, which included Interior Airways and later Alaska International.[102] In 1974, a young George W. Bush traveled to Fairbanks, Alaska, where he took a job working for Bergt. When asked by Russ Baker how exactly the younger Bush came to be in his employ, Bergt stated that it was as a favor to "someone from a Houston construction firm."[103] This becomes all the more curious when considering Bergt's claims that Alaska International became embroiled in intelligence work after the election of President Carter – in other words, right when Bush was purported to have been setting up his intelligence network. These were off-the-books operations, Bergt told Baker, "after Jimmy Carter went in, gutted the CIA, and almost ruined them."[104] He further alleged that his connection to the Agency persisted into the Reagan administration, and that his company had provided support to Southern Air Transport during the Contra years.

Who was the individual from the Houston construction firm that brought W. Bush to Bergt's attention? It's impossible to say, but one possibility is that it was Walter Mischer himself. Nothing directly linking the two men has yet been found, but they both shared a mutual association with Robert O. Anderson. In the early 1950s, Mischer began accumulating land near Lajitas, a small town in West Texas near the US-Mexico border, and Anderson followed suit in the 1960s by setting up his Big Bend Ranch. By the early 1980s, the two joined forces, with Anderson selling half of the ranch's ownership to Mischer with big plans to "syndicate the land" and sell "shares to selected colleagues in the Texas establishment."[105]Throughout this whole period, Anderson maintained an intriguing business contact: Clermont Club member Tiny Rowland, a figure that, as will be discussed later in this chapter and elsewhere in this book, was tied to American and Israeli intelligence services, and played a rather murky role in the Iran-Contra affair. First introduced by the shadowy tanker magnate and billionaire Daniel K. Ludwig, Anderson had sold his ownership of the British *Observer* to Rowland in 1983.[106] Several years later, Anderson departed ARCO to focus on his private company, Hondo Oil & Gas. According to the *New York Times*, the company was "equally owned by Mr. Anderson and the British conglomerate Lonrho P.L.C." – a global corporate empire overseen by Rowland.[107]

THE SAFARI CLUB

In his book on the Shackley-Wilson private CIA, Joseph Trento describes how this ensemble of quasi-official intelligence operatives forged a working partnership with a shadowy covert apparatus known as the Safari Club.[108] This was a meeting space for the heads of numerous intelligence agencies that were allied with the United States in those increasingly heated days of the Cold War. Organizers of the club included Kamal Adham, the director of Saudi intelligence, as well as his nephew and successor Turki bin Faisal al Saud. Accompanying them was General Nassiri, head of Iran's SAVAK; Ahmed Duleimi, the Moroccan intelligence director; and Alexandre de Marenches, the head of France's Service de Documentation Extérieure et de Contre-Espionnage (External Documentation and Counter-Espionage Service or SDECE). The motivating factor for the club's formation was similar to that which had spawned Shackley's group. The rise of a reformist tendency within US intelligence and the political system at large limited the ability of the CIA to operate as it once had. It was into that void that the Safari Club hoped to step.

Turki bin Faisal discussed the club and its activities during a speech at Georgetown University:

In 1976, after the Watergate matters took place here your intelligence community was literally tied up by Congress. It could not do anything. It could not send spies, it could not write reports, and it could not pay money.... In order to compensate for that a group of countries got together in the hope of fighting Communism and established what was called the Safari Club. The Safari Club included France, Egypt, Saudi Arabia, Morocco, and Iran. The principal aim of this club was that we would share information with each other and help each other in countering Soviet influence worldwide, and especially in Africa.[109]

Iranian journalist Mohammed Heikal, in *Iran: The Untold Story*, describes how bin Faisal's remarks reflected the development of a series of critical geopolitical alignments that had been emerging since the early 1970s.[110] The Saudi and Iranian governments were both turning toward Africa as a source of raw materials and as an emerging market. For them, there was a need to curb the influence of the Soviet Union on the continent, which was then being felt throughout the myriad of blossoming anti-colonial movements. These movements challenged the continued dominance of European powers, particularly that of France, whose African interests encompassed the global trade in uranium, diamonds, and gold. As a result, a triangular relationship began to take shape.

The backbone of the club involved not only intelligence sharing but also economic arrangements that parlayed into a lucrative arms trade. Egypt became a hotbed of Safari Club activity, with Cairo featuring its first "operation center." This center was "equipped to evaluate what was going on in Africa, identifying the danger spots, and to make recommendations for dealing with them."[111] At the same time, Saudi Arabia was lending its Egyptian allies large sums of money, which were then used to purchase French-produced weapons that soon flooded African conflict zones. Given that the Saudis provided the financing, Trento writes, they effectively ran the show. In order to function properly, the Safari Club required a banking apparatus to marshal and direct its economic resources. The vehicle of choice was the colossus of dark money and offshore finance known as the Bank of Credit and Commercial International, discussed at length in the next chapter. While nominally a Pakistani merchant bank, BCCI was also backed by the Saudi intelligence directorate, which in turn was closely integrated with the country's ruling elite. Likewise, BCCI maintained branches across Europe and the Middle East; in Cairo, a pivotal city for the Safari Club, the Egyptian branch of the Arab International Bank operated as a BCCI affiliate.

220

The Arab International Bank curiously appears as a footnote, albeit perhaps a significant one, in the history of the US savings and loan crisis. Employed at this offshore bank for some time as treasurer was Mario Renda, later renowned for depositing a flood of money from Teamsters union locals in New York City into various thrifts across the United States. Many of them were intimately intertwined with organized crime, and many also subsequently collapsed. According to the testimony of "Colombo family lieutenant" Lawrence Iorizzo, Renda had been "handling business for Paul Castellano," the boss of the Gambino crime family.[112] Prior to these interesting career turns, Renda had formed a business partnership with a man who was no stranger to the world of the BCCI, arms deals, and shadowy intelligence networks at-large: Adnan Khashoggi. The Safari Club owed much to Khashoggi. The name of the group had come from its first meeting place, the Mount Kenya Safari Club in Nanyuki, Kenya, which Khashoggi had purchased in the mid-1970s. Once a hangout of the older generation of Hollywood stars, the international jet set, and a slick-heeled group of globe-trotting American mobsters, the hotel and its surrounding acres had been purchased by the arms dealer for a mere $900,000. Among Khashoggi's first acts was to dial up the location's exclusivity: press reports from the time allude to his plans to close the resort and "use it all for himself."[113] This wasn't exactly accurate. Khashoggi's plan, it seems, was to market the facility to an even more select clientele – and to use it as the private meeting place for the sorts of figures who inhabited the same, strange netherworld.

Notably, Khashoggi was not the first intelligence-linked figure to be involved with the Mount Kenya Safari Club. Most accounts of the club note that its rise had been facilitated by its owners: William Holden, the actor and close friend of Ronald Reagan, and Ray Ryan, a professional gambler and businessman with extensive ties to the "hoodlum element."[114] They had acquired the properties around 1960; but a year earlier, they had visited the club in the company of columnist Robert Ruark – whose syndicated newspaper writings framed him as an international adventurer with a strong taste for the exotic – and Ruark's good friend Ricardo Sicre. As Ruark tells it, he and Sicre had convinced Holden and Ryan to purchase the Safari Club.[115] During World War II, Sicre had served in the OSS, participating in the North African and Mediterranean theaters in a covert group under the direction of Frank Ryan.[116] Outside of the world of intelligence, Ryan had been a prominent businessman involved in several import/export firms with a focus on textiles. These business skills came in handy after the war, when veterans of the OSS and the British intelligence apparatus – and a number of British merchant banks, Canadian industrialists, and US financiers – formed the World Commerce Corporation (WCC). Ryan served as the WCC's president and Sicre, as its vice president.

While the WCC remains largely unknown, there has been increased interest in its activities, and various writers and researchers have emphasized different aspects of the corporation.[117] Most focus on its function as a commercial cover for intelligence activities, while others such as Steven Snider have assessed the WCC in terms of the "special relationship" that exists between the US and the UK.[118] Anthony Cave Brown, the biographer of OSS founder and head William Donovan – one of the primary movers behind the scenes of the WCC – links the firm to efforts to rebuild European industry in the aftermath of World War II, while Ralph Ganis parses out the linkages between the WCC and the construction of the industrial infrastructure for NATO.[119] When the WCC was first created, it was reported that its purpose was to bring to an end the dollar shortages of the post-war era. Such a task was vital for the formation of an international economic order that was to be led by the US and its European allies. With holdings and interests in mining, oil, natural gas, film, shipping, agriculture, and tourism, the WCC did indeed pursue this goal. Was the Holden-Ryan development of the Mount Kenya Safari Club, carried out at the encouragement of WCC's vice president Ricardo Sicre, part of this international dollar-recycling effort?

The idea is not as outrageous as it might sound. As early as 1945, President Roosevelt and Juan Trippe – the founder of Pan American World Airways – were locked in discussions about the role international tourism and luxury resorts would play in attracting dollars to the developing world. Trippe was the brother-in-law of Edward Stettinius Jr., President Roosevelt's secretary of state, who had a spot on the WCC board until his untimely death in 1949. To accomplish the goals he had conceived with Roosevelt, Trippe organized Intercontinental Hotels. Decades later, Adnan Khashoggi tapped Intercontinental to manage the Safari Club.[120] Scratching the surface of Khashoggi's own Safari Club takeover also reveals the presence of intelligence assets. He had been introduced to the club by his public relations manager, Edward K. Moss, who had been a longtime member. Moss was also working as a consultant for the Kenyan government, while Khashoggi had his own business in the country – he was privy to the details of "a planned beach resort and a World Bank study that projected millions of dollars for the area."[121] These various strands converged at the Safari Club. As his biographer writes, Khashoggi felt that the locale "was a Shangri-La."[122]

As far back as 1962, Moss had connections to the CIA. That year he was cleared for ZR/MAJOR, a CIA operation that entailed "the exploitation of political consultants." While few details exist as to the exact purpose of the operation, it was run by the Political Action Group of the Covert Action Staff, which in turn was overseen by Cord Meyer.[123] It was not Moss' first encounter with the Agency: a handwritten memo states that he had "obtained a covert security approval in 1959."[124] Yet another CIA document refers to Moss as acting as the "assistant for raising funds against Castro and for public relations matters" to Tony Varona, the leader of the CIA-backed Cuban Revolutionary Council.[125] Varona is not only known for being one of the CIA's chief assets in their covert war against Castro's Cuba, he was also one of several figures who were connected to the Agency and organized crime figures Santo Trafficante and John Roselli. CIA files make it abundantly clear that Moss was working deeply within this nexus where organized crime and intelligence mixed. The aforementioned handwritten memo alludes to Moss' "long-standing 'mafia' connection" before noting that his "operation seems to be government contracts for the underworld and probably surfaces mafia money in legitimate business activities."[126] The Moss file reports a rumor that Julia Cellini, sister of Dino Cellini, was Moss' mistress and operated a "secretarial service" that was in reality a "front for Edward K. Moss' activities." Moss, furthermore, moved money from Dino Cellini to Varona – yet another clear example of CIA–organized crime collusion. Throughout the 1950s, Cellini was Meyer Lansky's point man in Cuba and helped manage several major National Crime Syndicate casinos: the Riviera Casino and the Tropicana Club. As noted in the last chapter, Cellini's activities brought him into close contact with Charles Tourine and Joe Nesline.

Peter Dale Scott points out that this nexus raises the specter of human trafficking and the deployment of sex as a means of political influence. The Cellini siblings were described in FBI files as active participants in the trade of narcotics and "white slavery rackets."[127] Scott adds that this "FBI report suggests an important shared interest between Moss and Khashoggi: sexual corruption."[128] More on Khashoggi's alleged role in sexual blackmail is discussed in the next chapter as well as chapter 11. Incredibly, the source of the information linking Moss to organized crime was none other than Edwin Wilson. A CIA internal memo drafted in 1973 states:

Wilson stated that he had met Moss in 1966 through Frank O'Connell, Washington representative of the Transport Workers Union. The memorandum also suggests that one of Wilson's business associates, Richard S. Cobb, was also having business contacts with Moss.... Wilson stated that 'subsequent investigation surfaced from [business analysis firm] Dun and Bradstreet and a verbal report from Dun and Bradstreet recognizing Moss' longstanding "Mafia" connections.' Moss' operation seems to be government contracts for the underworld and probably surfaces Mafia money in legitimate business activities.[129]

One cannot help but wonder if 1966 was really the earliest encounter between Wilson and Moss. As mentioned earlier, Wilson's early tenure in the Agency included a long stint operating under the auspices of the CIA's work with the AFL-CIO, which was overseen by Cord Meyer's International Operations Division. In March 1962, the International Operations Division merged with the Covert Action Staff, with Meyer maintaining control of both. The Covert Action Staff under Meyer was, as previously mentioned, the wing of the CIA that oversaw ZR/MAJOR, the operation that Moss had been cleared for. It is certainly plausible that Wilson and Moss crossed paths at this earlier stage. Further indications of the close-knit nature of this network of individuals comes through JM/WAVE, the Miami station that oversaw the Cuban exile operations to which Moss was also connected. Shackley and Clines, Wilson's closest CIA contacts, spent considerable time there.

This entire complex was hidden away in the shadows. Through Shackley, the Safari Club was linked with powerful forces within the domestic opposition to Carter. The president himself, writes Trento, "had never been briefed on the Safari Club."[130] This was despite advancing corruption within his own administration, as evidenced by certain Carter officials, such as Clark Clifford, playing a fundamental role in BCCI's penetration of the US banking system. By 1980, elements interwoven through the Safari Club network and Shackley's private CIA were mounting international opposition to Carter, laying the groundwork for the arrival of soon-to-become president Ronald Reagan.

Critical to this effort was a series of meetings held by Le Cercle, a quasi-formal group composed of representatives from conservative military, intelligence, and business circles in NATO countries. Since its inception in the 1950s, Le Cercle had been carefully nurtured by US, British, and French intelligence assets in tandem with German and Italian industrialists. The upcoming US election was a topic of conversation at a June 1980 Le Cercle meeting held in Zurich, with the minutes making reference to the "shattered remains of [Carter's] foreign policy" and a "discussion … about a series of appropriate measures to promote the electoral campaign of Presidential candidate Reagan against Carter."[131]

Among those attending this Le Cercle meeting was Donald Jameson, an old CIA hand who had retired to take a job at Tetra Tech, a contractor with extensive interests in the Middle East. Tetra Tech, which was suspected by authorities of being tied to BCCI, had been founded by another CIA veteran, James Critchfield. Both Critchfield and Jameson were close to Shackley, and both were attached to his Research International Associates – a key node in the private CIA network.[132]

Several days after this Le Cercle meeting, another participant, Brian Crozier – who, coincidentally, answered for many years to Meyer in the Covert Action Staff – met personally with Ronald Reagan in Los Angeles. Shortly thereafter, the French intelligence chief, Alexandre De Marenches, met with Reagan's new campaign manager, William Casey, in Paris. David Teacher, in his lengthy study of Le Cercle, points out that this meeting occurred a month prior to the infamous meetings in Madrid that are suspected to have led to the infamous October Surprise plot, whereby representatives of Reagan's campaign are said to have conspired with Iran to delay the release of hostages until after the 1980 election in order to influence that election's outcome. Teacher states: "De Marenches was well-placed to advise Casey on the Iranian hostage crisis; he had been the driving force behind the creation of the Safari Club, founded in 1976 to coordinate covert operations between the French, Iranian, Saudi, and Egyptian intelligence services."

CASEY'S EARLY WARS

William Casey is best remembered as the hawkish director of the CIA during the final stage of the Cold War – an individual who, to some, strove to reorient the Agency away from the direction it had taken under the Carter administration and, to others, somebody who permanently stained the Agency with the mark of scandal. It was under Casey's watch that the so-called Iran-Contra affair (a misnomer, designed to conceal the Reagan administration's drive toward global covert warfare) flourished. By the time he died in early May 1987 from a fast-moving brain tumor, the scandal had broken wide open, and, one by one, his former colleagues, underlings, and frontmen were being called to testify.

Casey's story, however, started long before Oliver North and Richard Secord arrived on the scene. It began with his education under the Jesuits at Fordham University in New York City, which had kindled a life-long animosity toward anything that bore the faintest hint of socialism and an affinity for the Knights of Malta, to which he belonged. According to Leo Cherne, who later led the CIA-financed International Rescue Committee, Casey was a prototypical Cold Warrior by the 1930s. "Bill, from the beginning, was to the right of Attila the Hun," said Cherne. When it came to the conflict unfolding in Spain, Casey "was one hundred percent for Franco ... to understand this, you had to understand his Catholicism."[133]

Cherne's early acquaintance with Casey had come through the Research Institute of America, an economic analysis and publishing venture both were involved in. While the RIA strove to be nonpartisan, Casey deeply opposed the Roosevelt administration's New Deal. The policies, he felt, smacked of socialistic impulses and restrained the free functioning of the private sector. This political orientation opened doors for Casey in certain circles of New York politics, while the analytic capabilities he had honed at the RIA opened others. In the short term, however, he worked at the law practice he had formed with his friend Jerry Doran called Backer, Casey, Doran and Siegel. When that did not pan out, he went to work at the Board of Economic Warfare.

The Board of Economic Warfare was one of many byzantine wartime bureaucracies that had been created to deal with the immense logistical quandaries posed by a truly global war effort. Casey joined the organization in September 1942 as a consultant, but he quickly grew bored with it. He then found himself in the Navy, but he found himself detailed to the Office of Naval Procurement, where he carried out basically the same tasks he had at the Board of Economic Warfare. Then he began to hear rumors about the Office of Strategic Service, led by William Donovan. As luck would have it, Jerry Doran had joined up with Donovan's law firm. Through this contact, Casey was able to arrange a meeting with Otto Doering – "Donovan's right hand man at the OSS" and also a senior partner at Donovan's law firm. Casey soon found himself in London, the base for all OSS operations in Europe.[134]

The OSS London station was overseen by David K. E. Bruce. Much has been made of the close-knit relationship between the OSS and the moneyed elite – America's practical aristocracy populated by dynasties such as the Mellons, Harrimans, DuPonts, and Morgans. Bruce, too, was a product of this world: he was married to Ailsa Mellon of the prominent

226

Pittsburgh family. Paul Mellon – Ailsa's brother – served in London under Bruce. Although Ailsa Mellon and David Bruce divorced in 1945, Bruce seems to have stayed in contact with the family. During the early days of his tenure as US ambassador to the United Kingdom, he was acquainted with one of the family's young heirs, William Mellon Hitchcock. As noted in chapter 4, both would play a role in the Profumo Affair.

Nominally, Casey was a rank-and-file member of the secretariat, a cog in the intelligence machinery who spent his time drafting reports to be passed to the upper brass. Perhaps because of Casey's experience in bureaucracy and background in research and analysis (or perhaps because of his economic ambitions), Casey and Bruce developed a close working relationship that propelled the future CIA director far beyond the ground floor of the OSS.

Through Bruce, he was promoted to the service's inner sanctum, the elite social matrix that made up the center of power within the intelligence apparatus. Soon, Casey was granted the title of chief of the OSS Secretariat in the European Theater of Operations – a position that made him "Donovan's troubleshooter" on the Continent.[135] Another well-connected OSS man at the London station – who later inherited Bruce's position – was J. Russell Forgan. Forgan hailed from the high-finance circles of Chicago. His father, David R. Forgan, and his uncle, James B. Forgan, served as presidents of the First National Bank of Chicago. Investors in this historic institution included Morgan and Harriman interests and James Stillman, a close ally of the Rockefeller family. James Forgan had also served on the first board of the Federal Reserve. Russell Forgan followed in his family's footsteps and ingratiated himself with the world of Chicago banking. Then, abruptly, in the mid-1940s, as World War II rumbled to a close, he and William Casey found themselves tasked with a very different kind of business. As Joseph Persico notes:

> General [Donovan] summoned his senior staff and told them that this war had forever ended the isolation of the United States. He directed an OSS colonel, J. Russell Forgan, to head up a committee, as he put it, "to study the need for our country to establish on a permanent basis, as an integral part of the military, a strategic intelligence agency." Bill Casey was to serve as the committee's secretary. The assignment was to bring Casey in at the creation of what would ultimately metamorph into the Central Intelligence Agency. As he would tell his staff at Langley thirty-seven years later, "I was there in the beginning. Nobody saw me. But I was there."[136]

After the war, Casey continued to inhabit intelligence, military, and defense circles. This can be seen in his often overlooked role in cofounding a national security think-tanked called the National Strategy Information Center (NSIC) in 1962. The NSIC was essentially an offshoot of a National Security Council propaganda outfit called the Institute for American Strategy, as evidenced by NSIC's cofounder, Frank Barnett, having served there as program director.[137] The NSIC maintained a presence in intelligence circles over the years and through Casey's time as CIA director. It accumulated familiar faces on its board of directors, including Thomas Moorer. Likewise, NSCI seminars on special operations and Cold War geopolitical activities were attended by such people as Ted Shackley and Oliver North.[138]

When he wasn't running Cold War propaganda organizations or practicing law, Casey spent his days pursuing a future in politics. He planted himself firmly in the wing of the Republican Party that was opposed to the Nelson and David Rockefeller centrist faction. His sympathies were with the so-called fiscal conservatives and the militant anti-Communists. He was in alignment with Roy Cohn's good friend William F. Buckley and his *National Review,* even going so far as to ghostwrite an anti-Rockefeller essay for the paper. "The thrust of Bill's article," Buckley later said, "was that Rockefeller wanted to lead New York State and then America away from anti-communism and towards collectivism."[139]

The political vehicle that Casey ultimately hitched himself to was Richard Nixon. Nixon, he reasoned, was a figure far removed from the sort of "Eastern establishment" cultural circles that had fostered politicians like Nelson Rockefeller. Furthermore, Nixon was an avid cold warrior and a friend of business. Casey went to work in an unofficial capacity for Nixon's ill-fated campaign against John F. Kennedy. While these efforts bore little fruit, he continued to spend the 1960s aiding Nixon's advance and turning down offers to work on the campaigns of Barry Goldwater and others.

Nixon's resurgence at the end of the 1960s was Casey's moment. He dumped money into the Nixon campaign's coffers and worked to organize a book titled *Nixon on the Issues.* He had expected that, in return for his efforts, the incoming administration would grant him some high-value position – but the long-awaited offer never came. Instead, Casey resorted to calling on go-betweens to help him find a position. One of these was his old OSS colleague, J. Russell Forgan, who was close to Maurice Stans, Nixon's financial manager and eventual head of the Committee for the Re-Election of the President. From 1965 to 1969, Stans had served as president of Glore Forgan, a prominent New York investment house led in part by Russell Forgan.[140] Casey's vision was singular and hewed closely to his geopolitical bona fides: he wanted a position at the top of the armed forces pyramid or in the State Department or the CIA. When he finally got an offer from Nixon, it was as *deputy director* of the CIA, a position beneath director Richard Helms, and Casey rejected it. According to Casey biographer Joseph Persico, the offer bordered on insult: "Dick Helms worked for Casey more than twenty-five years ago. He had been a junior officer in London when Casey was US intelligence chief for all of Europe."[141] He was equally reluctant about the next offer, but he eventually accepted. As a result, in 1971, he became the head of the Nixon administration's Securities and Exchange Commission (SEC). He held that post for two years, before holding a series of other positions, including that of Undersecretary of State for Economic Affairs (where he butted heads with Henry Kissinger), as chairman of the Import-Export Bank, and a spot on the Foreign Intelligence Advisory board. It is worth pausing for a moment, however, to examine Casey's tenure at the SEC, because it was there that he crossed paths with the infamous financial bandit Robert Vesco.

The "Detroit Kid"

Robert Vesco was one of the greats in the world of white-collar crime. He was renowned for his rapid rise and his subsequent fall – which forced him to become a country-hopping, yet incredibly wealthy, fugitive who courted right-wing paramilitaries, Colombian cartels, and Cuban Communists with equal ease. He was something of an enigma.

Mitchell WerBell III, the old OSS China hand who had become a gun for hire and arms merchant, suspected Vesco of being a CIA asset. He was described by Jim Hougan in his classic book *Spooks* as "Watergate's own Rosetta Stone."[142] His meteoric rise was fueled by his takeover – and subsequent looting – of an international mutual fund that was, at the very least, adjacent to both organized crime and the CIA. Not satisfied, he then tried to take control of Resorts International, the notorious Paradise Island hotel and casino that was tied to these *exact same* organized crime and intelligence networks.

The initial object of Vesco's takeover and looting was Investors Overseas Services (IOS), the brainchild of the "hippie" entrepreneur, B'nai B'rith activist, and self-proclaimed Trotskyite Bernie Cornfeld. On the surface, IOS was a peddler of mutual funds, with its salesmen traveling door-to-door across Europe and elsewhere hawking their products. These were modest beginnings for something that later became a global octopus. "Even before Vesco's advent on the scene," writes Hougan, "IOS bordered on the bizarre. It was an underground institution, the financial equivalent to Thomas Pynchon's *V*."[143] R. T. Naylor, an expert on offshore finance, sums up IOS: "If Bernie Cornfeld did not invent the modern technology of capital flight, he did far more than his contemporaries to put it to work in an imaginative, systematic, and profitable way."[144]

As Naylor points out, IOS' early successes were made possible by US-led economic policies. On the one hand, the status of the dollar as a reserve currency had opened up the nascent eurodollar markets and created the need for dollar recycling. IOS fit nicely into each. On the other hand, there was the IMF's encouragement for developing countries to loosen controls on capital flows. The flight of capital from these countries often saw that capital going right into investments in the United States and Europe, as well as into other developing zones. The IMF's policies often created a business boom, though not necessarily in the countries it was professing to help, and Cornfeld capitalized on these and related policies to turn IOS and its web of mutual funds into a veritable sponge for soaking up all of this now-available capital. IOS salesmen and couriers descended on developing countries, criss-crossed war zones, and forged alliances with dictators, offering investment opportunities and access to bank accounts in Luxembourg, Geneva, and the Bahamas.

In managing this ever-ballooning mass of hot money, Cornfeld and IOS cultivated a close working relationship with a very peculiar banker: Tibor Rosenbaum. As previously mentioned, the Geneva-based money-man's International Credit Bank was a favored repository for the funds of both Meyer Lanksy and the Mossad.[145] Rosenbaum even went so far as to take credit for being the person who first pointed out the benefits of a mutual fund scheme to Cornfeld. The result was the creation of IOS' first major financial entity, the International Investment Trust, which launched in 1962.

Rosenbaum was not the only figure involved with Mossad that Cornfeld had buddied up with. There was also Bruce Rappaport, the banker, tanker magnate, and financial criminal who was among William Casey's closest friends. According to criminologist Alan Block, Rappaport once bailed Cornfeld out of jail in Switzerland.[146] Importantly, IOS was supported by Bank van Embden, which owned a portion of Rappaport's own banking complex, Inter Maritime Bank. "In October 1970," Block notes, "British bankers discovered that Bank van Embden was either a subsidiary or an affiliate of Banque Occidentale, owned by James Goldsmith" – the Clermont Club member, corporate raider and another figure who would later appear repeatedly in the nexus that later surrounded Robert Maxwell and Jeffrey Epstein.[147]

While IOS was rapidly expanding internationally, an unrelated corporate complex, the International Controls Corporation, was carrying out a series of rapid acquisitions in the United States. At the helm of ICC was Robert Vesco. Vesco's main tactic was to borrow money to finance takeovers and then use the assets of the captured companies to pay off the loans. This ensured a stellar credit rating and, with a few strategic moves, Vesco was soon offering shares of his newly minted empire on the stock exchange.

Vesco, known as the "Detroit Kid," targeted troubled, mid-sized industrial outfits for his early acquisitions. One of his first ventures was Captive Seal, a manufacturer of parts for missile technology. The company had been floundering, but Vesco managed to turn it around by courting an investment capital firm called HH Industries – a co-owner of which was Baron Edmond de Rothschild.[148] To illustrate the incestuous nature of these business networks, this was the same Baron Rothschild who had organized the Israel Corporation – "Israel's largest investment company," designed to "encourage large-scale private investment in Israel" – with none other than Tibor Rosenbaum.[149]

It seems to have been the Rothschild connection that put IOS on Vesco's radar sometime between 1967 and 1968. According to Arthur Herzog, Vesco's biographer, Baron Rothschild had bragged to Henry Buhl III, then the newly minted president of the International Investment Trust, of the successes of Captive Seal.[150] Shortly thereafter, George Karlweiss – an agent of Edmond de Rothschild's Banque Privée – brokered an introduction of Vesco to Buhl. From there it was off to the races: at Buhl's discretion, IOS began to purchase ICC shares. Vesco was being propelled upward.

The Detroit Kid made his move when IOS began to feel a liquidity crunch. There was a certain irony to this: while IOS controlled an unfathomable sum of money, it was not always readily accessible for above-board economic purposes. Vesco offered to bail out IOS in exchange for a high degree of control over the company. What happened next was described by Jim Hougan as "a masterpiece of unarmed robbery.... A newly created

231

Bahamian subsidiary of International Controls – ICC Investments, Inc. – was the lender to IOS. What Vesco did was have ICC Investments borrow five million from a Wall Street brokerage house, the money to be repaid in six weeks. He then convinced the owner of Butler's Bank in the Bahamas (also undergoing a liquidity crisis) to lend ICC Investments five million dollars to repay the six-week loan."[151] From here, Vesco structured the loan agreement to IOS so that it would extend the five million to ease the liquidity crunch, minus $350,000 – which was used to cover the financing cost of the Wall Street brokerage. With the remaining money, Vesco took control of IOS and then directed the company to repay the loan that had been taken from Butler's Bank. Vesco, in other words, had used IOS' own funds to finance its takeover. Next, he began to systematically purge the board of older Cornfeld loyalists and effectively consolidated control over one of the world's largest offshore financial institutions. Finally, through a bizarre web of shell companies and fronts – organized with IOS money – Vesco began to sell off IOS assets, call in debts, and simply pocket large sums of money.

The systematic looting of IOS quickly caught the attention of Stanley Sporkin, head of the SEC's Enforcement Division. The way that Sporkin has told the story, the resulting SEC investigation was a noble effort that had been greenlit by his boss, William Casey. The SEC began to freeze Vesco's accounts abroad, with the goal of slowing the torrents of money that were flowing out of IOS (and by extension, the pockets of those who had bought IOS mutual funds). Yet, these successes were short lived. There was the matter of a $250,000 campaign contribution Vesco had made to Nixon's Campaign for the Re-Election of the President. Incredibly, a portion of this contribution was used to finance the Watergate break-ins.[152] Almost immediately, Casey began to pump the brakes on Sporkin's efforts. Vesco, meanwhile, sought a one-on-one meeting with Casey.

Questions have been raised regarding Casey's impartiality when it came to the IOS. The reason for this was a strange little company he had been involved with, starting in 1968, that was called Multiponics. The company would follow Casey like a ghost and rear its head to haunt him again and again. Multiponics – formerly named Ivanhoe Associates – was ostensibly organized "to engage in farming operations, agribusiness, and the acquisition of land."[153] A mere three years after it launched, Multiponics was bankrupt with hints of suspect activity everywhere. The company, for example, had acquired the mortgage debts of all of its organizers – Casey's included. Multiponics' investors were never informed of this function of the company. Nevertheless, the money they had put into Multiponics shares inevitably went, without their knowledge or consent, into paying down these mortgage debts. Helping to organize the Multiponics stock offering was none other than Glore Forgan – the firm of Casey's old OSS comrade J. Russell Forgan. Lawrence F. Orbe, "an advisor in the corporate finance department of Glore Forgan," maintained a spot on the board of Multiponics.[154]

The primary investor in Multiponics just so happened to be International Investment Trust, the leading mutual fund of IOS. What this meant is that Casey, as head of the SEC and the person ultimately in charge of the investigation into Vesco, had business interests that were intimately interwoven throughout Vesco's affairs. There is little doubt that Vesco understood the precarious position that Casey was in. It was later revealed that, while he had sought a back channel to Casey, he had also been preparing potential legal action against him. The purpose of Multiponics, Vesco argued, had been "to take over the personal interests of Mr. Casey and others in certain farming operations ... at values subsequently determined to be inflated."[155] Vesco, in other words, was charging that Casey, the Glore Forgan crew and their other colleagues in Multiponics had committed fraud against IOS. Intriguingly, Vesco's subsequent flight to Costa Rica – the beginning of his grand tour of the Caribbean and Latin America – occurred in February 1973, the same month that Casey resigned from the SEC. There is no evidence to suggest that the two events were related, although a subsequent "grand jury found evidence that [Casey's successor at the SEC, Bradford Cook] and Casey ... directly interfered" with the SEC's investigation into Vesco and IOS.[156]

Years later, an informant and US Customs contract agent named Joe Kelso arrived in Costa Rica on the trail of a fugitive drug dealer. While he never found his target, Kelso did discover Vesco's private jet, tucked away inside a hanger paid for by a shrimp company called Frigorificos de Puntarenas.[157] Frigorificos was, as stated in a CIA Inspector General's report, "among the companies that were used by the Department of State in the mid-1980s to channel humanitarian aid to the Contras."[158] The report goes on to acknowledge that the company and its operators, Frank Chanes and Moises Nuñez – the latter a "narcotics officer in the Government of Costa Rica" – were linked to the international transport of cocaine and the laundering of drug money, per US Drug Enforcement Administration (DEA) reports. The Kerry Committee report, meanwhile, further identified Ramon Milian-Rodriguez, a money launderer tied to the Colombian cartels, and Luis Rodriguez, a convicted narcotics trafficker, as other Frig-orificos principals.

That Vesco would appear in direct proximity to Colombian narcotics traffickers is not surprising. In the early 1980s, drug smuggler George Jung testified that Carlos Lehder, a high-level trafficker from the Medellin drug cartel, had partnered with Robert Vesco in moving cocaine through the Bahamas.[159] Lehder later confirmed Jung's claim. When he was called to testify in the 1991 trial against Manuel Noriega, Lehder identified Vesco as of one his partners in the Bahamas since the early 1980s.[160]

Inside "Billygate"

One of the scandals that dogged President Carter in the waning days of his administration was the so-called "Billygate" affair. "Billygate" was named for the president's brother, Billy Carter, and focused on the ties he had cultivated with the government of Libya. Billygate became a media circus throughout late 1979, as a Senate inquiry heated up and widespread dissent rippled through the Democratic Party. A *Christian Science Monitor* article from the summer of 1980 is particularly revealing, as it addresses the way the scandal prevented Carter from focusing more attention on Reagan during election season and describes the rise of an anti-Carter bloc within his party:

> Washington reporters are hearing from Democratic leaders all over the United States – in office or out, and usually in private – who say they would really prefer to have Carter step aside or be forced to step aside.
>
> This growing anxiety – "call it fear," one congressman says – is that the President will not only lose badly but will bring about the defeat of a lot of Democrats in marginal seats and possibly elect a GOP-controlled House and Senate.[161]

Billygate came about in the context of deepening tensions between the US government and Libya, and in particular via an effort launched by Gaddafi's government to influence the American population with the hopes of influencing American policy decisions. Under the leadership of Ahmad al-Shahati, the head of the Libyan Foreign Liaison Office, a program was organized to invite "prominent U.S. citizens and business organizations" to Libya.[162] In March, 1978, efforts were made to involve Billy Carter in the program. The connection that was established between the Libyans and Billy was rather tenuous: according to the Senate report on

234

the matter, Michele Papa, a Sicilian lawyer and founder of the Sicilian-Arab Association, told an Atlanta-based real estate broker named Mario Leanza that if "he could get Billy Carter to come to Libya, Leanza could make a lot of money."[163] Arrangements were made through mutual associates to establish contact between a Libyan ambassador and Billy, and Leanza did receive money for his role.

After Billy did make a trip to Libya, he helped arrange for a Libyan delegation to visit Georgia in early 1979. He acted as something of a "goodwill ambassador," and promoted plans for the formation of a "Libyan-Arab-Georgian friendship society."[164] Plans were also hatched for a commodity exchange program, where Libyans would purchase goods produced in Georgia and Billy would use his connections to help Libya sell its own commodities – namely, oil – on the open market. To help facilitate these arrangements, the Carter administration's director of the Office of Budget and Management, Bert Lance, recommended the services of a "knowledgeable London banker."[165] Lance would later tell investigators that he had recommended the Bank of Commerce and Credit International (BCCI).[166] As previously noted and as will be discussed in detail the next chapter, BCCI was an incredibly corrupt institution, with deep ties to a web of intelligence agencies and linkages to various covert operations, terrorist organization, drug smugglers, and money launderers.

The presence of BCCI suggests that more was likely going on behind the scenes – and Joseph Trento, in his history of the Shackley network, concurs. According to his sources in the intelligence community, "Israeli intelligence decided to compromise the president through his brother, Billy."[167] The job was outsourced to the private CIA, with Thomas Clines making arrangements to convince the Libyans "that Billy Carter should be put on their payroll as a goodwill ambassador. This would be devastating to President Carter and very useful to the Republicans in 1980."[168]

A dense nebula of backroom business dealings, power plays, and dirty tricks characterized the events that unfolded around the Billy Carter-Libya relationship. One way to begin exploring that nexus can be found through the Florida holdings of the powerful DuPont family, which by the 1970s and 80s had become involved with the CIA's aviation complex. The family's interest in the state were overseen by Alfred I. DuPont, who set up shop there in 1926. DuPont's early Florida affairs revolved around real estate investments, which soon developed into a sprawling empire with countless holdings that were eventually managed by the Alfred I. DuPont Testamentary Trust. Administrating this vast financial complex was Ed Ball, a prominent Florida financier whose sister Jessie had married Alfred DuPont. When DuPont died in 1935, the Trust was left in Jessie's hands – and Jessie turned it over to Ball.

Thanks to DuPont's accumulation of different holdings and assets, Ball controlled, according to Florida senator Claude Pepper, a "great machine which he operates and manipulates…. Every string which controls this vast empire runs through the fingers of Mr. Edward Ball."[169] Besides the real estate holdings, the railroads, the shipping companies, and the heavy industries, the major locus of Ball's influence and power was the control he wielded over the state's banking system. This had its origins in the 1930s, with the DuPont's takeover of Florida National banks, which were then used as the vehicle to buy up beleaguered lending institutions throughout the state. Soon, DuPont maintained – and Ball administered – a sprawling banking complex that held an estimated $530 million in deposits.[170]

The DuPont-Ball banks may have been intertwined with Paul Helliwell's banking network. A list of Florida National Group banks, published in the records of a 1964 US government inquiry into DuPont and Ball as part of a wider investigation into holding company practices, lists Helliwell's Bank of Perrine-Cutler Ridge as being owned by this umbrella group.[171] Also listed was Miami National Bank, the Helliwell-represented bank that had been set up with the aid of a Teamster pension fund loan.[172]

By the late 1960s, Ball's domination of Florida was drawing the ire of government regulators and politicians. Moves were being made to force the DuPont Trust to divest of a sizable chunk of its holdings. As a result, Ball turned to his friend Raymond Mason. Mason bought up some of Ball's real estate, and a proposition was made whereby the concern Charter Company would take control of the lucrative St. Joe Paper Company. The problem, however, was that Charter (at this point) was a much smaller company and lacked the capital requirements necessary to maintain St. Joe. A potential solution arose with a proposed takeover of Charter by Occidental Petroleum, the oil concern controlled by businessman Armand Hammer – who maintained a spot on the board of Ball's Florida National Bank of Jacksonville.[173] The sale of Charter to Occidental fell apart, though by no means ended the relationship between the two companies, which remained quite cozy. However, the failed acquisition also doomed Charter's planned purchase of St. Joe. Yet, in 1972, Charter and St. Joe swapped stock in one another. By this point, Ball had partially divested the DuPont Trust from Florida National Banks, while stepping down as chairman. However, they still maintained the dominant position, and he took up a new position as the bank's controlling "coordinator."[174] In the course of the Charter-St. Joe stock swap, Mason ended up controlling 8% of St. Joe and Ball controlled 22% of Charter.

The same year as the stock swap, Mason and Ball toyed with the idea of purchasing IOS. Just like the Occidental Petroleum affair, this buy-out never took place. According to Robert Vesco's biographer Arthur Herzog, Ed Ball had told Vesco "I had a dream. You and I slept together on a cold night. In the morning, you had all the blankets."[175] Still, Mason and Ball maintained close ties to Vesco, who, after becoming an international fugitive, cozied up to Gaddafi's government in Libya, which was an important source of crude oil for Charter. Interestingly, Armand Hammer was also a player in the world of Libyan oil – to quote from Edward Jay Epstein's book *Dossier*, the oil magnate:

> …managed in the 1960s to obtain a huge concession for Occidental in Libya by paying a multimillion-dollar bribe to a key official in the Libyan court. It was one of the few concessions in the Middle East not controlled by major international oil companies, and Hammer made a fortune that he then used to finance immense barter deals with the Soviet Union. He also used his Libyan oil to undermine the power of established oil companies, and in doing so, he radically changed the rules of the international oil business.[176]

How Charter entangled itself in the complex world of Libyan oil affairs cuts right to the core of the "Billygate" scandal, and possibly links to the wider web of "renegade" intelligence operations and private intelligence networks that have been the subject of this chapter. The lynchpin here, however, was a company called Carey Energy, headed by Edward Carey – the brother of New York governor Hugh Carey and the mob-linked petroleum seller Martin Carey. Hugh and Martin Carey are both discussed elsewhere in this book: Hugh in chapter 11, and Martin in chapter 7.

Alan Block notes that Carey and his oil business were "exceptionally close" to the Kulukundis clan, the Greek shipping dynasty, and its patriarch, Elias J. Kulukundis, who at this time was managing the Burmah Oil Tankers Corporation (a subsidiary of the major British oil concern, Burmah Oil, from which British Petroleum sprang).[177] As discussed in chapter 3, the interests of the Kulukundis family interlocked with those of Bruce Rappaport, while the family's in-laws and business partners, the Mavroleons, were later linked to Jeffrey Epstein and Ghislaine Maxwell (see chapter 15 for more on that connection). Through Elias' position at

Burmah Oil Tankers, the Kulukundis family maintained a presence near the center of power in the Bahamas. Burmah Oil and the Bahamas Development Corporation co-owned an oil transport facility, located in Freeport on Grand Bahama, while Kulukundis "maintained an apartment in New York for the use of Bahamian government officials."[178]

Carey Energy also had a presence in the Bahamas, where it owned the majority stake in a Freeport-based oil refinery called Borco and this facility would have been directly linked to the transport terminal controlled by Kulukundis. Borco processed crude oil from Libya and Iran – yet, somewhere along the way, Carey Energy had ran afoul of the Libyan government, as one of its holdings had defaulted on oil payments to the country's state-owned oil company. Facing bankruptcy, Carey began searching for a buyer for his company – and it caught the eye of Charter Oil.

How Carey Energy and Charter first connected is unclear. Through Carey's family connections, Carey Energy was plugged into the world of New York politics, while through the company's executive vice president, Jack McGregor, it had a line to the Carter family. McGregor, according to government documents related to the Billygate affair, was an informal advisor to Billy Carter during the time that the president's brother was making his own forays into Libyan business. Finally, through its presence in Libya, Carey Energy likely brushed up against the interests of Hammer and Vesco – both of whom moved in and out of the Charter Oil orbit.

Indeed, Vesco offered his "services" to Charter Oil – for a fee. He would use his leverage with the Libyans to put pressure on Carey to help move the negotiations along. In a statement given to congressional investigators, Charter Oil chief financial officer J. Steven Wilson stated that Vesco had contacted Raymond Mason concerning a potential acquisition by Charter of three former IOS subsidiaries that were then in liquidation. In June 1978, Wilson and other Charter executives traveled to the Bahamas to meet with Vesco. Wilson and Mason then paid a follow-up visit to the fugitive in September 1978, and then again in January 1979, when they were in the Bahamas "for the purpose of working on Charter's … acquisition of Borco."[179] The way that Wilson tells the story, there were never any plans to do business with Vesco due to the financier's precarious legal situation. Nevertheless, these meetings between Charter and Vesco did take place and, during at least one of them, the "Borco acquisition was discussed."[180] Then, in March of 1979 – shortly after Charter took control of Carey Energy – Vesco began calling Mason, "claiming that he had been instrumental" in the acquisition and was "entitled to a $5 million finder's fee."[181] Charter, for their part, claimed that they had never enlisted the aid of Vesco, and therefore were not required to make any payments.

While Charter's denial was accepted by the government, accusations to the contrary continued to arise. These were compounded by the fact that, in the wake of the purchase of Carey Energy, Billy Carter's friend Jack McGregor had taken a position at Charter. Several months later, in August of 1979, Billy Carter signed an agreement with Charter to help the company "obtain additional Libyan oil."[182] "Allegations have been made in the press," reads one intriguing footnote in the Senate report on "Billygate," "that Billy Carter's oil deal with Charter Oil was engineered by Robert Vesco as part of a larger scheme to influence the US government to deliver planes to Libya."[183]

The planes in question were Boeing jumbo jets and C-130 and Lockheed L-100 cargo transport aircraft. They had been ordered by Libya from American manufacturers but had been blocked due to an export ban to the country, which had been established by the Carter administration's State Department in fall of 1978.[184] Vesco had inserted himself into this mix, which sparked a series of plots and counterplots that caused considerable problems for the Carter administration between 1979 and 1980. "If they [the State Department] would release the airplanes," Vesco told co-conspirator James W. Brewer, "then the [unidentified] people in Washington can get paid [$7.5 million] out of the airplane deal and I can get paid [$7.5 million]."[185]

For years, Brewer had been an on-again, off-again special assistant for Shearn Moody Jr. while the latter was acting as head of ANICO. He also exemplified the Moody family's tendency to climb into bed with organized crime types: Brewer had a long history of associations with the criminal element, and was a repeat offender for his participation in fraud schemes. One such scheme had gotten him into trouble in 1978 and, in exchange for his freedom, Brewer had agreed to become an FBI informant. As one Senate report reads, Brewer "helped the Miami office of the FBI uncover offshore bank scandals involving phony or improperly used cashier's checks, letters of credit, or securities. He offered opportunities to individuals, 'targets' presumably predisposed to commit crimes and reported the targets conduct to the FBI."[186] Brewer, in other words, was moved around the board by the FBI like a chess piece and was used to set up sting operations against persons of interest.

One such target was James C. Day. A former Texas state representative, Day had become a lobbyist on Capitol Hill for ANICO, and had also cul-

tivated deeper organized crime ties. For example, one of his business partners was Leonard Capaldi, who was "alleged by law enforcement … to be
a major representative of the Houston [Texas] interests of several Midwest and Eastern mob families." During the early 1980s, he would again
emerge as a major borrower at Houston's Mainland Savings, where – as
will be discussed in the next chapter – Adnan Khashoggi and others tied
to intelligence operations could be found.[187] Day had cultivated contacts
deep within the halls of the Carter administration, and in April 1978, he
told Brewer that White House Chief of Staff Hamilton Jordan and DNC
chairman John C. White "were not too confident that Carter was going to
make it again and they were interested in deals to make money."[188]

The details of what happened next are muddled. Brewer claims that
Day asked him to contact Vesco to try and arrange something for Jordan
and White. However, according to Day, the plan to bring Vesco into the
mix was Brewer's idea. Regardless, Brewer, Day, and another ANICO aide
named James Wohlenhaus traveled to the Bahamas to meet personally
with Vesco. It was the first of several trips, with the issue of the planes
becoming an increasingly important focus for this unlikely crew. Day
brought the issue to White's attention and, immediately following an October trip to the Bahamas, the State Department released a handful of the
planes – and with the FBI, all the while, quietly observing the succession
of events.

Yet, there is also the possibility that the FBI had a hand in instigating
these very events. After the release of the planes, Vesco claimed to Day
that the Libyans had not paid him, and therefore Day himself could not
receive his agreed-upon cut. Day, meanwhile, suspected that Vesco had
in fact been paid. At this point, Day hoped to extricate himself from the
affair – but Brewer, perhaps at the request of the FBI, kept Day in play by
arranging for one of his associates, a man named James Feeney, to pay him
the money owed in exchange for a cut of future profits in dealings with
the Libyans, Vesco, and Carter administration officials. Incredibly, Day
himself knew that Brewer was an FBI informant.[189] What neither Brewer
and Day knew, however, is that Feeney himself was soon to become an
informant himself, this time for the Southern District of New York, which
was hoping to get a chance to nab Vesco.[190]

There's also the question of why ANICO featured so prominently in
this operation, with three associates of the company and the Moody family – Brewer, Day and Wohlenhaus – acting as the intermediaries between
Carter administration officials like White and Vesco. As previously men-

tioned, the Moody family had ties into the old power structure of the FBI via Hoover ally Roy Cohn and Shearn Moody Jr. was said to supply "many little boys of the night" to Cohn and other guests visiting his ranch who were so inclined. Cohn, by the time of Billygate and the plane affair, was gearing up to act as an informal advisor to soon-to-be president Ronald Reagan. As will be mentioned in chapter 10, Cohn was also reportedly involved in an effort to blackmail Carter during this period, via his chief of staff Hamilton Jordan over Jordan's alleged cocaine use at New York's Studio 54.

Importantly, both Shearn Moody and Cohn popped up in the course of the scheming: Cohn's law partner was representing Kevin Krown, who was under investigation along with Feeney by the Southern District of New York. In September, 1979, Brewer attended a dinner with Moody, Cohn, and Wohlenhaus, where both the investigation into Krown and Feeney and the plane affair were discussed. According to a Senate report, "Moody told Wohlenhaus that they 'were gonna go to the Federal D.A. and try to make a deal to get them off the hook on the hot check charges by telling the Libyan plane story and adding a bit to it.'"[191] Subsequently, "Krown wrote a scenario 'about all the players, the Brewers, the Feeneys, the Days, the Vescos,' and gave it to John Doyle, the Chief of the Criminal Division in the Southern District."[192] Given the political connections and orientation of Cohn and Moody, one cannot help but wonder if much of this was carried out to embarrass an already flailing Carter administration.

Unsurprisingly, it didn't take long at all for word of these schemes to reach the press. Vesco himself directly leaked information to Jack Anderson, who wrote twelve columns on the subject between September and October 1979. "They described how Vesco tried to wriggle free of the Justice Department's extradition requests by seeking the assistance of high level Carter officials including Hamilton Jordan."[193] To make matters worse for the administration, recordings Feeney made of his conversations with various conspirators were shown to the press by aides of Senator Orrin Hatch (who, as we will see, was connected to Adnan Khashoggi, the Bank for Commerce and Credit International, and other intelligence assets). As the *Washington Post* reported:

> An exotic cast appears in the tapes. The names, spoken by Feeney, Vesco, at least two other convicted swindlers, and Libyan diplomats, include Billy Carter and John C. White, chairman of the Democratic National Committee ... Hatch, in a phone interview,

said he wanted, no dissemination of unsubstantiated allegations, but thought reporters should be able to sample for themselves the technical"quality" of the tapes. The quality of the segment was excellent. The obviously sensitive tapes – raw files with a high potential to besmirch the reputations of possibly innocent persons and even to affect the presidential election campaign – had been closely husbanded by federal prosecutors for an investigation that began 19 months ago and has involved formal presentations to a grand jury since last fall.[194]

Vesco himself had told Senate investigators about the existence of the tapes, effectively widening the probe – just as he had done earlier with the Anderson leak. This raises the possibility that Vesco's role here was aimed at getting the US to drop its extradition efforts against him. Yet, if there was more to it than that, the next question is: who was Vesco working for or with? One possibility is that he was aiding Shackley's "private CIA" network, which of course maintained a deep presence in Libya throughout this whole period, allegedly had information concerning Billy Carter's business there, and had been involved in dirty tricks against the Carter administration.

There is at least one demonstrable link between the worlds of Vesco and that of Shackley where Libya is concerned. Deeply involved in the sale of IOS subsidiaries during the liquidation phase of the mutual fund's existence was Edward du Cann, a high-ranking official in the UK Conservative Party (among other things, du Cann played a key role in Margaret Thatcher's early political rise). By 1972, he was serving as the chairman of Keyser Ullman, a major British banking concern with interests across Europe and in the United States. Keyser Ullman was also tied to Jack Dellal, a Clermont Club member who would later fund a suspect, intelligence-linked company headed by Robert Maxwell's daughter, Christine (see Chapter 21).[195] "Du Cann," states his obituary concerning this period, "was at the heart of a mass of intricate – and generally shady – financial maneuverings."[196] Some of these included the tattered ruins of IOS. They also involved Lonrho, the massive international conglomerate controlled by the corporate raider Roland "Tiny" Rowland, another Clermont Club member. Keyser Ullman had become Lonrho's bank of choice, and du Cann was added to the company's board. He would eventually achieve the position as chairman, overseeing a sprawling network of corporate affiliates and subsidiaries that criss-crossed every economic sector – with a particular focus on mineral extraction in Africa. Lonrho and Tiny Rowland will be discussed more in the next chapter. For now, it's important to note that Rowland's ties to the world of intelligence and covert operations were plenty. He had deep ties to American, British, and Israeli intelligence services, and his African holdings often acted as cover for Mossad agents. He appeared repeatedly in the course of the Iran-Contra affair, and he had complex – sometimes harmonious, sometimes tense – relationships with figures like Adnan Khashoggi. Rowland was also close to Robert Maxwell, and reportedly helped peddle the bugged PROMIS software to his political contacts. All in all, Rowland was a well-heeled operator, known for his ruthless, buccaneering ways.

It is unsurprising, then, that Lonrho's tentacles reached into Libya, right up to the highest levels of its government. A Lonrho subsidiary, Tradewinds Air Holdings, maintained a heavy presence in the country, and counted among its board members Ahmed Gaddafadam, the cousin of and security advisor to Colonel Gaddafi (du Cann himself was another director).[197] Tradewinds became a subject of interest in British parliament, especially after a letter written to the British Secretary of State for Trade and Industry by Mohamed al-Fayed, chairman of Harrods department store and, for a time, the husband of Samira Khashoggi, Adnan Khashoggi's sister. Mohamed and Samira's son, Dodi Fayed, would later become romantically involved with Princess Diana of Wales and die with her in the infamous 1997 car crash.

Mohamed al-Fayed had been partners with Lonrho and Rowland for a period in the 1970s, but by the 1980s they had become bitter enemies, with Rowland seeking to carry out a hostile takeover of Mohamed's economic interests. In the letter, Mohamed outlined a series of charges against Lonrho. While most of these concerned their business practices, they also included allegations of arms dealing and ties with the infamous Edwin Wilson. To quote from Mohamed al-Fayed's letter:

> ...the Lonrho subsidiary Tradewinds has been named as the carrier in deals whereby ex-CIA agent, Edwin P. Wilson, shipped to Libya its weapons of terrorism. Wilson is presently serving 52 years in a US prison for his enterprise whilst, interestingly, a co-director in Tradewinds with Messrs Rowland, du Cann and [Robert] Dunlop, from April 1981 to May 1983, was the head of Libyan "security," Ahmed el Gaddafadam, a cousin of Colonel Gaddafi.
>
> Until 1983, Lonrho's 40 per cent partner in Tradewinds was Ashraf Marwan who, however, served only fleetingly as a director and it is possible that he was acting merely as a front for Libyan interests. It is something of a coincidence that Wilson should have

243

been arrested, Marwan sold his shareholding and Gaddafadam resigned as a director almost at the same time. A Sunday Times article of 1984 ... gave some background on the Marwan/Libya involvement and it is interesting that Gaddafadam cited Marwan's office as his address in the notification of his directorship to Companies House.[198]

To summarize: Tradewinds, a subsidiary of Tiny Rowland's Lonrho, was involved in Libya and was named as a player in arms dealings, including shipping weapons on behalf of Edwin Wilson – in other words, on behalf of Shackley's "private CIA." At the same time, Lonrho's chairman – and Tradewinds director – Edward du Cann had previously been involved in liquidations and acquisitions of IOS subsidiaries, thus placing him in the direct orbit of Robert Vesco. Vesco, at the same time that Shackley's group was active in Libya, became embroiled in not one *but two* potentially interrelated Libyan business and political affairs that reached into the Carter administration. The first of these was the strange dealings with Charter Oil, and the second was the plane affair. The latter in particular proved to be incredibly embarrassing for the administration, right at a time when a connected network of individuals and entities – including Shackley and his associates – were working to undermine Carter.

It is also worth noting that Charter Oil did not only have ties to the Carters via Jack McGregor and Billy Carter. In 1980, 13.7% of the common shares of Charter were held by American Financial Corporation, the Cincinnati, Ohio-based flagship company of Carl Lindner. According to press reports, Lindner was "advising Charter chairman Raymond Mason on some corporate ventures."[199] The secretive Lindner was a major Republican supporter, and was a particularly tight business associate of Max Fisher, who was described as having a "close, personal relationship" with Reagan and is regarded as Leslie Wexner's mentor.[200]

LEGAL AFFAIRS

A few short years before he became Reagan's campaign manager and prior the eruption of "Billygate," William Casey had returned to the world of private legal practice. He arrived at the offices of Rogers & Wells, one of New York City's impressive white-shoe law firms. Renowned for its litigation division, the "Rogers" of Rogers & Wells was William P. Rogers, who had been a longtime confidant of Richard Nixon and served as his Secretary of State until 1973. The "Wells," on the other hand, was John A.

Wells. During his tenure as head of Nixon's SEC, Casey had recruited Wells to oversee a committee evaluating the commission's policies and practices. It was just another step in a long friendship; Casey and Wells had been close since they had first met during Nixon's 1960 presidential campaign.

During the course of Casey's nomination for the leading position in the CIA, Rogers & Wells had furnished a list of clients with whom he had worked between 1976 and 1981.[201] A perusal of the list reveals some of Casey's close friends and business associates. It includes, for example, Antony Fisher, who cofounded a proto-Reaganomics think-tank called the Manhattan Institute for Policy Research with Casey. There was also Science Life Systems, which Casey had formed with William Simon, a fellow Knight of Malta, who had served as Nixon's Treasury Secretary and would later reappear in connection with the Covenant House controversy (discussed in chapter 10). Science Life Systems was a "chain of computerized fitness spas," which was pitched to the governing body of the Olympic Games as a service for athletes. Simon was, at the time, the treasurer of the Olympic Committee.[202] Another client of Casey's was Bear Stearns, the major New York investment bank. Casey's legal work on behalf of Bear Stearns coincided with the promotion of Alan Greenberg to the position of CEO, which he would maintain until the early 1990s. It also coincided with the arrival of Jeffrey Epstein, who rose rapidly through the ranks of the bank until his abrupt departure in 1981. This, curiously enough, was the same year that Casey left private law and returned to government service as CIA director.

A close examination of other Casey clients shows a distinctive pattern: the recurrent appearance of figures linked to organized crime, the world of intelligence, or both. One client that straddled both worlds was Deak & Co., an international banking and currency-trading firm run by Nicholas Deak. Deak, much like Casey, had served in the OSS, and his company maintained a close relationship with the CIA throughout the post-war epoch. An exposé of Deak & Co. published in the *New Republic* in 1976 stated: "Deak is said to have handled CIA funds in 1954 when the agency overthrew Iran's Premier Mohammad Mossadegh and restored the Shah to the throne. During the Vietnam war, Deak & Co. allegedly moved CIA funds through its Hong Kong office for conversion into piasters in Saigon's unofficial market. Deak officials in Hong Kong and Macao helped the CIA investigate Far East gold smuggling in the mid-1950s."[203]

Deak & Co. also had a side that angled toward organized crime. Between January 1977 and summer 1978, the bank maintained accounts for

Isaac Kattan. Kattan was subsequently identified by authorities as "the biggest drug financier in South America." He had worked closely with both the Cali and Medellin cartels since the 1970s, laundering the illicit profits produced by the lucrative drug trade through bank accounts in Miami and New York.[204] Deak accounts were among those being used for these purposes, and there is evidence that the firm might have been aware of what was happening. An Internal Revenue Service (IRS) audit revealed that Deak employees filed false currency-transaction reports – an anti-money laundering mechanism that tracked large-sum bank deposits – and sometimes even neglected to file the reports altogether.[205]

The Casey client list also included DWG Corp, NVF, and Sharon Steel, a trio of companies that were under the control of the man who invented the modern hostile takeover, Victor Posner. "He would spot a company whose assets he judged were underfunded, gain control, and milk it," read Posner's 2002 obituary in *The Economist*. "Some bits would be sold off, others would be closed. Previously unconsidered treasures, such as employees' pension funds, would be raided and reinvested in Posner's other companies," it added.[206] The three companies represented by Rogers & Wells reveals the diversity of Posner's holdings. DWG was a cigar manufacturer that has since become the Wendy's fast food chain, and NVF, formerly National Vulcanized Fiber, was the creator of forbon, a fiber used in guitar picks. Sharon Steel, meanwhile, had once been a booming industrial firm that had led the pack in Pennsylvania's steel industry.

Posner's seemingly innate talent in corporate buccaneering required easy access to capital. Because of this, by the mid-1970s, he had fallen in with the crowd around Michael Milken and Drexel Burnham Lambert. By the 1980s, he was one of the Milken's biggest customers, and it becomes difficult to perceive – at times at least – where Posner's interests and Milken's were separate. Another person in this circle that was particularly close to Posner was fellow Drexel Burnham Lambert client Ivan Boesky. Years later, when Boesky was dragged before the courts for his role in a stock-manipulation fraud case involving the Irish beer giant Guinness, none other than Max Fisher, whose ties to Leslie Wexner are detailed in Chapter 13, personally intervened on his behalf.[207] Notably, Clare Hazell, a former employee of Epstein's and an alleged key figure in the Epstein-Maxwell sexual trafficking/blackmail operation, married into the wealthy Guinness family in the early 2000s.[208]

Much like Robert Vesco, Posner crossed paths with the SEC during Casey's time there. The commission had brought a case against the corporate raider, spearheaded once again by Stanley Sporkin, for "dipping into employees' pension plans" at Sharon Steel.[209] However, the case seemed not to have soured relations between the SEC veteran and the dispersed gang of corporate raiders. In 1980, aside from Casey obtaining the Posner corporate accounts at Rogers & Wells' DWG, Posner's close friend Meshulam Riklis "worked out the guidelines with the SEC's then head of enforcement, Stanley Sporkin … and proceeded to take [his company] Rapid-American private."[210] As mentioned in Chapter 2, Rapid-American included the remnants of Lewis Rosenstiel's business empire, and Riklis acquired the Manhattan townhouse that Rosenstiel had bugged for blackmail purposes.

One close associate of Posner who is worth scrutinizing is the Miami real estate developer Armer E. White, who had been the finance chairman of the Dade County Reagan for President campaign in 1980. Casey was, of course, the manager of the national campaign.[211] It is likely that Posner and White initially encountered each other when Posner first became interested in Florida land development through his Security Management Corporation. Beginning in the 1960s, White was a constant fixture in Posner's world. Sometime in the 1960s, he became a director at DWG, and later he was granted a position on the board of Sharon Steel. By the 1970s, he was listed as a trustee of Posner's investment trust.[212]

What makes White important, beyond his prominent role within Posner's financial network, is the ties he maintained to organized crime. Many of these ties came through his real estate vehicle, Context Industries, which had benefited from the Florida land boom in the 1960s.[213] The real estate affairs of the Sunshine State had, historically, served as an investment outlet for organized crime. Unsurprisingly, Context soon found itself also swimming in those currents. The company retained Leonard Pelullo as a "consultant."[214] Pelullo, in turn, was identified in a New Jersey State Commission of Investigation report as being closely tied to the Nicodemo Scarfo crime family.[215] Scarfo, allied with the Philadelphia crime family, had been given control of Atlantic City when it was something of a backwater. Under his management, it was transformed into the upper East Coast's major gambling hub. Donald Trump's Atlantic City interests were built, in fact, with concrete supplied by Scarfo's companies.[216]

Pelullo seems to have brought the worlds of White and Scarfo together, with Context Industries making plans for the construction of hotels and casinos in Atlantic City.[217] He also served as a source of financing for

White's company: Context paid the mobster $80,000 to obtain loans that, when they arrived, totaled around $800,000.[218] The source of these loans was Sunshine State Bank, a shady Florida savings and loan in which Pelullo owned a 6 percent stake.[219] The full extent of Pelullo's borrowing from the S&L was immense and, upon its collapse, his outstanding debts were over $12 million. It was not the only financial outfit that made, ultimately unpaid, loans to Pelullo. Another was Florida's Great American Bank. Owned by former US ambassador to Switzerland Marvin Warner, it had been one of the banks used by the aforementioned Isaac Kattan to launder Colombian drug money.

An even more direct organized crime connection found in Casey's client list was SCA Services, a major waste-management company. While having all the pretenses of an above-board corporate firm – the SCA's directors and investors have been some of America's largest businessmen – the company has been dogged by repeated scandals, illustrating that its roots have remained squarely planted in the underworld. One such investor was Anthony Bentrovato, who became a "substantial SCA stockholder" after selling "a profitable garbage company to SCA in 1973 for $1.7 million worth of stock."[220] Two years later, Bentrovato was indicted in a mob-linked conspiracy involving kickbacks from the Teamsters pension fund. Indicted alongside him was Teamster official Anthony Provenzano – notable for having been at the center of the initial probe into the disappearance of Jimmy Hoffa.[221]

The association between a mobbed up waste-management owner like Bentrovato and a Teamster official like Provenzano is illustrative of the arrangement between the union and waste management. Waste management in New Jersey – the center of the SCA complex – fell under the auspices of Teamsters Local 945. The business agent for this local was Ernest Palmeri, who came "from a long line of organized crime figures." Palmeri had been placed in that position by Genovese capo Peter LaPlaca.[222]

Close to Palmeri was Crescent "Chris" J. Roselle, the general manager of a family-owned waste-management group that was sold to SCA. Roselle also operated a series of businesses with Anthony Gaess, the manager of a number of SCA subsidiaries. Both were involved, for example, with MSLA, a company that managed a large New Jersey landfill that housed toxic-waste. Linked to MSLA was "one of the region's largest waste contractors," Charles Macaluso. Close to corrupt Teamsters officials, Macaluso was by no means an ordinary businessman – according to the *New York Times*, he had been identified "in a Congressional report as a 'soldier' in the Tieri organized crime 'family.'"[223] That would be Frank Tieri, a boss in the Genovese family.

Perhaps fearing that these associations would come to light, SCA attorneys filed a legal document in 1978 arguing that Gaess was not involved with the company's subsidiaries. However, as Alan Block points out in *Poisoning for Profit*, the minutes of a corporate board meeting clearly indicate Gaess' position.[224] It is notable that this situation occurred during the time when Casey worked with SCA via Rogers & Wells. The connection to Gaess might have been obscured temporarily, but the connection between SCA and organized crime was later dragged into the media limelight in December 1980, when Gaess' associate Crescent Roselle was "shot multiple times with both .22 and .32 caliber weapons outside his company offices in Elizabeth, New Jersey."[225] This gangland-style murder occurred less than a week after an FBI informant gave testimony concerning ties between SCA and the mob.

In May 1981, New Jersey State Police Lt. Col. Justin Dintino testified that the Genovese and Gambino families exerted extensive influence across the New Jersey waste-management industry and had significant ties to SCA. When it came to SCA's president, Thomas Viola, Dintino suggested that he was not a member of organized crime. He was instead "an associate member of organized crime – a business associate."[226] Viola, meanwhile, was quickly prepping for his departure from SCA, and he opted to hire another familiar face to serve as his lawyer, Joseph Califano Jr., whose role in Watergate was discussed in the last chapter. The whole episode makes a brief appearance in Califano's autobiography:

> Though Viola denied any ties of organized crime, an SCA manager had been shot and killed a few months earlier and the garbage-collection business in New Jersey was suspected of being infiltrated by the mob. I was negotiating Viola's exit. He wanted me to meet him … in New York at the offices of Rogers & Wells, which had been retained to do an independent investigation of allegations of mob involvement in SCA. I flew to New York for negotiations, which dragged on into the early evening. Rogers & Wells had found that Viola had no mob connections, had cleaned up SCA, and removed any employees responsible for misconduct.[227]

Notably, a very close business associate of Leslie Wexner's, Frank Walsh of Walsh Trucking, would later become of interest to law enforcement for his ties to these same organized crime networks – specifically, the Genovese crime family's New Jersey branch. Walsh managed logistics for Wexner's company The Limited and, when Walsh was under investigation by the New York Organized Crime Task Force in 1984, all notices sent to Walsh in connection with that investigation were addressed to Frank Walsh Financial Resources at One Limited Parkway, Columbus, Ohio – the same address of Wexner's The Limited. The Walsh-Wexner relationship is revisited in greater detail in Chapter 13.

Two final Casey clients worth mentioning are Newfoundland Refining Company and Shaheen Natural Resources. This pair of firms represented the interests of John Shaheen, an independent oilman whose long-running association with Casey dated back to their days together in the OSS. Shaheen's official bio states that he had served as "aide to General Donovan, director of the Office of Strategic Services; Chief, Special Projects Branch in OSS Washington; OSS field service in European, Mediterranean, and Pacific Theaters."[228] Richard Harris Smith, in his history of the OSS, describes Shaheen's Special Projects Branch as a "completely autonomous" unit that answered directly to Donovan "outside of the regular OSS chain of command."[229]

Shaheen's activities brought him very close to the circle of OSS insiders that Casey had become acquainted with during his time in London. At the end of the war, for example, Donovan organized a committee to advise Hollywood on the production of spy-themed movies. The members of this special commission included David K. E. Bruce, J. Russell Forgan, Allen Dulles, and Shaheen. Their efforts successfully inserted a score of OSS veterans into the movie business, while also giving directors and producers a direct link to the inside world of wartime-intelligence operatives. Hollywood, as a result, became yet another milieu where the worlds of American intelligence intersected with organized crime.

Close connections to Nixon was something else Casey and Shaheen shared, with the latter being part of Casey's "Hardy Boys" clique. Shaheen, like Casey, had been involved with the Nixon campaigns of the 1960s. When Nixon had briefly returned to private law practice, Shaheen had been one of his clients. He was responsible for connecting Nixon with Joey Smallwood, the premier of the Canadian province of Newfoundland. Smallwood, meanwhile, was engaged in an effort to industrialize the remote province by courting European and American capital. Some of the firms he courted bore the unmistakable mark of organized crime – for example, the controversial John C. Doyle and his company, Canadian Javelin.[230] Doyle's company also included a close associate of Edgar Bronfman's, Mark Millard, as a major investor.[231] Doyle had also enticed

Shaheen, whose Newfoundland ventures were the two companies taken on by Casey as Rogers & Wells clients.

The Newfoundland venture was rocky for Shaheen. In 1976, his oil refinery went bankrupt, setting off a firestorm of legal problems and a domino effect that soon impacted his other businesses. He desperately tried to raise money from outside sources, at one point attempting to enlist – with the aid of Casey – the Kuwaiti National Petroleum Corporation to invest in his Newfoundland oil company. When that effort failed, Shaheen turned to the open market in a desperate search for sources of crude petroleum for refining in Newfoundland. It was then that he made contact with Cyrus Hashemi, an Iranian arms dealer with close ties to Iran's post-revolution government.

Anyone who has ever looked into the October Surprise plot will instantly recognize the name Cyrus Hashemi. Indeed, one could argue that the trail of events that led to that plot began with the encounter between Shaheen and Hashemi. According to the report prepared by the October Surprise Task Force, "Hashemi had been identified to Shaheen as someone with good contacts in the oil communities in Iran, Nigeria, and Tunisia. Following their introduction, Shaheen solicited Hashemi in securing contracts to purchase crude oil."[232] The report continues: "In 1980, Cyrus Hashemi assisted Shaheen in his bid to regain control of the Newfoundland refinery. According to O. Jackson Cook, an attorney who also assisted Shaheen in this effort, Hashemi assembled a group of investors who made money available to Shaheen to bid on the refinery. The FBI's electronic surveillance of Cyrus Hashemi confirms that Cyrus and Shaheen were in contact in late 1980 regarding the Newfoundland refinery."[233]

Hashemi also made an appearance in the Carey Energy affair, discussed earlier in this chapter. Roy Furmark, the "right-hand man" of Shaheen in the Newfoundland venture and a close associate of William Casey, testified during the course of the Iran-Contra hearings that he had encountered Hashemi in the Bahamas on the eve of Charter's acquisition of BORCO 198.[234] According to Furmark, Hashemi was operating as a "representative of the Iranian government," and had been invited to participate in the negotiations by a CIA asset named Roger Tamraz.[235] Many of Tamraz's other activities, including his connections to the Maxwells, will be discussed in chapter 16

Shortly after Shaheen became acquainted with Hashemi, he began making overtures to officials in the Carter White House and the CIA concerning schemes to free the hostages being held in Iran. While the CIA was reportedly uninterested in what Shaheen had conjured up – which involved a team of "cadres" led by an exiled Iranian general – the October Surprise Task Force report suggests that Hashemi was party to the plotting. An FBI report from the period mentions that "Shaheen stated that he mentioned [Cyrus] Hashemi to persons in the CIA because ... he determined that Hashemi might be able to play some role in either alleviating the hostage crises [sic] or in establishing a dialogue with the [Khomeini] government and the United States."[236]

The Task Force report then adds an ominous detail: "According to [FBI agent Louis] Stephens, Shaheen indicated during the interview that he mentioned Cyrus Hashemi to Casey, approximately twice to [William] Casey prior to Ronald Reagan's inauguration in January 1981."[237] The significance of this is that Cyrus' brother, Jamshid Hashemi, claimed that he was visited by William Casey and Roy Furmark in DC. The purpose of this meeting, he relayed, was to discuss the hostage crisis in Iran.

The October Surprise Task Force cast doubt on the legitimacy of Jamshid Hashemi's claims, citing the lack of independent corroboration. Far more complicated for the Task Force were the meetings in Madrid in July 1980. As previously mentioned, the Madrid meetings occurred a month after the fateful Le Cercle meeting where the Reagan campaign was discussed. With Le Cercle, the Safari Club, and Shackley's network all revolving around one another, we are left with a highly complex picture of elaborate inner power plays.

According to Jamshid, Casey, flanked by Donald Gregg and an unidentified man, attended two days of meetings with himself, his brother Cyrus, and Iranian officials in Madrid in late July concerning the hostages. Much of the debate relating to the October Surprise Task Force revolved around Casey having been in London for a World War II historical conference on the days when he was alleged to have been in Madrid. The Task Force noted that there were significant ambiguities in the conference attendance records, making it hard to know whether Casey could be consistently accounted for in London.

Madrid is only an hour and half from London by plane, conceivably giving Casey enough time to move between the cities in a relatively insignificant amount of time. While the media soundly rejected the possibility that this occurred, a State Department cable later emerged from this precise time period stating that Casey had indeed been in Madrid "for purposes unknown."[238] Interestingly, Jamshid Hashemi claimed to have used a series of aliases, including "Abdula Hashemi, "Jamshid Khalaj," and "Jamshid Parsa."[239] Throughout late July and August 1980, a series of names were logged into the guest records of the Hotel Ritz, where the meetings with Casey were said to have taken place. These names included "Abdululi Hashmi," "Jamshid Khalaj," and "Parsa Jamshid." These individuals appeared to have checked in and out repeatedly at odd intervals.

There was another name that appeared in the guest records, right alongside the probable aliases of Jamshid Hashemi. On July 23, a "Robert Gray" checked into the Hotel Ritz, and on July 25 he checked out.[240] Was "Robert Gray" actually Robert Keith Gray? Speculation swirled in the media, as Gray – at the time – was working on Reagan's campaign directly under Casey. The October Surprise Task Force eventually turned its attention to the possibility. They cleared him because his passport showed no evidence that he had been in Spain in summer 1980.

Others were not so convinced. Susan Trento, for instance, cites counterarguments made by former Gray employees that he had multiple passports. For Gray, a man who had multiple intelligence connections (as detailed in the last chapter), having multiple passports was hardly out of the question. There were also eyewitness accounts that suggested that Gray was indeed the "Robert Gray" who had stayed at the Ritz. According to Susan Trento, "network reporters followed through by showing a photograph of Gray to people at the hotel, who said they recognized him."[241]

ORIGINS OF THE IRAN DEAL

Bill Casey's appointment as director of Central Intelligence was hardly popular with many on the Hill and the broader political establishment. One particularly vehement opponent was Barry Goldwater, whom Casey had sparred with back in the 1960s. Casey had designated Goldwater as a candidate of an increasingly incoherent right-wing fringe, and Goldwater clearly held a grudge against the veteran spook. He proposed his own candidate: Bobby Ray Inman, the naval intelligence and NSA chief who had done much to disrupt the Shackley clique by shuttering Task Force 157. Goldwater even went so far as to personally lobby Reagan to appoint Inman rather than Casey. But he was only successful in getting Inman the number-two position at the Agency.

The split at the top of the intelligence hierarchy was part of a cascade of factional struggles that swept across Reagan's first term as president. Joseph Persico has described how quickly the CIA bureaucracy was polarized between the two men, eventually reaching a point where "Casey's staff and Inman's staff barely communicated."[242] Inman was blocked from participating in major operations, such as the early Contra-support operations, and Casey even went so far as to plant stories about Inman in the press. He devised a new division of labor in the Agency so that it gave Casey unfettered access to President Reagan – a privilege that Inman did not enjoy.

Joseph Trento argues, drawing on sources from within the intelligence community, that the rivalry between the two men was capitalized on by Casey's other rival, then vice president George H.W.Bush. Inman, already close to Bush, acted as his eyes and ears within the CIA. "Bush was walking a tightrope," Trento writes. "Inman considered himself a friend of Bush's and was reporting to Bush on Casey's activities within the CIA. At the same time, Inman's great rival, Shackley, was [also] reporting to Bush."[243] To make matters more complicated, Shackley and his core group of associates – Richard Secord and Thomas Clines, among others – were increasingly active in Casey's off-the-books operations, apparently walking a tightrope of their own between other rival factions.

Details scattered throughout Persico's biography of Casey add credence to Trento's claims. When Inman accepted the CIA job, for example, he wanted Bush present for the welcoming ceremony. "George Bush isn't welcome out here," Casey told him, alluding to the CIA. "Inman waited for an explanation, but none was forthcoming."[244] At another point, Casey flew into a rage on discovering that Inman had been frequently meeting with Bush and briefing him on intelligence matters.

Inman stepped down from his CIA post in 1981 and turned toward a career in the private sector. The presence of Bush's influence can be seen in some of his subsequent business affairs. Inman, in the mid-1980s, worked as the head of an electronics-industry holding company called Westmark, which in turned owned Tracor – a major defense contractor that produced electronics for weapons systems. The main group behind Tracor was a web of in-laws and business associates of Walter Mischer, the same Texas banker and real estate developer that Pete Brewton had found to have been involved with Bush in private-intelligence operations.[245]

There are other indications that Bush was operating his own intelligence web within the Reagan administration. Seymour Hersh, for example, charged that Bush, wary of Casey, set up a "team of military operatives" that "bypassed the national-security establishment – including the CIA – and wasn't answerable to congressional oversight."[246] According to Hersh, this team included Vice Adm. Arthur Moreau, then serving as assistant to the Joint Chiefs of Staff; Daniel Murphy, Bush's chief of staff; and Donald Gregg, the former CIA officer who had become Bush's advisor on national security. Gregg, as discussed earlier, had a history with Shackley and may have been involved in the October Surprise. According to Joseph Trento, Gregg served as a channel of communication between Bush and Shackley.[247]

Such was the reality of the Reagan administration. Despite the outward appearance of strength and unity, the internal dynamics were characterized by rivalry, factionalism, double-dealing, and, on occasion, moments of fragile cooperation. This was the heady environment that incubated the Iran-Contra affair, in which the US government violated several of its own laws in an attempt to covertly finance the Nicaraguan Contras in their fight against the country's Sandinista government. It was very much the legacy of the Shackley-Wilson private-intelligence network. Though Ed Wilson was, by this point, in prison for his Libyan escapades, old veterans of that network such as Clines, Secord, and even Gray were active in this new covert war.

Oliver North, Secord's primary partner in orchestrating many of the byzantine plots that characterized the Contra-support efforts, appears to have been operating on behalf of Casey, who had been blocked from overtly supporting the Nicaraguan rebels by Congress. For example, Casey directly intervened to keep North in the National Security Council when he was supposed to be rotated back to regular Marine duties. The close proximity of North to Casey adds credence to the allegations made by Seymour Hersh that Bush's own intelligence operations had leaked details to the press concerning North and Secord's arms sales to Iran.

Shackley himself was called to testify in the wake of the revelations of the scandal. He was never found to be connected with the affair, though subsequent statements by investigators suggest that, behind closed doors, there was doubt as to his professed innocence. The facts that he shared during his testimony were, however, quite revealing. In the course of his work for John Deuss, Shackley deployed the services of a former SAVAK agent named Novzar Razmara as a source of information on Middle East oil and the geopolitical situation surrounding the Iran-Iraq War. Through Razmara, Shackley was plugged into a network of former Iranian military officers who maintained some contact with the country's post-revolution government.

In November 1984, as the hostage crisis in Lebanon was mobilizing the National Security Council, Shackley traveled to Hamburg, Germany, with Razmara to meet with the former SAVAK general Manucher Hashemi (no relation to Cyrus and Jamshid Hashemi). The ostensible goal of this meeting was to introduce Shackley and Razmara to "interesting Iranians who were traveling in Europe at the time and from Iran."[248] Present for the meeting was Manucher Ghorbanifar, an arms dealer and shady businessman with ties to both the older pro-Shah military officers and the new intelligence apparatus of Khomeini's government.

There were numerous meetings over the course of that day, and many of the details about them are redacted in the publicly available version of Shackley's deposition. What is revealed is that Ghorbanifar approached Shackley with questions concerning the acquisition of TOW missiles – anti-tank guided missiles that the Iranians were seeking in hopes of turning the tide in their conflict with Iraq. Shackley claims that he rejected Ghorbanifar's overtures. Yet, TOW missiles were not the only thing on the arms dealer's mind. Ghorbanifar stated that "for a price he could arrange for the release of the US hostages in Lebanon through his Iranian contacts."[249]

Shackley's version of these events is somewhat difficult to believe: the TOW missiles that would be shipped to Iran were not to be used as a source of financing for the Contras but were to guarantee that Iran would utilize its influence to release the hostages held by Hezbollah in Lebanon. One of these hostages was, in fact, a CIA station head whom Shackley had been close to. These weapons sales were carried out by individuals all closely associated with Shackley, working in concert with Ghorbanifar. Yet, somehow we are supposed to believe that Shackley's 1984 meeting in Hamburg had happened just by chance. Also suspicious was that Shackley had written a memo on his meeting with Ghorbanifar and dispatched it to Lt. Gen. Vernon Walters at the State Department.

This memo was brought up during Robert McFarlane's deposition:

> **MR. COHEN:** You recall that Ted Shackley, back in 1984 sent a memo to Vernon Walters suggesting we have a new relationship with Iran. Were you aware of that?
>
> **MR. MCFARLANE:** No, sir.
>
> **MR. COHEN:** That that recommendation was discarded and that the memo was retyped in June of 1985, actually June 7 of 1985, it was sort of retyped and given to Michael Ledeen. Are you aware of that?
>
> **Mr. MCFARLANE:** No, sir.
>
> **Mr. COHEN:** That Michael Ledeen gave it to Oliver North?

Mr. MCFARLANE: I didn't know that.

Mr. COHEN: Are you aware of a John Shaheen?

Mr. MCFARLANE: The name is familiar. I believe he was associated with Mr. Khashoggi.

Mr. COHEN: Actually he was a very close friend of Bill Casey's. They served together in World War II in the OSS, and John Shaheen floated a possible hostage initiative on behalf of Cyrus Hashemi … that proposal was determined by the State Department to be unworthy of pursuit. Were you aware that was being done at the same time we had paper being prepared by – a recommendation by John Shaheen?

Mr. MCFARLANE: No sir, I don't.

Mr. COHEN: Were you aware that the State Department looked behind the Shaheen proposal and saw Mr. Ghorbanifar?[250]

Cyrus Hashemi, John Shaheen's contact who put the October Surprise conspiracy in motion, was indeed a close associate and business partner of Manucher Ghorbanifar, and the two would operate in the murky world of arms trafficking up until Ghorbanifar broke ties with him and partnered instead with Adnan Khashoggi. According to Gordon Thomas and Matt Dillon, Ghorbanifar and Robert Maxwell were well acquainted, having been introduced to each other by Cyrus Hashemi.[251]

Subsequently, both Khashoggi and Ghorbanifar were recruited by Israel to help traffic arms to Iran to bolster the country in its fight against Iraq, allowing the two enemies of the Jewish state to continue to weaken each other. Overseeing this operation was David Kimche, a former Mossad officer and at the time director general of Israel's Ministry of Foreign Affairs. Robert Maxwell, who was playing a supporting role in the plan, was also actively working on behalf of Israel intelligence. As will be detailed in Chapter 9, Khashoggi and Ghorbanifar were also connected, as was Maxwell, to the PROMIS scandal, also known as the Inslaw affair.

Shackley might have been privy to these complicated arrangements and designed his testimony concerning the 1984 Hamburg meeting to suppress knowledge of his role in them. In his memo, he had effectively offered Ghorbanifar's services to the State Department. Former CIA officer William Corson holds that he did this "because Israeli intelligence suggested it."[252] This sort of interplay between Shackley's network and the other factions detailed in this chapter with Israeli intelligence would be a recurring theme throughout the Reagan era and beyond.

Endnotes

1   Jerry Sanders, *Peddlers of Crisis: The Committee on the Present Danger and the Politics of Containment* (South End Press, 1999), 221.

2   Sanders, *Peddlers of Crisis*, 221.

3   Yvonne Dilling and Ingrid Rogers, *In Search of Refuge* (Pennsylvania: Herald Press, 1984), 220.

4   Ken Silverstein and Daniel Burton-Rose, *Private Warriors* (Verso, 2000), 215-16; Holy Sklar, *Washington's War on Nicaragua* (South End Press, 1988), 80.

5   Joseph John Trento, *Prelude to Terror: The Rogue CIA and the Legacy of America's Private Intelligence Network* (New York: Carroll & Graf, 2005), 72, http://archive.org/details/preludetoterror-r00tren.

6   Jonathan Kwitny, *The Crimes of the Patriots: A True Tale of Dope, Dirty Money, and the CIA* (W. W. Norton), 1987.

7   Kwitny, *Crimes of the Patriots*, 59-62.

8   Kwitny, *Crimes of the Patriots*, 115.

9   John Pilger, "The British-American Coup That Ended Australian Independence," *Guardian*, Oct. 23, 2014.

10   Joseph Trento, "FBI Probing Ex-Spy's Role in Task Force," *Wilmington Sunday News Journal*, October 5, 1980, https://www.cia.gov/readingroom/docs/CIA-RDP99-00498R000200010073-2.pdf.

11   Trento, *Prelude to Terror*, 73.

12   Peter Maas, *Manhunt: The Incredible Pursuit of a CIA Agent Turned Terrorist* (Random House, 1986), 59.

13   Trento, *Prelude to Terror*, 71.

14   Maas, *Manhunt*, 59.

15   Trento, *Prelude to Terror*, 74.

16   "Exposing the Libyan Link," *New York Times Magazine*, June 21, 1981.

17   Maas, *Manhunt*, 163.

18   William E. Schmidt, "Ex-Green Beret Is Convicted of Assault on Libyan Student," *New York Times*, December 5, 1981.

19   Peter Dale Scott and Jonathan Marshall, *The Iran-Contra Connection: Secret Teams and Covert Operations of the Reagan Era* (South End Press, 1987), 41.

20   "Theodore Shackley deposition," *Report of the Congressional Committees Investigating the Iran-Contra Affair,* One Hundredth Congress, First session, Washington, 1987, appendix B, Vol. 25, 15, https://www.maryferrell.org/php/showlist.php?docset=1949.

21   "Shackley deposition," 25-28.

22   "Shackley deposition," 14.

23   Trento , *Prelude to Terror*, 174.

24   David Stout, "Theodore Shackley, Enigmatic C.I.A. Official, Dies at 75," *New York Times*, December 14, 2002.

25   Philip Taubman, "Ex-C.I.A. Agent's Associates Run Arms Export Concerns," *New York Times*, September 6, 1981.

26   "Pseudonym: Ledbetter, Wallace," Mary Farrell Foundation, https://www.maryferrell.org/php/pseudodb.php?id=LEDBETTER_WALLACE.

27   Javier Blas and Jack Farchy, *The World for Sale: Money, Power, and the Traders Who Barter the Earth's Resources* (Oxford University Press, 2021), 89; *Fuel for Apartheid: Oil Supplies to South Africa* (Shipping Research Bureau Amsterdam, September 1990).

28   Susan Mazur, "John Deuss' Editors on Record on the Man," *Scoop News*, December 2, 2006.

29   Trento, *Prelude to Terror*, 230-31.

30   Terry Reed and John Cummings, *Compromised: Clinton, Bush, and the CIA* (S.P.I. Books, 1994), 542.

31   "Clines Interview," *Report of the Congressional Committees Investigating the Iran-Contra*

Affair, First Session, Washington, 1988, appendix A, Vol. 2, Source Documents, 179, https://www.maryferrell.org/php/showlist.php?docset=1949.

32   "Clines Interview," 179.

33   "Clines Interview," 179.

34   Edward T. Pound and Walter S. Mossberg, "Arms Sales to Egypt Yielded Huge Profits for Obscure New Firm," *Wall Street Journal*, October 1, 1982.

35   Peter Maas, "Oliver North's Strange Recruits," *New York Times Magazine,* January 18, 1987, https://www.nytimes.com/1987/01/18/magazine/oliver-norths-strange-recruits.html.

36   Taubman, "Ex-C.I.A. Agent's Associates."

37   Taubman, "Ex-C.I.A. Agent's Associates."

38   "Libya: Terrorism II [Terrorism: Libya 09/25/1986-09/30/1986]" Ronald Reagan Presidential Library Digital Library Collections, https://www.reaganlibrary.gov/public/digitallibrary/smof/nsc-politicalandmilitaryaffairs/north/box-105/40-633-1201554-105-022-2017.pdf.

39   Trento, *Prelude to Terror*, 148.

40   Trento, *Prelude to Terror*, 148.

41   Trento, *Prelude to Terror*, 148-149; David H. Halevy and Neil C. Livingstone, "Noriega's Pet Spy," *Washington Post*, January 7, 1990.

42   Halevy and Livingstone, "Noriega's Pet Spy."

43   Halevy and Livingstone, "Noriega's Pet Spy."

44   Peter Dale Scott and Jonathan Marshall, *Cocaine Politics: Drugs, Armies, and the CIA in Central America*, (Berkeley: University of California Press, 1998), 73–78.

45   Morgan Strong, "Mubarak, the Bag Man," *Consortium News*, March 3, 2011, https://www.consortiumnews.com/2011/030311b.html.

46   Jon Grambell, "UK Court Orders Gunrunner to Pay over $4.1 Million to UAE Emirate," ABC News, May 22, 2020, https://abcnews.go.com/International/wireStory/uk-court-orders-gunrunner-pay-41m-uae-emirate-70836616.

47   Trento, *Prelude to Terror*, 179.

48   Pete Brewton, *The Mafia, CIA, and George Bush* (S.P.I. Books, December 1992), 201.

49   Brewton, *The Mafia*, 201.

50   Brewton, *The Mafia*, 201.

51   Trento, *Prelude to Terror*, 179.

52   Jack Anderson, "Did Ex-CIA Agents Bug the Army?," *Washington Whirl*, October 18, 1981.

53   Anderson, "Did Ex-CIA Agents Bug the Army?"

54   Stephen Pizzo, Mary Fricker, and Paul Muolo, *Inside Job: The Looting of America's Savings and Loans* (Harper Collins, 1991), 119-120; Brewton, The Mafia, 200.

55   Pizzo, Fricker, and Muolo, *Inside Job,* 90-91.

56   Pizzo, Fricker, and Muolo, *Inside Job,* 91.

57   Brewton, *The Mafia, 160-64.*

58   Brewton, *The Mafia, 162.*

59   Brewton, *The Mafia*, 162.

60   Brewton, *The Mafia*, 162.

61   Brewton, *The Mafia*, 161.

62   "Vaughn R. "Bobby" Ross, Sr. Obituary," *The Advocate*, March 5, 2018, https://obits.theadvocate.com/us/obituaries/theadvocate/name/vaughn-ross-obituary?id=12105551.

63   James R. Woodrall, *Twelve Texas Aggie War Heroes* (Texas A & M University Press, 2015), 237.

64   Brewton, *The Mafia*, 163.

65   Pizzo, Fricker, and Muolo, *Inside Job*, 232.

66   Brewton, *The Mafia*, 155-57.

67   Brewton, *The Mafia*, 160.

68   Brewton, *The Mafia*, 5.

69   Brewton, *The Mafia*, 6-7; "Dan Kuykendall Deposition," *Report of the Congressional Com-*

mittees Investigating the Iran-Contra Affair, First Session, Washington 1988, appendix B, Vol. 15, 243-47.

70   Brewton, *The Mafia*, 6-7.

71   "[CTRL] S&L Fraud Suspect Found Dead; Suicide Possible in Corson Case," July 28, 2001, https://www.mail-archive.com/ctrl@listserv.aol.com/msg73302.html.

72   Brewton, *The Mafia*, 104.

73   Gordon Thomas and Martin Dillon, *Robert Maxwell, Israel's Superspy: The Life and Murder of a Media Mogul*, 1st Carroll & Graf ed (New York: Carroll and Graf, 2002), 78-79, https://archive.org/details/robert-maxwell-israels-superspy-thomas-dillon-2002.

74   Brewton, *The Mafia*, 105.

75   Jack Z. Smith, "Fund-raiser faces hard choice in '84," *Fort Worth Star-Telegram*, July 31, 1983.

76   Smith, "Fund-raiser faces hard choice in '84."

77   Rad Sallee and Kristen Mack, "Walter Mischer left mark on politics, real estate," *Houston Chronicle*, December 20, 2005, https://www.chron.com/news/houston-deaths/article/Walter-Mischer-left-mark-on-politics-real-estate-1637567.php.

78   Brewton, *The Mafia*, 12.

79   Eric C Orlemann, *LeTourneau Earthmovers* (MN: MBI, 2001), 124–25; William R Haycraft, *Yellow Steel: The Story of the Earthmoving Equipment Industry* (Urbana: University of Illinois Press, 2002), 180.

80   Van Craddock, "Marathon Manufacturing Co. Sold," *Longview News-Journal*, December 20, 1979.

81   Brewton, *The Mafia*, 33.

82   Brewton, *The Mafia*, 32.

83   Paul Burka, "Power," *Texas Monthly*, December 1987, 218.

84   See, for examples, "Camp Rio Vista Sold to Houston Group," *Kerrville Mountain Sun*, December 16, 1970; "Parker Drilling Firm Re-Elects Chairman," *Abilene Reporter-News*, December 29, 1981.

85   For a discussion how the Duncans launched Hines' career, see George Rodrigue, "Anatomy of a Super Mall," *D Magazine*, November 1, 1981, https://www.dmagazine.com/publications/d-magazine/1981/november/anatomy-of-a-super-mall/

86   "Joseph Patten, 73, Retired in '73 as Partner of Bear, Stearns & Co.," *New York Times*, April 20, 1978, https://www.nytimes.com/1978/04/20/archives/joseph-patten-73-retired-in-73-as-partner-of-bear-stearns-co.html; "Gulf Chiefs Beaten," *Spokane Chronicle*, June 8, 1982.

87   Martin Paredes, "Watergate and Mexico," *El Paso News*, May 17, 2017, https://elpasonews.org/2017/05/17/watergate-and-mexico/; Allen McDuffee, "Shady funds through foreign powers, digging up dirt, and an election won: the Nixon playbook," *Timeline*, November 16, 2017, https://timeline.com/richard-nixon-election-creep-c6002789b554.

88   George Bush, *All the Best, George Bush: My Life in Letters and Other Writings* (New York: Scribner, 1999), 82.

89   *The Structure of the U.S. Petroleum Industry: A Summary of Survey Data*. United States. Congress. Senate. Committee on Interior and Insular Affairs. Special Subcommittee on Integrated Oil Operations, 1976, 135.

90   "New Bank is Headed By Smith," *Kilgore News Herald*, October 3, 1978. Prior to its merger into Mischer's complex, one of the Bank of Texas' directors was Houston oilman Sidney Adger. In 1968, Adger approached Texas lieutenant governor Ben Barnes – identified above as an associate of Herman Beebe – about arranging for George W. Bush to enter into the National Guard as a means of preemptively avoiding the Vietnam War draft. See Jeff Horwitz, "I'm Very Ashamed," *Salon*, August 28, 2004, https://www.salon.com/2004/08/28/barnes_4/.

91   "People and Business," *New York Times*, February 23, 1977, https://www.nytimes.com/1977/02/23/archives/people-and-business-trial-begins-for-2-exofficials-of-penn-central.html

92   Russ Baker, *Family of Secrets* (Bloomsbury Press, 2010), 300, https://archive.org/details/familyofsecretsb0000bake_r7l6.

93   Baker, *Family of Secrets,* 300. Joseph Trento writes that the London merchant bank sub-sidiary of First International moved "petrodollars and BCCI money... for a variety of intelligence operations that would span the next decade, according to the Senate BCCI investigation and the Morgenthau New York BCCI investigation." Trento, *Prelude to Terror,* 139.

94   Glenn R. Simpson, "Riggs Had Longstanding Link to the CIA," *Wall Street Journal,* December 31, 2004, https://www.wsj.com/articles/SB110444413126413199.

95   "Riggs Bank guilty of money laundering," *NBC News,* January 27,2005, https://www.nbc-news.com/id/wbna6875033.

96   Kirk Johnson, "Clore Takes Over at Gulf," *New York Times,* June 9, 1982, https://www.ny-times.com/1982/06/09/business/clore-stock-takes-over-at-gulf.html. During the takeover, Clore retained the legal services of the New York City attorney Kenneth Bialkin. Bialkin, whose law firm Wilkie Farr & Gallagher saw charges brought against some of its members in connection to Robert Vesco's looting of IOS, was at this time the chairman of the Anti-Defamation League of B'nai B'rith. Interestingly, Robert Allen, who was ousted from control of Gulf Resources in the Clore takeover, was a recipient of the ADL's Torch of Liberty Award. See "Robert H. Allen: Business and Professional Background," https://utsystem.edu/sites/default/files/offices/board-of-regents/board-meetings/agenda-book-full/msa3-1-1996.pdf.

97   On John Murchison and his ties to First International and LTV, see "Briefs," *Scouting,* January/February 1979, 4. On Edwin L. Cox and his ties to First International and LTV, see Harry Hurt III, "The Most Powerful Texans," *Texas Monthly,* April 1976, 114.

98   "Post Edges Back Into LTV's Leadership Ranks," *Bradenton Herald,* June 14, 1970.

99   Robert E. Bedingfield, "Personality," *New York Times,* May 24, 1970, https://www.nytimes.com/1970/05/24/archives/personality-stewart-of-ltvgroup-leadership-seen.html.

100   Howard D. Putnam and Gene Busnar, *The Winds of Turbulence: A CEO's Reflections on Surviving and Thriving on the Cutting Edge of Corporate Crisis* (Howard D. Putnam Enterprise, 1995), 184.

101   Robert O. Anderson was at the Council on Foreign Relations from 1974 to 1980, while George H.W. Bush was there 1977-1979.

102   "Governor Tours Oil Drilling Site," *Fairbanks Daily News-Miner,* May 2, 1967; "Airline Puts Sleek New Charter Plane to Work," *Fairbanks Daily News-Miner,* November 9, 1967.

103   Baker, *Family of Secrets,* 320.

104   Baker, *Family of Secrets,* 321.

105   "State Secrets," *Texas Monthly,* July 1984, 196.

106   "All's Well That Ends Well," *The Observer,* May 23, 1993.

107   Andre Adelson, "Legendary Oilman Has a New Venture," *New York Times,* July 31, 1987, https://www.nytimes.com/1987/07/31/business/business-people-legendary-oilman-has-a-new-venture.html

108   Trento, *Prelude to Terror,* 102-6.

109   Trento, *Prelude to Terror,* 102.

110   See Mohammed Heikal, *Iran: The Untold Story – An Insider's Account of America's Iranian Adventure and Its Consequences for the Future* (Pantheon Books, 1982).

111   Heikal, *Iran: The Untold Story,* 124.

112   Stephen Pizzo, Mary Fricker, and Paul Muolo, *Inside Job: The Looting of America's Savings and Loans,* 1st Harper Perennial ed (New York, NY: Harper Perennial, 1991), 461.

113   "Fit for a Saudi", *Philadelphia Daily News,* October 12, 1977.

114   "RE: Alex Gus," FBI Airtel from Special Agent in Charge, Los Angeles, to FBI Director, February 9, 1961, NARA Record number 124-10199-10054, https://www.maryferrell.org/showDoc.html?docId=142286.

115   Robert C. Ruark, "Here's How Ray Ryan of Evansville Happened to Buy Hotel Kenya," *Evansville Press,* September 26, 1959.

116   Ricardo Sicre was a participant in a special OSS unit nicknamed the "Banana Boys," which carried out activities in Spain and Morocco. See Patrick K. O'Connell, *Operatives, Spies, and Saboteurs: The Unknown Story of the Men and Women of World War II's OSS* (Free Press, 2014), 27, 30, 43; Robin W. Winks, *Cloak & Gown: Scholars in the Secret War, 1939-41* (Yale University Press, 1996), 177. Overseeing the OSS Secret Intelligence apparatus, which handled 'cloak and dagger' operations, in

Spain was Frank Ryan. See, George C. Chalou (eds.), *The Secrets War: The Office of Strategic Services in World War II* (National Archives Trust Fund Board, 1992), 127.

117 On the World Commerce Corporation, see Anthony Cave Brown, *Wild Bill Donovan: The Last Hero* (Times Books, 1982), 795-800; Major Ralph Ganis, *The Skorzeny Papers: Evidence for the Plot to Kill JFK*, ePub (Hot Books, 2020), 293-300; S. William Snider, *A Special Relationship: Trump, Epstein, and the Secret History of the Anglo-American Establishment* (Independent, 2020), 97-150; Larry Loftis, *The Princess Spy: The True Story of World War II Spy Aline Griffith, Countess of the Romanones* (Atria Books, 2021), 222, 266.

118 Snider, *A Special Relationship*, 97-150.

119 Brown, *Wild Bill Donovan*, 795-800; Ganis, *The Skorzeny Papers*, 293-300.

120 Ronald Kessler, *The Richest Man in the World: The Story of Adnan Khashoggi* (Grand Central Publishing, 1986), 204.

121 Kessler, *Adnan Khashoggi*, 203.

122 Kessler, *Adnan Khashoggi*, 302.

123 "Memorandum for the Record, Subject: Report on Plots to Assassinate Fidel Castro," CIA, April 25, 1967, NARA Record Number 104-10213-10101, https://www.archives.gov/files/research/jfk/releases/104-10213-10101.pdf.

124 "World Commerce Corporation & the Safari Club," *Reciprocal Contradiction*, January 8, 2021, https://reciprocalcontradiction.home.blog/2021/01/08/world-commerce-corporation-the-safari-club/.

125 "Edward Moss' Mafia Connections," CIA Memo, May 14, 1973, NARA Record Number 104-101119-10406, https://www.maryferrell.org/showDoc.html?docId=14916.

126 "Edward Moss' Mafia Connections."

127 Peter Dale Scott, "The American Deep State, Deep Events, and Off-the-Books Financing," *Asia-Pacific Journal*, April 6, 2014, https://apjjf.org/2014/12/10/Peter-Dale-Scott/4090/article.html

128 Scott, "American Deep State."

129 "Edward Moss' Mafia Connections"

130 Trento, *Prelude to Terrror*, 169.

131 David Teacher, *Rogue Agents: The Cercle and 6I in the Private Cold War 1951-1991* (5th ed., 2017), 192.

132 Teacher, *Rogue Agents*, 189, 467.

133 Joseph Persico, *Casey: The Lives and Secrets of William J. Casey from the OSS to the CIA* (Viking, 1990), 42.

134 Persico, *Casey*, 84-85; "Otto Doering, Former O.S.S. Leader," *New York Times*, July 14, 1979, https://www.nytimes.com/1979/07/14/archives/otto-doering-former-oss-leader.html.

135 Persico, *Casey*, 61.

136 Persico, *Casey*, 61.

137 Teacher, *Rogue Agents*, 35-36. Teacher notes that the Institute for American Strategy had been organized by the American Security Council.

138 Teacher, *Rogue Agents*, 546.

139 Persico, *Casey*, 114.

140 Stu Bishop, "Stans: He Fixed the Books," *North American Congress on Latin America*, September 25, 2007, https://nacla.org/article/stans-he-fixed-books.

141 Persico, *Casey*, 131.

142 Jim Hougan, *Spooks: The Haunting of America: The Private Use of Secret Agents* (New York: Morrow, 1978), 222.

143 Hougan, *Spooks*, 169.

144 R. T. Naylor, *Hot Money and the Politics of Debt* (Linden, 1987), 19.

145 Naylor, *Hot Money*, 26-30.

146 Alan A. Block and Constance A. Weaver, *All is Clouded by Desire: Global Banking, Money Laundering, and International Organized Crime* (Prager, 2004), 36.

147 Block and Weaver, *Clouded by Desire*, 36.

148 Arthur Herzog, *Vesco: From Wall Street to Castro's Cuba – The Rise, Fall, and Exile of the King*

of White Collar Crime (Doubleday, 1987), 11-15.

149	"Israeli Corporation-Rosenbaum-International Credit Bank Controversy," US State Department cable, September 30,1974, https://wikileaks.org/plusd/cables/1974TELAV05552 b.html.

150	Herzog, *Vesco*, 30-31.

151	Hougan, *Spooks*, 176-77.

152	Robert Hutchinson, *Vesco* (Avon, 1976), 241.

153	Dan Dorfman, "Casey Misled Investors on Agribusiness, Judge Rules," July 15, 1981, *Chicago Tribune*.

154	Dorfman, "Casey Misled Investors"; In the Matter of *Multiponics, Incorporated, Bankrupt. machinery Rental, Inc. and Carl Biehl, Appellants, v. William W. Herpel, Trustee, et al.*, Appellees, 622 F.2d 709 (5th Cir. 1980).

155	Hutchinson, *Vesco*, 235.

156	Gary Miller and Andrew Whitford, *Above Politics: Bureaucratic Discretion and Credible Commitment*, 165; Alan A. Block and Patricia Klausner, "Masters of Paradise Island: Organized Crime, Neo-Colonialism, and the Bahamas," *Dialectical Anthropology* 12, no. 1 (1987): 85–102, https://doi.org/10.1007/BF00734790.

157	Gary Webb, *Dark Alliance: The CIA, the Contras, and the Cocaine Explosion* (Seven Stories Press, 2014), 303-5.

158	"Allegations of Connections Between Cia and the Contras in Cocaine Trafficking to the United States, Volume II: The Contra Story," Central Intelligence Agency Inspector General, Report of Investigation, October 8, 1998, https://irp.fas.org/cia/product/cocaine2/contents.html.

159	Peter Dale Scott and Jonathan Marshall, *Cocaine Politics: Drugs, Armies, and the CIA in Central America* (University of California Press, 1998), 95.

160	"Drug Trafficker Links Fugitive to Laundering," *Baltimore Sun*, November 26, 1991, https://www.baltimoresun.com/news/bs-xpm-1991-11-27-1991331037-story.html.

161	Godfrey Sperling Jr, "'Billygate' Stands in Way of Comeback for President," *Christian Science Monitor*, July 28, 1980, https://www.csmonitor.com/1980/0728/072837.html.

162	*Inquiry into the Matter of Billy Carter and Libya: Report Together with Additional Views*, US Senate, Ninety-Fifth Congress, Second Session, October 2, 1980, 1-2, https://www.intelligence.senate.gov/sites/default/files/961015.pdf.

163	*Inquiry into the Matter of Billy Carter and Libya*, 2.

164	*Inquiry into the Matter of Billy Carter and Libya*, 7.

165	*Inquiry into the Matter of Billy Carter and Libya*, 11.

166	*Inquiry into the Matter of Billy Carter and Libya*, 11, note 35.

167	Trento, *Prelude to Terror*, 160.

168	Trento, *Prelude to Terror*, 161.

169	Robert Sherrill, *Gothic Politics in the Deep South: Stars of the New Confederacy* (New York: Grossman, 1968), 146.

170	Gerard Colby, *Du Pont Dynasty: Behind the Nylon Curtain*, ePub (Open Road Media, 2014), 782.

171	*Hearing Before the Committee on Banking and Currency*, House of Representatives, Eighty-Eighth Congress, June 11, 1964, 188, https://www.google.com/books/edition/Hearings Reports and Prints of the Senat/9Tc4AAAAIAAJ.

172	*Hearing Before the Committee on Banking and Currency*, 188.

173	Elizabeth Hedderigg, "Nix Hints Charter Plays Major Role in Bankshares", *Tampa Bay Times*, February 18, 1970.

174	Colby, *DuPont Dynasty*, 796.

175	Herzog, *Vesco*, 143.

176	Edward Jay Epstein, *Dossier: The Secret History of Armand Hammer* (Random House, 1996), 23.

177	Alan A. Block and Constance Weaver, *All is Clouded by Desire: Global Banking, Money Laundering, and International Organized Crime* (Praeger, 2004), 20.

178	Black and Weaver, *All is Clouded by Desire*, 20.

179   *Investigation of Robert L. Vesco Hearings Before the Subcommittee on Improvements in Judicial Machinery of the Committee on the Judiciary,* United States Senate, Ninety-sixth Congress, Second Session, October 2, 3, 23, 24, December 2, and 3, 1980, 237, https://books.google.com/books/about/Investigation_of_Robert_L_Vesco.html?id=wHFAmuZlAqcC.

180   *Investigation of Robert L. Vesco,* 237.

181   *Investigation of Robert L. Vesco,* 238.

182   *Inquiry into the Matter of Billy Carter and Libya,* 13.

183   *Inquiry into the Matter of Billy Carter and Libya,* 11, note 37.

184   "Inquiry is Reported on Libya Plane Sale," *New York Times,* September 30, 1979, https://www.nytimes.com/1979/09/30/archives/inquiry-is-reported-on-libya-plane-sale-vesco-and-democratic.html; Yousseff M. Ibrahin, "U.S. Delays Sales Made to Libyans," *New York Times,* June 24, 1978, https://www.nytimes.com/1978/06/24/archives/us-delays-sales-made-to-libyans-curbs-on-others-studied-in-drive-on.html

185   *The Undercover Investigation of Robert L. Vesco's Alleged Attempts to Reverse a State Department Ban Preventing the Export of Planes to Libya,* Staff Report of the Committee on the Judiciary, United States Senate, September 1982, 6, https://www.google.com/books/edition/The_Undercover_Investigation_of_Robert_L/42eslxxc8RcC.

186   *The Undercover Investigation,* 4.

187   Brewton, *The Mafia, CIA and George Bush,* 50-53, 75.

188   *The Undercover Investigation,* 4.

189   *The Undercover Investigation,* 11.

190   *The Undercover Investigation,* 8-9.

191   *The Undercover Investigation,* 35.

192   *The Undercover Investigation,* 35.

193   *The Undercover Investigation,* 60.

194   Morton Minz, "Truth is Elusive in 'Plot' to Gain Release of C130s," *Washington Post,* August 18, 1980, https://www.washingtonpost.com/archive/politics/1980/08/18/truth-is-elusive-in-plot-to-gain-release-of-c130s/698dfd4a-00e8-4f91-926d-489dc9fc72e1/.

195   David Brewerton, "Jack Dellal Obituary," *The Guardian,* November 8, 2012, https://amp.theguardian.com/business/2012/nov/08/jack-dellal.

196   Nicholas Faith, "Obituary: Sir Edward du Cann, ex-politician and financier who helped elect Margaret Thatcher," *Independent,* September 8, 2017, https://www.independent.co.uk/news/obituaries/sir-edward-du-cann-tory-conservative-politician-financier-oily-margaret-thatcher-1922-committee-city-life-insurance-a7933726.html.

197   "Letter from Mr Mohamed Al-Fayed to The Rt Hon Paul Channon, MP Secretary of State for Trade and Industry," Select Committee on Standards and Privileges First Report, UK Parliament, February 1987, https://publications.parliament.uk/pa/cm199798/cmselect/cmstnprv/030ii/sp01100.htm.

198   "Letter from Mr Mohamed Al-Fayed."

199   "AFC on Charter Co.'s list of creditors," *Cincinnati Post,* April 23, 1984.

200   "Max M. Fisher: In Ronald Reagan's White House," https://maxmfisher.org/resource-center/photo/ronald-reagans-white-house.

201   Ronald Brownstein and Nina Easton, *Reagan's Ruling Class: Portraits of the Top One Hundred Officials* (Presidential Accountability Group, January 1982), 630-32.

202   Persico, *Casey,* 166.

203   Tad Szulc, "Deak & Co. Cited," *New Republic,* April 2, 1976, https://archive.org/details/nsia-DeakNicholas/nsia-DeakNicholas/Deak%20Nicholas%2005/. Nicholas Deak died under strange circumstances on November 19, 1985. He was shot to death at the Deak corporate offices in lower Manhattan. The gunman was a homeless woman named Lois Lang, who had arrived at the building earlier that day "asserting that she was part owner of the company and that 'an injustice had been done to her.'" Also killed by Lang was receptionist Frances Lauder (Margot Hornblower, "Deak-Perera Chairman Fatally Shot in Office," *Washington Post,* November 19, 1985, https://www.washingtonpost.com/archive/politics/1985/11/19/deak-perera-chairman-fatally-shot-in-office/c9133e93-e2e1-446d-8989-41ca8d7beed1/). It was subsequently reported that Lang was suffer-

ing from paranoid schizophrenia and had "believed the government had given her Deak-Perera in the 1940s. . . . When Deak & Co. filed for protection under federal bankruptcy laws last year, Lang became convinced that [Nicholas Deak] had mismanaged the firm, and decided to kill him." (Rick Hampson, "Woman Diagnosed as Paranoid and Schizophrenic, Psychiatric Report Says," *AP News*, November 21, 1985, https://apnews.com/article/911643acc47ca5b4ce77f8ac9a11c451).
Hank Albarelli notes: "Deak's killer, Lois Lang, as early as 1975, was confined to the Santa Clara Valley Medical Center under the care of the late Dr. Frederick Melges, a psychiatrist associated with the Stanford Research Institute, a longtime facility used by the CIA and US Army for behavior mod-ification experiments.... According to numerous medical journal articles written by Dr. Megles, his specialty was narco-hypnosis and the use of hypnosis to create dissociative states. Dr. Melges worked closely at Stanford with Dr. Leo Hollister, also deceased, who had been a CIA MK/ULTRA sub-contractor working with LSD and other drugs" [H. P. Albarelli, *A Secret Order: Investigating the High Strangeness and Synchronicity in the JFK Assassination* (Trine Day, 2013)].

204   Scott and Marshall, *Cocaine Politics*, 82.

205   "The Cash Connection: Organized Crime, Financial Institutions, and Money Laundering," President's Commission on Organized Crime, US Department of Justice, Office of Justice Programs, 1984, 42.

206   "Victor Posner obituary," *Economist*, March 7, 2002, https://www.economist.com/obitu-ary/2002/03/07/victor-posner.

207   "Letter from Max Fisher to Judge Morris Lasky on Behalf of Ivan Boesky," *Securities and Exchange Commission Historical Society*, September 28, 1987, http://www.sechistorical.org.

208   Richard Eden, "Countess of Iveagh, 46, Splits from £900m Guinness Heir," *Mail Online*, February 27, 2021, https://www.dailymail.co.uk/news/article-9306473/Countess-Iveagh-splits-Guinness-heir-one-Britains-biggest-divorces.html.

209   "Interview with Stanley Sporkin," *Securities and Exchange Commission Historical Society*, September 2003, http://3197d6d14b5f19f2f440-5e13d29c4c016cf96cbbfd197c579b45.r81.cf1.rackcdn.com/collection/oral-histories/sporkin092303Transcript.pdf.

210   Connie Bruck, *The Predators' Ball: The Inside Story of Drexel Burnham and the Rise of the Junk Bond Raiders* (New York, N.Y., U.S.A: Penguin Books, 1989), 58. Incredibly, Riklis had his own encounters with Robert Vesco and IOS. In 1971 it was reported that he offered $10 million to a "dissident" group of IOS shareholders loyal to Cornfeld. There might be a simple explanation for this apparent factional disput. Cornfeld had pressured Riklis to purchase, through Rapid American, "450,000 shares [of IOS] at $4 a piece"; it was suggested by those close to the fight that he wanted, with the $10 million commitment, "to be taken out of his stock position at cost, at which point he would drop the dissidents and step aside." See "I.O.S. Managers Score Riklis on Rebel Move," *New York Times*, August 19, 1971; and Hutchison, *Vesco*, 174.

211   Rebecca Thom, "2 Elected in Palm Beach; 2 in Run-off," *Sun-Sentinel*, February 3, 1988.

212   Brewton, *The Mafia*, 321.

213   According to Walter Beinecke Jr., White had been "manager or junior partner for [the] Mackle brothers." See "Interview with Walter Breinecke Jr., Samuel Proctor Oral History Project," Uni-versity of Florida, July 9, 1990, 129, https://ufdc.ufl.edu/UF00006970/00001/. The Mackle brothers were behind the General Development Corporation, the major land development corporation that helped develop Florida hotspots such as Key Biscayne, Deltona, and Port St. John. Another figure in the General Development Corporation was Lou Chesler, the Canadian-born mobster who acted as a front man for Meyer Lansky.

214   Susan Sachs, "Pelullo, Sunshine State Bank had most dealings," *Miami Herald*, October 9, 1986; On the Mackle Brothers, General Development Corporation, and Lou Chesler, see "General Development Corp," Mackle Brothers website, https://www.themacklecompany.com/general-de-velopment. On Lou Chesler and Meyer Lansky, see Jim Hougan, *Spooks*, 230-231.

215   Rick Green, "State Reinstated Boxing Promoter," *Hartford Courant*, October 28, 2004, https://www.courant.com/news/connecticut/hc-xpm-2004-10-28-0410280032-story.html.

216   Chris Frates, "Donald Trump and the Mob," *CNN*, July 31, 2015, https://edition.cnn.com/2015/07/31/politics/trump-mob-mafia/.

217   "Context in Accord for Casino Project," *New York Times*, June 8, 1979, https://www.ny-times.com/1979/06/08/archives/context-in-accord-for-casino-project.html. The project was even-tually abandoned.

218   Susan Sans, "Pelullo, Sunshine State Bank Had Most Dealings," *Miami Herald*, Oct. 4, 1986.

219   Pelullo's stake in Sunshine was organized through King Crown, a company that he had cofounded with the thrift's primary owner, Ray Corona. Corona's background may be relevant here: he had cut his teeth in the world of shadowy finance at Miami National Bank. This bank, in the late 1950s, had been bought by Louis Poller, a close associate of Sam Cohen, a veteran of the Detroit Pur- ple Gang and ally of Meyer Lansky. Poller's purchase of Miami National was carried out with the aid of a loan from the Teamsters Pension Fund: "Shortly thereafter, a coterie of Hoffa-Teamsters associates became directors of the bank, and loans became available for numerous mob-connected ventures" See: "Subject: Joseph Shimon," FBI, November 3, 1962, 34, https://www.maryferrell. org/showDoc.html?docId=116372; "Organized Crime: Stolen Securities," Senate Subcommittee on Government Operations, 1971, 708; Jeff Gerth, "Richard M. Nixon and Organized Crime," Penthouse, July 1974). Miami National also boasted a curious choice for legal counsel: the law firm of Helliwell, Melrose and DeWolf. This was the firm of OSS veteran and CIA banker Paul Helliwell, but work for the bank fell to Helliwell's associate Truman Skinner. Peter Brewton notes that Skinner frequently worked with Donald Berg – a business associate of Richard Nixon's good friend Bebe Rebozo – and Harold White in a series of Florida real estate ventures. Harold White, to bring this full circle, was the son of Pelullo's good friend Armer White. (Brewton p. 322-23)..

220   Alan A. Block and Frank R. Scarpitti, *Poisoning for Profit: The Mafia and Toxic Waste in America* (William Morrow & Co., 1985), 172.

221   "Provenzano and 2 Other Temaster Aides Indicted for Kickback Deal," *New York Times*, December 11, 1975, https://www.nytimes.com/1975/12/11/archives/provenzano-and-2-other-teamster-aides-indicted-for-kickback-deal.html.

222   William M. Adler, *Mollie's Job: A Story of Life and Work on the Global Assembly Line* (Scribner, 2000), 226; *Organized Crime Links to the Waste Disposal Industry: Hearings Before the House Subcommittee on Oversight and Investigations*, Department of Justice, Office of Justice Programs, May 28, 1981, 17-24, https://play.google.com/store/books/details?id=2TYhAAAAMAAJ.

223   Ralph Blumenthal, "Illegal Dumping of Toxins Laid to Organized Crime," *New York Times*, June 5, 1983, https://www.nytimes.com/1983/06/05/nyregion/illegal-dumping-of-toxins-laid-to-organized-crime.html.

224   Block and Scarpitti, *Poisoning for Profit*, 176.

225   *Hazardous Waste Enforcement: Report of the Subcommittee on Oversight and Investigations of the Committee on Energy and Commerce*, US House of Representatives, December 1982, 22.

226   *Hazardous Waste Enforcement*, 24.

227   Joseph A. Califano Jr., *Inside: A Public and Private Life* (Public Affairs, 2004), 391.

228   *Nominations to the US Advisory Commission on Information: Hearings*, Ninety-Second Congress, First Session, April 29 and June 8, 1971, 33, https://books.google.com/books/about/Nominations_to_the_U_S_Advisory_Commissi.html?id=t9cRAAAAIAAJ

229   Richard Harris Smith, *OSS: The Secret History of America's First Central Intelligence Agency* (Lyons Press, 2019), xiv.

230   See Walter Stewart, "John Doyle's Gamble with Millions: Heads He Wings, Tails You Lose," *Macleans*, February 1, 1969.

231   Mark Millard was director of Carl M. Loeb, Rhoades & Co. when it held over 28,000 shares in Canadian Javelin, while Millard himself held 1,000 shares in Doyle's company. See "Company officials report stock changes," *National Post* (Toronto), October 27, 1962. Edgar Bronfman, in his book *Good Spirits*, refers to Mark Millard as "my friend" and as "a senior executive at Carl M. Loeb, Rhoades & Company and my father-in-law John L. Loeb's partner". He goes on to say of Millar "I had enjoyed many successful business dealings with Mark over the years, and I trusted him deeply." See Edgar Bronfman, "Good Spirits: The Making of a Businessman," *New York Times*, 1998, https://archive.nytimes.com/www.nytimes.com/books/first/b/bronfman-spirits.html.

232   *Joint Report of the Task Force to Investigate Certain Allegations concerning the Holding of American Hostages by Iran in 1980*, US Congress, House Committee on Foreign Affairs, One Hundred Second Congress, Second Session, January 3, 1993, 120, https://books.google.com/books?id=x-pl1AAAAMAAJ.

233   *Task Force to Investigate Certain Allegations*, 120-21.

234   Deposition of Roy Furmark," *Report of the Congressional Committees Investigating the*

Iran-Contra Affair, Appendix B, Vol. 11: Depositions, 100 Congress, First Session, 1988, 19 https://www.maryferrell.org/showDoc.html?docId=146481#relPageId=43

235   "Deposition of Roy Furmark," 19

236   *Task Force to Investigate Certain Allegations*, 121.

237   *Task Force to Investigate Certain Allegations*, 122.

238   Robert Perry, "Debunking the Debunkers of October Surprise" (Excerpt from *America's Stolen Narrative*), FAIR, March 2013, https://fair.org/extra/debunking-the-debunkers-of-october-surprise/.

239   *Task Force to Investigate Certain Allegations*, 74.

240   *Task Force to Investigate Certain Allegations*, 130.

241   Susan Trento, *The Power House: Robert Keith Gray and the Selling of Influence and Access in Washington* (St. Martins, 1992), 129. https://archive.org/details/powerhouserobert00tren

242   Persico, *Casey*, 233.

243   Trento, *Prelude to Terror*, 216.

244   Persico, *Casey*, 232.

245   Brewton, *The Mafia*, 7. To make things more complicated, Tracor was in 1985 involved in a joint venture to produce and install hush kits for Boeing 707s. Customers of these particular hush kits included Buffalo Airways, one of the successors to Global International Airways formed by Farhad Azima. See Brewton, *The Mafia*, 318.

246   Seymour M. Hersh, "The Vice President's Men," *London Review of Books, Vol.* 41, no. 2, January 24, 2019, https://www.lrb.co.uk/the-paper/v41/n02/seymour-m.-hersh/the-vice-president-s-men.

247   Trento, *Prelude to Terror*, 214.

248   "Shackley deposition," 144.

249   *Report of the Congressional Committees Investigating the Iran-Contra Affair*, Vol. 1, 164, https://www.maryferrell.org/showDoc.html?docId=146504.

250   *Joint Hearings Before the House Select Committee to Investigate Covert Arms Transactions with Iran and Senate Select Committee on Secret Military Assistance to Iran and the Nicaraguan Opposition: Testimony of Robert C. McFarlane, Gaston J. Sigur, Jr., and Robert W. Owen*, One Hundredth Congress, First Session, May 11, 12, 13, 14, and 19, 1987, p. 244, https://archive.org/details/Iran-Contra-HearingsTestimonyTranscripts/1987-irn-0003-McFarlane-Sigur-Owen/.

251   Thomas and Dillon, *Israel's Superspy*, 145.

252   Trento, *Prelude to Terror*, 284.

CHAPTER 7

A KILLER ENTERPRISE

OUTLAW BANKS

"We must learn to 'feel' that BCCI is this *Power*," read a bizarre memo once circulated by the Bank of Commerce and Credit International, better known as BCCI. That "power" was a reference to the image printed in light tones behind the text – a print of Michelangelo's famous *Creation of Adam*, the fresco painting that adorns the ceiling of the Sistine Chapel. It shows God, surrounded by angels and with his finger outstretched, reaching toward the first man, Adam, imbuing him with the gift of life. In continuing the reference to Michelangelo's depiction of the divine spark, the memo stated that BCCI is "not merely a group of branches, a set of facts and figures. Since, BCCI is a power, a spirit, a Desire – it is all encompassing and enfolding – it relates itself to cosmic power and wisdom, which is the will of God."[1]

Founded in 1972, BCCI certainly wielded considerable power in its day, though its power was hardly of a spiritual or benevolent variety. When it finally collapsed after a nearly two-decades run, thanks to forced closures brought about by regulators and law enforcement, so too did the "planetary Ponzi scheme" it had been running.[2] At the time of its collapse in 1991, *TIME* ran a lengthy story describing the bank as the "dirtiest bank of them all."[3] The authors of that article, Jonathan Beaty and S. C. Gwynne, also wrote that Robert Morgenthau, Manhattan's district attorney, had stated that he received no help from the Justice Department when he launched his own investigation into the bank.

Obfuscation and protection from the highest levels of power were defining characteristics of BCCI. The bank's founder, Agha Hasan Abedi, who had a penchant for occult ramblings and mind games, surrounded himself with a bevy of politicians, community leaders, business giants, powerful criminals, and spooks.[4] Prior to the formation of BCCI, Abedi, a Pakistani banker, had been an economic advisor to Sheikh Zayed bin Sultan Al Na-hyan. Sheikh Zayed had been the driving force behind the formation of the United Arab Emirates and was the union's first leader. According to one person close to Abedi, he had been the one who had first planted the idea of what would become the UAE in Sheikh Zayed's mind.[5]

Abedi was something of a cosmopolitan, an internationalist, and an opponent of classical colonialism in the developing world. At the same time, he opposed socialist currents sweeping across the Middle East and elsewhere. A self-described liberal, he first conceived of BCCI as a "world bank, a global bank for the third world."[6] With backing from Sheikh Zayed, the Saudi royal family, and probably the Saudi intelligence service, what developed was something else entirely. BCCI's expertise was in money laundering, capital flight, fraud, and much, much worse.

While the conventional narrative presents BCCI as an enterprise whose origins lay in Pakistani-Saudi networks of power, influence, and finance, there have also been allegations that the bank's origins also involved the CIA. A 1992 report published in *Newsweek* cites an anonymous former officer of BCCI and its predecessor, United Bank, as well as a close associate of Abedi's, who asserted that Abedi "had worked with the CIA during his United Bank days and that the CIA had encouraged him in his project to launch BCCI, since the agency realized that an international bank could provide valuable cover for intelligence operations."[7] This same source specifically mentioned Richard Helms, CIA director from 1966 until 1973, as having been involved in the bank's creation. He told *Newsweek*, "What I have been told is that it wasn't a Pakistani bank at all. The guys behind the bank weren't Pakistani at all. The whole thing was a front."[8]

According to Beaty and Gwynne, the bank's organizational structure was divided between two very different worlds. On the front-facing side, "more conventional departments of [BCCI] handled such services as laundering money for the drug trade and helping dictators loot their national treasuries." On the back end, meanwhile, was something that was called the "black network," which reportedly continued after the demise of the bank. This black network "operates a lucrative arms-trade business and transports drugs and gold," engages in sex trafficking and maybe even murder-for-hire. In some cases, it even helps shape the military capacities of entire nations.[9]

Thus, BCCI supported the work of A.Q. Khan, a Pakistani nuclear physicist and engineer known as the father of Pakistan's nuclear weapons program. This work had begun after India tested the "Smiling Buddha," their own nuclear weapon, in 1974 and it was carried out under the auspices of Khan Research Laboratories. The clandestine laboratory operated several front groups, one of which was the Ghulam Ishaq Khan Institute of Engineering Sciences and Technology. A "philanthropic" arm of BCCI, the BCCI Foundation, provided funding for this institute.[10]

According to Beaty and Gwynne, BCCI obtained, on behalf of Pakistan and Iraq, an experimental weapon called a "Columbine head."[11] Columbine heads were allegedly a type of thermobaric bomb, better known as a "fuel air explosive," as they suck in the surrounding air to create a powerful explosion.

It was not all bombs, however, when it came to BCCI's activities in Abedi's home country. The bank also played an important role in tightening relations between Pakistan and states in the Persian Gulf. The economic development of Saudi Arabia and Abu Dhabi had been built on the massive flow of cheap labor from Pakistan. There was a reciprocal flow of money from those states back to Pakistan through migrant remittances, that is, money sent by laborers to their families at home.

In the developing world, remittances are often a complicated issue, with the lack of strong banking sectors and financial regulations resulting in everything from overcharging for financial transactions to outright theft. BCCI stepped into this world and soon made itself the primary conduit for the flow of such money. It was a win-win for all parties: the functioning of this system solidified the use of Pakistani labor by states in the Persian Gulf, while Pakistan received in-flows of foreign currencies. It was good for BCCI, too: the remittance float was registered on BCCI's balance sheets, allowing the bank to appear far more cash-rich than it really was.[12]

Other services that BCCI provided for the Arab ruling families included the procurement of "Pakistani prostitutes … typically teenage girls, known as 'singing and dancing girls.'"[13] When discussing these types of activities, the Congressional report on BCCI came close to revealing the bank/black network dichotomy discussed by Beaty and Gwynne in *TIME*. The head of BCCI's Pakistan operations was a close friend of Abedi named Sani Ahmad. Nazir Chinoy, BCCI's general manager for France and Africa, told investigators that "Sani was the trusted man for things no one else was supposed to know. We were the technocrats. Sani Ahmed would handle the things we wouldn't, like get girls. If anyone paid anyone any money [as a bribe], Sani would have been the one to do it."[14] BCCI's role in sex trafficking, including of minors, is discussed in chapter 11.

Early on, BCCI saw a pipeline into the US financial system as being necessary to its success. The earliest attempts to cement this connection saw Abedi court American Express. This plan was abandoned when American Express demanded significant influence over BCCI's internal activities. Abedi then pivoted toward Bank of America, one of the largest American banks that, since the 1960s, had been active in the Eurodollar trade. Bank of America became a large stakeholder in BCCI, holding some 30 percent of the stock, and a number of the bank's officials joined the BCCI board.

Bank of America later sold that 30 percent, expressing concern over BCCI's activities. It looked like Bank of America was engaging in due diligence, but appearances were deceiving. As the Congressional BCCI report pointed out, Bank of America "would in fact retain correspondent banking relations with BCCI, continually seek additional business from BCCI, collude in least one of BCCI's purchase of foreign banks through nominees in South America, and earn a great deal of money from the relationship until BCCI's closure."[15]

Ultimately, Bank of America's sale of the shares simply allowed BCCI to further develop its complicated web of front companies, proxies, and offshore entities that it used to mask its activities. The bank turned to ICIC (Overseas) Limited, set up in the Caymans by BCCI, to act as a clearinghouse to sell shares of BCCI subsidiaries.[16]

Beyond their relationship with Bank of America, BCCI's major penetration of the US financial system came through the bank's involvement with Bert Lance, a prominent banker from Atlanta and a close friend of Jimmy Carter. He served as an advisor to Carter's 1976 presidential campaign and was subsequently named director of the Office of Management and Budget (OMB). However, Lance was soon forced from his post under the cloud of scandal. In the words of the Congressional BCCI report, "By September 21, 1977, when Bert Lance tendered his resignation from the position of director of the [OMB] to President Jimmy Carter, Lance had become the most notorious banker in the United States."[17]

Lance's notoriety was directly related to the National Bank of Georgia, of which Lance had become president in 1975. His time there was marred by controversy. For instance, he had particularly tense relations with the bank's parent company, Financial General Bankshares (FGB), "for making loans which both exceeded his lending limit and were not secured by collateral."[18] These activities, as well as similar ones that Lance had carried out at other banks, haunted him during his time at the OMB, particularly when Carter asked Congress "to suspend ethics rules that would have forced Lance to sell 190,000 shares of stock he owned in National Bank of Georgia. He based his request on the ground that Lance would lose $1.6 million if he was forced to sell, because the bank's stock was depressed."[19] His request instead resulted in a sweeping investigation into Lance's banking practices.

Lance was also violating regulations by engaging in other financial activities while serving in public office. FGB's major stockholder and controller, Gen. George Olmsted, was under orders from the Federal Reserve to unload his stock due to laws governing holding companies. He approached Lance for help, and Lance began the hunt for buyers for their holdings in FGB and National Bank of Georgia.

Olmsted is an intriguing figure, and his history in banking might shed some light on why FGB was such a hot commodity in the 1970s. During World War II, Olmsted wore many hats, with involvement in everything from managing lend-lease arrangements to working in intelligence in the China-Burma-India theater. After the war, he took control of International Bank in Washington, DC, and built a business empire with extensive holdings in other banks, real estate, and insurance companies. It was through International Bank that he bought his controlling stake in FGB. Another major International Bank holding was the Cayman Islands-based Mercantile Bank & Trust. Mercantile was one of the many banks that composed Paul Helliwell's dark money network, and it owned a stake in his Castle Bank & Trust.[20]

During his last days as director of OMB, Lance put Olmsted in touch with J. Middendorf, who had served as Secretary of the Navy and as ambassador to the Netherlands under President Nixon. Middendorf was also close to Carter, who had offered to retain him as Navy Secretary. Middendorf opted instead for a career in the private sector. He was immediately intrigued by Lance's plan, and the "Middendorf Group" was put together to take over FGB.

The Middendorf Group consisted of prominent business figures like Jackson Stephens, the Arkansas kingmaker behind Stephens, Inc.; the banker Jorge Pereira; and Armand Hammer of Occidental Petroleum. Stephens, discussed in greater detail in the next chapter, was particularly important to the whole chain of events involving FGB and its takeover by BCCI. He had known Lance since at least 1975, likely through their mutual support for Jimmy Carter, whom Stephens had allegedly known since their days at the Naval Academy. Stephens and Lance continued to work together on selling-off FGB even after the Middendorf Group fell apart. Reportedly, Stephens was involved in the bank's convoluted affairs because he "wanted FGB to use a company he controlled, Systematics Inc., for its data processing business."[21]

Other prospective buyers had different motives. Armand Hammer, for example, saw a gold mine of valuable information that could be leveraged for political and economic gain. FGB "had outstanding loans to more than one hundred US senators and congressmen.... Hammer explained that all these congressional borrowers had submitted statements to the bank that revealed their precise financial status, including their debts, earnings, real estate holdings, other assets.... Hammer had blackmail in mind."[22] As will be mentioned in Chapter 9, Hammer's father had been a spy for Soviet intelligence, and suspicions that he too had a relationship with the security-intelligence apparatus of the USSR dogged Armand Hammer for years. This makes his interest in using FGB for the "financial blackmail" of American senators and congressmen particularly significant.

However, Hammer eventually abandoned his takeover scheme and sold off his shares to BCCI frontmen. It is possible that his encounter with the bank was not a one-off event, however, as throughout the 1970s, roughly one million shares in Hammer's Occidental Petroleum were held by one of BCCI's agents, Ghaith Pharaon. In a *New York Times* blurb on the arrangement, Pharaon was described as Occidental's representative in Saudi Arabia.[23] Later, Occidental partnered with the London-based Attock Oil Co. Ltd., which was led by a handful of BCCI players. These included Pharaon and Kamal Adham, the former Saudi intelligence chief and co-founder of the Safari Club.[24]

BCCI came to be involved with FGB only after the Middendorf Group had begun to split apart. The primary agents in the BCCI takeover of FGB were Lance, Stephens, and Eugene Metzger, a Washington attorney who had formerly served in the Justice Department and the Office of the Comptroller of the Currency. It appears that BCCI was first interested in the FGB subsidiary, National Bank of Georgia. During a meeting with a BCCI representative in Little Rock, Arkansas, Stephens and Lance suggested that they purchase FGB. Shortly thereafter, the pair, joined by Metzger, began to accumulate large holdings of FGB stock, purchased on both the open market and from individual shareholders. These shares were then sold to investors operating on behalf of BCCI, including Kamal Adham.

By January 1978, BCCI had secretly gained control of 20 percent of FGB. Facing a hostile takeover, the bank's leadership hit back with a lawsuit aimed at Abedi, Lance, Metzger, Stephens, and Stephens' companies Stephens Inc. and Systematics.[25] The US Securities and Exchange Commission launched its own suit, charging securities fraud. To defend itself against this legal onslaught, the "Lance group" retained the services of Clark Clifford and Robert Altman. According to Clifford and Altman, this was their first interaction with BCCI. Their timeline may not have been entirely truthful, however, considering the contents of a *Washington Post* article from December 1977. In the article, Altman is quoted as saying that Lance was involved with "Middle Eastern financial interests" and had set up for them "a holding company to direct their capital into banks and other U.S. investments."[26]

The SEC suit was settled quickly, but the challenge posed by FGB tossed roadblock after roadblock in BCCI's path. The battle dragged on for a year before a Maryland judge ruled in favor of FGB, stating that the bank could not be acquired via hostile takeover. BCCI was blocked but not defeated. Clifford selected three of his close associates to act as hidden proxies for BCCI's interests and managed to get them onto the board of FGB. One of these individuals, former Senator Stuart Symington, was also made the chairman of a company, registered in the Netherland Antilles, called Credit and Commerce American Holdings N.V. Credit and Commerce American Holdings' stock was owned by various BCCI principals, and it acted as the holding company for Credit and Commerce American Investments B.V..

Another man involved in Credit and Commerce American Holdings was Mohammed Rahim Motaghi Irvani, an Iranian billionaire and a business partner of former CIA director Richard Helms.[27] Irvani, referred to in the BCCI Affair as "BCCI's lead front-man in the original takeover" of FGB, was directly assisted by Helms in these efforts. As a result, media reports later noted that "U.S. Senate investigators are examining dealings between Helms and Irvani that it said raise questions about the CIA's knowledge of BCCI's evolution into a criminal organization."[28]

Helms and Irvani also had interlocking business interests with Roy Carlson, the Bank of America executive who had overseen the bank's 1972 purchase of 30 percent of BCCI's shares. In 1975, Carlson left Bank of America to oversee the business interests of Irvani.[29] Years later, Carlson became vice president at Helm's consulting firm.[30] Both Carlson and Abedi also had documented ties to BCCI. Carlson had accompanied Abedi on business trips, while Irvani had been recruited into BCCI's affairs directly by Abedi himself.[31]

This maze-like structure of offshore companies hid the ultimate controlling body, which of course was BCCI. By forming yet another layer, a dummy company set up beneath Credit and Commerce American Holdings, BCCI was able to evade the prohibition of regulators and finally take control of FGB. Clifford and Altman relayed to regulators that these new purchasers were in no way connected to BCCI, and despite the overwhelming abundance of evidence that they *were* BCCI proxies, the Federal Reserve and other regulators began the approval process. In this sudden about-face, the US government appeared to be simply ignoring the obvious.

Catherine Austin Fitts, former assistant secretary for housing–federal housing commissioner at the US Department of Housing and Urban Development during the George H.W.Bush administration and an investment banker with the Hamilton Securities Group and Dillon, Read & Co., was placed on the board of First American Bankshares (the name of FGB following its takeover by BCCI) following the collapse of BCCI in 1991. She later stated that, after reading through troves of documents regarding the bank's activities prior to its implosion, it was clear that there was "no way" its clandestine activities were carried on without the full knowledge of the Federal Reserve, specifically the Federal Reserve Bank of New York, and the White House.[32] Did such knowledge extend back to when BCCI finally gained control of FGB?

After the takeover, FGB was rechristened First American Bankshares, and an impressive plan for growth was launched. Clifford stated that he wanted First American "to be one of the twenty biggest banks in the country," and, by 1989, it held over $11.5 billion in assets.[33] It also embarked on a close working relationship with its hidden parent company. Dozens of BCCI subsidiaries held accounts at First American branches, and Abedi arranged for BCCI managers to take top positions at the bank.
Meanwhile, Abedi courted US politicians and developed a particularly close bond with Jimmy Carter.

As BCCI burrowed deeper into the US financial system, Abedi and his close cohorts became involved with the Carter Presidential Center. Abedi, Adnan Khashoggi, and Clifford were all large donors to the center, and BCCI became a mega-donor to a third world development project set up by Carter called Global 2000. Abedi was selected to serve as co-chairman of Global 2000, while Carter himself was the acting chairman.[34]

Another politically connected philanthropic outfit that BCCI became connected to was called the Chiefs of Police National Drug Task Force (COP), which received money from First American.[35] The head of COP was the Utah senator Orrin Hatch, who became a defender of BCCI during its collapse and who had ties to a number of its principals. Another figure involved in COP was Randy Anderson, the son of DC journalist Jack Anderson whose roles in Watergate and the Profumo Affair were discussed in previous chapters.

First American's board included Robert Keith Gray, who joined shortly after the bank was renamed.[36] Seven years later, in 1988 – after Gray had rejoined Hill & Knowlton, with his Gray and Company becoming a subsidiary of the firm – H & K was retained by BCCI after the bank was indicted in Tampa for drug-money laundering. As part of its campaign to distance BCCI's image from illicit activity, H & K "disseminated materials discrediting persons and publications whose statements were later proved accurate about BCCI's criminality."[37]

As for FGB's/First American's subsidiary, National Bank of Georgia – it was purchased by BCCI front man and business partner of Armand Hammer, Ghaith Pharaon. While the Office of the Comptroller of the Currency expressed concern over the purchase, the regulators ultimately allowed these transactions to go through. Roy Carlson, the former Bank of America executive who first forged ties between that bank and BCCI, was "recruited by Abedi to run the National Bank of Georgia" after it was purchased by Pharaon.[38] Several years later, Pharaon resold the bank to none other than First American.

Pharaon, it should be mentioned, maintained significant political connections of his own. Just prior to his first encounter with Bert Lance, he had bought a large block of stock in the Main Bank of Houston, Texas. Another Arab investor was the Saudi billionaire Khalid bin Mahfouz, the power behind the prominent National Commercial Bank. Like Pharaon, bin Mahfouz was extremely close to BCCI and even owned shares in the bank. Later, in 1986, plans were underway for bin Mahfouz to take over both BCCI, and Credit and Commerce American Holdings, but internal auditors for National Commercial raised too many questions about the arrangement.[39]

Other investors in Main Bank alongside Pharaon and bin Mahfouz included John Connally, the former governor in Texas who was soon to become a major player in the world of defrauding savings and loans. There was also James R. Bath, a close friend of George W. Bush and, according to his former partner, Bill White, a CIA asset who had been personally recruited by George H.W.Bush in 1976, when Bush was director of the Agency.[40]

Bath had a long career in aviation, real estate, and finance. Early on, he became a vice president at the Texas division of Atlantic Aviation, which was controlled by the powerful DuPont family. This was followed by Bath/Bentsen Interests, a real estate development company that he co-founded with Lan Bentsen, the son of future Clinton treasury secretary, Lloyd Bentsen Jr. In 1976, the year he was reportedly recruited by G. H.W. Bush and the CIA, he created Jim Bath and Associates. Almost immediately thereafter, Bath's career took a rapid, upward ascent: "He was named as trustee for Sheikh Salem bin Laden of Saudi Arabia. ... Bath's job was to handle all of bin Laden's North American investments and operations."[41] He also was made the trustee for bin Mahfouz's US investments.

Russ Baker, in *Family of Secrets*, recounts how Bill White told him that Bath's recruitment by G. H.W.Bush was intimately connected to the growing relationship between Saudi Arabia and Texas oil.[42] Bath, it seems, was something of a middle man for these two parties – and his presence alongside the two BCCI-linked individuals, Khalid bin Mahfouz and Ghaith Pharaon, should be understood in that context.

BCCI's reach extended far beyond Saudi Arabia, Pakistan, and the United States, as it was truly global in scope. The bank maintained, for example, a presence in the People's Republic of China. During the "reform and opening up" of the PRC under the leadership of Deng Xiaoping, BCCI was the second foreign bank to open branches in the country. It "secured substantial deposits from the Chinese government and its business affiliates"; according to the BCCI Affair, Chinese officials and government entities lost around $500 million when the bank collapsed.[43] BCCI also maintained joint ventures with other businesses within China. One of these was the China-Arab Bank, a joint venture with the Abu Dhabi Investment Authority.

At the time, the relationship between the PRC and the Soviet Union was considerably strained – and yet BCCI was in the USSR as well. In an appendix to the BCCI Affair titled "Matters for Further Investigation," the joint activities of BCCI and the Foreign Trade Mission of the Soviet Union in London was highlighted as significant, but little information was added. The report states that "obtaining the records of those financial transactions would be critical to understanding what the Soviet Union under Brezhnev, Chernenko, and Andropov was doing in the West."[44]

One clue as to USSR-connected activities was reported by Jonathan Beaty and S. C. Gwynne in their book on BCCI. Beaty was told by a German arms dealer, whom they refer to as "Heinrich," that the Soviets were buying Western high technology via BCCI – in this instance the Navstar GPS system.[45]

Throughout the third world, BCCI presented itself as a development bank. This allowed it to gain intimate access to governments, emerging markets, and the financing systems that they required. It was the "second largest of all lenders to the Congo," while in Cameroon it developed close ties to the country's finance ministry – and bribed them to take high-interest loans from the bank.[46] The *BCCI Affair* charges that BCCI cultivated relationships with the United Nations outpost and the US embassy in Cameroon as well. In Nigeria, meanwhile, BCCI cozied up to the nation's central bank and apparently traveled with their top financial functionaries throughout the world. One witness reported that, at a meeting of the World Bank in Seoul, they had observed "one of the BCC[I] officers with a lot of cash, handing it out to the staff of the central bank of Nigeria."[47]

In Jamaica, BCCI became the intermediary between the state and the world financial system. It handled "essentially every foreign current account of Jamaican government agencies."[48] US government agencies were involved in this corruption of the Jamaican government, as BCCI became "involved in financing all of Jamaica's commodity imports from the United States under the U.S. Commodity Credit Corporation."[49] The CCC itself was no stranger to skullduggery. As will be seen, it was implicated – along with BCCI and several connected banks – in the transfer of armaments and munitions to Iraq at the height of the Iran-Iraq War.

Through the Gulf Group – headed by Abbas, Mustafa, and Murtaza Gokal – BCCI had a foothold in global shipping. Abedi was particularly close to Abbas Gokal, the main figure in Gulf's shipping lines. He had courted him early on in BCCI's existence, and an ever-escalating series of loans fueled the Gokal's maritime interests, allowing the family to quickly control an impressive fleet. The Gulf Group and BCCI were so fundamentally interwoven, acting as practical extensions of one another, that when BCCI collapsed, the resulting shockwaves profoundly destabilized Gulf.[50]

Like Ghaith Pharaon, Abbas Gokal sometimes acted as a front man or proxy for BCCI. In 1975, for example, he attempted to acquire Chelsea National Bank, a small New York City bank. Regulators very quickly recognized that Gokal had practically no familiarity with the ins and outs of bank ownership – and they saw how closely tied he was to BCCI. In 1976, Gokal admitted that, upon acquiring the bank, he had planned to bring in a BCCI management team to run its operations.[51]

In the early 1980s, Gokal approached the intelligence/organized crime-linked Bruce Rappaport with an offer to buy 50 percent of his Inter Maritime Bank. Rappaport declined the offer and instead sold 19.9 percent of the bank's shares to the Gulf Group and added Abbas to his board of directors[52] Later, when he was shuffled off to prison for his fraudulent activities with BCCI, Abbas' personal secretary went to work for Rappaport.

Was Gokal fronting for BCCI in Rappaport's organization? It seems likely, as Rappaport himself maintained numerous ties to the bank. One of his top money managers, the Swiss banker Alfred Hartmann, was himself a BCCI frontman, while Rappaport held a significant stake in the illustrious Bank of New York, which was one of BCCI's correspondent banks. Bert Lance, meanwhile, had mentioned Rappaport in his testimony before the official BCCI inquiry, stating that he believed that Rappaport had been dispatched by William Casey, Rappaport's close friend, to spy on him and keep tabs on BCCI. "Lance said that Rappaport maintained contact with him for a period of years until the death of Director [William] Casey," the *BCCI Affair* states, before adding that Lance "failed to mention in his testimony that despite his suspicions of Rappaport, he arranged with him to have one of his sons work in the financier's New York bank."[53]

Both Rappaport and BCCI were also engaged in various activities in the oil-rich nation of Oman. BCCI had been active there since 1973, when, together with Bank of America, it set up the National Bank of Oman. Peter Truell and Larry Gurwin, in *False Profits*, note that the National Bank of Oman "became one of BCCI's biggest units, with fifty-five branches."[54] Tellingly, the *BCCI Affair* suggests that "BCCI may have been moving money through the National Bank of Oman to fund the war in Afghanistan," before adding that the National Bank of Oman and its CEO, Qais-Al Zawawi, also did business with CIA director Casey's associate, Bruce Rappaport.[55]

Interestingly, one of the most active players in Oman's oil market was John Deuss, the enigmatic oil trader whom Ted Shackley had gone to work for after leaving the CIA. In fact, Deuss reportedly hired Shackley specifically to help him operate in Oman.[56] According to one of Deuss' associates, journalist Susan Mazur, Deuss' main contact in Oman was Qais-Al Zawawi of the National Bank of Oman. Could there have been a connection with the purported use of the bank by the CIA to finance the Afghan Mujahideen? It is certainly possible. As mentioned in the last chapter, there are rumors that EATSCO, the freight forwarder managed by Shackley's crony Thomas Clines, was involved in the movement of arms and other war supplies to the Mujahideen.

Yet another major player in Oman during this period was a firm called Tetra Tech International. Once a subsidiary of Honeywell, Tetra Tech was run by former CIA officer James Critchfield, who was not only an old Middle East hand, but also a close associate of Shackley. In 1979, Tetra Tech was "given supervisory control … over the operations of [eleven] government ministries."[57] Major construction projects, the management of ports, the telecommunication infrastructure, the post office, and food inspections were just a handful of the things that Tetra Tech controlled in Oman. In addition, as noted in the last chapter, Donald Jameson, a CIA veteran who went to work for Tetra Tech, had been one of the attendees of the Le Cercle meeting tied to the October Surprise plot.

As the *BCCI Affair* makes clear, investigators also suspected a potential connection between Tetra Tech International and the similarly named Tetra Finance, a Hong Kong-based financial outfit that was closely integrated with the Hong Kong Deposit and Guaranty Company.[58] Playing an active role in each of these institutions was John Shaheen, one of William Casey's "Hardy Boys" and a central figure in the October Surprise plot. Shaheen was paid by each bank to broker deposits and to court wealthy Arabs to join their boards. Individuals who maintained a post on the board of each included Hassan Yassin, Kamal Adham's successor as Saudi intelligence chief and a cousin of Adnan Khashoggi. Another was Al Mazrui, the head of the Abu Dhabi Investment Authority and director at BCCI.

Once again, BCCI appears, albeit surrounded by heavy fog, in the background of the covert conflicts of the 1980s. The support for the Mujahideen was just one of many such instances. Another is the Iran-Contra affair. A global web of operations and cooperating and competing factions, each with logistical networks dedicated to arms dealing, drug smuggling, and money laundering, the complexity of Iran-Contra is simply mind-boggling. Despite its involution, at nearly every level of these interlocking components and operations, one invariably finds the tendrils of BCCI.

BLACK EAGLE

When the Kerry Commission on terrorism, narcotics, and international operations was underway in the early 1990s, longtime BCCI executive Amjad Awan was one of the witnesses called to testify.

Awan told the commission that he had acted as the banker for Manuel Noriega, the strong-man who had first come to power in Panama in 1983. Noriega would deposit "$3 million at a time in $100 bills" in BCCI, while Awan would disperse "$20,000 payments to Panamanian politicians at Noriega's request."[59]

Furthermore, according to Awan, Clark Clifford's partner Robert Altman had personally intervened to obscure the massive flow of Noriega-connected funds into BCCI. As BCCI collapsed and regulators and politicians subpoenaed internal bank documents, Altman hid them by having them relabeled as "attorney work product."[60]

A sizable chunk of Noriega's wealth came from his deep involvement in the Latin America drug trade. According to Carlos Lehder, the Medellin cartel boss who had worked closely with Robert Vesco in the Bahamas, Noriega reached an agreement with Pablo Escobar and other Medellin leaders that made Panama a transshipment point for Colombian cocaine destined for the US. In exchange for "$1000 for each kilogram of cocaine and a percentage of every dollar of drug proceeds flown to Panamanian banks," Noriega was purported to have guaranteed the safe passage of drug flights in and out of various airstrips across the country.[61]

Partial corroboration of Lehder's claims comes from Steven Kalish, an American drug smuggler who worked closely with Noriega's pilot, Cesar Rodriguez. Kalish was made a partner in Servicios Turisticos, a Panamanian airline owned by Rodriguez and Noriega, and was given "special military protection for shipments of money into the country."[62] According to Kalish, the relationship between Noriega and the Medellin cartel did not fully blossom until 1984, when he arranged for some of their cohorts to be released from Panamanian jail.

Noriega was also a CIA asset and had been since 1967, becoming the Agency's eyes and ears in Panama. He became particularly close to George H.W.Bush when the future president was director of the CIA. Peter Dale Scott and Jonathan Marshall write that, in 1976, "CIA director George Bush arranged to pay Noriega $110,000 for his services [and] put the Panamanian up as a house guest of his deputy CIA director."[63] Noriega enjoyed a similar camaraderie with Bush's rival, CIA director William Casey, who is alleged to have met with Noriega repeatedly in Washington, DC.

That Noriega served as both *de facto* drug baron and the CIA's man in Panama became an issue for the US during the early 1980s, when Casey launched the first operations to support the Nicaraguan Contras in their fight against the ruling Sandinistas of Nicaragua. According to various journalists writing in the late 1980s this operation was code-named "Black Eagle."[64]

Howard Kohn and Vicky Monks, in their 1989 *Rolling Stone* article on the operation, stated that, very early on, Casey recruited Israel's Mossad "to arrange for the acquisition and shipping of weapons to the Contras."[65] As noted in the last chapter, Mossad had its own man in Panama, Michael Harari, who worked as an arms trafficker and security consultant for Noriega. The "Harari network," as it was later dubbed, overlapped with the drug smuggling networks that were operated in Panama by the Medellin cartel. Though he was no longer officially in the employ of Mossad by this point, Harari's activities were funded to the tune of $20 million from Israel.[66]

José Blandón, one of Noriega's top advisors, later told journalists that Harari had worked with Duane Clarridge, the head of CIA operations in Latin America, and Donald Gregg, Vice President Bush's National Security Advisor, to establish a network of bases for logistical support of the Contra conflict. Kohn and Monks appear to corroborate Blandón's story, writing that the vice president's office did have a role in the Black Eagle operation and that the man on the ground had been Donald Gregg. They add that the airstrips in Panama utilized by the CIA were the same as those being used by the Medellin cartel and that the arrangement between these parties had first been set up by Israel.

Independent accounts show that the prime years that Black Eagle was purported to have been running, 1982 and 1983, were busy ones for the US and Israel.[67] In November 1982, the US government admitted to supporting rebel forces in Nicaragua. By March of the following year, the CIA had set up a $50 million intelligence apparatus in Latin America that was largely focused on Nicaragua, and US military advisors were placed in Honduras to advise the main Contra group, the Fuerza Democrática de Nicaragua or FDN. In the summer of 1983, the *New York Times* reported that Israel, at the urging of the US, was providing arms, confiscated from the PLO in Lebanon to the Contras.

In 1984 and 1985, Black Eagle began to fall apart. This was in no small part thanks to Noriega. As Kohn and Monks noted:

> While helping to raise funds for the contras, Noriega was pursuing a favorite pastime – adding to his store of potential political-blackmail material. An insatiable collector of "negative information" about both friends and foes, Noriega is known to have hidden

video and audio equipment in government offices to record meetings and phone calls. Early in the Black Eagle operation, according to Blandón, Noriega began to compile a dossier about the role of Bush and his staff. In the dossier is said to be copies of status reports sent to Gregg and videotapes of meetings held in Noriega's office, plus a special report that Blandón prepared about Black Eagle on Noriega's orders.[68]

With Noriega acting increasingly bold, tensions reportedly developed between US and Israeli operators throughout Latin America, each worried that the other would hang them out to dry if the link between the pro-Contra efforts and the Medellin drug flights was revealed.

Another issue was the increasing unpopularity of the Contra war in the US. Beginning in 1982, a series of laws passed by Congress limited the ability of the Reagan administration to provide military aid to Contra groups. This reached its apex with the 1984 Boland Amendment, which prohibited all US military aid to the Contras and hampered the CIA's Nicaraguan operations. With a crisis mounting, Casey began to search for an alternative system that would allow him to continue the covert war. Soon, with the aid of his new protégé Oliver North, "the Enterprise" would be up and running.

The Enterprise appears to have been named as such because it was fundamentally a money-making endeavor, and its numerous tendrils and interlocking components cut across as many business ventures as they did covert operations. It was also an offshoot – if not a direct continuation – of Shackley's private-intelligence apparatus. Richard Secord, who had been involved in the overbilling scam at the Pentagon that provided funding for EATSCO, was one of North's right-hand men in the Enterprise's money networks. Joining him was Albert Hakim, another veteran of Shackley's world, as was Thomas Clines. As alluded to previously, the arms-for-hostage deals that ultimately torpedoed the Enterprise's activities had come to North's attention from a complex changing of hands. It had originated, however, in a meeting between Shackley and Iranian interests.

North, a marine and veteran of the Vietnam War, was apparently recruited into Shackley's network in the early 1980s. In 1981, he joined the National Security Council (NSC), and in 1983 – right in the middle of Black Eagle – he became the NSC's deputy director for political-military affairs. During his first two years at the NSC, however, he was an assistant to Robert "Bud" MacFarlane, who soon became Reagan's National Security Advisor. MacFarlane's career had depended on his development and maintenance of connections to prominent players. For instance, he had served as military assistant to Henry Kissinger and accompanied him on his secret trips to China. At the end of the 1970s, he was appointed by John Tower to head the US Senate Committee on Armed Services, and in 1981 he became an assistant to Alexander Haig. Tower's critical role in the subversion of US national security by aiding Robert Maxwell in the PROMIS scandal is detailed in chapter 9. Notably, Tower and Maxwell had first been brought together by Henry Kissinger.

According to Joseph Trento, MacFarlane's early work for Kissinger had been arranged by his mentor, Col. Jack Brennan, who was Nixon's last chief of staff.[69] Brennan and MacFarlane had stayed in touch over the years, and, at some point, North, while working under MacFarlane, was introduced to Brennan's associate, Lt. Col. James M. Tully. Tully was close to Shackley and Secord.

Trento writes that he was told by Marine colonel and sometimes CIA asset William Corson that North had informed him about his growing ties to this crowd, who were then being used to operate off-the-books operations for the CIA and the National Security Council. "It was then that I realized what had happened," Corson reportedly said. "These dumb bastards got sucked into the old Ed Wilson crowd: Shackley, Secord, Clines. The administration had let these guys in the tent, and it was only a matter of time before they owned the circus."[70]

THE STRUCTURE OF THE ENTERPRISE

The basis for the Enterprise was a company founded by Richard Secord and Albert Hakim in 1983 called Stanford Technology Trading Group International (STTGI). It was one of many similarly-named companies that the pair had set up. They had formed the nearly identical Stanford Technology Corporation in the 1970s, and had since set up StanTech Services S.A.; Stanford Technology Corporation Services, S.A.; and Scitech, S.A, among others. A year after STTGI was formed, North introduced Secord to Adolfo Calero, the leader of the FDN, the CIA's preferred Contra group. An arrangement was made where, thanks to a sizable cash donation from Saudi Arabia, STTGI would buy arms and resell them to the Contras.

This basic business arrangement rapidly ballooned during 1985 and 1986. Throughout 1985, Manucher Ghorbanifar (who, as previously noted, had brought an arms-for-hostages deal to Shackley), Israel's David Kimche, and Michael Ledeen met multiple times to discuss the possibility of an arrangement between the Reagan administration, Israel, and Iran. Ledeen often reported back to McFarlane, who was by then National Security Advisor, on these meetings. At the end of August of that year, a US arms package – including 100 TOW missiles – was dispatched to Iran via Israel.[71] The initial financing for this shipment, which was routed through his accounts at BCCI, was provided by Adnan Khashoggi.

Ledeen was, at this time, operating from North's office at the NSC, though he later claimed that North was unaware of the arms sales. North, he continued, was busy trying to arrange for the freeing of the hostages in Lebanon. Ledeen was likely dissembling: according to the Tower Report, McFarlane told President Reagan that Israel has "taken it upon themselves" to sell arms to Iran in order to try to get hostages released.[72] Roughly a month after this first arms sale, Kimche contacted McFarlane with news that one of the hostages was to be released, and more would follow. Records show that North was tasked with handling this situation.

By October, North was holding meetings with Ledeen and Ghorbanifar as well as Al Schwimmer and other players on the Israeli side of the operation in DC. The arms sales continued smoothly for the next several months. January 1986 was when the operation took on another dimension. During the course of a meeting between Oliver North, Edwin Meese, and Amiram Nir, Israeli prime minister Shimon Peres' top counterterrorism advisor, Nir reportedly suggested to North that funds from the arms sales could be diverted to support the Contras. Shortly after this meeting, funds now destined for the Contras began to be routed through the Enterprise's byzantine maze of corporate shell and holding companies.

The Enterprise maintained dozens of accounts held in the names of various dummy companies, usually in Swiss banks such as Credit Suisse. The primary receiving accounts, which dispersed money outward into the corporate compartments set up for the ongoing operations, included Energy Resources International, Lake Resources Inc., and the Hyde Square Park Corporation.[73] North's Israeli co-conspirators may have had access to these accounts as well.[74]

In order to manage this complex web, the Enterprise retained the services of Willard Zucker and the Geneva company he worked for, Compagnie de Services Fiduciaire or CSF. Zucker, a US tax lawyer, "had provided Hakim with financial services since the mid-1970s, when Hakim still lived in Iran."[75] Zucker's connection to these players is made all the more interesting because of his background. He had been affiliated with Investors Overseas Services and had gained a seat on the mutual fund's board during the ouster of its founder, Bernard Cornfeld.[76] There are various rumors and suggestions that Zucker was one of Vesco's proxies whom he arranged to get onto the IOS board.

Zucker's role in Vesco's takeover was obliquely referenced in a letter he wrote to Hakim concerning a trip he took to Seattle to discuss a series of business ventures with other Enterprise partners. Zucker states in the letter that he had met a businessman from Colorado who was involved in a venture with the politically connected oilman John M. King. The man offered to send Zucker materials relating to the venture, but Zucker declined. He added to Hakim that King "hates my guts because I helped bring down King Resources, the Colorado Corporation."[77]

IOS had been involved with King Resources in some oil-and-gas ventures in the late 1960s, while King Resources acted as one of IOS' biggest clients. King was close to Edward Cowett, IOS' general counsel, director, and a member of its executive team. When IOS began to fall apart, Cowett conspired to help King take control of the company from Cornfeld. It was not meant to be. King failed and his King Resources slid into bankruptcy, while Vesco, King's competitor, claimed the mutual fund.

In June 1982, CSF set up a Bermuda-based subsidiary called CSF Investments Ltd. Legal work for this company was carried out by Conyers Dill & Pearman – one of the preeminent firms specializing in offshore finance, with outposts across the Caribbean, London, and Hong Kong. The firm's cofounder, Nicholas Bayard Dill, was a powerful presence in Bermuda politics. He and his law partner, James Pearman, were directors of Coastal Caribbean Oils & Minerals Ltd. According to the National Security Archive's Iran-Contra chronology, Secord owned stock in this same company in the early 1980s.[78] Later, when Contra support operations were fully underway, CSF Investments was used to acquire aircraft.

The Enterprise maintained numerous companies to manage the aviation wing of the Contra support operations. Southern Air Transport (SAT), the CIA proprietary airline utilized in the Contra airlift that was previously Air America (and before that, Civil Air Transport), worked closely with an Enterprise dummy company, registered in Panama, called Albon Values Corp. David Rogers, a journalist for the *Wall Street Journal*, wrote that "public records in Panama City list employees in the Geneva firm, [CSF], as principals in Albon Values Corp.... Roland Farina, an accountant at CSF, and Jacques Mossaz, an attorney at the Swiss firm, are listed as principal officers in Albon Values, which was registered by a Panama City law firm, Quijano & Associados, frequently used by CSF."[79]

Costa Rica was one of the main staging grounds for North's pro-Contra operations. Land belonging to John Hull, an American rancher, was the main location for the Contra airlift. Hull, who reportedly received a $10,000 monthly retainer from the Enterprise, claimed to have been the CIA's main liaison with the Contras between 1982 and 1986.[80] His involvement in covert operations seems, however, to have begun before 1982. Two years earlier, a far-right paramilitary group used his ranch as their base to launch an attack on a left-wing Costa Rican radio station.[81] Hull was also reportedly close to the Free Costa Rica Movement, that country's branch of the World Anti-Communist League.

In frequent contact with Hull was Robert Owen, who had been selected by North to serve as his own liaison to the Contras. Owen – unsurprisingly – had ties to Shackley that went back to the Vietnam War, and through him he had met Neil Livingstone.

Livingstone, as discussed, had been involved in Panama with Michael Harari, which opens the possibility that he may have been involved with Black Eagle. After Owen served a stint on the staff of Senator Dan Quayle, Livingstone recruited him to work at Gray and Company, the PR firm set up by Robert Keith Gray during his time away from H & K.[82]

Under the auspices of a PR campaign for the Contras, Livingstone set up a nonprofit organization called the Institute for Terrorism and Subnational Conflict, located in the Washington, DC, offices of the American Security Council. What it was really designed to do, according to the Congressional report on the Iran-Contra affair, was to act as an Enterprise cut-out to pay Owen for his work.[83] To receive these funds, Owen set up his own organization, the Institute for Democracy, Education, and Assistance (IDEA).

The same day that IDEA was formed, Owen set up a sister organization, the Council for Democracy, Education and Assistance.[84] One of the council's directors, aside from Owen, was a retired Air Force general, John Flynn, who had reportedly been recruited by Hull to serve in that role. The council took in some $66,000 in donations for the Contras, all reportedly from the fundraising activities of conservative activist Carl "Spitz" Channell. In 1984, Channell had organized a tax-exempt foundation for the purpose of soliciting donations. This foundation, the National Endowment for the Preservation of Liberty was North's vehicle of choice for garnering private donations for the Contras and other worldwide "freedom fighters" being backed by the Reagan administration.

Through the National Endowment for the Preservation of Liberty, money provided by wealthy donors courted by North and his associates

– individuals like Texas oilman Nelson Bunker Hunt, Ellen Garwood, the daughter of a prominent New Deal-era administrator, and prolific confidence man E. Trine Starnes – would be flushed into an offshore banking system.[85] Channell's partner was a PR man by the name of Richard Miller, who maintained a company called International Business Communications. Money from the National Endowment for the Preservation of Liberty would flow to International Business Communications, which in turn would deposit the money into bank accounts in the Cayman Islands under the name of "I.C., Inc." I.C., Inc. would then move the money to Enterprise bank accounts in Switzerland belonging to Lake Resources.[86]

Another fundraising apparatus utilized by the Enterprise was Citizens for America.[87] Founded by conservative activist Lewis Lehrman, Citizens for America was, for a time, run by the infamous lobbyist Jack Abramoff. Citizens for America's executives met personally with President Reagan. The organization would reappear during the Franklin child abuse scandal in Nebraska (discussed in chapter 10), as Lawrence King, the man at the center of that sexual-abuse ring, was a board member of and donor to Citizens for America during the Contra years.

By 1985, cracks in the Boland Amendment were forming, and the covert apparatus was ready to take full advantage of the opportunities at hand. Congress was still blocking "lethal aid," but it authorized the State Department to move "humanitarian" supplies to the Contras. A special organization, the Nicaraguan Humanitarian Assistance Office (NHAO) was set up under the leadership of Ambassador Robert Duemling. From the outset, the NHAO was an extension of the Enterprise. It provided money to Owen's IDEA, and Owen himself became an NHAO consultant. The CIA, meanwhile, recommended and vetted the companies that the office utilized to move the aid.[88]

This vetting process brought in a number of intriguing partners. One of these was the shrimp company Frigorificos de Puntarenas and its sister firm, Ocean Hunter. As previously discussed, Frigorificos was found to have been footing the bill for the storage of Robert Vesco's aircraft in Costa Rica and was itself run by representatives of the Colombian drug cartels. One principal of both companies, Luis Rodriguez, was found by the FBI to have been "funding the Contras through 'narcotics transactions.'"[89]

At the same time that the State Department was unlocking funds for Frigorificos and its principals were busy at work in the blossoming cocaine trade, North, Owen, and rancher Hull were working closely with those behind Frigorificos and Ocean Hunter on developing maritime warfare capacity for the Contras.[90] Memos written by Owen refer to Frig-orificos/Ocean Hunter ships being used as "motherships" for these operations. Incredibly, they also reference a "DEA person who might help with the boats."[91]

Another curious pair of companies that simultaneously received NHAO funds, got tapped by the Enterprise for military support, and were implicated in drug-running operations were SETCO Aviation and Hondu Carib. Hondu Carib had been formed by Frank Moss, who had been a pilot for SETCO. According to the report of the Kerry Commission on narcotics trafficking, SETCO "had a long-standing relationship with the largest of the Contra groups, the Honduras-based FDN."[92] The aviation company, importantly, had been set up by "Honduran cocaine trafficker Juan Matta Ballesteros."[93] Matta, described in the press as the "boss of bosses of Mexico's cocaine industry," mainly partnered with the Cali cartel, which, by the 1990s, had overtaken the Medellin cartel as the dominant drug empire in Colombia.[94]

Matta and other members of his organization, the Guadalajara, were implicated in the kidnapping, interrogation, brutal torture, and murder of DEA agent Enrique "Kiki" Camarena, which took place in early February 1985. The cartel boss who had personally ordered the kidnapping of Camarena, Felix Gallardo, was reported to have bragged in court that he had "[supplied] arms to the Contras" and had brought together a network of drug traffickers "to finance their [the Contras] cause during 1983 and 1984, in exchange for protection."[95]

Phil Jordan, former director of the DEA's El Paso Intelligence Center, later reported that he was informed by Mexican authorities that "CIA operatives" were present for the interrogation and torture of Camarena and had made tape recordings of the agent's final hours.[96] Hector Berrellez, the DEA agent who led the investigation into Camarena's death, stated that the CIA provided the DEA with those tapes. Camarena was first kidnapped by members of La Dirección Federal de Seguridad (DFS), a now-shuttered Mexican intelligence agency and secret police. When Felix Gallardo was boasting of his ties to the Contras, he also claimed that Contras were being trained at a law-enforcement training facility maintained by the DFS, which was acting as a front for the CIA.[97]

Frigorificos and Ocean Hunter, SETCO and Hondu Carib – these are just a few of the CIA-vetted companies that were recommended to the State Department for the delivery of "humanitarian aid" to the Contras. There was also Vortex, a Miami-based aviation concern run by Michael

B. Palmer. The Kerry Commission report notes that, at the time Vortex was getting NHAO contracts for supply runs, "Palmer was under active investigation by the FBI in three jurisdictions in connection with his decade-long activity as a drug smuggler, and a federal grand jury was preparing to indict him in Detroit."[98] One of Vortex's employees in this period, Joseph Haas, "was suspected of involvement in drug trafficking and had been a suspected marijuana trafficker since 1984."[99] He had also been a CIA contract agent but was "'taken off' CIA's payroll" in 1987 "because he had gone to work for a US law enforcement agency."[100]

Vortex was brought to the NHAO's attention by Pat Foley, described in the Kerry Commission report as the "president of Summit Aviation."[101] What the report left out, however, was that Foley had been (or had continued to be) a CIA operative and had earlier flown 747s on behalf of Flying Tiger Lines, the aviation company set up by the Chennaults and where Robert Keith Grey had maintained a spot on the board.[102] Summit Aviation, too, had a fascinating history: it had been founded by Richard C. du Pont Jr., a member of the illustrious DuPont chemicals family and the son of one of the great boosters of aviation in the 1930s. Besides Summit, Richard Jr. served as a director at Edward du Pont's Atlantic Aviation, where the aforementioned CIA asset and Bush ally, James R. Bath, had served as vice president.

In September 1983, a Cessna 404 twin-engine propeller plane entered the airspace of the Nicaraguan capital of Managua and began a miniature bombing run. The aircraft was quickly shot down, and Sandinista authorities found that it had been dispatched from Costa Rica. A subsequent investigation in the US press revealed that the plane had come from a company called Investair Leasing Corporation, headed by the former vice president of the CIA proprietary airline Intermountain Aviation. Before its doomed flight, it had been purchased by Summit Aviation, which had modified it with bombing capabilities and machine guns.

SINGLAUB AND GEOMILITECH

The bombing attempt carried out by Summit Aviation foreshadowed some of the later activities of the Enterprise. For example, there was the case of Civilian Materiel Assistance (CMA), a militia group – likely a cover for members of the 20th Special Forces Group – that managed a Contra-support network and conducted cross-border raids with Contra forces from Honduras into Nicaragua.[103] The CMA's active presence in the conflict was revealed in 1984 when one of its helicopters was shot down, killing two of the group's members. Despite the exposure, the CMA's head, Thomas Posey, continued the Contra support operations and was linked to arms deals taking place at John Hull's ranch.

Working closely with the CMA, and then later with the Enterprise, was Gen. John K. Singlaub. Singlaub was a veteran of the old OSS China network, which means that his entry into the world of covert activities took place alongside seasoned operators such as Paul Helliwell and E. Howard Hunt. After the war, he continued his military career while serving as one of the CIA's clandestine warriors, popping up in special operations the world over. By the late 1970s, he departed from a high-ranking military position to protest Carter administration policies. It parallels the attitude of Shackley, with whom Singlaub was reportedly associated in Vietnam.

During the 1980s, Singlaub headed the US Council for World Freedom, the US branch of a global network of spies, criminals, Nazi exiles, fascist operators, and death squad leaders belonging to the World Anti-Communist League.[104] By 1984, he was serving as the chairman of the league itself. Prior to this, some of the leading lights of the organization included Roger Pearson, an anthropologist who maintained ties to groups such as Willis Carto's Liberty Lobby. Another was Swiss attorney Pierre Schifferli, who was rumored to have been involved in arranging massive weapon deals for UNITA in Angola.[105] When he wasn't arranging falsified end-user certificates for arms transfers or cavorting with a group called the Pinochet Foundation, Schifferli worked as one of the attorneys retained by Bruce Rappaport to represent the interests of Inter Maritime Bank.

The World Anti-Communist League and the US Council for World Freedom were interlaced with a host of like-minded pressure groups, dark-money fronts, private-intelligence apparatuses, and closed-door meeting places. These groups pressed for rolling back Cold War policies and boosting defense spending. More specifically, they pushed for the continuation and deepening of covert wars across the world; free trade policies, and other packages beneficial to multinational corporations; and the curtailing of civil and labor rights. Some of these, such as the American Security Council, appear to have participated in psychological operations aimed at the domestic population of the United States as well as abroad. Others, such as the Council for National Policy, helped broker the cozy relationship between evangelical Christians and the emergent New Right. High Frontier lobbied for the Strategic Defense Initiative, while the US Strategy Council brought together intelligence operatives with representatives of the Unification Church to coordinate policy and public relations activities, particularly through the Unification Church-controlled *Washington Times.*

Another group that operated in close proximity to the World Anti-Communist League was the Western Goals Foundation, a private-intelligence outfit set up by Congressman Larry McDonald in 1978. McDonald envisioned Western Goals as a clearinghouse, working in tandem with other private groups and law enforcement agencies to collect and share information on domestic groups deemed threatening to prevailing power structures. They engaged in propaganda via book publishing and, at one point, "solicited funds to create a computer database on American subversives."[106] During the 1980s, Western Goals fell under the control of Spitz Channell, who used it as one of the vehicles for private fundraising on behalf of the Contras.[107] Notably, Western Goals' effort to create a database on "American subversives" would be realized as part of the "Continuity of Government" protocol, which was developed by key players in the Enterprise and Iran-Contra and is discussed in chapter 9 in the context of the PROMIS scandal.

A Western Goals letter from 1983 lists a number of intriguing individuals comprising the advisory board. There was John Singlaub himself, as well as Adm. Thomas Moorer from the Nixon days. At this point, Moorer worked at both the American Security Council and H & K. Another Western Goals advisor was Roy Cohn. A 1982 *New York Times* article states that Cohn joined the foundation after being satisfied that it had "no ties to the right-wing John Birch Society" – despite Western Goals founder Larry McDonald having been a John Birch leader, and Cohn's fellow advisory board member Roger Milliken having funded the society.[108]

Cohn's interest in Western Goals may have been tied to the wider pro-Contra networks that were coalescing across the United States in the early 1980s. At the time, Cohn was serving as an attorney to his close friend Rupert Murdoch. (Robert Parry has written that the two first became close due to their mutual support for Israel.) According to *New York Magazine*, "Whenever Roy wanted a story stopped, item put in, or story exploited, Roy called Murdoch."[109] After Murdoch bought the *New York Post*, Cohn "wielded the paper as his personal shiv."[110]

At the same time, Cohn was forging close ties with the director of the US Information Agency, Chad Wick, even hosting a luncheon in Wick's honor that was widely attended by influential figures in the conservative press, as well as US senators and representatives. Soon after, then CIA director William Casey was spearheading an extensive propaganda campaign to shore up public support for Reagan's Latin American policies, including support of the Contras.

This domestic effort was technically illegal, which caused the CIA to outsource the job to the private sector. As Robert Parry reported in 2015, Wick took the lead in obtaining private funding for the effort, and, just a few days after Wick promised to find private support, Cohn brought Rupert Murdoch to the White House. Parry later noted that, after this meeting, "documents released during the Iran-Contra scandal in 1987 and later from the Reagan Library indicate that Murdoch was soon viewed as a source for the private funding" for the propaganda campaign.[111]

After that meeting, Murdoch became the top media ally of this Casey-directed propaganda effort and also became increasingly close to the Reagan White House. Murdoch, as a consequence, benefited greatly from Reagan's policies and his friendship with the administration, which allowed Murdoch to increase his US media holdings and to create the Fox Broadcasting Corporation in 1987.

In addition, Singlaub was named as a "consultant" to a Florida-based company called GeoMiliTech Consultants Corporation (GMT), which had been put together by Barbara Studley, a beauty queen turned conservative talk show host in Florida. Studley had also operated as a lobbyist and had worked at the Pentagon. The National Security Archive's Iran-Contra *Chronology* suggests that Studley may have even set up GMT at the behest of Singlaub, as he was reported to have "suggested" to Studley that she start the company in 1983.[112]

GMT worked with various arms dealers to source and transport munitions to conflict zones such as Nicaragua and Afghanistan. Among the arms dealers it worked with were Ernest Werner Glatt and his sometimes partner, Samuel Cummings. Cummings, by way of his company Interarmco, was a longtime weapons merchant for the CIA. Cummings' brother-in-law was none other than Senator John Tower, who in December 1986 was tapped by President Reagan to oversee the initial inquiry into the Iran-Contra affair.[113] This was a conflict of interest of immense proportions. In addition, Tower, at the time, was close to Robert Maxwell, who had his own role in the Iran arms deals of this period and was actively working for Israeli intelligence. Also, by this point, Maxwell had secured Tower a place on the payroll of Israeli intelligence.

It is not surprising, then, that GMT had extremely close ties to Israel.[114] The outfit's executive vice president, Ron Harel, was a "veteran of the Israeli Air Force who specialized in 'tactical cargo and light and early warning aircraft.'"[115] He managed GMT's overseas offices, which was conveniently located in Tel Aviv.

A sister company to GMT, Global Technologies Ltd., was also stationed in Israel and was overseen by Joel Arnon, an Israeli diplomat and military officer who was also a vice president of GMT. Global Technologies was located in Tel Aviv's Asia House, a striking Bauhaus-style building that housed various diplomats and embassies. Asia House had been owned by the Israeli billionaire Shaul Eisenberg, who – as mentioned in chapter 3 – enjoyed close relations with the Israeli intelligence and security apparatus. In addition, GMT's Israeli offices utilized the banking services of Israel Discount Bank. In 1986, portions of the money that were provided to Frigorificos and Ocean Hunter was deposited in Israel Discount Bank.[116]

Incredibly, there appears to have been ties between GMT and the clandestine activities of Robert Maxwell and those in his orbit. Key here was Nicholas Davies, the globe-trotting foreign editor for Maxwell's *Daily Mirror* – where he was often known by the nickname that his boss had bestowed upon him: "Mister Sneaky."[117] According to Ari Ben-Menashe, Davies, like Maxwell, worked on behalf of Mossad, having been recruited in the 1970s from Strategic Intelligence Services, a British intelligence front led by a Special Air Service veteran named Anthony Pearson.[118] By the 1980s, Davies – with Maxwell's knowledge – was using his *Daily Mirror* duties to act as a cover for his involvement in Mossad-sanctioned arms trafficking

Besides the *Mirror*, Davies also acted as the manager and representative of the Ora Group, "an Israeli company based in London."[119] Headquartered at Davies' London home, Ora was set up with the aid of Ari Ben-Menashe, and operated as a key node in global arms flows. Among the "clients" that received arms – in this case weapons from the Soviet bloc – with the help of Davies and Ora was GMT.[120] In his book *Profits of War*, Ben-Menashe reprinted a number of internal documents illustrating the role played that Davies played in these affairs, including communications between Ora and GMT.[121]

Davies vigorously denied the allegations made by Ben-Menashe, and the *Daily Mirror* made a number of counter-allegations, including the charge that the documents in question were forgeries. Another contested claim was that Davies had traveled to Ohio to meet with arms dealers.[122] Davies went out of his way to claim that he had never been to Ohio, yet this was quickly proven to be false by various journalists.[123] Likewise, the

British Observer turned up other Ora-related documents, which included a telex from Davies to "renowned American arms merchant, Richard J. Breneke [*sic*]."[124] Brenneke, as discussed in this chapter, managed an offshore financial apparatus utilized by the American and Israeli intelligence assets active in Operation Black Eagle. Brenneke would later state that he had met Davies, but did not know that he was involved with the *Daily Mirror*.[125]

Like all other shadow companies and strange entities that surrounded the Enterprise and Robert Maxwell's broader network, GMT was involved with the complicated world of offshore banking. To carry out their operations, Studley called on the services of Jean de la Giroday, a managing director at Geneva's Banque Cantrade, itself a subsidiary of Union Bank of Switzerland with branches in Geneva and on the Isle of Jersey. Together, Studley and Giroday set up a company called Consulentia Ltd.; GMT's principals were told to avoid maintaining records of this company's existence. Consulentia is just one of the many enduring mysteries of this intricate web: while GMT's Consulentia was set up in 1984, Robert Vesco stated that, when he was looting IOS, he utilized the "Consulentia sub of Banque Cantrade" in 1970.

In summer 1985, GMT was involved in the acquisition of arms on behalf of the Contras. According to the chronology published by the National Security Archives, Studley and Singlaub arranged "a $5 million shipment of AK-47 and RPG grenade launchers from Europe to Honduras onboard a 15,000-ton Greek flag freighter."[126] The arms may have been sourced from Eastern Bloc countries like Poland or Bulgaria, as Studley wrote to North in October of that year, "vociferously complaining that another arms dealer, Mario [Delamico], who was associated with the Florida arms dealer Ron Martin, was essentially horning in on their sources of Soviet-style armaments."[127]

Several months after the October letter, in late December 1985, Studley and Gen. Daniel Graham – the vice chairman of Singlaub's US Council for World Freedom and a close associate of CAUSA, the political arm of the Unification Church – attended a meeting with CIA director Casey. An unnamed CIA officer who was present at this meeting was asked by Congressional investigators if the meeting had involved a discussion of a complicated three-way trading scheme, developed by GMT as a means of sustaining finances and equipment for covert operations. The investigators described this scheme as "a circular arrangement in which a trading company would be established to supply freedom fighter movements which Congress was unwilling to support for one reason or another.... Israel would sell certain things, military equipment, to the People's Republic of China, who would supply Soviet arms, which would then be brokered.... Israel would be benefited by the United States through a high technology support or other compensation."[128]

A schematic outline of this trading arrangement that was entered into evidence shows the destination for the arms sourced from China.[129] They would go to US-backed rebels in Afghanistan, Angola, Nicaragua, and Cambodia. GMT, in other words, was proposing the creation of a multinational economic arrangement that would bind together the US, Israel, and China through a series of credit extensions, technology transfers, and arms deals.

It is quite possible that this was the ultimate plan for what the Enterprise was intended to become, though the official narrative holds that this arrangement was never completed. It seems clear that certain elements of the plan did go into motion. Israel and China intensified economic and political relations in the 1980s and both actively collaborated with the US in covert operations. Chief among these was the arming of the Mujahideen in Afghanistan. Jeffrey Epstein was later alleged to have been involved in such arms deals, specifically those involving the Mujahideen. It appears that he may have facilitated major facets of something very similar to GMT's US-Israel-China plan in collaboration with members of the Clinton White House, Chinese weapons firms and Southern Air Transport in the mid to late 1990s (more on this in chapter 17).

GMT's other claim to fame was that it appears to have been involved in some of the very first arm deals with Iran, ones that predated the Enterprise's formation but took place alongside the CIA-Mossad relationship during Operation Black Eagle. The plan was a swap: "trade 200 tanks for Iran's US-built F-14 fighter aircraft," which had been sold to Iran in the 1970s.[130] Per this plan, Israel would have served as a cut-out for the tanks. It is quite possible that the scheme originated on the Israeli side of GMT. According to Alan Block, it was the first thing that Ron Harel had been involved with when he joined the company.

It is also possible that this was the groundwork for later arms-for-hostages arrangements. GMT worked closely with Israel Aircraft Industries (IAI), a major defense contractor for the Israeli military discussed previously in chapter 3. The founder of Israel Aircraft Industries, Adolph "Al" Schwimmer, had been heavily involved in weapons arrangements with Iran during the rule of the shah, and these arrangements had continued in secret after the Islamic Revolution. According to many press reports, it was Schwimmer who first concocted the idea to trade arms in exchange for the (attempted) release of hostage William Buckley.[131]

EDMOND SAFRA'S FUNNY BANK

Besides BCCI and Credit Suisse, another set of banks utilized by the Enterprise were Republic National Bank, headquartered in New York City, and Trade Development Bank, headquartered in Geneva and sold to American Express in 1983. Both of these banks were controlled by Edmond Safra, a Lebanese-Brazilian businessman who hailed from a long line of bankers. By the early 1990s, Safra was a billionaire, with Republic National among the five largest banks in New York. Both Safra and his bank, however, were dogged by controversy. Safra himself died under suspicious circumstances after his bank was implicated in large-scale money laundering and the possible theft of "stabilization credits" provided by the IMF to a financially devastated, post-Soviet Russia.

A decade earlier, Republic National Bank was named – but never indicted – as having participated in a money-laundering network called "La Mina," which was the subject of a sweeping federal investigation called Operation Polar Cap.[132] La Mina, which washed money for Colombian drug cartels, was composed of a circular daisy chain of banks, mines, gold refineries, precious metal brokers, and jewelry stores and provided the financial infrastructure for "airplane manufacturers and fixed-base operators" as well as "aircraft used to ferry drugs."[133]

Unsurprisingly, one of the banks that factored into the La Mina daisy chain was BCCI. Elsewhere, Safra's Trade Development Bank did business with loyal customers of BCCI such as Altaf Nazerali, a high-flyer in the world of securities fraud.[134]

Trade Development Bank and Republic National Bank are discussed in the fourteenth chapter of the Congressional report on Iran-Contra.[135] There, Republic National is described as having "handled many of the Enterprise's wire transfers." Besides these sorts of transfers, the bank was further involved in a clandestine cash delivery system that took place "outside bank channels." Nan Morabia, an officer at Republic National's International Division, her husband Elliot, and their son David were utilized by the Enterprise's money manager, Willard Zucker, to "make cash drops to Hakim, Secord, and others on their behalf."[136] Zucker would contact the Morabias with the amount required and tell them which individual the money was intended for. Then, that amount was deposited in an account at Trade Development Bank under the name "Codelis." Sometimes, the money drops would take place at Republic National Bank itself. On at least one occasion, Robert Owen received $7,000 from Morabia at the bank in New York City.

Nan Morabia's FBI 302 (i.e., summary of the FBI's interview with her) states that she had known Zucker for "approximately 8 to 10 years" and that his "account at [Republic National] was already established when she began working in the International section."[137] She added that CSF maintained accounts at Trade Development Bank and that Safra had "contact with Zucker in Geneva." She was not able to identify to the FBI, however, any potential business relations between Safra and Zucker, although she made clear that she assumed that such business did actually take place.

Yet, there were direct business relations between Republic National and CSF that were separate from – but by no means unconnected to – the Enterprise. In the summer of 1985, for example, CSF organized a Geneva-based company on behalf of Republic National called Republic New York Corporation Air Transport Services S.A.[138] The purpose of this company was to maintain a private aircraft on behalf of Safra's bank. At the end of 1985, the ownership of the plane was transferred out of the CSF-managed company to a Swiss aviation company called Aeroleasing S.A., which continued to maintain the plane on behalf of Republic National.

Aeroleasing was one of the aviation companies contracted by the Enterprise to ferry personnel around the world for various purposes. The Enterprise's expenditure lists included in the Congressional Iran-Contra final report show that, under a section titled "Mid-East (Iran Arms)," a total of $226,998 had been paid to the company. The ultimate costs were likely much higher. In his testimony, Secord stated, "We owe an aeroleasing firm in Europe, I am told, about $60,000. Something like that. We still owe the firm Southern Air Transport, here in the United States, quite a bit of money. I think it is something just under $100,000. We can't pay them."[139]

Gordon Thomas, in his biography of Robert Maxwell, states that Safra and Maxwell had enjoyed a long-lasting friendship. They particularly enjoyed, Thomas writes, dining "on board the *Lady Ghislaine* when the yacht berthed opposite Safra's home in Monte Carlo."[140] Their relationship was not all pleasure, however. According to Thomas, Safra allowed Maxwell to use Republic National Bank accounts to launder money coming from Eastern Europe.

When Maxwell was active in the Eastern Bloc, his primary base of operations was Bulgaria. There, as will be noted in more detail in chapter 9, Maxwell was deeply involved in the thorny *Cold War issue* of tech transfers – the often-illicit movement of high technology from the West to the Soviet sphere. This likely brought him into contact with Kintex, a state-owned trading company that had been organized by the Darzhhavna Sigurnost, the Bulgarian intelligence apparatus that was closely aligned with and ultimately answerable to the KGB. A CIA report on Kintex said it was a "central coordinator" of smuggling activities, with a "clandestine charter" to facilitate smuggling for Arab and Balkan drugs and arms traffickers and to "collect items of science and technology interest in the West."[141]

Kintex was more than willing to deal arms to right-wing insurgencies as much as left-wing ones, with clients including those who opposed Soviet-backed forces. These included the Christian Falangists of Lebanon, the Grey Wolves of Turkey, and even the Contras of Nicaragua. Also closely tied to Kintex was Mohammed Shakarchi, a prominent Geneva-based currency trader and the owner of Shakarchi Trading. Shakarchi, who from his offices near the Zurich airport ran "the most sophisticated currency exchange and commodity trading operations in Switzerland" and courted state officials in Soviet-allied Bulgaria while being, at the same time, involved in the CIA's covert support for the Mujahideen in Afghanistan. Between 1981 and 1989, a CIA front company called Argin purchased millions of dollars' worth of rare currencies from Shakarchi, which were sold to raise money for the rebels.[142]

One of Shakarchi's US partners was Capcom, a commodity-futures firm that "was created by the former head of BCCI's Treasury Department … who capitalized it with funds from BCCI and BCCI customers."[143] This wasn't the only familiar face engaging in funny banking with Shakarchi. A classified DEA report stated that Shakarchi's currency-exchange services were "utilized by some of the world's largest trafficking organizations to launder the proceeds of their drug-trafficking activities" and that part of his network included accounts at Safra's Republic National Bank.[144] Mohammed Shakarchi's father, Mahmoud, was reportedly close to Safra.

Safra's name can also be found in Jeffrey Epstein's contact book, though the banker's last name is misspelled as "Saffra." There are two phone numbers listed for Safra and no addresses. Another individual in the book with ties to Safra, albeit through a rather circuitous route, is Michael de Picciotto. Picciotto, who had five phone numbers listed in Epstein's contact book, has been associated with Engel & Völkers, the massive German real estate company and, since 2020, has served on the board of Aston Martin. He got his start, however, working at Union Bancaire Privée, a Swiss bank controlled by his family. He had joined as the managing director for their

London offices in 1988 and eventually became "responsible for UBP's global financial activities."[145]

Union Bancaire Privée began life as Compagnie de Banque et d'Investissements of Geneva, founded by Edgar de Picciotto. Edgar, the uncle of Michael de Picciotto, came from a family with a long history in both banking and European diplomacy. The Picciotto family was fairly close to the Safras, and like Edmond Safra, Edgar de Picciotto was born in Lebanon. As their respective banking enterprises bloomed, the two became friends. In the late 1980s, when American Express disposed of Trade Development Bank, the Geneva bank that had formerly belonged to Safra, it was Edgar who bought it.[146] The merger of Trade Development Bank and Compagnie de Banque et d'Investissements led to its reformation into Union Bancaire Privée.

Edgar de Picciotto was also, according to SEC filings, a member of the board of advisors to Quantum Industrial Holdings, a division of the complicated investment network of George Soros. Quantum Industrial Holdings held the majority of the shares of Quantum Industrial Partners, one of the advisors to which was George Soros' brother Paul Soros. Paul's son, Peter Soros, appears in Epstein's black book with addresses in New York City and London and ten phone numbers.

Another item appearing in Epstein's notebook that ties into this network is Aeroleasing. Both of Epstein's books contain lists for the aviation company, for both its Geneva and Zurich locations.

THE MAINLAND SAVINGS CONNECTION

When US arms began flowing to Iran at the end of August 1985, it was Adnan Khashoggi who advanced the initial capital – through his BCCI bank accounts – to put the thrust of the plan in motion. The initial "bridge financing" was $1 million, followed shortly thereafter by an additional $4 million.[147] Khashoggi subsequently claimed that this $5 million, "plus an additional $2.5 million whose purpose was unclear" came from a loan provided by Roland "Tiny" Rowland, the well-heeled British tycoon, corporate raider, and member of the Clermont Club who was briefly discussed in the last chapter. While Rowland's connection to Iran-Contra affair is well documented – and will be discussed shortly – he denied the validity of Khashoggi's claims.

While this denial might simply be a case of Rowland trying to put distance between himself and the affair, it happens that shortly prior to the initiation of the arms transfers, Khashoggi came into $5 million via a surprising route: Mainland Savings, a Houston-based savings and loan. Mainland Savings, one of the S&Ls that collapsed spectacularly over the course of the 1980s, was plugged into a wider network of crooked land developers, organized crime associates, and other denizens of the murky world of covert operations.

Khashoggi's ties to Mainland Savings dated back to 1977, when Mario Renda, an ambitious New Yorker with dreams of wealth and power, stepped off a plane in Riyadh, Saudi Arabia. He was then a partner in IPAD – the International Planners and Developers Construction Consortium – that hoped to gain a lucrative contract to build concrete homes in Jidda.[148] Khashoggi, it was reasoned, would be the key to unlocking the deep pockets of wealthy Saudis and, after a meeting with Renda, the arms dealer committed himself to the venture. While IPAD's ambitions were ultimately never realized, it resulted in a long-lasting relationship between Khashoggi and Renda.

After IPAD fizzled out, Renda leveraged the contacts he gained through his introduction into Khashoggi's inner circle and secured a position as the treasurer of Arab International Bank. Interestingly, in 1973, this bank had formed a joint venture with Lonrho, the corporate monolith controlled by Tiny Rowland.[149] Arab International Bank's specialty was certificates of deposits (CDs): it would use vast petrodollar reserves to shop CDs around the world, seeking out the locations that had the highest rates of return. Renda positioned himself front and center in these efforts, which provided him with the idea for his next venture. In 1978, he returned to New York City and formed Arabas Inc., a "one-man firm" that was intended to broker deposits, likely on behalf of Arab clients.[150]

The timing was fortuitous. Against the backdrop of early 1980s deregulation fever, Renda became connected to Martin Schwimmer. Schwimmer, rumored to be a money-launderer for the Lucchese crime family, managed the pension funds for several New York unions, including Teamsters Local 810, which was reportedly close to organized crime interests.[151] A plan was then hatched: Renda and Schwimmer would begin brokering deposits of union pension fund money into S&Ls across the United States, collecting along the way commissions from lending institutions and fees from the unions. Arabas was renamed First United Fund, and soon Renda and Schwimmer were moving billions into a string of savings and loans.

By the end of the decade, Renda and Schwimmer had deposited money in 130 S&Ls, all of which collapsed. Renda's CDs were linked directly to massive borrowing at each of these institutions, which were generally unpaid. In addition, quite frequently, the borrowing was carried out by an interlinked network of organized crime associates. That collusion was undeniable. Besides the accusations of Schwimmer's involvement with the Lucchese family, Renda was rumored to have "controlled a lot of money being loaned for the benefit of Paul Castellano," the powerful head of the Gambino family and, until 1985, the chairman of the Commission, the Mafia's governing body.[152] Notably, Castellano was one of several organized crime figures who were clients of Roy Cohn.[153]

Khashoggi stayed close to Renda throughout these developments. One notable example of this involved a mobster by the name of Lawrence Iorizzo, the president of the mob-linked Vantage Petroleum Company. Iorizzo was close to Martin Carey, the brother of New York governor Hugh Carey and oilman Edward Carey. Vantage had taken over Carey's Petroleum Combustion International, which by that point had already carried out numerous dealings with Iorizzo. Iorizzo would later testify that Martin Carey had been involved in bootlegging gasoline with him and that the profits from these operations had been funneled into Hugh Carey's re-election campaigns.[154]

Iorizzo, in other words, was clearly politically connected, and this was what had caught Renda's attention. Renda had wanted to help Khashoggi, who at the time was struggling to get the proper permits to build a helicopter landing pad at his home just outside New York City. An associate of Renda by the name of Leslie Winkler "told Iorizzo that ... Renda might be able to assist Iorizzo in getting a fat oil contract if Iorizzo used his powers of 'persuasion' in New York to help Khashoggi.... Renda said if Iorizzo could 'remove these obstacles,' Khashoggi would be most appreciative."[155]

At the same time that they were concocting a way to get Khashoggi's helipad up and running, Renda and Iorizzo agreed to embark on a classic bank bust-out scheme, akin to what Renda and Schwimmer were doing with the savings and loans. Renda would make deposits at a bank, which would then make loans to a Panamanian shell company controlled by Iorizzo – loans that would never be repaid.[156] The shell company that Iorizzo used was called Houston Holdings, and it had been purchased by Iorizzo from Steven Sandor Samos, a lawyer who maintained a lucrative trade in off-the-shelf Panamanian companies.[157] Iorizzo and Samos had been introduced by Renda's friend Leslie Winkler, and one of Samos' primary business associates was a Florida banker named Ray Corona – the partner of Leonard Pelullo in Sunshine State Bank.[158]

Samos also made an appearance in the Iran-Contra affair. Southern Air Transport purchased a Panamanian company called Amalgamated Commercial Enterprises, which it used to "purchase and maintain planes carrying supplies to the contras."[159] ACE was one of Samos' off-the-shelf companies, and all of the company's officers were employed by International Management and Trust Corp., a company run by Samos. Another noteworthy link involves how ACE utilized bank accounts at the Banco de Iberoamerica, a location that Samos was accused of using as a conduit for drug money laundering.[160] Banco de Iberoamerica was a subsidiary of the Arab Banking Corporation, a major international bank headquartered in Bahrain that offered floating rate notes on the open market on behalf of BCCI.[161]

Among the S&Ls where Renda and Schwimmer were brokering deposits of union pension fund money was Houston's Mainland Savings. This same S&L became embroiled in a series of overly complicated financial transactions with Khashoggi and a slew of business partners, the origins of which go back to 1974.[162] That was when Khashoggi purchased a large tract of property adjacent to the Galleria, a major shopping hub in downtown Houston that had been developed with the aid of the Marcos family of the Philippines. Khashoggi acted as front man for Imelda Marcos on more than one occasion.[163] Khashoggi let the land sit bare until 1979, when he was joined by Clint Murchison Jr., scion of the Dallas oil family. With $15 million in financing courtesy of Texas Commerce Bank, the pair embarked on an ambitious development plan.

The plans never came to fruition and, three years later, Murchison exited the scheme. Khashoggi began looking for buyers for the land and began cooking up other real estate schemes. One of these was in Aspen, Colorado, where he and a developer named John Roberts planned to purchase property using a $44 million loan from Commerce Savings, plus an additional $14 million from San Jacinto Savings. In a now-obvious pattern, this money disappeared into the black void of Khashoggi's finances. What was left was a staggering debt owed to a string of banks and S&Ls.

Mainland Savings, flush with deposits from Khashoggi's friend Mario Renda, offered an ambitious way out of these problems by purchasing Khashoggi's Galleria-adjacent property for the grossly inflated sum of $68 million dollars. Of this, $22 million would be put up by Mainland itself, with the remainder provided by a loan from Austin-based Lamar Savings. The plan was: "The $30 million in prior loans from Texas Commerce Bank and San Jacinto Savings would be paid off. Khashoggi would buy

$10 million in preferred stock at Mainland and use $12 million as a down payment to buy foreclosed loans real estate (called 'cash for trash'), thus boosting its capital and keeping regulators at bay. That left $16 million for miscellaneous costs and Khashoggi."[164]

A problem arose when Mainland could only get Khashoggi's property valued at $55 million, short of the $68 million that they had originally hoped for. They were able to inflate the loan up to $58 million, which covered most of the debts and miscellaneous costs – except for the $10 million that was to be used by Khashoggi to buy Mainland stock and bad assets. Luckily for Mainland, Khashoggi had additional properties next to the Galleria-adjacent tract in question, which he had financed through S&L borrowing. Khashoggi was issued lines of credit by Mainland that were marked for developing those properties, but they were actually used to cover the missing $10 million. But there was something else: "On the same day, Mainland signed a $5 million letter of credit to Khashoggi."[165]

The deal between Mainland and Khashoggi over these lines of credit was reached on August 1, 1985, just weeks before the arms transfers to Iran were underway. These transfers, of course, relied on a $5 million advance from Khashoggi. As Pete Brewton notes, the $5 million line of credit from Mainland vexed regulators and attracted the attention of the FBI. It was then discovered that Mainland's executives had worked to conceal it from the S&L's board of directors. Khashoggi later denied that the $5 million came from Mainland, instead claiming that Tiny Rowland had been the source of the funds. However, as mentioned, Rowland denied this. Mainland, for its part, insisted the money was a guarantee to Khashoggi for his purchase of $10 million in Mainland stock – $10 million, it must be reiterated, that was coming from Mainland itself.

It might be tempting to write the Mainland events off as a curiosity, another dead end in the hall of mirrors that is the Iran-Contra affair. There are, however, other ties between Mainland and Lamar Savings – the institution that loaned Mainland the bulk of the money for the Khashoggi deal – and the netherworld of BCCI and intelligence agencies. Besides Khashoggi, one of the major borrowers at both of these savings and loans was Mounzer Hourani, a Lebanese-American from Utah with extensive interests in Texas real estate.[166] Hourani might have had intelligence connections. "A former high-ranking officer at Lamar Savings," writes Brewton, "said that Hourani claimed to have ties to the Mossad."[167]

Ties to Israeli intelligence or not, Hourani was certainly linked to Utah's Orrin Hatch, who, as mentioned, was tightly connected to BCCI and to First American. Hatch stated that he had known Hourani "from the mid-1980s and was partly based on their shared devotion to the Mormon faith."[168] Hourani, meanwhile, told *NBC News'* Mark Hosenball that he had joined with Hatch and BCCI insider Mohammed Hammoud on "various private schemes to free US hostages held by terrorists in Lebanon."[169]

In 1986, Hourani was in hot water over his borrowing at Mainland, which by that point had collapsed and had been taken over by the Federal SavingS&Loan Insurance Corporation. Hatch appears to have tried to intervene directly, penning a letter to the federal institution stating that a possible "resolution" could be found with respect to Hourani's problems.[170] Four years later, as BCCI began to fumble toward collapse, Hatch once again acted as Hourani's lobbyist. He reached out to the beleaguered bank requesting that they lend money to Hourani for a series of real estate ventures in Illinois, Minnesota, and Texas.[171] Hourani himself then sent a proposal for financing. It is not clear if any proposed loans were ever actually provided.

Hatch has one more connection to figures in this saga. In 1985, during the peak of his Mainland borrowing and the initiation of the Iran weapons sales, Khashoggi arrived in Salt Lake City, Utah, with grand plans to build "two gold-colored 43 story office towers that would dwarf the nearby Mormon Church office building, the tallest structure in town."[172] Khashoggi had been a presence in Salt Lake City since the 1970s, and this increased significantly during the 1980s. Yet, by 1987, construction on the towers had been abandoned and Khashoggi had fled Utah, leaving numerous unpaid loans and broken promises in his wake.

It was during this period, Hatch stated, that he had met Khashoggi. Details on their relationship are scarce, but, according to Hatch, their association was the senator "extending the courtesies he would to any big investor in Utah."[173]

"A PAN-EUROPEAN PLOT"

A key aspect of the covert operations of the Reagan era that is frequently overlooked is that, with respect to the complex trafficking of arms to Iran, Oliver North and the Enterprise were dipping their toes into a much wider swamp of political and economic corruption, arms trafficking, and money laundering on a truly colossal scale. As the conflict between Iraq and Iran heated up, companies, banks, intelligence agents, and smugglers poured arms and military materials into both sides of a bloody war.

Despite laws barring such activities, the conflict in the Middle East was a boom time for many. For instance, there was the so-called powder cartel, a "pan-European plot" to move propellant powder for artillery and other armaments to Iran.[174] At the top of this cartel was Bofors-Nobel, the Swedish arms combine that is now the Swedish subdivision of the massive UK-based defense contractor BAE Systems. Bofors had a close relationship with Iran that predated the revolution. In the early 1970s, the company entered into a business agreement with the country to build an armaments factory. Relations between the two were suspended following the revolution. However, a dip in Bofors' balance sheet, a product of the downsizing of the Swedish military, led the company to embark on the lucrative path of embargo busting.

Moving propellant powder to Iran required numerous partners, complicit shipping agents, and payoffs to officials. The primary mechanism for coordinating this network was the European Association for the Study of Safety Problems in the Production and Use of Propellant Powders, a public relations group organized and set up by Bofors and other European weapons manufacturers following a series of disastrous plant explosions.[175] This provided a convenient cover for these various arms merchants to come together, arrange the logistics for weapons orders, disperse the proceeds, and even inflate prices of their wares.

The Bofors powder cartel made extensive use of Italian companies for arranging shipping and payments. Soon, Italy had become the primary locus of this subterranean arms trade. In an October 1990 exposé in *Euromoney* magazine, the role of the French arms manufacturer Luchaire in the trafficking of arms to Iran was dissected.[176] Luchaire had two subsidiaries based in Italy, SEA and Consar, which were used to arrange the movement of weapons through the Islamic Republic of Iran Shipping Lines. The ships would log false destinations and then make their way to Iran via secret routes. The arms loaded on these ships were not only sourced from Luchaire, as SEA and Consar acted as intermediaries for numerous European companies involved in the trade.

One such firm was Defarm, which was actively collaborating with Bofors in the illicit movement of propellant powder.[177] The founder of Defarm was Nicola Dubini, who had cofounded Consar before he sold it to Luchaire. Another firm was a Portuguese arms brokerage called Defex, described in testimony as having a "close relationship" with Richard Secord, after having been introduced by Thomas Clines.[178] It became one of the companies utilized by the Enterprise. According to Albert Hakim,

Defex sourced weapons from Eastern Bloc arms manufacturers and merchants, which were then purchased and resold to the Contras.

Behind these moves were various European banks, some shadowy and others well known. On the shadowy side, there was International Bankers Incorporated, which issued lines of credit to SEA and Consar.[179] The Italian branch of International Bankers Incorporated was located in a building owned by the scandal-plagued Banco Ambrosiano, which had been set up by Jean-Maxime Lévêque in 1982. Lévêque had previously been the president of Crédit Commercial de France, a sizable French bank that, incidentally, had lent Adnan Khashoggi large sums for his Salt Lake City ventures.[180] The major shareholders of International Bankers Incorporated included the Saudi businessman Akram Ojjeh, a friend of Adnan Khashoggi's, and Robert Maxwell.[181]

More well-known was the French merchant bank Banque Worms, which was nationalized by the Mitterand government in 1982. During the period when the French state owned the bank, it held 23 percent of Luchaire and aided in financing the flow of arms and powder.[182] Joining Banque Worms in these efforts was a renowned Italian bank, Banca Nazionale del Lavoro. The interactions were complex, as R. T. Naylor has described in *Patriots and Profiteers*:

> Bank Melli [the Iranian bank handling their side of the financing] would order its Italian correspondent banks to issue LCs [lines of credit] on behalf of Luchaire's Italian subsidiaries, which sent them to Italy's Banca Nazionale del Lavoro.... BNL would use the original LCs as security to issue their own LCs in favour of the Luchaire parent firm in France. That firm sent the LCs to Banque Worms for negotiation. When the goods were loaded up on board ships, Banque Worms would present its LCs to BNL for payment, and BNL would do likewise with the correspondent banks of Bank Melli. The use of back-to-back letters of credit was a simple but effective device for breaking up the money trail.[183]

London was another major hub for these activities, with various arms merchants playing a role in the flow of weapons as far back as 1981. Chief among these were Ben Banerjee, an arms dealer and owner of BR&W Industries, and his close associates Michael and Leslie Aspin. According to *Die Welt*, Banerjee and Michael Aspin were involved in negotiations between Oliver North and several representatives from the Iranian government in 1984 over the sale of $264 million worth of TOW missiles. Subsequently, evidence was entered as part of a British court case that showed that Banerjee's BR&W Industries did indeed attempt to move 1,250 TOW missiles to Iran, which were obscured in customs invoices as "lift trucks."[184]

These customs invoices were handled by BCCI, and they were "accompanied by telexes and letters on BCCI stationary of a nature and type ordinarily used by BCCI, showing BCCI providing counter guarantees and letters of credit involving the 'lift trucks.'"[185] What is more, according to Michael Aspin's brother, Leslie, these TOW missile sales were indeed part of North's operation. Leslie Aspin further claimed that he and North had opened three joint bank accounts at the Paris branch of BCCI to launder money for these sales and that one of these accounts was under the name "Devon Island." The Senate subcommittee investigating BCCI learned that BCCI Paris did indeed have a Devon Island account, but they were unable to acquire internal documentation for this branch.

The use of suspect invoice techniques, such as classifying TOW missiles as "lift trucks," seemed to be a habit of Michael Aspin's. In the early 1980s, he was working closely with a British arms dealer named Leonard Hammond, who also manufactured machine gun parts through his company, Delta Engineering. Hammond and Aspin used Delta Engineering to move machine guns to the Middle East and Africa, with a particular focus on South Africa. By 1981, they were moving arms to Iran.[186] Frequently, these arms flows were mislabeled on invoices as "hydraulic lifting tools."

Aspin and Hammond had a particularly close relationship with Kuehne & Nagel, a large German freight-and-logistics company.[187] When the arms dealers moved a thousand rifles to South Africa in 1980 – invoiced as "hi-lift hydraulic machinery spares" – K & N's subsidiary Air Cargo handled the freight. In 1981, K & N worked with Aspin and Hammond in moving weapons destined for Iran. K & N, according to Aspin, played a role very similar to that which BCCI would later play in moving TOW missiles in 1984. He told Spiegel that "the management of Kuehne & Nagel knew about the illegal arms transports, planned the routes with necessary intermediaries, issued documents and change information."[188]

In 1981, right as these operations were being developed, Kuehne & Nagel was acquired by Tiny Rowland's Lonrho.[189] Were these two events connected? It is impossible to say for sure, but there is reason to suspect that this was the case. As previously mentioned, one Lonrho freight cargo subsidiary has been identified as a participant in Edwin Wilson's covert activities in Libya on behalf of the Shackley network. Lonrho obtained K & N shortly after the loss of that cargo company.

In addition to Italy and the UK, Belgium was a major node in this wide-ranging European network. Of particular interest are the allegations made in the ATLAS dossier, a confidential report drafted by the Belgian Gendarmerie in November 1994. ATLAS makes a series of startling accusations concerning an entity that they describe as "the Nebula" – a network of Belgian businessmen, politicians, and criminals who were involved in arms trafficking, diamond smuggling, drug running, and the like. At the center of the Nebula was Felix Przedborski, a businessman and Belgian diplomat who, since 1978, lived in Costa Rica, where he maintained dual citizenship.

There is a small, but steady stream of press reports independent of the ATLAS dossier that have linked Przedborski to various forms of corruption. Notably, in 1978, Italian police found drugs in a vehicle belonging to the Costa Rican embassy, with one of Przedborski's employees at the wheel. That same year, one of Przedborski's close associates who was serving as Monaco's diplomat to Costa Rica, was arrested in connection with drug trafficking.[190]

When the Costa Rican newspaper *La Nación* published a series of articles probing Przedborski's connection to various criminal enterprises – based largely on reports already published by European journalists – "Don Felix," as he was known, responded litigiously. In the end, *La Nación*'s journalist, Herrera Ulloa, was charged with criminal defamation and forced to pay Przedborski "a fine equivalent to 120 days' wages."[191]

The ATLAS dossier names numerous individuals in Przedborski's network. Among these were his son Daniel, a Geneva lawyer who was poised to take over his father's complex. Interestingly, Daniel Przedborski, from 1984 through 2019, had worked at the law firm of Pierre Schifferli – Bruce Rappaport's attorney who, as mentioned, had been head of the World Anti-Communist League. Documentation from several lawsuits suggests that Daniel worked directly on some of Rappaport's affairs.

These are not the only familiar faces that appear in the dossier. In a list of banks used by the "Przedborski Group" for money laundering is Republic National Bank, with a note beside it stating that "in this bank it is a certain Safra who would be responsible for special transfers."[192] This, of course, refers to Edmond Safra, thus directly linking the Przedborski Group to Contra support operations and to Republic National. The ATLAS dossier further links the Przedborski Group or Nebula to these support operations: "It is said that some of the weapons of Irangate would have been transferred to the Contras of Nicaragua by this network."[193]

ATLAS identifies one of the lesser-known members of the Nebula as Bruno Goldberger, a purported real estate broker from Brussels. It adds that Goldberger worked "for a certain Globus Group," but the investigators who penned the document stated that they were unfamiliar with this entity. This was likely the Bulgarian state-owned trading company Globus. In *Evil Money*, Rachel Ehrenfeld cites a DEA report from 1989 that states that Globus "was formerly known as Kintex" – the Bulgarian firm tied to Safra's friend Mohammed Shakarchi and, possibly, Robert Maxwell.[194] The DEA report states Ehrenfeld recounted that "Globus transmitted Middle Eastern drug money to Switzerland via Shakarchi."[195]

Przedborski's time in Costa Rica overlapped with the country being used a major hub for the Enterprise's pro-Contra efforts. The ATLAS dossier charges that, while he was serving as a diplomat, Przedborski had embarked on a major business venture: the construction of a "tourist real estate project" in the Santa Elena region of Costa Rica.[196] Intriguingly, North was also using the dense jungles of Santa Elena as cover for secret airstrips that were used for Contra support flights.[197]

Other connections to the Enterprise's operations can be seen via another bank mentioned as being part of Przedborski's network. This was Geoffrey's Bank in Belgium, described in the dossier as a conduit for arms-smuggling payments. Geoffrey's Bank had also been intimately connected to some of Roy Cohn's suspect business activities (see chapter 4). Geoffrey's Bank was controlled by Arno Newman, a friend of Cohn's, and his son, Geoffrey, for whom the bank was named. According to Belgian journalist Willy van Damme, the Newmans were closely connected to Pierre Salik, a clothing manufacturer with close ties to Israel's Mossad.[198] Salik, importantly, was named in the ATLAS dossier as a member of Przedborski's core group: it states that Salik's daughters "were promised in marriage to the two sons of Przedborski," though this never took place for reasons unknown.

A frequent visitor to Geoffrey's Bank – and a close associate of both the Newmans and Pierre Salik – was Jacques Monsieur, described as one of Europe's biggest arms dealers.[199] Like Salik, Monsieur was close to Israeli intelligence. For instance, in 1986, Belgian authorities recovered documentation outlining his contacts with both Mossad and Iran. When he was arrested in Turkey in 2002, in part for having sold "embargoed American spare parts and aviation technology to Iran," numerous press reports identified him as having been an active participant in the Iran-Contra affair.[200]

Willy van Damme writes that Monsieur's introduction to the world of arms trafficking came through a partner of the Newmans named David

Benelie. As noted in chapter 4, David Benelie was really David Azulay, the brother of Avner Azulay.[201] Avner, a former Mossad agent, is best known as the business partner of the notorious commodities dealer Marc Rich, who himself worked closely with Israeli intelligence. Azulay was put in charge of the Marc Rich Foundation, the philanthropic appendage of Rich's empire. The foundation has maintained outposts in Zug, Switzerland and in Israel.

Rich has other ties to individuals and entities that populate this netherworld. There are rumors – albeit ones that are difficult to substantiate – that he was close to fellow oil trader John Deuss, who retained the services of Ted Shackley while Shackley was running his "private CIA." There are more demonstrable ties between Rich and Rappaport's Inter Maritime Bank and BCCI. In 1984, for example, the Rothschild Bank in Zurich loaned Rich the astronomical sum of $50 million Swiss francs. The managing director of the bank at that time was Alfred Hartmann, the money manager for Inter Maritime and a frequent BCCI front man.[202]

To complete the circle, the report of the US inquiry into BCCI states:

> Marc Rich remains one of the most important figures in international commodities markets, and remains a fugitive from the United States following his indictment on securities fraud. BCCI lending to Rich amounted to tens of millions of dollars. Moreover, Rich's commodities firms were used by BCCI in connection with BCCI's involving in US guarantee programs through the Department of Agriculture. The nature and extent of Rich's relationship with BCCI requires further investigation.[203]

Others named in the ATLAS dossier as involved in Przedborski-linked arms trafficking suggested Przedborski's group had close connections to the heights of Belgian political power. Featuring prominently among these names was Paul Vanden Boeynants, a meat-packing magnate who had been prime minister from 1966 to 1968 and again from 1978 to 1979. In the interim period, he served as Belgium's defense minister, where he presided over a series of controversial arms deals and a weapons buildup. An adamant cold warrior, Vanden Boeynants moved among the webs spun by groups such as Le Cercle and the World Anti-Communist League.

Vanden Boeynants had a particularly controversial relationship with Roger Boas, another figure whose name appears extensively in the ATLAS dossier. Boas oversaw the Belgian weapons manufacturer ASCO, which profited handsomely during Vanden Boeynants' years as defense minister. *De Morgen* reported that "as soon as the politician came to Defense in 1972, his company had probably not missed a single defense contract. ASCO ... saw its profits increase tenfold in the 1970s."[204] Many of these deals bore the unmistakable signs of corruption, and allegations of bribes and kickbacks, embezzlement and money-laundering, harassment and intimidation often followed in their wake.[205]

There were also the accusations that Vanden Boeynants and Boas made use of a highly connected call girl ring headed by Fortuna Israel, better known as "Madame Tuna." According to *De Morgen*, Madame Tuna was placed on the payroll of one of Boas' ASCO subsidiaries, where her job title was listed as "decorator."[206] This ring had connections to other familiar faces. Madame Tuna, it seems, was also an associate of Adnan Khashoggi, who reportedly called upon her services for help in obtaining lucrative contracts through subterfuge and blackmail. Boas was reported to have been introduced to Khashoggi and Akram Ojjeh – an investor, alongside Robert Maxwell, in International Bankers Incorporated – by the madame herself.

A direct line between this network of connections and the early 1980s flow of weapons to Iran may well exist. Named in the ATLAS dossier as a member of Przedborski's group was Abraham Shavit, Boas' general manager at ASCO. The dossier describes Shavit as the "right arm of Roger Boas."[207] Shavit was well connected in Israel. For instance, in the 1970s, he served as the president of the Manufacturer's Association of Israel and, afterward, had a stint as the chairman of El Al, Israel's chief airline company that was involved in CIA-Mossad airlifts in the 1980s, including Operation Moses, and has also operated as a front company for Israeli intelligence. He was also reportedly a former Israeli intelligence officer and a close associate of Manuel J. Pires, a CIA-employed arms trafficker.[208] Pires would later be identified as one of the Enterprise's middlemen in the Iranian arm sales.

Prior to the Enterprise's operations, in January 1983, ASCO's Malta branch was involved in the transfer of "aircraft parts, weapons and ammunition" to Iran via a contact at Bank Melli.[209] Two ASCO Malta invoices for these show that the shipments were underwritten with a line of credit from BCCI's branch on Brompton Road in London. According to Gary Sick, one of ASCO's liaisons to Iran for these types of arrangements was the arms dealer Hushang Lavi – one of the witnesses who claimed to have inside knowledge of William Casey's October Surprise activities.[210]

Guns for Iraq

Support for the Iran weapons arrangements was not universal within the Reagan administration and dissenting voices rippled through the corridors of powers. While such dissenters were unable to stop the virtually uncontrollable cascade of events, many of these individuals used the fallout from the scandal to concentrate their political power. Chief among these was George P. Shultz, President Reagan's Secretary of State. During the inquiry into the activities of the Enterprise, Shultz turned over significant documentation to investigators and provided detailed testimony. The official Iran-Contra report states that Shultz used the opportunity afforded by the scandal to "to regain control over counterterrorism policy. Following a strenuous bureaucratic struggle, Shultz persuaded President Reagan to prohibit arms transfers to Iran and to announce that the Department of State would take the lead on such counterterrorism and diplomatic matters in the future."[211]

Shultz testified that he only had fragmentary knowledge of the arms sales and that he had learned fairly late that they had taken place. Senate investigators found, however, that Shultz was far more knowledgeable about what was taking place than he had initially let on. Likewise, he had knowledge of the Iran sales far earlier than what he testified. Nonetheless, the record showed that his opposition to the sales was consistent. What is not mentioned, however, is that Shultz had interests involving Iran's bitter enemy – Saddam Hussein's Iraq.

Early on in his tenure as secretary of state, Shultz dispatched Donald Rumsfeld, who at the time was working as an executive in the private sector, to Iraq to meet with Saddam. The first of these meetings took place in December 1983, with a follow-up meeting in March 1984. Declassified documents illustrate the purpose of the visits was to move the US and Iraq toward normalizing relations, despite official condemnations of Saddam's use of chemical weapons.[212]

Shultz, however, had other things on his mind when he dispatched Rumsfeld. Before he had become Secretary of State, Shultz had been an executive at the construction giant Bechtel. Prior to Bechtel, he had served in multiple positions in the Nixon administration, first as Labor Secretary, then as the Director of the Office of Management and Budget, and finally as Treasury Secretary.[213] He was not the only Bechtel figure high up within the Reagan administration. Caspar Weinberger, who had served alongside Shultz in Nixon's OMB, had also moved to Bechtel. Shultz and Weinberger carried on a multi-decade feud that spilled over into the Reagan administration. Weinberger, unlike Shultz, was a major booster of the Enterprise and had played a role in the Iran weapons transfers.

Bechtel, in the early 1980s, had launched an ambitious, multibillion-dollar project in the Middle East that sought to establish an oil pipeline that would move crude from Kirkuk, Iraq to the port of Aqaba, Jordan, on the banks of the Red Sea. A now-declassified memo from Rumsfeld, sent to the State Department during his December 1983 trip stated that he had "raised the question of a pipeline through Jordan. He [Saddam] said he was familiar with the proposal. However, he was concerned about the proximity to Israel as the pipeline would enter the Gulf of Aqaba."[214]

Weighing heavily on Saddam's mind was Israel's Operation Opera in June 1981, when Israeli military aircraft bombed an unfinished nuclear power plant. The Iraqis would be on the hook for sizable loans connected to Bechtel's project, and the possibility that Israel might destroy the pipeline would place a major burden on Iraq's wartime finances.

The Bechtel pipeline negotiations became something of a boondoggle, rife with subterfuge and intrigue. It intersected in odd ways with the Iran-Contra project, and formed something of a parallel – if not an entirely opposing – operation. In the spring of 1984, Iraq and Jordan agreed to grant Bechtel a contract for pipeline construction that was dependent on several conditions. These included $500 million in financing from the US government; an agreement that American oil companies would take a sizable chunk of the oil moved by the pipeline; and that not only Bechtel, but American banks and the Export-Import Bank, would be involved in the guarantees for the project.[215] As Alan Block points out, the rationale for these demands was simple: put the US government and American businesses on the hook for the project, and they would act as a buffer against Israel.

The agreement operated smoothly until Iraq made an additional demand. It wanted "a 'force majeure clause' that would free Iraq from its obligation to pay interest on construction loans in the event of Israeli aggression."[216] With this demand threatening to derail the whole project, an interesting figure interjected himself into the middle of the negotiations: Bruce Rappaport, Casey's good friend and a BCCI insider. Interestingly, one of the directors of Rappaport's Inter Maritime Bank, until 1979, had been a former consultant for Bechtel.

Rappaport wanted a discount on oil transported by the pipeline in exchange for guarantees from Shimon Peres that Israel would leave the pipeline alone. To sweeten the deal, Rappaport was prepared to grant Israel a portion of his profits from this oil deal. The deal with Israel would require two elements: a written security guarantee and an insurance fund for the pipeline set up by Israel. Israel, through Rappaport's intercession, agreed to the former but not the latter, and so the tanker magnate reached out to the Reagan administration for leverage over Israel. He turned to two attorneys he was close to, Samuel Pisar – the powerful attorney whose client list has included Armand Hammer and Robert Maxwell – and E. Robert Wallach. Wallach, in turn, brought Rappaport to the attention of Reagan's Attorney General Edwin Meese. Meese, in turn, managed to bring the National Security Council into the mix, which believed that US government entities like the Overseas Private Investment Corporation could be used to organize the insurance fund.

Several years of torturous negotiations began, with Rappaport acting as a back channel between the US and Israel. One letter, written by Peres, was passed from Rappaport to Wallach to Meese and stated that the Israeli politician would discuss the matter with Shultz himself. It was ultimately for naught. The NSC backed out of the project under the leadership of Admiral John Poindexter, curiously one of Oliver North's chief allies and a major player in the movement of arms to Iran.

Despite this failure, in 1986, Rappaport received a sizable sum of money. Shultz concocted a plan to elicit a $10 million donation from the Sultan of Brunei for the Contras. Elliot Abrams was dispatched to handle the money transfer, and he provided an account number at Credit Suisse bank in Geneva for the deposit. It was presented as an account for the Enterprise's Lake Resources, but when the money was transferred, it ended up in an account controlled by Rappaport. It was later written off as a mistake, with several numbers in the account flipped around and thus "coincidentally" depositing the money with Rappaport. Rappaport, for his part, would deny that he ever received the money – though some of his top personnel, as well as Bert Lance, later told Alan Block that Rappaport had indeed received the funds. Lance stated that the money was used for "pay-offs," while Jerry Townsend – a CIA officer who worked for Rappaport – said that Secord had personally asked him to try to recover the money.

The Bechtel pipeline negotiations were unfolding against a backdrop of what has been described as a geopolitical "tilt" designed to "draw Iraq permanently into the camp of America's Gulf allies."[217] A key component of this tilt was the expansion of lines of credit provided to Iraq that were arranged and guaranteed by the Commodity Credit Corporation (CCC),

a New Deal–era public corporation set up to provide financing and pro-
tections for the US agricultural sector. Ostensibly, the CCC credits to Iraq
were to be used strictly for agricultural purchases, with the US adding
additional nonagricultural credits via the Export-Import Bank, the same
entity involved in the Bechtel pipeline negotiations. The primary bank
used to issue these credits was the Atlanta branch of Banca Nazionale del
Lavoro (BNL) – the Italian bank that, as mentioned earlier, was working
with Banque Worms in financing arms transfers to Iran.

In 1989, BNL-Atlanta was raided by the FBI, and revelations soon followed that the bank had been providing massive loans to Iraq that were
"far in excess of the amounts reported to the Federal Reserve."[218] These
loans, in turn, were being used by Iraq to purchase weapons. Beside the
CCC-guaranteed lines of credit that were mixed in with BNL's lending,
the possibility was raised that the CCC itself – with or without its knowledge – had acted as an underwriter of arms deals. An investigation into
what was dubbed "Iraqgate" led to the verdict that there was, in fact, no
conspiracy on the part of the CCC and the Reagan administration to arm
Iraq. Yet, the overlap in time with the Bechtel negotiations and Donald
Rumsfeld's trips to Iraq seems to paint a different picture.

The Export-Import Bank is just one direct connection between the
CCC/BNL affair and the Bechtel pipeline negotiations. Another was the
connection that came from Rappaport himself – his close associate at Inter Maritime Bank, Alfred Hartmann. Hartmann, mentioned earlier in relation to the loans provided to Marc Rich, also maintained a high-ranking
position at BNL. Given that Hartmann tended to appear at banks as a representative of BCCI, this may indicate a relationship between BNL and
BCCI. Indeed, in 1991, the *New York Times* reported that BNL-Atlanta
had been receiving massive transfers of money from BCCI and its subsidiary First American Bankshares.[219] These transfers, which were happening
at the same time as the Iraq loans, appeared to have been made in order to
keep the BNL branch afloat.

In the US Congressional hearings that investigated Iraqgate, the relationship between BCCI and BNL's Italian leadership was further eluci-
dated. According to a written statement provided by the head of BNL's
North American operations, BNL's former managing director, A. Ferrari
– who resigned in 1981 after his membership in the notorious P2 Masonic lodge was revealed – had been close to "Pakistani nationals connected
to BCCI."[220] The statement further identified Ferrari as a close friend of
Roberto Calvi, the head of Banco Ambrosiano who wound up dead under

exceedingly murky circumstances. It also added that Ferrari and the head of BNL's international division, A. Florio, had worked closely with the corruption-plagued Vatican Bank. Finally, the statement charged that Ferrari and Florio exclusively handled BNL's "relationship with people like [Ghaith] Pharaon and Marc Rich."[221]

BCCI and BNL appeared together again in relation to a strange firm called Allivane International Group, which was described in a UK parliamentary inquiry as a "ghost company."[222] Allivane was, like BNL, a participant in the Bofors-led powder cartel that moved propellant powder, munitions, and weapons parts. At the same time, Allivane was participating in multiple illicit weapons deals with Iraq, and, by 1993, the company's leadership was wanted for questioning in the US in relation to the BNL-Atlanta loans.[223] Leaders included Allivane's founder, Terry Byrne, who had previously worked at a company called International Signal and Control and, before that, a "New Jersey firm called Rexon Corp."

Rexon was subsequently placed under investigation for, among other things, providing artillery-fuse parts to Iraq. International Signal and Control, meanwhile, had been founded by James Guerin who was linked, by the UK inquiry, to the Chilean arms dealer Carlos Cardoen, and who between 1984 and 1988 provided minerals used in munitions to Iraq.[224] Ari Ben-Menashe, the former Israeli intelligence officer, has charged that Margaret Thatcher's son Mark Thatcher was also close to Cardoen and had used this connection to broker the sale of armaments to Iraq. At the time, Thatcher was living in Texas, where he had cultivated contacts that included former Senator John Tower.[225]

While the relationship between Allivane and BNL remains vague, what is certain is that BCCI was working closely with both companies. It reportedly held several different accounts at BCCI during the mid-1980s and, in 1987, BCCI was "prepared to ensure the sale of 50,000 sets of fuses" by Allivane.[226] Invoices obtained by British parliamentarians further indicated a business relationship between Allivane and a company called Space Research Corporation, which had been tied in other reports to Allivane's successor Rexon Corp, to Carlos Cardoen and Mark Thatcher, and to BCCI.[227]

Space Research Corporation is best remembered for the man behind the company: Gerald Bull, a Canadian-born engineer and artillery expert who, prior to his 1990 assassination in the doorway of his Brussels apartment, had designed weapons systems for the Iraqis and the Chinese. He had also brokered the sale of arms to South Africa. Yet, his most famous effort was Project Babylon.

Commissioned by the Iraqi government, Project Babylon was intended to construct a series of space guns, based on Bull's earlier designs for launching satellites into orbit. These guns would be used to fire projectiles high into the atmosphere or near-earth orbit in order to reach targets far beyond the range of normal artillery equipment.

The ownership structure of Space Research Corporation was fascinating. In the late 1960s, it was jointly controlled by the Great West Saddlery Company and Arthur D. Little, the Boston corporate consultancy firm and think tank. The CEO of Arthur D. Little at the time was General James Gavin. In 1982, Gavin, along with Clark Clifford's partner Robert Altman, joined the board of Financial General Bankshares. Great West Saddlery had been a defunct company taken over by Edward and Peter Bronfman – the nephews of Samuel Bronfman – and they transformed it into an investment vehicle.[228] The acquisition of companies by way of Great West Saddlery was financed through Edper Investments, a holding company owned by the brothers. Edper, in turn, had been financed through the sale of Seagram's stock held by Edward and Peter Bronfman.

When the Iraqgate scandal began to break in the early 1990s, attention turned to former Secretary of State Henry Kissinger because, in 1985, he had taken a spot on the international advisory board of BNL. Furthermore, Kissinger's corporate consultancy firm, Kissinger Associates, counted the Italian bank as a client. Kissinger Associates, which had been set up in the early 1980s with seed money provided by a syndicate of large Wall Street firms led by Goldman Sachs, stacked its partner list with many prominent individuals. Lawrence Eagleburger held a spot at the firm from 1985 through 1989, right between stints as Reagan's Undersecretary of State for Political Affairs and George H.W.Bush's Deputy Secretary of State. Eagleburger had a long history with Kissinger, having served as his special assistant way back in the Nixon administration. Another Kissinger assistant from this period was Brent Scowcroft, who also ended up at Kissinger Associates before becoming Bush's National Security Advisor in 1989.

Both Eagleburger and Scowcroft were linked by government investigators and by the press to BNL, despite their protestations that they had played no role in the Iraq weapons deals. "On three occasions between 1986 and 1989," Rep. Henry B. Gonzalez of Texas recounted, "Mr. Scowcroft briefed the BNL board on international political and economic developments."[229] Once back in government, Scowcroft pushed for the expansion of the Commodity Credit Corporation's Iraq program, and enlisted his underlings in the NSC to provide political pressure to ensure this came to pass.

Eagleburger, meanwhile, was identified as having been present at meetings between BNL managers and Kissinger Associates in 1987. Though he denied interactions with BNL, events during the year prior to this meeting suggest that Eagleburger was being less than honest. In 1986, LBS Bank, the US subsidiary of Yugoslavia's Ljubljanska Banka, was set up in New York City, and Eagleburger joined the board of directors. Roughly 2 percent of LBS' business was carried out with BNL, and it had even purchased some of the loans that the Italian bank had made to Iraq.[230] Two years after it had opened its doors, LBS Bank was implicated in a money-laundering scheme connected to the transfer of high technology to the Eastern Bloc.[231]

Kissinger also had personal ties to George P. Shultz. As with Eagleburger and Scowcroft, the relationship between the men formed during the Nixon administration. Kissinger attested, "For decades, George and I talked practically every Sunday," and that if "in a position to choose a president, I would select George Shultz."[232] When Shultz first accepted the position as Reagan's Secretary of State, Kissinger was the first person he consulted.[233] Reportedly, this consultation pertained directly to developing a roadmap for Middle East policy. It seems likely that the question of Iraq was among the subjects discussed.

Besides the personal relationship between Kissinger and Shultz, there was a line running from Kissinger Associates to Bechtel via William E. Simon, a director at the firm who had served as a consultant to the construction giant. He also served on the board of Tamco, a corporate concern of the Gouletas family, who are discussed in relation to Jeffrey Epstein in chapter 11, and was also connected to Covenant House and AmeriCares, discussed in chapter 10. Simon further maintained a position as chairman of an investment vehicle controlled by Suliman Olayan, a Saudi investor who had embarked on major joint ventures with Bechtel.[234] Simon, too, had a long history with Kissinger. For instance, he had served as Shultz's successor as Nixon's Treasury Secretary, and while there he developed what Kissinger later described as an "affectionate comradeship" with the Secretary of State.[235]

Each of these facts is certainly suggestive. When put together, a portrait emerges of a network – wrapped inside the Reagan administration but extending beyond it into companies such as Kissinger Associates, Bechtel, and BNL – that was working to not only promote the "tilt" to

Iraq but was actively aiding Iraq in its fight against Iran. Particular institutions such as BNL – and BCCI – appear to have worked both sides of the conflict, supplying money and logistical support for the flow of arms to Iran and Iraq alike.

Seen from this perspective, the Bofors-led powder cartel, which was interlinked with the activities of the Enterprise, was just one element in a truly international network of money laundering, backroom deals, and arms trafficking. This tapestry, in turn, was the backdrop for the dark maneuvers of factional infighting that cut across the governments of the countries involved.

To bring these matters full circle, it is worth turning to the matter, left unresolved in the official inquiry, of the ties of Kissinger Associates to BCCI. In 1986, a consultant with Kissinger's firm, Sergio de Costa, was recruited by BCCI to aid in the takeover of a bank in Brazil.[236] Before the ink had dried on the paperwork, de Costa began to lobby Kissinger Associates to take BCCI on as a client. He found an ally at Kissinger Associates in Alan Stoga, a former chief economist at the First National Bank of Chicago – an institution historically linked to Rockefeller interests. Stoga – who had reportedly attended the 1987 meeting with BNL where Lawrence Eagleburger was also present – later communicated extensively with BCCI principals and even, on a handful of occasions, met with them in person.

When the BCCI inquiry was underway, Kissinger Associates painted a picture in which Stoga had pushed for the firm to take on BCCI on as a client, while Kissinger had been more reticent. This narrative was shaped by the files and communiqués that the firm had turned over to investigators, indicating that Stoga's talks with BCCI terminated in December 1988. Yet, the files turned over by BCCI itself complicated this picture: they showed that Stoga was still meeting with BCCI representatives a month later, in January 1989. Kissinger Associates stated that Stoga reiterated at this meeting that the talks could not continue, but BCCI's files stated that, at the meeting, it "was established that it is in our interest for both parties to continue with conversations. As such, the door for an eventual relationship remains open."[237]

With BCCI's compounding notoriety and eventual collapse, a working relationship between the bank and Kissinger Associates was never cemented. Kissinger Associates did, however, make an "unofficial" recommendation for BCCI by referring them to the New York law firm of Arnold & Porter.[238] One of the partners at Arnold & Porter, named directly on the referral to BCCI, was William D. Rogers, who had served beneath Kissinger in 1976 as the Undersecretary of State for Economic Affairs. Rogers had subsequently helped Kissinger set up Kissinger Associates and was serving on the board at the time that the Arnold & Porter recommendation was being made.

RIVALRIES

Buried deep within the pages of testimony, declassified documentation entered into evidence, and summaries that make up the bulk of the published Iran-Contra proceedings, there are faint traces and hints of an internecine bureaucratic feud that trickled down into Contra-support operations. Scattered throughout this documentation, one finds references to an entity called "the Supermarket," based out of Honduras. A leading military official stationed in Latin America, General John R. Galvin, described the Supermarket as a place where "a lot of weapons ... from somewhere overseas" were stored.[239] An unnamed CIA officer who was called to testify, meanwhile, called the Supermarket a "private organization" that was operating in league with "international arms dealers."[240]

The independent counsel's final report (also known as the Walsh report) identifies the figures behind the Supermarket as Ron Martin and Colonel James McCoy, the latter having recruited the former sometime in late 1984. McCoy was a "former US military attaché to Nicaragua," while Martin was "a Miami-based arms dealer who had been the focus of investigation by the Bureau of Alcohol, Firearms and Tobacco for many years."[241] The report adds that Martin had "at one time been charged with providing arms illegally to narcotics traffickers."[242]

The Supermarket actually predated the Secord-led Contra airlift that had been set up at North's behest. This is clearly illustrated in the Walsh report and is alluded to by Howard Kohn and Vicki Monks in their reporting on Iran-Contra that appeared in *Rolling Stone*. Kohn and Monks write that, while Operation Black Eagle was breaking down and the Enterprise was being assembled, William Casey "turned to a third weapons smuggling operation."[243] Martin and McCoy were not part of Casey's network of operatives; they were instead "entrepreneurs who had learned about the Contra slush fund and hoped to profit from it."[244]

As the Enterprise swung into motion, a significant rivalry developed between the two groups. North's personal notebooks illustrate that the Supermarket became a growing concern for the Enterprise during 1985. That spring, North wrote down information about Martin and McCoy's operation that Secord had gleaned from Rafael Quintero, the CIA-trained Cuban exile who had become involved with the Shackley network in the 1970s. Among the information listed was that Martin was wanted in Guatemala for "criminal activity" and that Defex – the Portuguese arms dealing outfit that Secord was close to – would not do business with them.

North also noted that there was "possible Martin interference w/ Puerto Cortez [sic] delivery." This was a reference to an Enterprise-organized weapons shipment from Portugal destined for Puerto Cortés in Honduras, which Martin had learned about through his own network of sources. He dispatched the Supermarket's chief agent, the Cuban American Mario Delamico, who posed as one of Secord's employees in order to obtain a cargo manifest from the ship, the *Erria*, when it docked. Martin later stated that he "used the manifest and other documents that Dellamico [sic] took from the *Erria* to convince [Mario] Calero that Secord was 'ripping off' the Contras."[245]

Other notes made by North show that he was interested in where the money for the Supermarket had come from in the first place. On July 12, 1985, he wrote that he had received information that the "[Honduran] Army plans to seize all [weapons] when supermarket comes to a bad end," and that "$14 [million] to finance [the Supermarket] came from drugs."[246] Despite the relationship between North's operations and drug traffickers, he used this link of the Supermarket's financing to drugs – with Noriega allegedly being the connection here – to warn others to avoid them. North later stated that he was being guided in these decisions by William Casey himself.

Evidence of Martin's wider involvement with the Latin America drug trade comes through his choice to employ Theodore Klein, a Miami criminal-defense lawyer, as his attorney. Klein had previously represented Jack DeVoe, a pilot and owner of a charter airline service that operated as a front for a Colombian-led cocaine-smuggling operation. DeVoe had entered the world of drug smuggling in 1970 and, by the 1980s, he was in league with a powerful drug smuggler named Pepe Cabrera, a partner of Carlos Lehder.[247] When it came to laundering the proceeds of this smuggling operation, DeVoe looked to Jack Freeman – a veteran of Paul Helliwell's law firm and, for a time, the in-house counsel for Castle Bank & Trust.[248]

According to Theodore Klein, Felix Rodriguez – a longtime actor in CIA shadow operations who was then connected to the Enterprise – had some sort of "business relationship" with the Supermarket.[249] This particular connection may help determine who might have been the actual benefactors of the Supermarket. By 1986, significant tensions had built up between Rodriguez and North, but the Walsh report shows extensive contact between Rodriguez and Donald Gregg, the former CIA official who had become Vice President Bush's National Security Advisor.

Rodriguez had first been introduced to North through William R. Bode, a State Department official who might have also been an asset for the CIA.[250] That same day, Rodriguez met with Gregg to discuss "his [Rodriguez's] interest in going to El Salvador." Gregg promised to make introductions between Rodriguez and key people and reported the meeting to Vice President Bush as soon as it concluded. Less than a month later, Gregg arranged for a meeting between Rodriguez and Bush to discuss counterinsurgency operations in El Salvador.[251]

When Rodriguez was running the Enterprise's Contra resupply operations from El Salvador, working under him as the day-to-day operations manager was CIA-trained Cuban exile Luis Posada Carriles. Posada was a real piece of work – during the 1970s, he had been one of the founding members of the Cuban exile terrorist group CORU, but he had maintained a close connection with US organized crime figures like Lefty Rosenthal before CORU existed. In the decade prior to his recruitment as a cog in the Enterprise's machinery, he had been identified as "big time trafficker" of Colombian cocaine into Miami.[252]

Records indicate that North was kept abreast of Rodriguez's repeated meetings with Gregg, but it is doubtful that he knew everything that was being discussed between the two. The Walsh report indicates that Rodriguez used those opportunities to express his misgivings about North and the Enterprise, at one point telling Gregg that North was "involved in the Edwin Wilson group."[253]

Whether or not this referred to something earlier in North's career, or simply to the presence of old Shackley network operators like Secord and Clines in the Enterprise, is not clear. However, the role being played by Clines in the Enterprise troubled Rodriguez to no end. The two had been friends going back to the Bay of Pigs, but they had split up over the covert involvement with Libya. Gregg wrote notes about this split that were later entered into evidence during the Iran-Contra hearings. He also noted that "Tom Clines = snake! (would sell his mother)."[254]

In Joseph Trento's *Prelude to Terror* – largely based on interviews he carried out with Edwin Wilson, Thomas Clines, and others from that nexus – he recounts that it had been Clines who had first introduced and brought Wilson and Rodriguez together in 1973. Wilson, in turn, put Rodriguez in touch with the infamous arms dealer Sarkis Soghanalian, who at the time was looking for somebody to train the Falangists in Lebanon. According to Soghanalian, Wilson told him to take Rodriguez to Lebanon and "don't bring him back ... get rid of him."[255]

As the tension built between North and Rodriguez, Rodriguez appeared to have been leveraging his contact with Bush via Donald Gregg. The Walsh report states that, in early 1986, Rodriguez was causing "continual problems" by boasting of his "very close relationship with the Vice President and a number of his people."[256] On January 9, North wrote in his notebook "Felix talking too much about VP connection." Several months later, notes made by North's assistant Robert Earl added a few more pieces to the puzzle. During a meeting between NSC staffers and representatives (including Gregg) of the Office of the Vice President, Earl wrote the following: "Felix needs to be eased out w/honor," "Felix claims working w/ VP blessing for CIA," "Mario Delameco [sic], Miami = Felix contact," and "Calero–Martin link = a problem too."[257]

The relationship between Rodriguez and the Supermarket on one side, and between Rodriguez and Bush on the other, raises an important question: was Vice President Bush the ultimate backer of Martin and McCoy's operation? If so, it would likely reflect the ongoing power struggle, first addressed in the last chapter, between Casey and Bush. Casey, after all, was the ultimate backer of the Enterprise, having effectively outsourced CIA activities to North and the remnants of the Shackley network.

There is also other evidence that links Bush to the Supermarket. Howard Kohn and Vicki Monks, for example, noted that the Supermarket was popular among influential Contra supporters in Miami, precisely where Jeb Bush was doing private fundraising for the Contras and, according to a Customs report, was involved in gunrunning on behalf of the fighters.[258] Intriguingly, *Newsweek* reported in 1988 that it had obtained an NSC report stating that "disclosure of 'covert black money' flowing into Honduras to fund military projects 'could damage' Vice President Bush."[259]

There are also questions of potential connections to Robert Corson, the Houston land developer and rumored CIA asset who was the son-in-law of Bush's friend (and potential intelligence cut-out) Walter Mischer. Corson, as discussed in the last chapter, was identified by controversial whistleblower Richard Brenneke as his partner in money-laundering activities. Importantly, Brenneke further stated that Corson and the Supermarket's Ron Martin were business partners and had even jointly owned a casino in the Canary Islands for several years in the early 1980s.[260] Also suggestive is a complex real estate deal in Florida that involved a thrift, controlled by Corson, called VisionBanc. VisionBanc and several other S&Ls lent money to Mike Adkinson, a reputed arms dealer, to buy up property in the Florida panhandle from St. Joe Paper Company, then controlled by DuPont interests.[261]

When the deal was settled, the money from VisionBanc, never to be paid back, was swiftly tucked away in the Isle of Jersey branch of Bank Cantrade. This was the same bank where Jack Freeman was hiding the proceeds from Jack DeVoe's drug smuggling – and, as mentioned earlier, DeVoe used the same attorney, Theodore Klein, as Ron Martin. It was also the same bank from which GeoMiliTech had drawn its offshore finance managers.

A much more direct linkage comes in the figure of S. Cass Weiland, a Houston lawyer who was retained by Corson. Weiland appears extensively in North's notebooks, mostly in conjunction with figures circulating around the Supermarket. In 1984, North was following a project in Belize that involved both Weiland, then serving as counsel to the Senate Permanent Subcommittee on Investigations, and a Cuban exile named Sergio Brull.[262] Brull appeared later in the notebooks as a key contact for Martin and for John Molina, a Cuban American businessman who was shot to death in Panama in October 1987.

Molina, in the 1970s, was the president of UniBank, the Panamanian subsidiary of the WFC Corporation – the CIA-linked drug smuggling operation and money laundromat – that was co-owned by the First National Bank of Louisville.[263] After WFC went bust, Molina continued to operate in the underworld and eventually became the chief banker for the Supermarket.

If Robert Corson, as Pete Brewton argues, was part of an intelligence apparatus that was tied up with George H.W. Bush, then Corson's connections to banks and to individuals linked to the Supermarket becomes indicative of a pattern. Tellingly, Belize, the country where Weiland and Martin's associate Brull was active, was a primary node for the drug-smuggling ring in which DeVoe was involved. According to a UPI report, "cocaine was flown to Belize and islands in the Caribbean, then to processing points in the United States.... The pure cocaine was then brought to Miami where it was diluted and eventually distributed for street sales throughout the United States."[264]

Brull was mentioned in a 1986 FBI interview given by Richard Secord that concerned an investigation that had been launched into the activities of Jack Terrell. Terrell, using the name "Colonel Flaco," had worked with the Contras through his position in Civilian Materiel Assistance, the militia outfit used to train and assist the fighters that was connected to Singlaub, among others.[265] He subsequently became a whistleblower, turning over information to Florida authorities linking Oliver North, Robert Owen, and John Hull to gun running and drug smuggling. This was prior to revelations about the Enterprise that followed the doomed flight of Eugene Hasenfus in October 1986.

Terrell also provided information to the media. In June 1986, he appeared on a television show called *West 57th*, where he made allegations that the Contra-support flights were also being used to move drugs into the US. Several days later, North met with assistant FBI director Oliver "Buck" Revell to discuss identifying Terrell as a terrorist suspect – one with potential ties to Nicaraguan intelligence, to boot! This was a clever move on the part of North. In 1984, North organized a special group within the NSC called the Terrorist Incident Working Group (TIWG), which in turn spawned a secretive subunit called the Operations Sub-Group (OSG). This apparatus, dedicated to counterterrorism activities, was made up of North's allies across various agencies – including Buck Revell.

By designating Terrell a terrorism suspect, the FBI's counterterrorism operation was plugged directly into the NSC through Revell, allowing North to have a direct means of monitoring the whistleblower. On July 17, 1986, North sent a memo to Admiral Poindexter stating that, concerning Terrell, the "FBI has notified the Secret Service and is preparing a counterintelligence/counter-terrorism operation plan for review by OSG-TIWG tomorrow."[266]

The FBI interviewed Secord just under a week later, on July 23, 1986. He told the agents that Terrell's allegations were part of a "concerted effort" by an interconnected group of individuals. Operating in "collusion" with Terrell, Secord continued, was "Sergio Brulle [*sic*], a Cuban-American with a commercial business, a (FNU) [first name unknown] Gomez, whom he described as a bad Cuban involved with drug running."[267] Secord, in other words, was linking Terrell to the Supermarket, since Brull was tied to Martin. Gomez might have been none other than Felix Rodriguez, who frequently went under the alias "Max Gomez."

This statement raises more questions than it answers. By tying Terrell to the Supermarket, was Secord trying to place Martin and McCoy's outfit under FBI counterterrorism surveillance? Or was there truth to this statement? If it was the latter, then it would seem that the Supermarket could have been trying to expose the Enterprise in the press and to US law enforcement. This would directly parallel the claims later made by

Seymour Hersh: that a secret intelligence apparatus, run from the Office of the Vice President, had leaked information to the press concerning the missile sales to Iran.

Information and insider knowledge, it seems, was the weapon of choice in the shadow wars fought behind and beneath the bloody covert operations of the Reagan era.

Endnotes

1   Sen. John Kerry and Sen. Hank Brown, *The BCCI Affair: A Report to the Committee on Foreign Relations*, One Hundred Second Congress, Second Session, US Senate, December 1992, 41, https://play.google.com/store/books/details?id=CoKC-Sxb9kIC.

2   Jonathan Beaty and S. C. Gwynne, "BCCI: The Dirtiest Bank of Them All," *TIME*, July 29, 1991, https://content.time.com/time/subscriber/article/0,33009,973481-1,00.html.

3   Beaty and Gwynne, "BCCI: The Dirtiest Bank."

4   The *BCCI Affair* recounts that "Abedi's philosophy was often an obscure mix of Islamic mysticism, focusing on the links between the individual, the family, and the universe; and self-help motivational pitches" (Kerry and Brown, *BCCI Affair*, 41). Beaty and Gwynne cite BCCI employees who stated that Abedi would do strange tricks at the bank's training seminars. "He would hold a piece of paper in his hand and tell them to concentrate on an ink spot in the middle of it, making it grow and shrink in size. As it turned out, there was no ink spot, but he made them believe it." Jonathan Beaty and S. C. Gwynne, *The Outlaw Bank: A Wild Ride into the Secret Heart of BCCI* (Ramjac Inc, 1991), 266-67.

5   Peter Truell and Larry Gurwin, *False Profits: The Inside Story of BCCI, the World's Most Corrupt Financial Empire* (Houghton Mifflin, 1992), 11.

6   Truell and Gurwin, *False Profits*, 11.

7   "The BCCI-CIA Connection: Just How Far Did It Go?," *Newsweek*, December 6, 1992, https://www.newsweek.com/bcci-cia-connection-just-how-far-did-it-go-195454.

8   "The BCCI-CIA Connection."

9   Beaty and Gwynne, "BCCI: The Dirtiest Bank of Them All."

10   Christopher O. Clary, "The A. Q. Khan Network: Causes and Implications," thesis, Naval Postgraduate School, Monterey, CA., Dec. 2005.

11   Beaty and Gwynne, *Outlaw Bank*, 255, 262.

12   Beaty and Gwynne, *Outlaw Bank*, 139.

13   Kerry and Brown, *BCCI Affair*, 34.

14   Kerry and Brown, *BCCI Affair*, 34.

15   Kerry and Brown, *BCCI Affair*, 46.

16   Kerry and Brown, *BCCI Affair*, 59.

17   Kerry and Brown, *BCCI Affair*, 128.

18   Kerry and Brown, *BCCI Affair*, 128.

19   Kerry and Brown, *BCCI Affair*, 128.

20   Alan A. Block and Constance Weaver, *All Is Clouded by Desire: Global Banking, Money Laundering, and International Organized Crime* (Praeger, 2004), 41.

21   Truell and Gurwin, *False Profits*, 40.

22   Edward Jay Epstein, *Dossier: The Secret History of Armand Hammer* (Random House, 1996), 321-22.

23   Douglas W. Cray, "People and Business," *New York Times*, December 27, 1974.

24   Rob Wells, "BCCI Links to Oil Industry," *AP News*, August 26, 1991, https://apnews.com/article/228b9990df1c5f952c542cf256d0fd17.

25   Truell and Gurwin, *False Profits*, 43.

26   Kerry and Brown, *BCCI Affair*, 128, 134.

27   On Irvani and Credit and Commerce Holdings, see *The BCCI Affair: Hearings Before the Subcommittee on Terrorism, Narcotics and International Terrorism of the Committee on Foreign Relations*, One Hundred and Second Congress, First Session, August 1, 2, and 8, 1991, Part 1, p. 114; On Irvani and Richard Helms as business partners, see "The BCCI-CIA Connection: Just How Far Did It Go?" *Newsweek*, December 6, 1991, https://www.newsweek.com/bcci-cia-connection-just-how-far-did-it-go-195454.

28   "Ex-CIA Leader Aided Bcci Effort, Report Says," *Deseret News*, February 16, 1992, https://www.deseret.com/1992/2/16/18968049/ex-cia-leader-aided-bcci-effort-report-says-br.

29   "Ex-CIA Leader Aided BCCI."

30   "Ex-CIA Leader Aided BCCI."

31   Douglas Frantz, "BCCI: Odd Bank with Air of Cult: From its Roots in Pakistan until its Closure by Regulators, the Institutions Story Is One of Secretive Clients, Powerful Friends, and Global Fraud," *Los Angeles Times*, Sept. 3, 1991, https://www.latimes.com/archives/la-xpm-1991-09-03-mn-1965-story.html; Kerry and Brown, *BCCI Affair*, 145.

32   Whitney Webb, "The Genesis and Evolution of the Jeffrey Epstein, Bill Clinton Relationship," *MintPress News*, August 23, 2019, https://www.mintpressnews.com/genesis-jeffrey-epstein-bill-clinton-relationship/261455/.

33   Truell and Gurwin, *False Profits*, 73.

34   Truell and Gurwin, *False Profits*, 84.

35   Truell and Gurwin, *False Profits*, 376.

36   Scott Chase and Chapin Wright, "BANKING, FINANCE," *Washington Post*, June 29, 1981, https://www.washingtonpost.com/archive/business/1981/06/29/banking-finance/8893eab1-954c-458e-b9dd-1b0de7554f92/.

37   Kerry and Brown, *BCCI Affair*, 523.

38   Frantz, "BCCI: Odd Bank."

39   Kerry and Brown, *BCCI Affair*, 179.

40   Beaty and Gwynne, *Outlaw Bank*, 228.

41   Pete Brewton, *The Mafia, CIA and George Bush* (SPI Books, 1992), 221.

42   Russ Baker, *Family of Secrets* (Bloomsbury Press, 2010), 296-97.

43   Kerry and Brown, *BCCI Affair*, 486.

44   Kerry and Brown, *BCCI Affair*, 612.

45   Beaty and Gwynne, *Outlaw Bank*, 238-45.

46   Kerry and Brown, *BCCI Affair* 93-94.

47   Kerry and Brown, *BCCI Affair* 99.

48   Kerry and Brown, *BCCI Affair* 98.

49   Kerry and Brown, *BCCI Affair*, 101.

50   Philip Shendon, "BCCI's Best Customer Is Also Its Worst Customer," *New York Times*, August 6, 1991.

51   Truell and Gurwin. *False Profits*, 35.

52   Block and Weaver, *Clouded by Desire*, 86.

53   Kerry and Brown, *BCCI Affair*, 482.

54   Truell and Gurwin, *False Profits*, 18.

55   Kerry and Brown, *BCCI Affair*, 320.

56   Susan Mazur, "Caspian Tales: John Deuss, Oil, Spooks and Cohibas," *Scoop Independent News*, November 29, 2007, https://www.scoop.co.nz/stories/HL0711/S00443/caspian-tales-john-deuss-oil-spooks-cohibas.htm.

57   Christopher Dicky, "US Firm, Headed by Ex-CIA Man, Provides Oman More Than Stability," *Los Angeles Times*, April 27, 1986.

58   On Tetra Tech and Tetra Finance, see Kerry and Brown, *BCCI Affair*, 319. On Tetra Finance, John Shaheen, and BCCI links, see Kerry and Brown, *BCCI Affair*, 315-18.

59   William J. Eaton, "Senate Told of Noriega-BCCI Cover-Up," *Los Angeles Times*, July 31, 1992, https://www.latimes.com/archives/la-xpm-1992-07-31-mn-4549-story.html.

60   Eaton, "Senate Told of Noriega-BCCI Cover-Up."

61   Ricardo Castillo, "Convicted Trafficker Describes Noriega's Links to Drug Cartel," *Washington Post*, Nov. 20, 1991, https://www.washingtonpost.com/archive/politics/1991/11/20/convicted-trafficker-describes-noriegas-links-to-drug-cartel/50a6668d-242e-4b66-805f-e611ed11715c/.

62   Peter Dale Scott and Jonathan Marshall, *Cocaine Politics: Drugs, Armies, and the CIA in Central America* (University of California Press, 1998), 68.

63   Scott and Marshall, *Cocaine Politics*, 66.

64   See Howard Kohn and Vicky Monks, "The Dirty Secrets of George Bush," *Rolling Stone*, November 3, 1988, https://www.rollingstone.com/politics/politics-news/the-dirty-secrets-of-george-bush-71927/; John Cummings and Ernest Volkman, "Snowbound," *Penthouse*, July 1989.

65   Kohn and Monks, "Dirty Secrets."

66   Scott and Marshall, *Cocaine Politics*, 74.

67   Armstrong, Scott, Malcolm Byrne, Thomas S. Blanton, Laurence Chang, Glenn Baker, and National Security Archive, *The Chronology: The Documented Day-to-Day Account of the Secret Military Assistance to Iran and the Contras* (NY: Warner, 1987), 12, 13, 15, 19, 26, 24, 33, https://archive.org/details/chronologydocume00arms.

68   Kohn and Monks, "Dirty Secrets."

69   Joseph John Trento, *Prelude to Terror : The Rogue CIA and the Legacy of America's Private Intelligence Network* (New York : Carroll & Graf, 2005), 276, http://archive.org/details/preludetoterrorr00tren.

70   Trento, *Prelude to Terror*, 277.

71   Armstrong et al, *The Chronology*, 148.

72   Armstrong et al, *The Chronology*, 152.

73   *Final Report of the Independent Counsel for Iran/Contra Matters, Volume 1: Investigations and Prosecutions*, United States Court Of Appeals for the District of Columbia Circuit, August 4, 1993, chap. 8, https://irp.fas.org/offdocs/walsh/chap_08.htm.

74   Armstrong et al, *The Chronology*, 237.

75   *Final Report*, chap. 8.

76   Edward Cowan, "Board Defeat Angers Cornfeld," *New York Times*, July 2, 1970.

77   *Joint Hearings Before the House Select Committee to Investigate Covert Arms Transactions with Iran and Senate Select Committee on Secret Military Assistance to Iran and the Nicaraguan Opposition*: Testimony of Robert C. McFarlane, Gaston J. Sigur, Jr., and Robert W. Owen, One Hundredth Congress, First Session, May 11, 12, 13, 14, and 19, 1987, p. 451, https://archive.org/details/Iran-ContraHearingsTestimonyTranscripts/1987-irn-0003-McFarlane- Sigur-Owen/.

78   Armstrong et al, *The Chronology*, 16.

79   David Rogers, "Panama Records Show Strongest Link between Swiss Firm, Airlift to Contras," *Wall Street Journal*, January 30, 1987.

80   Scott and Marshall, *Cocaine Politics*, 13.

81   Scott and Marshall, *Cocaine Politics*, 87.

82   Susan B. Trento, *The Power House: Robert Keith Gray and the Selling of Access and Influence in Washington* (St. Martin's Press, 1992), 262-63.

83   *Final Report*, chap. 13, https://irp.fas.org/offdocs/walsh/chap_13.htm.

84   Armstrong et al, *The Chronology*, 79.

85   E. Trine Starnes, on January 30, 1986, was invited to the White House to meet personally with President Reagan, Spitz Channell, Elliot Abrams, and others. The special event was for individuals who had donated $30,000 or more to the National Endowment for the Preservation of Liberty. Starnes seems to have had ties to the circles around George H.W.Bush. He was reportedly part of the group of S&L borrowers around Robert Corson and John Riddle, referenced elsewhere here. He was also the second biggest borrower at Silverado Savings, the Colorado thrift where Neil Bush sat on the board of directors. "On September 30, 1986, exactly eight months after Starnes made his contribution to the Contra cause, he and his associates received three loans from Silverado Savings totaling $77.5 million" (Brewton, *The Mafia*, 258).

86   *Final Report*, chap. 13, https://irp.fas.org/offdocs/walsh/chap_13.htm.

87   Sidney Blumenthal, "Reagan Doctrine's Passionate Advocate," *Washington Post*, December 17, 1986, https://www.washingtonpost.com/archive/politics/1986/12/17/reagan-doctrines-passionate-advocate/750d4579-a2f0-4f72-826c-33966e8b5e64/.

88   *Allegations of Connections between CIA and the Contras in Cocaine Trafficking to the United States, Vol. 2, The Contra Story*, "Pilots, Companies, and Other Individuals Working for Companies Used to Support the Contra Program," Oct. 8, 1998, https://irp.fas.org/cia/product/cocaine2/pilots.html.

89   Scott and Marshall, *Cocaine Politics*, 11.

90   Scott and Marshall, *Cocaine Politics*, 118-19.

91   Scott and Marshall, *Cocaine Politics*, 118.

92   Drugs, Law Enforcement and Foreign Policy: A Report Prepared by the Subcommittee on Terrorism, Narcotics and International Operations, Committee on Foreign Relations, United States Senate, December 1988, 44, https://www.ojp.gov/ncjrs/virtual-library/abstracts/drugs-law-enforcement-and-foreign-policy.

93   Scott and Marshall, *Cocaine Politics*, 42.

94   "The Cali Cartel: The New Kings of Cocaine," US Department of Justice, November 1994, *https://www.ojp.gov/pdffiles1/Digitization/152436NCJRS.pdf*.

95   Scott and Marshall, *Cocaine Politics*, 41.

96   "US Probing Claims That CIA Operative, DEA Official Betrayal Led to Murder of Agent: Report," Fox News, February 28, 2020, https://www.foxnews.com/us/dea-agent-kiki-camarena-murder-investigation.

97   Scott and Marshall, *Cocaine Politics*, 41.

98   *Drugs, Law Enforcement and Foreign Policy*, 48.

99   *Allegations of Connections*, "Pilots, Companies, and Other Individuals Working for Companies Used to Support the Contra Program."

100   *Allegations of Connections*, "Pilots, Companies, and Other Individuals Working for Companies Used to Support the Contra Program."

101   *Drugs, Law Enforcement and Foreign Policy*, 49.

102   Gerald Colby, *DuPont Dynasty: Behind the Nylon Curtain*, ePub (Open Road Media, 2014), 1154.

103   FBI files on Civilian Materiel Assistance obtained by Edmund Berger via the Freedom of Information Act request tie the CMA to the 20th Special Forces Group. Beyond this, allegations have been made that the CMA, during the Contra years, obtained "surplus U.S. military equipment from the 20th Special Forces Unit of the US Army in Alabama" ("Declarations of the Plaintiff's Counsel, filed by the Christic Institute," US District Court, Miami, Florida, March 31, 1988, 80).

104   On the World Anti-Communist League, see Scott Anderson and Jon Lee Anderson, *Inside the League: The Shocking Expose of How Terrorists, Nazis, and Latin American Death Squads Have Infiltrated the World Anti-Communist League* (Dodd Mead, 1986); and Russ Bellant, *Old Nazis, the New Right and the Republican Party: Domestic Fascist Networks and Their Effect on Cold War Policy* (South End Press, 1991).

105   Block and Weaver, *Clouded by Desire*, 108.

106   Chip Berlet, *The Hunt for the Red Menace: How Government Intelligence Agencies and Private Right-Wing Groups Target Dissidents and Leftists as Subversive Terrorists and Outlaws* (Political Research Associates, 1994), https://politicalresearch.org/sites/default/files/2018-10/huntred-1994.pdf.

107   Holly Sklar, *Washington's War on Nicaragua* (South End Press, 1999), 82.

108   Albin Krebs and Robert Thomas Jr., "Notes on People: Roy Cohn Joins Board of Anti-Communist Group," *New York Times*, May 15, 1982.

109   Frank Rich, "The Original Donald Trump," *New York Magazine*, April 2018, https://nymag.com/intelligencer/2018/04/frank-rich-roy-cohn-the-original-donald-trump.html.

110   Rich, "Original Donald Trump."

111   Robert Parry, "How Roy Cohn Helped Rupert Murdoch," January 28, 2015, https://consortiumnews.com/2015/01/28/how-roy-cohn-helped-rupert-murdoch/.

112   Armstrong et al, *The Chronology*, 321.

113   On Samuel Cummings and John Tower, see Emma North-Best, "John Tower's FBI File Reveals Role in Iran-Contra Cover-Up," *Muckrock*, January 9, 2017, https://www.muckrock.com/news/archives/2017/jan/09/john-towers-fbi-file-reveals-role-in-iran-contra-cove/.

114   The following information on GMT, unless stated otherwise, comes from Alan A. Block, "The Origins of Iran-Contra: Lessons from the Durrani Affair," in Frank Bovenkirk and Michael Levi, *The Organized Crime Community: Essays in Honor of Alan A. Block* (Springer Science, 2007), 12.

115   Bovenkirk and Levi, *The Organized Crime Community*, 12.

116   Scott and Marshall, *Cocaine Politics*, 76.

117   Roy Greenslade. *Maxwell's Fall: An Insider's Account* (Simon & Schuster, 1992), 133

118   Ari Ben-Menashe. *Profits of War: Inside the Secret U.S.-Israeli Arms Network* (Sheridan

Square Press, 1992), 112

119   Ben-Menashe. *Profits of War*, 115.

120   Ben-Menashe. *Profits of War*, 155-156.

121   Ben-Menashe. *Profits of War*, 360-361.

122   Among Davies' contacts in Ohio was "William Johnson, managing director of the now-defunct Armtec International Columbus" – a very intriguing location, given the importance of Columbus, Ohio in this book. Glenn Frankel, "Media Baron Sues Seymour Hersh", *Washington Post*, October 25, 1991, https://www.washingtonpost.com/archive/lifestyle/1991/10/25/media-baron-sues-seymour-hersh/c16c29e2-04ba-4038-9fff-08113fa33b77/. See also "Book: Ohioans would-be arms dealers", *Lancaster-Eagle Gazette*, October 28, 1991.

123   Russell Davies. *Foreign Body: The Secret Life of Robert Maxwell* (Bloomsbury, 1995), 152-153.

124   John Merritt, "Davies: fresh evidence on arms deals", *The Observer*, October 27, 1991.

125   Merritt, "Davies."

126   Armstrong et al, *The Chronology*, 321.

127   *Report of the Congressional Committees Investigating the Iran-Contra Affair*: Testimony of unnamed CIA Officer, Appendix B, Vol. 10, 610, https://www.google.com/books/edition/Report_of_the_Congressional_Committee_In/MB15AAAAMAAJ.

128   *Report of the Congressional Committees*, Appendix B, Vol. 10, 612.

129   *Report of the Congressional Committees*, Appendix B, Vol. 10, 691

130   Block, "Origins of Iran-Contra," 15.

131   Jonathan Marshall, Peter Dale Scott, and Jane Hunter, *The Iran-Contra Connection: Secret Teams and Covert Operations in the Reagan Era* (South End Press, 1987), 175.

132   Rachel Ehrenfeld, *Evil Money: Encounters Along the Money Trail* (Harper Business, 1992), 70.

133   Ehrenfeld, *Evil Money*, 113.

134   Truell and Gurwin, *False Profits*, 174-75. Nazerali's partner in securities fraud schemes was Irving Kott. Kott was an associate of Willie Obront, a "Montreal meat merchant who once made front-page headlines across Canada after a public inquiry named him as a key money launderer for the Cotroni mafia." During the 1970s, Obront had moved to the US, where his associates included a Meyer Lansky front man named Barry Ressler. See Tu Thahn Ha, "Montreal Butcher Was a Banker for the Mafia," *The Globe and Mail*, July 31, 2019, https://www.theglobeandmail.com/canada/article-montreal-butcher-was-a-banker-for-the-mafia/.

Obront also had ties to the Bronfman family. Pete Newman writes that "although he vehemently denies any venal implications in his friendships, Mitchell Bronfman was condemned in 1977 by having the Quebec Police Commission inquiry into organized crime as having had an 'almost brotherly relationship' with Willie Obront, a convicted kingpin of Montreal's underworld." See Peter Newman, *The Bronfman Dynasty* (McClelland and Stewart, 1978), 225.

135   *Final Report*, chap. 14, https://irp.fas.org/offdocs/walsh/chap_14.htm.

136   *Final Report*, chap. 14

137   "FBI 302 - Record of Nan Morabia Interview," FBI, November 6, 1987, https://archive.org/details/FBI302NanMorabia1.

138   John Tagliabue, "The White House Crisis; Small, Quiet Building in Geneva Had Wide Use," *New York Times*, December 3, 1986.

139   *Report of the Congressional Committees Investigating the Iran-Contra Affair*, Testimony of Richard Secord, Appendix B, Vol. 24, 242, https://archive.org/details/Iran-ContraHearingsTestimonyTranscripts/1987-irn-0001-Secord/.

140   Gordon Thomas, *Robert Maxwell, Israel's Superspy: The Life and Murder of a Media Mogul* (De Capo Press, 2003), 37-38.

141   "Illicit Narcotics Threats," Compiled by Office of the Deputy Director of the CIA for Robert McFarlane, May 1984, https://www.cia.gov/readingroom/docs/CIA-RDP-86M00886R000800010012-3.pdf.

142   Ehrenfeld, *Evil Money*, 142.

143   Kerry and Brown, *BCCI Affair*, 567.

144   Jonathan Marshall, *The Lebanese Connection: Corruption, Civil War, and the International Drug Traffic* (Stanford University Press, 2012), 160.

145   "Michael De Picciotto Biography," http://michaeldepicciotto.com/biography/.

146   Kurt Eichenwald, "American Express to Sell Geneva Bank for $1 Billion," *New York Times*, December 29, 1989.

147   Armstrong et al, *The Chronology*, 148.

148   Stephen Pizzo, Mary Fricker, and Paul Muolo, *Inside Job: The Looting of America's Savings and Loans* (Harper Perennial, 1991), 113.

149   *International Petrodollar Crisis: Hearings Before the Subcommittee on International Finance of the Committee on Banking and Currency*, House of Representatives, Ninety-Third Congress, Second Session, July and August 1974, 229, https://fraser.stlouisfed.org/title/international-petrodollar-crisis-225/fulltext.

150   Pizzo, Fricker, and Muolo, *Inside Job*, 115.

151   Pizzo, Fricker, and Muolo, *Inside Job*, 115-16; Brewton, *The Mafia*, 44-46.

152   Brewton, *The Mafia*, 45-46.

153   David Cay Johnston, "Just What Were Donald Trump's Ties to the Mob?," *POLITICO Magazine*, May 22, 2016, https://www.politico.com/magazine/story/2016/05/donald-trump-2016-mob-organized-crime-213910.

154   Sydney Schanberg, "Gas Tax Cash and Re-Electing a Governor," *New York Newsday*, December 4, 1987.

155   Pizzo, Fricker, and Muolo, *Inside Job*, 165.

156   Pizzo, Fricker, and Muolo, *Inside Job*, 165-66.

157   Brewton, *The Mafia*, 190-91. Iorizzo was introduced to Samos by Eric D'Antin, a confidence man with aristocratic pretensions. D'Antin is described in various press reports and court cases as a "Mexican Duke who works as a banker in London," a "petroleum broker," an "Austrian duke," and an "agent" of textile magnate Joseph Koret. In the 1980s D'Antin was married to Michaela von Habsburg, the daughter of Otto von Habsburg. See "The Princess and the P (for Press), *Daily News, (New York)*, December 11, 1980. Also, Michaela's former sister-in-law, Francesca von Habsburg, is listed in Jeffrey Epstein's black book.

158   Samos was married to Alma Robles Chiari, the heiress from a prominent and politically well-connected family. In 1977, Alma and Samos' partner, Ray Corona, attempted to purchase the National Bank of South Florida. The bank, a well-known drug laundromat located in Hialeah, was for sale by the First National Bank of Louisville. It had previously been owned by the WFC Corporation, which was partnered with First National Bank of Louisville in the ownership of Panama's UniBank, through which loans were granted to individuals and institutions. When WFC began to collapse in the late 1970s, First National Bank of Louisville was exposed to a compounding liquidity crunch. To compensate, WFC turned National Bank of South Florida over to First National Bank of Louisville, and in order to recoup losses First National Bank of Louisville placed it for sale. See James Ring Adams, *The Big Fix: Inside the S&L Scandal : How an Unholy Alliance of Politics and Money Destroyed America's Banking System* (New York: Wiley, 1991), 72–84.

        Other potential buyers for National Bank of South Florida from First National Bank of Louisville included Gustavo Villoldo, a CIA-trained Cuban exile who was suspected of being a front man for the WFC's founder, Guillermo Hernandez-Cartaya. Villoldo would later resurface in the covert Contra support operations. According to Peter Dale Scott and Jonathan Marshall, Villoldo was sent in 1983 "into Central America by Vice President Bush's national security advisor Donald Gregg to advise the Contras on military strategy." This would closely conform to reporting on Operation Black Eagle. Later, during the feud between the Enterprise and the Supermarket, Oliver North toyed with the idea of using Villoldo to take the Supermarket's Mario Delamico "out of the picture." See Scott and Marshall, *Cocaine Politics*, 29, 59.

159   Armstrong et al, *The Chronology*, 171.

160   Brewton, *The Mafia*, 192; Scott and Marshall, *Cocaine Politics*, 197n60.

161   *Major Financial Institutions of Continental Europe 1990/91* (Graham & Trotman Limited 1990), 179, https://doi.org/10.1007/978-94-011-3022-6; *The BCCI Affair: Hearings Before the Subcommittee on Terrorism, Narcotics, and International Operations of the Committee on Foreign Relations*, United States Senate, One Hundred Second Congress, First Session, August 1, 1991, 475, part 1,

https://books.google.com/books?id=8DLDVLJN_sUC.

162   Brewton, *The Mafia*, 53-57.

163   James S. Henry, *Blood Bankers: Tales from the Global Underground Economy* (Basic Books, 2005), 48.

164   Brewton, *The Mafia*, 55.

165   Brewton, *The Mafia*, 56.

166   On Hourani and Lamar, see Brewton, *The Mafia*, 130-31; on Hourani and Mainland, see Truell and Gurwin, *False Profits*, 375-77.

167   Brewton, *The Mafia*, 130.

168   Truell and Gurwin, *False Profits*, 376.

169   Brewton, *The Mafia*, 131.

170   Truell and Gurwin, *False Profits*, 377.

171   Truell and Gurwin, *False Profits*, 376.

172   Michael Isikoff, "Deals of Developer Khashoggi Building Frustration in Utah," *Washington Post*, January 4, 1987.

173   Truell and Gurwin, *False Profits*, 377.

174   R. T. Naylor, *Patriots and Profiteers: Economic Warfare, Embargo Busting, and State-Sponsored Crime* (McGill-Queen's University Press, 2008), 244.

175   Naylor, *Patriots and Profiteers*, 246.

176   "Illegal Arms to Iran: How the Banks Broke the Rules," *Euromoney*, October 1, 1991, https://www.euromoney.com/article/b1dfgmpypmxgbc/illegal-arms-to-iran-how-the-banks-broke-the-rules.

177   "In Un' Agenda I Nomi Dell' Iraq – Connection," *La Repubblica*, September 13, 1989, https://ricerca.repubblica.it/repubblica/archivio/repubblica/1989/09/13/in-un-agenda-nomi-dell-iraq.html.

178   *Report of the Congressional Committees Investigating the Iran-Contra Affair: Depositions*, Appendix B, Volume 3, One Hundredth Congress, First Session, 1988, 861, https://www.google.com/books/edition/Report_of_the_Congressional_Committees_I/u1_-pOKeFe8C.

179   "Illegal Arms to Iran: How the Banks Broke the Rules."

180   John De Belot, "International Bankers: Jean Maxine Leveque Takes the Field," *Les Echos*, March 2, 1992, https://www-lesechos-fr.translate.goog/1992/03/international-bankers-jean-maxime-leveque-prend-du-champ-921859?_x_tr_sl=fr&_x_tr_tl=en&_x_tr_hl=en&_x_tr_pto=sc; *Report of the Congressional Committees Investigating the Iran-Contra Affair, Depositions*: Testimony of Emanuel A. Floor, Appendix B, Volume 10, One Hundredth Congress, First Session, 1988, 486, https://www.google.com/books/edition/Report_of_the_Congressional_Committee_In/MB15AAAAMAAJ.

181   Gaetner Gilles, "The Other Lyonnais Scandal," *L'Express*, May 18, 2005, https://www-lexpress-fr.translate.goog/informations/l-autre-scandale-du-lyonnais_607863.html?_x_tr_sl=fr&_x_tr_tl=en&_x_tr_hl=en&_x_tr_pto=sc; "Mansour Ojjeh Obituary," *The Times*, June 9, 2021, https://www.thetimes.co.uk/article/mansour-ojjeh-obituary-spbm52bpl.

182   "Illegal Arms to Iran."

183   Naylor, *Patriots and Profiteers*, 254.

184   Kerry and Brown, *BCCI Affair*, 314.

185   Kerry and Brown, *BCCI Affair*, 313.

186   "Unusual Behavior," *Der Spiegel*, February 10, 1983, https://www.spiegel.de/politik/unuebliches-gebaren-a-52408d0c-0002-0001-0000-000014022410.

187   "Unusual Behavior."

188   "Unusual Behavior."

189   "Lonrho's Foothold in Forwarding," *The Guardian*, June 29, 1981,

190   "Felix Przedborski: diplomaat en groot-officier met een loodzwaar strafblad," *De Tijd*, https://www.tijd.be/algemeen/algemeen/felix-przedborski-diplomaat-en-groot-officier-met-een-loodzwaar-strafblad/5159483.html.

191   "Attacks on Press in 2004 – Costa Rica," *Refworld*, February, 2005, https://www.refworld.

org/docid/47c566d1c.html; Inter-American Court of Human Rights: The *La Nación* Newspaper Case," February 18, 2004, https://cpj.org/wp-content/uploads/2004/06/Costa19feb04_Amicus-Brief.pdf.

192   *ATLAS Dossier*, Translation provided by Institute for the Study of Globalization and Covert Politics, 15, https://isgp-studies.com/belgium-la-nebuleuse-atlas-dossier-and-dutroux-x-files.

193   *ATLAS Dossier*, 6.

194   Ehrenfeld, *Evil Money*, 144.

195   Ehrenfeld, *Evil Money*, 144.

196   *ATLAS Dossier*, 20.

197   Doyle McManus, "Secret Airstrips Links CIA, State Department, to Contra Aid," *Los Angeles Times*, March 1, 1987.

198   Willy van Damme, "Mossad–Een vrijgeleide in België," February 27, 2013, https://willyvandamme.wordpress.com/2013/02/27/mossadeen-vrijgeleide-in-belgi/.

199   Van Damme, "Mossad."

200   Alain Lallemand, "Jacques Monsieur Arrested in Turkey," *Center for Public Integrity*, May 14, 2002, https://publicintegrity.org/accountability/jacques-monsieur-arrested-in-turkey/; Alain Lallemand, "The Field Marshal," *International Consortium of Investigative Journalists*, November 15, 2002, https://www.icij.org/investigations/makingkilling/field-marshal/

201   Van Damme, "Mossad."

202   Block and Weaver, *Clouded by Desire*, 110-11.

203   Kerry and Brown, *BCCI Affair*, 612.

204   "Call Girls, Tax Fraud and Weapons," *De Morgen*, January 10, 2001, https://www.demorgen.be/nieuws/callgirls-fiscale-fraude-en-wapenhandel~b6c633de/.

205   René Haquin, "Bribes at VDB?," *Le Soir*, Sept. 28, 1988, https://www.lesoir.be/art/pots-de-vin-a-vdb_t-19880928-Z01062.html.

206   "Call Girls, Tax Fraud and Weapons."

207   *ATLAS Dossier*, 15.

208   Jack Colhoun, "BCCI: The Bank of the CIA," *Covert Action Quarterly*, Spring, 1993, 41, https://archive.org/details/covert_action_44; Block, "Origins of Iran-Contra."

209   Colhoun, "BCCI: The Bank of the CIA," 40-42.

210   Gary Sick, *October Surprise: America's Hostages in Iran and the Election of Ronald Reagan*, 1st ed (New York: Times Books, 1991), 220.

211   *The Investigation of State Department Officials: Shultz, Hill and Platt: Final Report*, ch 24, https://irp.fas.org/offdocs/walsh/chap_24.htm.

212   Dana Priest, "Rumsfeld Visited Baghdad in 1984 to Reassure Iraqis, Documents Show," *Washington Post*, December 19, 2003, https://www.washingtonpost.com/archive/politics/2003/12/19/rumsfeld-visited-baghdad-in-1984-to-reassure-iraqis-documents-show/2aaa6f-bc-59bd-46e7-86ca-8ca84fa1c0f4/.

213   The long history of Shultz at Bechtel is discussed in Sally Denton, *The Profiteers: Bechtel and the Men Who Built the World* (Simon & Schuster, 2016).

214   "Bechtel in Iraq: Shultz and Rumsfeld," *Zfacts*, https://zfacts.com/zfacts.com/p/170.html.

215   The pipeline negotiations and Bruce Rappaport's role in them is discussed at length in Block and Weaver, *Clouded by Desire*.

216   Block and Weaver, *Clouded by Desire*, 74.

217   Steven Hurst, *The United States and Iraq since 1979: Hegemony, Oil and War* (Edinburgh University Press, 2009), 52, https://www.jstor.org/stable/10.3366/j.ctt1r27xm.

218   George Lardner Jr., "Bush Aides Ethics Questioned over Loans to Iraq," *Washington Post*, April 29, 1992, https://www.washingtonpost.com/archive/politics/1992/04/29/bush-aides-ethics-questioned-over-loans-to-iraq/f85edf9c-269e-48c7-9654-47ce34be09fa/.

219   Kurt Eichenwald, "BCCI Once Lent Money to Bank Tied to Iraq Loans," *New York Times*, July 11, 1991.

220   *Hearings Before the Committee on Banking, Finance and Urban Affairs*: Testimony of Former Employees of the Banca Nazionale Del Lavoro, November 9, 1993, Vol. 4, 176, https://archive.

org/details/testimonyofforme1994unit/page/176/mode/2up.

221   Testimony of Former Employees of the Banca Nazionale Del Lavoro, 176.

222   "Arms Exports (Iraq)," Hansard, UK Parliament, House of Commons, November 23, 1992, https://api.parliament.uk/historic-hansard/commons/1992/nov/23/arms-exports-iraq.

223   "Update on BNL Investigation," Congressional Record, House of Representatives, January 21, 1993, https://irp.fas.org/congress/1993_cr/h930121-bnl.htm.

224   Douglas Frantz, "Sale of US Bomb Material to Iraq Probed," Los Angeles Times, February 1, 1993, https://www.latimes.com/archives/la-xpm-1993-02-01-mn-979-story.html.

225   "Around the Nation: Thatcher's Son to Stay in Dallas Flat after All," New York Times, April 25, 1986.

226   "Arms Exports (Iraq)."

227   The connections between Cardoen, Bull, and Mark Thatcher are made by Ari Ben-Menashe, Profits of War: Inside the Secret U.S.-Israeli Arms Network (Sheridan Square Press, 1992).

228   Newman, Bronfman Dynasty, 244-45.

229   Lardner Jr., "Bush Aides Ethics Questioned."

230   Henry, Blood Bankers, 348.

231   Walter Pincus, "Kissinger's Clients May Be Revealed," Washington Post, February 11, 1989.

232   Henry A. Kissinger, "A Remembrance of George P. Shultz," October 17, 2021, https://www.hoover.org/research/remembrance-george-p-shultz-henry-kissinger.

233   Don Oberdorfer, "Kissinger's New Team," Washington Post, August 24, 1982, https://www.washingtonpost.com/archive/politics/1982/08/24/kissingers-new-team/c313bd33-2912-4855-8efb-73674d5c56dd/.

234   L. J. Davis, "William Simon's Pacific Overtures," New York Times Magazine, December 27, 1987, https://www.nytimes.com/1987/12/27/magazine/william-simon-s-facific-overtures.html; Laton McCartney, Friends in High Places: The Bechtel Story – The Most Secret Corporation and How It Engineered the World (Ballantine Books, 1988), 187, 210.

235   Henry Kissinger, Years of Renewal, ePub (NY: Simon & Schuster, 1999), 1294.

236   Kerry and Brown, BCCI Affair, 92.

237   Kerry and Brown, BCCI Affair, 560.

238   Kerry and Brown, BCCI Affair, 560.

239   Report of the Congressional Committees Investigating the Iran-Contra Affair, Testimony of Gen. John R. Galvin, Appendix B, Vol. 11, 1988, 582, https://www.google.com/books/edition/Report_of_the_Congressional_Committees_I/w8U9sKdxC3wC.

240   Report of the Congressional Committees Investigating the Iran-Contra Affair, Testimony of unnamed CIA Officer, appendix B, Vol. 5, 1988, 148, https://www.google.com/books/edition/Report_of_the_Congressional_Committee_In/6ft4AAAAMAAJ.

241   Final Report, chap. 21 (CIA Subject #1), https://irp.fas.org/offdocs/walsh/chap_21.htm.

242   Final Report, chap. 21.

243   Kohn and Monks, "Dirty Secrets."

244   Kohn and Monks, "Dirty Secrets."

245   Final Report, chap. 21.

246   Final Report, chap. 21.

247   Organized Crime and Cocaine Trafficking, President's Commission on Organized Crime, November, 1984, 252, https://www.google.com/books/edition/Organized_Crime_and_Cocaine_Trafficking/iPghAAAAMAAJ; "Smuggler Convicted in Case Implicating Governments," UPI, July 6, 1986, https://www.upi.com/Archives/1988/07/06/Smuggler-convicted-in-case-implicating-governments/4859584164800/.

248   Brewton, The Mafia, 286.

249   Kohn and Monks, "Dirty Secrets."

250   Final Report, chap. 29 (Donald P. Gregg), https://irp.fas.org/offdocs/walsh/chap_29.htm; Webb, Dark Alliance, 339.

251   Final Report, chap. 29

252   On Posada, see Webb, Dark Alliance, 253-55; and Scott and Marshall, Cocaine Politics,

31. Posada has been identified as an associate of Philip (or Phillip) Arthur Thompson, a hitman, suspected serial killer, and FBI informant. Thompson, during the 1980s, turned up in the Wackenhut-Cabazon arms joint venture at the Cabazon Indian Reservation in Southern California. As discussed in chapters 8 and 9, this venture was intimately tied to, among other things, Iran-Contra and the Inslaw affair. Thomspon had been involved in the security side of the arrangement and had acted as bodyguard for Michael Riconosciuto. Cheri Seymour writes that "Philip Arthur Thompson was originally sent in by Patrick Moriarty … (Patrick Moriarty was Michael's father's partner of 40 years)." Cheri Seymour, *The Last Circle: Danny Casolaro's Investigation into the Octopus and the PROMIS Software Scandal*, 1st ed (Walterville, OR: TrineDay, 2010), page 301

253   *Final Report*, chap. 29.

254   *Final Report*, chap. 29.

255   Trento, *Prelude to Terror*, 54.

256   *Final Report*, chap. 29.

257   *Final Report*, chap. 29.

258   Kohn and Monks, "Dirty Secrets."

259   Colhoun, "BCCI: The Bank of the CIA," 17.

260   Brewton, *The Mafia*, 94.

261   Brewton, *The Mafia*, 331-57. Mike Adkinson, when he was not dealing arms, was a real estate developer from Houston. Sometime in the early 1980s, he had fallen in with a group of wealthy Kuwaitis. He began fronting for their real estate interests in Texas and was traveling in and out of the Middle East in this period. This was when he reportedly became involved in gunrunning, and Iraq was identified to have been one of the destinations of the arms he brokered. Adkinson stated that his "rise to stardom" was thanks to Herman Beebe, the crooked S&L player with ties to organized crime and the CIA. According to Brewton's sources, Adkinson was something of a front man for Beebe. One of their operations was Skyways Aviation.

262   Brewton, *The Mafia*, 94.

263   Robert Parry, *Lost History: Contras, Cocaine, the Press, and 'Project Truth'*, (Media Consortium, 1999), 160.

264   "Authorities Claim Breakup of Largest Cocaine Ring," *UPI*, May 2, 1984.

265   On Jack Terrell and Oliver North's counterintelligence operations against him, see Peter Dale Scott, "North, Iran-Contra, and the Doomsday Project: The Congressional Cover-Up of Continuity of Government Planning," *Asia-Pacific Journal*, February 21, 2011; and Edmund Berger, "Iran-Contra and Domestic Counter-Intelligence Networks," *Reciprocal Contradiction*, May 19, 2021, https://reciprocalcontradiction.home.blog/2021/05/19/iran-contra-and-domestic-counter-intelligence-networks/.

266   *Report of the Congressional Committees Investigating the Iran-Contra Affair*, Supplemental, Minority and Additional Views, Vol. 2, 1321, https://www.google.com/books/edition/Report_of_the_Congressional_Committees_I/Fp2wJHOda6IC.

267   *Report of the Congressional Committees Investigating the Iran-Contra Affair*, Source Documents, Appendix A, Vol. 1, 859, https://books.google.com/books?id=hCYlFcNbYtsC.

CHAPTER 8

CLINTON CONTRA

SEAL, THE SMUGGLER

On October 5th, 1986, the Enterprise took a mortal blow. At 9:50 AM, a C-123K military transport aircraft took off from the Ilopango military base, carrying a stockpile of rifles, ammunition, and explosives in its hull. These were to be air-dropped into the Nicaraguan jungle for the Contras – but the plane never made it to its destination. It was instead shot down by Sandinista forces, killing three of the four man crew. The sole survivor, Eugene Hasenfus of Wisconsin, was subsequently captured. Under interrogation, he began to detail what he knew of the wide-ranging plot to arm the Contra rebels.

The first official communication surrounding the plane came through Felix Rodriguez, who alerted Samuel Watson, an aide to Vice President Bush, that an aircraft had gone missing. A day later, on October 6th, Rodriguez contacted Watson again with an update. Soon, Oliver North was bound for El Salvador. Meanwhile, cover stories were being drafted in a desperate attempt to provide an alternative explanation of events. Despite their efforts, North and the Enterprise were out of luck and, within days, congressmen were calling for inquiries into the crash, the FBI began nosing around Southern Air Transport's Miami offices, and the press started to run stories about different aspects of their clandestine activities. It was all unraveling at a fast pace.

As with most things related to the Enterprise, mystery begat more mystery. Hasenfus, for example, had been hired to serve as a crewman on the doomed C-123K by a company called Corporate Air Service, which was registered in Pennsylvania but had offices in Miami. Corporate Air was "revealed to be a phantom company," and its Miami location was actually Southern Air Transport's headquarters at the Miami Airport.[1]

The history of the C-123K was itself a tangled web. In 1983, it had been purchased from the US Air Force by Harry Doan, the proprietor of a Florida aviation company called Doan Helicopters. It had been picked up by the Enterprise in March 1986, via a front company called Udall Research Corporation. Udall, registered in Panama, was also involved in the construction of the airstrip in the Santa Elena region of Costa Rica. Papers recovered from North's safe described Udall as an "operating company."[2]

Udall was not alone in acquiring this C-123K from Doan. It had previously fallen into the hands of one Adler Barriman "Barry" Seal, the commercial pilot-turned-drug smuggler and CIA asset. Seal had picked up the plane, used it for drug smuggling flights, and then returned it to Doan Helicopters in July 1985. Seal, importantly, was connected to the same criminal figures that had been woven into the covert Contra support network. Beginning in 1981, Seal had begun to ferry cocaine on behalf of Jorge Ochoa, one of the Medellin cartel's founding members. In a few years, Seal's Medellin smuggling had expanded considerably. With police attention mounting in his home state of Louisiana, Seal set up a new base of operations in rural Arkansas.

The location that Seal selected was the Intermountain Municipal Airport in Mena, Arkansas, near the Arkansas-Oklahoma border. Mena was a small, unassuming town; yet, throughout the 1980s, the area encircling the airport became a hotbed of intrigue. In 1989, journalist John Cummings, in one of the first articles written on Seal in Mena, wrote that "Seal had virtually taken over a local aircraft repair-and-modification operation at the airport, and the good citizens of Mena began to notice some strange goings on: landings at night, tight security around Seal's planes, a hangar converted into a virtual fortress."[3] There were also sightings of what appeared to be airdrops, the construction of airstrips deep in the woods beyond the airport, and even darker rumors that whatever was happening was sanctioned by the CIA.

The report of the Kerry Commission on narcotics later stated that "[a]ssociates of Seal … were … targets of grand jury probes into narcotics trafficking." Yet, these cases were dropped despite the "strong protests of State and federal law enforcement officials.. … The apparent reason," the report continues, "was that the prosecution might have revealed national security information."[4]

Jack Anderson wrote in the *Washington Post* that, after Seal died in 1986, IRS investigators descended upon Mena and seized records and other documents from the smuggler's offices there. The IRS was keeping its report "under wraps," but Anderson relayed its name: "Contra Mena Connection."[5] The absence of a public release of this report allowed a comprehensive firewall to be set in place, permitting investigators to quietly detail the story of Seal and that of Iran-Contra.

That the plane shot down in Nicaragua had been used by Seal was written off as mere coincidence, with the intermediary figure, Harry Doan, acting as a convenient buffer. Unfortunately for the proponents of this narrative, the specter of Seal appears throughout the official documentation of the Iran-Contra case.

A May 1983 US Customs report noted that an aircraft piloted by Frank Moss and owned by his Hondu Carib aviation company was involved in drug smuggling linked to Barry Seal. As previously mentioned, Moss and his aviation companies were entangled, not only with the Enterprise's Contra support efforts, but with repeat allegations of drug trafficking. Those allegations rang true in the case of this plane, tail number N90201, which made at least one airdrop of "large quantities of marijuana and cocaine at an isolated farm near Baton Rouge, Louisiana. The farm's address Rt. 6, Box 282E in East Baton Rouge, Louisiana, belong[ed] to Adler [Barry] Seal…"[6] Given Moss' ties to Matta's drug trafficking operations, it seems likely that Seal himself was part of these wider smuggling networks. It would also align Seal with the Cali cartel in addition to his earlier Medellin ties, which paints a complicated picture of the unstable alliances and power competitions that raged beneath the surface of this covert world.

Journalist Daniel Hopsicker, in his biography of Barry Seal, writes that he obtained documents from the trafficker's widow which show that, in the 1980s, Seal was doing business with Summit Aviation. As mentioned in the previous chapter, Summit was controlled by the DuPont family, and was managed by Patrick Foley, a veteran of the CIA and Flying Tiger Line. It was Summit that had provided a small aircraft that was utilized for a bombing run in Nicaragua, while it was Foley who had recommended a drug-smuggling pilot to the State Department for the transportation of "humanitarian supplies" to the Contras. Foley, Hopsicker writes, was a "Seal associate whose name and number are in Barry's files."[7]

Summit was involved in the acquisition and trade of Beechcraft King Air, turboprop planes known for their flexibility and versatility. Seal, likewise, maintained his own King Air plane, and one, sporting the tail number N6308F, had a particularly interesting provenance. It was owned by Greycas Inc., a Phoenix, Arizona-based subsidiary of Greyhound Lines, the bus company. Greycas leased the plane to a company called Systems Marketing Inc., reportedly a subsidiary of another firm named Military

Electronics.[8] Systems Marketing provided the plane to Gene Glick, a real estate developer who, in turn, leased it to Seal.

According to Hopsicker, Glick "leased not just this but several other of Barry Seal's planes and helicopters as well, during the time Seal was most active in drug and weapons smuggling. Other documents we uncovered revealed that Glick was also actively helping Seal purchase ocean-going vessels... "[9]

Hopsicker reproduced an FAA form showing the leasing of the aircraft from Greycas to Systems Marketing. The form identified Systems Marketing's vice president as a Leonard F. Lavoie. Press reports at the time suggested that Lavoie, at this time, was also affiliated with an aviation company called Skyways Travel & Tours, while his early career had revolved around Arizona real estate. During the 1970s, Lavoie had been the treasurer for the Halwin Corporation, which had been founded by a man named Allen Winter.[10] Winter, notably, was a "known racketeer" who, prior to relocating to Arizona, had operated out of the Seattle area and had been particularly close to Dave Beck – Jimmy Hoffa's mob-linked predecessor as president of the Teamsters union.[11]

Both Winter and Lavoie had previously worked for the major Phoenix, Arizona, construction firm Del E. Webb Development Company.[12] Del Webb had developed major projects like Sun City, the famous retirement community; yet, what the builder and his company were best known for was their role in building and owning a number of Las Vegas casinos. Unsurprisingly, this brought him into close contact with organized crime interests, and to Bugsy Siegel and Meyer Lansky in particular – as well as to J. Edgar Hoover. According to Anthony Summers, Hoover – who rubbed shoulders with Webb at places like the Hotel Del Charro, a favorite haunt of mob-linked Texas oil bigwigs like Clint Murchison – appears to have protected the builder. "Hoover," said Justice Department attorney William Hundley, "gave Webb a pass. He was his buddy."[13]

Hundley added that "No bugs went in on Webb's places."[14]

It's unsurprising, then, that Webb himself came to own a number of casinos – including the Sahara, which he had acquired with loans from major Wall Street entities like Lehman Brothers and Morgan Guaranty.[15] He also ended up with the Thunderbird Hotel and the Flamingo, which means that the money of Del E. Webb Development Company had also freely mingled with that of the Moody family's American National Insurance Company (ANICO).

That Lavoie appears in the chain of custody that delivered a plane from Greycas into the hands of Barry Seal illustrates, once again, the integration of organized crime networks into those of the intelligence community. It also makes one wonder if Gene Glick, the builder who acquired the plane from Systems Marketing before leasing it to Seal, was himself tied into Del Webb's network.

Greycas itself was involved in large-scale financial crimes that also seemed nebulously linked to individuals in Seal's orbit: it was bilked for truly massive sums of money by a prolific confidence man by the name of Sheldon Player. Hopsicker writes that: "Player would sell Greycas heavy machine tools, lease them back, and then pretend to sublease the expensive devices to end-users."[16] Sheldon would pocket the money – or perhaps move it on behalf of other parties – by siphoning it away into offshore bank accounts. According to Arthur Johnson, in his book *Breaking the Banks*, Player's preferred offshore banker was Gordon Aiton of Bank Intercontinental Ltd.[17] The true owners of Bank Intercontinental, located in the Cayman Islands, are unfortunately unknown, though Aiton himself was the Cayman's former inspector general of banks.[18]

A second company controlled by Aiton, Investment Consultants Limited, was also involved in Sheldon Player's activities. Intriguingly, Hopsicker reproduced a document from this very company, showing that Aiton was in communication with Barry Seal.[19] The document in question concerned payments and insurance for Seal's Lear Jet.

About a year after Moss' airdrops at Seal's farm, Seal had become deeply involved in a curious DEA sting operation. What made this sting so odd was that its goal was propagandistic in nature: it was intended to produce concrete evidence of collusion between the Sandinistas and the Medellin cartel. In June 1984, Seal flew – allegedly – into Nicaragua, where he picked up a load of cocaine. The pickup was covertly filmed and photographed, but the ongoing DEA operation quickly derailed.[20] General Paul F. Gorman of the US Military Southern Command, publicly announced that evidenced had been found linking the Sandinistas to drug traffic. However, corroboration that Seal indeed met with Sandinistas has never been produced. While Seal wasn't named by Gorman, he was fingered in an exposé on the story published by the *Washington Times*.

This whole series of events raises a number of questions. The Southern Military Command had been linked to arms flows to the Contras, while the *Washington Times* was owned by the Unification Church – the China Lobby-aligned sect that, at the time, was involved in private fundraising for the rebels. As Peter Dale Scott and Jonathan Marshall note in their book *Cocaine Politics*, Seal and the photos from this odd DEA operation were featured prominently in North's notebooks and personal diaries at the time, and North had gone out of his way to acquire copies. One note recorded by North, based on a report from the CIA's Duane Clarridge, stated that "DEA thinks CIA linked info to Gorman."[21] Did the Enterprise, or the CIA, or some other party, intentionally disrupt the DEA operation?

Barry Seal's life was ultimately cut short by a hail of gunfire in Baton Rouge on February 19th, 1986. The official story is that the smuggler had been taken out by hitmen dispatched by the Medellin cartel, who had placed a bounty on Seal when it became known that he was involved with the DEA. It's possible, however, that there were other actors in play.

As Daniel Hopsicker reported, rumors have abounded that the source of the hit was really the CIA, or Oliver North, or even George H.W. Bush. It was alleged, for instance, that Seal had considerable evidence of the Vice President's sons, George W. and Jeb Bush, receiving a large amount of cocaine.[22] Bob Thommasson, a Louisiana State Police officer, told Hopsicker that the FBI had taken charge of the crime scene and removed boxes from the trunk of Seal's car – boxes that contained "very very compelling documents and tapes."[23]

There is also the question of the weapon used in the hit. It had been sourced from Jose Coutin, the owner of a gun store and fashion boutique in Miami.[24] Coutin had been one of many CIA-trained Cuban exiles, having served in Brigade 2506, though it is unknown if he participated in Bay of Pigs. In the 1980s, he was deeply involved in Contra support activities – and had been flipped into acting as an FBI informant. Through the information that he provided to the Bureau, we know that he was acquainted with a number of key players. These included the principals of Frigorificos, the Colombian cartel front company contracted by the State Department; the CIA and cartel-linked rancher in Costa Rica, John Hull; Tom Posey of Civilian Materiel Assistance, the militia-special forces group tied to the Enterprise and to John K. Singlaub; and Jack Terrell, the early Iran-Contra whistleblower.[25]

Barry Seal's untimely death didn't put an end to the goings-on in Mena, however. Russell Welch, a state police investigator who had been monitoring Seal, noted that in 1987 there was a spate of "new activity at the [Mena] airport with the appearance of … an Australian business … and C-130s had appeared."[26]

There were in fact two Australian companies, Southern Cross Aviation Inc. and Multi-Trade, that had set up shop in Mena in the immediate post-Seal years.[27] Southern Cross was an aircraft ferrying company with an apparent specialty in moving C-130s, while Multi-Trade was an aircraft interiors business. The two shared several common principals, who in turn took an active interest in the aircraft being stored at Mena. One of Multi-Trade's executives, a former Australian air force pilot named Glen Conrad, held a stake in one C-130 that he subsequently sold to a company in Florida called African Air Trans Inc. Florida business records show that African Air was owned by Henry A. Warton, a fairly well-known pilot and smuggler with known ties to the CIA. African Air Trans Inc. is mentioned again in the next chapter as the C-130 it bought was tied to another CIA-linked company, E-Systems.

In December 1988, the C-130 took off from Mena, destined for somewhere in Africa. It was seized by US Customs in Florida. Press reports from 1991 state that the plane had been "accused of violating regulations on trafficking arms," and that Warton's company was actually a dummy front set up to obscure the real owner. The plane had actually been acquired, the article continues, by "an unnamed Israeli living in Panama who set up a fake American corporation and mortgage on the aircraft to 'cover his ass.'"[28]

Several years later, in the summer of 1991, another C-130 linked to Mena met an odd fate. It crashed on a runaway in Luanda, the capital city of Angola, killing all onboard – including Chuck Hendricks, a 34 year old aircraft mechanic from Arkansas.[29] Hendricks' parents, who lived in Mena, set out to learn what happened to their son, only to be confronted with a web of mysteries. The C-130 had been owned by a Delaware company called CZX Productions, and the crew had been hired by a German firm called Unitrann International. Both of these companies, in turn, were controlled by a shadowy German aviation specialist named Dietrich Reinhardt.

Reinhardt's name will be instantly recognizable to those familiar with the Iran-Contra affair. One of the companies he controlled, St. Lucia Airways, had been utilized by the Enterprise to ferry weapons to the Middle East. According to Albert Hakim, St. Lucia was a CIA proprietary firm.[30] If Reinhardt was involved with aircraft from Mena as late as 1991, it seems that whatever was taking place in Arkansas was an ongoing operation.

Down in Arkansas

Hot Springs, Arkansas, was, to quote Roger Morris, the "Geneva of organized crime in the 1920s and 30s. It's where the barons, the gangster bosses came to meet."[31] That association certainly continued through the decades. Influence over the city, considered a neutral territory for the different, often-competing criminal gangs, families and outfits, was held by Owney Madden, a New York gangster whose distinctive nickname was "The Killer." Madden was reportedly something of an ambassador for Meyer Lansky and counted among his close associates Frank Costello, who popped up in Hot Springs from time to time. New Orleans crime boss Carlos Marcello was reported to have held significant influence over Hot Springs as well.

There is some evidence, albeit circumstantial, that a young Bill Clinton might have had contact with these forces while he was growing up in Arkansas. The man that Clinton had often referred to as "the most commanding male presence in his life" and a "father figure" was his uncle, Raymond Clinton.[32] Outwardly, Uncle Raymond ran a profitable car dealership, but he was also known to have engaged in various vices and backroom wheeling and dealing. According to a former Arkansas FBI agent, Raymond "ran some slot machines that he had scattered about town," while close business associates have admitted that the car dealer had "considerable dealings in the underworld."[33]

Along the way, Raymond began to collect political power. He cultivated ties to the state's Democratic Party, but also political figures in surrounding states, like Alabama's George Wallace.

These ties paid off in a big way for Bill Clinton in 1968. It was a big year for Bill: he had just won a Rhodes Scholarship to Oxford University in the United Kingdom, and he was on the verge of being drafted. Being shipped off to war in Vietnam would have derailed Oxford entirely – and so Uncle Raymond leapt into action. Using his political connections, he was able to secure for Bill a draft deferral.[34]

Uncle Raymond tended to crop up at opportune moments such as these, where Clinton's political destiny seemed to hang in the balance. In 1974, when Bill embarked on his first political campaign for Arkansas' House of Representatives, Raymond arranged for a $10,000 loan for his nephew from the First National Bank of Hot Springs. While Bill would lose the race, two years later he secured a position as Arkansas' Attorney General. This was the springboard for his next venture, the 1978 campaign for governor. This campaign was a success, thanks in no small part to loans and donations from Arkansas' economic elite. Here, once again, one could find the name of Raymond Clinton.

In addition to the assistance provided by Uncle Raymond and his friends, Clinton may have had other benefactors who helped shape his early political education, if not his career itself. There are hints, rumors, and intimations of a relationship with the CIA during the 1970s, particularly during his year at Oxford, which had been secured with the aid of Raymond. A former CIA officer told Roger Morris and Sally Denton that he had seen Clinton's name on a list of informants used by the Agency's Operation CHAOS – the surveillance program aimed at the anti-war and civil rights movements. Another officer stated that "part of Clinton's arrangement as an informer had been further insurance against the draft."[35] Reportedly, Clinton was regularly debriefed by the CIA, who he supplied with information concerning activist groups on British campuses.

The underworld figures like Barry Seal who haunted Mena seemed to always operate with much less than six degrees of separation from Clinton during his time as the state's governor. In his 1999 confessional expose, *Cross-fire: Witness in the Clinton Investigation,* former Arkansas policeman turned personal driver and security guard for Bill Clinton, L.D. Brown, recounts how Clinton encouraged him to seek out a post at the CIA.[36] Clinton allegedly went so far as to edit the essay Brown wrote for this employment application. The essay topic was drug smuggling in Central America. Upon receiving his application, the CIA put Brown in touch with none other than Seal.

Seal was far from being the only affiliate of Oliver North running a Contra-connected operation in Arkansas. Terry Reed, who had worked for North since 1983, claimed to have been put in touch with Seal by North and established a base just 10 miles north of Mena – in Nella, Arkansas – where "Nicaraguan Contras and other recruits from Latin American were trained in resupply missions, night landings, precision paradrops and similar maneuvers," according to Alexander Cockburn and Jeffrey St. Clair.[37]

Reed charges that another figure in this circle (with particularly close ties to Seal) was Dan Lasater.[38] Lasater was the ultimate Little Rock operator. During the day, he was renowned for his lucrative bond brokerage business, Lasater and Company; while, after nightfall, he had a reputation as a party animal. Lasater was plugged into the world of Arkansas cocaine, something he shared with his close friend, Roger Clinton. Roger was, of course, the brother of then-Governor Bill Clinton. It was revealed during the course of the Whitewater investigations that Roger Clinton had even spent several years working for Lasater.[39]

Just like his close friends, scandal seemed to follow Lasater. In 1977, his private jet turned up in Las Vegas with Jimmy Chagra, a prominent drug trafficker, onboard. (Two years later, Chagra contracted hitman Charles Harrelson to assassinate Federal Judge John H. Wood Jr. in San Antonio, Texas.)[40]

Several years later, in 1984, Lasater purchased a ski resort in a remote northern corner of New Mexico. According to journalists Denton and Morris, Lasater "was given free rein to use Bill Clinton's name commercially to help promote the isolated development." They continue:

> Undercover law enforcement agents later found the resort a center for drug running, what US customs called a "large controlled-substance smuggling operation and large-scale money-laundering activity." While Lasater held "Arkansas Week" at the resort with Governor Clinton's endorsement and entertained politicians from Santa Fe as well as Little Rock, local New Mexico sheriffs were hearing reports from Angel Fire reminiscent of Mena – strange nighttime traffic, sightings of parachute drops, even hikers' accounts of a "big black military-type cargo plane" seeming to come out of nowhere and swooping low and almost silently over a deserted mountain meadow near the remote ski area.[41]

Rumors of drug trafficking, money laundering, powerful military connections and the shadowy presence of military activity grew throughout the latter half of the 1980s and into the early 1990s. A tantalizing early reference to an "Arkansas project" connected to the Iran-Contra affair can be found in a legal declaration drafted by Daniel Sheehan in connection with the lawsuit he brought against the Enterprise on behalf of journalists Tony Avirgan and Martha Honey.[42]

This "project" was reportedly a scheme to set up a training facility for anti-Communist insurgents – in this case, Laotian tribesmen. A key witness in Sheehan's lawsuit, Gene Wheaton, identified some of the backers of this project as Rick Wade, a private citizen from Alaska; William Bode, a State Department employee whose name appeared in Oliver North's personal notebooks; and Vaughn Forrester, an assistant to the pro-Contra Congressman William McCollum; and CIA officer Carl Jenkins. "Some managers of the Daisy Air Rifle Company," writes Sheehan, "provided property in western Arkansas for the training camp."[43]

That there was interest in training Laotian tribesmen for anti-communist purposes isn't as strange as it might sound. In the early 1980s, prior to the spin-up of the Enterprise, the National Security Council ran an off-the-books operation aimed at supporting Laotian anti-communists that was financed via private donations to a slew of POW-MIA groups.[44] Many of the donors – including Nelson Bunker Hunt and Ellen Garwood – would subsequently emerge as major private donors to the Enterprise.

And much like the case of private donations to the Contras, money for the Laotian operation moved through familiar banks. One of these was none other than Seoul branch of BCCI. This money, as reported in a memo by Senate investigator John Mattes, "was used to arm Laotian resistance groups in a covert network 'run by members of the NSC.'"[45]

Rick Wade, the private citizen named by Wheaton, had been active in the POW/MIA movement, and was likely connected to the NSC's operations. During the 1980s, he had developed contacts with aides to Vang Pao, the Hmong opium warlord that had been so close to Ted Shackley and his team a decade prior. He became a lobbyist for the Hmong in Washington and elsewhere, and would meet with figures like Ellen Garwood and Robert Owen in order to garner materiel support for the tribesmen.[46]

Gene Wheaton himself is an intriguing figure. A former Army criminal investigator and intelligence agent, Wheaton was on the periphery of the internal core of the Enterprise, and was thus privy to many covert operations unfolding during the 1980s.[47] His name appears within North's notebooks alongside those of Carl Jenkins, the CIA officer who had served under Shackley at JM/WAVE and in Laos.

Wheaton and Jenkins were close friends and business associates – they were both attached, at one point in the mid-1980s, to an air freight company called National Air Cargo – and it was through Jenkins that Wheaton found himself enmeshed in the world of the Enterprise. Jenkins, as mentioned in chapter 6, was connected with Charles Haynes and Vaughn "Bobby" Ross via a web of companies likely linked to covert operations. Ross, in turn, was a close associate of Barry Seal.

Attempts to investigate Clinton's role in these sorts of operations and more broadly in the Iran-Contra affair were scuttled by Clinton's confidantes, who consistently denied he played a role in the scandal. According to the *Wall Street Journal*, former IRS investigator William Duncan teamed up with Arkansas State Police Investigator Russell Welch in what became a decade-long battle to bring the matter to light.[48] Yet, of the nine separate state and federal probes into the affair, all were shut down.

Duncan would later say of the investigations, "[They] were interfered with and covered up, and the justice system was subverted." A 1992 memo from Duncan to high-ranking members of the attorney general's staff notes that Duncan was instructed "to remove all files concerning the Mena investigation from the attorney general's office." The attorney general, serving under George H.W.Bush, at that time, was William Barr. As mentioned before, Barr had been a former CIA officer before then joining the Agency-linked law firm of Shaw, Pittman, Potts & Trowbridge.

Reed alleged that one of the CIA's point men in the Arkansas operations was a man who claimed to be the general counsel for Southern Air Transport and went by the name Robert Johnson. Johnson seemed to give Governor Clinton his marching orders, and was particularly incensed when Bill's wayward brother, Roger Clinton, was busted in 1985 for peddling cocaine. As previously mentioned, Roger's penchant for cocaine was one he shared directly with Lasater, who testified that the two had frequently indulged in the drug together.

Johnson reportedly told Clinton that he was "Mr. Casey's fair-haired boy" and that Arkansas had been the CIA's "greatest asset." Johnson went on to deliver to Clinton the following message: "Mr. Casey wanted me to pass on to you that unless you fuck up and do something stupid, you're No. 1 on the short list for a shot at the job that you've always wanted. You and guys like you are the fathers of the new government. We are the new covenant."[49]

According to Terry Reed, who witnessed these happenings, he would later learn that Robert Johnson was none other than William Barr. These allegations place Barr's use of the alias Robert Johnson in an interim period where little is known about Barr's activities – he had served as Deputy Assistant Director for Legal Policy in the Reagan White House until September 1983, and then had joined President Bush's Justice Department in 1989. As previously discussed, it was between the months of September and October 1983 that Casey's pre-Enterprise support for the Contras began moving in a concrete way, and it was also in this same period that Manuel Noriega had entered the picture. The answers that Barr provided to the Senate Judiciary Committee states that between 1983 and 1989, he had returned to the CIA-linked firm of Shaw, Pittman, Potts & Trowbridge, and in 1985 had become a partner at that firm.[50]

As for Roger Clinton, after he was released from prison in 1986, he went to work at Calumet Farms, a Horse Farm in Lexington, Kentucky.[51] Calumet's owner, J.T. Lundy, had been a longtime friend and business partner of Lasater, who was something a big name in the inner circle of Lexington's elite. Lundy boasted his own roster of organized crime contacts. One figure who flickered in and out of Calumet was Robert Libutti, a brash "New Jersey gambler, racehorse consultant" and associate of the Gambino crime family.[52] All in all, it was an interesting environment for a politician's brother out on parole who was ostensibly seeking to clean up his act.

Just across the street from Calumet were a pair of curious horse farms. One was owned by Nelson Bunker Hunt, of the Dallas Hunt family, who had been one of Oliver North's prominent private Contra donors. Next door was Murty Farms, purchased in 1984 by fellow Texan – and fraternity brother of Nelson Hunt – George Aubin.[53] Aubin was part of the savings and loan crowd down in Texas, and was something of a mentor to a mega-borrower named John Riddle. Besides looting S&Ls, Riddle had a taste for aviation, which was expressed through his ownership of a company called First Western Airline. According to Ari Ben-Menashe, First Western "was used as a cutout by the Israelis and the CIA to transport American arms to the Middle East."[54]

Additional information about the Mena operations was provided in a deposition given by the controversial Iran-Contra whistleblower Richard Brenneke. His allegations, made in the summer of 1991, were recently summarized in a lawsuit filed on behalf of Linda Ives, the mother of Kevin Ives. Kevin's body was found, along with that of his friend Dan Henry, on train tracks near Alexander, Arkansas, under exceedingly strange circumstances.[55] According to this summary, Brenneke claimed that he had flown "10 to 12 flights of a C-130 into the Mena, Arkansas, airport" and "took guns and paramilitary forces from Mena to Panama."[56] Cocaine was being flown back from Latin America to the Mena airport, where it was dispersed to, among others, representatives from New York City organized crime.

One of the most fascinating parts of Brenneke's allegations is that he moved money that had been paid by the organized crime figures for the drugs into accounts in a Panamanian bank held in the name of International Fund for Mergers and Acquisitions (IFMA), a company where he was acting as vice president. IFMA was reportedly not only utilized by the CIA, but by Michael Harari, Mossad's man in Panama, to launder money and arrange arms shipments in Latin America.[57] The company's president was Ramon d'Onofrio, a businessman with a long track record of shady deals and bankruptcies.[58] A *New York Times* article identified d'Onofrio as a business associate of Alfred Buhler, a lawyer from Lichtenstein, who was reported by the paper as being protected by the CIA itself.[59]

Another d'Onofrio business partner was Charles Hurwitz, the big-time corporate raider who, from his humble beginnings as a prominent commodities trader Bache & Co., had developed extensive holdings ranging from the Kaiser Aluminum Corporation to Arkansas real estate to the United Financial Group (UFG), the largest S&L in Texas.[60] Hurwitz filled

UFG's asset sheets with junk bonds peddled by Drexel Burnham Lambert, which also owned a 10% stake in the S&L. This wasn't Hurwitz's only involvement with the Drexel Burnham junk bond kings: a sale of $450 million worth of junk bonds were sold to help a Hurwitz company, Maxxam, take over California's Pacific Lumber.[61]

UFG was subsequently bought by the New York bonds trader and financier Lewis Ranieri, who appears in Jeffrey Epstein's contact book with eight phone numbers and two addresses listed. Ranieri is best known for his role in developing the first market for mortgage-backed securities.

Hurwitz, while he was still riding high on Drexel's runaway junk bond train, developed several business ventures with the mob-linked S&L bigwig from Louisiana, Herman Beebe.[62] As mentioned in the previous chapter, Beebe had, during the 1970s, owned a warehouse where explosives destined for Cuban exiles were stored – explosives that were meant to be moved by Barry Seal, prior to a Customs sting.

Herman Beebe had a tendency to appear at the same S&Ls where Mario Renda could also be found. Renda, as noted in the previous chapter, was Adnan Khashoggi's friend with a penchant for seeding fraudulent borrowing with Teamster pension fund deposits. A list of banks controlled or suspected of being controlled by Beebe from a 1985 Comptroller of the Currency report included Mainland Savings of Houston. This is the same S&L where Renda had brokered deposits and where Khashoggi had involved himself in an aforementioned series of bewildering deals. Were Renda and Beebe operating in concert?

A smoking gun is hard to discern, but the two both hung out – and arranged deals – at the La Costa resort in Southern California. La Costa, as noted in chapter 1, had long been a mob hang-out; it had been built with the aid of Teamster pension fund loans, and Burton Kanter was listed as the resort's agent at the time it was incorporated.

Beebe had other potential ties to Iran-Contra. The same Comptroller of the Currency report that named Beebe-linked banks also listed Palmer National Bank in Washington DC.[63] If Beebe did control Palmer, it was hidden. The bank's founder was Stefan Halper, a DC bureaucrat who had held various positions within the Nixon, Ford, and Reagan administrations. Halper's father-in-law was Ray Cline, the old OSS and CIA veteran who, at the time, was working with John Singlaub of GeoMiliTech.

Palmer was also where the National Endowment for the Preservation of Liberty, the Contra fundraising apparatus set up by Spitz Channell on behalf of the Enterprise, held its bank accounts. According to internal

NEPL documents acquired by Pete Brewton from the National Security Archives in DC, the NEPL maintained accounts at only one other bank: Irving Trust, the New York City-based commercial bank. Irving Trust was also the major financier, alongside Drexel Burnham Lambert, of Charles Hurwitz's Pacific Lumber takeover.[64] Irving Trust which subsequently be purchased by Bank of New York with the aid of Bruce Rappaport. Bank of New York and Rappaport's Inter Maritime Bank (IMB) would become intertwined when the stake held by BCCI in IMB was purchased by BNY.

Irving Trust also maintained a branch in Little Rock, Arkansas. In the late 1970s, an intern at this branch was James T. Riady, the son of a prominent Indonesian banker and businessman named Mochtar Riady. Together, the Riady family, originally from China's Fujian province, and their close relationship with another giant of Arkansas business, Jackson Stephens, would become crucial to understanding what exactly was happening in Arkansas during Clinton's time as governor.

BANK BUILDING

The last time we encountered Jackson Stephens, he was aiding BC-CI's takeover of First General Bankshares – later rechristened as First American Bankshares – and its subsidiary, National Bank of Georgia. He had been brought into the fold through his friendship with one of NBG's big shareholders who had been courted by BCCI, Bert Lance, who Stephens had brought to Arkansas with some of BCCI's representatives for negotiations over the purchases.

When Lance began searching for buyers of his NBG stock, BCCI wasn't the only interested party that he brought to Stephens' attention. There was also Mochtar Riady, a politically-connected Indonesian banker and financier who commanded the Bank of Central Asia, "the third largest private banking firm in Indonesia" that held some $100 million in assets.[65] In the years to come, the wealth of Mochtar and his son, James Riady, would swell into the billions, all marshaled under the auspices of an umbrella corporation called the Lippo Group. Their meteoric ascension was thanks in no small part to the strategic partnership the Riadys had with Jackson Stephens and Stephens Inc., which developed soon after the Indonesians dropped out of the NBG purchase.

How Riady first entered the picture is telling. According to various press reports, Riady had been introduced to Stephens by Bert Lance, while Lance had first come into contact with Riady through an introduction made by Robert B. Anderson, a once-well regarded figure in politics who had become a specialist in offshore banking. Anderson and Riady, meanwhile, had been brought together several years prior by an unnamed executive from New York City's Chemical Bank.[66]

Chemical, at the time, had established a significant presence in southeast Asia: it had opened branches in Hong Kong; maintained business operations in Singapore; and in Indonesia, it had embarked in a joint venture with the Riady family. Chemical Bank would ultimately maintain a long-running alliance with Riady interests. In 1988, their joint venture expanded when they teamed up with Royal Bank of Scotland and Jardine Fleming (a Hong Kong partnership between the merchant houses Jardine Matheson and Robert Fleming & Co.) to set up the Multinational Finance Corp, or Multicor. According to Mochtar, Multicor was set up first and foremost to "expand Bank Central Asia's financing channels and financing capabilities."[67]

While Riady was toying with buying into National Bank of Georgia, commentators and regulators began to suspect that something else was afoot. One common concern was that Riady wasn't acting alone, and that he was serving as a front for Indonesian political interests that hoped to gain political and economic leverage in the United States.

Interestingly, in this same period, William Casey had a series of dealings with Indonesian interests. These activities later came back to haunt Casey during his confirmation hearings for the CIA, when he was questioned if he had failed to register as a foreign agent for Indonesia.[68]

When he was working in the private sector as an attorney for Rogers & Wells – a time discussed extensively in chapter 6 – Casey took on as clients a complex of interrelated Indonesian interests.[69] There was Pertamina, the country's state-owned oil company, and the Ramayana Indonesian Restaurant in New York City. There was also Indonesian Enterprises Inc., a holding company that had been set up for the restaurant. Pertamina was the major interest in this holding company, holding all of its Class B stock. Indonesian Enterprises issued Class A stock, in turn, to various banks and oil companies that were doing business with Pertamina.

Holders of Class A stock included Bruce Rappaport's InterMaritime Bank, which was engaged in a convoluted succession of fraudulent tanker chartering deals with Pertamina.[70] Elias Kulukundis, mentioned previously as a close business associate of Edward Carey, was also involved in these chartering activities. Investment capital from Kulukundis and Rappaport further mingled in the tanker companies of a "mystery man" named Steven Davids-Morelle, whose Tankers International Navigation

Corporation joined Pertamina's tanker chartering and in the purchase of Indonesian Enterprises Inc. stock.

Was there any sort of connection between Casey's relationship with Indonesian interests and Anderson's encounter with the Riadys? The picture is murky, and records of Anderson's own Indonesian activities isn't readily accessible. What is certain, however, is that Anderson was another member, alongside Rappaport, of Casey's "Hardy Boys" clique, which is certainly suggestive that some sort of collusion was taking place. Furthermore, the list of Indonesian Enterprises, Inc.'s Class A stockholders includes Dresser Industries – the Texas oil concern closely intertwined with Bush family interests – where Anderson had sat on the board of directors.

It is worth diving a little deeper into Anderson's biography before returning to Stephens and Riady, because it is both an illustrative case of high-level political corruption and also intersects in numerous ways with key figures in this ongoing history. With a background in law, Anderson had served in a number of mid-level bureaucratic positions in Texas in the 1930s, including stints as the state's Assistant Attorney General and as the state tax commissioner. In 1937, he became the general counsel for the W.T. Waggoner estate, headquartered in Vernon, Texas. The Waggoner estate was a large ranching empire that extended its reaches into banking and various other industries, real estate development and the like.

The Waggoner family, like many of the great Texas clans, was a source of political clout, and Anderson was soon found mingling with the Texan elite. One impressive early encounter was his purchase of the KTBC radio station, which he then sold to Claudia Alta "Lady Bird" Johnson, Lyndon Johnson's wife, in 1943. It subsequently became a major source of revenue for the Johnson family. Anderson also acted as a lobbyist for powerful Texas oil interests, and was particularly close to early industry giants like Sid Richardson, Clint Murchison, and the Bass family. He could also be found at the helm of the Mid-Continent Oil and Gas Association of Texas, which brought together a wide range of businessmen involved in all different aspects of oil production.

At the urging of these deep-pocketed petroleum interests, Anderson was brought into the Eisenhower administration. In 1953, he was made Secretary of the Navy, and a year later he moved and became the Deputy Secretary of Defense. In 1955, he left government and took a position as president of Ventures Ltd., a Canadian mining company controlled mostly by American and British industrial and financial interests, before returning to the public sector again as Eisenhower's Secretary of the Treasury. There, he arranged for lucrative tax relief packages for Texas oil. By 1961, he was back in the private sector again, this time managing his own business consultancy – the Anderson Group – located at Rockefeller Plaza. He also joined on as a limited partner at Carl M. Loeb, Rhoades & Co., the Wall Street brokerage firm that was closely interlinked with Bronfman interests (the Loeb-Bronfman connection will be discussed in chapter 11).

During his time with Loeb, Rhoades & Co., Anderson developed two important connections. The first was to Bank of America, which was central to the later development of BCCI. In 1964, Anderson joined forces with Bank of America and Belgium's Banque Lambert to set up the World Banking Corporation, an offshore facility in Bermuda that was set up for dealing in the emerging Eurodollars market.[71] That same year, he joined Bank of America's council of advisors.

He also forged ties with Rockefeller interests. He had been connected to the Rockefellers during his time in the Eisenhower administration – if not earlier, given the presence of the Rockefeller family in Texas. Then, during the mid-1960s, he became an investment advisor for Standard Oil of Indiana. In 1969, this led Anderson, acting on behalf of Standard, to set up an investment consortium in partnership with Maurice Tempelsman, a major player in the international diamond market, that would push for American-led interests in the Congo.[72]

Tempelsman, interestingly, had ties to American intelligence. With numerous interests across Africa, he recruited veterans of the Agency to navigate that world. As Arthur Levy points out, "In the 1960s Tempelsman hired as his business agent the CIA station chief in Kinshasa, Larry Devlin, who helped put Mobuto into power and afterward served as his personal advisor".[73]

There was yet another line leading from Tempelsman to Casey's "Hardy Boys" that was independent of Anderson. According to Alan Block, one of Rappaport's top lieutenants, Jerry Townsend, was a "former" CIA officer who had worked in Turkey, Zambia, and Burundi with Tempelsman. Block adds that "Tempelsman was part of Rappaport's group, according to Townsend."[74]

Then there were the ties between Anderson and the banking circles around BCCI. In the early 1980s, he was found on the board of the Paris-based Saudi European Bank, which was owned by the BCCI-linked Saudi European Investment Corporation N.V. Other principals in the Saudi European Bank included John Connally, the former governor of Texas and George Shultz's predecessor in the Nixon administration as Treasury

Secretary. When Connally was running against Reagan in the early days of the Republican presidential campaign against Carter, Bechtel had initially backed him before switching to support the eventual president. Connally, at that point, embarked on a voyage as a real estate developer, partnering with the infamously corrupt Ben Barnes – also a former Texan politician – in deals that involved tapping a slew of savings and loans for fraudulent loans.

The S&L connection to Saudi European was strong. Its board also counted with the presence of Charles Keating, whose American Continental Corporation and Lincoln Savings and Loan, pumped out bad loans at an astounding rate after the Reagan administration led the deregulation of the S&L industry. Keating and Connally were close, with the banker having served at first as Connally's West coast finance chairman during his political campaign, followed by a shorter stint as campaign manager. Interestingly, one of Connally's campaign workers, Joyce Downey, later went to work for Connally and Barnes before relocating to Arizona, where she worked as the office manager for John Singlaub's US Council for World Freedom, the American branch of WACL.[75] USCWF happened to be located next door to the headquarters of Keating's American Continental Corporation.

In 1984, Keating's Lincoln Savings invested $18 million into Saudi European's holding company, the Saudi European Investment Corp.[76] Keating then joined Saudi European's international advisory board, while Saudi European began issuing lines of credit to Keating's companies. According to a report in the Los Angeles Times, the "bank and its parent company acted as sham financiers and buyers in Keating's efforts to book profits at Lincoln."[77] A subsidiary of Lincoln called Amcor Investments – which was involved in several complicated real estate arrangements with John Connally – sold an option it held to Saudi European in order to buy a "profits interest" in General Oriental Securities Limited, an offshore corporation set up by the corporate raider Sir James Goldsmith for takeover purposes.[78] Goldsmith, as previously mentioned, was part of the Clermont Club and was also one of the main businessman, along with Robert Maxwell, sought out by Rothschild Inc. to help the elite banking family expand its influence in the US financial system.[79]

In December 1986, Keating, utilizing a subsidiary of his American Continental Corporation called Dungiven, organized a Bahamian investment corporation called Trendinvest.[80] Joining the board of directors was one of the busiest man in shadow banking, Alfred Hartmann, who could also be found alongside Anderson, Keating and Connally at the Saudi European Bank. Among the other stakeholders in Trendinvest was Gesellschaft Fur Trend Analysen, a West German firm that specialized in computerized currency trading, and Royork and Company, a subsidiary of the Royal Bank of Canada. Through this offshore vehicle, Keating was able to funnel tens of millions of S&L money out the United States – money that, in the end, had to be paid back by the US taxpayer. Thus, the fact that Riady's meeting of Bert Lance, and by extension Jackson Stephens, was made by Anderson, reveals the type of networks that enabled the Riady-Stephens partnership.

The story of Jackson Stephens is inseparable from Arkansas' longest running and most prestigious law firm, Rose Law. Rose's beginnings went back to the 1820s, when Arkansas was still a territory instead of a state. One of its founders was Robert Crittenden, a Kentucky-born lawyer who had been appointed by President James Monroe to act as the governor of the Arkansas territories. His partner was Chester Ashley, one of Arkansas' very first senators. From these beginnings, Rose Law was woven into the fabric of the state itself, and remained closely tied to the Arkansas' political and economic elite.

Arkansas, to quote journalist L.J. Davis, boasted a "ruling oligarchy, a small and relatively powerless middle class and a disenfranchised, leaderless populace."[81]

Through the 1970s and into the late 1980s, a period which saw Stephens' star rise in Arkansas, Rose was headed by C. Joseph Giroir. In addition to his status as a high-powered attorney, Giroir was a specialist in securities. In the 1960s, Giroir worked far from Arkansas, in the offices of the Securities and Exchange Commission in Washington, DC. While little is known about his activities in the capital, what is certain is that, when he returned to his home state, he brought with him an adamantly pro-business outlook and a drive for modernization.

Once settled at Rose, he went about upgrading Rose's home-spun inclinations for the nascent information age. "He brought the firm billable hours, computers and high-premium securities work, then got in trouble with his side business – buying and selling banks while wearing too many hats for his shallow pockets, and using Rose lawyers to do the work."[82]

One particularly controversial banking escapade in which Giroir was embroiled involved a string of borrowing from a fraud-riddled savings and loan in Pine Bluff, Arkansas, called FirstSouth. Regulators were intrigued by whatever relationship Giroir had with the S&L. While he was dipping into their loan basket, he had also become a stakeholder in First-South and was writing legal advice to the S&L on paper with a Rose Law letterhead.[83] FirstSouth, by the time it collapsed in 1986, had doled out a big pile of loans that were never paid back. Among their biggest borrowers – and defaulters – was Clint Murchison Jr., the organized crime-linked Texas oil player.[84]

A small group of lawyers who worked under Giroir would later become powerful actors in state and federal politics and, while at Rose, they were involved with the firm's strangest dealings. This group was composed of Webster Hubbell, who would become Associate Attorney General under President Clinton; Clinton's future White House counsel Vince Foster; and the soon-to-be First Lady, Hillary Rodham Clinton. This trio, like their boss, had an appetite for shady business dealings. All three were partners in a company called Midlife Investors, which had been set up in the early 1980s by E.F. Hutton. "Hubbell, Foster and Rodham Clinton each kicked in $15,000 and named each other – rather than their spouses – as beneficiaries."[85] Through Midlife, the trio dumped money into companies being targeted by corporate takeover artists like James Goldsmith.

Clinton in particular liked to haunt the corporate boardrooms and offices, often spending more time working on business affairs than the daily law work demanded by Rose. As L.J. Davis writes,

> She was only one of two Rose partners to act as a corporate director, serving at various times on the boards of four companies and earning $64,700 in 1991 from director's fees alone. (Her 1991 salary from Rose was in the vicinity of $110,000; her husband earned $35,000 and got to live in a free house.) She was on the board of Wal-Mart, a Rose client that Stephens had launched on the road to glory. (Rodham Clinton also owned $80,000 worth of Wal-Mart stock.) She served Southern Development Bancorp, a holding company created to give development loans in rural Arkansas, which, according to the *Washington Post*, paid Rose somewhere between $100,000 and $200,000 in fees. In 1989 she joined the board of TCBY yogurt company, which occupies the tallest building in Little Rock. TCBY then proceeded to pay Rose $750,000 for legal work during the next few years.[86]

Such was the backdrop to the grand ambitions of Stephens and Riady for a sprawling business complex. Not satisfied with playing in Arkansas alone, the pair made a very early stop-over in Macau, where they bought up massive blocks of stock in the storied Seng Heng Bank, which allowed them to gain full control over the company.[87] The sellers had been the trio of Cheng Yu-tung, Ho Yin, and Lu Daohe. Cheng had been the founder of two interlinked Hong Kong-based conglomerates, Chow Tai Fook Enterprises and New World Development Company Limited. Through these two large corporations, he had become one of the city's richest individuals. Cheng was very close to Stanley Ho, another Hong Kong billionaire who held the monopoly over Macau's casino industries. In 1989, Stephens and Riady, curiously enough, sold Seng Heng to STDM, a company controlled by Stanley Ho.[88] Ho will appear again later, in chapter 16, as one of his close business partners, Ng Lap Seng, was a key figure in the so-called Chinagate scandal of the mid-1990s.

Cheng's associate in Seng Heng, Ho Yin, is worth examining briefly. Like Cheng and Stanley Ho, Ho Yin was another Hong Kong-based businessman with numerous Macau holdings. What he was most infamous for, however, was his role in Macau's illicit gold trade, which flourished due to international regulations governing gold markets from the end of World War II through the early 1970s. His particular largess derived from the ties he had cultivated with the nascent Chinese Communist Party, having made contacts with Mao and Zhou Enlai shortly after the revolution.[89]

His work managing funds for the Party earned him a spot among the so-called "Red Fat Cats," and he even held a position on the Standing Committee of the Chinese National People's Congress. In Macau, meanwhile, he ran multiple public companies and for a time served as vice president of the Macau Legislative Assembly. He also ran numerous businesses, including multiple banks, through which his gold trade flowed. Among these banks was Seng Heng. Until 1974, when gold trading was deregulated, "$40-50 million worth of gold passed through the narrow door of Seng Heng annually."[90] All in all, this made a very interesting purchase on the part of Stephens and Riady.

Seng Heng wasn't the only bank the duo bought in 1983. That was also the year they began purchasing the stake held by Midland, Texas, oilman John Hendrix in the First Arkansas Bankstock Corporation (FABCO). As part of the deal, FABCO issued additional stock that could be purchased exclusively by Stephens and Riady; combined with Hendrix's holding, Stephens Inc. and Lippo achieved control over FABCO as a joint venture.[91] This takeover granted them control over a wide network of Arkansas banks that were held by FABCO. These included Worthen Bank &

Trust Co of Little Rock, First National Bank of Hots Springs, the National Credit Corp of Pine Bluff, and the First National Bank of Mena.[92]

That the latter bank was located in the same town where the CIA had set up shop and where drug smuggling was taking place raises all sorts of questions.

However, at the same time, the acquisition of these banks was part of a wider effort by Stephens and Riady to build out an Arkansas banking empire. They turned to Joseph Giroir, the head of the Rose Law Firm, to lobby for changes in state laws that restricted the range of activities that bank holding companies could carry out.[93] Giroir then purchased several banks, which were subsequently sold to Stephens and Riady. For his efforts, Giroir received money, a large block of Worthen stock, and a spot on Worthen's board. Rose Law became counsel to Worthen, and the bank itself was transformed into something of a flagship for Stephens' interests.

Clinton's Development Machine

In late 1984, Governor Bill Clinton unveiled an ambitious economic development plan for the state of Arkansas. It was a sterling example of Clinton's commitment to a "pro-business" vision of government, and a direct foreshadowing of the sorts of economic policies that would become the norm during his time as US president. As one Arkansas newspaper put it, Clinton's agenda "would wed some state agencies, their activities, funds and fund sources to efforts of the private sector."[94] It included the creation of a science and technology hub to "seed the birth of new firms, industries and innovations in Arkansas," and a capital fund that would "aggressively lend higher risk capital to … member banks."[95]

The centerpiece of Clinton's plan, however, was the transformation of Arkansas Housing Development Authority, established in the 1970s, into the Arkansas Development Finance Authority (ADFA). The transition was more than a cosmetic change – the mandate for the new agency was to "do in the field of business development what it does in the field of housing development." A month later, in January, Clinton outlined how the ADFA would work. It would "sell a wide range of tax-exempt revenue bonds to generate revenue. The money would then be passed to financial institutions for low-interest economic development loans."[96]

The fortunes of Jackson Stephens became intimately entangled with the activities of the AFDA. Stephens Inc., for example, was frequently utilized by the ADFA to underwrite the bonds it issued.[97] Stephens' Worthen Bank, meanwhile, sometimes acted as the trustee for loans made by the ADFA.[98] The bank itself directly interlocked with the agency itself: the president of the Worthen branch in the city of Pine Bluff, Arkansas, James Stobaugh, sat on the ADFA board. To make matters even more incestuous, one of the recipients of a major ADFA loan, Arkansas Freightways, was a freighter company in which Stephens Inc. held the controlling stake.[99] Rose Law, of course, was Arkansas Freightways' legal representative of choice.

The ADFA seems to have had a particularly close relationship with Beverly Enterprises, a subsidiary of Stephens Inc. that managed a national nursing home chain. Bobby Stephens (no familial relation to Jackson Stephens), the vice president of Beverly Enterprises, sat alongside Stobaugh on the board of the ADFA. Unsurprisingly, Beverly Enterprises profited handsomely from ADFA bond issuance, and retained the services of Rose Law. Several Rose Law associates, including Webster Hubbell, owned stock in Beverly.[100] Beverly would later pop up in the Inslaw Affair – discussed in the next chapter – due to allegations that it was using the infamous, compromised version of the PROMIS software.

Besides Stephens Inc., the ADFA was a great economic boon for Clinton's friend Dan Lasater and his bond business, Lasater & Company. Larry Nichols, the ADFA's marketing director who had been dismissed by the governor, charged that the agency had been "set up by Clinton for Dan Lasater."[101] The reason for Nichols' dismissal is intriguing: the press had learned that he had been using ADFA phones to make long-distant calls to Contra leaders, which he insisted had been authorized by ADFA head Wooten Epes. While there might have been a bit of hyperbole and vindictiveness to Nichols' allegation, it is true that Lasater & Co. acted as an underwriter for bonds issued by the agency.[102] There seems to have been a high degree of competition between Stephens Inc. and Lasater & Co. when it came to these underwriting contracts, but there was at least one direct link between the two companies. Michael Drake, formerly of Stephens Inc, was the vice president of Lasater & Co.

The ADFA's first industrial development loan was granted to a strange company in Russellville, Arkansas called Park-On-Meter, Inc, or POM for short. It was another clear-cut example of Arkansas nepotism: the law firm that handled the legal work on the loan was Rose Law, while POM's founder and president was Seth Ward II – the brother-in-law of Webster Hubbell. Alexander Cockburn, who penned a series of articles on POM, noted that "Worthen Bank ... appeared among the institutions that from time to time had liens on POM."[103]

In *Compromised*, Terry Reed and John Cummings wrote that the initial ADFA loan to POM was intended for the expansion of their industrial capacities in connection with a subcontract the company had gained from Iver Johnson's Arms, a New Jersey-based firearms manufacturer.[104] In addition to parking meters, POM was dipping into the armament business: on behalf of Iver Johnson's, Reed and Cummings claimed, POM was constructing bolts and carrier assemblies for M16 rifles. Iver Johnson's, in turn, had been tapped by the CIA for covert weapons production, and the M16s were ultimately destined for the Contras in Nicaragua.

Howard Schneider, a journalist for the *Washington Post*, found that the "Iver Johnsons company near Little Rock, which the book [*Compromised*] portrays as being the center of the gun-manufacturing effort, did ship a load of weapons to Nicaragua through a Mexican distributor" – precisely the arrangement that Reed and Cummings described.[105] POM itself was found to have had a contract to make gun parts on behalf of Iver Johnson's, though Seth Ward Jr. told the *Post* that it had been firing pins, not bolts. Iver Johnson's, for its part, identified the arms as M1 rifles, not M16s.

Gary Webb observed a stark similarity between the gun manufacturing operation in Arkansas and a similar operation that had taken shape on the Cabazon Indian Reservation in Riverside County, California.[106] What had started off as a takeover of the tribe as part of a plan to develop a gambling hub by John Philip Nichols, a mobster with reputed CIA ties, had transformed into an intricate joint venture with the Wackenhut Corporation and a handful of other firms (at least one of which was a direct CIA cut-out company) to develop weapons systems.[107] Some of these, such as a line of light-weight machine gun pistols, were intended to be provided to the Contras.

These activities at Cabazon were at the center of journalist Danny Casolaro's investigation into the network that he dubbed "the Octopus" and Cabazon played a key role in the Inslaw affair or PROMIS scandal – the subject of the next chapter.

Contra leader Eden Pastora – who later ran afoul of the Enterprise and was the target of an assassination attempt in May 1984 – attended at least one weapons demonstration at Cabazon. The list of those present for this demonstration included John Vanderwerker, a CIA research and development specialist, G. Wayne Reeder, a crooked developer close to Nichols (Reeder, incidentally, was a major S&L borrower with close connections to Herman Beebe), and Earl Brian, a close friend of Ronald Reagan and the controlling interest behind several tech firms.[108] Brian, who was purported to have arrived at the demonstration with Reeder, would emerge as a central player in the Inslaw Affair.

Michael Riconosciuto, a chief witness in that case, was also present at the demonstration, and would subsequently charge that the alterations made to Inslaw's PROMIS software were made at Cabazon.

Riconosciuto further attested to personal knowledge of Contra-oriented weapons development taking place at POM in Arkansas. He told Alexander Cockburn that POM had entered into an arrangement with Wackenhut and Stormont Labs, a California-based genetics research and pharmaceutical company, "to develop chemical and biological weapons that could be deployed in chemical guerrilla warfare."[109]

An Army "chemical unit" was purported to have supplied POM with "chemical agents," while the parking meter manufacturer, as part of its end of the arrangement, prototyped explosive devices such as grenades and bombs that would disperse the chemicals.

Internal documentation from Cabazon Arms, the joint venture between Wackenhut and the Cabazon tribe, does allude to Stormont Labs in the context of "agents and production techniques related to biological war." The document in question, obtained by Casolaro and today logged in an archived collection of his surviving papers, was a letter from Nichols to a Harry Fair at Tactical Technology in Arlington, Virginia. That would be the Tactical Technology Office of the Pentagon's DARPA, which Fair was connected to in the mid-1980s.[110]

Mentioned elsewhere in the papers of the Cabazon-Wackenhut joint venture was a company called the First Intercontinental Development Corporation (FIDCO), described by author Cheri Seymour as a purported National Security Council front company.[111] Directors of FIDCO included Michael McManus, an attorney who served as an assistant to Reagan's chief of staff, George K. Pender and Kenneth Roe of Burns & Roe, and Clinton Murchison Jr.[112] As mentioned earlier, Murchison Jr. himself was in and out of Arkansas, borrowing heavily from the Rose Law-linked FirstSouth savings and loan.

When questioned about Riconosciuto's claims, Ward Jr. told a journalist from *The Nation* that POM wasn't in the chemical warfare business. The company was instead busy making "re-entry cones for the nuclear warheads on MX missiles and nozzles for rocket engines."[113] Intriguingly, the US Army's 354th Chemical Company, since April 1981, had been located in Russellville, Arkansas. This unit maintained property directly adjacent to POM's industrial complex.[114]

Riconosciuto told Alexander Cockburn and Bryce Hoffman, a journalist for *The Nation*, that since 1981, POM had been in the business of making drop tanks – auxiliary fuel tanks attached to the exteriors of aircraft – for C-130s. However, Cockburn and Hoffman were not able to confirm via the FAA, which regulates tank manufacturing, that POM was an authorized producer. Cockburn writes that when Hoffman contacted the FAA, "the official with whom he spoke apparently misunderstood his question on drop tank regulations and assumed he was a prospective manufacturer. 'Oh! So you must have one of those Southern Air Transport contracts.'"[115]

OFFSHORED

One of the weirder intersections in the ADFA complex was between the development agency and the Coral Reinsurance Company, which had been set up in the offshore haven of Barbados. Reinsurance is basically insurance for insurance companies: it allows company A (in this case, the primary insurance firm) to offload portions of its risk onto company B (the reinsurance company). The reasons for this are multifold. It offers a buffer or protection for the insurance company from risks, while also – and perhaps more importantly – allowing insurance companies to engage in expanded business practices that might otherwise have been blocked by government regulations requiring particular asset to risk ratios. Often, insurance companies will set up their own reinsurance companies for this exact purpose. In order to hide the ownership structure, offshore havens are selected to create these companies.

This is exactly how Coral functioned. It took debt and other risks off the books of its parent, though this parent was hidden through proxies. On the other side of this firewall, in actual control of Coral, was American International Group (AIG), the international insurance and finance monolith that, during the 2008 financial crisis, was bailed out by the US government to the tune of $180 billion dollars. In the Financial Crisis Inquiry Report, published in 2011, AIG was identified as having a lengthy history of engaging in overly risky ventures, frequently carried out with little to no hedging or protection.[116] AIG's creation of Coral is just one example of this.

In order to hide its connection to Coral, AIG had called upon the resources of Goldman Sachs, which in turn did the actual legwork in setting up the reinsurance company. Overseeing this operation was the head of Goldman's stock and bonding trading department, Robert Rubin.[117]

Rubin would subsequently serve as co-chairman of Goldman, starting in 1990, before transitioning to a storied career in public service. At the beginning of 1993, Bill Clinton – now president – appointed him as the director of his National Economic Council. A year later, Rubin was sworn in as Clinton's Treasury Secretary. He served in that position until 1999 and, upon leaving the government, he went to work at Citigroup. As will be noted in chapter 16, Rubin was the person who signed off on Jeffrey Epstein's first visit to the Clinton White House in early 1993.

Goldman Sachs organized Coral in such a way that AIG would not appear as a stockholder. Instead, stocks would be spread around to a small and select group who had been handpicked by Goldman. One of these was Samuel Zell, a shady property-flipper from Chicago who had ties to the Gouletas family, whose significant ties to Epstein are detailed in chapter 12, as well as to Burton Kanter. In 1976, Zell and Kanter, along with a handful of other associates, were indicted for hiding money gained from real estate deals in Helliwell and Kanter's Castle Bank.[118]

The ADFA, however, was the largest holder of stock in Coral Reinsurance.[119] It fueled its purchase in Goldman's private offering with a hefty, multi-million dollar loan from the Chicago branch of Japan's Sanwa Bank, which had a history of money laundering allegations. For instance, Sanwa's Los Angeles branch had been a depository for money pilfered by the Marcos family of the Philippines.[120] Interestingly, Terry Reed and John Cummings write in *Compromised* that the ADFA loan to Park-on-Meter was purchased by Fuji Bank of Japan.[121] Fuji Bank has a history of involvement with Sanwa Bank, and the two banks have undertaken several different merger projects since the 1970s.

What brought the ADFA to the attention of Goldman Sachs and AIG? It is strange that a fairly obscure state government development agency, albeit one teeming with ties to intelligence networks and criminal enterprises, would be selected by these major Wall Street businesses to effectively underwrite AIG's reinsurance apparatus. The answer is that the deal was arranged through the ADFA's powerful insider, Jackson Stephens. It turns out that Stephens boasted all sorts of business connections with AIG. For example, an offshore company called Beverly Indemnity was doing some work underwriting policies issued by AIG. Beverly Indemnity was itself something of a hidden subsidiary of Beverly Enterprises, and was run by Beverly's general counsel, Robert Pommerville.[122]

The nursing homes managed by Beverly Enterprises were insured by National Union Fire and Home Insurance of Pittsburgh, an insurance company 100% owned by AIG.[123] National Union Fire and Home had its own connections to the world of offshore insurance hijinks. According to financial journalist Lucy Komisar, the AIG subsidiary was providing insurance to Victor Posner's NVF Corp. via an offshore company called Chesapeake Insurance.[124] Posner's NVF, as mentioned in chapter 6, had been one of the firms represented by William Casey in the years just prior to his time as Reagan's CIA director. Importantly, Reagan offered the position of deputy director of the CIA to Maurice Greenberg, then the head of AIG. Greenberg, who had maintained longstanding ties to the agency, declined the offer.[125]

Greenberg's ties to the CIA are nested within a wider history of involvement of AIG with the world of intelligence. These ties stretched back to the earlier years of the company, when it was known as American International Underwriters, and was overseen by the company's founder, Cornelius Vander Starr. Starr had set up a string of insurance companies across the Asia and the Pacific region, which became key nodes in the wartime intelligence apparatus. Starr himself went to work for the OSS, which brought him into contact with other "China hands" like Paul Helliwell. These insurance companies were deployed as cover for OSS agents, many of whom had started off as Starr's employees.[126] In addition, AIG's longtime general counsel, Duncan Lee, had served in the OSS as the special assistant to William Donovan. After the war, he went to work as counsel for the CIA's Civil Air Transport. Incredibly, Lee was eventually outed as having acted as a mole for Soviet intelligence within the OSS.[127]

The connection between Starr and Helliwell was of particular importance. In 1963, Helliwell and Inge Gordon Mosvold – a frontman for Daniel K. Ludwig, the mysterious billionaire shipping magnate – set up the Bank of the Caribbean Limited. It was something of a paper bank, established and then left on the shelf. During the mid-1960s, it was picked up by American International Underwriters and rechristened as Underwriters Bank Limited. The directors of the bank were all individuals connected to Helliwell and Kanter's Castle Bank, signaling that the insurance complex that would become AIG was woven into the same hot money networks utilized by the CIA and organized crime.[128]

That Sam Zell, with his own dealings with Kanter and Castle Bank, would end up alongside the ADFA as a stockholder in AIG's Coral Reinsurance suggests that these networks are in fact linked directly together. Also instructive is the fact that Paul Helliwell himself seems to have been involved in the very first offshore reinsurance companies, which he set up on behalf of George Eccles (who sat on the board of the Moody-controlled American National Insurance Company, or ANICO).[129] AIG, meanwhile, took credit itself for developing the practice of offshoring re-insurance companies.[130] Given the intertwined history of Helliwell and AIG, it is possible that both stand together at the genesis of these deceptive financial tactics.

BCCI RETURNS

Jackson Stephens liked to spread around his money and political influence. He was not content trafficking just with the Clintons and Arkansas interests, even if they were being propelled at a rapid pace toward the White House. He was also intent on cozying up to their counterparts in the Republican Party – the Bush family. In the late 1980s, Stephens was a member of the Bush-led "Team 100" project, which was a coterie of deep-pocketed GOP donors who had contributed at least $100,000 to the party (a *Washington Post* article on the Team 100 noted that donors included "major Drexel Burnham Lambert clients Frank Lorenzo, Ronald Perelman, T. Boone Pickens, and Saul Steinberg").[131] During this same time period, Stephens' wife Mary Anne served as the co-chair of the Bush for President campaign's Arkansas wing.[132]

Few cases, however, are as telling as the encounter between Jackson Stephens and Harken Energy, a small oil company oddly full of influential principals – the best known among them being George W. Bush, who was both a stakeholder and director. The story of Stephens and Harkens brings, among other things, BCCI back into the picture, and also sets the stage for the deepening relationship between BCCI-linked individuals and the banking networks down in Arkansas.

Harken was created in July 1973. The company was incorporated in California by two Wall Street traders, Phil Kendrick Jr. and Henry L. Mulligan.[133] Their early target was Australia, which was viewed at the time as a place with untapped drilling potential. They soon entered into a consortium alongside Esso and Exxon and, before long, Harken had a dozen wells producing a modest amount of crude. In 1983, Kendrick and Mulligan unloaded Harken to a syndicate led by a pair of New York attorneys, Alan and Wayne Quasha. A sizable share of Harken stock was purchased by an offshore company called North American Resources (NAR). NAR was a joint venture of the Quashas and the Richemont Group.

Richemont is based in Switzerland, but first began in South Africa under the leadership of its founder, Antony Rupert. Richemont had been formed on the basis of Rupert's predecessor company, set up in 1947, called the Rembrandt Group. Rembrandt had been closely tied to European financial interests. For example, Edmund L. Rothschild, then chairman of N.M. Rothschild, had served on the board of Rembrandt. Even the initial fortune that Rupert used to set up Rembrandt can ultimately be traced back to European origins. In 1943, he had become the head of the South African subsidiary of the Distillers Company, the Scottish alcohol and pharmaceutical giant that, as noted in chapter 2, was intimately connected to the Bronfmans.

The Quashas, meanwhile, are perhaps even more interesting than their South African business partner. Alan and Wayne Quasha worked at the law firm founded by their father, William Quasha, who – throughout the 1970s and 1980s – operated from his base in the Philippines. Jonathan Kwitny, in his classic work, *Crimes of the Patriots*, linked Quasha directly to Nugan Hand, the Australian bank that was utilized by Ted Shackley, Edwin Wilson, and others in their network. General LeRoy Manor, a counter-insurgency specialist, had become the chief of staff for the US Military Pacific Command before retiring and taking a position running the Nugan Hand office in the Philippines. He tapped Quasha to serve as the office's attorney.[134]

Nugan Hand's Philippines office was closely tied to the country's corrupt leader, Ferdinand Marcos. General Manor had known Marcos since his days in the US Pacific Command, when the two negotiated over the land rights for American military bases in the Philippines. Kwitny adds that "Marcos' brother-in-law, Ludwig Rocka, actually shared the Nugan Hand office suite, and Rocka's International Development & Planning Corporation took over the suite after Nugan Hand's collapse."[135] Rocka himself moved money through the bank, while Ferdinand Marcos and his wife, Imelda, were rumored to do the same. Quasha himself appears to have had ties to the Marcos family. When Marcos was facing stiff political opposition in 1986, he penned a controversial statement in support of the leader.[136]

It was subsequently revealed that the Marcos family hid away massive amounts of money and gold, pilfered from the Filipino citizenry, the public coffers, and the country's gold mines, in secret Swiss bank accounts – namely, those at the Union Bank of Switzerland.[137] According to Kwitny, Union Bank of Switzerland also appeared in the course of the Nugan Hand affair: "Bernie Houghton [one of the bank's founders] was well acquainted with a traveling official of the Union Bank, and had brought him around to Nugan Hand representatives in Asia to make introductions."[138]

David Armstrong, who penned an expose of Harken in *Z Magazine* in 1991, noted that Union Bank of Switzerland maintained connections to other figures involved with the oil company. Harken was closely connected to a Denver, Colorado-based company called Frontier Oil & Refining Co. – where Alan Quasha served as chairman of the board – which was taken over in the late 1980s by the Richemont Group's Antony Rupert. Armstrong writes that "When Rupert acquired Frontier in a leveraged buyout in 1988, he announced an $85 million 'revolving credit facility' with Union Bank of Switzerland, replacing all of refiner's previous 'working capital facilities.'"[139]

Union Bank of Switzerland also had a history with one of Harken's more surprising investors: the billionaire hedge fund manager George Soros. Shortly after the Quasha-Rupert takeover of Harken in 1983, Soros became the next biggest shareholder in the company after them. In 1984, an arrangement was made where Harken would act as the "exclusive agent and manager of Soros Oil Inc."[140]

Two years later, Harken would gain two additional – and equally surprising – shareholders. For one, there was the Harvard Management Company, the body set up under the auspices of the Harvard Corporation to manage the elite university's investments. Less than a decade later, Harvard and Soros would be found alongside each other again in arranging the privatization and looting of Russia state-owned industries shortly after the collapse of the Soviet Union.

As Russ Baker has shown, the longtime head of the Harvard Corporation, Robert G. Stone, was intimately familiar with the elite circles where business and intelligence mixed. Intriguingly, the president of the Harvard Management Corporation, Michael Eisenson, stated that "There were not too many degrees of separation between Stone and the Quashas."[141]

There were also not too many degrees of separation between Stone and the Quasha's partner, Antony Rupert. Stone's father-in-law was Godfrey A. Rockefeller, a cousin of the better-known David, Nelson and Laurance brothers and a college friend of George H.W. Bush. In the late 1960s and early 1970s, Godfrey played a central role in organizing the World Wildlife Fund (WWF); according to a memorial published by the fund after his death in 2010, he had even hired their "first staff and chief scientist."[142] This would have certainly brought Godfrey into direct contact with Rupert, as the Southern African businessman had been personally recruited into the organization by Prince Bernard of the Netherlands in 1968.[143]

Also joining Harken in 1986 alongside Harvard was the son of God-frey's friend – George W. Bush. It was also the year that Harken bought up Spectrum7, a beleaguered oil company that had been formed from a merger between Bush Exploration – set up originally as Arbusto Ener-gy by George W. Bush in 1977, with investment capital provided in part by CIA asset Jim Bath as well as the oil concerns of Ohio businessmen William DeWitt Jr. and Mercer Reynolds III.[144] Spectrum was reported-ly barely even an oil producer, "less concerned with recovering oil than in creating tax shelters. The company specialized in selling limited part-nerships, which generated generous write-offs before the tax laws were revised in 1986."[145]

Russ Baker writes that within several years of the deal between Bush Energy and Spectrum, DeWitt and Reynolds were "on the ground floor" of an insurance and reinsurance company called Midwest Employers Ca-sualty Company (MECC).[146] Stephens Inc. – which, as noted above, was actively connected to the world of reinsurance – was one of the big stock-holders in MECC.

When Spectrum was purchased by Harken, Bush, formerly Spectrum's CEO, joined Harken's board of directors. He also received a sizable chunk of Harken stock, and a high-dollar consultancy fee that he continued to receive after he went to work on his father's presidential campaign in the late 1980s. In December 1988, Bush took a low-interest loan out from Harken, which he used to purchase more of the company's stock. As the 1980s drew to a close, Harken had drawn itself even deeper into the orbit of Bush-connected interests. It organized a commodities trading subsid-iary, which formed a close working relationship with Enron.[147] Enron's president, Kenneth Lay, had been a big supporter of George H.W. Bush since the 1980 election, and the company would later become one of George W. Bush's greatest political benefactors.[148]

However, it was in 1987, before Bush re-upped his Harken stock, that the company crossed paths with Clinton's and Bush's backer, Jackson Ste-phens. After the Spectrum7 buy-out, Harken had a debt problem, and was in need of further financing in order to resolve its core issues. They turned to Stephens Inc., which quickly went to work and brought in the Union Bank of Switzerland.[149] Union Bank bought up Harken stock via Stephens, but soon the bank ran into a "regulatory snag." The stock was then moved to another client of Stephens Inc., Sheikh Abdullah Taha Bakhsh, who was a close business associate of two BCCI insiders: Khalid bin Mahfouz and Ghaith Pharaon. Union Bank of Switzerland, for its part, had its own

BCCI ties. Together with the criminal bank it owned a Swiss bank called Banque de Commerce et de Placements (BCP). Representing BCCI interests at BCP was the ubiquitous Alfred Hartmann.[150]

Despite these efforts, by 1989, Harken was in trouble yet again. The commodity trading subsidiary proved disastrous, costing Harken some $17 million in losses by the end of that year. Soros exited at the same time, and along the way managed to convince Harken to sell their stake in the lucrative Crystal Oil Company of Louisiana to his Quantum Fund N.V. Harken's future was now uncertain, as the company faced a cash shortage. Yet, suddenly, in January 1990, it landed an inexplicable oil deal with the mineral-rich country of Bahrain. David Armstrong wrote that the deal gave "Harken the exclusive exploration, development, production, transportation and marketing rights to most of Bahrain's offshore oil and gas reserves. The territories covered by the pact lie sandwiched between the world's largest oil field, off the shore of Saudi Arabia, and one of the biggest natural gas fields, off the shore of Qatar."[151]

The cast behind Harken's landing of this deal, which came at such a crucial time for the company, is full of the usual suspects. There was David Edwards, who acted as a go-between for Harken and Bahrain. He had previously worked for Stephens Inc. and had been involved in the Harken-Union Bank of Switzerland negotiations. There was Bahrain's prime minister, Sheikh Khalifa bin-Salman al-Khalifa, whose brother was a BCCI stockholder in 1990.[152] And there was also the US ambassador to Bahrain, Charles Hostler. He was reportedly close to BCCI frontman Mohammed Hammoud, who, as discussed previously, was tied up in various business and political ventures with Senator Orrin Hatch and Adnan Khashoggi. And what about Abdullah Taha Bakhsh, the man who ended up with Union Bank of Switzerland's Harken shares? In October 1990, the *New York Times* reported that he had "acquired a 9.6 percent stake in the Worthen Banking Corporation, a bank holding company based in Little Rock, Arkansas."[153]

Endnotes

1   Armstrong, Scott, Malcolm Byrne, Thomas S. Blanton, Laurence Chang, Glenn Baker, and National Security Archive, *The Chronology: The Documented Day-to-Day Account of the Secret Military Assistance to Iran and the Contras* (NY: Warner, 1987), 516, https://archive.org/details/chronologydocume00arms.

2   Paul Houston and Michael Wines, "Papers from North Safe Trace Cash; Diagrams Suggest a Network of Groups to Aid the Contras," *Orlando Sentinel*, February 28, 1987, https://www.orlandosentinel.com/news/os-xpm-1987-03-01-0110250206-story.html.

3   John Cummings and Ernest Volkman, "Snowbound," *Penthouse*, July, 1989.

4   *Drugs, Law Enforcement, and Foreign Policy: A Report Prepared by the Subcommittee on Terrorism, Narcotics and International Operations*, Committee on Foreign Relations, December 1988, 121, https://babel.hathitrust.org/cgi/pt?id=pst.000014976124.

5   Jack Anderson and Dale Van Atta, "Legacy of a Slain Drug Informer," *Washington Post*, February 28, 1989, https://www.washingtonpost.com/archive/local/1989/02/28/legacy-of-a-slain-drug-informer/41b5c1bf-ba53-48f4-87d8-afd6bcbc15ce/.

6   *Drugs, Law Enforcement, and Foreign Policy: A Report*, Volume 4, 285.

7   Daniel Hopsicker, *Barry and the Boys: The CIA, the Mob, and America's Secret History* (Madcow Press, 2006), 270.

8   Hopsicker, *Barry and the Boys*, 270.

9   Hopsicker, *Barry and the Boys*, 271.

10   "Lavoie Appointed Halwin Treasurer," *Arizona Republic*, September 12, 1971.

11   Sally Denton and Roger Morris, *The Money and the Power: The Making of Las Vegas and Its Hold on America*, 1947-2000, 1st ed (New York: Alfred A. Knopf, 2001), 233, https://archive.org/details/moneypowermaking00dent.

12   "Lavoie Appointed Halwin Treasurer"; Don G. Campbell, "Just Like Big Boys: Trust Lets Little Guy Put His Funds to Work in Tough Real Estate Field," *Arizona Republic*, June 27, 1971.

13   Anthony Summers, *Official and Confidential: The Secret Life of J. Edgar Hoover* (New York: Pocket Star Books, 1994), 266, https://archive.org/details/officialconfide000summ.

14   Summers, *Official and Confidential*, 266.

15   Denton and Morris, *The Money and the Power*, 233.

16   Hopsicker, *Barry and the Boys*, 274.

17   Arthur Johnson, *Breaking the Banks* (Lester & O. Dennys Publisher, 1987), 187.

18   James Fleming, "Probing the Cayman Islands Connection," *Maclean's*, August 29, 1983, https://archive.macleans.ca/article/1983/8/29/probing-the-cayman-islands-connection.

19   Hopsicker, *Barry and the Boys*, 425.

20   Peter Dale Scott and Jonathan Marshall, *Cocaine Politics: Drugs, Armies, and the CIA in Central America* (University of California Press, 1998), 101-102.

21   Scott and Marshall, *Cocaine Politics*, 101.

22   Hopsicker, *Barry and the Boys*, 263.

23   Hopsicker, *Barry and the Boys*, 371.

24   Gary Hines, "Defense to Present Case in Seal Murder Trial," *UPI*, May 12, 1987, https://www.upi.com/Archives/1987/05/12/Defense-to-present-case-in-Seal-murder-trial/8621547790400/.

25   Scott and Marshall, *Cocaine Politics*, 14; Coutin and his ties are discussed at length in "Declaration of Plaintiff's Counsel, Tony Avirgan and Martha Honey v. John Hull, Rene Corbo," https://archive.org/details/DeclarationOfPlaintiffsCounselTonyAvirganAndMarthaHoneyV.JohnHullReneCorboEtAl.

26   Sally Denton and Roger Morris, "The Crimes of Mena," *Penthouse*, July, 1995.

27   Jo Chandler and Jan Roberts, "The Shadowy Fate of an RAAF Hercules," *The Age*, July 1, 1991.

28   Chandler and Roberts, "The Shadowy Fate."

29   Jack Anderson and Dale Van Atta, "Angola Plane Crash Tangled in Mystery," *Washington Post*, December 30, 1991, https://www.washingtonpost.com/archive/sports/1991/12/30/angola-plane-crash-tangled-in-mystery/2d51ee0c-db96-4b4a-bc96-63acc560803c/.

30   For a lengthy discussion about Reinhardt, St. Lucia, and the CIA, see Don Rogers, *Hotel Hercules: Flying CIA and UN Missions from Jamba to Phnom Penh* (Transarms Editions, Chicago), 2015, https://ipisresearch.be/wp-content/uploads/2017/02/Hercules_v004.pdf.

31   "Roger Morris Interview," *PBS Frontline*, June 13, 1996, https://www.pbs.org/wgbh/pages/frontline/shows/choice/bill/morris1.html.

32   Sally Denton and Roger Morris, *Partners in Power: The Clintons and their America* (Regnery Publishing, 1999), 40.

33   Denton and Morris, *Partners in Power*, 40.

34   Denton and Morris, *Partners in Power*, 80-82.

35   Denton and Morris, *Partners in Power*, 104.

36   L. D. Brown, *Crossfire: Witness in the Clinton Investigation*, 1st ed (San Diego, Calif: Black Forest Press, 1999), 101.

37   Alexander Cockburn and Jeffrey St. Clair, *Whiteout: The CIA, Drugs, and the Press* (London: Verso, 1998), 328, https://archive.org/details/whiteoutciadrugs00cock.

38   Terry Reed and John Cummings, *Compromised: Clinton, Bush and the CIA* (S.P.I. Books, February 1, 1994), 58.

39   "Investigation of the Whitewater Development Corporation and Related Matters," US Senate Special Committee to Investigate the Whitewater Development Corporation and Related Matters (1997), 111.

40   Jimmy Chagra utilized as his bodyguards members of "The Company," an entity described in FBI files as a network of former US special forces soldiers, police officers, and US Customs officials involved in drug smuggling and other illicit activities. The Company was set up and operated by Bradley Bryant and Andrew Thornton II, with a base of operations in rural Kentucky (Thornton was a former Lexington, Kentucky narcotics detective). Sally Denton's reporting on The Company illustrates that their connections went very high in the world of Kentucky politics, even extending to the office of governor John Y. Brown. If this all sounds very reminiscent of what was taking place in Arkansas at the exact same time, it probably wasn't coincidence. Brown was close to both Clinton and Lasater (Lasater stated that he had been first introduced to cocaine by Jimmy Lambert, a business partner of Brown who was close to The Company). Bill and Hillary Clinton and Lasater traveled together on Lasater's private plane to the 1983 Kentucky Derby, and while there Lasater passed "a paper bag containing $300,000 in cash" to Brown via Lambert. In a strange line leading back to the world of Ted Shackley's "private CIA" network, Denton writes in her book that the ATF strongly suspected that The Company was tied to Edwin Wilson and Frank Terpil's activities.

On The Company, see Sally Denton, *The Bluegrass Conspiracy* (Avon, 1990). On Lasater's money pass, see Denton and Morris, *Partners in Power*, 419-20.

41   Denton and Morris, *Partners in Power*, 421.

42   "Declaration of Plaintiff's Counsel," 297.

43   "Declaration of Plaintiff's Counsel," 297-98.

44   Michael Ross, "Probe Links 'Reagan Doctrine' to Covert Aid to Laos Rebels," January 23, 1993, *Los Angeles Times*, https://www.latimes.com/archives/la-xpm-1993-01-23-mn-1607-story.html.

45   Ross, "Probe Links."

46   See Paul Hillmer, *A People's History of the Hmong* (Minnesota Historical Society Press, 2015).

47   For a good overview on Gene Wheaton, see "Bill Kelly's 2021 CAPA Conference Presentation on Gene Wheaton and Carl Jenkins," *JFKcountercoup*, December 20, 2021 https://jfkcountercoup.blogspot.com/2021/12/bill-kellys-2021-capa-conference.html.

48   Micah Morrison, "The Mena Coverup," *Wall Street Journal*, March 3, 1999, https://www.wsj.com/articles/SB920421328276427000.

49   Reed and Cummings, *Compromised*, 277.

50   "United States Senate Committee on the Judiciary Questionnaire for Non-Judicial Nominees," https://www.judiciary.senate.gov/imo/media/doc/William%20Barr%20Senate%20Questionnaire%20(PUBLIC).pdf

51   Josh Tyrangiel, "O Brother, Where Art Thy Standards?," *TIME*, July 9, 2001, https://content. time.com/time/subscriber/article/0,33009,1000277,00.html.

52   Anne Hagedorn Auerbach, *Wild Ride: The Rise and Tragic Fall of Calumet Farm, Inc., America's Premier Racing Dynasty* (Holt Papersbacks, 1995), 175.

53   Pete Brewton, *The Mafia, CIA and George Bush* (S.P.I. Books, 1992), 143. Though their time in the fraternity was separated by a few decades, Hunt and Aubin were both members of Kappa Sigma. Brewton shows that many of the S&L looters in Texas were connected to this fraternity.

54   Brewton, *The Mafia*, 150-151. John Riddle was another member of the Kappa Sigma fraternity. He engaged in many business arrangements with Robert Corson, the suspected CIA asset who had ties to the Supermarket.

55   "Complaint for Freedom of Information, filed by R. David Lewis on August 4, 2016, as part of Linda Ives V. United States of America," US District Court for the Eastern District of Arkansas Western Division, https://arktimes.com/wp-content/uploads/2019/03/pdf-ivessuit.pdf.

56   "Complaint for Freedom of Information," 17.

57   Jane   Hunter,   "Cocaine   and   Cutouts: Israel's   Unseen   Diplomacy,"   The Link,   Vol.   22,   No.   1,   January-March   1989,   https://ameu.org/getattachment/7ab-1cd1b-ba2c-41da-8d09-8483bce764dc/Cocaine,-Cutouts-Israel-s-Unseen-Diplomacy.aspx.

58   Brewton, *The Mafia*, 106-107.

59   Jeff Gerth, "European Tied to Illegal Acts is Shielded by C.I.A.," *New York Times*, February 8, 1983,   https://www.nytimes.com/1983/02/08/us/european-tied-to-illegal-acts-is-shielded-by-cia. html.

60   Brewton, *The Mafia*, 80-81.

61   Ned Daly, "Ravaging the Redwood: Charles Hurwitz, Michael Milken and the Costs of Greed," https://multinationalmonitor.org/hyper/issues/1994/09/mm0994_07.html.

62   Brewton, *The Mafia*, 80.

63   The Comptroller Report on Herman K. Beebe is reprinted in full in Stephen Pizzo, Mary Fricker, and Paulo Muolo, *Inside Job: The Looting of America's Savings and Loans* (Harper Perennial ,1991), 497-511.

64   Daly, "Ravaging the Redwood."

65   Hobart Rowen, "Man Seeking Lance Stock No Newcomer to World of Finance," *Washington Post*, September 1, 1977, https://www.washingtonpost.com/archive/politics/1977/09/01/man-seeking-lance-stock-no-newcomer-to-world-of-finance/048e8147-3eac-4a54-8b20-c0d7d3df0e9b/.

66   Peter Waldman, "Lippo's Arkansas Ties Win Benefits if Not Many Contracts," *Wall Street Journal*, October 16, 1996, https://www.wsj.com/articles/SB84541484812670000.

67   Mochtar Riady, *Mochtar Riady: My Life.* (Wiley, 2016), 101.

68   See, for example, "Casey Cleared in Foreign Agent Case," *UPI* April 9, 1982, https://www. upi.com/Archives/1982/04/09/Casey-cleared-in-foreign-agent-case/8185387176400/.

69   Alan A. Block, *All is Clouded By Desire: Global Banking, Money Laundering, and International Organized Crime.* (Praeger, 2004), 28-32.

70   This is discussed at length in Block, *All is Clouded By Desire*, 16-32.

71   Donald White, "What Makes Stocks Go Up?," *San Francisco Examiner*, January 29, 1964; "In Bahamas, Banking is Second Only to Tourism," *New York Times*, March 3, 1977.

72   David Gibbs, *The Political Economy of Third World Intervention: Mines, Money, and U.S. Policy in the Congo Crisis* (University of Chicago Press, 1991), 182-184.

73   Arthur Levy, *Diamonds and Conflict: Problems and Solutions* (Novinka Books, 2003), 67.

74   Block, *All is Clouded by Desire*, 85.

75   Brewton, *The Mafia*, 366.

76   *Investigation of Lincoln Saving and Loan, Hearings Before the Committee on Banking, Finance, and Urban Affairs*, House of Representatives, One Hundred First Congress, First Session, 1990, 212-15, https://www.google.com/books/edition/Investigation_of_Lincoln_Savings_Loan_As/kGUzAAAAIAAJ.

77   James Granelli, "French Bank off the Hook in Keating Suit," Los *Angeles Times*, June 17, 1992, https://www.latimes.com/archives/la-xpm-1992-06-17-fi-599-story.html.

78   *Investigation of Lincoln Saving and Loan*, 46.

79   William H. Meyers, "Megadealer for the Rothschilds," *New York Times*, December 4, 1988, https://www.nytimes.com/1988/12/04/magazine/meagdealer-for-the-rothschilds.html.

80   *Investigation of Lincoln Saving and Loan*, 456; Block *All is Clouded By Desire*, 111.

81   L.J. Davis, "The Name of the Rose: An Arkansas Thriller," *New Republic*, April 4, 1994.

82   Terry Carter, "From Bum's Rush to Bum Rap," *ABA Journal,* July, 1998.

83   Davis, "The Name of the Rose."

84   Pizzo, Fricker and Muolo, *Inside Job*, 468-69.

85   Davis, "The Name of the Rose."

86   Davis, "The Name of the Rose."

87   "Banking Is Different in Arkansas," *St. Louis Post-Dispatch*, September 12, 1984; Mochtar Riady, *My Life*, 170.

88   Patrick Huen, Jean Jinghan Chen, Ming-Hau Liu, *Seng Heng Bank: History and Acquisition by Industrial and Commercial Bank of China* (Palgrave Macmillan, 2021), 25.

89   Bertil Lintner, *Blood Brothers: The Criminal Underworld of Asia* (Palgrave Macmillian, 2003), 102.

90   Lintner, *Blood Brothers*, 101.

91   "FABCO announces Stephens group transactions," *The Times* (Shreveport), October 22, 1983; "Fabco Announces 473,000-share sale," *Baxter Bulletin*, Februay 17, 1984.

92   "FABCO Readies Stock Purchase," *The Commercial Appeal*, October 30, 1983.

93   Davis, "In the Name of the Rose."

94   "Gov. Clinton Outlines Job Development Plan," *Baxter Bulletin*, December 12, 1984.

95   "Gov. Clinton Outlines Job Development Plan."

96   "Clinton Wants to Spend State's Surplus Millions," *The Commercial Appeal*, January 6, 1985.

97   Davis, "In the Name of the Rose."

98   Alexander Cockburn, "Air Cocaine: the Wild, True Story of Drug Running, Arms Smuggling, and Contras at the Backwoods Airstrip in Clinton's Arkansas," *Counterpunch*, November 4, 2016.

99   Michael J. Goodman and John M. Broder, "Arkansas Lending Agency Benefited Clinton Donors," *Los Angeles Times*, June 29, 1992.

100   See Alexander Cockburn, "Hillary Clinton's Great Nursing Home Rip-Off," *Counterpunch*, February 19, 2016; Goodman, Broder, "Arkansas Lending Agency Benefited Clinton Donors." Beverly also directly interlocked with Worthen, the bank's chairman, Curtis Bradford, for a director at Beverly.

101   Davis, "In the Name of the Rose."

102   Lasater's connections to the ADFA are discussed at length in the Investigation of the Whitewater Development Corporation and Related Matters report.

103   Cockburn, "Air Cocaine."

104   Reed and Cummings, *Compromised*, 169-172.

105   Howard Schneider, "Clandestination: Arkansas," *Washington Post,* July 21, 1994, https://www.washingtonpost.com/archive/lifestyle/1994/07/21/clandestination-arkansas/e2c39f46-602b-4f4c-91fd-1ce94c743d69/.

106   Gary Webb, *Dark Alliance: The CIA, the Contras and the Crack Cocaine Explosion* (Seven Stories Press, 1998), 114-115.

107   This is discussed at length in works such as Cheri Seymour, *The Last Circle: Danny Casolaro's Investigation into The Octopus and the PROMIS Software Scandal*, ePub (Trine Day, 2010).

108   G. Wayne Reeder appears to have been involved in several ventures involving Herman Beebe. According to Beebe's right-hand man Dale Anderson, the two probably met at the La Costa resort, which was also likely the point of contact between Beebe and Khashoggi's friend Mario Renda. Reeder also got $14 million from Silverado Savings and Loan, where Neil Bush, son of George H.W. Bush, sat on the board. On Reeder and Beebe, see Pizzo, Fricker and Muolo, *Inside Job*, 332. On Reeder and Silverado, see Brewton, *The Mafia*, 261.

Reeder was also reportedly close to C.H. and Jake Butcher, brothers from Knoxville whose banking empire went bottom-up in the 1980s due to a blizzard of fraudulent loans and overspending. According to one source, Reeder posted C.H.'s bail money when the Tennessee banker went down for fraud. See David Martin, "He's No Angel," *The Pitch*, September 14, 2004.

A 1987 interview with Michael Riconosciuto, founded in the papers of journalist Danny Casolaro, also mentions the Reeder/Butcher link. A reference in the document is made to "the Butchers and the Joe Duncan affair that involved the letter from Meese's wife." This refers to an incident where Edwin Meese's wife wrote a letter declaring that she and her husband supported Joseph Duncan, the son of Tennessee congressman John J. Duncan, who had become mired in legal issues due to his association with the Butchers. The Duncan family controlled a Knoxville, Tennessee thrift called Knox Federal Savings and Loan Associate, and in 1981 had apparently conspired to transfer control of the lending institution to the Butcher brothers. In exchange, C.H. Butcher arranged to have large, outstanding debts Duncan owed to United American Bank of Knoxville—owned by Jake Butcher—forgiven. See Philip Shenon, "Meese's Wife Writes to Judge in Praise of Convicted Friend," The New York Times, November 6, 1987; John E. Yang, U.S. Sues Congressman, 2 of his Sons for Roles in Collapse of Tennessee Bank," *Wall Street Journal*, November 11, 1987).

The Butcher brothers are worthy of deeper scrutiny. They appear as major players in James Ring Adam's book *The Big Fix: Inside the S&L Scandal* (Wiley, 1990). Adams writes that Jake Butcher "was a close friend of President Jimmy Carter and Carter's confidant, the Georgia banker Bert Lance" (p. 87). Lance, on one occasion, was a guest of honor at a dinner at Jake's illustrious mansion, named "Whirlwind" (p. 88). According to one of insiders to Butcher's banking world, another dinner guest at times was Bruce Rappaport (p. 192). Yet another close associate of the Butchers that is named by Adams—and something that is reflected in numerous newspaper society pages from the 1980s—was Kentucky governor John Y. Brown. On John Y. Brown, drug smuggling, and the connection to Clinton and Lasater, see endnote 40 above.

109   Cockburn, "Air Cocaine."

110   An overview of Fair's biography can be found at the website for the Institute for Strategic and Innovative Technology: https://isitaustin.org/downloads/Fair_bio.html.

111   Seymour, *The Last Circle*, 74.

112   A US Trade and Development Program datasheet from August, 1982 lists a "Frank Pindar" from Burns & Roe as a contractor on an electricity program for the country of Belize. Burns & Roe is named as having been contracted by USAID. Also named on the project is Sergio Brull, discussed in the last chapter in connection with the Supermarket. The datasheet can be viewed at https://archive.org/details/201611171611.

113   Cockburn, "Air Cocaine."

114   Department of the Army Lineage and Honors: 354th Chemical Company, https://history.army.mil/html/forcestruc/lineages/branches/chem/354cmco.htm. "Lineage and Honors Information:354th Chemical Company," *United States Army Center of Military History*, https://history.army.mil/html/forcestruc/lineages/branches/chem/354cmco.htm.

115   Alexander Cockburn, "The Secret Life of a Parking Meter Manufacturer," *The Nation*, March 16, 1992.

116   *The Financial Crisis Inquiry Report: Final Report of the National Commission on the Causes of the Financial and Economic Crisis in the United States*, The Financial Crisis Inquiry Commission, January 2011, 352, https://www.govinfo.gov/content/pkg/GPO-FCIC/pdf/GPO-FCIC.pdf.

117   "The Crimes of Mena: Gray Money," *Arkansas Gazette*, date unknown; Lucy Komisar, "Cooking the Insurance Books," *The Komisar Scoop*, November 2004, https://www.thekomisarscoop.com/2004/11/cooking-the-insurance-books/.

118   Brewton, *The Mafia CIA and George Bush*, 245.

119   "The Crimes of Mena: Gray Money"; Lucy Komisar, "The Fall of a Titan," *AlterNet*, March 17, 2005, https://www.thekomisarscoop.com/2005/03/the-fall-of-a-titan/; John Crudele, "AIG's Coral Insurance Woes Add Up," *New York Post*, March 31, 2005, https://nypost.com/2005/03/31/aigs-coral-insurance-woes-may-add-up/.

120   Bob Drogin and Henry Weinstein, "Marcos, Manila Reportedly Strike a Deal," *Los Angeles Times*, November 2, 1991, https://www.latimes.com/archives/la-xpm-1991-11-02-mn-689-story.html.

121   Cummings and Reed, *Compromised*, 248.

122   "The Crimes of Mena: Gray Money."

123   "The Crimes of Mena: Gray Money."

124   Komisar, "The Fall of a Giant."

125   R.T. Naylor, *Satanic Purses: Money, Myth and Misinformation in the War on Terror* (McGill-Queen's University Press), 2006.

126   Ron Shelp, *The Fallen Giant: The Amazing Story of Hank Greenberg and the History of AIG* (Wiley, 2006), 93-95; Richard Harris Smith, *OSS: The Secret History of America's First Central Intelligence Agency* (Lyons Press, 2005), 244.

127   On Lee and Civil Air Transport, see Smith, *OSS*, 253. On Lee as a Soviet spy, see John Haynes and Harvey Klehr, *Venona: Decoding Soviet Espionage in America* (Yale University Press, 2000), 104-107.

128   This is discussed in Alan A. Block, *Masters of Paradise: Organized Crime and the Internal Revenue Service in the Bahamas* (Routledge, 1991) 182.

129   *Insurance Industry: Hearings Before the Subcommittee on Antitrust and Monopoly, Committee on the Judiciary*, United States Senate, Eighty-Sixth Congress, Second Session, part 10, 1958, p. 5927, https://books.google.com/books?id=mZ-rRADfew0C.

130   Komisar, "The Fall of a Giant."

131   Charles R. Babcock, "George Bush's Ruling Class," *Washington Post*, January 24, 1989, https://www.washingtonpost.com/archive/politics/1989/01/24/gop-discloses-names-of-big-donors/5f97af2e-0d67-4adb-aee1-7f738367c4b3/.

132   Craig Unger, *House of Bush, House of Saud: The Secret Relationship Between the World's Two Most Powerful Dynasties* (Scribner, 2004), 120.

133   David Armstrong, "Global Entanglements: The Political Economy of a Texas Oil Co.," *Z Magazine*, November 1991. Accessed via https://quixoticjoust.blogspot.com/2017/03/remembering-harken-money.html.

134   Jonathan Kwitny, *The Crimes of the Patriots: A True Tale of Dope, Dirty Money and the CIA* (W.W. Norton & Co, 1987), 36.

135   Kwitny, *The Crimes of the Patriots*, 37.

136   "U.S. Businessmen Distance Themselves from Pro-Marcos Statement," *UPI*, February 21, 1986, https://www.upi.com/Archives/1986/02/21/US-businessmen-distance-themselve-from-pro-Marcos-statement/8923509346000/.

137   See Ellen Guerrero, "Official Claims Marcos Shipped Tons of Gold to Switzerland," *AP News*, August 14, 1991, https://apnews.com/article/e2c5ce3f218206be6e9813db1754928a; Henry Weinstein, "Swiss Accounts Frozen in Marcos Case," *Los Angeles Times*, September 30, 1997, https://www.latimes.com/archives/la-xpm-1997-sep-30-me-37657-story.html; "Marcos Family Mum on Swiss Bank Withdrawal," *PhilStar Global*, March 14, 2001, https://www.philstar.com/headlines/2001/03/14/90035/marcos-family-mum-swiss-bank-withdrawal.

138   Kwitny, *Crimes of the Patriots*, 259.

139   Armstrong, "Global Entanglements."

140   John Dunbar, "A Brief History of Bush, Harken, and the SEC," *Center for Public Integrity*, October 16, 2002, https://publicintegrity.org/environment/a-brief-history-of-bush-harken-and-the-sec/.

141   Baker, *Family of Secrets*, 343.

142   World Wildlife Fund, "In Memorium: Godfrey A. Rockefeller," https://web.archive.org/web/20160404232506/ https://www.worldwildlife.org/press-releases/in-memoriam-godfrey-a-rockefeller.

143   World Wildlife Fund, "Our History," https://www.wwf.org.za/our_people/our_history/.

144   Dunbar, "A Brief History."

145   Dunbar, "A Brief History."

146   Baker, *Family of Secrets*, 332.

147   Dunbar, "A Brief History."

148   *Enron: The Bush Connection* (Democracy Now, 2006), https://www.democracynow.org/2006/5/26/enron_the_bush_connection.

149   Peter Truell and Larry Gurwin, *False Profits: The Inside Story of BCCI, The World's Most Corrupt Financial Empire* (Houghton Mifflin, 1992), 370.

150   Block, *All is Clouded By Desire*, 112.

151   Armstrong, "Global Entanglements."

152   Truell and Gurwin, *False Profits*, 370.

153   "Investor Acquires 9.6% of Worthen", *New York Times*, October 13, 1990 https://www.nytimes.com/1990/10/18/business/company-news-investor-acquires-9.6-of-worthen.html

CHAPTER 9

HIGH TECH TREASON

THE MAKING OF A MAXWELL

Born in what is now part of Ukraine, "Robert Maxwell" was the last in a series of names used by Jan Ludvick Hoch, with his earlier aliases including the names Abraham Hoch, Jan Ludvick, and Leslie Du Marier. The name Robert Maxwell emerged at the behest of one of his superiors in the British military, which Maxwell had joined during World War II. He left the village of his birth prior to the war, when the Third Reich began its expansion, and made his way to Britain. Maxwell's parents and his siblings are believed to have died in the Holocaust.

Robert Maxwell was involved with the British intelligence service MI6 during the war and, after the war, was befriended by Count Frederich vanden Huevel, who had worked closely with Allen Dulles during the war.[1] Dulles went on to be the first civilian director of the CIA and, during the war, was busy running interference for prominent Nazis and actively undermining FDR's "unconditional surrender" policy for senior Nazi leadership.[2]

The chaos of post-war Europe allowed Maxwell to plant the seeds for what would become his future media empire. Thanks to his contacts with Allied Forces in post-war Berlin, he was able to acquire the publishing rights for prominent European scientific journals and, in 1948, those interests were folded into the British publishing company Butterworth, which had long-standing ties to British intelligence.[3] In the early 1950s, the company was renamed Pergamon Press, and this company soon became the cornerstone of Maxwell's media empire.

Pergamon's access to prominent academics, scientists, and government not only led to Maxwell acquiring great wealth but also attracted the interest of various intelligence agencies – British, Russian, and Israeli among them – all of which attempted to recruit Maxwell as an asset or as a spy. When MI6 attempted to recruit Maxwell for the service shortly after the war, it concluded, after conducting an extensive background check, that Maxwell was a "Zionist – loyal only to Israel."[4] His subsequent relationship with MI6 was choppy and largely opportunistic on both sides, with Maxwell later laying some of the blame for his financial troubles on MI6's alleged attempts to "subvert" him. Yet, it would not be until the early 1960s that Maxwell was formally approached and successfully recruited by Israeli intelligence, which sought to make use of his access to the various prominent businessman and world leaders that he had cultivated while growing his media empire.[5]

A few years after being officially recruited as an asset of Israeli intelligence, Maxwell ran for public office, becoming a member of the British Parliament for the Labour Party in 1964. His bid for re-election failed, which left him out of office by 1970. Around that same time, he also lost control of Pergamon Press, after a failed takeover attempt by Saul Steinberg prompted a government inquiry into Maxwell's management of the company. That inquiry concluded that Maxwell "is not, in our opinion, a person who can be relied on to exercise proper stewardship" of a publicly held company.[6] Nevertheless, Maxwell reacquired control of the company a few years later in 1974.[7]

Having nearly lost everything, Maxwell devoted his time to consolidating control over an ever-growing web of interlocking companies, trusts, and foundations that now encompassed much more than media concerns. During this time, he also began developing deep ties to prominent politicians, businessmen, and their fixers, a group that Maxwell proudly referred to as his "sources." Among these early "sources" were soon-to-be UK prime minister Margaret Thatcher; Israel's biggest arms dealer and one of its powerful oligarchs, Shaul Eisenberg; financial behemoths such as Edmund Safra; and master manipulators such as Henry Kissinger. Another early "source" was George H.W.Bush, who was then part of the Nixon administration and would soon serve as CIA director before becoming Reagan's vice president and then US president himself.[8]

Maxwell's sources and influence extended well beyond the West, with many of his most prominent contacts residing in Eastern Europe and in the Soviet Union. He had cozy relationships with dictators, intelligence officials, and even organized crime lords such as Semion Mogilevich, sometimes referred to as the "boss of the bosses" of the Russian mafia.[9] It was none other than Robert Maxwell who orchestrated the entry of Mogilevich-connected companies into the United States, a move that was accomplished after Maxwell successfully lobbied the state of Israel to grant Mogilevich and his associates Israeli passports, thereby allowing them easier access to US financial institutions.[10]

The expansion of Maxwell's prominent contacts paralleled the growth of his media empire. By 1980, he had acquired the British Printing Corporation, which he renamed the Maxwell Communication Corporation. Just a few years later, he bought the Mirror Group, publisher of the British tabloid the *Daily Mirror*.[11] This was followed by his acquisition of publishers like MacMillan and later the *New York Daily News*. Money "borrowed" from some Maxwell-owned companies was allegedly used to finance Mossad activities in Europe and elsewhere; then, the funds were restored before the absence was noticed by company employees not privy to these operations. Maxwell later derailed this well-oiled system by dipping into these same funds to finance his own ostentatious and salacious habits as well as attempts to further expand his already bloated media empire well beyond its means.

During this period, Maxwell's ties to Israeli intelligence deepened in other ways, particularly during the time when Yitzhak Shamir was prime minister. Shamir, previously a leader of a terrorist group known as Lehi or the Stern Gang, deeply loathed the United States, a sentiment he confided to Maxwell during one of Maxwell's visits to Israel.[12] Shamir told Maxwell that he blamed the Americans for the Holocaust because of the US' failure to support the transfer of European Jews to Palestine prior to the war.[13] Shamir's very negative views about the US likely informed Israel's more aggressive espionage operations that targeted the US during this time and in which Maxwell prominently figured.

A BROKEN PROMIS

One of the most brazen and successful operations ever conducted by Israeli intelligence on a global scale involved its sale of a bugged software program to governments, corporations, and major financial and scientific institutions around the world. That software program, known as the Prosecutor's Information Management System or PROMIS, was originally created and marketed by Inslaw Inc., a company created by former NSA official Bill Hamilton and his wife Nancy.

In 1982, Inslaw leased its revolutionary PROMIS software to the US Justice Department, then headed by Edwin Meese III, Ronald Reagan's most trusted advisor, Attorney General and, later, an advisor to Donald Trump following the 2016 election. The success of the software, which allowed integration of separate databases and information analysis on a previously unimaginable scale, eventually caught the attention of Rafi Ei-tan, the notorious and legendary Israeli spymaster as well as the handler of the *"most damaging spy"* in American history, Jonathan Pollard.[14] Eitan, at the time, was serving as the then-head of the now defunct Israel intel-ligence service known as Lekem (sometimes written as Lakam), which focused specifically on espionage related to scientific and technical in-formation and discoveries. Eitan *had first learned* of PROMIS some time in 1982. That December, using the alias Dr. Ben Orr, Eitan entered the US and unsuccessfully attempted to attend an official demonstration of PROMIS.[15] He returned in February of the following year and was given a demonstration of a new version of the software, advanced PROMIS, by Bill Hamilton himself.[16] During that trip, a former Inslaw employee then working at the Department of Justice, C. Madison "Brick" Brewer, gave "Dr. Orr" a copy of the software.[17]With the software in his possession, Eitan sought to to install a "trapdoor," also often referred to as a back door, into the software. He would then orchestrate the marketing of this mod-ified version of PROMIS throughout the world, providing Israeli intelli-gence with a direct window into the operations of its enemies and allies. According to the testimony of ex-Israeli intelligence official Ari Ben-Me-nashe, he, on Eitan's orders, *contacted* an Israeli American programmer living in California.[18] That programmer then planted a "trapdoor" or back door into the software that would grant the Eitan-led Lekem covert ac-cess to any database connected to a device on which the software was installed.To help market the compromised version of PROMIS, Eitan sought out a man named Earl Brian. Brian was a long-time associate of Ronald Reagan who had previously worked for the CIA in covert oper-ations, beginning with the Vietnam-era Phoenix program, and had been in charge of Reagan's healthcare program when Reagan was governor of California.[19] It was through his healthcare-related ventures that Brian had first met Eitan.[20] In 1982, however, Brian was attempting to build a new business empire, this one focused on technology. It was later disclosed that Attorney General Ed Meese's wife, at the time, was a major investor in two companies controlled by Earl Brian and those investments had been made with money loaned to Meese's wife by a close associate of Brian's.[21] In speaking with Rafi Eitan, Brian acknowledged the revolutionary effi-cacy of PROMIS. The software could track anything, specifically money and people. Instead of praising its innovative approach to data analysis, Brian expressed his frustration that the software enabled US federal investigators to successfully track and target money laundering and other financial crimes. He also expressed frustration that he had been left out of the profits on PROMIS, the development of which he had followed closely for several years.[22]As their conversation wore on, Eitan and Brian *hatched a plan* about how to best utilize and market the modified version of PROMIS.[23] This agreement between Eitan and Brian eventually led to two different versions of bugged PROMIS software, one bugged by Israel for the main purpose of spying on the operations of foreign governments and intelligence services and one bugged by CIA-linked entities and individuals for the main purpose of engaging in financial espionage and money laundering. However, what would later become known as the Inslaw affair, sometimes also called the PROMIS scandal, began first with the version of PROMIS that had been stolen and then modified by Israel. With the bugged version of PROMIS ready, Brian attempted to use his company Hadron Inc. to market the bugged PROMIS software around the world, though he first had tried to buy out Inslaw to do so. When that effort failed, Brian launched a second effort to buy out Inslaw using a company called SCT that had been financed by Allen & Co., the company of the organized crime-linked Charles and Herbert Allen who were, among other things, business partners of Leslie Wexner's mentors Max Fisher and A. Alfred Taubman (see chapter 13).[24] *Wired* described Allen & Co. as having "close business ties to Earl Brian."[25] As will be noted in chapter 12, another figure associated with Earl Brian was Allan Tessler, the lawyer for the Epstein-connected Gouletas family who was added to the board of Wexner's The Limited in the late 1980s. Notably, Allen & Co. owned a significant amount of common stock in Earl Brian's Hadron.[26] Unsuccessful and unable to buy out the Hamiltons, Brian turned to his close friend, then-Attorney General Ed Meese, whose wife, as previously mentioned, had also invested in Brian's business ventures. Soon, the Justice Department abruptly refused to make the payments to Inslaw that had been stipulated by the contract. They were essentially using the software for free, which Inslaw claimed was theft.

Meese's actions forced Inslaw into bankruptcy and Inslaw *subsequently sued* the Justice Department, with a US court later finding that the Meese-led department "took, converted, stole" the software through "trickery, fraud, and deceit."[27] With Inslaw out of the way, Brian sold the bugged software to Jordan's and Iraq's intelligence services, a major boon for Israel, and to a handful of companies. Despite this, Eitan was unsatisfied with Brian and Hadron and their progress in selling the software. He quickly turned to the person he thought could most effectively market and sell PROMIS to governments of interest all over the world: Robert Maxwell.[28]

THE SPY AND THE SALESMAN

Maxwell's prominent roles in the PROMIS software scandal and the Iran-Contra affair during the 1980s were facilitated by his purchase of numerous Israeli companies, several of which were either fronts or "providers of services" for Israeli intelligence. The most notable of these was Scitex, where Yitzhak Shamir's son Nachum was a major executive throughout the 1990s and early 2000s, and Degem, a computer company with a large presence in Central and South America as well as in Africa.[29]

According to Gordon Thomas and Martin Dillon, even before Maxwell's purchase of Degem, it had been used by Mossad as a cover for agents, particularly assassins, who would use its offices as a cover before conducting kidnappings and murders of individuals linked to groups with ties to or sympathies for Israel's enemies, particularly the PLO.[30] Some of the most notable events occurred in Africa, where Mossad assassins used Degem as cover to launch killings of members of the African National Congress. In Latin America, Degem was also used as cover for the Mossad to infiltrate terrorist and narco-terrorist organizations such as Peru's Sendero Luminoso (known in English as the Shining Path) and Colombia's National Liberation Army or ELN.[31]

Through Degem and other Maxwell-owned companies based in Israel and elsewhere, Maxwell marketed PROMIS so successfully that Israeli intelligence soon had access to the innermost workings of innumerable governments, intelligence services, and corporations around the world. Many of Maxwell's biggest successes came in selling PROMIS to dictators in Eastern Europe, Africa, and Latin America. Following the sale, and after Maxwell collected a handsome pay check, PROMIS' unparalleled ability to track and surveil anything – from cash flows to human movement – was used by these governments to commit financial crimes with greater finesse and also to hunt down and disappear dissidents. Israeli intelligence, of course, watched it all play out in real time.

In Latin America, for instance, Maxwell sold PROMIS to *military dictatorships in Chile and Argentina. There, PROMIS was* used to facilitate the mass murder that characterized Operation Condor, as the friends and families of dissidents and so-called subversives were easily identified using PROMIS.[32] PROMIS was so effective for this purpose that, just days after Maxwell *sold the software* to Guatemala, its US-backed dictatorship rounded up 20,000 "subversives" who were never heard from again. Of course, thanks to their backdoor in PROMIS, Israeli intelligence knew the identities of Guatemala's disappeared before the victims' own families. Israel, along with the United States, was also *intimately involved* in the arming and training of many of the same Latin American dictatorships that had been sold the bugged PROMIS software.[33]

Though Israeli intelligence found obvious use for the steady stream of sensitive and classified information, their biggest prize was yet to come – top secret government laboratories in the United States. Eitan *tasked Maxwell* with selling PROMIS to US labs in the Los Alamos complex, including Sandia National Laboratory, which was (and is) at the core of the US nuclear weapons system.[34] Notably, Maxwell's eventual sale of PROMIS to these laboratories occurred during the same period in 1984 when Eitan tasked one of Israel's top nuclear experts with supervising Jonathan Pollard's espionage of U.S. nuclear secrets on Israel's behalf.

In order to plot how he would accomplish the sale of PROMIS to Los Alamos, Maxwell consulted one of his "sources," none other than Henry Kissinger. Kissinger told him that. in order to sell PROMIS to these sensitive laboratories, he needed to enlist the services of then-Senator for Texas John Tower, who was the then-head of the Senate Armed Services Committee.[35] At the time, Tower was searching for lucrative opportunities as the sun was setting on his Senate career. Maxwell quickly struck a deal with Tower and then, using Mossad money, *paid Tower $200,000* for his services, which included opening doors – not just to the Los Alamos complex, but also to the Reagan White House.[36] Tower would arrange a trip for Maxwell to travel to Sandia National Laboratory, where he would market PROMIS. Unlike most other PROMIS sales, this one would not be handled by Degem, but a US-based company called Information on Demand.

Robert Maxwell had purchased Information on Demand from its founder, Sue Rugge – a former librarian – through the Pergamon Group in 1982. This was also the very year plans were made by Rafi Eitan and Earl Brian to subvert PROMIS.[37] Its offices were just a few doors down from the home of Isabel Maxwell and her first husband Dale Djerassi, the son of the scientist credited with creating the birth control pill.

According to FBI files obtained by Inslaw Inc. via a FOIA request in the 1990s, San Francisco's FBI field office began to look into Information on Demand, just a year after Maxwell had acquired it. The San Francisco office's interest in the company was aroused in October 1983 and the FBI subsequently interviewed Rugge about the business and its activities.[38] She

387

told the FBI that the company's sources "include over 250 computer data bases" and that company uses these to "locate single facts as well as provide answers to complex questions dealing with such areas as comprehensive marketing research, custom data summaries, sophisticated literature searching, current awareness service and global information capability."

One of these databases included Lockheed's Dialog database and "the Defense Technical Center which is connected to the Department of Defense (DOD) which contains classified information." She asserted, however, that the company "has no password for access and further no need for access." Elsewhere in the document, it notes that Information on Demand claimed to not to have had any access to classified information "to the best of their knowledge," but did "[include] information concerning government and various available means of tapping government information databases."

The FBI asked Rugge about one client of the company in particular, whose name and identifying information is redacted in its entirety, but notes that this mysterious client had worked with Information on Demand since at least 1973. Subsequent efforts by Inslaw Inc. and others to learn the identity of the redacted client have been unsuccessful since 1994.

Notably, just one month before the FBI opened an investigation into Information on Demand and interviewed Sue Rugge, another related Maxwell-owned firm, Pergamon International Information Corporation (PIIC), *had sent a letter* to then-CIA Director Bill Casey, offering to provide the agency with access to patent databases.[39] The only redacted portion of the letter is the identity of PIIC's Executive Vice President, who had written the letter to Casey. After Rugge had been interviewed, FBI interest in Information on Demand peaked in June 1984, when a formal investigation was opened. This took place after two employees of Sandia National Laboratory, who worked in technology transfer, approached the Bureau over Information on Demand's efforts to sell PROMIS to the laboratory.[40] Those employees were compelled to contact the FBI after obtaining information from employees of the National Security Agency (NSA) regarding "the purchase of Information on Demand Inc. by one Robert Maxwell, the owner of Pergamon International." The specific information on this purchase from the NSA is included in the report but redacted in its entirety. Two months later, one of the Sandia employees followed up with the Bureau, suggesting that the NSA and FBI jointly investigate Information on Demand, but was essentially stonewalled and told to take it up with FBI headquarters. The FBI case file is specifically coded as a foreign counter-intelligence investigation, suggesting that the case was opened because the FBI was made aware of the alleged involvement of a foreign intelligence service in some aspect of Information on Demand's activities that related specifically to the "dissemination, marketing, or sale of computer software systems, including but not limited to the PROMIS computer software product."[41] It also noted that Maxwell himself had previously been the subject of a "security investigation" conducted by the FBI from 1953 until 1961. Notably, 1961 is the year that Maxwell was formally recruited as an Israeli intelligence asset. The FBI investigation likely focused on Information on Demand's ties to Mossad, which were later reported by author Gordon Thomas. Per Thomas, the money used to run and operate Information on Demand's California office "would come out of one of the Mossad accounts in Credit Suisse."[42]

In early August 1984, FBI headquarters and other higher-ups in the Ed Meese-led Department of Justice, which itself was complicit in the whole sordid PROMIS affair, ordered the New Mexico office to halt its investigation into Information on Demand, Maxwell, and PROMIS. The cover-up, oddly enough, continues today, with the FBI *still refusing, decades later*, to release documents pertaining to Robert Maxwell and his role in the PROMIS scandal.[43]

Several months following the shuttering of the FBI investigation into Information on Demand, in February 1985 Robert Maxwell again returned to Sandia National Laboratories, signing the contract for the sale of PROMIS and listing himself as President and CEO of Information on Demand. A few months later, he passed that role on to his daughter Christine, who served as the company's president and CEO up until her father's death in 1991, according to *her résumé*.[44] Upon the collapse of his business empire shortly after his demise, which also resulted in the closure of Information on Demand, Christine created a company called Research on Demand that offered similar services and specialized "in Internet – and Big Data analytics-related market studies for companies in the Telecoms." In addition, Isabel Maxwell, who lived in close proximity to the company's offices in Berkley, CA, told *Haaretz* that she had also worked for Information on Demand, which she refers to as "her sister's company," following her 1989 divorce from Dale Djerassi.[45]

THE CIA AND PROMIS

As previously mentioned, there were eventually two different modified versions of PROMIS containing different backdoors – the first having been developed by Israeli intelligence and the second having been developed by CIA-linked entities and individuals. The CIA version appears to have been focused mainly on the banking industry while the Israeli/Lekem version seemed to have been mainly marketed to intelligence agencies and other parts of the public sector that dealt with classified state information.

Though some authors have tried to paint the CIA's acquisition of PROMIS as having happened well after Eitan's theft of the software, it has since emerged that the Agency was offered a government copy of PROMIS as far back as 1981, thanks to a government memo obtained by Emma Best. Best wrote that, despite the CIA having denied buying the software:

> This memo [...] shows that the Agency was offered the PROMIS software along with a list of other pieces of government owned software and the hardware necessary to run them. Since CIA didn't disclose this or search those records, it's unknown if they acquired an initial copy of the software this way. Even if it did not, it undermines their claims to have fully cooperated and searched every reasonable record and Agency component as they didn't search their software requisition records.
>
> The Department of Justice also repeatedly stated that, aside from a notable exception, they didn't provide copies of PROMIS to anyone else or distribute it throughout the government. These memos, however, show that the software was being offered throughout the federal government from the beginning, making versions of the software readily acquirable for anyone in the government to review or toy around with prior to Earl Brian and Edwin Meese's scheme to defraud INSLAW while modifying (i.e. inserting backdoors) and distributing the software through the U.S. and overseas.[46]

This timeline muddles the conventional narrative and raises the possibility that the supposedly "dueling" versions serving Israeli intelligence and US intelligence were perhaps more inter-related and collaborative in nature as opposed to competitive, as some authors like Gordon Thomas have claimed. Ari Ben-Menashe, in an interview for this book, attested to the collaborative nature between both the Israeli and CIA's version of PROMIS, with Robert Maxwell himself engaging in unspecified collaborations related to the CIA version of PROMIS.

The CIA version of PROMIS was modified by a man named Michael Riconosciuto, who altered the software at Cabazon Indian Reservation near Indio, California. At the reservation, Riconosciuto had worked for Wackenhut (now G4S Security), which – at the time – provided security for critical infrastructure and high security government facilities. Wacken-hut, in 1981, had entered into a joint venture with the Cabazon Band of Mission Indians, which was focused on establishing a "production facility, called 'Cabazon Arms,' on the one square mile of Cabazon-owned desert land near Indio."[47] This joint venture was briefly discussed in the previous chapter. In speaking to author Cheri Seymour, Riconosciuto noted that the company's board of directors was stuffed with former top figures in US intelligence and law enforcement. Riconosciuto corroborated to Sey-mour that he had been the one to modify PROMIS and he also fingered Earl Brian as the mastermind of the scheme. "A man named Earl Brian was spearheading a plan for worldwide use of the software, but essentially, the modified software was being pirated from the owners, Bill and Nancy Hamilton," Riconosciuto had told Seymour.[48] Riconosciuto alleges that he was targeted by the government after signing an affidavit to assist the Hamiltons' case. In that document, he had stated his role in the modifica-tion of the PROMIS software.

The modification of PROMIS was hardly Riconosciuto's first interac-tion with intelligence or even with Earl Brian. Per Seymour, Riconosciuto had been recruited by the CIA while at Stanford University and Riconos-ciuto "and Earl Brian had traveled to Iran in 1980 and had paid $40 mil-lion to Iranian officials to persuade them not to let the hostages go before the presidential election," a scheme better known as the October Surprise (see Chapter 6).[49] Per Riconosciuto, Brian's role in the October Surprise was related to his theft of PROMIS. He later testified that the software "was stolen as a favor to software-company executive Earl Brian, a friend of Meese's, for Brian's help in persuading the Iranian government to hold on to the embassy hostages until the 1980 election was over."[50]

Regardless of exactly when US intelligence developed and began using a bugged PROMIS, the software was subsequently developed for many uses, including on nuclear submarines of the United States and the Unit-ed Kingdom and for tracking of nuclear material inventories and long-range ballistic missiles. However, one of the most unsettling uses of the software, on which both the US and Israel collaborated, was its use to keep track of dissident Americans.

This use of PROMIS was spearheaded by Oliver North. North had de-cided to turn PROMIS' power against Americans, particularly perceived dissidents. Beginning in 1982, as part of the highly classified Continuity of Government (COG) program, North used the PROMIS software at a 6,100-square-foot "command center" in the Department of Justice, as well as at a smaller operations room at the White House, to compile a list of American dissidents and "potential troublemakers" if the COG protocol were to ever be invoked.[51] According to a senior government official with a high-ranking security clearance and service in five presidential administrations who spoke to *Radar* in 2008, this was:

> A database of Americans, who, often for the slightest and most trivial reason, are considered unfriendly, and who, in a time of panic might be incarcerated. The database can identify and locate perceived 'enemies of the state' almost instantaneously.[52]

In 1993, *Wired* described North's use of PROMIS in compiling this database as follows:

> Using PROMIS, sources point out, North could have drawn up lists of anyone ever arrested for a political protest, for example, or anyone who had ever refused to pay their taxes. Compared to PROMIS, Richard Nixon's enemies list or Sen. Joe McCarthy's blacklist look downright crude.[53]

The COG program defined this "time of panic" as "a national crisis, such as nuclear war, violent and widespread internal dissent, or national opposition to a US military invasion abroad," whereby the government would suspend the Constitution, declare martial law, and incarcerate perceived dissidents and other "unfriendlies" in order to prevent the government's (or then-serving administration's) overthrow.[54] This secretive database has often been referred to as "Main Core" by government insiders and it still exists today. Journalist Christopher Ketcham, citing senior government officials, reported in 2008 that, at that time, Main Core was believed to contain the names of as many as 8 million Americans.[55] Since then, it is highly likely that the number of Americans included in the Main Core database has grown considerably.

Author and investigative journalist Tim Shorrock also covered other disturbing aspects of the evolution of Main Core back in 2008 for *Salon* and further noted that Main Core, at the time, was said to contain "a vast amount of personal data on Americans, including NSA intercepts of bank and credit card transactions and the results of surveillance efforts by the FBI, the CIA, and other agencies."[56]

Bill Hamilton of Inslaw had told Shorrock at the time that he believed that "U.S. intelligence uses PROMIS as the primary software for searching the Main Core database" and had been told as much by an intelligence official in 1992 and an NSA official in 1995.[57] Dan Murphy, former deputy director at the CIA, had told Hamilton that the NSA's use of PROMIS was "so seriously wrong that money alone cannot cure the problem." "I believe in retrospect that Murphy was alluding to Main Core," Hamilton had told Shorrock.[58]

In 2019, citing a former US intelligence official with direct knowledge of the U.S. intelligence community's use of PROMIS and Main Core from the 1980s to 2000s, I reported that Israeli intelligence played a role in the U.S. government's deployment of PROMIS as the software used for the Main Core domestic surveillance database system.[59] Per this source, Israeli intelligence remained involved with Main Core at the time of the August 1991 death of journalist Danny Casolaro. This same official told me that, shortly before his death, Casolaro had obtained copies of computer printouts from the PROMIS-based Main Core domestic surveillance database system from NSA whistleblower Alan Standorf, among other items. Standorf was found murdered a few months before Casolaro's lifeless body was discovered in a hotel room.[60]

The source also stated that Main Core's contents had been used for the political blackmail of members of Congress and their staff, journalists, and others by Walter Raymond, a senior CIA covert operator in psyops and disinformation who served on President Reagan's National Security Council after Main Core was created.[61] If used for this purpose by Raymond in the 1980s, it is highly likely that Main Core has also been used by other individuals with access to the database for blackmailing purposes in the years since. In addition to their collaboration on Main Core, there is also the possibility that the CIA and Israel's Lekem collaborated and shared at least some of the intelligence reaped from the different versions of PROMIS. As previously detailed, Israeli intelligence and the CIA were already collaborating on major aspects of Iran-Contra during this same period. Yet, these networks also appear to have been intimately involved with the sale of the PROMIS software themselves.

For instance, one connection of Iran-Contra to PROMIS can be seen in the visit Contra leaders made to Cabazon for weapons demonstrations, which was mentioned in the previous chapter. Another clear example of overlap is Robert Maxwell. Yet, another and arguably the most compelling evidence for the overlap can be found in a 1985 letter written by William Bradford Reynolds, Assistant Attorney General in the Civil Rights Division, to William F. Weld, then-the US Attorney in Boston. The letter told Weld that PROMIS (misspelled as Promise in the letter) was being provided to Sheik Khalid bin Mahfouz, a Saudi billionaire and banker who had owned a personal 20% stake in BCCI and was mentioned in connection with BCCI in Chapter 7.

That letter states the following:

> Dear Mr. Weld: As agreed Messrs. Manichur [sic] Ghorbanifar, Adnan Khashoggi, and Richard Armitage will broker the transaction of Promise [sic] software to Sheik Khalid bin Mahfouz for resale and general distribution as gifts in his region contingent upon the three conditions we last spoke of. Promise [sic] must have a soft arrival. No paperwork, customs, or delay. It must be equipped with the special data retrieval unit. As before, you must walk the financial aspects through Credit Suisse into National Commercial Bank [which bin Mahfouz chaired]. If you encounter any problems contact me directly. Sincerely, WM. Bradford Reynolds, Assistant Attorney General Civil Rights Division.[62]

This letter implicates key figures involved in Iran-Contra weapons deals, i.e. Khashoggi and Ghorbanifar, as also selling PROMIS software for covert purposes. In this case, they were specifically selling it to a man tied to the banking industry, more specifically BCCI. As it turns out, the global banking industry was a major target of the bugged PROMIS software. As will be mentioned shortly, this was partially facilitated by BCCI and affiliated entities as BCCI was known to use PROMIS and had other connections to its illicit uses.

One of the key companies involved with the bugged PROMIS' entry into the global financial system was tied to a major figure in BCCI's entry into the American financial system, Jackson Stephens, discussed in the previous chapter as well as chapter 7. While Israel's bugged version of PROMIS was being marketed worldwide by Robert Maxwell and his front companies, the CIA's equivalent was marketed, in part, by the Jackson Stephens-owned Systematics.

Systematics was a data-processing company that, like other prominent Stephens-owned firms, was represented by the Rose Law Firm, which – as noted in the last chapter – had deep ties to the Clinton family and its political machinery. Two partners in the Rose Law Firm who would later serve in the Clinton administration, Vince Foster and Webster Hubbell, went on to acquire significant financial interests in Systematics through ownership in Alltel, which acquired Systematics in the early 1990s.[63] Notably, Rose had also represented Systematics as part of a lawsuit related to the efforts of Jackson Stephens and others to bring BCCI into the American financial system. As noted in chapter 7, Systematics was a defendant alongside Jackson Stephens, another Stephens owned company Stephens Inc., Agha Hasan Abedi, Bert Lance, and Eugene Metzger relating to their hostile takeover attempt of FGB. Rose Law represented Systematics in this lawsuit. As was also noted in chapter 7, Stephens had been involved in BCCI's affairs because he "wanted FGB to use a company he controlled, Systematics Inc., for its data processing business."[64]

Unlike Maxwell's fronts used to market PROMIS, Systematics was more focused on selling software and data-processing services to financial institutions than governments and intelligence agencies. Acquired by Stephens in the 1960s, Systematics primarily serviced banks and, by the 1990s, was "one of the leading vendors in the United States and, reportedly, in some 40 foreign countries, of computer software and services for the banking industry."

According to former *Forbes* assistant editor James Norman in his book *The Oil Card: Global Economic Warfare in the 21st Century*, Systematics was also "a primary vehicle or front company for the National Security Agency in the 1980s and early 1990s to market and implant bugged software in the world's major money-center banks and clearinghouses as part of the Reagan/Bush 'follow the money' effort to break the Soviets."[65] The late journalist Michael Ruppert and others have asserted that this "bugged software" was none other than the PROMIS software. Ruppert specifically cited Systematics as "a primary developer of PROMIS for financial intelligence use."[66]

Norman, in his reporting which was censored by *Forbes*, alluded to the role of National Security Council member Norman Bailey in urging the involvement of the NSA in surveilling the flow of money through SWIFT, Fedwire, CHIPS, and other financial transfer mechanisms. In his censored report, Norman wrote that Bailey "confirms that within a few years the National Security Agency ... had begun vacuuming up mountains of data by listening in on bank wire traffic. It became a joint effort of several Western governments with the Israelis playing a leading role." Norman further noted that the NSA's ability to spy on financial transactions was directly enabled by Systematics.

As will be discussed in greater detail in chapter 16, Norman had learned that one of the main individuals overseeing this NSA program for Systematics was Vince Foster of Rose Law and subsequently the deputy White House counsel during Bill Clinton's first term until his death in 1993.

Yet, Norman's censored report, later published in *Media Bypass* magazine, went even further and revealed that Systematics not only aided NSA surveillance of the financial system, it was also intimately linked to money laundering efforts:

> Systematics has had close ties to the NSA and CIA ever since its founding, sources say, as a money-shuffler for covert operations. It is no secret that there were billions of dollars moving around in "black" accounts – from buying and selling arms to the Contras, Iran, Iraq, Angola and other countries to paying CIA operatives and laundering money from clandestine CIA drug dealing. Having taken over the complete computer rooms in scores of small U.S. banks as an "outsource" supplier of data processing, Systematics was in a unique position to manage that covert money flow. Sources say the money was moved at the end of every day disguised as a routine bank-to-bank balancing transaction.[67]

Norman also alleges that Jackson Stephens' efforts to bring BCCI into the US were related to this situation:

> Systematics' money-laundering role for the intelligence community might help explain why Jackson Stephens tried to take over Washington-based Financial General Bankshares in 1978 on behalf of Arab backers of the Bank of Credit and Commerce International. BCCI's links to global corruption and intelligence operations has been well documented, though many mysteries remain.
>
> According to a lawsuit filed by the Securities and Exchange Commission, Stephens insisted on having then-tiny Systematics brought in to take over all the bank's data processing. Representing Systematics in that 1978 SEC case: Hillary Rodham Clinton and Webster Hubbell. Stephens was blocked in that takeover. But FGB, later renamed First American, ultimately fell under the domination of BCCI through Robert Altman and former Defense Sec. Clark Clifford. According to a technician who worked at First American in Atlanta, Systematics became a key computer contractor there anyway.[68]

A 1995 document sent on behalf of Inslaw's founders to then-independent Counsel Ken Starr by Inslaw lawyer Elliot Richardson supports several of Norman's claims.[69] That document states that Systematics had "covertly implanted [software] into the computers of its bank customers" that allowed "allied intelligence agencies surreptitiously to track and monitor the flow of money through the banking system" and had done so at "the behest of the U.S. National Security Agency (NSA) and its partner in Israeli intelligence."[70] Inslaw also stated that the software was used by these same intelligence agencies in the "laundering of money, especially drug profits."

Systematics did, in fact, appear to have ties to Israeli intelligence, as Richardson asserts. The company was known to have a subsidiary in Israel that, according to a former Israeli intelligence officer, was operated by contractors for the Mossad and sold software to banks and telecommunications companies.[71] According to Richardson's letter, that Israeli subsidiary of Systematics also had a Massachusetts-based front company, which was partially owned by a former U.S. intelligence official named Harry Weschler. Furthermore, Systematics also had dealings with Israel's PROMIS salesman *par excellence*, Robert Maxwell. According to Bill Hamilton of Inslaw as cited by Cheri Seymour, Systematics entered into a joint venture with Robert Maxwell, who was allegedly acting on Israel's behalf. In that venture, Maxwell and Systematics sold bugged versions of PROMIS to five banks, most of which were Swiss.[72] This again suggests that the "CIA version" of PROMIS was more of a complement to the "Israeli version" Robert Maxwell was best known for marketing, rather than a competitor. It also further hints at collaboration between Israeli and US intelligence for the purpose of placing backdoors into global financial flows.[73]

This focus on obtaining a secret window into the in and out-flows of the global banking system enabled not only the covert tracking of funds, but presumably allowed funds to be covertly hidden and financial crimes to be effectively covered up or rendered invisible. This was likely why BCCI employed the PROMIS software after its theft by the DOJ, as one of its subsidiaries, First American Bank, reportedly "filtered PROMIS money" (i.e., laundered the money generated from the sale of the stolen PROMIS software), according to the late journalist Danny Casolaro.[74]

Returning to the matter of Vince Foster, the Hamiltons of Inslaw have also provided considerable evidence that Foster's distress prior to his 1993 death appears to have been related to concerns about litigation involving Systematics and PROMIS.[75] James Norman, the previously mentioned journalist who was then writing for *Forbes*, reported in 1995 that Foster had been known to be under counterintelligence surveillance at the time of his death. Norman has also stated that it was suspected at the time that an adversarial government, allegedly the Chinese, had bought "high-level code, encryption, and other secrets via Foster's Swiss bank account and Israeli banks" and that *Forbes* had declined to publish these allegations (and by extension Norman's reporting on the matter) because, among other concerns, they didn't want to make any public statements about Systematics' role in the affair.[76] As will again be noted in chapter 16, another assistant editor of *Forbes* at the time, alongside Norman, was the daughter of Harry Weschler, the former CIA official who partially owned the Israeli subsidiary of Systematics. Norman subsequently intimated that this connection played a role in the censoring of his reporting.

Vince Foster's death, which many regard as suspicious despite it being officially labelled a suicide, is discussed in more detail in chapter 16, as the very event that marked one of Jeffrey Epstein's earliest visits to the Clinton White House makes an odd appearance in Foster's controversial "suicide note."

E-SYSTEMS

Another company that surfaces in the allegations surrounding Systematics and the Inslaw affair is E-Systems, a Dallas-based defense contractor specializing in computer software and systems. Authors James Norman and J. Orlin Grabbe have both discussed E-Systems as having a particularly close relationship with Systematics. However, the CEO of Alltel, a successor company to Systematics has denied that any such relationship exists.[77] Among the claims made by Grabbe and Norman is that sensitive E-Systems computer code ended up in the hands of Israel a mere thirty days after it was first deployed by the NSA.[78]

While parsing out the details of the connections between E-Systems and Systematics is difficult, E-Systems did maintain a tight connection with another corporation located at the heart of the Inslaw affair: Wackenhut. William Raborn, who had served as director of the CIA under President Lyndon Johnson, joined the board of directors of Wackenhut in 1971.[79] Press reports show that by at least 1977, he had also joined the board of E-Systems. Wackenhut annual reports illustrate that, for a time, he served on the board of these companies simultaneously.

E-Systems' connections to the intelligence community are long-standing. The company began in the 1960s as LTV Electrosystems, a wholly-owned subsidiary of Ling-Temco-Vought (LTV), the Texas-based defense contractor that was then rapidly expanding due to military contracts related to the Vietnam War.[80] As discussed in chapter 6, LTV shared multiple connections with First International Bancshares, the CIA-linked bank that George H.W. Bush joined in 1976. LTV Electrosystems held a major share of the defense contracts that LTV received, having been consolidated with another major LTV subsidiary, LTV Military Electronics Division.[81] In 1972, LTV Electrosystems was spun off as an independent company, and rechristened as E-Systems under the leadership of John W. Dixon, its new president and chairman.

As the presence of William Raborn on its board shows, E-Systems maintained a cozy relationship with the CIA and other US intelligence agencies. E-Systems has attempted to keep this relationship under wraps, with much of the company's projects shrouded under confidentiality agreements. Nevertheless, there have been occasions when the company's intelligence ties have bubbled up to the surface. In 1994, for example, *Washington Post* journalist John Mintz wrote that:

> CIA employees who are experts in high technology are "automatic hires" for the firm, a former CIA official said. "E-Systems made it a point to say, 'When you retire, come work for us.'" ... "E-Systems has one of the more unique relationships with the agency," he added, calling it "chummy."
>
> A staff member of a congressional intelligence committee said E-Systems is "virtually indistinguishable" from the agencies it serves. "Congress will ask for a briefing from E-Systems, and the [CIA] program manager shows up," he said. "Sometimes he gives the briefing. They're interchangeable."[82]

Among the known collaborations between E-Systems and the Agency included the construction of "ground stations in China" used to "eavesdrop on Soviet satellites in flight" – the information from which was then "shared with China."[83] In another notable instance, taking place in 1975, E-Systems purchased Air Asia, one of the CIA's proprietary airlines that was hidden as a civilian-staffed aviation company.[84] The sale garnered considerable controversy at the time as E-Systems only paid $1.9 million for the front company, despite the fact that Air Asia's net worth was calculated to be approximately $3.4 million at the time of sale.[85]

Several years later, in 1977, E-Systems became involved in Operation Condor, a DEA and US Customs supported Mexican government initiative to crack down on the ballooning drug trade. It was a completely different operation than the notorious South American operation of the same name.

On hand to support Condor was the CIA, with Evergreen International Aviation providing Mexican authorities with planes and pilots.[86] That same year, Evergreen had absorbed Intermountain Aviation, a CIA proprietary airline, and placed the "former head of all CIA air operations" on its board of directors. E-Systems was contracted to provide maintenance for Evergreen's planes actively participating in Condor, a task no doubt related to the company's wider contracts with US Customs for electronic technology and aircraft maintenance for drug interdiction purposes.[87]

Remarkably (and perhaps unsurprisingly), Condor was an abject failure, and it effectively allowed the drug trade to continue unabated. Where planes were supposed to be spraying herbicides on drug crops, the tanks were frequently found to instead contain water, while officials involved with the program had a tendency to shake down "drug cultivators in exchange for protection from spraying."[88]

Tom Farer notes that Condor in fact encouraged the deepening centralization and concentration of the drug trade within a small handful of powerful cartel-linked groups. "As a result of this policy initiative," he writes, "the Mexican drug industry came under the control of entrepreneurial organizations that were fewer in number, stronger in resources, and more dangerous to society and government."[89] Chief among the drug traffickers that rose in prominence in this time was Felix Gallardo and his criminal associate, Juan Matta Ballesteros. As noted in chapter 7, both of these figures were linked to Contra support activities and, in the case of Matta, to CIA-linked aviation companies.

E-Systems may have also been linked to the activities of both Ted Shackley and his team and that of Robert Vesco in Libya. As discussed in chapter 6, a point of intersection between these two networks was the British company Lonrho, its infamous leader Tiny Rowland, and his right-hand man Edward Du Cann. To briefly recap: Du Cann, whose duties extended beyond Lonrho to act as a liquidator for the Vesco-looted Investors Overseas Services (IOS), sat on the board of a Lonrho freight subsidiary called Tradewinds, which was accused of running arms into Libya on behalf of Shackley's close associate, Edwin Wilson. At this same time, Vesco was involved in a number of Libyan affairs, several of which blew back on the Carter administration – an administration despised by Shackley and a number of his "former" CIA colleagues. One of these was an attempt to get embargoed planes released to Libya, which included a number of C-130 aircraft.

At around this same time, E-Systems was in talks to update a number of C-130s, located in Australia, that a group of individuals was attempting to sell to Libya.[90] This group was led by L.T. "Bill" Ransom, head of a Texas-based aircraft broker firm called Global Jet Sales, and included Max

Park of Parmax, Inc. (which shared addresses with Ransom's Global Jet); Stanley Mann, a petroleum broker; and Admiral E.L. "Whitey" Feightner, an aviation consultant and retired military officer.[91] Also involved was Jack Richards, an aircraft broker from Oklahoma City. Richards' firm, Onyx Aviation, was later named during the Iran-Contra hearings as one of the firms that had provided aircraft for the Contras in Nicaragua.[92]

Ransom's attempts to sell the C-130s to Libya ultimately fell apart, and it isn't clear if E-Systems ended up working on the aircraft. The route the planes ended up taking, however, is still quite interesting. Aviation records show that a number of these planes passed from the hands of Ransom and Park to Ford & Vlahos, a powerful San Francisco law firm.[93] The "Ford" in Ford & Vlahos was John Ford, who had ties to another aviation company, T & G Aviation, based in Chandler, Arizona.[94] Chandler is a suburb of Phoenix roughly an hour's drive from Marana, where the aforementioned CIA-linked Evergreen Aviation maintained its aircraft maintenance center.[95] According to whistle-blower Gary Eitel (himself a former Evergreen pilot), T & G-owned aircraft "were doing work for Southern Air and Evergreen in Saudi Arabia and Abu Dhabi" that was disguised as contract work for Bechtel.[96]

From Ford & Vlahos, the C-130s ended up in a number of intriguing locations. Records show that a number ended up in the hands of an aviation concern owned by the Aboitiz family in the Philippines, who had grown particularly wealthy and powerful under the Marcos regime.[97] Another was sold to AVIACO of Bogotá, Colombia, a company described in the press as part of the "'air wing' of the Colombian cartels," having been "involved in [drug] smuggling since 1982."[98] Yet another ended up parked at Mena, Arkansas, before being bought by a Miami company, African Air Trans.[99] This is the same C-130 that was discussed in the previous chapter, having been seized by Customs for arms trafficking violations. As discussed in that chapter, African Air Trans was itself a front for an "unnamed Israeli living in Panama."

The question remains: was the initial attempt, which involved E-Systems, to sell these C-130s to Libya part of the broader calculus involving that country by Vesco, Shackley, and others? Answers to this question remain elusive, though there is one provocative tie that suggests these may all have been interrelated incidents.

Stanley Mann, the member of Ransom's group that attempted the initial C-130 sale, was closely connected to and had provided financing for Andrew Racz, the head of Racz International, a subsidiary of the Philips,

Appel & Walden brokerage house in New York.[100] Declassified US State Department cables show that Racz was also associated with Tiny Rowland (as well as Henry Kissinger), and had acted as a back-channel between the government and the Lonrho chief concerning African affairs.[101]

THE MAN WHO KNEW TOO MUCH

Not only was the PROMIS scandal linked with the US Department of Justice, the CIA, and Israeli intelligence, but major elements of organized crime could also be found in its web. For instance, one of the key figures involved in the PROMIS scandal was Robert Booth Nichols. Nichols served on the board of First Intercontinental Development Corporation (FIDCO) alongside Clint Murchison Jr., a business tycoon with organized crime connections; and Robert Maheu, the private investigator who was an intermediary between the CIA and organized crime and who author Lisa Pease has linked to the 1968 assassination of Robert F. Kennedy.[102] Maheu was FIDCO's vice president while Nichols was the company's Senior Vice President and Chairman of the Investment Committee.[103] FIDCO, per Riconosciuto, was "an NSC [National Security Council] corporate cut-out […] created to be the corporate vehicle to secure the financing for the reconstruction of the cities of Beirut and Damour in Lebanon." Riconosciuto further alleged that, in his dealings with FIDCO in the Middle East, he "came in contact with the PROMIS software" via a system from "IBM Tel Aviv."[104]

In 1981, Nichols formed Meridian Arms with a man named Peter Zokosky. Meridian would later join Wackenhut in its Cabazon-related activities. Michael Riconosciuto had also been Meridian's vice president on the board of directors alongside Nichols and Zokosky for a brief period.[105] Meridian Arms was a subsidiary of Meridian International Logistics, and that company's board of directors included Nichols, Zokosky and Eugene Gianquinto. Gianquinto was notably the president of the Home Entertainment Division of MCA, the entertainment giant that was later acquired by the Bronfmans' Seagram Company and reincorporated as Universal Studios. One of MCA's top executives, as noted in chapter 1, was Lew Wasserman, who was deeply connected to organized crime, particularly through Moe Dalitz, and was largely responsible for Ronald Reagan's political career.[106] When Reagan took office, the Department of Justice had been probing MCA's ties to organized crime, but – thanks to help from Reagan's Attorney General Ed Meese – the probe was squashed. The Wasserman-Reagan relationship and Wasserman's organized crime ties are discussed in more detail in the next chapter. Another member of the MCA board at this time, Senator Howard Baker, would also later "advise" Robert Maxwell about his entry into New York in the early 1990s, alongside John Tower and Robert Keith Gray. Baker was also a business partner of Maxwell's at that time (see Chapter 15 for more).[107]

According to Cheri Seymour, both Gianquinto of MCA and Nichols of Meridian "had a close working relationship with the Justice Department" and Gianquinto, in a recorded FBI wiretapped conversation referenced by Seymour, took credit for contacting Meese to have the DOJ's MCA-organized crime probe quashed in the early 1980s.[108] One of the special prosecutors for the Justice Department who had worked on the MCA case, Richard Stavin, obtained documents that identified Nichols as "a money launderer with ties to the Gambino crime family and the Yakuza [Japanese organized crime]."[109]

Per Seymour, Nichols also had ties to Ferdinand Marcos of the Philippines, having "reportedly laundered between $50-200 million" on his behalf.[110] Nichols was also investigated by the FBI in the late 1970s for money laundering for Marcos as well as drug smuggling.[111] That investigation also found evidence that Nichols had also sold weapons to the Marcos government and other foreign governments. Much of his money laundering activities, including those on behalf of the Marcos family reportedly involved the Swiss banking system. The FBI found that Nichols had claimed to have had access to "highly sophisticated computers in Switzerland with detailed information on a number of subjects," suggesting that Nichols may have been using PROMIS as part of his Swiss laundromat.[112]

Nichols, according to the FBI report, had also claimed "to have highly placed sources in numerous foreign government agencies which can detect any investigation initiated against him. One of these individuals was supposedly a United States Senator with much seniority whom Nichols claimed to utilize in the trafficking of narcotics and money laundering."[113] Given that Nichols, via Eugene Gianquinto, was just one degree of separation from Senator Howard Baker, who was also on the board of the organized crime-linked MCA and later engaged in suspect business activities with Robert Maxwell, the Tennessee senator seems like a potential suspect.

Nichols also loomed large in the tragic fate of journalist Danny Casolaro. Casolaro had been investigating an international crime syndicate he termed "the Octopus" at the time of his death in 1991. Casolaro believed that this "Octopus" involved powerful individuals in the private and public sectors as well as the criminal underworld and that they were collectively responsible for some of the biggest scandals of the 1980s, including Iran-Contra, BCCI and the theft of the PROMIS software.

"Dan dealt in this nebulous, shadowy world," Dick O'Connell, a friend of Casolaro's and publisher of *Washington Crime News Services* said in mid-August 1991 to the *Associated Press*. "He was saying 'they' took that INSLAW software and sold it overseas and took the profits from that and turned it into arms for the Contras. … That's what he was working on and he told me he thought BCCI was the conduit for all of these money transactions."[114]

Cheri Seymour notes that Casolaro's work on "the Octopus" had "encompassed the October Surprise story, the Inslaw computer software case, the Iran/Contra affair, the BCCI scandal, and MCA entertainment corporation, all overlapping and interconnecting into one network." Before his death, Casolaro had called this network "a dirty CIA 'Old Boy' network" that, per Seymour, "had begun working together in the 1950s around the Albania covert operations. These men had gotten into the illegal gun and drug trade back then and had continued in that business ever since."[115]

Shortly before his death, Casolaro had told friends and family that he was close to concluding his investigation. Several people close to him had seen documents involving money transfers involving BCCI and the World Bank to people involved in these scandals, such as Earl Brian and Adnan Khashoggi.

In July 1991, something strange happened and Casolaro suddenly became "somewhat alarmed." It appears to have been a threat from Robert Booth Nichols, who had initially been a source for Casolaro, before warning him "If you continue this investigation, you will die." Casolaro, later that same month, learned from former DOJ special prosecutor Richard Stavin that Nichols was deeply enmeshed in organized crime networks as well as intelligence networks.[116]

Shortly thereafter, on August 5th, 1991, Michael Riconosciuto contacted Bill Hamilton and asked him to use his sources to dig up info on a man named Mike Abbell.[117] Abbell had worked at the Department of Justice in the early 1980s, where he was director of the Office of International Affairs before going into private legal practice.[118] Hamilton ultimately passed the task of investigating Abbell over to Casolaro, who contacted his own sources about ties between Abbell, Robert Booth Nichols, and Gilberto Rodriguez, an early leader of the Cali cartel. The Cali cartel's connections to Contra support efforts and to E-Systems were discussed in chapter 7 and earlier in this chapter, respectively. Years later, in 1994, Abbell's law offices were raided by the FBI in connection with an investigation to Cali cartel money laundering and Abbell was subsequently charged and convicted for being directly involved in the cartel's activities.[119]

The following day, Casolaro traveled to Martinsburg, Virginia, to meet with some sources to get the final piece of the puzzle and "bring back the head of the Octopus." Two days after arriving in Martinsburg, Casolaro was found dead in his hotel room and his briefcase full of his research notes and evidence was missing. His death was ruled a suicide.

Many, including Casolaro's family, do not believe that Casolaro committed suicide. A week before his death, Casolaro told his brother he had been receiving death threats and the manner in which he died, deep slashes in his arms, was not consistent with Casolaro's well-known squeamishness around even minor amounts of blood. Speculation only grew following the FBI investigation, given that the FBI lied to Congress, pressured its own agents not to question whether it was a suicide, and lost 90 percent of its files related to Casolaro's death – among other glaring inconsistencies.[120]

In a 1994 letter provided to *me in 2019* by Inslaw Inc., Inslaw lawyer Charles Work told then-Assistant Attorney General John Dwyer that one of Inslaw's confidential sources in government had stated that Casolaro had been injected with a substance that deadened his nerves from the neck down, explaining the apparent lack of struggle on Casolaro's part, and that the substance used had come from the US Army inventory.[121]

The person who had arranged Casolaro's final meeting before his death was a US military intelligence officer named Joseph Cuellar. Prior to Casolaro's death, Cuellar had promised to arrange a meeting between Casolaro and Peter Videnieks, "a Department of Justice contracting official with responsibility for the PROMIS software" who was a close associate of Earl Brian.[122] Videnieks, before joining the Department of Justice, had previously worked as a contracting officer at US Customs during the years of Operation Condor and was in a position where he could have handled contracts related to E-Systems and Evergreen International.

The same year that Casolaro died, there were several other suspicious deaths involving people directly connected to the PROMIS scandal or involved in Casolaro's investigation of "the Octopus" – including Alan Standorf, one of Casolaro's sources;[123] Robert Maxwell, father of Ghislaine Maxwell and the intelligence-linked salesman of the bugged PROMIS software;[124] and John Tower – the former Texas senator who assisted Maxwell in selling the bugged PROMIS software to the Los Alamos laboratories.[125] Other aspects of Robert Maxwell's death are dealt with in Chapter 15.

Around this same time, the PROMIS scandal or Inslaw Affair itself became too unruly, especially after several Congressional investigations concluded wrongdoing by the Justice Department and called for a special prosecutor to be appointed. That appointment was made by none other than the then-Attorney General under George H.W. Bush, William Barr. As previously mentioned in Chapter 8, Barr had not only had an alleged role in major aspects of Iran-Contra under the alias Robert Johnson, but he had begun his career at the CIA. As will be discussed in Chapter 11, Barr's employment with the CIA overlapped with his father's decision to hire Jeffrey Epstein at the Dalton School, which would prove essential in Epstein's rise to prominence in these same networks.

Early on, Barr essentially stonewalled Congress by denying Congressmen access to "privileged" documents related to PROMIS and Inslaw Inc., much like he had done years earlier when he stonewalled the Church Committee on behalf of the CIA. As a result, a Congressional hearing was held in December 1990 on Barr's continued refusal to make the documents available.[126] After considerable political pressure, Barr moved to appoint a special counsel to "investigate" the Inslaw affair, appointing a retired judge from Chicago named Nicholas Bua to serve in that role in September 1992.[127] Bua authored a 267-page report, which he completed in early 1993, that claimed to find no credible evidence to support the Hamilton's allegations and the report has been widely criticized as a "whitewash" of the whole situation.[128]

After Inslaw's Bill Hamilton distributed Inslaw's heavily detailed rebuttal of the "Bua report" to members of House Judiciary Committee, Congressmen Jack Brooks (D-TX) and Charlie Rose (D-NC) attempted to force an investigation of the Justice Department as it related to PROMIS as well as an investigation into the death of journalist Danny Casolaro and the payment of reparations to the Hamiltons. Despite their best efforts, and the continued efforts of the Hamiltons through the decades, the PROMIS scandal, Casolaro's death, and other matters that swirl around the entity Casolaro called "the Octopus" remain largely uninvestigated by the federal government (and most of mainstream media) to this day.

CDC and Tech Transfers

As previously mentioned, prior to Casolaro's death, those close to the journalist had seen documents involving money transfers involving the World Bank to people involved in these scandals, such as Earl Brian and Adnan Khashoggi. In addition, it was reported by economist and author J. Orlin Grabbe that this particular version of PROMIS in use by the World Bank was being used to track wire transfers "in connection with a money-laundering operation that went from BCCI London through the World Bank and into Caribbean institutions."[129]

The role of the World Bank in the PROMIS scandal has been largely unexplored. However, the trail left by the company that managed PROMIS for the financial institution, Control Data Corporation, itself leads to a different, yet parallel operation involving technology transfers to the Soviet Union. Both Robert Maxwell and, subsequently, the Gouletas family, close associates of Jeffrey Epstein, would have their own run-ins with the company.

Control Data Corporation was originally formed in 1946 under the name Engineering Research Associates (ERA). ERA had been created by a group of engineers who had worked for a wartime Naval division involved in code-breaking and cryptography called the Communications Supplementary Activity. The core ERA team eventually broke away from the original company and formed Control Data Corporation (CDC) in September 1957. From the beginning, CDC was a major defense contractor.

During the 1970s, CDC computers were installed at Sandia National Laboratories, which would become the target of Robert Maxwell's marketing of PROMIS roughly a decade later. CDC had developed special code expressly for the products it sold to Sandia, which – as previously mentioned – dealt with aspects of the US nuclear program.[130] CDC computers, also containing specially designed code, were also present at Oak Ridge Laboratories, which also played a role in development of the nuclear program.

CDC also had a long-standing relationship with the Soviet Union's nuclear laboratories and facilities during this same period. Congressional hearings from the mid-1970s revealed that:

> In 1968, a second-generation Control Data Corporation 1604 system was installed at the Dubna Soviet Nuclear Facility near Moscow. In 1972 [CDC] sold the Soviet Union a third-generation CDC 6200 system computer. For these systems, [CDC's] operating statement had improved by about $3 million dollars in the past three years. And the Soviet Union has gained 15 years in computer technology.[131]

As seen here, CDC's business in the USSR raised concerns that the company was engaging in technology transfers to the United States' ostensible arch-enemy at the height of the Cold War. Such concerns would continue to follow the company for decades.

Around this same period, in the early 1970s, CDC acquired the Commercial Credit Corporation (CCC), which had nearly gone bankrupt during the calamitous bankruptcy of Penn Central in 1970. That bankruptcy, the nation's largest until the collapse of Enron several decades later, is discussed in greater detail in the next chapter.[132] In the years that followed, CDC and its newly acquired subsidiary CCC would become involved with the networks of Shackley's "private CIA" and "rogue" CIA agent (and alleged sex blackmailer) Edwin Wilson.

As previously detailed in Chapter 7, CCC played a key role in the creation of Global International Airways, a company created in the late 1970s by Farhad Azima, an Iranian businessman reportedly tied to Iran's pre-revolutionary intelligence service – SAVAK. That airline had been launched with the aid of a "multi-million dollar loan from the Commercial Credit Corporation" and was allegedly tied to Shackley's network as well as Air America (known by this time as Southern Air Transport). Global International Airways had worked with EATSCO, the company tied to the Shackley-Cline "Private CIA" network that served as a "middle man" in arms deals.

Also noted in Chapter 6 is the fact that CDC itself, around 1976 or so, had directly hired Edwin Wilson as a consultant with the hopes that Wilson's contacts could help the company "unload some outdated computers on Third World countries." However, CDC appears to have leveraged Wilson's abilities for much more, as the "rogue" CIA agent was accused of bugging the US Army's Materiel Command on behalf of the company. Considering these associations and activities, CDC was likely much more than just a computer company and its public claims that the company was not involved in illicit, high-technology transfers to the Soviet Union seem dubious at best.

After the aforementioned Congressional hearing in 1974, CDC made an apparent move at increasing its role in technology transfers, despite political concern. By the late 1970s, they had established a new subsidiary called Worldtech, described in the press as "a division of Control Data Corp that does research and consulting on, and brokering of, technology transfers."[133]

Once Worldtech was established by CDC, it entered into a joint venture in 1979 with Greek publisher George Bobolas that was called Worldtech Hellas Ltd., where 70% was owned by Bobolas and 20% was owned by CDC. The owner of the remaining 10% was not disclosed in reports at the time.

A 1979 letter from one of Bobolas' companies to A. Afonin, identified as a "representative of the State Committee for Foreign Economic Relations of the USSR Council of Ministers," proposed the creation of a "joint development company using Worldtech for 'world-wide technology transfer' and stressed that 'Worldtech Hellas Ltd. will give a lot of help' to 'technology transfer on an international base.'"[134] After journalist Paul Anastasi published information about Bobolas and called him a "KGB agent of influence," one of his companies, Bobtrade, asserted that "no improper transfer of high technology was involved," while CDC moved to dissolve their partnership, likely due to bad publicity.[135]

Around the time that Worldtech was being created, CDC's then-executive vice president, Robert D. Schmidt, was part of the American Committee on US-Soviet Relations (ACUSR, previously the American Committee on East-West Accord). Other members at the time, specifically in 1977, included Robert Maxwell's lawyer and confidant, Samuel Pisar (stepfather to future US Secretary of State Anthony Blinken), as well as Thomas Watson Jr. of IBM, who would become US ambassador to the Soviet Union in 1979.[136] Another member was Paul Ziffren, previously discussed in Chapter 1 as a major figure in the organized crime networks that ran through Hollywood, including those tied up with Lew Wasserman and MCA. Ziffren's and Wasserman's families would later intermarry.

By the mid-1980s, Occidental Petroleum executives Armand Hammer and William McSweeney would also join the ACUSR. ACUSR member Samuel Pisar also represented Hammer's business interests. As previously mentioned in Chapter 7, Hammer served as a back channel between the Americans and the Soviets and had been involved in the entry of BCCI into the US financial system. Also noted was the fact that he had originally sought to acquire FGB himself for the purpose of financially blackmailing US politicians. It is also worth mentioning again that Hammer's father, Julius Hammer, had once served as a Soviet spy.[137]

Another member of the ACUSR was Joseph Filner, president of Noblemet International (later Newmet Corporation). Filner was extensively involved in USSR-US tech transfers. Filner's Noblemet created a joint venture for the purpose of tech transfers, which was called Multi-Arc. By 1984, CDC's Worldtech had become "a worldwide marketing representative for Multi-Arc."[138]

CDC would later recruit Minnesota governor Rudy Perpich after Perpich lost his re-election campaign in 1979. Perpich, a dentist by training, would specifically work for CDC overseas as "vice president and executive consultant to Control Data Worldtech Inc."[139] The *New York Times*, reporting on his hire by CDC in January 1979, stated that Perpich was expected to be based in Yugoslavia, but he said he could find himself in Hungary, Bulgaria or Rumania [sic]."[140] Robert Maxwell was also intimately involved with tech transfers in Eastern Europe, specifically in Bulgaria, which is discussed at the end of this chapter. Perpich, after working for Worldtech, would win another term as Minnesota's governor in 1983.

CDC would also recruit another influential politician, Walter Mondale, who was hired by CDC right after he left office as Jimmy Carter's vice president. CDC hired Mondale as a legal consultant and retained his services for $2,000 per month (about $6,360 in 2022 dollars).[141] Simultaneously, Mondale was also a consultant to Allen & Co, the company of the organized crime-linked Charles and Herbert Allen mentioned throughout this book. Mondale was not only a consultant to, but also a close friend of the Allen brothers. The Allen brothers also worked closely with organized crime interests as well as Leslie Wexner's "mentors" Max Fisher and Alfred Taubman (discussed in detail in chapter 13). As previously mentioned earlier in this chapter, Allen & Co. had a close business association with Earl Brian and had financed one of his attempts to buy out Bill Hamilton's Inslaw.

By 1983, CDC was providing its services to the World Bank's computer center and, that same year, the PROMIS software was found to be in use at that specific facility to keep track of wire transfers of money. This is according to a sworn statement that Inslaw Inc. obtained from David McCallum in 1995. In 1983, McCallum was working for CDC at the World Bank.

In my correspondence with Inslaw's Bill Hamilton, he stated the following: "According to an article in the *International Banking Regulator* dated January 17, 1994, U.S. Justice Department officials delivered the VAX version of PROMIS to the World Bank in 1983. The World Bank, as an international institution, is outside the reach of discovery of the U.S. courts. For its part, the World Bank declares that it has been unable to find any evidence that it ever possessed the VAX version of PROMIS."[142] Hamilton also relayed that he had once been informed of a connection between CDC and PROMIS that involved the Deputy Attorney General under Ed Meese, D. Lowell Jensen. However, he could no longer remember the specifics of that connection.

As previously mentioned, among the connections Danny Casolaro revealed to those close to him in the days and weeks before his death, he had specifically mentioned the World Bank. There was talk specifically about money transfers involving BCCI and the World Bank to individuals such as Earl Brian and Adnan Khashoggi. Given that the documentation of those transfers mysteriously disappeared from Casolaro's hotel room at the time of his death, CDC's apparent involvement with the World Bank's use of PROMIS takes on increased significance.

Also significant is the role CDC played during the 1990 visit of Mikhail Gorbachev, the then-leader of the Soviet Union, to the United States. During that trip, Gorbachev visited CDC headquarters alongside Rudy Perpich as well as Robert Maxwell. The Gorbachevs arrived in Minnesota immediately after a summit meeting in Washington with then-President George H.W. Bush.[143]

According to a report from the Minnesota Historical Society:

> Gorbachev most likely agreed to the visit [Minnesota] because several Minnesota-based corporations – especially the computer firm, Control Data Corporation – had long done business in the Soviet Union. When the corporation's officials learned that Gorbachev was interested in a post-summit tour, they passed the word to Perpich, who had worked for Control Data between his two terms as governor. Albert Eisele, who had been a consultant for Control Data and, earlier, was Vice President Walter Mondale's press secretary, drafted the governor's letter inviting the Gorbachevs. Former Control Data CEO Robert Price personally delivered the letter to the Soviet embassy on February 26, 1990.[144]

During the visit, Gorbachev attended a lunch at the governor's mansion, where Robert Maxwell and Rudy Perpich joined groups of Soviet and American officials. One of the American officials present was Condoleezza Rice, the future Secretary of State who was then a National Security Council staff member. Afterwards, there was a press conference where Robert Maxwell, in characteristic bombastic fashion, "announced that he would donate $50 million to help create a private research institution to be called the Gorbachev-Maxwell Institute of Technology." Maxwell said that the donation was "contingent on Perpich raising matching funds."[145] The institute was never launched.

After visiting Minnesota, Gorbachev next visited Silicon Valley, where he spent the week "trying to perfect the art of winning acceptance and investment from the captains of capitalism." A *Washington Post* article on his visit quoted John Sculley, then-head of Apple Computers as saying, "I think Gorbachev got to us ... We'll all be thinking about business with the Soviet Union in a way we wouldn't have if he hadn't come."[146]

MAXWELL AND MULTI-GROUP

Robert Maxwell's involvement in intelligence-linked technology transfers was considerable and went far beyond his tangential involvement with Control Data Corporation, as detailed above. The most important of these involved Maxwell's relationship with Bulgarian intelligence and his role in an operation known as "Neva."

Maxwell had long been interested in Bulgaria, even before he was first brought into Mossad's fold in the early 1960s. In one of his earliest meetings with Vladimir Kryuchkov, the KGB chief and one of the most powerful of Maxwell's "sources," Maxwell had "raised the possibility that Bulgaria might be a country where he could invest his money away from prying eyes in the City of London and Wall Street." Kryuchkov later granted him permission to establish a "financial bunker in the Bulgarian capital, Sofia."[147] Maxwell, years later and after he established a close relationship with Bulgarian leadership and the top figures in its intelligence service, would go on to sell the bugged PROMIS software to Bulgarian intelligence, the proceeds of which were laundered and eventually made available to finance Mossad's "black" operations.[148]

Out of Maxwell's associations with Bulgarian intelligence came a program called Neva. Neva, per Gordon Thomas, was "designed to be the single largest program for the mass-scale theft of US technology" and sought to "plunder every Western industrialized nation."[149] The program was operated by Bulgarian intelligence, whose agents would steal technology and bring it into Bulgaria, "usually under diplomatic cover."[150] Bulgarian companies owned by Maxwell would then re-engineer the stolen equipment and then those companies would resell those products to other Eastern bloc countries.

One of the men who developed Neva alongside Maxwell, Ognian Doinov, president of the Bulgarian Chamber for Industry and Trade from 1980 to 1984 and Bulgaria's Vice Premier from 1984 to 1986, claimed that Bulgarian intelligence agents involved in Neva had been covertly working "in Silicon Valley and other key technology centers" in the United States, as well as in Britain and other Western countries. There, they would steal "technology blueprints, actual software, even computers."[151]

According to Gordon Thomas, Robert Maxwell created an umbrella of companies for use in Neva within six months. Thanks to Maxwell, Thomas writes, "The country had become [...] the center of a thriving economy based upon whole-scale theft and money laundering." This growing business empire, Thomas asserts would later "grow into one of the most powerful crime syndicates in the world, embracing the Russian Mafia, the crime families of Bulgaria and, far away across the Atlantic, those in New York and, on the other side of the world, the crime families of Japan and Hong Kong."[152]

The beginnings of this crime syndicate can be found in the umbrella corporation that would combine the companies Maxwell had created to operate Neva – Multi-Group. Multi-Group would go on to "control a significant percentage of the global profits from gas, telecommunications, oil, gambling, and money laundering."[153] It would later emerge that Neva companies, many of which were now part of Multi-Group, were used as cover by Mossad with Maxwell's blessing.[154]

John Patrick O'Neill, FBI executive agent-in-charge in New York until 2001, would later say the following about Maxwell and Multi-Group:

> …in many ways Maxwell was at the heart of the global criminal network. Beginning with his Bulgarian connection he showed how to structure a network that grew into financially powerful criminal corporations whose power would extend to the South American drug cartels, the Tongs and the Triads, the Russian Mafia and the Japanese Yakuza. They were all there before. But the way Robert Maxwell set up things up, they would all come together in Multi-Group in its early years. His last contribution was not that he just robbed his pension funds. It was that he was the man who set in motion a true coalition of global criminals.[155]

Another Maxwell company that was based in the US has been suspected of playing some role in the Neva program. In 1985, Maxwell created Pergamon-Brassey, registering the company in McLean, Virginia. He and his son Kevin were listed as directors. Two years later, in 1987, the company underwent a major shake-up and former Senator John Tower, who had been a major accomplice of Maxwell's in the PROMIS scandal, became chairman of its board.[156] Prominent former generals of the US and British militaries were also added to the company's board.

According to Bill Hamilton of Inslaw Inc., Pergamon-Brassey seemed to have more connections to PROMIS aside from Robert Maxwell and John Tower:

> In 1987, Pergamon-Brassey hired two senior computer-systems executives who resigned at the same time from the Meese Justice Department's Justice Data Center. The proprietary IBM mainframe

version of PROMIS had been operating at the Justice Data Center since the early eighties. George Vaveris resigned his estimated $90,000 a year Senior Executive Service position as director of the Justice Data Center to become vice-president for technical services at the tiny Pergamon-Brassey. He told a colleague at the Justice Department his new salary would be in excess of $200,000 a year.[157]

Pergamon-Brassey was a specialist company, with no more than six employees on its payroll at any given time. While it did publish books on topics related to national security and intelligence, it primarily dealt with software; software that some suspect may have been part of Maxwell's sprawling, Neva-related operations.[158]

A year after Pergamon-Brassey was revamped and Tower installed as its chairman, Maxwell became involved with the notorious Russian mobster Semion Mogilevich. Mogilevich was part of a plan that had been pitched to Maxwell and designed by Vladimir Kryuchkov. Gordon Thomas relays that plan as follows:

> Even more fearful at the pace at which perestroika was accelerating, Kryuchkov said that for the KGB to remain a potent force he wanted to establish "over six hundred commercial enterprises." They would all have links to the West. Just as Maxwell's companies provided cover for Mossad's katsas, Kryuchkov envisaged his companies would provide similar protection for KGB operatives. […]
>
> The six hundred companies would each employ a quota of senior party members to provide them with an income during the difficult days ahead in the transition from Communism to capitalism. Through genuine trading links, the companies would obtain access to the very heart of capitalism: Wall Street and the City of London and the Bourses of Western Europe. Its staffs would then learn the innermost secrets of the West's banking system, the wellspring of all capitalism. Eventually it might even be possible to destabilise Western economies – and pave the way for the return of Communism.[159]

The year he met Maxwell, in 1988, Mogilevich was granted an Israeli passport thanks to Maxwell's lobbying of Israel's government on his behalf. With this passport, Mogilevich soon established a web of seemingly legitimate companies in Israel, the United States, and the United Kingdom which were used to launder his illicit profits from his considerable involvement in weapons deals, drug trafficking, and human trafficking. A year after meeting Maxwell, Mogilevich's criminal profits grew considerably, reaching an estimated $40 billion annually. [160]

Maxwell subsequently became a business partner of Mogilevich's as well as Ivo Janchev, a Bulgarian intelligence officer linked up with Mogilevich and other organized crime figures in the Eastern bloc. Janchev was also allegedly a part of Kryuchkov's plan and was tasked with acting as "the front man to make contact with several Russians with businesses in the West."[161]

Maxwell would ultimately play a crucial role in allowing these organized crime interests to enter into the world of "respectable" international finance. It is unknown if anything ever resulted from Kryuchkov's plan, but Maxwell's connections to Mogilevich, Janchev, and other unsavory characters would undeniably have a considerable impact on the expansion of the mobsters' legitimate and illegitimate businesses and foster the expansion of the "global criminal network" that Maxwell had helped spawn through Multi-Group.

FROM COLD WARS TO HOT MONEY

According to Tom Bower's biography of Maxwell, the tycoon spent a considerable amount of time in Moscow in 1991. There, he was negotiating the purchase of approximately $1 billion worth of gold.[162] The sellers were reportedly KGB officers, and the outcome of the exchange has been shrouded in secrecy. Per the account in Bower's book, Maxwell went to Moscow to secure the gold, only to discover that it had been "lost."[163] Other versions of the tale suggest that Maxwell wasn't acting alone, and that he was once again operating in tandem with the Mossad. According to this account, the gold actually found its way to Israel – not an uncommon destination for assets that had flowed out of the Eastern bloc during and after the collapse of the Soviet Union.

Throughout 1991, stories of massive outflows of Soviet gold circulated about, with many naming sums considerably higher than the $1 billion that Maxwell was purportedly seeking to acquire. In spring of that year, a report appeared in the *Manchester Guardian* that a "'package' worth $12 billion" was moved from the USSR outside of "normal export channels."[164] Several months later Grigori Yavlinski, the Russian economist tapped by Gorbachev to help oversee Soviet economic reforms, told stunned world leaders at a G-7 summit that Russia's gold reserves had dwindled from 2,000-3,000 tons to 240 tons.[165] Even before the Soviet Union collapsed, looting was taking place on a colossal scale.

According to Claire Sterling's book *Thieves World*, an army of strange and dubious figures descended upon Europe in 1991, offering to sell off massive amounts of Russian gold. One of these figures, subsequently well-known in conspiracy circles for his questionable claims, was an American mob-linked conman named Leo Wanta. In league with several mafioso and other "faceless investors," Wanta blanketed trading houses across the globe "with faxed offers to sell two thousand tons of gold."[166] At the same time, Roberto Coppola, an Italian boasting credentials identifying him as a member of the Knights of Malta, was likewise trying to sell off the exact same amount of gold. According to a source for Sterling that she refers to only as "Mr. X," "Roberto Coppola was the source of all the gold that Wanta was offering."[167]

Were there any links between the Wanta-Coppola gold sales and Maxwell's attempts to buy up Soviet gold? One tantalizing possibility can be found in the ATLAS dossier, discussed in chapter 7, which outlined a criminal network connected to the corrupt Belgian-Costa Rican diplomat Felix Przedborski. The dossier names an American company called New Republic as one of the vehicles through which Przedborski's group laundered money, mostly profits accrued through arms and drug trafficking.[168] Documents reproduced by Sterling in her book show that Wanta was offering the gold through his US-based company, New Republic/USA Financial Group, Ltd.[169]

There were a number of ties, albeit links one or two steps removed, between Przedborski's group and Maxwell's network. There is the fact, for instance, that Bruce Rappaport called upon the legal resources of a law office where Przedborski's son was a partner. Rappaport and Maxwell had a number of mutual associates that included attorney Samuel Pisar, banker Edmond Safra, and Russian mobster Simeon Mogilevich. Along similar lines, the ATLAS dossier identified Safra's Republic National Bank as one of its money laundering outlets. There was also the reason the dossier had been drafted in the first place: the looting-induced collapse of a company called Comuele S.A. by the associate of the Przedborski group. According to the dossier, Comuele had been taken over by "Russians," and injected with money from Israel.[170] During the 1980s, Comuele was owned by Lonrho, the corporate flagship of Maxwell's friend Tiny Rowland.[171]

Throughout the later period of the Cold War, the intelligence services of the Eastern bloc established trading companies and corporate fronts, often obscured behind walls of ownership, through which they could simultaneously conduct espionage operations and obtain hard currency for cash-starved states. East Germany's KoKo was one example, as was Kintex in Bulgaria (which Maxwell certainly would have done business with).

These and entities like Bulgaria's Multi-Group subsequently became the conduits through which capital flowed out of the Eastern bloc as the Soviet Union buckled and collapsed. Maxwell's role in Multi-Group shows his direct involvement in these activities. As discussed earlier in this chapter, Maxwell had struck a deal with KGB chief Vladimir Kryuchkov to help manage the secret service's economic fronts in Europe and elsewhere.[172] The 1991 gold deals likely arose from precisely these sorts of strategic alignments.

Another KGB front that became a vehicle for capital flight that was tied to the Maxwell family was Nordex, based in Vienna and launched with the ostensible purpose of exporting fertilizer. The full details of the relationship between Nordex and the Maxwells will be discussed in chapter 16, but for now it is enough to mention that the firm's founder, Grigori Loutchansky, had been a rising star in the Latvian Communist Party under the sponsorship of Boris Pugo, the soon-to-be chairman of the Latvian section of the KGB.[173] Perhaps importantly, Pugo had been closely tied to KGB chief Vladimir Kryuchkov, who – according to Gordon Thomas – was the one who reached out to Maxwell concerning corporate cover for Soviet economic espionage operations.[174]

After a stint in prison for theft, Loutchansky landed a job as the fertilizer exporter for Adahzi, a state-owned import-export company. In 1989, after a year at Adahzi, he launched Nordex, which soon boasted numerous subsidiaries; these were dedicated to shipping and freight transport and were organized along with joint ventures with late Soviet companies. Soon Nordex was swimming in the world of offshore finance, with "multi-million dollar transfers with obscure companies, incorporated in tax havens such as Ireland, Lichtenstein, and the Isle of Man" making up a significant chunk of its shadowy business activity.[175] It also indulged in global black market trades. According to intelligence sources cited by Andrew and Leslie Cockburn, Nordex was deeply "involved in arms, drugs, the whole nine yards."[176] This also entailed the trade of nuclear materials such as uranium, plutonium, and beryllium.

Reports in the Swiss press identify Nordex's co-founder as none other than Marc Rich, an allegation reiterated in US government documents.[177] Bruce Raphael writes in his book *King Energy*, that Rich utilized Nordex to snap up Russian oil refineries that were being auctioned off during the post-Soviet economic transition.[178] Yet another player in Nordex was the

Swiss attorney Iso Lenzlinger, known for his status as a "financial juggler" who had "sat on over 100 boards of directors" and spent time as the secretary of Zug, Switzerland's official trade association.[179] According to press reports, "Lenzlinger maintained connections with western and eastern secret service agents."[180] One of his clients had been Guenther Forgber, the Stasi's front-man in running the West German trading company KoKo.[181] In a set of circumstances reminiscent of Control Data Corporation's Eastern bloc activities, Forgber was involved in the acquisition and transfer of high technology from the West.[182]

During the 1990s, Nordex's money laundering activities linked it with a company, registered in New Jersey and active in New York City and London, called Benex International Co., Inc. Benex's offices, located in the New York borough of Queens, "shared the same building with two companies connected to … Loutchansky."[183] Authorities investigating Russian mob-linked money laundering activities also found the fingerprints of Marc Rich at Benex. Wire transfers were discovered between Benex and "Glencore of Rich"—though the transactions took place after Rich had departed from Glencore.[184] Both Rich and Glencore denied that they had done any sort of business with Benex.

The most glaring connections between Nordex and Benex were found in Europe. During the mid-1990s, Benex moved as much as $9 billion through a handful of companies in Paris, all of which shared the same office. The most important of these was Kama France, controlled by brothers Igor and Oleg Berezovsky (whether they were related to the better-known Russian oligarch Boris Berezovsky is unknown) and owned by a Swiss company called Kama Trade AG. Italian investigators found that Kama Trade was "said to be a member of the Nordex group of companies."[185] One of Kama's "substantial shareholders" was a man named Andreas Marissov, a director and shareholder in another firm called IFS Fracht-Service—a subsidiary of Nordex.[186] Finally, Kama Trade was managed by Lenzlinger & Partners, a trust headed by the aforementioned Iso Lenzlinger.[187]

Benex also arose in investigations into the financial activities of Maxwell's most notorious criminal associate, Simeon Mogilevich. Money had been moved through bank accounts held by Benex to YBM Magnex International, a Pennsylvania company that had merged with a large Hungarian firm "that sold industrial magnets and military hardware."[188] YBM was firmly under the control of Mogilevich, and had been capitalized with funds from Arigon Ltd., the "heart of his criminal empire."[189] Within four years of its launch, YBM grew to a billion dollar company, and embarked on an ambitious plan to use the Canadian stock market as a means of money laundering via a publicly-traded shell company. That effort, however, was unsuccessful.

Benex was just one part of a vast and much more complicated money laundering network that encompassed Mogilevich and a number of Russian oligarchs as well as newly-minted private banks operating in the wildly unregulated markets of the former Soviet Union. The company had been formed by Peter Berlin and his wife, Lucy Edwards, an officer in the Eastern European Division of Bank of New York (BONY).

When Benex moved hot money on behalf of Nordex and Mogilevich, it was using accounts the pair had set up at the bank, and at their offices in Queens. Berlin and Edwards had installed BONY's wire-transfer technology, Micro/Ca$h-Register, on their computers. When the pair were finally busted for money laundering activities, Edwards confessed that she had been working under the assumption that what they had been doing was "consistent with the practice of [BONY's] Eastern European Division."[190]

A lawsuit brought against BONY in the Southern District Court of New York disclosed that BONY executives were themselves close to Mogilevich. The head of the bank's Eastern European Division, Natasha Gurfinkel, was revealed to "have contacts with Mogilevich" via her husband, Konstantin Kagalovsky. Interestingly, Konstantin, a former Soviet economist, was Russia's representative to the IMF from 1992 through 1995, and was very close with the teams carrying out the privatization of former state-owned enterprises.[191] According to the suit, BONY's security personnel contacted the bank's chairman and CEO, Thomas Renyi, concerning these ties. "Renyi," reads the legal complaint, "'interviewed' Gurfinkel about the matter, and no action was taken."[192]

BONY's connection to the former Eastern bloc arose from the close relationship between the bank and Bruce Rappaport. Between 1989 and 1990, BONY purchased the stake held in Rappaport's Inter Maritime Bank (IMB) by BCCI front-men, leading IMB to be rechristened as Bank of New York-Inter Maritime Bank (BONY-IMB).[193] Immediately following this restructuring, Rappaport went about increasing his business in the Soviet Union. In August 1990, Rappaport met with Gorbachev in Moscow to discuss a series of joint ventures between the Inter Maritime complex and Soviet state-owned enterprises. Curiously, this meeting took place just one month after the encounter between Gorbachev and Maxwell in Minnesota.

Soon, a number of joint ventures were announced. Most involved collaborations with Soviet shipbuilding enterprises, which were set up to boost the Eastern bloc's export capacities. Others were to be dedicated to port construction, cruise lines, and to oil and gas exploration in Siberia.[194] With Paul Helliwell's old banking partner Burton Kanter working hard on the legal dimensions, IMB-BONY fostered ties to a number of Soviet-controlled banking entities. Correspondent banking relations were set up between a handful of joint-stock banks and IMB-BONY, which only increased in number when the Soviet Union relaxed laws restricting private banking enterprises.

This became the backbone of BONY's push eastward. The Eastern European Division was established and Gurfinkel was installed as its head. Soon, she was "working closely with BONY-IMB personnel" and meeting personally with a number of "banking executives throughout Russia and Eastern Europe."[195] She put the Micro Ca$h-Register technology on display, and illustrated to interested parties how it could "route US dollar denominated currency to a web of offshore banking entities."[196] Just as BONY-IMB had done before, BONY began to accumulate a vast number of Russian correspondent banks.

One particularly interesting bank that BONY and BONY-IMB were tied to was the European Union Bank (EUB), which had been named as a money laundromat used by Russian organized crime figures. With operations set up in Antigua, EUB had been established by Alexander Konanykhine, who just a few years prior had organized the All-Russian Exchange Bank (AREB) at the behest of the KGB. Through AREB, Konanykhine "aided and abetted the movement of approximately $300 million [or up to] $1 billion, to the West, from November 1991 through May 1992."[197] When Konanykhine turned his attention to Antigua, BONY and BONY-IMB weren't the only Rappaport-linked entities that he did business with. EUB also maintained ties to Rappaport's own Antiguan bank, Swiss-American, which he had set up with Burton Kanter and Marvin Warner – the close friend and business partner of Edward DeBartolo. As will be noted in chapter 13, Edward DeBartolo was not only a close business associate of Leslie Wexner, but also a major associate of organized crime.

BONY's Eastern European banking activities took on sophisticated technological dimensions. Besides Micro Ca$h-Register, the bank took steps to develop what it called "cyphergrams," an encrypted communication system to allow for more direct interactions between BONY, its correspondent banks, and the offshore network of banks and businesses that they used to move money.[198] Similarly, databases were developed that provided code-names for the participants, tabulated ownership shares in offshore entities, and tracked money dispersal. This and the other systems were marketed to various Russian banks in BONY's client list.

Both the cyphergrams and the database systems were part of an effort to help develop a technique created by Gurfinkel, the manager of Inkombank (one of BONY's largest Russian banking clients), and a mysterious individual named Bob Klein, called "prokutki", or "spinning around.'" As the Southern District of New York suit against BONY described it, "spinning around" was an elaborate means of laundering money around the world:

> After a major "investment" was placed by a Russian customer with Inkombank or one of its satellite offshore companies, BONY would execute a series of electronic funds transfers (EFTs) from the Inkombank U.S. dollar accounts to specific offshore front companies and bank accounts. Usually, several layers of these electronic funds transfers to offshore entities were executed in succession, hence the name "spinning around." The ultimate goal of the "spinning around" scheme was to obscure and disguise the true origin of the funds being moved through the BONY accounts. The "spinning around" scheme allowed Inkombank's customer to evade payment of Russian taxes and duties, and provided the ability to launder proceeds from illegal acts. The conspirators generated "commission" payments, or "skim," based on a percentage of the total amount of money moved through the network out of Russia. The commissions, also referred to as "consulting fees," were ultimately diverted for the benefit of the conspirators through BONY to offshore entities.[199]

To make matters even more complicated, the existence of Bob Klein himself remains an open question. In various legal declarations and investigations, he has been described as "a close associate and representative of both Rappaport and [BONY chairman Thomas] Renyi."[200] Two BONY employees testified under oath that they had met Klein, but neither any BONY-IMB office logs nor BONY internal paperwork ever mentioned his name.

Alan Block and Constance Weaver, authors of the most definitive work on Rappaport and his decades of corruption, concluded that Klein was something of a fiction deployed to obscure the inner-workings of BONY's criminal activities. "We … have met the man who invented Klein," they write. While they don't name this individual, they do pass along the ominous statement that he gave them: "How can we ever know who someone really is in any case – Passports can be faked – Records can be forged – How can we really know?"[201]

This financial maze came crumbling down in August 1998, thanks to an untimely intervention by a surprising party: Republic National Bank (RNB), the bank controlled by Maxwell's close friend Edmond Safra. RNB drafted a "suspicious activities report" and turned it over to the treasuries, outlining evidence of strange transactions between RNB, BONY, and a handful of companies – including Benex.[202] On August 5th, Lewis Shiliro at the Justice Department sent a letter to Dov Schlein, chairman of RNB, thanking him for the bank's report. In the letter, Shiliro wrote that RNB had assisted "the New York Office of the Federal Bureau of Investigation in an ongoing major money laundering investigation."[203]

Suspicions have been raised about the supposed altruism of RNB, a bank that, as discussed in other chapters, was linked to Iran-Contra, Colombian cartel money laundering, the Przedborski group, and drug traffickers operating in the Middle East. Indeed, Block and Weaver write that RNB "had been obnoxiously crooked for some time," and may have taken "the 'high road' in order to protect itself."[204] In order words, RNB was getting out ahead of an FBI probe that might have exposed whatever banking affairs it was indulging in with BONY and its affiliates.

RNB itself had a long history of involvement with both Russian organized crime figures and with the troubled Russian economy in the years that followed the end of the Cold War. It held accounts, for example, used by Shabtai Kalmanovitch, a "Russian-Israeli entrepreneur" and insider to the world of the Russian-American mob operating from Brighton Beach.[205] Kalmanovitch brought with him, unsurprisingly, ties to the world of intelligence services. During the height of the Cold War, he was tied closely to the KGB and Mossad, and like Maxwell appears to have served as a back-channel between them and other intelligence agencies.[206] There have other been allegations that Kalmanovitch had served as a point of contact for Jonathan Pollard, the infamous Israeli spy operating within the US intelligence community.[207]

At the beginning of 1992, the US Federal Reserve began an ambitious project of injecting money into Russia by selling dollars to its leading banks. RNB was the Fed's principal agent in these transactions, which saw RNB obtaining dollars from the central bank, which would then be transported by courier to Russia to be sold. The sum of these dollars was soon in excess of $80 billion, far outstripping "the value of all the Russian rubles in circulation."[208] While the ostensible goal of the Federal Reserve was to preserve the beleaguered Russian banking industry, the flood of dollars was a boon for organized crime. Many of the banks that were on the receiving end of the trade were controlled by criminal enterprises, and not an insignificant portion of these funds was being funnelled into offshore zones by laundering webs like the one operated by BONY.

With the dollar flows leaving Russia at a rapid rate, and the general problem of large-scale capital flight, Russia was teetering on the brink of crisis by 1998. These factors were compounded by the Asian financial crisis, which led to a global dip in the supply of oil and other mineral resources and caused a decline in exports. At its climax, Russia faced a run on its banks. In response, the IMF put in motion an emergency "stabilization credit" for Russia valued at $11.2 billion, $4.8 billion of which was made immediately available to the country's central bank.[209] Yet within a month, the Russian financial crisis had set in, and RNB was alerting authorities about suspicious transactions. The reason for the former, and almost certainly the latter, was that the IMF credits had vanished into the financial void.

Following a forensic analysis of the complex webs of transfers involving the $4.8 billion credit, Russia's prosecutor-general, Yury Skuratov, announced that the lion's share of the funds had gone to commercial banks, who then used their correspondent banking relations to siphon the money back out of Russia.[210] Aiding and abetting this theft, he continued, was BONY. Meanwhile, in Czechoslovakia, investigators began tracing transactions between BONY and Komercini Bank. They were "certain these transactions were a part of the money-laundering operation of IMF funds."[211] Soon, independent investigations into BONY and the IMF credit were underway in financial centers from London to Zurich.

BONY was not the lone recipient of the money. The Russian Ministry of Finance charged that portions of the money had flowed into an account held at RNB that was used to "sell currency on foreign exchanges."[212] According to the Russian paper *Novaya Gazeta*, Edmond Safra was spooked by the financial crisis that had ensued, and began turning evidence over to the FBI. This timing here certainly overlaps with that of RNB blowing the whistle on BONY, while Safra was reported to have had "periodic conversations with FBI representatives [that] lasted almost a year."[213]

Oleg Lurye, a journalist for *Novaya Gazeta*, subsequently reported that in the fall of 1999, Safra was visited at his French estate by the Russian oligarch Boris Berezovsky, one of Russia's wealthiest individuals and a part of Boris Yeltsin's inner circle. Numerous press reports show that, by August of that year, the probes into BONY's money laundering had ensnared Berezovsky.[214] According to Lurye, Safra and Berezovsky had an increasingly angry conversation that lasted several hours, "after which Safra fled in panic to his heavily fortified Monte Carlo residence."[215]

Several months later, at the beginning December, Safra was dead. The official cause of death was suffocation from a fire in his Monte Carlo estate that had been caused by exceedingly bizarre circumstances. His bodyguards – many of whom were veterans of Mossad – were not present that night.[216] In early reports, "two hooded intruders" entered Safra's residences. They were fought off by one of Safra's nurses (and former Green Beret), Ted Maher, although he was stabbed in the process.[217] Maher then ushered Safra and his fellow nurse, Vivian Torrente, into a secure room, and proceeded to attempt to alert the authorities through, oddly enough, the only means at his disposal: starting a fire in a waste basket to set off the fire alarms. For whatever reason, it took the fire department and the police two and half hours to arrive on the scene. By the time they arrived, Safra and Torrente had already succumbed to the fire's fumes.[218]

The story very quickly changed. In the end, the court found that Maher himself was to blame. As the story goes, the military veteran had hoped to impress Safra by staging the attack and setting the fire. To make it seem more realistic, he had stabbed himself. Once in court, stories swirled that Maher was troubled and that his behavior had become increasingly erratic and lawyers speculated this was linked to a family history of schizophrenia. "[W]e can exclude with certainty all [conjectures] of any international conspiracy," declared the Safra family attorney, before adding that "The fact that Maher is unstable became apparent to us only after the accident."[219] Others were not convinced. According to *Vanity Fair* journalist Dominick Dunne, an associate of the Safra family told him that "Among friends, we avoid talking about it. It might not be what it is."[220]

What really happened that night in Monaco will likely never be known. However, Safra's fate closely parallels the murky death of his friend, Robert Maxwell, nearly a decade prior, amid a similar whirlwind of strange transactions and Eastern European intrigue. While other giants moving in these same shadows – like Bruce Rappaport – managed to slip away, the deaths of Maxwell and Safra are something like bookends to the 1990s, the decade when the US and its allies emerged victorious from the Cold War and everything belonging to the defeated went up for sale.

Endnotes

1   Gordon Thomas and Martin Dillon, *Robert Maxwell, Israel's Superspy: The Life and Murder of a Media Mogul*, 1st Carroll & Graf ed (New York: Carroll and Graf, 2002), 40-41, https://archive.org/details/robert-maxwell-israels-superspy-thomas-dillon-2002.

2   David Talbot, *The Devil's Chessboard: Allen Dulles, the CIA, and the Rise of America's Secret Government*, ePub (New York, NY: Harper Perennial, 2016), 12.

3   Stephen Buranyi, "Is the Staggeringly Profitable Business of Scientific Publishing Bad for Science?," *The Guardian*, June 27, 2017, https://www.theguardian.com/science/2017/jun/27/profitable-business-scientific-publishing-bad-for-science.

4   Thomas and Dillon, *Israel's Superspy*, 41.

5   Thomas and Dillon, *Israel's Superspy*, 51.

6   Leslie Wayne, "Socialist Millionaire: Robert Maxwell; Fighting to Be the Tabloid King on London's Fleet Street," *New York Times*, November 11, 1984, https://www.nytimes.com/1984/11/11/business/socialist-millionaire-robert-maxwell-fighting-be-tabloid-king-london-s-fleet.html.

7   Dennis Barker and Christopher Sylvester, "Robert Maxwell Obituary," *The Guardian*, November 6, 1991, https://www.theguardian.com/politics/1991/nov/06/obituaries.

8   Thomas and Dillon, *Israel's Superspy*, 41.

9   Robert Friedman, "The Most Dangerous Mobster in the World," *The Village Voice*, May 26, 1998, https://www.villagevoice.com/1998/05/26/the-most-dangerous-mobster-in-the-world/.

10   Thomas and Dillon, *Israel's Superspy*, 37.

11   Barker and Sylvester, "Maxwell Obituary."

12   "Paper Breaks Taboo on Shamir, Nazi Link ; *Jerusalem Post* Cites Stern Gang Past, Hits Stance on Peace Now," *Los Angeles Times*, March 7, 1989, https://www.latimes.com/archives/la-xpm-1989-03-07-mn-330-story.html; "Yitzhak Shamir: The Well-Liked Terrorist," *Consortium News*, July 2, 2012, https://consortiumnews.com/2012/07/02/yitzhak-shamir-the-well-liked-terrorist/.

13   Thomas and Dillon, *Israel's Superspy*, 35.

14   Philip Giraldi, "The Truth of Jonathan Pollard," *The American Conservative*, December 2, 2015, https://www.theamericanconservative.com/articles/the-truth-of-jonathan-pollard/.

15   Thomas and Dillon, *Israel's Superspy*, 54.

16   Thomas and Dillon, *Israel's Superspy*, 58.

17   Thomas and Dillon, *Israel's Superspy*, 60.

18   Thomas and Dillon, *Israel's Superspy*, 63.

19   Thomas and Dillon, *Israel's Superspy*, 65; Richard L. Fricker, "The INSLAW Octopus," *Wired*, January 1, 1993, https://www.wired.com/1993/01/inslaw/.

20   IThomas and Dillon, *Israel's Superspy*, 65

21   Emma North-Best, "The Undying Octopus: FBI and the PROMIS Affair Part 1," *MuckRock*, May 16, 2017, https://www.muckrock.com/news/archives/2017/may/16/FBI-promis-part-1/.

22   Gordon Thomas, *Gideon's Spies: The Secret History of the Mossad*, 4th ed (New York: Thomas Dunne, 2007), 197-98, https://archive.org/details/gideonsspiessecr00thom.

23   Thomas and Dillon, *Israel's Superspy*, 67.

24   Fricker, "The INSLAW Octopus."

25   Fricker, "The INSLAW Octopus."

26   "INSLAW'S Analysis and Rebuttal of the BUA Report," https://cdn.preterhuman.net/texts/law/rebuttal.txt.

27   Fricker, "The INSLAW Octopus."

28   Thomas and Dillon, *Israel's Superspy*, 68.

29   Alison Leigh Cowan, "Wall Street; Israeli Stocks' Post-Shamir Rally," *New York Times*, July 19, 1992, https://www.nytimes.com/1992/07/19/business/wall-street-israeli-stocks-post-shamir-rally.html.

30   Thomas and Dillon, *Israel's Superspy*, 36-7.

31   Thomas and Dillon, *Israel's Superspy*, 36-7.

32   Thomas and Dillon, *Israel's Superspy*, 81.

33   Eitay Mack, "Forget Trump: Israel's Sordid History of Supporting Dictatorships," *972 Magazine*, August 27, 2017, https://www.972mag.com/forget-trump-israels-sordid-history-of-supporting-dictatorships/.

34   Thomas and Dillon, *Israel's Superspy*, 92.

35   Thomas and Dillon, *Israel's Superspy*, 90.

36   Thomas and Dillon, *Israel's Superspy*, 92.

37   Thomas and Dillon, *Israel's Superspy*, 54-55.

38   "Letter to the Director of the FBI, SUBJECT: Robert Maxwell," FBI Documents obtained by INSLAW through FOIA, p. 13-15, https://unlimitedhangout.com/wp-content/uploads/2022/05/FBIInvestigationMaxwellPROMISSales.pdf.

39   "Letter to CIA Director William Casey," Pergamon International Information Corporation, September 6, 1983, https://www.cia.gov/readingroom/docs/CIA-RDP85B01152R000600710072-7.pdf.

40   Emma North-Best, "Sir Robert Maxwell's FBI File Is Getting More Classified by the Minute," MuckRock, June 28, 2017, https://www.muckrock.com/news/archives/2017/jun/28/sir-robert-maxwells-fbi-PROMIS/.

41   North-Best, "Sir Robert Maxwell's FBI File."

42   Thomas and Dillon, *Israel's Superspy*, 96.

43   North-Best, "Sir Robert Maxwell's FBI File."

44   "Christine Maxwell Resume," https://web.archive.org/web/20200205024502/https://personal.utdallas.edu/~cym110030/Christine_Maxwell-CV_2013Feb.pdf.

45   Mary Sagi-Maydan and Yehoshua Sagi, "Comfortable in Her Skin," *Haaretz*, February 13, 2002, https://www.haaretz.com/2002-02-13/ty-article/comfortable-in-her-skin/0000017f-f6fb-d5bd-a17f-f6fb5de60000.

46   Emma North-Best, "Memo Shows the CIA Was Offered PROMIS Software in 1981," *MuckRock*, December 18, 2018, https://www.muckrock.com/news/archives/2018/dec/18/promis-81-memo/.

47   Cheri Seymour, *The Last Circle: Danny Casolaro's Investigation into the Octopus and the PROMIS Software Scandal*, 1st ed (Walterville, OR: TrineDay, 2010), 38, 41.

48   Seymour, *Last Circle*, 38-39.

49   Aaron Kesel, "Octopus PROMIS: The Conspiracy Against INSLAW Software, And The Murders To Cover Up A Scandal Bigger Than Watergate," *Activist Post*, September 30, 2019, https://www.activistpost.com/2019/09/octopus-promis-the-conspiracy-against-inslaw-software-and-the-murders-to-cover-up-a-scandal-bigger-than-watergate.html.

50   Kesel, "Promise."

51   Fricker, "The INSLAW Octopus."

52   Scott Horton, "'Main Core': The Last Round-Up: Sidney Blumenthal on the Origins of the Republican Party, the Fallout from Clinton's Emails, and His New Biography of Abraham Lincoln," *Harper's Magazine*, May 21, 2008, https://harpers.org/2008/05/main-core-the-last-round-up/.

53   Fricker, "The INSLAW Octopus."

54   "Context of '1980s; Oliver North Uses PROMIS Software to Track Dissidents,'" *History Commons*, https://web.archive.org/web/20170626063208/www.historycommons.org/context.jsp?item=northpromis80.

55   Horton, "'Main Core': The Last Round-Up."

56   Tim Shorrock, "Exposing Bush's Historic Abuse of Power," *Salon*, July 23, 2008, https://www.salon.com/2008/07/23/new_churchcomm/.

57   Shorrock, "Exposing."

58   Shorrock, "Exposing."

59   Whitney Webb , "The CIA, Mossad and "Epstein Network" Are Exploiting Mass Shootings," *MintPress News*, September 6, 2019, https://www.mintpressnews.com/cia-israel-mossad-jeffrey-epstein-orwellian-nightmare/261692/.

60   Webb, "The CIA."

61   Webb, "The CIA."

62   Seymour, *Last Circle*, 52.

63   Elliot L. Richardson, "Letter to Kenneth Starr," February 7, 1995, https://www.archives.gov/files/research/kavanaugh/releases/docid-70105136.pdf.

64   Peter Truell and Larry Gurwin, *False Profits: The Inside Story of BCCI, the World's Most Corrupt Financial Empire* (Boston: Houghton Mifflin, 1992), 40.

65   James R. Norman, *The Oil Card: Global Economic Warfare in the 21st Century*, 1st ed (Oregon: Trine Day, 2008), 101.

66   Michael C. Ruppert, *Crossing the Rubicon: The Decline of the American Empire at the End of the Age of Oil* (Gabriola, BC: New Society Publishers, 2004), 172.

67   James Norman, "Fostergate," Document 3, *Media Bypass Magazine*, August 1995, https://archive.org/details/VinceFoster-NSA-Banking-Transactions-Spying

68   Norman, "Fostergate," Document 3.

69   Richardson, "Letter to Starr."

70   Richardson, "Letter to Starr."

71   Richardson, "Letter to Starr."

72   Seymour, *Last Circle*, 272.

73   Richardson, "Letter to Starr."

74   Emma North-Best, "Recently Released Evidence Shows FBI May Have Investigated Danny Casolaro's Death Through 2017," *MuckRock*, May 20, 2018, https://www.muckrock.com/news/archives/2018/may/20/casolaro-update/.

75   Richardson, "Letter to Starr."

76   Normal, *The Oil Card*, 101.

77   Norman, "Fostergate," Document 1, 6.

78   Norman, "Fostergate," Document 28.

79   "2 Military Chiefs Join Wackenhut," *Fort Lauderdale News*, November 5, 1971.

80   "E-Systems Inc. History," Funding *Universe*, http://www.fundinguniverse.com/company-histories/e-systems-inc-history/.

81   "E-Systems Inc. History"

82   John Mintz, "The Secret's Out: Covert E-Systems Inc. Covets Commercial Sales," *Washington Post*, October 24, 1994, https://www.washingtonpost.com/archive/politics/1994/10/24/the-secrets-out-covert-e-systems-inc-covets-commercial-sales/3deadc17-4bd2-41bd-b607-9fa493458fb8/.

83   Mintz, "The Secret's Out."

84   Mintz, "The Secret's Out." On Air Asia and the CIA, see Alan Axelrod, *Mercenaries: A Guide to Private Armies and Private Military Companies* (SAGE Publications, 2013), 142-43.

85   "CIA front company sold for less than network worth," *Des Moines Register*, July 13, 1977.

86   Peter Dale Scott and Jonathan Marshall, *Cocaine Politics: Drugs, Armies, and the CIA in Central America* (University of California Press), 37-8.

87   Scott and Marshall, *Cocaine Politics*, 38.

88   Scott and Marshall, *Cocaine Politics*, 88.

89   Thomas J. Farer, *Transnational Crime in the America* (Routledge, 1999), 195.

90   Jim Fuquay, "Fort Worth group tried to buy planes for Libya," *Fort Worth Star-Telegram*, December 7, 1980.

91   Fuquay, "Fort Worth group tied to buy planes for Libya."

92   *Report of the Congressional Committees Investigating the Iran-Contra Affair: Depositions*, Appendix B, Volume 3, One Hundredth Congress, First Session, 1988, 176, https://www.google.com/books/edition/Report_of_the_Congressional_Committees_I/u1_-pOKeFe8C.

93   Geoff Goodall, "Warbirds Directory, Version 6: Lockheed," http://www.goodall.com.au/warbirds-directory-v6/lockheed.pdf.

94   In 1993, T & G sold two aircraft to a Mexican aviation company called Aero Postal, which was subsequently discovered to have been flying cocaine into the US on behalf of the "Tijuana-based cartel of the Arellano Felix Family." T & G's sale to Aero Postal had been "financed by a Mexican bank, which was assured of repayment by the Export-Import Bank of the United States."

These planes had first been acquired by the Arizona aviation company from Valley National Bank of Arizona, a firm that was also providing loans to Charles Keating's American Continental Corporation. Ari Ben-Menashe alleges that he had been instructed on behalf of his Israeli intelligence handlers to deposit $4 million into an account at Valley National Bank belonging to Earl Brian, as part of the October Surprise pay-offs. Ben-Menashe notes that he suspected that the source of these funds was "drug profit money from Central America."

For T & G sale to Aero Postal, see "Arizona Firm Sold Military Plane to Cartel-Linked Carrier," *San Diego Source*, April 15, 1998.

On T & G, Aero Postal and Valley National Bank, see *Review of the U.S. Forest Service Firefighting Aircraft Program Hearing Before the Subcommittee on Specialty Crops and Natural Resources of the Committee on Agriculture*, House of Representatives, One Hundred Third Congress, First Session, August 5, 1993, 74, https://www.google.com/books/edition/Review_of_the_U_S_Forest_Service_Firefig/_a0eAAAAMAAJ.

On Valley National Bank and Charles Keating, see *Investigation of Lincoln Savings & Loan Association, Hearings Before the Committee on Banking, Finance, and Urban Affairs*, House of Representatives, One Hundred First Congress, First Session, 781, https://www.google.com/books/edition/Investigation_of_Lincoln_Savings_Loan_As/vSyjyvbmeqMC.

On Ari Ben-Menashe's allegations, see Ari Ben-Menashe, *Profits of War: Inside the US-Israeli Arms Network* (Sheridan Square Press, 1992), 77.

Del E. Webb, the organized crime-linked Arizona developer who shaped Las Vegas, had close ties to Valley National Bank, and had even sat on the bank's board of directors. Judith Nies, *Unreal City: Las Vegas, Black Mesa, and the Fate of the West* (Public Affairs, 2014), 15.

As discussed in chapter 8, a former Webb employee, Leonard Lavoie, had set up a company called Systems Marketing that leased a Beechcraft King Air that ended up in the hands of Barry Seal.

95   On the transfers between Ransom's group and Ford & Vlahos, see Goodal, "Warbirds Directory." On John Ford and T & G Aviation, see "Ford & Vlahos v. ITT Commercial Finance Corp," Court of Appeals, First District, Division 4, California, December 20, 1993, https://caselaw.findlaw.com/ca-court-of-appeal/1848036.html; and "*Gary R, Eitel V. Roy D. Reagan* (Declaration)," US District Court of Oregon, https://en.wikisource.org/wiki/Eitel_vs_Reagan_(declaration).

96   "Gary R. Eitel V. Roy D. Reagan (Declaration)."

97   On the transfers to Aboitiz concernse, see Goodall, "Warbirds Directory". On the Aboitiz family and Marcos, see Albert F. Celoza, *Ferdinand Marcos and the Philippines: The Political Economy of Authoritarianism* (Praeger, 1997), 96.

98   "Aerial Drug Smuggling Broken," *Washington Post*, June 30, 1994, https://www.washingtonpost.com/archive/politics/1994/06/30/aerial-drug-smuggling-broken/49b0356c-6296-4c7a-b107-86af5f5dc299/.

99   Goodall, "Warbirds Directory."

100   "Hunts reportedly finish sale of Bache Holdings," *Associated Press*, October 23, 1980. Tim Carrington, *The Year They Sold Wall Street* (Houghton Mifflin Company, 1985), 170.

101   "Declassified State Department Cable," US Department of State, July, 1977, https://archive.org/details/StateDeptcable1977-162169.

102   Seymour, *Last Circle*, 71; For Maheu and RFK, see Lisa Pease, *A Lie Too Big to Fail: The Real History of the Assassination of Robert F. Kennedy*, Kindle (Feral House, 2018).

103   Seymour, *Last Circle*, 95-6.

104   Seymour, *Last Circle*, 74-5.

105   Seymour, *Last Circle*, 71.

106   Seymour, *Last Circle*, 349.

107   Seymour, *Last Circle*, 349.

108   Seymour, *Last Circle*, 348.

109   Seymour, *Last Circle*, 204.

110   Seymour, *Last Circle*, 105.

111   Seymour, *Last Circle*, 307.

112   Seymour, *Last Circle*, 380.

113   Seymour, *Last Circle*, 380.

114   David Wilkison, "Journalist Investigating Bank Was Second To Die," *AP News*, August 15, 1991, https://apnews.com/article/e2fc70d3fe4808d7e34529c7173eeee7.

115   Seymour, *Last Circle*, 41.

116   Seymour, *Last Circle*, 204.

117   Seymour, *Last Circle*, 12.

118   Seymour, *Last Circle*, 6.

119   Seymour, *Last Circle*, 6; *United States v. Abbell*, US District Court for the Southern District of Florida, April 3, 1997, https://law.justia.com/cases/federal/district-courts/FSupp/963/1178/1645124/.

120   Emma North-Best, "The Danny Casolaro Primer: 13 Reasons to Doubt the Official Narrative Surrounding His Death," *MuckRock*, March 15, 2018, https://www.muckrock.com/news/archives/2018/mar/15/danny-casolaro-primer/.

121   "Correspondence between John Dwyer and Charles Work," March 1994, https://www.mintpressnews.com/wp-content/uploads/2019/08/Letters-Casolaro-Death.pdf.

122   Seymour, *Last Circle*, 58.

123   Karen Yurconic, "Army Secrecy Surrounds Standorf Death," *The Morning Call*, February 6, 1991, https://www.mcall.com/news/mc-xpm-1991-02-07-2786588-story.html.

124   Martha M. Hamilton, "Robert Maxwell's Death at Sea Gives Birth to a Big Mystery," *Washington Post*, December 23, 1991, https://www.washingtonpost.com/archive/politics/1991/12/23/robert-maxwells-death-at-sea-gives-birth-to-a-big-mystery/9f95c17d-fe11-4e45-9b19-50147764bfc2/.

125   Keith Schneider, "Plane Crash in Georgia Kills 23, Including Former Senator Tower," *New York Times*, April 6, 1991, https://www.nytimes.com/1991/04/06/us/plane-crash-in-georgia-kills-23-including-former-senator-tower.html.

126   *Congressional Hearing On The Attorney General's Refusal To Provide Congressional Access To "Privileged" Inslaw Documents*, Subcommittee on Economic and Commercial Law, Committee on the Judiciary, One Hundred First Congress, Second Session, 1990, https://archive.org/details/CongressionalHearingOnTheAttorneyGeneralsRefusalToProvideCongressionalAccessToPr/.

127   "Profile: Nicholas Bua," History Commons, https://web.archive.org/web/20210127190739/http://www.historycommons.org/entity.jsp?entity=nicholas_bua_1.

128   Joel Sucher, "The Octopus Lives: How Danny Casolaro's 'Suicide' Foreshadowed Our Current Dystopia," *CovertAction Magazine*, October 10, 2021, https://covertactionmagazine.com/2021/10/10/the-octopus-lives-how-danny-casolaros-suicide-foreshadowed-our-current-dystopia/.

129   Norman, "Fostergate," Document 37.

130   *Energy Research Abstracts*, Vol. 5, 1980, 1745, https://books.google.com/books?id=qN-wvAAAAMAAJ.

131   *Hearings Before the Committee on Finance: The Trade Reform Act of 1973*, United States Senate, Ninety Third Congress, Second Session, Vol. 11, parts 2-4, 1974, 1494, https://books.google.com/books/about/The_Trade_Reform_Act_of_1973.html?id=GuPPAAAAMAAJ.

132   Per CCC, they were not actually involved with Penn Central directly. Instead, the company was just stuck holding worthless Penn-issued commercial paper that bigger banks (like the Rockefeller-linked First National City Bank of New York) were allowed to cash in at the Federal Reserve following Penn Central's bankruptcy. See Robert U. Ayres, *The Bubble Economy: Is Sustainable Growth Possible?* (Cambridge, Massachusetts: The MIT Press, 2014), 112.

133   Craig R. Waters, "Silicon Steppe," *Inc.com*, January 1, 1984, https://www.inc.com/magazine/19840101/1407.html.

134   Gordon Crovitz, "Pericles, Greece Needs You Back," *Wall Street Journal*, June 19, 1984, https://archive.org/details/CIA-RDP90-00845R000201300017-4.

135   Crovitz, "Pericles, Greece Needs You Back."

136   *Hearings Before the Committee on Foreign Relations on Nomination of Paul C. Warnke*, Ninety-Fifth Congress, First Session, 1977, 187–90, https://www.govinfo.gov/content/pkg/CHRG-95shrg83872O/pdf/CHRG-95shrg83872O.pdf.

137   "The Riddle of Armand Hammer," *New York Times*, November 29, 1981, https://www.ny-

times.com/1981/11/29/magazine/the-riddle-of-armand-hammer.html.

138   Waters, "Silicon Steppe."

139   Frank J. Prial, "Business People," *New York Times*, January 10, 1979, https://www.nytimes.com/1979/01/10/archives/business-people-exgov-perpich-joins-control-data-johnson-trusjoist.html.

140   Prial, "Business People."

141   Charles R. Babcock, "Citizen Mondale's Transition Made Him a Conglomerate," *Washington Post*, November 6, 1983, https://www.washingtonpost.com/archive/politics/1983/11/06/citizen-mondales-transition-made-him-a-conglomerate/dcac9467-8c59-45e7-a786-0a0738959eb2/.

142   Email correspondence between the author and Bill Hamilton of Inslaw Inc., May 2022

143   Greg Gaut and Marsha Neff, "Red Stars Over Minnesota," *Minnesota History*, Winter 2009, http://collections.mnhs.org/mnhistorymagazine/articles/61/v61i08p346-359.pdf.

144   Gaut and Neff, "Red Stars."

145   Gaut and Neff, "Red Stars."

146   David Remnick, "In U.S., Gorbachev Tried to Sell a Dream," *Washington Post*, June 6, 1990, https://www.washingtonpost.com/archive/politics/1990/06/06/in-us-gorbachev-tried-to-sell-a-dream/a1e19e21-3e21-4241-ae67-17a47d763598/.

147   Thomas and Dillon, *Israel's Superspy*, 84-5.

148   Thomas and Dillon, *Israel's Superspy*, 83.

149   Thomas and Dillon, *Israel's Superspy*, 160.

150   Thomas and Dillon, *Israel's Superspy*, 161.

151   Thomas and Dillon, *Israel's Superspy*, 161.

152   Thomas and Dillon, *Israel's Superspy*, 162-63.

153   Thomas and Dillon, *Israel's Superspy*, 163.

154   Thomas and Dillon, *Israel's Superspy*, 163-64.

155   Thomas and Dillon, *Israel's Superspy*, 163.

156   "WASHINGTON TALK: Guest List; Early Risers Get Eggs, Bacon and Tower," *New York Times*, May 19, 1989, https://www.nytimes.com/1989/05/19/us/washington-talk-guest-list-early-risers-get-eggs-bacon-and-tower.html.

157   Thomas and Dillon, *Israel's Superspy*, 170.

158   Thomas and Dillon, *Israel's Superspy*, 170.

159   Thomas and Dillon, *Israel's Superspy*, 172-73.

160   Thomas and Dillon, *Israel's Superspy*, 173.

161   Thomas and Dillon, *Israel's Superspy*, 173.

162   Tom Bower, *Maxwell: The Final Verdict* (London: HarperCollins, 1995), 373.

163   Bower, *Maxwell*, 373.

164   Claire Sterling, *Thieves' World: The Threat of the New Global Network of Organized Crime* (New York: Simon & Shuster, 1994), 175.

165   Sterling, *Thieves' World*, 175.

166   Sterling, *Thieves' World*, 195-96. Wanta's confederates in gold-selling and other fraudulent activities tied to speculation on the troubled Russian ruble included Jack Tremonti, the owner of a company registered in Oklahoma called Global Tactical Solutions, and his close associate Martin Gulewicz. Both individuals had ties to Detroit organized crime circles, and Gulewicz had been indicted for drug trafficking (Sterling, *Thieves World*, 187.) In 1978, Tremonti was described in a Tennessee newspaper as a "Detroit meat dealer" who was doing time in prison for "larceny of interstate meat shipments." This article goes on to describe how representatives of Tremonti were involved in an attempted marijuana trafficking operation that was busted as part of a sting. Reportedly, Tremonti himself was "an informant for the federal government." See Ralph Dawson, "Setup deal told by pot defendant," *The Tennessean*, April 26, 1978. Wanta, Tremonti, and Gulewicz were joined by Michael Preisfreund, a banker and currency trader from Finland whose family had been longtime suppliers for the Russian military. Preisfreund "knew most of the powerful men in old Russia and had access to the highest levels of Russian governmental and military personnel." Sterling, *Thieves' World*, 186.

167	Sterling, *Thieves' World*, 195.

168	*ATLAS Dossier*, Translation provided by Institute for the Study of Globalization and Covert Politics, 10, https://isgp-studies.com/belgium-la-nebuleuse-atlas-dossier-and-dutroux-x-files.

169	Sterling, *Thieves' World*, document insert. According to a 1999 lawsuit, Wanta was using New Republic in the late 1980s to "make payments from the corporate accounts for his own benefit" and to "avoid collection of outstanding tax warrants." State of Wisconsin v. Leo F. Wanta, No. 98-0318-CR, February 4, 1999, https://caselaw.findlaw.com/wi-court-of-appeals/1309687.html.

170	*ATLAS Dossier*, 11. The dossier names one of the Russians involved as Mike Brandwain, head of an Antwerp-based firm called M & S International. M & S, according to Robert Friedman, was part of "a heroin ring of French Connection proportions" that moved the drug from Thailand to the US by way of Europe. This ring was operated by the Russian-American gangster Boris Nayfeld, who by the early 1990s was a frontman for the Ukrainian mob boss Marat Balagula. Notably, one of Balagula's more notorious criminal conspiracies involved "import[ing] gasoline to Sierra Leone, which was brokered through the Spanish office of Marc Rich by Rabbi Ronald Greenwald." Robert I. Friedman, *Red Mafiya: How the Russian Mob Has Invaded America*, ePub (Warner Books, Inc, 2000), 65, 103.

171	Dun & Bradstreet, *D&B Who Owns Whom* (Gap Books, 1989), 41.

172	Thomas., *Robert Maxwell*, p. 172-173

173	Andrew Cockburn and Leslie Cockburn, *One Point Safe*. Anchor Books, 1997, 1st Anchor Books ed (New York: Anchor Books, 1997), 108.

174	Thomas and Dillon, *Israel's Superspy*, 172-73.

175	S.C. Gwynne and Larry Gurwin, "The Russian Connection," *TIME*, Vol. 148, No. 3, July 8, 1996, 35.

176	Andrew Cockburn and Cockburn, *One Point Safe*, 1st Anchor Books ed (New York: Anchor Books, 1997), 106.

177	"Rich Worked with Russian Mafia?" *Swissinfo*, June 13, 2002, https://www.swissinfo.ch/ger/arbeitete-rich-mit-russen-mafia-/2764916,

178	Bruce Raphael, *King Energy: The Rise and Fall of an Industrial Empire Gone Awry* (iUniverse, 2000), 537-38.

179	"Zug lawyer involved in criminal proceedings," *Zentralplus*, June 18, 2014, Zuger Anwalt in Strafverfahren verwickelt zentralplus.

180	"Zug lawyer involved in criminal proceedings."

181	Thomas Scheuer, "The Millions of the Mielke Advocate," *Focus Magazine*, No. 43, 1999, https://www.focus.de/politik/deutschland/die-millionen-des-mielke-advokaten-vereinigung-skriminalitaet_id_1927402.html.

182	"Transfer of United States High Technology to the Soviet Union and Soviet Bloc Nations: *Hearings Before the Permanent Subcommittee on Investigations of the Committee on Government Affairs* ,US Senate United States Senate Committee on Government Affairs, Ninety- Seventh Congress, Second Session, 1982, 413, https://www.google.com/books/edition/Transfer_of_United_States_High_Technolog/k8SvVaSpa34C.

183	"Rich Linked to Money Laundering."

184	"Rich Linked to Money Laundering."

185	*Loutchansky v. Times Newspapers Ltd. & Ors. England and Wales High Court* (Queen's Bench Division), December 12, 2002, https://www.casemine.com/judgement/uk/5a8ff7b-860d03e7f57eb175b

186	*Loutchansky v. Times Newspapers*.

187	*Report of the Procura della Repubblica di Bologna: Direzione distrettuale antimafia*, Archived at the Transborder Corruption Archive, p. 109, https://tbcarchives.org/wp-content/uploads/spider-web2.pdf.

188	Friedman, *Red Mafiya*, 252, 245.

189	Friedman, *Red Mafiya*, 244, 240.

190	Alan Block and Constance Weaver, *All is Clouded by Desire: Global Banking, Money Laundering, and International Organized Crime* (Praeger, 2004), 166.

191	"In Re Bank of New York Derivative Litigation," United States District Court Southern District of New York, 22, https://www.mail-archive.com/ctrl@listserv.aol.com/msg65701/BONY-AMC.pdf.

192   "In Re Bank of New York," 22.

193   Block and Weaver, *All is Clouded by Desire*, 97-99.

194   Block and Weaver, *All is Clouded By Desire*, 100-5.

195   "In Re Bank of New York," 22.

196   "In Re Bank of New York," 22.

197   Block and Weaver, *All is Clouded by Desire*, 131.

198   "In Re Bank of New York," 24.

199   "In Re Bank of New York," 24.

200   "In Re Bank of New York," 23.

201   Block and Weaver, *All is Clouded by Desire*, 190.

202   Block and Weaver, *All is Clouded by Desire*, ch. 8.

203   *Russian Money Laundering: Hearing Before the Committee on Banking and Financial Services*, US House of Representatives, One Hundred Sixth Congress, First Session, September 21, 22, 1999, 414.

204   Block and Weaver, *All is Clouded by Desire*, 166.

205   Friedman, *Red Mafiya*, 65, 67.

206   Robert I. Friedman, "The Fixer," *New York Magazine*, June 19, 1995, 63-64. Friedman quotes one individual familiar with Kalmanovitch as saying that "Wherever you looked in the world, Kalmanovitch knew the spookiest, the dirtiest, the weirdest people. Paraguayan ex-Nazis, New York mafiosos, South African neo-fascists, US congressmen, CIA agents—spooks of every description."

207   Friedman, "The Fixer," 64.

208   Friedman, *Red Mafiya*, 206.

209   Press Release: IMF Approves Augmentation of Russia Extended Arrangement and Credit under CCFF; Activates GAB. International Monetary Fund, July 20, 1988, https://www.imf.org/en/News/Articles/2015/09/14/01/49/pr9831.

210   Natalya Shulyakovskaya, "Skuratov Says IMF Billions Sold on the Sly," *St. Petersburg Times*, September 17, 1999.

211   Block and Weaver, A*ll is Clouded by Desire*, 147.

212   "Russiagate, ecco le prove," *La Repubblica*, October 6, 1999.

213   "Если Касьянов приедет в Швейцарию, его вызовут к следователю?" *Novaya Gazeta*, July 24, 2000, https://web.archive.org/web/20131202222313/http://old.novayagazeta.ru/data/2000/52/00.html.

214   "NY Bank in Money Laundering Inquiry," *The Irish Times*, August 20, 1990; "A Mess of Mafia Money – Fact or Fancy?," *Jerusalem Post*, Septembr 3, 1999.

215   "Newspaper Scandal Over IMF Diversion Expands," Monitor, Vol. 6, Issue 144, July 25, 2000, https://jamestown.org/program/newspaper-scandal-over-imf-diversion-expands/.

216   Dominick Dunne, "Death in Monaco," Vanity Fair, December, 2000, https://web.archive.org/web/20160301221519/https://www.vanityfair.com/culture/2000/12/dunne200012.

217   Dunne, "Death in Monaco."

218   David Kohn, "Murder in Monaco: An American On Trial," *CBS News*, July 8, 2003, https://www.cbsnews.com/news/murder-in-monaco-an-american-on-trial/.

219   Dunne, "Death in Monaco."

220   Dunne, "Death in Monaco."

CHAPTER 10

GOVERNMENT BY BLACKMAIL: THE DARK SECRETS OF THE REAGAN ERA

"ROY COULD FIX ANYONE IN THE CITY"

Iran-Contra, PROMIS, BCCI, and related schemes of the Reagan era are clear examples of how the alliance between intelligence networks and organized crime resulted in both national and international business rackets with criminal elements. Such conspiracies largely succeeded thanks to individuals at the highest levels of government, particularly in the Justice Department, who worked to protect these rackets and the bad actors behind them.

Much of the "dirty laundry" of these different criminal enterprises would be mopped up in the early 1990s by none other than William Barr, who started his career at the CIA and served as George H.W. Bush's Attorney General. Barr would play a major role in covering up Iran-Contra, PROMIS, and BCCI, as seen in his pardoning of Iran-Contra criminals, his patronage of the Bua report, and his thwarting of indictments related to BCCI's 1991 collapse, respectively.

Some have explained these specific scandals away, painting them as blights of the Reagan-Bush administrations and treating these intelligence-organized crime rackets as isolated incidents. However, instead, it appears that these intelligence-organized crime networks were so central to the national power structure by the time Reagan took office that the more well-known scandals of the era can be seen as "business as usual" for the period. Yet, lurking beneath Iran-Contra and other scandals that rocked the Reagan administration, there were darker and more nefarious activities that reached the highest levels of power during the same period, but received considerably less media attention.

These other, lesser known scandals and crimes of the era show that, during the reigns of Reagan and Bush Sr., the rot reached all the way to the

White House. Key power brokers in this sordid milieu included individuals intimately involved in the world of sex blackmail, who often bragged about their ability to "fix" and "manipulate" any politician or powerful individual they sought to influence, for the benefit of intelligence agencies, organized crime, as well as their own personal gain.

One figure emblematic of this side of Reagan era politics is none other than Roy Cohn, whose ties to sex blackmail, organized crime, and the centers of American political power were already explored in detail in Chapters 2 and 4. By the late 1970s, Roy's "favor bank" system, modeled after the system used by the organized crime-linked Generoso Pope, had led him to grow in both power and influence, especially politically.

For instance, Cohn's birthday party in 1979 was attended by "the important officials of the Democratic, Republican, and Conservative parties, most of the city's major elected officials, a number of congressmen, the Chief Judge of the District Court, and Roy's usuals," who included his close friends Si Newhouse, William Safire, and Donald Trump, among others.[1] The party was hosted at the infamous Studio 54, whose owners were Cohn's clients.[2] Studio 54 was known for its wild parties, semi-naked performers, and culture of open drug use, with *Vanity Fair* once describing it as "the giddy epicenter of 70s hedonism, a disco hothouse of beautiful people, endless cocaine, and every kind of sex."[3] The politicians, journalists, and celebrities invited to Cohn's exclusive parties, including those at Studio 54, were said to be those who "had open accounts in Cohn's 'favor bank.'"[4]

Cohn regularly took "judges, elected officials, men and women of money and influence" to the club.[5] On at least one occasion, Cohn allegedly used a story about a government official's drug use at Studio 54 for political purposes. The official was Hamilton Jordan, Jimmy Carter's chief of staff, and Cohn was widely believed to be the person who leaked details of Jordan's alleged cocaine use at the club to the *New York Times*.[6]

As his political star rose, Cohn's ties to organized crime not only deepened, but became more public. He gained a reputation as a lawyer for kingpins of organized crime, counting major mobsters like Tony Salerno of the Genovese crime family and Carmine Galante of the Bonanno crime family among his rolodex of clients from the city's, and nation's, underworld.

Cohn had also developed even more powerful media connections than those he had first gained in his youth. Among Cohn's closest friends during this time was Barbara Walters, to whom Cohn often referred to as his "fiancée" in public, and whom he later introduced to the head of the US Information Agency, Chad Wick, as well as other high rollers in the Reagan White House.[7] Yet, Walters was just one of Cohn's powerful friends in the media, a group that also included Abe Rosenthal, executive editor of the *New York Times*; William Safire, long-time *New York Times* columnist and *New York Magazine* contributor; and George Sokolsky of the *New York Herald Tribune, NBC,* and *ABC.*[8]

Cohn was also the attorney and friend of media mogul Rupert Murdoch, and Cohn's role in involving Murdoch in Contra-related propaganda on behalf of the US government was discussed in Chapter 7. Cohn also continued to lean on his life-long friend since high school, Si Newhouse Jr., to exert media influence.[9] Newhouse's media empire had also grown in power and influence – it now counted among its assets publications such as *Vanity Fair, Vogue, GQ, The New Yorker,* and numerous local newspapers throughout the United States, as well as major interests in cable television. *New York Magazine* later noted that "Cohn used his influence in the early '80s to secure favors for himself and his Mob clients in Newhouse publications."[10]

Cohn's media confidants, like journalist William Buckley of *The National Review* and *Firing Line,* often attacked Cohn's political enemies – particularly long-time Manhattan District Attorney Robert Morgenthau – in their columns, using Cohn as an anonymous source. Buckley – along with Barbara Walters, Alan Dershowitz, and Donald Trump – would later serve as character witnesses for Cohn during his 1986 disbarment hearings and all but Buckley would later draw controversy for their subsequent connections to Jeffrey Epstein.[11]

With connections like this, it's no wonder that Stanley Friedman – a law partner of Cohn, who was later imprisoned over a kickback and bribery scandal while serving as New York's deputy mayor – told journalist Marie Brenner in 1980 that "Roy could fix anyone in the city."[12] Roy Cohn's "favor bank" and his unique position as a liaison between the criminal underworld, the rich and famous, and top media influencers made him a force to be reckoned with. In particular, however, it ensured his success as a major "political fixer" and his power in this regard reached its zenith during Ronald Reagan's 1980 presidential campaign.

In 1979, a year before the election, the *New York Daily News* reported that Cohn had "emerged as the city's preeminent manipulator. A one-man network of contacts that have reached into City Hall, the mob, the press, the Archdiocese, the disco-jet set, the courts and the backrooms of the Bronx and Brooklyn where judges are made and political contributions are arranged."[13]

Former Congressman Neil Gallagher later remarked to Cohn's biographer Nicholas Von Hoffman that Cohn "was very important in the whole

Reagan setup – look at the number of judges who owed him allegiance through their appointments. Even today you've got people sitting on the federal bench who kid, but they don't kid, that Roy was their rabbi."[14]

Cohn's involvement in Reagan's 1980 campaign would be critical and, decades later, would also influence the political style and campaigns of Cohn's protégé – Donald Trump. During the 1980 campaign, Cohn would also meet another of his protégés, Roger Stone. Cohn infamously instructed Stone to leave a hefty bribe tucked in a suitcase at the door-step of the Liberal Party's headquarters during the 1980 campaign, a "dirty trick" that helped Reagan win the state of New York.[15] During this campaign, Cohn would also meet Paul Manafort – an associate of Stone's – and introduce both to Donald Trump. Manafort would later serve as Trump's 2016 campaign manager.

Cohn's law partner, Tom Bolan, was also an influential force in the Reagan campaign and later chaired Reagan's transition team in 1980.[16] Reagan then named Bolan, whom he considered a friend, as a director of the Overseas Private Investment Corporation, the government's develop-ment finance institution. Bolan was also the New York finance co-chair-man for the Reagan campaign in both 1980 and 1984. He was also close to others in Cohn's circle, such as William F. Buckley Jr., Donald Trump, and Rupert Murdoch.[17] In 1989, roughly three years after Cohn's death, Bolan attended a party on Robert Maxwell's yacht, the *Lady Ghislaine*, alongside Donald Trump and literary agent Mort Janklow (who repre-sented Ronald Reagan and two of Cohn's closest friends: journalists Wil-liam Safire and Barbara Walters), among others.[18]

Furthermore, Bolan, like Cohn, was instrumental in securing federal judgeships for several individuals who would later become influential, including future FBI Director Louis Freeh. Freeh would later be hired by Epstein associate, lawyer and Harvard professor Alan Dershowitz, to "investigate" the Epstein scandal, where he allegedly harassed Epstein vic-tims, and was also involved in the cover-up of the Penn State child mo-lestation and abuse scandal.[19] Cohn was also able to get friends of clients appointed as federal judges, including Donald Trump's sister, Maryanne Trump Barry.[20] After Barry was appointed as a federal judge, Trump called Cohn to thank him for pulling strings on his sister's behalf.[21]

Though Cohn was not given a public position in the Reagan admin-istration, he was not merely a "dirty trickster" who worked in the shad-ows of the Reagan campaigns. In fact, he worked closely with some of the more visible faces of the campaign, including the then-manager of Reagan's 1980 campaign and later CIA director, William Casey. According to Christine Seymour – Cohn's long-time switchboard operator from the late 1960s up until his death in 1986, who listened in on his calls – Casey and Cohn were close friends and, during the 1980 campaign, Casey "called Roy almost daily."[22]

In the early 1990s, Seymour would attempt to write a book about the calls she overheard working for Cohn. News of the book was published by the *New York Post* in 1994 in a column by Cindy Adams, who wrote that Seymour "monitored every call in or out, knew everything, everyone, knew where all the bodies were buried." Five months later, Seymour was killed in a suspicious car accident, leaving her book unfinished. When Seymour's collaborator on the book, Jeffrey Schmidt, learnt of Seymour's death and the circumstances surrounding it, "he panicked, took a box of the notebooks [that contained details of Cohn's calls], and burned them."[23]

Seymour, before her death, had also noted that one of Cohn's other most frequent phone pals and closest friends was Nancy Reagan and she was also one of his clients.[24] Reagan, whose influence over her husband was well-known, was so close to Cohn that it was largely his death from AIDS that led her to "encourage her husband to seek more funding for AIDS research."[25] Ronald Reagan himself was also a friend of Cohn's and, according to late journalist Robert Parry, "lavished favors on Cohn, including invitations to White House events, personal thank-you notes, and friendly birthday wishes" over the course of his presidency.[26]

Given that Reagan heavily courted the evangelical right and promoted "family values" as president, the close ties between not only himself, but his inner circle, with Cohn may seem odd. However, Reagan, like Cohn, had deep ties to the same organized-crime factions that were among Cohn's clients and affiliates of the same Mafia figures close to Cohn and his network. One of the men credited as Reagan's mentor was Lew Wasserman, who was long alleged to have close ties to the mob, as noted previously in chapter 1.[27]

Wasserman, the long-time president of MCA and a well-known Hollywood mogul, is known for not only advancing Reagan's film and television career, but also for supporting his successful push to become president of the Screen Actors Guild, which later helped Reagan launch his political career. In addition, MCA was a major financier of Reagan's successful gubernatorial bid in 1966 and, not long after Reagan became president, his administration controversially shut down a massive Department of Justice (DOJ) probe into MCA's ties to organized crime.[28] According to

Shawn Swords, a documentary filmmaker who explored Reagan's ties to MCA:

> Ronald Reagan was an opportunist. His whole career was guided by MCA – by Wasserman and [MCA founder] Jules Stein, who bragged that Reagan was malleable, that they could do what they wanted with him.... That thing about Reagan being tough on [organized] crime – that's a fallacy.[29]

Swords' characterization of this relationship is supported by an unnamed Hollywood source cited in a declassified DOJ document, who called Reagan "a complete slave of MCA who would do their bidding on anything."[30]

What elements of organized crime were connected to Wasserman? As a young man, Lew Wasserman joined the Mayfield Road Gang, which was run by Moe Dalitz, a close friend of Meyer Lansky who, per the FBI, was a powerful figure in Lansky's criminal enterprise, second only to Lansky himself among members of the Jewish mob.[31] As previously mentioned in Chapter 4, Cohn's involvement in the United Dye case revealed that he had been involved with Dalitz's network since at least the early 1960s.

Lew Wasserman would later marry Edith Beckerman, whose father was Dalitz's lawyer.[32] As noted in chapter 1, Wasserman's closest friend and lawyer, Sidney Korshak, also had close ties to Dalitz and once partnered with Lansky in the Acapulco Towers Hotel.[33] Notably, the magazine *New West* stated in 1976 that Korshak was the "logical successor to Meyer Lansky."[34] Korshak, as a lawyer, fit a niche similar to that occupied by Roy Cohn and gained a reputation as a bridge between organized crime and "respectable" society.[35]

In addition, the DOJ probe into MCA that the Reagan administration quashed had reportedly been launched after the Justice Department learned that an influential member of the Gambino crime family, Salvatore Pisello, was doing business with the massive entertainment company.[36] At that time, the boss of the Gambino crime family, Paul Castellano, was a client of Roy Cohn.[37] As noted in the previous chapter, an MCA board member with ties to organized crime and the network behind the Inslaw Affair, Eugene Gianquinto, had bragged that he was responsible for the scuttling of DOJ probe in a wiretapped phone call.

Another figure intimately involved with Reagan's 1980 presidential campaign was Robert Keith Gray, whose activities were discussed in detail in Chapter 5. As previously mentioned, Gray was said to have been a friend of Cohn's, but the exact nature of their relationship is murky. However, Gray, like Cohn, was involved with Reagan's unsuccessful bid for the presidency in 1976 and then, like Cohn, worked closely with Casey during the 1980 campaign. Gray later "boasted of his close relationship with the CIA's William Casey; Gray used to say that before taking on a foreign client, he would clear it with Casey," according to *Newsweek*.[38]

Gray would go on to co-chair Reagan's Inauguration Committee and afterwards would return to the PR business, taking on several clients, including Saudi arms dealer Adnan Khashoggi and the Mossad-linked hedge fund manager Marc Rich.[39] At the same time, Roy Cohn would also take on Khashoggi as a client. Shortly thereafter, as will be discussed in the next chapter, Jeffrey Epstein would also take on Khashoggi as a client, which coincided with the genesis of the Iran-Contra Affair.

It certainly is an odd coincidence that three men tied in different ways to sexual blackmail would all begin to circle around a man like Khashoggi, who was alleged to have used sex blackmail himself, within the same short span of time. However, it begins to look a bit less like a coincidence when one considers that, by the late 1980s, several organizations tied, not only to key factions of the Reagan administration, but also to aspects of the Iran-Contra Affair, would be tied to child sex abuse, sex trafficking, and sex blackmail.

More overlap in these networks can be seen at a May 2, 1983 "testimonial dinner" hosted by B'nai B'rith's Banking and Finance Lodge at the Grand Hyatt hotel in New York. [40] The hotel, at the time, was a project between Donald Trump, Cohn's protégé, and the organized crime-linked Pritzker family discussed in chapter 1. The Trump-Pritzker partnership began to dissolve around 1993 and formally ended in 1996.

This "testimonial dinner" was in Roy Cohn's honor. The dinner's invitation states that it took "special pride" in "this well-deserved public tribute" to Cohn because he has been a "tenacious champion of Israel's right to exist in peace and security and of American economic political support" for Israel as well as his "deep-rooted commitment of purpose on behalf of his fellow man."[41] It was also noted that he had received honors from the Jewish National Fund and Federation of Jewish Philanthropies. The latter group, three years later, would merge with the United Jewish Appeal, which was intimately connected to the philanthropic activities of Leslie Wexner and Wexner's mentor Max Fisher at the time (see chapters 13 and 14). The dinner invitation also notes that Cohn has been "a long-time member of [the] Banking and Finance Lodge of B'nai B'rith – continuing a tradition established by his father, Justice Albert Cohn, who was president of the organization's New York-New England district."[42]

That Albert Cohn was a high-ranking member of B'nai B'rith, i.e. the president of its most influential chapter, has some significance. As early as 1878, the *New York Times* referred to the B'nai B'rith organization as "one of the most powerful secret organizations in the United States" that "now exercises an immense influence in all matters of common interest to the Jewish community."[43] "To bind its member more closely together," the article continues, "the seal of secrecy was stamped upon its proceedings, thereby following the example of the Masonic and other secret fraternities." Though a history of B'nai B'rith is beyond the scope of this book, if indeed – as claimed in this 19th century article – the secret society's origins were noble, by the 20th century, and definitely by the 1980s, its leadership had become dominated by powerful men with organized crime and/or intelligence connections. An early example would be Albert Cohn, whose ties were detailed in chapter 4, serving as head of B'nai B'rith's most powerful chapter.

At the time B'nai B'rith was hosting this dinner for Cohn, the organization's board of overseers included individuals with organized crime connections, such as Edmond Safra and Edgar Bronfman, as well as Leslie Wexner's mentor Max Fisher. As will be noted in chapter 14, B'nai B'rith played a critical role in the creation of Wexner's main philanthropic organization, the Wexner Foundation.

What's perhaps more significant about this dinner are the honorary chairmen – eight close friends of Cohn that populated his inner circle. Some have already been mentioned at length in relation to Cohn, including Donald Trump, Rupert Murdoch, and Stanley Friedman. Others, such as George Steinbrenner were also well-known friends and clients of Cohn. Another, Gerald Schoenfeld, was described as a "the most influential figure in the theater business" credited with "reinvigorating" Broadway.[44]

Another honorary chairman, Maxwell Rabb, had previously been a secretary to president Eisenhower's cabinet, where he was succeeded by Robert Keith Gray and to whom Rabb left his secretary.[45] After leaving the White House, Rabb was involved in a business deal with organized crime-connected investors like Jack Cooper and frontmen for Meyer Lansky.[46] He also served on the board of directors of a company founded by Lansky frontman Louis Chesler.[47] At the time of the 1983 dinner, Rabb was US ambassador to Italy and was later accused of involvement in aspects of Iran-Contra. He was also described by the *New York Times* as "a long-time acquaintance" of one of Roy Cohn's clients at the time – Adnan Khashoggi.[48]

Aside from these, other chairmen included Edward Regan, who was comptroller of the State of the New York from 1979 to 1993 under Governors Hugh Carey (discussed in chapters 6 and 12) and Mario Cuomo. Regan's connection to Cohn is troubling, given Regan's role as state comptroller. Also troubling is Regan's apparent political ethos.

As noted in his 2014 obituary in the *New York Times*:

> In 1988, prosecutors investigated Mr. Regan's fund-raising practices after the disclosure of a memo written by a top aide advocating a policy under which "those who give will get" – suggesting, perhaps, that financial firms that provided the bulk of the comptroller's campaign contributions would receive state business.[49]

The last honorary chairmen and intimate of Cohn may be the most significant, at least in the context of this book – Alan C. Greenberg, then chairman of Bear Stearns. As will be detailed in the next chapter, Greenberg played perhaps the most crucial role of all in the early rise of Jeffrey Epstein into the networks of the New York elite.

Other close friends of Cohn could be found on the dinner tribute committee, including Tom Bolan, Cohn's law partner, and William Safire. Other members of that committee included Charles Allen of Allen & Co.; Ron Perelman, the corporate raider closely tied to Drexel Burnham Lambert; Ron Lauder, of the Estee Lauder fortune then serving as Reagan's Undersecretary of Defense; representatives of Israel Discount Bank (see chapter 7) and Leumi Bank (see chapter 3) and several sitting Congressmen and Senators, including Strom Thurmond, Jack Kemp, and Arlen Specter.

COVENANT HOUSE AND AMERICARES

In 1968, a Catholic priest named Bruce Ritter asked his superiors for permission to take homeless teenagers, boys and girls, into his home in Manhattan.[50] Per Ritter's account, they agreed and, during a snowstorm in 1969, he sheltered six runaway teenagers by hosting them in his apartment.[51] Ritter's activities would later grow into a large, privately funded agency that still exists today, called Covenant House, which offers a variety of service to homeless and runaway youth.

Roughly two decades after founding the organization, Ritter was accused of having sexual relationships with some of the teenagers and young adults he had taken in, and of spending Covenant House funds on lavish gifts and payments to the vulnerable teenagers he was alleged to have groomed and exploited.[52] As a result, Ritter was forced to resign from Covenant House in February 1990.

The main allegation that dogged Ritter, first published by the *New York Post*, related to claims that Ritter had paid off a male prostitute with Covenant House funds in exchange for sex. Four more young men later spoke to *The Village Voice* and the *New York Times*, repeating similar claims and with some alleging that their sexual relationship with Ritter had begun while they had received services through Covenant House.[53]

One of those alleged victims, Darryl Bassile, was 14 at the time. Bassile later wrote an open letter to Ritter a year after the allegations about the priest's predatory behavior were published in the *New York Post*. His letter stated: "You were wrong for inflicting your desires on a 14-year-old.... I know that someday you will stand before the one who judges all of us and at that time there will be no more denial, just the truth."[54]

As the allegations made their way through the press, nearly half of the charity's board resigned in relatively short order. According to the *New York Times*, the resignations were related, not just to the sex-related allegations, but also to the discovery of "a secretive fund set up by Father Ritter that made loans to two board members, who have since resigned, and to others."[55] Notably, Charles M. Sennott, the *Post* reporter who wrote the first story about Ritter's accusers, would later state that "the secular powers more than the archdiocese or the Franciscans protected him [Ritter]."[56]

Sennott's report was attacked viciously by columnists in other New York media outlets, powerful politicians including then-Governor of New York Mario Cuomo, and Cardinal John O'Connor. The Archdiocese of New York, now led by O'Connor, intervened to "broker a deal" between Ritter and the Manhattan District Attorney Robert Morgenthau. O'Connor's predecessor, Cardinal Francis Spellman, had been a close friend of Roy Cohn and alleged attendee of the Plaza Hotel "blackmail parties" involving Cohn, Hoover, and Rosenstiel (see Chapters 2 and 4).

Though accusations swirled around Ritter and were the subject of several media reports, he was never charged, as "Manhattan District Attorney Robert Morgenthau said there was not enough evidence of financial misconduct to charge him with a crime."[57] Notably, Covenant House decided to hire the "CIA of Wall Street" Kroll Associates, the firm so deeply connected to Thomas Corbally (see chapter 4), to "independently investigate" possible financial wrongdoing.[58] Kroll Associates, its longstanding US and Israeli intelligence links and Robert Maxwell's hiring of the firm prior to his 1991 death are discussed in Chapter 15. For now, it is important to note that the intelligence-linked investigative firm has produced "limited hangout" investigations of individuals connected to the networks explored in this book, such as Adnan Khashoggi and Imelda Marcos, and had previously been hired by Drexel Burnham Lambert in an effort to help Michael Milken's case.[59]

In the case of Covenant House, Kroll Associates claimed that "none of the allegations, when viewed individually, can be proved beyond any question," while also claiming that the "cumulative" evidence against Ritter was "extensive."[60] As for Ritter himself, he denied the charges and had told Sennott by phone that he had been "set up" by "organized crime."[61]

Ritter's claims for being "set up" seem dubious, however, when one considers that his main patron was Robert Macauley, Bush Sr.'s roommate at Yale and a long-time friend of the Bush family.[62] According to reports, Macauley was the key figure behind Covenant House's rise and his own interest in "humanitarian aid" coalesced around the time he began his relationship with Ritter.[63]

Macauley, who first met Ritter in 1977, was described by the *New York Times* as "instrumental" to Covenant House fundraising after he joined its board and especially after he became its chairman in 1985. Indeed, with Macauley as chair, Covenant House's operating budget grew from $27 million to $90 million and its board came to include powerful individuals including top executives at IBM, Chase Manhattan Bank, and Bear Stearns.[64] Their alliance, among other things, led Macauley and Ritter to be jointly granted an audience with Pope John Paul II in Rome in 1982.[65]

Macauley was also alleged to have played a major role in courting several "other wealthy or well-connected people," including former government officials, such as William E. Simon – Treasury Secretary under Nixon and Ford – and investment bankers from Salomon Brothers and Bear Stearns, among others.[66] Notably, Simon was also connected to Kissinger Associates and Bechtel (see Chapter 7) as well as the Epstein-connected Gouletas real estate family, as he served on the board of the Gouletas family company Tamco (see Chapter 12).

Macauley also introduced Ritter to George H.W. Bush and, through J. Peter Grace, Ritter met Ronald Reagan. Both Bush and Reagan publicly praised Ritter during the Reagan administration, including during the 1984 State of the Union address, which Ritter attended and where Reagan praised Ritter as an "unsung hero."[67] Grace, who was not only deeply involved in AmeriCares but also donated heavily to Covenant House, once chaired the board of a reported CIA front named the American Institute of

Free Labor Development (AIFLD) and was also the former head of United Fruit/United Brands, which had CIA links during his tenure.[68] United Fruit/United Brands would later be led by Eli Black, father of corporate raider and Epstein associate Leon Black, and – after Black's alleged suicide – would be controlled by Leslie Wexner's "mentors" Max Fisher and Alfred Taubman (See Chapters 13 and 14). Macauley's organization, the AmeriCares Foundation, which was later accused of funnelling money to the Contras in Central America, was one of the main sources of funding for Covenant House. Bruce Ritter himself was also tied to AmeriCares, serving as Vice President of AmeriCares until he was forced to resign from Covenant House.

Despite Macauley's denials that AmeriCares funded the Contras, the *Hartford Courant* reported in 1991 that AmeriCares "sent more than $291,000 in food and medicine to Nicaragua and $5,750 in cash to [Contra leader Mario] Calero in 1985."[69] Its board members, aside from Grace and Macauley, included Trilateral Commission co-founder and National Security Advisor to Carter, Zbigniew Brzezinski, former Republican Senator Gordon J. Humphrey, and George H.W. Bush's brother, Prescott.[70] After George H.W. Bush died, AmeriCares stated that he had been "instrumental in founding the health-focused relief and development organization."[71] Another AmeriCares board member, who Macauley would later bring to Covenant House, was William E. Simon, the aforementioned former U.S. secretary of the treasury. Simon also ran the Nicaraguan Freedom Fund, which sent aid to the Contras and was also tied to Rev. Sun Myung Moon's Unification Church.[72] AmeriCares was also funded by the Unification Church and was deeply connected to the Catholic organization, the Knights of Malta.[73] William Simon, Roy Cohn's law partner Tom Bolan, and former CIA director William Casey were also members of this group. At the time, the president of the Knights of Malta's American branch was J. Peter Grace.[74]

AmeriCares was also known to have connections to U.S. intelligence. As the *Hartford Courant* noted in 1991: "Knowledgeable former federal officials, many with backgrounds in intelligence work, help AmeriCares maneuver in delicate international political environments." Also suggestive of intelligence connections is the fact that AmeriCares "frequently used" the CIA-linked Southern Air Transport for many of its flights, including flights it made during the Gulf War to Kuwait and to Iran in the early 1990s.[75] Southern Air Transport, a few years later, would become intimately involved with Leslie Wexner's The Limited and Jeffrey Epstein (see the end of this chapter and Chapter 17).

Once the Macauley-Ritter alliance was cemented, Covenant House seemed to become enmeshed in similar intelligence-linked networks. For instance, as Covenant House grew into an international organization, its first branch in Central America was opened in Guatemala and was headed by Roberto Alejos Arzu, a CIA asset whose plantation had been used to train the troops used in the CIA's failed "Bay of Pigs" invasion of Cuba.[76] Arzu was also an associate of the former U.S.-backed dictator of Nicaragua, Anastasio Somoza, and a member of the Knights of Malta.[77] Alejos Arzu also worked directly for AmeriCares and was tied to several Central American paramilitary groups.[78]

Intelligence community sources cited by *Franklin Cover-Up* author John DeCamp asserted that the Alejos Arzu-led branch of Covenant House procured children for a pedophile ring based in the United States.[79] A few years later, Mi Casa, another US-run charity in Guatemala that George H.W. Bush had personally toured with his wife Barbara in 1994, was accused of rampant pedophilia and child abuse.[80]

THE SECRETS OF LARRY KING AND CRAIG SPENCE

Bruce Ritter was not the only man accused of preying on minors that would have contacts nestled deep within the national power structure and with institutions involved in Contra financing. Around the same time as Ritter's downfall, a sordid child sex trafficking and abuse network began to be exposed. Centered in Omaha, Nebraska, it is remembered today as the "Franklin Scandal." The man at the center of this scandal was Lawrence "Larry" King, a prominent local Republican activist and lobbyist who ran the Franklin Community Federal Credit Union until it was shut down by federal authorities in November 1988.

According to journalist and author Nick Bryant, the earliest mention of King in the press was 1973, when the *Omaha Sun* reported that King had served in the Air Force from 1965 to 1969, where he worked as an "information specialist" and handled "top secret" military communications. After an honorable discharge from the Air Force, he began studying for a career in the banking industry. At age 25, he joined a "management training program" at First National Bank in Omaha. Unsatisfied, he quit the bank in August 1970 and, later that year, Larry's father was offered the reins of the faltering Franklin Community Credit Union. His father declined, but suggested the Credit Union hire his son as its manager. The

1973 *Omaha Sun* article, as cited by Bryant, lauded King for his supposed industriousness and work ethos at Franklin.[81]

Eventually, and many years before the Credit Union collapsed, King began to use its funds as "his personal, bottomless ATM." His personal wealth greatly increased and King soon began making major political connections, mainly in the Republican Party, which King had joined in 1981.[82]

King soon founded and later chaired the Nebraska Frederick Douglas Republican Council, which threw a reception honoring King in 1983 for his "service to the Republican party both locally and nationally." He became involved in the National Black Republican Council, where he held several positions, as well as the Planned Parenthood Federation of America, where he served as "Secretary/Treasurer." Author Nick Bryant has noted that King seemed "particularly interested in children" as he also became involved with the child-oriented organizations Camp Fire Girls, the Girls Club, and Head Start during this period.[83]

By the late 1980s, King was hosting parties attended by major political figures, such as Supreme Court Justice Clarence Thomas as well as Congressmen Jack Kemp (a friend of Cohn's) and Hal Daub. Daub, who represented Nebraska, "had a stint on Franklin's Advisory Board," according to Nick Bryant.[84] King also donated to Daub and held a fundraiser for him while also generously donating to Republican Kay Orr's campaign for Nebraska governor. In 1982, King sang the Star Spangled Banner at a National Black Republican Council dinner attended by Ronald and Nancy Reagan and he would go on to sing the national anthem at the 1984 Republican convention in Dallas. King's political connections continued to grow, leading him to form the Council of Minority Americans. A gala hosted by the Council included former President Gerald Ford, Jack Kemp, and Alexander Haig (mentioned throughout Chapter 5) on its "host committee."[85]

These deep connections to the Republican power base in the 1980s also led King to apparently become involved in the financing of Nicaragua's Contras. Hints of King's ties to Contra financing networks first emerged in a May 1989 article in the *Omaha World Herald*, which states that: "In the 6 1/2 months since federal authorities closed Franklin, rumors have persisted that money from the credit union somehow found its way to the Nicaraguan contra rebels."[86] The possibility that King's fraudulent credit union was covertly funding the Contras was supported by subsequent reporting by the *Houston Post's* Pete Brewton, who discovered that the CIA, in conjunction with organized crime, had secretly borrowed money from various savings and loans (S&L) institutions to fund covert operations.[87] One of those S&Ls, Silverado, had Neil Bush, George H.W. Bush's son, on its board and it had done business with King's organization.

Another link between King and the Iran-Contra affair is King's donation of over $25,350 to an organization affiliated with the Reagan administration, Citizens for America, which sponsored speaking trips for Oliver North and Contra leaders.[88] The group was said to have been "one of the conservative Washington-based groups that advised former Lt. Col. Oliver L. North and helped develop a base of citizen support for him."[89] Other groups in this orbit included the aforementioned AmeriCares. The then-chairman of the group, Donald Devine, stated that they "supported the Reagan administration's effort to supply the Contras with US military aid," but did not directly "funnel money to the rebels."[90]

An officer at Citizens for America at the time was David Carmen, who – after leaving the group – ran a public relations firm called Carmen, Carmen & Hugel with his father Gerald, who had also been appointed by Reagan to head the General Services Administration and then appointed to a subsequent ambassadorship, and the former head of covert operations at the Casey-led CIA, Max Hugel.[91]

A 1989 article from the *Omaha World Herald* stated that King's donation of $25,350 netted him access to Citizens for America's "founders club."[92] Other members of the group's founders club included Ivan Boesky, the insider trader tied to Drexel Burnham Lambert, and the corporate raider T. Boone Pickens. Boesky boasted longstanding ties to Max Fisher, a mentor of Leslie Wexner's.[93] Pickens was a major shareholder in Occidental Petroleum, which was run by Armand Hammer and somewhat involved in BCCI's entry into the US financial system (See Chapter 7).[94]

King made the $25,350 donation in 1987 and also made other "gifts" to the organization. A lawsuit filed against King by the National Credit Union Administration alleged that the large donation had been made with money he had looted from the Franklin Credit Union.[95] King's donations to Citizens for America made up roughly half of the approximate $55,000 King spent on political donations in total before Franklin's collapse.[96]

King's criminal activities extended far beyond the looting of the Credit Union he managed, although it would be the investigation into the Credit Union that would help expose his other acts. In reality, King was a key "pimp" in an "interstate pedophile network" that trafficked mostly vulnerable children, particularly orphans from Boys Town Nebraska, across the United States.[97]

Hints of this emerged in the *New York Times* in 1988, which cited Nebraska State Senator Ernie Chambers as having been "told of boys and girls, some of them from foster homes, who had been transported around the country by airplane to provide sexual favors, for which they were rewarded," as part of King's activities.[98] The *New York Times* also cited various law enforcement sources as stating that money-laundering and drugs were also part of the investigations. King's pedophile ring in Omaha allegedly involved many of the city's most powerful men, including Harold Andersen, publisher of the *Omaha World Herald* and friend of fellow Nebraskan Robert Keith Gray, as well as Omaha Police Chief Robert Wadman.[99] Then-Attorney General of Nebraska Robert Spire was also a "friend" of King's who attended King-hosted parties. Spire was later accused of "sitting on" allegations related to King's criminal activities.[100]

Several of the witnesses critical to the story of the Franklin Scandal – Alisha Owen, Paul Bonacci, Danny King, and Troy Boner – independently told investigators that they were abused in other ways, not just sexually, by Larry King's network. Per their accounts, they were also victims of sadistic physical abuse, which included suffering from whippings, knife wounds, and cigarette burns.[101] Some of the witnesses revealed that they had seen other children at King's "parties" and "orgies" who had claimed to have been kidnapped from their homes, some as young as twelve. At least one told of a child whose molestation, torture, and subsequent murder were all filmed by King and a group of adults.[102]

While King was mainly based in Omaha, he was also active in Washington DC, where he maintained a $5,000 per month residence off of Embassy Row.[103] Intimately related to King's DC activities was a man named Craig Spence. Spence had gotten his start as a press assistant for the Governor of Massachusetts before joining *ABC News* as a Vietnam War correspondent. According to some of his fellow Vietnam correspondents, Spence appeared to have an "inside track on seemingly clandestine information." He later moved to Tokyo, where he forged a business relationship with a Japanese politician named Motoo Shiina.

Shiina, after and during his relationship with Spence, was accused of "passing US military secrets to the Soviets." Notably, Shiina appears to have been a member of the Trilateral Commission, the body founded by David Rockefeller and Zbigniew Brzezinski, which has been accused of pursuing policies that involve the transfer of US technology to China and Russia under the guise of "normalizing" relations and building a "new international economic order."[104] In 1991, Shiina co-authored a book published by the Trilateral

Commission entitled *Global Competition After the Cold War: A Reassessment of Trilateralism* with Kurt Biedenkopf and Joseph S. Nye Jr.[105] Nye later went on to head the North American branch of the Trilateral Commission.

In the 1980s, after Shiina was accused of passing "military secrets" to the Russians, it was subsequently suggested by a member of Congress that Spence himself may have been involved in this alleged transfer of sensitive technology to China and Russia. Shortly thereafter, Shiina and Spence parted ways bitterly in 1983. Spence later stated that two bank transfers Shiina had sent him had come "into the country illegally from Hong Kong."[106] Spence had used the money to purchase a lavish property in the DC area, which would become central to his story.

Once established in DC, Spence became a prominent lobbyist. In the early 1980s, before he parted ways with Motoo Shiina, he described himself as an "international business consultant, party host, registered foreign agent" and a "research journalist."[107] His clients included "a number of American multinational companies." Much like Jeffrey Epstein, Spence was often compared to Jay Gatsby, the mysterious, wealthy figure from the well-known Fitzgerald novel *The Great Gatsby*. A 1982 *New York Times* article written about Spence said "what most impresses, if not benefits, his clients is his ability to master the social and political chemistry of this city, to make and use important connections and to bring together policy makers, power brokers, and opinion shapers at parties and seminars." It then stated that "there seems to be an inexhaustible demand in Washington for the sort of thing Mr. Spence offers."[108]

The *Times* also noted that Spence's "personal phone book and party guest lists constitute a 'Who's Who' in Congress, Government, and journalism" and that Spence was "hired by his clients as much for whom he knows as what he knows." Spence also had a reputation for throwing lavish parties, which the *Times* described as "glitter[ed] with notables, from ambassadors to television stars, from senators to senior State Department officials."[109] "According to Mr. Spence," the *Times* article continues, "Richard Nixon is a friend. So is [former Attorney General under Nixon] John Mitchell. [CBS journalist] Eric Sevareid is termed 'an old, dear friend.' Senator John Glenn is 'a good friend' and Peter Ustinov [British actor and journalist] is 'an old, old friend.'"[110] Notably, Jeffrey Epstein claimed to be friends with John Mitchell while Ustinov wrote for *The European* newspaper soon after it was founded in 1990 by Robert Maxwell, and where Ghislaine Maxwell also held a position.[111] Glenn, who represented Ohio, later flew on Jeffrey Epstein's jet to attend a birthday dinner for one of Ohio's richest political donors, Leslie Wexner.[112] Roy Cohn, William Casey, and Roy Cohn's journalist friend William Safire were just some of the other attendees at Spence's festivities. Cohn, it turns out, was another "good friend" of Spence's and Spence had hosted at least one birthday party for Roy Cohn at his DC area home.

It was revealed just seven years after the *New York Times* published its doting profile of Spence that his "glittery parties for key officials of the Reagan and Bush administrations, media stars, and top military officers" had been bugged in order "to compromise guests." According to the explosive report published by the *Washington Times*, Spence was linked to a "homosexual prostitution ring" whose clients included "government officials, locally based U.S. military officers, businessmen, lawyers, bankers, congressional aides, media representatives, and other professionals."[113] Spence also offered cocaine to his guests as another means of acquiring blackmail.

According to the report, Spence's home "was bugged and had a secret two-way mirror, and ... he attempted to ensnare visitors into compromising sexual encounters that he could then use as leverage." One man who spoke to the *Washington Times* said that Spence sent a limousine to his home, which took him to a party where "several young men tried to become friendly with him." According to John DeCamp, Spence was known to offer his guests young children for sex at his blackmail parties.[114]

Several other sources cited by the *Washington Times*, including a Reagan White House official and an Air Force sergeant who had attended Spence-hosted parties, confirmed that Spence's house was filled with recording equipment, which he regularly used to spy on and record guests, and his house also included a two-way mirror that he used for eavesdropping.[115]

The report also documented Spence's alleged connections to US intelligence, particularly the CIA. According to the *Washington Times* report, Spence "often boasted that he was working for the CIA and on one occasion said he was going to disappear for awhile 'because he had an important CIA assignment.'" He was also quite paranoid about his alleged work for the agency, as he expressed concern "that the CIA might 'double-cross him' and kill him instead and then make it look like a suicide."[116] Not long after the *Washington Times* report on his activities was published, Spence fell from grace and was later found dead in the Boston Ritz Carlton. His death was ruled a suicide.

The *Washington Times* report also offers a clue as to what Spence may have done for the CIA, as it cited sources that said Spence had spoken of smuggling cocaine into the US from El Salvador, an operation that he claimed involved US military personnel.[117] Given the timing of these comments from Spence, Spence's powerful connections, and the CIA's involvement in the exchange of cocaine for weapons in the Iran-Contra scandal, his comments could have been more than just boasts intended to impress his party guests.

One of the most critical parts of the scandal surrounding Spence, however, was the fact that he had been able to enter the White House late at night during the George H.W. Bush administration with young men whom the *Washington Times* described as "call boys."[118] After his fall from grace, Spence later stated that his contacts within the White House, which allowed him and his "call boys" after-hours access, were "top level" officials and he specifically singled out George H.W. Bush's then-National Security Advisor Donald Gregg.[119] Gregg had worked at the CIA since 1951 before he resigned in 1982 to become National Security Advisor to Bush, who was then vice president. Gregg denied Spence's allegations.

Prior to resigning from his post at the CIA, Gregg had worked directly under William Casey and, in the late 1970s, had worked alongside a young William Barr in stonewalling the Pike Committee and the Church Committee, which investigated the CIA beginning in 1975.[120] Among the things that these committees were tasked with investigating were the CIA's "love traps," or sexual blackmail operations used to lure foreign diplomats to bugged apartments, complete with recording equipment and two-way mirrors.[121] Gregg's role in Iran-Contra and other events during the Reagan years are discussed in Chapter 7.

The *Washington Times* article on this affair, stated that there was an official inquiry into Spence's activities and blackmail. However, it appeared to imply that the Department of Justice official managing the inquiry had a conflict of interest. It states:

> The office of US Attorney General Jay B. Stephens, former deputy White House counsel to President Reagan, is coordinating federal aspects of the inquiry but refused to discuss the investigation or grand jury actions.
>
> Several former White House colleagues of Mr. Stephens are listed among clients of the homosexual prostitution ring, according to the credit card records, and those persons have confirmed that the charges were theirs.
>
> Mr. Stephens' office, after first saying it would cooperate with *The Times'* inquiry, withdrew the offer late yesterday and also declined to say whether Mr. Stephens would recuse himself from the

case because of possible conflict of interest.

At least one highly placed Bush administration official and a wealthy businessman who procured homosexual prostitutes from the escort services operated by the ring are cooperating with the investigation, several sources said.

Among clients who charged homosexual prostitutes services on major credit cards over the past 18 months are Charles K. Dutcher, former associate director of presidential personnel in the Reagan administration, and Paul R. Balach, Labor Secretary Elizabeth Dole's political personnel liaison to the White House."[122]

Despite the names that surfaced in connection with Spence, including several different White House connections, it seems that – following his fall from grace and death – interest in the case disappeared and was largely memory-holed, not unlike what would follow years later in the Jeffrey Epstein case.

The information contained within the *Washington Times* reports was subsequently corroborated by Henry Vinson, who operated the "largest gay escort service ever uncovered in DC." Vinson had been significantly involved with Spence in Washington, DC and had received "thousands and thousands of dollars a month" from Spence at his escort service. Vinson claimed that he had been invited by Spence to his home "on numerous occasions" and that Vinson witnessed Spence flaunt his predilection for "cocaine and little boys." "He [Spence] was definitely a pedophile," Vinson would later tell Nick Bryant.[123]

Spence had also showcased his blackmail equipment to Vinson. Vinson, as quoted in Bryant's *Franklin Scandal*, stated:

Spence showed me the hidden, secret recording devices that were scattered throughout his home.... Spence often alluded to the fact that he was connected to the CIA, and it was obvious to me that he was very well connected. There were people at his home who said they were CIA, and at least one or two Secret Service agents – I believe that it was some of the CIA operatives who installed Spence's blackmail equipment. Much of Spence's influence came from the House of Representatives and the Senate, and he told me he was blackmailing Congressmen. I believe that Spence was blackmailing both for the CIA and for his own personal purposes.[124]

Vinson alleged that former CIA director William Casey was also a "personal friend" of Spence and attended his parties. Vinson additionally alleged that Casey had been one of his patrons, in addition to Spence,

452

and had begun requesting gay escorts from Vinson in 1986. Vinson stated that Casey's "preferred escort was an eighteen-year-old with minimal body hair and a slender swimmer's physique." Vinson asserted that Casey had requested underage escorts, which Vinson declined to provide.[125] It would be Vinson's refusal to supply underage escorts to Craig Spence that would bring about his downfall and subsequent arrest.[126]

Vinson also told Nick Bryant that Spence and Larry King were "partners" and "hooked up with the CIA," stating specifically that "King and Spence were in business together, and their business was pedophilic blackmail." "They were transporting children all over the country. They would arrange for children to be flown into Washington, DC and also arrange for influential people in DC to be flown out to the Midwest and meet these kids."

Paul Rodriguez, one of the *Washington Times* journalists who had helped expose Spence, also later told Nick Bryant that Spence and King had been partners, stating "I was told by several prostitutes along with law enforcement that there were connections between Craig Spence and Larry King. The allegations were that Spence and King hosted parties and were involved in a variety of nefarious activities: the allegations included Spence and King hosting blackmail sex parties that included minors and illegal drug use." Bryant also corroborated the Spence-King connection with Rusty Nelson and Paul Bonacci, who had both met Spence through King on different occasions.[127]

Per Vinson, Larry King had confided in him that he had clients who liked to torture and even kill children: "King said they had clients who actually liked having sex with kids as they tortured or killed the kid. I found that totally unbelievable." After Vinson said this to Nick Bryant, he asked Bryant later on in the interview if King's disclosure had indeed been true.[128] He was unaware at the time that other evidence, including witness testimony, had suggested that it was.

FROM OMAHA TO COLUMBUS: EXECUTIVE JET AVIATION

Larry King, before the Franklin Credit Union and related scandals completely unraveled, made extensive use of an airline called Executive Jet Aviation (EJA). King appears in the July 1987 issue of *Jet* magazine, where he was being congratulated personally by EJA executives Joseph B. Campbell and Skip Hockman "for being the passenger aboard the EJA jet that flew the company's 1 millionth mile of service" and was even "presented a model of the aircraft" on which he had flown. *Jet* also described King as being "a frequent user of EJA's service."[129] When EJA was later roped into a Congressional inquiry, accusations of the airline's alleged involvement in procuring girls for clients made their way into the questioning of company executives, as did allegations of the girls' exploitation for the purposes of blackmail.[130]

EJA was founded as Executive Jet Airways in 1964 by Brig. Gen. Olbert "Dick" Fearing Lassiter, an Air Force officer who was "known for his lust for excitement and fast living," characteristics which earned him the nickname "Rapid Richard."[131] EJA was originally founded in Delaware, but Lassiter quickly moved the company to Columbus, Ohio. Lassiter had been stationed in Columbus at Lockbourne Air Force Base, now known as Rickenbacker Airport, and was still a part of the Air Force when he incorporated EJA. Lassiter allegedly relocated EJA to Columbus mainly because "of the friendships he had made there."[132]

EJA's initial board of directors included actor Jimmy Stewart, former Assistant Secretary of the Navy James H. Smith, and former chairman of the Rockefeller family's Standard Oil branch in New Jersey, Monroe J. Rathbone.[133] At the time of its founding, it was "a closely held secret" that EJA had been financed by the American Contract Company, a wholly owned subsidiary of the Pennsylvania Railroad.

In 1965, the company adopted the name Executive Jet Aviation and created a subsidiary based in Switzerland. The Swiss subsidiary was largely led by Paul Tibbets, who served as its executive vice president and general manager.[134] Tibbets, who had also been on the founding board of EJA, is best known as the pilot of the Enola Gay when it dropped an atomic bomb on the Japanese city of Hiroshima at the close of World War II. By 1967, Tibbets and others left EJA. Tibbets allegedly left because "he believed some things that were going on [at the airline] were flagrantly illegal."

That same year, the parent company of the American Contract Company, the Pennsylvania Railroad, merged with the New York Central Railroad to form the Penn Central Transportation Company, better known as Penn Central. Rockefeller interests and Clinton Murchison Sr. were among those with financial stakes in New York Central and its subsidiaries at the time. The railroad also did significant business, including mergers and acquisitions, with individuals closely tied to the CIA-linked David Baird Foundation (see Chapters 1 and 4).[135] Penn Central would collapse in 1971, becoming one of the biggest bankruptcies in US history and what Peter Dale Scott referred to as "bankruptcy fraud with organized crime overtones."[136]

It would later emerge that Bruce Sundlun, a Washington attorney with past ties to Lassiter who was also on the EJA board of directors, would be responsible for the "covert" marriage between Pennsylvania Railroad/Penn Central and EJA. Their joining was performed by Glore Forgan at Sundlun's behest. Glore Forgan's vice president was General Charles Hodge, a Wall Street broker who was also the chief investment advisor to Penn Central and sat on the board of EJA.[137] As mentioned in Chapter 6, Glore Forgan was the same firm used by William Casey in his business ventures related to Multiponics.

The Penn Central link to EJA eventually emerged when Lassiter attempted to obtain a certificate that would have allowed him to operate larger aircraft. The Civil Aeronautics Board, which had a previous ruling forbidding a railroad from controlling an air carrier, discovered the tie and determined that the railroad had put around $22 million into the company. They then blocked Lassiter's request for the certificate and ordered the railroad to divest from EJA. Lassiter then proceeded as follows:

> Since he was barred from using the larger jets for domestic operations, Lassiter leased them to International Air Bahama, a Lichtenstein corporation he had persuaded a number of foreign investors to organize, which offered cut-rate service between Nassau and Luxembourg. However, although money was being made, lease money wasn't getting back to Executive Jet. The money Lassiter raised, said Tibbets, allowed him to live like a millionaire."[138]

Despite the Civil Aeronautics Board's ruling, Penn Central money continued to flow into EJA, albeit via a more convoluted route. This was reportedly made possible, according to the *New York Times*, by Lassiter arranging "dates" for the aforementioned Charles Hodge as well as David Bevan, Penn Central's CFO, so that the two men would "continue the flow of railroad funds to Executive Jet."[139] Both Hodge and Bevan were on the EJA board. The *Times* goes on to quote an official complaint, which stated: "The steady flow of Penn Central money to Executive Jet was maintained by Lassiter's procuring of young women to accompany Bevan and Hodge on various junkets in the United States and Europe."[140]

Paul Tibbets was also quoted as saying that "A weakness for beautiful women contributed to his [Lassiter's] problems, according to more than one magazine article that appeared while EJA's difficulties were making headlines."[141] Lassiter reportedly maintained furnished apartments in New York City and elsewhere in the US, as well as foreign cities that included Rome, where some of these women would allegedly accompany him.

In 1970, Bruce Sundlun, the attorney on the EJA board of directors who first connected the company to Penn Central, raided EJA's offices as the company began its descent. In the course of that raid, Sundlun reportedly came across "a large stack of color photographs" that showed Lassiter "in the company of various young women, all of them very pretty and amply endowed."[142]

During inquiries about the collapse of Penn Central, as previously mentioned, the congressional hearings involved lines of questioning directed at Lassiter about the procurement of women for Bevan and Hodge, which was allegedly performed by J.H. Ricciardi. Ricciardi had testified in 1968 that he had procured these women "to relieve the pressure they were exerting on Mr. Lassiter to get the company into the black."[143] Ricciardi also sued EJA over fees he claimed were owed to him for his efforts to procure women, which Ricciardi said he did at Lassiter's request. Lassiter denied Ricciardi's allegations and accused Ricciardi of "blackmail."[144]

In addition, at those same congressional hearings that followed Penn Central's implosion, Congressman J.W. Wright Patman (D-TX) stated that EJA's role in the Penn Central collapse raised "most serious questions about the involvement of the commercial banking industry in the strange and far-flung operations of Executive Jet Aviation [...] Commercial banks made massive amounts of credit available to Executive Jet Aviation for what appeared to be highly questionable – if not at times illegal – activities."[145]

After Penn Central's 1970 collapse, it re-emerged in 1977, not as a railroad company, but as an "energy, recreation, and real estate company."[146] A year later, it was disclosed that corporate raider Saul Steinberg, mentioned in Chapters 8 and 9 and who had previously tried to acquire Robert Maxwell's Pergamon Press, had obtained 7.9 percent of the new incarnation of Penn Central, which grew to 13 percent a year later.[147] Cincinnati financier Carl Lindner Jr. obtained 30 percent of the company between 1981 and 1982, which included Steinberg's position. Lindner became chairman of Penn Central in 1983.[148] The broker for these trades was Drexel Burnham Lambert's Michael Milken. Also involved was Randall Smith Jr., then at Bear Stearns who later went on to become a prominent "vulture capitalist."[149]

Lindner Jr. was also, at the time, intimately involved in Meshulam Riklis' Rapid-American, which – as mentioned in Chapter 2 – contained the remnants of Lewis Rosenstiel's business interests.[150] He was also seemingly connected to Jack DeVoe, the cocaine smuggler mentioned in Chapter 7, as DeVoe maintained his planes at a club and airstrip that Lindner owned.[151] In addition, the year after Lindner became chairman of Penn Central, Lindner Jr. would be given the reins of United Brands, a company with CIA links, by Leslie Wexner's "mentor" Max Fisher and his associates (see Chapter 13).

As for Executive Jet Aviation, it was foreclosed upon before reopening with Bruce Sundlun in charge. Paul Tibbets would return to the company around the same time and would succeed Sundlun as president in 1976. In 1984, with Tibbets still serving as president, EJA was acquired by Richard Santulli. Previously, Santulli had served as president of Goldman Sachs' leasing division, which bought helicopters and airplanes and then leased them to companies. Santulli left in 1980 to create his own leasing company, RTS Capital Services.[152] EJA became a subsidiary of RTS and was later renamed as NetJets. It was during this era of EJA that Lawrence King, of Franklin Scandal fame, became a "frequent user of EJA's service", which – as previously mentioned – brought him into close contact with EJA executives.[153]

In 1993, at least two EJA pilots were recruited by Leslie Wexner's The Limited, or Lbrands. One of these pilots, Eric Black, had been an EJA pilot starting in 1988, then working for an EJA subsidiary in Miami – Executive Jet Management – transporting checks for the Federal Reserve. He returned to EJA's Columbus location in 1993, before being hired as a pilot for The Limited in August 1993. Black is now the Lead Captain for Lbrands flights.[154] Another pilot, Mike Crater, also joined The Limited from EJA, where he had worked since 1986, in August 1993.[155]

1993 was a curious time in the activities of The Limited, particularly as it relates to its air freight concerns. As will be detailed in Chapter 17, in May of that year, The Limited was courted by a company called Polar Air Cargo, which sought to install itself at the Rickenbacker airstrip, once home to the Air Force Base where Lassiter had been stationed when he created Executive Jet. Polar Air Cargo, as reported by the *Columbus Dispatch*, was a joint venture of NedMark Transportation, Polaris Aircraft Leasing Corporation, and the now infamous CIA-linked airline Southern Air Transport.[156] At the time, more than half of Polar Air Cargo's employees had formerly worked for Flying Tiger Line, which – as noted in Chapter 5 – was tied to Anna Chennault and Robert Keith Gray. Though Polar Air Cargo's efforts would be for naught, The Limited, with direct input from Jeffrey Epstein, would be largely responsible for the relocation of Southern Air Transport to Rickenbacker in 1995.

Endnotes

1   Nicholas Von Hoffman, *Citizen Cohn*, 1st ed (New York: Doubleday, 1988), 402.

2   Gabriel H. Sanchez, "29 Pictures That Show Just How Insane Studio 54 Really Was," *Buzz-Feed News*, https://www.buzzfeednews.com/article/gabrielsanchez/pictures-that-show-just-how-insane-studio-54-really-was.

3   Bob Colacello, "Studio 54's Cast List: A Who's Who of the 1970s Nightlife Circuit," Vanity Fair, September 4, 2013, https://www.vanityfair.com/news/1996/03/studio-54-nightclub-new-york-city.

4   Tate Delloye, "Roy Cohn: New Documentary Explores the Man Who Made Donald Trump," *Mail Online*, March 14, 2019, https://www.dailymail.co.uk/news/article-6809557/Roy-Cohn-Donald-Trumps-ruthless-homophobic-attorney-partied-Studio-54-died-AIDS.html.

5   Von Hoffman, *Citizen Cohn*, 403.

6   Von Hoffman, *Citizen Cohn*, 405-407.

7   Frank Rich, "Roy Cohn was the Original Donald Trump," *Intelligencer*, April 29, 2018, https://nymag.com/intelligencer/2018/04/frank-rich-roy-cohn-the-original-donald-trump.html.

8   Rich, "Original Donald Trump."

9   Rich, "Original Donald Trump."

10   Rich, "Original Donald Trump."

11   Barbara Walters' name can be found in Epstein's black book of contacts. See "Epstein's Black Book," https://epsteinsblackbook.com/names/barbara-walters; Rich, "Original Donald Trump."

12   Alan Feuer, "Up From Politics, Almost," *New York Times*, October 1, 2004, https://www.nytimes.com/2004/10/01/nyregion/up-from-politics-almost.html; Marie Brenner, "How Donald Trump and Roy Cohn's Ruthless Symbiosis Changed America," *Vanity Fair*, June 28, 2017, https://www.vanityfair.com/news/2017/06/donald-trump-roy-cohn-relationship.

13   Von Hoffman, *Citizen Cohn*, 414.

14   Von Hoffman, *Citizen Cohn*, 334.

15   Jeffrey Toobin, "The Dirty Trickster," *The New Yorker*, May 23, 2008, http://www.newyorker.com/magazine/2008/06/02/the-dirty-trickster; Mark Ames, "Behind the Scenes of the Donald Trump – Roger Stone Show," *Pando*, August 11, 2015, https://web.archive.org/web/20190730062318/https://pando.com/2015/08/11/behind-scenes-donald-trump-roger-stone-show/.

16   Sam Roberts, "Thomas A. Bolan, Understated Force in New York Law, Dies at 92," *New York Times*, May 17, 2017, https://www.nytimes.com/2017/05/16/nyregion/thomas-bolan-dead-roy-cohn-law-partner.html.

17   Roberts, "Thomas A. Bolan,"; Wanda Carruthers, "Tom Bolan, Famed Attorney and Roy Cohn's Law Partner, Dies," *Newsmax*, May 14, 2017, https://www.newsmax.com/Newsfront/Tom-Bolan-dies-lawyer-conservative/2017/05/14/id/790052/.

18   "Donald Trump and Ghislaine Maxwell on Her Dad's (Robert) Yacht in May 1989," *St. Louis Post-Dispatch*, May 17, 1989, https://www.newspapers.com/clip/9383143/donald-trump-and-ghislaine-maxwell-on/.

19   David Ingram, "Sex Claim Filing Against Dershowitz a Mistake, Say Florida Lawyers; Defamation Claims Settled," *Insurance Journal*, April 12, 2016, https://www.insurancejournal.com/news/southeast/2016/04/12/404808.htm; Victor Thorn, "Louis Freeh: The Cover-up Goes National," *American Free Press*, June 22, 2012, https://americanfreepress.net/web-exclusive-louis-freeh-the-cover-up-goes-national/.

20   Carruthers, "Tom Bolan,"; Marcus Baram, "Eavesdropping on Roy Cohn and Donald Trump," *The New Yorker*, April 14, 2017, http://www.newyorker.com/news/news-desk/eavesdropping-on-roy-cohn-and-donald-trump.

21   Baram, "Eavesdropping."

22   Baram, "Eavesdropping."

23   Baram, "Eavesdropping."

24   Becky Little, "Roy Cohn: From Ruthless 'Red Scare' Prosecutor to Donald Trump's Mentor," *HISTORY*, March 6, 2019, https://www.history.com/news/roy-cohn-mccarthyism-rosenberg-trial-donald-trump.

25   James Michael Nichols, "Hillary Clinton Apologizes After Shocking Praise For Nancy Reagan's 'AIDS Activism,'" *HuffPost*, March 11, 2016, https://www.huffpost.com/entry/hillary-clinton-nancy-reagan-aids-activism_n_56e31770e4b0b25c9181e002.

26   Robert Parry, "How Roy Cohn Helped Rupert Murdoch," *Consortium News*, January 28, 2015, https://consortiumnews.com/2015/01/28/how-roy-cohn-helped-rupert-murdoch/.

27   Jerry Oppenheimer, "President Reagan's Mafia Ties Revealed in Explosive New Documentary," *Mail Online*, May 21, 2014, https://www.dailymail.co.uk/news/article-2635094/EXCLUSIVE-Revealed-MAFIA-helped-Ronald-Reagan-White-House-Shocking-documentary-reveals-Mob-connections-catapulted-presidency-probe-thwarted-highest-levels.html.

28   Oppenheimer, "President Reagan's Mafia Ties,"; Tina Daunt, "New Doc Alleges Ronald Reagan Blocked Probe Into Lew Wasserman's Mafia Ties," *The Hollywood Reporter*, June 12, 2014,   https://www.hollywoodreporter.com/news/politics-news/new-doc-alleges-ronald-reagan-711288/.

29   Oppenheimer, "President Reagan's Mafia Ties."

30   Oppenheimer, "President Reagan's Mafia Ties."

31   Carl Sifakis, *The Mafia Encyclopedia*, 3. ed (New York: Checkmark Books, 2005), 132.

32   Mike Barnes, "Edie Wasserman, Wife of Lew Wasserman, Dies at 95," *The Hollywood Reporter*, August 18, 2011, https://www.hollywoodreporter.com/news/general-news/edie-wasserman-wife-lew-wasserman-225101/.

33   Gus Russo, *Supermob: How Sidney Korshak And His Criminal Associates Became America's Hidden Power Brokers* (New York: Bloomsbury, 2008), 158.

34   *New West*, Volume 1, p. 27, https://www.google.com/books/edition/New_West/6SkcAQAAIAAJ.

35   Nick Tosches, "The Man Who Kept The Secrets," *Vanity Fair*, April 6, 1997, https://www.vanityfair.com/news/1997/04/The-Man-Who-Kept-The-Secrets.

36   Oppenheimer, "President Reagan's Mafia Ties."

37   David Cay Johnston, "Just What Were Donald Trump's Ties to the Mob?," *POLITICO Magazine*, May 22, 2016, https://www.politico.com/magazine/story/2016/05/donald-trump-2016-mob-organized-crime-213910.

38   Newsweek Staff, "The Bcci-Cia Connection: Just How Far Did It Go?," *Newsweek*, December 6, 1992, https://www.newsweek.com/bcci-cia-connection-just-how-far-did-it-go-195454.

39   Susan Trento, "Lord of the Lies; How Hill and Knowlton's Robert Gray Pulls Washington's Strings," *Washington Monthly*, September 1, 1992, https://www.thefreelibrary.com/Lord+of+the+lies%3B+how+Hill+and+Knowlton%27s+Robert+Gray+pulls...-a012529888.

40   "B'nai B'rith Testimonial Dinner in Honor of Roy Cohn," May 2, 1983, https://consortiumnews.com/wp-content/uploads/2015/01/Cohn-Dinner.pdf.

41   "B'Nai B'rith Dinner."

42   "B'Nai B'rith Dinner."

43   "The Order of B'Nai B'rith," *New York Times*, March 31, 1878.

44   Bruce Weber, "He Relit Broadway: Gerald Schoenfeld Dies at 84," *New York Times*, November 25, 2008, https://www.nytimes.com/2008/11/26/theater/26schoenfeld.html.

45   Barbara Gamarekian, "Washington Talk: Career Secretaries; Wielding Power Discreetly," *New York Times*, May 14, 1987, https://www.nytimes.com/1987/05/14/us/washington-talk-career-secretaries-wielding-power-discreetly.html.

46   Jonathan Marshall, *Dark Quadrant: Organized Crime, Big Business, and the Corruption of American Democracy: From Truman to Trump*, ePub, (Lanham: Rowman & Littlefield, An imprint of The Rowman & Littlefield Publishing Group, Inc, 2021), 245.

47   Dan E. Moldea, *Interference: How Organized Crime Influences Professional Football*, 1st ed (New York: Morrow, 1989), 93–95, 451 note 8.

48   E. J. Dionne Jr, "US Envoy Denies Discussing Iran Arms," *New York Times*, December 1, 1986, https://www.nytimes.com/1986/12/01/world/us-envoy-denies-discussing-iran-arms.html.

49   Robert D. McFadden, "Edward V. Regan, Longtime New York State Comptroller, Dies at 84," *New York Times*, October 19, 2014, https://www.nytimes.com/2014/10/19/nyregion/edward-v-regan-longtime-new-york-state-comptroller-dies-at-84-.html.

459

50   "Rev. Bruce N. Ritter,"*Bishop Accountability.org*, https://www.bishop-accountability.org/assign/Ritter_Bruce_N_ofm.conv.htm.

51   Tracy Connor, "Scandal-Scarred Founder of Covenant House Dead at 72," *New York Post*, October 12, 1999, https://nypost.com/1999/10/12/scandal-scarred-founder-of-covenant-house-dead-at-72/.

52   Steve Cuozzo, "This NYC Priest's Dramatic Downfall Was Just the Beginning of Perv-Priest Scandals," *New York Post*, September 13, 2018, https://nypost.com/2018/09/13/this-nyc-priests-dramatic-downfall-was-just-the-beginning-of-perv-priest-scandals/.

53   Cuozzo, "Priest's Dramatic Downfall."

54   Cuozzo, "Priest's Dramatic Downfall."

55   M. A. Farber, "Ritter Inquiry Leading Many To Quit Board," *New York Times*, May 1, 1990, https://www.nytimes.com/1990/05/01/nyregion/ritter-inquiry-leading-many-to-quit-board.html.

56   Cuozzo, "Priest's Dramatic Downfall."

57   Anthony Ramirez, "Rev. Bruce Ritter, 72, the Founder of Covenant House for Runaway Children," *New York Times*, October 13, 1999, https://www.nytimes.com/1999/10/13/nyregion/rev-bruce-ritter-72-the-founder-of-covenant-house-for-runaway-children.html.

58   Kroll Associates' role is discussed in detail in Peter J. Wosh, *Covenant House: Journey of a Faith-Based Charity* (Philadelphia: University of Pennsylvania Press, 2005), 184-88, 192, 207-210.
        It is also mentioned in New York Magazine. Christopher Byron, "High Spy," *New York Magazine*, May 13, 1991, 72, https://books.google.cl/books?id=COkCAAAAMBAJ&pg=PA72.

59   "Limited hangout" is intelligence jargon for a form of propaganda in which a selected portion of a scandal, criminal act, sensitive or classified information, etc. is revealed or leaked, but avoids telling the whole story. This may be done to establish one's credibility as a critic of something or somebody by engaging in criticism of them while, in fact, they are aiding the covering up by omitting more damaging details. Other motives may include the intention to distance oneself publicly from something using innocuous or vague criticism even when ones own sympathies are privately with them; or to divert public attention away from a more heinous act by leaking information about something less heinous. Byron, "High Spy,"; Kurt Eichenwald, "Drexel Burnham Fights Back," *New York Times*, September 11, 1988, https://www.nytimes.com/1988/09/11/business/drexel-burnham-fights-back.html.

60   Charles M Sennott, *Broken Covenant* (New York: Windsor Pub., 1994), 14, https://archive.org/details/brokencovenant00senn.

61   Cuozzo, "Priest's Dramatic Downfall."

62   Ann Marsh, "Americares' Success Hailed, Criticized," *Hartford Courant*, August 10, 1991, https://www.courant.com/news/connecticut/hc-xpm-1991-08-11-0000213209-story.html.

63   Marsh, "Americares' Success."

64   Cuozzo, "Priest's Dramatic Downfall."

65   Marsh, "Americares' Success."

66   Farber, "Ritter Inquiry."

67   Staff, "Rev. Bruce Ritter, 72, Founder of Covenant House, Dies," *Buffalo News*, October 12, 1999, https://buffalonews.com/news/rev-bruce-ritter-72-founder-of-covenant-house-dies/article_5d8b7652-4204-599a-9507-2eefadc9aea6.html.

68   "Cryptonym: ZRSIGN," Mary Ferrell Foundation, https://www.maryferrell.org/php/cryptdb.php?id=ZRSIGN&search=AIFLD; "United Fruit-C.I.A. Link Charged," *New York Times*, October 22, 1976, https://www.nytimes.com/1976/10/22/archives/united-fruitcia-link-charged.html.

69   Marsh, "Americares' Success."

70   Marsh, "Americares' Success."

71   Bill Flood, "Connecticut Reacts to Loss of 'Native Son', 41st U.S. President George H.W. Bush," fox61.com, December 1, 2018, https://www.fox61.com/article/news/local/outreach/awareness-months/connecticut-reacts-to-loss-of-native-son-41st-u-s-president-george-h-w-bush/520-0270014d-288b-4da7-bd12-3c60188a2a76.

72   Marsh, "Americares' Success."

73   Marsh, "Americares' Success."

74   Marsh, "Americares' Success."

75   Marsh, "Americares' Success."

76   Matthew Phelan, "Seymour Hersh and the Men Who Want Him Committed," *Salon*, February 28, 2011, https://www.salon.com/2011/02/28/seymour_hersh_whowhatwhy/.

77   Kris Hundley and Kendall Taggart, "No Accounting for $40 Million in Charity Shipped Overseas," *Tampa Bay Times*, https://www.tampabay.com/news/business/no-accounting-for-40-million-in-charity-shipped-overseas/2162553/.

78   Phelan, "Seymour Hersh."

79   John W. DeCamp, *The Franklin Cover-Up: Child Abuse, Satanism, and Murder in Nebraska* (Lincoln, Neb: AWT, 1992), 180.

80   Deborah Sontag, "L.I. Man Who Runs Home for Boys In Guatemala Is on Trial in Absentia," *New York Times*, April 12, 1997, https://www.nytimes.com/1997/04/12/nyregion/li-man-who-runs-home-for-boys-in-guatemala-is-on-trial-in-absentia.html.

81   Nicholas A. Bryant, *The Franklin Scandal: A Story of Powerbrokers, Child Abuse and Betrayal*, First edition (revised for softcover) (Waterville, OR: Trine Day, 2012), 32–33.

82   Bryant, *Franklin Scandal*, 35-36

83   Bryant, *Franklin Scandal*, 36.

84   Bryant, *Franklin Scandal*, 36-37.

85   Bryant, *Franklin Scandal*, 37-38.

86   Robert Dorr, "King Donated $25,350 to Aid Lobbying Group," *Omaha World Herald*, May 21, 1989.

87   For more information see: Pete Brewton, *The Mafia, CIA, and George Bush* (S.P.I. Books, Dec. 1992).

88   Bryant, *Franklin Scandal*, 37.

89   Dorr, "King Donated $23,500."

90   Dorr, "King Donated $23,500."

91   Harry Bernstein, "Former CIA Man Now Battling Unions," *Los Angeles Times*, February 18, 1987, https://www.latimes.com/archives/la-xpm-1987-02-18-fi-2605-story.html.

92   Dorr, "King Donated $23,500."

93   Max Fisher, "Letter to Morris Lasker," September 28, 1987, https://www.sechistorical.org/collection/papers/1980/1987_0928_FisherLaskerBoesky.pdf.

94   "Wall Street's Top Earners: Your Pain, Their Gain," *Forbes*, April 15, 2008, https://www.forbes.com/2008/04/15/paulson-falcone-earners-biz-wall-cz_js_0415wallstreet.html.

95   Dorr, "King Donated $23,500."

96   Dorr, "King Donated $23,500."

97   Warwick Middleton, MD, "An Interview with Nick Bryant: Part I – The Franklin Scandal," August 7, 2019, https://news.isst-d.org/an-interview-with-nick-bryant-part-i-the-franklin-scandal/.

98   William Robbins, "A Lurid, Mysterious Scandal Begins Taking Shape in Omaha," *New York Times*, December 18, 1988, https://www.nytimes.com/1988/12/18/us/a-lurid-mysterious-scandal-begins-taking-shape-in-omaha.html.

99   Bryant, *Franklin Scandal*, 87.

100   Bryant, *Franklin Scandal*, 98.

101   Bryant, *Franklin Scandal*, 158.

102   Bryant, *Franklin Scandal*, 158-59.

103   Robbins, "Scandal in Omaha."

104   Patrick Wood, "Flashback – How The Trilateral Commission Converted China Into A Technocracy," *Technocracy News*, April 22, 2016, https://www.technocracy.news/trilateral-commission-converted-china-technocracy/.

105   "Joseph S Nye Resume," https://apps.hks.harvard.edu/faculty/cv/JosephNye.pdf.

106   Bryant, *Franklin Scandal*, 280-84.

107   Phil Gailey, "Have Names, Will Open Right Doors," *New York Times*, January 18, 1982, https://www.nytimes.com/1982/01/18/us/have-names-will-open-right-doors.html.

108   Gailey, "Have Names."

109   Gailey, "Have Names."

110   Gailey, "Have Names."

111   Lee Siegel, "In Short: Nonfiction," *New York Times*, May 21, 1995, https://www.nytimes.com/1995/05/21/books/in-short-nonfiction-231795.html.

112   Jacob Shamsian, "John Glenn Was a Passenger on Jeffrey Epstein's Private Jet in 1996, According to Unsealed Flight Records," *Insider*, August 9, 2019, https://www.insider.com/john-glenn-flew-on-jeffrey-epstein-private-jet-2019-8.

113   Michael Hedges and Jerry Seper, "Power Broker Served Drugs, Sex at Parties Bugged for Blackmail," *Washington Times*, June 30, 1989, sec. Final.

114   John W. DeCamp, *The Franklin Cover-Up: Child Abuse, Satanism, and Murder in Nebraska*, ePub (Nebraska: AWT, 1992), 169.

115   Hedges and Seper, "Power Broker Served Drugs."

116   Hedges and Seper, "Power Broker Served Drugs."

117   Hedges and Seper, "Power Broker Served Drugs."

118   Paul M Rodriguez and George Archibald, "Homosexual Prostitution Inquiry Ensnares VIPs with Reagan, Bush 'Call Boys' Took Midnight Tour of White House," *Washington Times*, June 29, 1989, https://govcrime.wordpress.com/2011/03/02/washington-times-call-boy-article-1989/.

119   Jerry Seper and Michael Hedges, "Spence Arrested in N.Y., Released; Once-Host to Powerful Reduced to Begging, Sleeping in Park," *Washington Times*, August 9, 1989, https://govcrime.wordpress.com/2011/04/13/spence-arrested-in-n-y-released-once-host-to-powerful-reduced-to-begging-sleeping-in-park/.

120   "What the CIA Tells Congress (Or Doesn't) about Covert Operations: The Barr/Cheney/Bush Turning Point for CIA Notifications to the Senate," *NSA Archive*, February 7, 2019, https://nsarchive.gwu.edu/briefing-book/intelligence/2019-02-07/what-cia-tells-congress-or-doesnt-about-covert-operations-barrcheneybush-turning-point-cia.

121   Jack Anderson and Les Whitten, "CIA Love Traps Lured Diplomats," *Washington Post*, February 5, 1975, http://jfk.hood.edu/Collection/White%20Materials/Security-CIA/CIA%201025.pdf.

122   Rodriguez and Archibald, "Homosexual Prostitution Inquiry."

123   Bryant, *Franklin Scandal*, 293, 295.

124   Bryant, *Franklin Scandal*, 296.

125   Henry W. Vinson, *Confessions of a D.C. Madam: The Politics of Sex, Lies & Blackmail*, First Edition (Oregon: Trine Day, 2014), 118–19.

126   Bryant, *Franklin Scandal*, 296-300.

127   Bryant, *Franklin Scandal*, 284.

128   Bryant, *Franklin Scandal*, 296-97.

129   "Skybound Business Exec," *Jet*, July 6, 1987, 28, https://books.google.com/books?id=_LEDAAAAMBAJ.

130   Joseph R Daughen and Peter Binzen, *The Wreck of the Penn Central*, First edition (Boston: Little, Brown, and Company, 1971), 202-04, https://archive.org/details/wreckofpenncentr00daug.

131   "Paul Tibbets: A Rendezvous with History (Part 3)," *Airport Journals*, June 1, 2003, http://airportjournals.com/paul-tibbets-a-rendezvous-with-history-part-3/.

132   "Paul Tibbets."

133   "Paul Tibbets."

134   "Paul Tibbets."

135   John J. McCloy, chairman of the Rockefeller-dominated Chase Manhattan Bank, became an 'important financial ally' of Clint Murchison, Sr., and Sid Richardson when the two Texans became (through Alleghany Corp.) major stockholders in the New York Central Railroad, later merged into Penn Central." See Peter Dale Scott, *Deep Politics and the Death of JFK* (University of California Press, 1996), 136.

In addition, the founder of Alleghany and the architect of its takeover of New York Central via the use of Richardson and Murchison as proxies, Robert R. Young, was a client of the Baird Foundation. "...Mr. Young disclosed that Mr. David G. Baird, 'a good friend of his, had approached the [Chesapeake and Ohio Railroad] to sell its Central stock to an investing group before it sold the block to Messrs. Murchison and Richardson'" See: Tax-Exempt Foundations and Charitable Trusts, Their

Impact on Our Economy: United States House Select Committee on Small Business, 1963, 57-58.

Penn Central money was put into Great Southwest via Penphil, a private investment operation set up by the railroad's CFO David Bevan and General Charles J. Hodge, the railroad's chief investment officer. See: Associated Press, "$21-Million Fraud."

"...control of Great Southwest was tightly centered in the Rockefeller and Wynne families" See: The Penn Central Failure and the Role of Financial Institutions: Staff Report of the Committee on Banking and Currency, 1970, 30.

136   Scott, *Deep Politics*, 284.

137   Daughen and Blinzen, *The Wreck of Penn Central*, 161.

138   "Paul Tibbets."

139   The Associated Press, "$21-Million Fraud At Penn Central Is Charged to 3," *New York Times*, January 5, 1972, https://www.nytimes.com/1972/01/05/archives/21million-fraud-at-penn-central-is-charged-to-3-bevan-exfinance.html.

140   AP, "$21-Million Fraud."

141   "Paul Tibbets."

142   Daughen and Blinzen, *The Wreck of Penn Central*, 176.

143   Michael C. Jensen, "Pennsy Is Scored in a House Report," *New York Times*, December 21, 1970, https://www.nytimes.com/1970/12/21/archives/pennsy-is-scored-in-a-house-report-jet-aviation-units-history.html.

144   Daughen and Blinzen, *The Wreck of Penn Central*, 204.

145   Jensen, "Pennsy is Scored."

146   Robert J Cole, "Saul Steinberg: Gunning for Penn Central," *New York Times*, November 11, 1979, https://www.nytimes.com/1979/11/11/archives/saul-steinberg-gunning-for-penn-central.html.

147   Cole, "Saul Steinberg."

148   Daniel F. Cuff, "Business People; Lindner Chairman of Penn Central," *New York Times*, May 20, 1983, https://www.nytimes.com/1983/05/20/business/business-people-lindner-chairman-of-penn-central.html.

149   Hilary Rosenberg, *The Vulture Investors* (New York: J. Wiley, 2000), 12.

150   Cuff, "Business People."

151   For DeVoe's relationship to Ocean Reef, see: *Organized Crime and Cocaine Trafficking Record of Hearing IV*, President's Commission on Organized Crime, November 27-29, 1984, https://www.ojp.gov/ncjrs/virtual-library/abstracts/organized-crime-and-cocaine-trafficking. Additional corroboration can be found in Scott, *Deep Politics*, 335.

152   "How Richard Santulli Became The Father of Fractional Ownership," *International Aviation HQ*, January 26, 2022, https://internationalaviationhq.com/2022/01/26/richard-santulli-netjets/.

153   "Skybound Business Exec," *Jet*.

154   Eric Black, LinkedIn, Accessed June 28, 2022, https://www.linkedin.com/in/eric-black-660a01126/details/experience/.

155   Mike Crater, LinkedIn, Accessed June 28, 2022, https://www.linkedin.com/in/mike-crater-2aa9316/.

156   "Cargo Service Targets City – Polar Plans to Land Weekly Flights at Rickenbacker Starting Sunday," *Columbus Dispatch*, May 12, 1993, https://dispatch.newsbank.com/doc/news/10E0D9C54B7D92F8.

List of Abbreviations

ACUSR – American Committee on US-Soviet Relations

ADFA – Arkansas Development Finance Authority

AFL-CIO – American Federation of Labor and the Congress of Industrial Organizations

AIA- Aviation Industries Association

AIFLD – American Institute of Free Labor Development

AIG– American International Group

ANICO – American National Insurance Company

AREB – All-Russian Exchange Bank

BCCI – Bank of Credit and Commerce International

BCP – Banque de Commerce et de Placements

BNL – Banca Nazionale del Lavoro

BONY – Eastern European Division of Bank of New York

BONY-IMB – Bank of New York-Inter Maritime Bank

BSC – British Security Coordination

BWC – Bank of World Commerce

CAT – Civil Air Transport

CCC – Commercial Credit Corporation

CDC – Control Data Corporation

CIA – Central Intelligence Agency

CMA – Civilian Materiel Assistance

CMC – Centro Mondale Commerciale

COG – Continuity of Government

COI – Office of the Coordinator of Information

COP – Chiefs of Police National Drug Task Force

CORDS – Civil Operations and Revolutionary Development Support

CORU – Coordination of United Revolutionary Organizations

CPD – Committee on the Present Danger

CRP – Committee for the Reelection of the President

DEA – US Drug Enforcement Administration

DFS – La Dirección Federal de Seguridad

DIA – Defense Intelligence Agency

DNC – Democratic National Committee

DOD – Department of Defense

DOJ – Department of Justice

EATSCO – Egyptian-American Air Transport and Services Corporation

EJA – Executive Jet Aviation

ERA – Engineering Research Associates

EUB – European Union Bank

FABCO – First Arkansas Bankstock Corporation

FBI – Federal Bureau of Investigation

FBN – Federal Bureau of Narcotics

FGB – Financial General Bankshares (aka First American Bankshares)

FIDCO – First Intercontinental Development Corporation

GMT – GeoMili Tech Consultants Corporation

HUMINT – Nitze's program for a naval human intelligenceIAHC – Italo-American Hotel Corporation

IAI – Israel Aerospace Industries

IAI – Israel Aircraft Industries

ICB – International Credit Bank

ICLR – International Computerized Land Research

IDEA – Institute for Democracy, Education, and Assistance IDF – Israel Defense Force

IFMA – International Fund for Mergers and Acquisitions

IMB – Inter Maritime Bank

IOS – Investors Overseas Services

IRS – Internal Revenue Service

IRT – International Research and Trade KMT – Nationalist Chinese the Kuomintang

LTV – Ling-Temco-Vought

MCA – Music Corporation of America

MECC – Midwest Employers Casualty Company

NAR – North American Resources

NHAQ – Nicaraguan Humanitarian Assistance Office

NSA – National Security Agency

NSC – National Security Council

NSIC – National Strategy Information Center

NVA – North Vietnamese Army

OMB – Office of Management and Budget ONI – Office of Naval Intelligence

OPC – Office of Policy Coordination

OSG – Operations Sub-Group

OSS – Office of Strategic Services

PEC – Palestine Economic Corporation

PIIC – Pergamon International Information Corporation

PLO – Palestine Liberation Organization

RNB – Republic National Bank

SAG – Screen Actors Guild

SAT – Southern Air Transport

SDECE – France's External Documentation and Counter-Espionage Service

SDNY – Southern District of New York

SEC – Securities and Exchange Commission

SGS – Société Générale de Surveillance

SIG – Special Interrogation Group

SOE – Special Operations Executive

SSI – System Services International

STTG – Stanford Technology Trading Group International

TF–157 – Task Force 157

TIWG Terrorist Incident Working Group

TRADEVCO – Liberian Trade and Development Corp

UFG – United Financial Group

WCC – World Commerce Corporation WWF – World Wildlife Fund

YAF – Young Americans for Freedom

DOCUMENTS

Document 1: GeoMiliTech's circular trading arrange-ment with, the US, Israel and China.
https://www.google.com/books/edition/Report_of_the_Congressional_Committees_I/H8S6dlhvqp8C?hl=en

UNCLASSIFIED   59

1   document at the present time, does this cause you to
2   recall that any of these matters were discussed by
3   Studley with the Director at that December 20 meeting,
4   namely the idea of creating a circular arrangement in
5   which a trading company would be established to supply
6   freedom fighter movements which Congress was unwilling to
7   support for one reason or another and that Israel would
8   sell certain things, military equipment, to the People's
9   Republic of China, who would supply the Soviet arms,
10   which would then be brokered to the freedom fighters, and
11   that Israel would be benefitted by the United States
12   through a high technology support or other compensation?
13   Do you recall anything?
14   A   What's the question?
15   Q   Well, the question is were the matters that I
16   have just described discussed by Studley at that meeting?
17   A   To the best of my knowledge, they were not,
18   no.
19   Q   Do you recall the same day as the meeting with
20   Studley that the Director called Richard Secord for a
21   meeting?
22   A   No, I don't.
23   Q   Let me show you a document which we've been
24   provided by the CIA, which we are informed is a summary
25   of the Director's meeting log and telephone log with

UNCLASSIFIED

Document 2: Schematic of the circular trading agreement

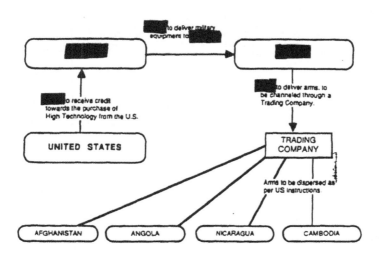

UNCLASSIFIED 3 WAY TRADE   N   5519

CONTINUATION OF INTERVIEW OF NANCY MORABIA   PAGE   2

to Europe again and was joined there by her son, MARC who resides in London. Together they went with Mr. ZUCKER and his family to the opera festival in Varona, Italy. There they were joined by ROLAND FARINA (ZUCKER's administration assistant) and his family.

Mrs. MORABIA knew that Mr. ZUCKER had an office in Bermuda but she did not know the purpose of the office. Manager of this office is EVELYN REPIQUET and she is assisted by MARTHA (last name unknown). Mrs. MORABIA said she knew that Mr. ZUCKER had various real estate deals in Florida and Texas and that possibly Ms. REPIQUET monitored these accounts. Mrs. MORABIA said she has met Ms. REPIQUET in New York on approximately five occasions but she (MORABIA) has never been to Bermuda.

In dealing with CSF Mrs. MORABIA said there was at one time a pouch system to the Trade Development Bank, Geneva, Switzerland, which at that time was an affiliate of RNB (which is owned by Mr. SAFRA). Mr. SAFRA is originally from Beirut and is part of the Sephardic (ph) Group (Jewish). Mrs. MORABIA has been to cocktail parties and dinners with the SAFRA's but has never discussed the CSF account with Mr. SAFRA. She does know that SAFRA has contact with ZUCKER in Geneva but does not know of any business between the two. She "assumes" there probably is because they both live in Geneva. Mrs. MORABIA said she has never seen any documents between ZUCKER and SAFRA.

At this time Mrs. MORABIA proceeded to relate information concerning cash transactions or making cash available. This was during a period of time from 1984 to sometime in 1986. During the latter part of 1984 or early 1985 she received a call from ZUCKER who needed funds of $10,000 or so and wondered if she had any sources who would have the money available. She told ZUCKER that she would contact her source to see if there was a possibility of obtaining the money. Her source would then tell her whether money was available and she would then tell ZUCKER. If money was available ZUCKER would tell her where to deliver the money. As an example: Room 1202 at the Hotel Helmsley or Hotel Hilton and give the time. Sometimes ZUCKER, when he knew money was available would tell her that either ALBERT HAKIM or RICHARD SECORD would call to give her instructions. She said she has never met either gentleman. Mrs. MORABIA said that her source (who she declined to identify) would tell her when the money had been delivered and that a like amount of funds should be transferred to an account at the Trade Development Bank in Geneva named CODELIS. Mrs. MORABIA said that she participated in approximately six transactions of this type. The largest amount transferred was $60,000 and the smallest was $5,000. The typical transfer was about $10,000 to $15,000. In

Document 3: Section of the Nan Morabia FBI 302 that discusses Edmond Safra.
https://archive.org/details/FBI302NanMorabia1/mode/1up?view=theater

```
4203      ALBERT HAKIM
          LEDGER                      FROM 01 01 86 TO 06 12 86

A/C.   NAME & DESCRIPTION                        DOC NO CONTRA

5608001   HYDE PARK SQUARE                        (SUITE)
   3 10 INT ON CALL                              770801
   6 10 COMMERCIAL TULIN                         009801
   6 10 ARTURO JOSE CRUZ PORRAS                  684301
   6 10 TDB GENEVE STC CORP.                     406601
   6 10 BANK CHARGES                             640401
   6 10 BANK CHARGES                             640401
   6 10 BANK CHARGES                             640401
   6 10 BANK CHARGES COMPLT                      640401
   6 10 BANK CHARGES COMPLT                      640401
   8 10 JILA H. LANKARANI                        640201
   8 10 CIE SERV. FID. INV ENERGY SFR 3000       640801
   8 10 CIE SERV. FID. AEROLEASING SFR 874       400501
   8 10 BANK CHARGES                             640401
   8 10 FROM CALL                                5608101
  10 10 INTEREST ON CALL                         770801
  14 10 CONSULAR                                 640201
  14 10 BANK CHARGES                             640401
  14 10 REIMBURSEMENT CSF                        402801
  14 10 REIMBURSEMENT CSF                        660401
  15 10 CIE SERV. FID. REMBT CASH AH             640201
  15 10 BANK CHARGES                             640401
  17 10 INTEREST                                 770801
  20 10 FROM CALL                                5608101
  20 10 TO MEMO EYTAN                            604201
  20 10 BANK CHARGED                             640401
  22 10 C.S.F. REMBT AEROLEASING SFR 3060        608501
  22 10 C.S.F. REMBT PRELEVT CASH                640201
  22 10 BANK CHARGES                             640401
  22 10 CHECK TOM GREEN                          605701
  22 10 BANK CHARGES                             640401
  27 10 WITHDRAWAL CASH ROBERT DUTTON            640201
  27 10 CIE SERV. FID. REMBT CASH A.H.           640301
  27 10 BANK CHARGES                             640401
  27 10 SERFID REMBT SFR 701 AVION FRANCK        640201
  27 10 HAEFELIN - UBS                           400501
  28 10 TRANSFER TO DOLMY                        5603001
```

Document 4: An Enterprise ledger that mentions Aeroleasing. https://www.maryferrell.org/showDoc.html?docId=146470#relPageId=325&search=Aeroleasing

South Ken
0207-741 6212

The Home Office
0207-273 2124

SWITZERLAND (SW)

Bristol Hotel
10 rue du Mart-Blanc
Geneva, Switzerland 1201
4122-732-3800
4122-738-8039
331-42-669-145 Paris

The Corveglia Club
010 41 6234864

The Steffani
010 41 82 22101

TRAVEL (T)

Aero Leasing
(1) 814 3700 (Zurich)
(22) 984510 (Geneva)

Air France
1-800-237-2747
0820 820 820
1023994264 frequent flier (GM)
1023994343 frequent flier number (JE)

Air Hansen
(Helicopter)
0252-390-089
0252-860-287

American Airlines
Key Leonard
Special Services:
Val Cushing - Gatwick
293 567 783
75261 9047
800 433 7300
1-800-882-8880 AA Frequent Flyer Dept.
340 774 6464 St T Brenda Boone
(special sev
305 526 7710 Susan Michado Miami special se

American Express
American Express
1-800-297-6453
1-800-297-3276 Membership Rewards
877 877 0987x57323 Amad Abdullah (Cent. Travel)
877 877 0987x6775 Ian Roche (Cent. Cards)

AT&T
1-800-225-5288

British Airways
001 800 247 9297
0845 779 9977uk
91086094 Pin 9919 club number
91859156 club member (JE)
0208-759 6511 Claire McArdle
0208-564 1880 Jilly Rutherford
718 425 5585 Roz Ollvier/Special Services
718 425 5654 Alan Jacobson/special services
212 452 5353 Roz home (emergencies)

718 553 5585 Penelope Foy
(special services
718 425 5585 Bernelle Berry - Spec. Rep.

Citicar
3515 37th Avenue
Long Island City, NY 10021
718-707-9090
800-456-3548
718-361-9800 Ellen/Tackle
800-456-3548 Toll-Free Number
718-361-8834 when ph system is down

Concord Tickets
David Gladwin
19 Main Street, Keyworth
Nottingham NG12 5AA, UK
0115 9372455 (t)
0115 9376930 (t)
012 931-0490 (Fisher) Susie Simon (h)
212 268-8088 (Wilpon) Michael Holtz

Continental Airlines
001 800 525 0280
#SM147662 frequent flier number (GM)

Delta Airlines
001 800 323 2323
2102103435 frequent flier number (GM)
1-800-325-1999 Flight information number
2001009253 frequent flier number (JE)

Delta Dash
1-800-638-7333

DHL Courier
800-225-5345

Flight Options
26180 Curtiss-Wright Parkway
Cuyahoga County Airport
Cleveland, OH 44143
877 357 1263 (w)
216 797 3325(wf)

Flyaway
081-759 1567/2020

Frequent Flyer Clubs
Delta One Pass
001 713 952 1530
001 800 221-1212
#2102103435 frequent flier number

Garnero, Jr., Mario B.
011 55 11 9970 1020
Email:
mbgarnero@brasilinvest.co
646 251 2211 (p) Europe
011 331 4720 1584 Paris

Helicopters
Jean-Jacques Moinel
Nice Helicopters
Aeroport Nice Cote d'Azur
Terminal 1
06281
Nice, Cedex 3,
04 93 21 34 32
04 93 21 35 64 (f)
Email:
nicehelicopteres@wanadoo.
06 14 356 353 (p)

Document 5: The same Aeroleasing appears in Jeffrey Epstein's black book.

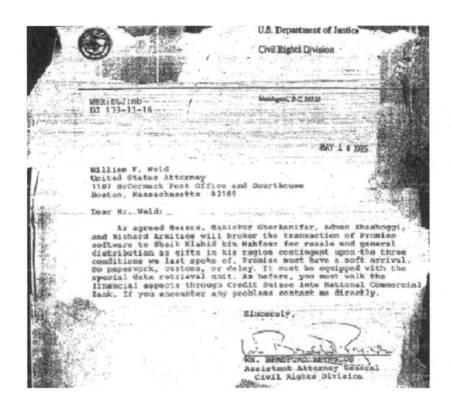

Document 6: Letter to William Weld from Assistant Attorney General Bradford Reynolds detailing the sale of PROMIS for financial purposes to Sheik Klahid bin Mahfouz and how Manucher Ghorbanifar, Adnan Khashoggi and Richard Armitage were to broker the deal.

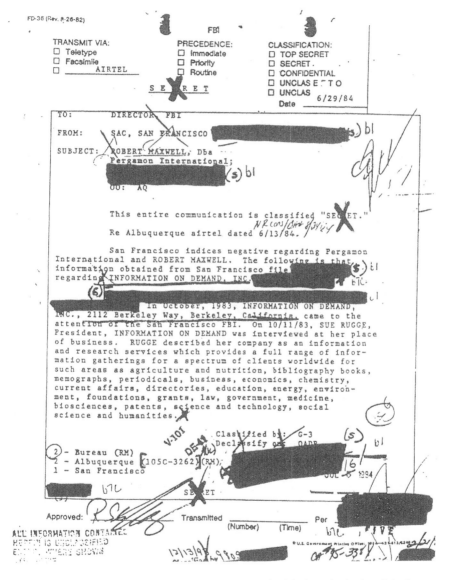

FD-36 (Rev. 8-26-82)

FBI

TRANSMIT VIA:
☐ Teletype
☐ Facsimile
☐ _____ AIRTEL

PRECEDENCE:
☐ Immediate
☐ Priority
☐ Routine

CLASSIFICATION:
☐ TOP SECRET
☐ SECRET .
☐ CONFIDENTIAL
☐ UNCLAS E F T O
☐ UNCLAS

S E C R E T

Date 6/29/84

TO: DIRECTOR, FBI

FROM: SAC, SAN FRANCISCO

SUBJECT: ROBERT MAXWELL, Dba
          Pergamon International;

OO: AQ

            This entire communication is classified "SECRET."

            Re Albuquerque airtel dated 6/13/84.

            San Francisco indices negative regarding Pergamon
International and ROBERT MAXWELL. The following is that
information obtained from San Francisco file
regarding INFORMATION ON DEMAND, INC.

                        In October, 1983, INFORMATION ON DEMAND,
INC., 2112 Berkeley Way, Berkeley, California, came to the
attention of the San Francisco FBI. On 10/11/83, SUE RUGGE,
President, INFORMATION ON DEMAND was interviewed at her place
of business. RUGGE described her company as an information
and research services which provides a full range of information gatherings for a spectrum of clients worldwide for
such areas as agriculture and nutrition, bibliography books,
memographs, periodicals, business, economics, chemistry,
current affairs, directories, education, energy, environment, foundations, grants, law, government, medicine,
biosciences, patents, science and technology, social
science and humanities.

                              Classified by: G-3
                              Declassify on: OADR

② - Bureau (RM)
2 - Albuquerque (105C-3262)(RM)
1 - San Francisco

                              S E C R E T

Approved: _____ Transmitted _____ Per _____
                                      (Number)   (Time)

Document 7: Pages 13-34 of FBI investigation records of the investigation into Robert Maxwell and Information on Demand, obtained via FOIA by Bill Hamilton.

SF [REDACTED] S 61

RUGGE advised that INFORMATION ON DEMAND's (IOD) sources include over 250 computer data bases which provide information in two main categories, research and document delivery.

According to RUGGE, all data bases that IOD has access to provide only public source information and nothing of a known or sensitively classified nature. She explained that it is a data base called the Defense Technical Center which is connected to the Department of Defense (DOD) which contains classified information, however, IOD has no password for access and further no need for access.

RUGGE advised that requests of IOD are approximately 50% business related and 40% technical and medicine related. She advised that IOD taps most publicly available computerized data bases including Lockheed's Dialog, System Development Corporation's Orbit, the New York Times Information Bank, the National Library of Medicine's MEDLARS, and the Bibliographic Retrieval Service.

Relative to research, RUGGE advised that IOD provides information to the business, technical, and professional communities, as well as to individuals. According to RUGGE, IOD can locate single facts as well as provide answers to complex questions dealing with such areas as comprehensive marketing research, custom data summaries, sophisticated literature searching, current awareness service, and global information capability.

Relative to document delivery, RUGGE advised that IOD locates photocopies or acquires published information in any form, whether they are manuals, conference papers, patents, or theses, as well as reports, catalogues, brochures, articles, etc. She advised that requests are received at IOD by telephone, mail, and electronically, and that information is sent to clients by the same means.

RUGGE advised that under the law and government heading, IOD has access to the American Statistics Index (ASI) and Congressional Information Service (CIS), the Commerce Business Daily, the Congressional Record Abstracts, the Criminal Justice Periodical Index, the Federal Index,

- 2 -

Document 7: Pages 13-34 of FBI investigation records of the investigation into Robert Maxwell and Information on Demand, obtained via FOIA by Bill Hamilton.

S E **X** R E T

SF [REDACTED] 5 b1

the Federal Register Abstracts, Labor Law, Illegal Resource
Index, the National Criminal Justice Reference Service
(NCJRS), the State Publications Index, the U. S. Government
Contact Awards (USGCA), and Votes.

(S)

According to RUGGE, the [REDACTED] has
been a client of IOD for at least ten years and it would
be impossible to recall all the information requested by
them, except for the last year, as records are not kept
beyond that period. RUGGE advised she does not know if
any of the requests of the [REDACTED]

(S) [REDACTED] RUGGE expressed a genuine willingness to
cooperate with the FBI and offered to provide the FBI
(S) all information available to her relative to requests
made by the [REDACTED] during the last year.
Additionally she advised that if for some reason a
(S) future request by the [REDACTED] was deemed
inappropriate by the Bureau, she would refuse to fill
that order. RUGGE advised she would prefer to continue
business with the [REDACTED]

c1

RUGGE presented a representative sampling most
recent request from the [REDACTED]

(S)

(S

- 3 -
S E **X** R E T

Document 7: Pages 13-34 of FBI investigation records of the investigation into Robert
Maxwell and Information on Demand, obtained via FOIA by Bill Hamilton.

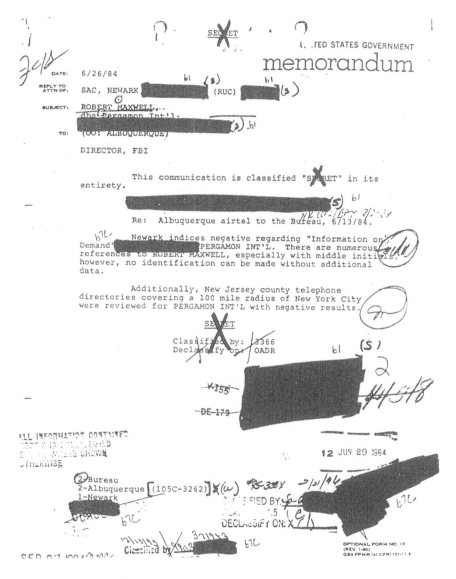

Document 7: Pages 13-34 of FBI investigation records of the investigation into Robert Maxwell and Information on Demand, obtained via FOIA by Bill Hamilton.

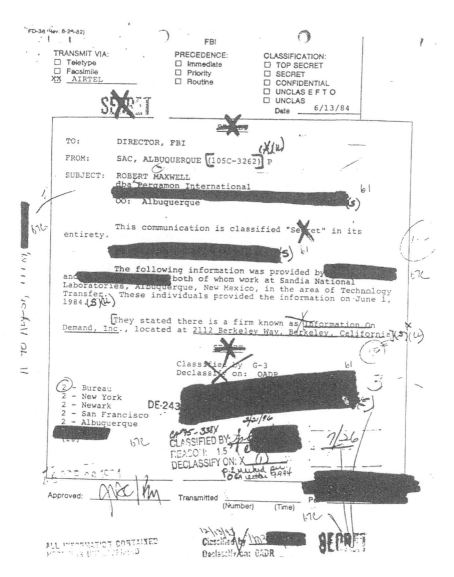

Document 7: Pages 13-34 of FBI investigation records of the investigation into Robert Maxwell and Information on Demand, obtained via FOIA by Bill Hamilton.

SECRET

AQ [105C-3262]

4704, with Telephones (415) 644-4500 and (800) 227-0750. The president of this firm is a woman known as SUE RUGGE. The nature of this firm is that it is a firm which has compiled data base information and for a fee will provide them to customers. The data base information relates to a wide variety and to the best of their knowledge is not classified in any manner. However, it includes information concerning government and various available means of tapping government information data bases. The information provided by the Sandia employees was received from employees of the National Security Agency (NSA) and has to do with the purchase of Information On Demand, Inc., by one ROBERT MAXWELL, the owner of Pergamon International, a British information firm. According to NSA,

The information received from these Sandia employees is

computerized data bases on behalf of the Soviets.

Albuquerque indices are negative regarding Pergamon International, ROBERT MAXWELL, Information On Demand, Inc.

According to the Sandia employees, there is a New Jersey Pergamon International Office; however, they did not know where it was located.

LEADS

NEW YORK CITY DIVISION

AT NEW YORK CITY, NEW YORK

Search indices regarding Pergamon International, ROBERT MAXWELL, Information On Demand, Inc.

NEWARK DIVISION

AT NEWARK, NEW JERSEY

Will check indices as set forth for New York Office.

SECRET

- 2 -

Document 7: Pages 13-34 of FBI investigation records of the investigation into Robert Maxwell and Information on Demand, obtained via FOIA by Bill Hamilton.

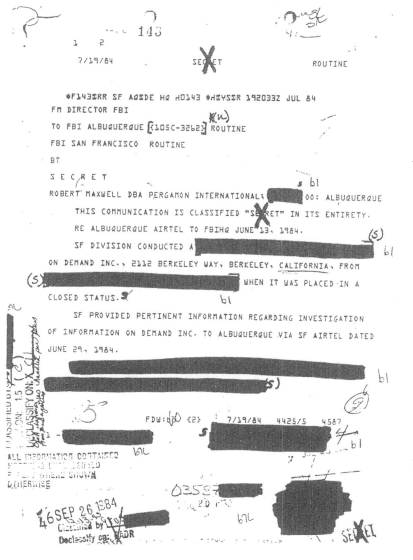

7/19/84   SECRET   ROUTINE

#F143SRR SF AGEDE HQ HO143 #HEYSER 192033Z JUL 84
FM DIRECTOR FBI
TO FBI ALBUQUERQUE [105C-3262] ROUTINE
FBI SAN FRANCISCO ROUTINE
BT
S E C R E T
ROBERT MAXWELL DBA PERGAMON INTERNATIONAL;   OO: ALBUQUERQUE
    THIS COMMUNICATION IS CLASSIFIED "SECRET" IN ITS ENTIRETY.
    RE ALBUQUERQUE AIRTEL TO FBIHQ JUNE 13, 1984.
    SF DIVISION CONDUCTED A
ON DEMAND INC., 2112 BERKELEY WAY, BERKELEY, CALIFORNIA, FROM
                                        WHEN IT WAS PLACED IN A
CLOSED STATUS.
    SF PROVIDED PERTINENT INFORMATION REGARDING INVESTIGATION
OF INFORMATION ON DEMAND INC. TO ALBUQUERQUE VIA SF AIRTEL DATED
JUNE 29, 1984.

FDW: (2)   7/19/84   4425/S   4587

ALL INFORMATION CONTAINED

Document 7: Pages 13-34 of FBI investigation records of the investigation into Robert Maxwell and Information on Demand, obtained via FOIA by Bill Hamilton.

477

PAGE THREE

NOTE:

ALBUQUERQUE DIVISION RECEIVED INFORMATION FROM TWO
EMPLOYEES OF SANDIA NATIONAL LABORATORIES OF ALBUQUERQUE, N.M.,
THAT A COMPANY NAMED INFORMATION ON DEMAND HAD BEEN PURCHASED
BY A ROBERT MAXWELL, OWNER OF PERGAMON INTERNATIONAL, A BRITISH
INFORMATION FIRM. THE TWO EMPLOYEES ADVISED THEY HAD LEARNED
FROM NSA

ALBUQUERQUE IS PROVIDED WITH RESULTS OF INDICES SEARCH.

Document 7: Pages 13-34 of FBI investigation records of the investigation into Robert Maxwell and Information on Demand, obtained via FOIA by Bill Hamilton.

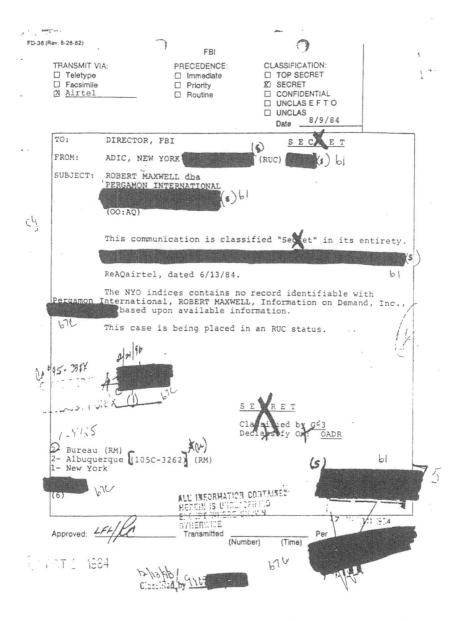

FD-36 (Rev. 8-26-82)

FBI

TRANSMIT VIA:
☐ Teletype
☐ Facsimile
☒ Airtel

PRECEDENCE:
☐ Immediate
☐ Priority
☐ Routine

CLASSIFICATION:
☐ TOP SECRET
☒ SECRET
☐ CONFIDENTIAL
☐ UNCLAS E F T O
☐ UNCLAS

Date 8/9/84

TO: DIRECTOR, FBI   S E C R E T

FROM: ADIC, NEW YORK   (RUC)

SUBJECT: ROBERT MAXWELL dba
          PERGAMON INTERNATIONAL

          (OO:AQ)

This communication is classified "Secret" in its entirety.

ReAQairtel, dated 6/13/84.

The NYO indices contains no record identifiable with
Pergamon International, ROBERT MAXWELL, Information on Demand, Inc.,
based upon available information.

This case is being placed in an RUC status.

S E C R E T

Classified by G-3
Declassify On: OADR

2- Bureau (RM)
2- Albuquerque [105C-3262] (RM)
1- New York

ALL INFORMATION CONTAINED
HEREIN IS UNCLASSIFIED
EXCEPT WHERE SHOWN
OTHERWISE

Approved: _____   Transmitted _____   Per _____
                              (Number)   (Time)

Classified by _____

Document 7: Pages 13-34 of FBI investigation records of the investigation into Robert
Maxwell and Information on Demand, obtained via FOIA by Bill Hamilton.

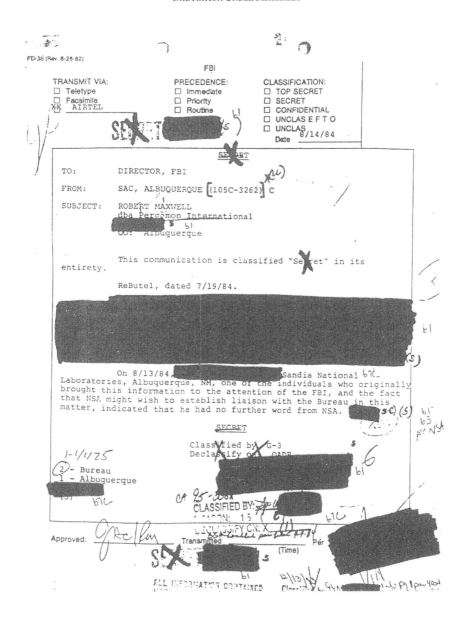

FD-36 (Rev. 8-26-82)

FBI

TRANSMIT VIA:
☐ Teletype
☐ Facsimile
XX AIRTEL

PRECEDENCE:
☐ Immediate
☐ Priority
☐ Routine

CLASSIFICATION:
☐ TOP SECRET
☐ SECRET
☐ CONFIDENTIAL
☐ UNCLAS E F T O
☐ UNCLAS

Date 8/14/84

SECRET

TO: DIRECTOR, FBI

FROM: SAC, ALBUQUERQUE (105C-3262) C

SUBJECT: ROBERT MAXWELL
dba Pergamon International
OO: Albuquerque

This communication is classified "Secret" in its entirety.

ReButel, dated 7/19/84.

On 8/13/84, [redacted] Sandia National Laboratories, Albuquerque, NM, one of the individuals who originally brought this information to the attention of the FBI, and the fact that NSA might wish to establish liaison with the Bureau in this matter, indicated that he had no further word from NSA.

SECRET

Classified by G-3
Declassify on OADR

2 - Bureau
1 - Albuquerque

CLASSIFIED BY:

Approved: _____ Transmitted _____ Per _____
(Time)

Document 7: Pages 13-34 of FBI investigation records of the investigation into Robert Maxwell and Information on Demand, obtained via FOIA by Bill Hamilton.

AQ [105C-3262] (u)

bl b3
for NSA

_____ appeared to be rather non-specific and c)(s)
at this point there was no indication that it was current information.
It was the speculation shown during the course of the conversation
that this might be dated information which relates to the data
furnished by FBIHQ concerning_____

(s) bl

Until such time as NSA re-establishes contact and expresses
further interest in this matter, Albuquerque is taking no further
action and this matter is being placed in a closed status. (u)

The personnel at Sandia National Laboratories were told
that if NSA has a desire to establish contact with the FBI in this
matter, a logical step would be to contact FBIHQ and pursue it through
that channel. There is a chance they will come to Albuquerque in
September and possibly they may be in touch with FBI, Albuquerque.
If this occurs, FBIHQ will be apprised of any pertinent data received. (u)

2

PAGE TWO DE HQ 0143 S E C R E T

C BY: 5006; DECL:OADR

8T

Document 7: Pages 13-34 of FBI investigation records of the investigation into Robert
Maxwell and Information on Demand, obtained via FOIA by Bill Hamilton.

AQ [105C-3262] (U)

<u>SAN FRANCISCO DIVISION</u>

<u>AT SAN FRANCISCO, CALIFORNIA</u>

Will search indices as set forth for New York Office.

<u>REQUEST OF THE BUREAU</u>

Requested to search indices regarding the firms and individuals as set forth in the New York lead.

- 3* -

Document 7: Pages 13-34 of FBI investigation records of the investigation into Robert Maxwell and Information on Demand, obtained via FOIA by Bill Hamilton.

4-22 (Rev. 7-1-83)

FEDERAL BUREAU OF INVESTIGATION
Records/Operations Sections

_____ , 19___

☐ Name Searching Unit, 4543, TL# 115
☐ Service Unit, 4054, TL# 225
☐ Special File Room, 5991, TL# 122
☐ Forward to File Review, 5447, TL# 143
☐ Attention
☐ Return to _____ 4425 242
                    Supervisor, Room, TL#, Ext.

Type of Search Requested: (Check One)
☐ Restricted Search (Active Index - 5 & 20)
☐ Restricted Search (Active & Inactive Index - 5 & 30)
☑ Unrestricted (Active & Inactive Index)

Special Instructions: (Check One)
☑ All References (Security & Criminal)
☐ Security Search
☐ Criminal Search
☐ Main _____ References Only
☐ Exact Name Only (On the Nose)
☐ Buildup   ☐ Variations
☐ Restricted to Locality of _____

Subject _____ Robert Maxwell
Birthdate & Place _____
Address _____

Localities _____

R# _____ Date 6/15   Searcher Initials
Prod. _____

FILE NUMBER	SERIAL
1 - 9440	
1 - 13195	
105 - 99072	
105 - 210759	
105 - 236925	
157 13923	
170 - 7059	
174 - 7381	
105 - 318403 - 240 - 58x1	
65 - 67359 - 1	
- 6	
65 - 74117 - 56 17	
- 121 #D	
105 - 72776 - 4	
105 - 91885 - 8x Ep67	
105 - 120958 - 27, 28, 29	
- 30, 33	
105 - 165490 - 2	
105 - 203693 - 1	

IAN ROBERT

Document 7: Pages 13-34 of FBI investigation records of the investigation into Robert Maxwell and Information on Demand, obtained via FOIA by Bill Hamilton.

4-22 (Rev. 7-1-83)

FEDERAL BUREAU OF INVESTIGATION
Records/Operations Sections

June 25, 19 81

☐ Name Searching Unit, 4543, TL# 115
☑ Service Unit, 4854, TL# 225
☐ Special File Room, 5991, TL# 122
☐ Forward to File Review, 5447, TL# 143
☐ Attention
☐ Return to

Supervisor, Room, TL#, Ext.

Type of Search Requested: (Check One)
☑ Restricted Search (Active Index - 5 & 20)
☐ Restricted Search (Active & Inactive Index - 5 & 30)
☐ Unrestricted (Active & Inactive Index)

Special Instructions: (Check One)
☑ All References (Security & Criminal)
☐ Security Search
☐ Criminal Search
☐ Main _____ References Only
☐ Exact Name Only (On the Nose)
☐ Buildup ☐ Variations
☐ Restricted to Locality of _____

Subject
Birthdate & Place
Address

Localities

R# _____ Date _____ Searcher Initials _____
Prod. _____

FILE NUMBER   SERIAL

DECLASSIFIED BY

ON

ALL INFORMATION CONTAINED
HEREIN IS UNCLASSIFIED

ALL INFORMATION CONTAINED
HEREIN IS UNCLASSIFIED
EXCEPT WHERE SHOWN
OTHERWISE

Classified by
Declassify on: OADR

Document 7: Pages 13-34 of FBI investigation records of the investigation into Robert Maxwell and Information on Demand, obtained via FOIA by Bill Hamilton.

A-22 (Rev. 7-1-83)

FEDERAL BUREAU OF INVESTIGATION
Records/Operations Sections

_____, 19____

☐ Name Searching Unit, 4543, TL# 115
☑ Service Unit, 4664, TL# 225
☐ Special File Room, 5991, TL# 122
☐ Forward to File Review, 5447, TL# 1 ~~SECRET~~ b7C
☐ Attention
☐ Return to _____ 4425 242
Supervisor, Room, TL#, Ext.

Type of Search Requested: (Check One)
☐ Restricted Search (Active Index - 5 & 20)
☐ Restricted Search (Active & Inactive Index - 5 & 30)
☑ Unrestricted (Active & Inactive Index)

Special Instructions: (Check One)
☑ All References (Security & Criminal)
☐ Security Search
☐ Criminal Search
☐ Main _____ References Only
☐ Exact Name Only (On the Nose)
☐ Buildup   ☐ Variations
☐ Restricted to Locality of _____

Subject _____
Birthdate __Place_____ b7C
Address _____

Localities _____

R# _____ Date 6/25 Searcher Initials K.T.
Prod. _____

FILE NUMBER	SERIAL

65-2358x   b7C
DECLASSIFIED BY _____
ON 07/21/96

391983
LL INFORMATION CONTAINED
HEREIN IS UNCLASSIFIED
_____   b7C

ALL INFORMATION CONTAINED
HEREIN IS UNCLASSIFIED
EXCEPT WHERE SHOWN
OTHERWISE.

12/21/93   b7C
Classified by _____
Declassify on OADR   ~~SECRET~~

Document 7: Pages 13-34 of FBI investigation records of the investigation into Robert Maxwell and Information on Demand, obtained via FOIA by Bill Hamilton.

San Francisco taking no further action.

Document 7: Pages 13-34 of FBI investigation records of the investigation into Robert Maxwell and Information on Demand, obtained via FOIA by Bill Hamilton.

.-4-750 (Rev. 12-14-88)

FEDERAL BUREAU OF INVESTIGATION
FOIPA DELETED PAGE INFORMATION SHEET

___2___ Page(s) withheld entirely at this location in the file. One or more of the following statements, where indicated, explain this deletion.

☐ Deletions were made pursuant to the exemptions indicated below with no segregable material available for release to you.

Section 552		Section 552a
☐ (b)(1)	☐ (b)(7)(A)	☐ (d)(5)
☐ (b)(2)	☐ (b)(7)(B)	☐ (j)(2)
☐ (b)(3)	☐ (b)(7)(C)	☐ (k)(1)
_____	☐ (b)(7)(D)	☐ (k)(2)
_____	☐ (b)(7)(E)	☐ (k)(3)
_____	☐ (b)(7)(F)	☐ (k)(4)
☐ (b)(4)	☐ (b)(8)	☐ (k)(5)
☐ (b)(5)	☐ (b)(9)	☐ (k)(6)
☐ (b)(6)		☐ (k)(7)

☐ Information pertained only to a third party with no reference to you or the subject of your request.

☐ Information pertained only to a third party. Your name is listed in the title only.

☒ Documents originated with another Government agency(ies). These documents were referred to that agency(ies) for review and direct response to you.

_____ Pages contain information furnished by another Government agency(ies). You will be advised by the FBI as to the releasability of this information following our consultation with the other agency(ies).

_____ Page(s) withheld for the following reason(s):_____

_____

☐ For your information: _____

_____

☒ The following number is to be used for reference regarding these pages:

___163 B - HQ - 1002741 - 1_____

Document 7: Pages 13-34 of FBI investigation records of the investigation into Robert Maxwell and Information on Demand, obtained via FOIA by Bill Hamilton.

4-750 (Rev. 12-14-88)

XXXXXX
XXXXXX
XXXXXX

FEDERAL BUREAU OF INVESTIGATION
FOIPA DELETED PAGE INFORMATION SHEET

_____ Page(s) withheld entirely at this location in the file. One or more of the following statements, where indicated, explain this deletion.

☐ Deletions were made pursuant to the exemptions indicated below with no segregable material available for release to you.

Section 552		Section 552a
☐ (b)(1)	☐ (b)(7)(A)	☐ (d)(5)
☐ (b)(2)	☐ (b)(7)(B)	☐ (j)(2)
☐ (b)(3)	☐ (b)(7)(C)	☐ (k)(1)
_____	☐ (b)(7)(D)	☐ (k)(2)
_____	☐ (b)(7)(E)	☐ (k)(3)
_____	☐ (b)(7)(F)	☐ (k)(4)
☐ (b)(4)	☐ (b)(8)	☐ (k)(5)
☐ (b)(5)	☐ (b)(9)	☐ (k)(6)
☐ (b)(6)		☐ (k)(7)

☐ Information pertained only to a third party with no reference to you or the subject of your request.

☐ Information pertained only to a third party. Your name is listed in the title only.

☐ Documents originated with another Government agency(ies). These documents were referred to that agency(ies) for review and direct response to you.

_____ Pages contain information furnished by another Government agency(ies). You will be advised by the FBI as to the releasability of this information following our consultation with the other agency(ies).

_____ Page(s) withheld for the following reason(s): _____

☒ For your information: _Serial 2 was missing from the file_
if/when it is found it will be forwarded to you

☒ The following number is to be used for reference regarding these pages:

_163 B - HQ - 1002741 - 2_

XXXXXX
XXXXXX
XXXXXX

XXXXXXXXXXXXXXXXXXXXXXX
X   DELETED PAGE(S)   X
X NO DUPLICATION FEE X
X   FOR THIS PAGE   X
XXXXXXXXXXXXXXXXXXXXXXX

FBI/DOJ

Document 7: Pages 13-34 of FBI investigation records of the investigation into Robert Maxwell and Information on Demand, obtained via FOIA by Bill Hamilton.

4-760 (Rev. 12-14-88)

XXXXXX
XXXXXX
XXXXXX

FEDERAL BUREAU OF INVESTIGATION
FOIPA DELETED PAGE INFORMATION SHEET

___2 8___ Page(s) withheld entirely at this location in the file. One or more of the following statements, where indicated, explain this deletion.

☐ Deletions were made pursuant to the exemptions indicated below with no segregable material available for release to you.

Section 552		Section 552a
☐ (b)(1)	☐ (b)(7)(A)	☐ (d)(5)
☐ (b)(2)	☐ (b)(7)(B)	☐ (j)(2)
☐ (b)(3)	☐ (b)(7)(C)	☐ (k)(1)
_____	☐ (b)(7)(D)	☐ (k)(2)
_____	☐ (b)(7)(E)	☐ (k)(3)
_____	☐ (b)(7)(F)	☐ (k)(4)
☐ (b)(4)	☐ (b)(8)	☐ (k)(5)
☐ (b)(5)	☐ (b)(9)	☐ (k)(6)
☐ (b)(6)		☐ (k)(7)

☐ Information pertained only to a third party with no reference to you or the subject of your request.

☐ Information pertained only to a third party. Your name is listed in the title only.

☒ Documents originated with another Government agency(ies). These documents were referred to that agency(ies) for review and direct response to you.

_____ Pages contain information furnished by another Government agency(ies). You will be advised by the FBI as to the releasability of this information following our consultation with the other agency(ies).

_____ Page(s) withheld for the following reason(s): _____

_____

☐ For your information: _____

_____

☒ The following number is to be used for reference regarding these pages:

___163 B - HQ - 1002741 - 3___

XXXXXX
XXXXXX
XXXXXX

XXXXXXXXXXXXXXXXXXXXXX
X   DELETED PAGE(S)   X
X NO DUPLICATION FEE X
X   FOR THIS PAGE   X
XXXXXXXXXXXXXXXXXXXXXX
FBI/DOJ

Document 7: Pages 13-34 of FBI investigation records of the investigation into Robert Maxwell and Information on Demand, obtained via FOIA by Bill Hamilton.

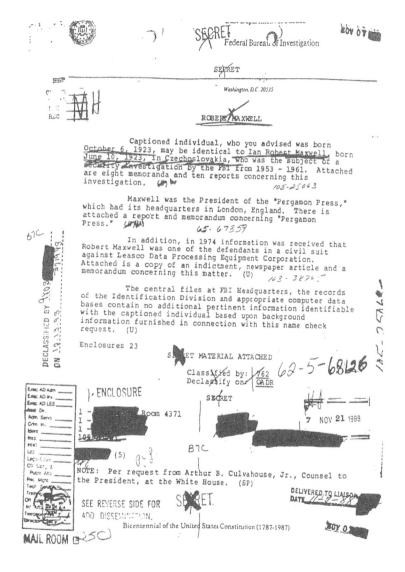

SECRET

Federal Bureau of Investigation

SECRET

Washington, D.C. 20535

ROBERT MAXWELL

Captioned individual, who you advised was born October 6, 1923, may be identical to Ian Robert Maxwell, born June 10, 1923, In Czechoslovakia, who was the subject of a security investigation by the FBI from 1953 - 1961. Attached are eight memoranda and ten reports concerning this investigation. (S) (U)

Maxwell was the President of the "Pergamon Press," which had its headquarters in London, England. There is attached a report and memorandum concerning "Pergamon Press." (S) (U)

In addition, in 1974 information was received that Robert Maxwell was one of the defendants in a civil suit against Leasco Data Processing Equipment Corporation. Attached is a copy of an indictment, newspaper article and a memorandum concerning this matter. (U)

The central files at FBI Headquarters, the records of the Identification Division and appropriate computer data bases contain no additional pertinent information identifiable with the captioned individual based upon background information furnished in connection with this name check request. (U)

Enclosures 23

SECRET MATERIAL ATTACHED

Classified by: 762
Declassify on: OADR

1- ENCLOSURE

SECRET

1 - Room 4371
1 -
1 -
105-

(5)

B7C

NOTE: Per request from Arthur B. Culvahouse, Jr., Counsel to the President, at the White House. (SP)

SEE REVERSE SIDE FOR SECRET.
AND DISSEMINATION.

Bicentennial of the United States Constitution (1787-1987)

MAIL ROOM

Document 7: Pages 13-34 of FBI investigation records of the investigation into Robert Maxwell and Information on Demand, obtained via FOIA by Bill Hamilton.

A Partnership Including
Professional Corporations
1850 K Street, N.W.
Washington, DC 20006-2296
202-887-8000
Facsimile 202-778-5087

Boston
Chicago
Los Angeles
Miami
Newport Beach
New York
Tallinn (Estonia)
Vilnius (Lithuania)
Washington, D.C.

Associated (Independent) Offices
London
Paris

McDermott, Will & Emery

Including the practice formerly carried on by Lee, Toomey & Kent

Charles R. Work
Attorney at Law
202-778-8030

March 14, 1994

John C. Dwyer, Esq.
Assistant Associate Attorney General
U.S. Department of Justice
10th Street and Constitution Avenue, N.W.
Washington, D.C. 20530

Dear Mr. Dwyer:

This is a follow-up letter to the meeting at my office on Tuesday morning, March 1, 1994 between my clients, William and Nancy Hamilton of INSLAW, myself, Mr. Stephen Zipperstein, First Assistant U.S. Attorney for Los Angeles, FBI Special Agent Scott Erskine, and my co-counsel, Michael Friedlander and Philip Kellogg.

You explained at the outset of the meeting that Messrs. Zipperstein and Erskine are reviewing the death of investigative journalist, Danny Casolaro, as part of the Justice Department's review of the June 1993 investigative report on INSLAW by its Special Counsel, Nicholas J. Bua.

We regard as significant the confirmation from Special Agent Erskine during the meeting that a maid at the Sheraton Hotel in Martinsburg, West Virginia, had seen a mean leave Mr. Casolaro's hotel room the Saturday morning of the death. According to Special Agent Erskine, the local police took a statement from the hotel maid in which she gave an eyewitness description of the man she saw leaving the room.

It is our understanding that the description is as follows:

> A male in his 30's, with an excellent sun tan, wearing a fashionable tee-shirt, dark slacks, and deck shoes.

We recall press accounts of Mr. Casolaro's death, which describe him waiting in the hotel bar on Thursday evening for a dark-skinned man. Could that have been the same man whom the

Document 8: A letter from Inslaw Inc.'s lawyer Charles Work to Assistant Associate Attorney General John C. Dwyer regarding the circumstances around the death of journalist Danny Casolaro, March 1994.

John C. Dwyer, Esq.
March 14, 1994
Page 2

maid saw leaving Mr. Casolaro's room Saturday morning and whom she describes as having "an excellent sun tan"?

I will now deal with the answers to the several requests to INSLAW for information that were made during the meeting.

Mr. Zipperstein raised the question of whether any of INSLAW's confidential sources have alleged that Mr. Casolaro was drugged before he was allegedly murdered. As Mr. Hamilton replied, INSLAW was told by one confidential source that a drug known as ethyl alcohol absolut was administered to Mr. Casolaro before he was allegedly killed. This source told INSLAW that the drug was administered by injection into the area just above Mr. Casolaro's spine in order to deaden the nerves below his head. INSLAW was also told that the inventory lot number for the drug administered to Mr. Casolaro was 6810-00-242-3645 and the composition code was ACS-C2-H5OH-FW-46 IGL SA-C-11-84.

A forensic pathologist, Dr. Kit Green, who worked at the CIA for 18 years, claims that the alleged inventory lot number indicates that the drug came from a U.S. Army inventory. Dr. Green's address is 1409 Cedar Bend, Bloomfield Hills, MI 48013.

Attachment A is a copy of the 27-page computer printout labelled "Criminal Division Vendor List." A procurement official for the Justice Department, in response to a question from a fact checker for a national magazine, acknowledged that this list is from the Criminal Division and that a special security clearance is normally required to gain access to it. Upon information and belief, this is a list of commercial organizations that serve as "cutouts" for the Justice Department's own covert intelligence agency, i.e., for the Criminal Division's Office of Special Investigations (OSI). As noted in the February 14, 1994 Addendum, a preliminary analysis has produced information consistent with these claims.

Attachment B is a set of documents relating to Mr. George Pender. Mr. Casolaro had described Mr. Pender to my client as a Los Angeles businessman to whom both Earl Brian and Peter Videnieks effectively reported in connection with the dissemination of stolen copies of the PROMIS software to intelligence entities. As Mr. Hamilton explained during the meeting, Mr. Casolaro, in the final several weeks of his life, confirmed to Mr. Hamilton that he was planning to visit a sensitive facility in Washington, D.C. that Mr. Casolaro said was associated with Mr. Pender. Mr. Hamilton had conveyed to Mr. Casolaro a warning form Mr. Charles Hayes not to visit the facility in question because it could result in Mr. Casolaro's death. According to INSLAW sources, the facility in question

Document 8: A letter from Inslaw Inc.'s lawyer Charles Work to Assistant Associate Attorney General John C. Dwyer regarding the circumstances around the death of journalist Danny Casolaro, March 1994.

John C. Dwyer, Esq.
March 14, 1994
Page 3

is a four story townhouse on Jackson Place just behind Blair
House that was used for White House "dirty tricks" during the
Reagan and Bush Administrations, that was staffed by ex-CIA
employees and that was equipped with computer equipment and
crypto communications devices used to access very sensitive
U.S. Government intelligence, law enforcement and national
security databases on American citizens.

At Mr. Zipperstein's request, INSLAW agreed to make
additional inquiries about whether any of its confidential
sources, in the Justice Department, U.S. intelligence agencies
or elsewhere, would agree to speak with Mr. Zipperstein about
anything they claim to know about Mr. Casolaro's death.

We are, of course, aware that Mr. Zipperstein served one
or more tours of duty in the Justice Department's Criminal
Division. You know from our meeting with you on December 16,
1993 and from earlier written submissions about the INSLAW
case, how concerned we are about having any career Criminal
Division lawyer included in any sensitive aspect of the Justice
Department's review of the INSLAW affair.

We have explained more than once that most of our sources
refuse to believe that the Justice Department can effectively
investigate itself. It is even more difficult to persuade our
sources to meet with an attorney who was recently part of the
Criminal Division, which, we have been told, was the nerve
center for the malfeasance against INSLAW.

It would help us to persuade our sources to come forward
if we knew more about Mr. Zipperstein's service in the
Department, and if we could argue that his contacts with
persons involved in the INSLAW matter were relatively minimal.
The following information would be helpful: (1) What were the
dates and associated duties of the various periods of Mr.
Zipperstein's service in the Justice Department's Criminal
Division; (2) What are the dates and associated duties of the
various periods of Mr. Zipperstein's service in the U.S.
Attorney's Office for Los Angeles; (3) What involvement, if
any, has Mr. Zipperstein had with the Criminal Division's
Office of Special Investigations (OSI) in general or Mr. Neil
Sher, in particular; (4) What involvement, if any, has Mr.
Zipperstein had with the Justice Command Center; (5) What
involvement, if any, has Mr. Zipperstein had with the Justice
Department's Office of Security and Emergency Planning or Mr.
D. Jerry Rubino; (6) What involvement, if any, has Mr.
Zipperstein had with either the PROMIS software, the INSLAW
affair, or any investigation by the Justice Department or an
external agency into any aspect of the INSLAW affair; (7) What

Document 8: A letter from Inslaw Inc.'s lawyer Charles Work to Assistant Associate Attorney General John C. Dwyer regarding the circumstances around the death of journalist Danny Casolaro, March 1994.

John C. Dwyer, Esq.
March 14, 1994
Page 4

involvement, if any, has Mr. Zipperstein had with either of two
former top Criminal Division officials from California, D.
Lowell Jensen and Stephen Trott; (8) What involvement, if any,
has Mr. Zipperstein had with the pending criminal investigation
by his U.S. Attorney's Office in Los Angeles of Earl W. Brian
and Financial News Network (FNN) for possible securities fraud;
and (9) In light of the claim by some of INSLAW's sources, that
disclosure of information to unauthorized persons could subject
them to penalties, what security clearances are currently held
by Mr. Zipperstein, FBI Special Agent Erskine, and yourself?

One point requires clarification. During the meeting, FBI
Agent Erskine read from the notes that he had been taking
during the meeting. As Mr. Hamilton pointed out to FBI Agent
Erskine, the notes significantly misconstrued Mr. Hamilton's
statements about Mr. Casolaro during the meeting. FBI Agent
Erskine's notes quoted Mr. Hamilton as stating during the
meeting that Mr. Casolaro had been "embarrassed" by his
inability to develop evidence during the initial several months
of the investigation. What Mr. Hamilton had, in fact, said,
was that Mr. Casolaro appeared to have a fairly healthy psyche
because he was not embarrassed to admit his frustrations about
obtaining evidence during the initial few months of his
investigation that began in August 1990. As Mr. Hamilton
stated, Mr. Casolaro was as comfortable talking about the
problems of the investigation as he was talking about the
eventual successes of his investigation.

Finally, since our meeting of March 1, 1994, Mr.
Richardson received a letter from you dated March 7, 1994. In
that letter you requested copies of the following documents:

>   (1) "[A] document published by the same Underseas Systems
>   Center in 1987 that revealed that its PROMIS is not only
>   operating at the land-based 'test facility' in Newport,
>   but is also operational on board both attack class and
>   'boomer' class submarines." [Addendum, p. 8.]

>   (2) "Justice Department documents that INSLAW obtained
>   years later in litigation discovery suggest[ing] that
>   Vaveris actually assisted Videnieks in perpetrating the
>   sham dispute." [Addendum, p. 7.]

Attachments C and D are in response to the aforementioned
requests.

Document 8: A letter from Inslaw Inc.'s lawyer Charles Work to Assistant Associate Attorney General John C. Dwyer regarding the circumstances around the death of journalist Danny Casolaro, March 1994.

John C. Dwyer, Esq.
March 14, 1994
Page 5

    If we can be of any further assistance, please do not
hesitate to call.

                         Sincerely yours,

                         Charles R. Work

CRW/ps
Enclosures
cc: Stephen Zipperstein, Esq., First Assistant, U.S.
     Attorney's Office for Los Angeles
     Mr. Scott A. Erskine, FBI Supervisory Special Agent
     Philip L. Kellogg, Esq.
     Michael E. Friedlander, Esq.

\09483\017\50CORCRW.021

Document 8: A letter from Inslaw Inc.'s lawyer Charles Work to Assistant Associate Attorney General John C. Dwyer regarding the circumstances around the death of journalist Danny Casolaro, March 1994.

D/A Registry
83-4162

Pergamon
International
Information
Corporation

September 6, 1983

Executive h□p....

83-4436

Director of Central Intelligence
Central Intelligence Agency
Washington, DC 20505

Sir:

    Pergaman International Information Corporation is an elec-
tronic publishing company with a special interest in computerized patent information. We are exclusive North American
representatives for the International Patent Documentation
Center in Vienna Austria (INPADOC). INPADOC was founded
jointly by the Austrian government and the World Intellectual
Property Organization, a specialized agency of the United
Nations, to serve as a central authority for the collection and
dissemination of official patent information from around the
world. At present, patent documents from over fifty national
and regional patent offices are represented in the INPADOC
files.

    Because national patent laws require complete disclosure of
the inventor's research, patent information represents the
state of the art in any technology and is perhaps the most
sensitive indicator of technical and scientific developments trends
around the world. Information from the INPADOC files can tell
you when and where such development are taking place and who or
what organizations are responsible. Studies by the U.S. Patent
and Trademark Office and others have determined that 80-90 per
cent of the informaton disclosed in patents is not published in
any other scientific or technical literature.

    A number of special features make the INPADOC files
particularly useful as an information resource. For example,
titles of patents from Japan, the Soviet Union and most Eastern
bloc countries are translated into English. Furthermore,
INPADOC is unique in its comprehensive coverage of Eastern bloc
and third world countries. Coverage for most of these
countries dates from 1973.

    This information can be supplied to the CIA in whole or in
part, and in any one of several formats, e.g., online, magnetic
tapes or microfiche. We would be pleased to meet with

DCI
EXEC
REG

1340 Old Chain Bridge Road, McLean, Virginia 22101 (703) 442-0900, Telex: 90-1811

Document 9: Letter from Pergamon International Information Corporation to CIA director Bill Casey, September 1983.

contained less than half as many names as the list he provided during the committee's subsequent investigation. In its December report on Casey, the committee said that Casey told them he had mistakenly supplied a list of only his clients for the previous two years which he had already supplied to the Office of Government Ethics, though the Committee's questionnaire calls for clients of the previous five years. Casey's original list, and the revised list follow:

Original Client List

Diamond Distributors, Inc.
Bear, Stearns & Co.
Capital Cities Communications
Est. of Jos. E. Ridder, Dec'd
Charles Atwood
Cox & Company
John Foglia Sr.
Kephart Communications Inc.
Environmental Research & Technology
Fidelity Management & Research
Anthony G. A. Fisher
Sidney Colen
Jeremiah Burns, Inc.
Resource Asia
Parr Meadows Racing Association Inc.
Robert Ross
Litco Corp. of New York
Long Island Trust Co.
Promenade Magazines, Inc.
Dr. Irving I. Dardik
Mitchell P. Kobelinski
Fitch Investors Service, Inc.
Armor Products Inc.
Jack Farber
Lauraine G. Smith
Nassau County
King Kullen Grocery Stores
Energy Transition Corp.
Andrew Duell
Milton Zipper
Saudi American Lines Company
The Institute for Economic Affairs
Gladding Corp.
The Wachenhut Corporation
Philip J. Sagona
Housatonic Valley Paper Co.
Servo Corporation of America
Semiconductor Specialists Inc.
S.G. Warburg & Co. Ltd.
Korvettes Inc.
Edward Swanson

Document 10: List of William Casey's legal clients from 1976 until his appointment as CIA Director in January 1981, from the book *Reagan's Ruling Class: Portraits of the President's Top One Hundred Officials* (pgs. 629-632). https://archive.org/details/reagansruling-cla0000brow

Florida Condominium Corp.
The Alternative Educational

REVISED CLIENT LIST

(List of Clients furnished by Rogers & Wells
with respect to which William J. Casey,
who was then affiliated with the firm,
had billable time or otherwise received credit
during the period 1976-1981.)

Alexander & Alexander
The Alternative Education
American Society of Allied Health Professions
H. W. Anderson Products
Armor Products Inc.
Associated Press
Charles N. Atwood
Parley Augustsson
BRS Inc.
Virginia Bacon
Banque de Paris
Ford Bartlett
Bear, Stearns & Co.
Bessemer Trust Company
Sidney B. Bowne & Son
Elwood D. Boynton
Broad Hollow Development
Jeremiah Burns, Inc.
Caesar's World
Capital Cities Communications, Inc.
Central American Pipeline
City of New York
Sidney Colen
Continental Hotels Corporation
Covert & Associates, Inc.
Cox & Company
DWG Corporation
Deak & Co. Inc.
Diamond Distributors, Inc.
Andrew Duell
E.T.P.M.
Energy Transition Corp.
Environmental Research & Technology
Jack Farber
Fidelity Management & Research Corp.
Film Corporation of America
Anthony G. A. Fisher
Fitch Investors Service, Inc.
Florida Condominium Corp.

Document 10: List of William Casey's legal clients from 1976 until his appointment as CIA Director in January 1981, from the book *Reagan's Ruling Class: Portraits of the President's Top One Hundred Officials* (pgs. 629-632.) https://archive.org/details/reagansruling-cla0000brow

NATIONAL SECURITY

John Foglia
Connie Francis
Mr. and Mrs. Abraham Friedberg
Fulbright & Jaworski (D.C.)
Gamble-Skogmo
Gladding Corp.
Government of Indonesia
Graphic Controls Corp.
Estate of Leonard W. Hall
Housatonic Valley Paper Co.
The Institute of Economic Affairs
International Crude Oil Refining Inc.
Kennecott Copper
Kephart Communications, Inc.
King Kullen Grocery Stores
Mitchell P. Kobelinski
Koren-DoResta
Korvettes
Nicholas Krapf
Litco Corporation of New York
Lockheed Aircraft
Long Island Forum for Technology
Long Island Trust Company
Dominique Maillard
Mastercraft Corp.
Merrill Lynch Hubbard
Merrill Lynch International Bank
Merrill, Lynch, Pierce, Fenner & Smith
Miles Laboratories, Inc.
Moore, Schley, Cameron & Company
U. V. Muscio
NAB Manufacturing Company
NVF Corporation
Nassau County
National Telephone Company
Newfoundland Refining
New York State Employees Retirement Fund
Norse Petroleum A/S
Old Lane International
Owens-Illinois Glass Mfg. Co.
Oyster Bay Foodtown
PAN AM World Airways
Parr Meadows Racing Association
Pertamina
Peter Piffath
J. T. Potter
Maxwell M. Powell
Promenade Magazines, Inc.
Pullman, Inc.
Republic of Korea

Document 10: List of William Casey's legal clients from 1976 until his appointment as CIA Director in January 1981, from the book *Reagan's Ruling Class: Portraits of the President's Top One Hundred Officials* (pgs. 629-632). https://archive.org/details/reagansruling-cla0000brow

REAGAN'S RULING CLASS

Resource Asia
Reynolds Construction Company
Estate of Joseph E. Ridder
Robert Ross/East-Europe Domestic International Sales Corp.
SCA Services, Inc.
Philip J. Sagona
Saudi American Lines
Scientific Life Systems (Dr. Irving Dardik)
Howard Sears, Jr.
Semiconductor Specialists, Inc.
Servo Corporation of America
Shaheen Natural Resources
Abraham Shames
Sharon Steel Company
Sloan Valve Company
Lauraine G. Smith
Edward Swanson
Tennessee Partners, Ltd.
Ter Bush & Powell, Inc.
Trubin, Sillcocks, Edelman
Twentieth Century Fox
Walter Van der Waag
Joseph F. Virdone
Wachenhut Corp.
S. G. Warburg & Company, Ltd.
David Westerman
Wilmer, Cutler & Pickering
Milton Zipper

Casey's financial disclosure form, listing assets and liabilities was also revised as the year went along. In his January 8, 1981 filing with the Office of Government Ethics, Casey and his wife listed assets of at least $3.085 million, including holdings of $100,000 or greater in: Prentice Hall, C&D Associates, Capital Cities Communications, Philip Morris, Raychem Corp., Amarex, Inc., Apache Corp., Dome Petroleum, Kerr McGee, Southland Royalty, Standard Oil of Indiana, Superior Oil, and Schlumberger Ltd. The couple reported holdings of $50,000 or more in Georgia Pacific, Data Point Corp., IBM, Englehard Minerals & Chemicals, Atlantic Richfield, Mesa Royalty Trust Unit, Halliburton, Intel Corp., and two trusts related to Southland; with smaller holdings in Exxon, Alcoa, DuPont, Amax, Armco, and other firms. He listed no liabilities, nor any gifts.

In August, 1981, though, Casey amended his filing to add 10 additional assets worth more than $145,000, and several liabilities (loan guarantees) worth $472,000 as well as a direct liability of $18,000. A few weeks earlier Jeff Gerth of the *New York Times* revealed that Casey had received as a gift a $10,000 interest in Penverter Partners, a computer technology firm. Casey was given the stock by Carl G. Paffendorf, who described himself as a frequent business associate.

Unlike his two predecessors, George Bush and Admiral Stansfield Turner, who placed their holdings in blind trusts, Casey has kept control of his stocks. "I don't see why I should be picked on," Casey said when we asked about his decision. "The law is the law; it's a clear cut law as to what you have to do with your stocks and I'm

Document 10: List of William Casey's legal clients from 1976 until his appointment as CIA Director in January 1981, from the book *Reagan's Ruling Class: Portraits of the President's Top One Hundred Officials* (pgs. 629-632). https://archive.org/details/reagansruling-cla0000brow

CONFIDENTIAL

15 MAY 1985
AN-128-85

GMT LTD.
4 WEIZMAN ST.
TEL-AVIV

RE: YOUR ENQUIRY/MILITARY EQUIPMENT
----

1.   THANK YOU FOR YOUR ENQUIRY.

2.   WE ARE GLAD TO INFORM YOU THAT WE ARE ABLE AND WILLING
     TO PROVIDE YOU WITH THE FOLLOWING:

	ITEM	QUANTITY	PRICE PER UNIT	TOTAL PR.
1	AK-47 M-70 AUTOMATIC RIFLE WOODEN OR FOLDING BUTT (EACH RIFLE COMES WITH 2 EMPTY MAGAZINES, 1 SLING, 1 CLEANING KIT	5000	US$210.00	US$1,050,000.00
2.	SPARE MAGAZINES FOR AK-47	50,000	US$9.00	US$450,000.00
3.	7.62 39 MM REGULAR AMMUNITION	5,000,000	US$0.11	US$550,000.00
4.	60 MM MORTARS (COMMANDO TYPE)	100	US$1,550.00	US$1,.00
5.	60 MM MORTAR SHELLS	5,000	US$32.00	US$160,.
6.	81 MM MORTERS	100	US$5,250.00	US$.
7.	81 MM MORTAR SHELLS	2,000	US$52.00	US$104,000.00
8.	ANTI-PERSONNEL MINES (SIMILAR TO CLAYMORE TYPE)	1,000	US$68.00	US$68,000.00

1

Document 11: Letter from Nicholas Davies (also signed "Davis") to GMT Ltd., dated May 15, 1985. From Ari Ben-Menashe's *Profits of War*.

CONFIDENTIAL

3. ALL THE ABOVE ITEMS ARE NEW AND OF YUGOSLAV MAKE AND ~~~~~~
   ACCOMPANIED BY SUPPLIERS QUALITY CERTIFICATE.

4. PRICES SET ARE F.O.B. YUGOSLAV PORT AND DO NOT COVER TRA~~~~
   CARGO COSTS OR INSURANCE.

5. DELIVERY OF GOODS IS GUARANTEED TO BE MADE WITHIN
   (POSSIBLY WITHIN 45 DAYS) OF OPENING OF AN ~~~~
   DIVISABLE AND TRANSFERRABLE LETTER OF CREDIT FOR THE ~~~~
   US$~~,~~~-~~~.~~ IN OUR FAVOR CONFIRMED BY A PRIME EUR~~~
   OR PAYMENT IN CASH AGAINST CONTRACT.

6. LETTER OF CREDIT SHOULD BE VALID FOR 75 DAYS AND A ~~
   ~~~~TIATION PERIOD AND BE RELEASABLE IN EUROPE UPON ~~~~
   OF:

   A. BILL OF LAIDING /FORWARDING AGENT'S RECEIPTS
   B. COMMERCIAL INVOICES (3 ORIGINALS)
   C. PACKING LIST

7. IF NECESSARY, ITEMS CAN BE INSPECTED BY A WEST EUROPEAN NATI~~~~
   IN YUGOSLAVIA AFTER TRANSACTION ARRANGEMENTS HAVE BEEN COMPLE~~~
   (TRAVEL COSTS WILL NOT BE COVERED).

8. GUARANTEES FOR THE DELIVERY OF THE ABOVE ITEMS CAN BE MADE AND
   WE WILL BE WILLING TO PUT UP A BOND OF 3.5% OF THE TOTAL VALUE
   OF YOUR PURCHASE IN YOUR FAVOR WITH A PRIME EUROPEAN BANK UP~~
   COMPLETION OF DEAL ARRANGEMENTS.

9. WE UNDERSTAND THAT A VALID AND ACCEPTABLE END USER'S CERTIFICATE
   WILL BE PROVIDED BY YOU.

10. THE TERMS OUTLINED ABOVE ARE VALID UNTIL 15 JUNE 1985.

11. DUE TO THE NATURE, WEIGHT AND VOLUME OF THE ABOVE GOODS ~~~~
    WEIGHT APPROX. 200 TONS. TOTAL VOLUME APPROX. 250 CUBIC ~~~~
    WE SUGGEST THAT THE ABOVE ITEMS WILL BE TRANSPORTED BY A ~~~~
    ~~~SEL WHICH WILL REACH A YUGOSLAV PORT ON A DATE MUTUALLY
    AGREED UPON. IF NECESSARY, TRANSPORT OF GOODS CAN BE ARRANGED B~
    US AGAINST ADDITIONAL PAYMENT.

12. WE ARE LOOKING FORWARD TO COMPLETING THIS DEAL SUCCESSFULLY AND
    TO DOING FURTHER BUSINESS WITH YOU.

                    FAITHFULLY,

                    NICHOLAS DAVIS
                    UK CONSULTANT

2

Document 11: Letter from Nicholas Davies (also signed "Davis") to GMT Ltd., dated May 15, 1985. From Ari Ben-Menashe's *Profits of War*.

INDEX

Index

505

Hull, John 288, 289, 292, 327, 344, 373
Humphrey, Gordon J. 444
Hundley, William 342, 461
Hunt, E. Howard 17, 174, 176, 177, 179, 181, 184, 201, 292
Hunt, H. L. 155
Huntley, Clarence 165
Hunt, Nelson Bunker 289, 348, 351
Hurwitz, Charles 351, 352, 353, 375
Hussein, Saddam 314
Hyatt Development Corp 30-32,

I

Icthyan Associates 139
Information on Demand 387-389
Inman, Bobby Ray 202-204, 253, 254
Inslaw 210, 257, 338, 362-364, 383-385, 387, 388, 392, 396-398, 404-406, 410, 413, 429, 430, 438
Institute for Democracy, Education, and Assistance (IDEA) 288, 289
Inter Maritime Bank (IMB) 34, 84-86, 231, 280, 292, 312, 315, 317, 353, 419-421
Intermountain Aviation 291, 399
International Computerized Land Research (ICLR) 34, 35
International Controls Corporation (ICC) 231, 232
International Credit Bank (ICB) 75, 76, 86, 89, 92
International Fund for Mergers and Acquisitions (IFMA) 351
International Maritime Services 84
International Research and Trade (IRT) 205, 206
International Youth Federation for Freedom 156
Intra Bank 77, 78, 79
Investors Overseas Services (IOS) 29, 85, 229-233, 237, 238, 242, 244, 261, 265, 286, 287, 296, 400
Iorizzo, Lawrence 221, 303, 334
Iran-Contra affair 17, 73, 78, 79, 124, 130, 150, 160, 162, 163, 204-206, 208, 212-214, 216, 219, 225, 243,

255, 258, 260, 267, 281, 287, 288, 293, 294, 298, 299, 301, 304, 305, 311, 314, 315, 322, 324, 332, 333, 335-338, 341, 344, 345, 348, 349, 351, 352, 386, 393, 394, 401, 404, 406, 422, 427, 433, 439, 440, 447, 451
Iran: The Untold Story 220, 261
Irving Trust 353
Israel Aerospace Industries (IAI) 73, 297
Israel and the Bomb 83, 95
Israel Defense Force (IDF) 69, 81, 83
Italo-American Hotel Corporation (IAHC) 92
Ivanov, Eugene 131, 132, 135
Iver Johnson's Arms 363
Ives, Kevin 351
Ives, Linda 351, 375

J

Jackson, Andrew 106
Jameson, Donald 206, 225, 281
Janchev, Ivo 415
Janklow, Mort 436
Jardine, Francis 206
Jardine-Matheson 12, 13
Jaworski, Leon 189, 190, 198
Jenkins, Carl 212, 348, 349, 374
Jensen, D. Lowell 410
Jewish Telegraph Agency 90
JM/WAVE 161-163, 206, 210, 224, 349
John Birch Society 170, 293
John Paul II (Pope) 443
Johnson, Arthur 343, 373
Johnson, Claudia Alta "Lady Bird" 355
Johnson, Lyndon 114, 121, 165, 355, 398
Johnson, Robert (Barr) 350, 406
Jones, Clifford 76, 184
Jordan, Hamilton 240, 241, 434
Jordan, Phil 290
Joseph E. Seagram's and Sons Limited 47
Joseph J. Cappucci Associates 208, 209, 210

McClintock, Michael 165, 196
McCollum, William 348
McCord, James 173, 174, 176, 177, 181, 182, 184, 188
McCoy, Alfred 4, 12, 18, 37, 38, 162, 163, 195, 322, 325, 327
McDonald, Larry 293
McDonald, Miles 104, 105
McElroy, James 204
McFarlane, Robert 256, 257, 267, 286, 331, 333
McGowan, James 35, 68
McGregor, Jack 238, 239, 244
McLaughlin, Edward 58
McLendon, Gordon 183, 184
McManus, Michael 336, 364
McSweeney, William 409
M.D. Anderson Foundation 189
Media Bypass 396, 427
Meese, Edwin 286, 316, 377, 383-385, 389-391, 402, 403, 410, 413
Mega Group 25, 70, 116
Mellon, Ailsa 226, 227
Mellon family 5, 33, 129
Mellon, Paul 227
Mena, Arkansas 340, 344, 345, 347-349, 351, 361, 373, 374, 377, 378, 401
Menzies, Stewart 6, 7
Mercantile Bank & Trust 273
MERRIMAC 176
Merthan, Lawrence 154
Metta, Michele 87, 91, 92, 96-98
Metzger, Eugene 274, 275, 395
Meyer, Cord 223, 224
MI5 82, 129, 132, 146
MI6 SIS [the Secret Intelligence Service 6, 131, 381, 382
Miami National Bank 21, 83, 157, 236
Miami News 71, 94
Middendorf Group 273, 274
Midwest Employers Casualty Company (MECC) 371
Milken, Michael 130, 246, 375, 443, 456
Millard, Mark 250, 266
Miller, Richard 289

Milliken, Roger 293
Mintz, John 399, 427
Mischer, Walter 213-216, 218, 219, 254, 260, 325
Mitchell, "Billy" 186
Mitchell, John 449
Mitterand 308
MK-ULTRA 15, 174
Mogilevich, Semion 80, 81, 95, 382, 383, 414-416, 418, 419
Moldea, Dan 28, 29, 40, 459
Molina, John 326
Mollenhoff, Clark 168, 196
Mondale, Walter 410, 411, 430
Money and the Power, The 37, 103, 142, 195, 373
Monks, Vicky 283, 322, 325, 330, 331, 337, 338
Monroe, James 358
Monroe, Marilyn 56, 133, 171
Monsieur, Jacques 311, 336
Moody family 137, 239, 240, 241, 342
Moody Jr, Shearn 137, 157, 239, 241
Moody, William Lewis Jr. 137, 157, 239, 240, 241, 342, 368
Moorer, Thomas H. 167, 169-171, 179, 180, 228, 293
Morabia, Elliot 298
Morabia, Nan 298, 299, 333
Moran, James 104, 105
Morgan, Jeff 32, 40
Morgans 6, 226
Morgenthau, Robert 121, 122, 124, 125, 261, 269, 435, 442
Moriarty, John "Jack" 191, 192, 193, 338
Morris, Roger 37, 103, 142, 157, 195, 345, 347, 373, 374
Mossad 31, 75, 83, 87, 88, 91, 95, 96, 124, 145, 206, 209, 230, 243, 257, 283, 295, 297, 305, 311-313, 336, 351, 383, 386, 387, 389, 397, 412-415, 422, 424, 425, 426, 439
Moss, Edward K. 222-224, 262, 290, 341, 343
Mosvold, Inge Gordon 367

Made in the USA
Monee, IL
07 January 2023

24731046R00302